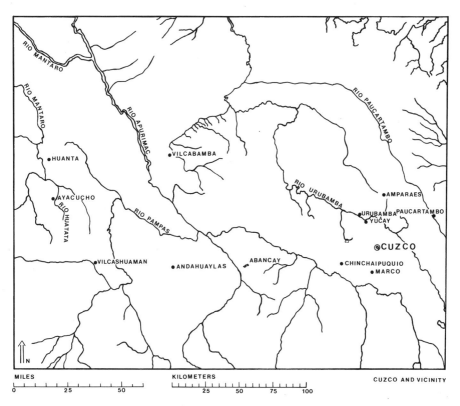

MILES
0   25   50

KILOMETERS
25   50   75   100

CUZCO AND VICINITY

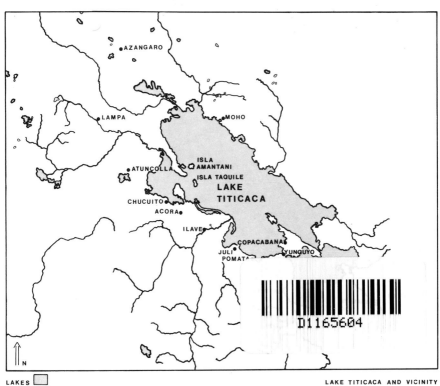

LAKES
MILES
0   25   50

KILOMETERS
0   25   50   75   100

LAKE TITICACA AND VICINITY

The Inca and Aztec States, 1400–1800
Anthropology and History

This is a volume in

STUDIES IN ANTHROPOLOGY

Under the consulting editorship of
E. A. Hammel, University of California, Berkeley

A complete list of titles appears at the end of this volume.

The Inca and Aztec States 1400–1800

Anthropology and History

EDITED BY

George A. Collier
Department of Anthropology
Stanford University
Stanford, California

Renato I. Rosaldo
Department of Anthropology
Stanford University
Stanford, California

John D. Wirth
Department of History
Center for Latin American Studies
Stanford University
Stanford, California

1982

ACADEMIC PRESS

A Subsidiary of Harcourt Brace Jovanovich, Publishers

New York   London
Paris   San Diego   San Francisco   São Paulo   Sydney   Tokyo   Toronto

ACADEMIC PRESS, INC.
111 Fifth Avenue, New York, New York 10003

United Kingdom Edition published by
ACADEMIC PRESS, INC. (LONDON) LTD.
24/28 Oval Road, London NW1 7DX

Library of Congress Cataloging in Publication Data

Main entry under title:

The Inca and Aztec states, 1400-1800.

   (Studies in anthropology)
   Includes index.
   1. Aztecs--Politics and government--Addresses,
essays, lectures. 2. Incas--Politics and government--
Addresses, essays, lectures. 3. Indians of Mexico--
Government relations--Addresses, essays, lectures.
4. Indians of Mexico--Politics and government--
Addresses, essays, lectures. 5. Indians of South
America--Andes--Government relations--Addresses,
essays, lectures. 6. Indians of South America--Andes--
Politics and government--Addresses, essays, lectures.
I. Collier, George Allen, Date   . II. Rosaldo,
Renato. III. Wirth, John D. IV. Series: Studies in
anthropology (Academic Press)
F1219.76.P75152   306'.08997   82-6760
ISBN 0-12-181180-8   AACR2

PRINTED IN THE UNITED STATES OF AMERICA

82 83 84 85   9 8 7 6 5 4 3 2 1

To
Evon Z. Vogt
and
John J. Johnson,
teachers, colleagues, friends

Contents

Contributors   xv
Preface   xvii

Introduction.   In the Shadow of Empire: New Directions in Mesoamerican and Andean Ethnohistory

George A. Collier

Challenges for the Comparative Study of Empire   2
New Directions in Ethnohistoric Research   4
New Generalizations about Mesoamerican and Andean Empire   8
References   18

PART I   A Comparative Model

1 The Political Economy of the Aztec and Inca States

Pedro Carrasco

Editors' Introduction   23
Economic Organization   24
Political System   33
Points of Contrast   36

Notes   39
References   39

PART II   Aztec State Formation

2   Patterns of Empire Formation in the Valley of Mexico, Late
Postclassic Period, 1200–1521

Edward E. Calnek

Editors' Introduction   43
Introduction   43
Early Development of the City-State System   46
The Formation of Dynastic Groups   48
Empire Formation   54
Organization of Empires   56
The Tribute System   58
Summary   59
References   60

3   Dynastic Succession and the Centralization
of Power in Tenochtitlan

J. Rounds

Editors' Introduction   63
Fraternal Succession and the Corporate Dynasty   67
Selection of the Successor   75
The Role of the Stand-in in the Maintenance of Continuity   78
Summary and Conclusions   83
Notes   84
References   86

PART III   Inca State Administration and Colonization

4   Inca Policies and Institutions Relating to the Cultural
Unification of the Empire

John Howland Rowe

Editors' Introduction   93
Introduction   93

Education and Language   95
Yanaconas, Camayos, and *Mitimas*   96
Chosen Women   107
Religion   108
Policies Perpetuating Local Differences   110
Consequences   111
Notes   114
References   115

5   Inca Decimal Administration in the Lake Titicaca Region

Catherine J. Julien

Editors' Introduction   119
The Inca Tribute System and the Role of Decimal
    Administration   121
The Lupaca Case   127
Decimal Administration in the Lupaca Province   133
The Labor Assignment of the Lupaca Province   135
The Role of Local Power under Centralized Authority   141
Notes   144
References   147

6   The Infrastructure of Inka Control in the Peruvian
    Central Highlands

Craig Morris

Editors' Introduction   153
Communication, Administration, and the Supply
    of the State Operations   156
The Link between State and Region   165
Concluding Comment   168
References   170

7   The Formation of Tawantinsuyu: Mechanisms of
    Colonization and Relationship with Ethnic Groups

Franklin Pease G.Y.

Editors' Introduction   173
Patterns of Migration   176

Consent and Redistribution   181
Three Examples of Tawantinsuyu   184
Notes   190
References   194

8   The *Mitimas* of the Cochabamba Valley:
    The Colonization Policy of Huayna Capac

Nathan Wachtel

Editors' Introduction   199
The Origin of the *Mitimas* of Cochabamba   201
The Land Distribution of Huayna Capac   205
The Organization of Work and the Distribution of Produce   213
Conclusions: Comparative Perspectives   217
Notes   222
Appendix 1: List of *Suyos* Assigned by Huayna Capac   226
Appendix 2: *Interrogatorio de J. Polo de Ondegardo*   229

9   The *Mit'a* Obligations of Ethnic Groups to the Inka State

John V. Murra

Editors' Introduction   237
La Visita General of 1549   239
Xagua's Testimony of 1562   249
La Visita General of 1571   251
Two Lupaqa Testimonies   254
Summary and Conclusion   256
Notes   257
References   260

PART IV   The Imposition of Spanish Governance

10   The Spanish and Indian Law: New Spain
Woodrow Borah

Editors' Introduction   265
Changes Brought to Indian Society by Spanish Rule   268
Indian Cases   274

Proposals for Reform   277
Reforms   283
Notes   285
References   285

11   The Social Significance of Judicial Institutions in an Exploitative Society: Huamanga, Peru, 1570–1640

Steve J. Stern

Editors' Introduction   289
Toledo's Reforms: A "Mixed Blessing" for Colonizers   292
Indian Legal Battles   293
The Opportunity: Cleavages within the Colonial Elite   297
From Defense to Manipulation   299
Effects of Judicial Politics: The Colonial Elite   305
Effects of Judicial Politics: Andean Society   307
Notes   312
Appendix: Official Counts of Huamanga Tributary Populations, 1570—1635   317

12   Exploitation as an Economic System: The State and the Extraction of Surplus in Colonial Peru

Karen Spalding

Editors' Introduction   321
Socioeconomic Structure in Colonial Peru   322
Tribute   328
Mita   331
Repartimiento de Mercancías   332
Summary and Conclusions   338
Notes   340

PART V   Indigenous Culture and Consciousness

13   Spiritual Conflict and Accommodation in New Spain: Toward a Typology of Aztec Responses to Christianity

J. Jorge Klor de Alva

Editors' Introduction   345
Authenticity of Conversions   346

Accommodation in the Christianization Process   351
Nepantlism   353
Incomplete Conversion   355
Coercion, Dissimulation, and Resistance   357
Conclusion   362
References   363

14 Views of Corporate Self and History in Some Valley of Mexico Towns: Late Seventeenth and Eighteenth Centuries

James Lockhart

Editors' Introduction   367
Levels of Indigenous Awareness   368
The Written Sources   370
Retention of Preconquest Elements   375
Incorporation of Postconquest Elements   386
Notes   393

15 Nahuatl Literacy

Frances Karttunen

Editors' Introduction   395
Introduction   396
Preconquest Precedents   397
Postconquest Developments   400
The Implications of Nahuatl Literacy   408
Appendix   415
References   416

16 Bureaucracy and Systematic Knowledge in Andean Civilization

R. Tom Zuidema

Editors' Introduction   419
Introduction   420
Hucha   425
The Straightness of *Ceques*   434
The Use of Tables in Andean Culture   445

Conclusions   449
References   454

Afterword   459
Renato I. Rosaldo

Index   465

Contributors

Numbers in parentheses indicate the pages on which the authors' contributions begin.

Woodrow Borah (265), Department of History, University of California, Berkeley, California 94720

Edward E. Calnek (43), Department of Anthropology, University of Rochester, Rochester, New York 14627

Pedro Carrasco (23), Department of Anthropology, State University of New York at Stony Brook, Stony Brook, New York 11794

George A. Collier (1), Department of Anthropology, Stanford University, Stanford, California 94305

Catherine J. Julien (119), Institute of Andean Studies, Berkeley, California 94709

Frances Karttunen (395), Linguistics Research Center, University of Texas, Austin, Texas 78712

J. Jorge Klor de Alva[1] (345), Merrill College, University of California at Santa Cruz, Santa Cruz, California 95064

James Lockhart (367), Department of History, University of California, Los Angeles, California 90024

[1] Present address: San Jose State University, San Jose, California 95192.

Craig Morris[2] (153), Department of Anthropology, American Museum of Natural History, New York, New York 10024

John V. Murra (237), Department of Anthropology, Cornell University, Ithaca, New York 14853

Franklin Pease G. Y. (173), Pontífica Universidad Católica del Perú, Lima 21, Peru

Renato I. Rosaldo (459), Department of Anthropology, Stanford University, Stanford, California 94305

J. Rounds (63), Socio-Behavioral Research Group, University of California, Los Angeles, California 90024

John Howland Rowe (93), Department of Anthropology, University of California, Berkeley, California 94720

Karen Spalding (321), Department of History, University of Delaware, Newark, Delaware 19711

Steve J. Stern (289), Department of History, University of Wisconsin—Madison, Madison, Wisconsin 53706

Nathan Wachtel (199), Ecole des Hautes Etudes en Sciences Sociales, Centre de Recherches Historiques, 75270 Paris, Cedex 06, France

R. Tom Zuidema (419), Department of Anthropology, University of Illinois at Urbana-Champaign, Urbana, Illinois 61801

---

[2] Present address: Department of Anthropology, Cornell University, Ithaca, New York 14853.

Preface

The 3-day Indianist conference held at Stanford in December 1978 was broadly conceived and ambitious. Historians and anthropologists from the United States, Latin America, and Europe considered a wide range of topics covering both pre- and postconquest America, drawing from both Andean and Mesoamerican examples. Papers were circulated and then debated at the conference. To prepare this final, published version the editors held a follow-up session in June 1979 at the Institute for Advanced Study in Princeton, where the conference papers and debates were brought into sharper focus.

The comparative approach was extensively discussed at the Stanford conference. Some felt that the juxtaposition of roughly parallel structures was a useful way to pinpoint more precisely both the similarities and differences in the Andean and Mesoamerican experiences. A number of participants felt that comparison can be extremely useful in posing new questions and in opening up new avenues of investigation. Still others asked whether the two archipelagoes of the Andean and Mexican civilizations were really linked by more than the shared fact of Spanish conquest. Mesoamericanists, who work a field more thoroughly researched than their Andean counterparts, seemed less hesitant to generalize and ask comparative questions. Thus, the willingness of Pedro Carrasco and James Lockhart to compare the two cultures stood in contrast to the cautions urged by John Rowe, who observed that even the Spanish colonial experiences were different, and to the admonitions of John Murra, who thought more should be learned about the Andean specifics before generalizing.

Themes arising from this debate are discussed in the Introduction. Suffice it to say here that the idea of comparing the imperial history, tributary relationships, religious and civil hierarchies, and political economies of the two states is still controversial. In the spirit of Carrasco's lead essay, some scholars may want to move forthrightly into comparison. Others, such as the Andean scholars who took part in the conference debates, may want to study discrete parts of Indian societies that lacked a written record into colonial times, and for which much of the evidenciary base available in Mexican studies is either completely lacking or incomplete. At the same time, the recent advances in Andean studies are striking, as this collection reveals.

Discussion of new research on the Spanish colonial period also highlighted the challenge of comparison. Just as the accumulating case studies of eighteenth- and nineteenth-century landed systems in Latin America stress the time–place specific nature of the hacienda, so the new research on postconquest Spanish–Indian relationships is turning up a wide range of interactions. There is no single hacienda model; there is no single colonial society. Yet the template of the modern world's first bureaucratic empire was consequential. This legalistic, hierarchical, late Medieval culture pervaded the viceroyalties of New Spain and Peru. Certainly there are interesting questions to be raised about the sequencing and timing of colonial rule.

Clearly, the study of Native American states and Indianist societies under Spanish rule is eliciting highly dynamic research. Governments, scholars of comparative colonial history, students of other world areas, and the general public all want to know what this experience meant and still means. Comparative analysis seems to hold great promise, although by no means all the conferees agreed that enough basic research has been done to support such an effort.

There was much more agreement on the need for new periodizations. While incorporating the fact of conquest and the demographic catastrophe for Native Americans that followed, research now points not only to the survival of Indian institutions, but also to their elaboration and development under and within the structures of colonial rule. This brings into focus the existence of continuities among generations, within villages, and across regions. From this perspective, the value of projecting postcolonial Indian structures backward is handled in the chapter by Nathan Wachtel. Andean studies are enriched by this approach, which considers the conquest less as the crucial break between historical epochs and more as another benchmark for calibrating social and institutional change. New insights into the direction and rate of change in Indian societies are also coming out of Mesoamerican studies. The use of new linguistic evidence by Karttunen and Lockhart is a case in point.

The Native American state structures were enveloped by the Spanish, but these were new empires in rapid evolution. Parts of these complex imperial structures survived and even flourished well into the seventeenth and eighteenth centuries. New time lines to reflect continuities and change of this sort have not been fully worked out. It is clear that historians and anthropologists can no longer justify a division of labor based on the arrival of the Europeans. The Indian perspectives now being apprehended do not fit neatly into pre- and postcolonial periods. In fact, the willingness to accept new time spans as well as new techniques was clearly demonstrated at the conference.

Interdisciplinary research on Native American states and Indianist societies is well established, as is shown by the debates and this volume. It is not that the disciplinary lines mean little. It is that problems and questions examined here are best approached through the use of interdisciplinary methods and concepts. The fruitfulness of this approach is shown in the chapter by Karen Spalding, who examines the postconquest economy of Peru through lenses polished by both historians and anthropologists.

This conference brought together junior and senior scholars whose principal frame of professional reference has been regional studies. Thus, the research and writing presented come from specialists with a long-standing commitment to the regional approach. The argument for area studies receives strong confirmation in this volume. With confidence in the continuing vitality of this approach, and in anticipation of the many insights and innovations still to come out of it, the Center for Latin American Studies was pleased to host this conference.

A word about editorial format: the editors have chosen to allow for differences in bibliography and citation demanded by different problems and areas of our collaborators' research. Generally, contributors have followed conventions closest to their fields of anthropology and history. John Rowe and Catherine Julien have introduced a special system of double citation for rare source materials enabling readers to locate references to them in more than one published edition.

Generous funding from the National Endowment for the Humanities enabled us to bring leading scholars to Stanford and to prepare this edited volume. We want to thank James Lockhart for his helpful comments on the conference model and on the editing project. Pedro Carrasco, Karen Spalding, and John Elliott shared their valuable insights and assistance with the editors at our Princeton meeting. At Stanford, Erick Langer forged a useful transcript of the debates, while the Dickinson Symposium Fund enabled us to involve students in this open conference. We wish to thank Mary Berg and Elborg Forster for help with translations and Rosa Mendoza de Rick and Jane Becker Dill for help in planning and drafting maps. Nancy Donham gave us valued editorial advice. We also appreciate the care and attention that the staff at Academic Press gave to the production of this volume.

G. A. C.
R. I. R.
J. D. W.

Introduction

In the Shadow of Empire: New Directions in Mesoamerican and Andean Ethnohistory

George A. Collier

The civilizations of central Mesoamerica and the Andes pose both a challenge and an opportunity for the comparative study of civilization because they developed independently of counterparts in Europe, the Near East, and Asia. They challenge us to arrive at an authentic understanding by means of concepts and interpretation that do not distort the facts to fit an alien analytical scheme. They provide an opportunity to test independent cases for generalizations about civilization. Much that has been written about the Incas and the Aztecs in a comparative vein has seized the opportunity without first meeting the challenge.

Writing at the close of the 1960s about Andean and Mesoamerican ethnohistory and social history, three of the contributors to this volume—James Lockhart, Karen Spalding, and John Murra—identified a trend in their fields. This trend was setting aside modeling and comparison in favor of extending fundamental understanding of these social systems through time and space by means of interdisciplinary examination of new sources. A decade later we have asked these scholars and several of their colleagues to assess what the fields of anthropology and history now show the two regions to have shared during the period spanning the ascendance of the Incas and Aztecs, their conquest, and their colonial rule—and thus to reconsider problems of generalization and comparison.

The results have been a dramatic redirection of studies of the

THE INCA AND AZTEC
STATES, 1400–1800

1

indigenous empires to stress the importance and enduring character of their sub-imperial organization. By examining the polities overshadowed by empire, these studies shed new light on how the empires compared in their constitution, in how they arose, and in what were the limits to their growth and development.

Challenges for the Comparative Study of Empire

The manner in which scholars now regard generalization and comparison has to be understood in light of the two reasons for which they initially set them aside. First, one cannot generalize about what one does not understand. As new sources and strategies for exploring these civilizations brought entirely unexplored aspects of indigenous social and cultural life to view, writers in the 1960s came to question many older views of indigenous and colonial imperial institutions. Second, they grew increasingly impatient with the anachronistic application of social science models rooted in the problems and perspectives of the nineteenth and twentieth centuries to the era surrounding the conquest of America. For example, James Lockhart (1972) deplored the "development" paradigm's naive interpretation of the colonial era as one of traditional society prior to modernization. Karen Spalding (1972) decried the inaccurate view of colonial Indian societies as simple peasantries stripped of their preconquest elite superstructure. She argued that anthropologists tended to foster this view by extrapolating from their synchronic analyses of contemporary Indian pueblos back to the colonial era. John Murra (1970) dismissed the typological classifying of Andean society as socialist (Baudin 1928), hydraulic (Wittfogel 1955), or slave-based (Choy 1960). These classifications generalized too blatantly from *au courant* theories of the socioeconomic history of the Old World with too little regard for Andean realities. Lockhart (1972:33) summed up the discontent:

> Social science ideas can serve to inspire interpreters as well as any others—but no better. . . . Unsophisticated work on insufficient sources with the newest European methods and concepts is, as Rolando Mellafe . . . has said, nothing but an amusing intellectual game.

Willingness to generalize and compare thus makes sense to the degree that empirical understanding of these civilizations in their own terms has matured.

This volume brings together such new understanding of these civilizations and their later development and illustrates the strategies with which anthropologists and historians have pursued the understanding. Let me identify some of the strategies that have proved most significant by way of suggesting how they enabled Pedro Carrasco, whose comparison of Inca and Aztec political economy opens this volume, to accomplish his task.

Instead of using the familiar chroniclers who gave overall descriptions of native society, scholars have been shifting their attention toward the analysis of case materials. This has meant shifting their interest from the imperial centers to regional sub-imperial constituents and to the use of local administrative records from the early Spanish period. Carrasco and other ethnohistorians of Mesoamerica have been publishing documents and analyses of materials from within and outside the Valley of Mexico (Carrasco 1963a,b, 1966, 1969a,b, 1970, 1976, 1977, 1980; Calnek 1978; Olivera 1978; Reyes 1977). In addition to traditional chronicles, they have been using such sources as tribute-payers' lists, land suits, and parochial marriage records. When Carrasco and his colleagues (Carrasco *et al.* 1976; Carrasco and Broda 1978) applied similar methods to source materials from other localities, they were able to sort out the features common to local and regional systems of Mesoamerican stratification because their strategy allowed empirical generalization from large numbers of cases that had been studied by comparable methods.

As Carrasco demonstrates in his present contribution, such steps enable a reconsideration of imperial organization from the fresh perspectives afforded by sub-imperial studies, and in a manner that invites comparison of one thoroughly understood imperial system with another. Carrasco suggests that the political economies of the Inca and Aztec empires developed differing degrees of centralization based on the stratification that both civilizations shared, especially at the level of fundamental, sub-imperial constituencies. In both civilizations societies were of a type fusing polity, economy, and stratification in social relations between estates. Land and labor were the principal factors of production in both areas. A dominant or ruling estate organized relations of production politically, each society being stratified into producers and managers with distinctive obligations and rights. Although producers held land that they worked for household subsistence, they always owed labor services and sometimes goods to members or institutions of the dominant estate, which held other categories of land worked by these labor services. The dominant elites managed the surplus to maintain their status, partly through ostentatious presentations of goods, and partly for public works, which accounted for most of the circulation of goods. Markets played only a minor role in circulation and were not media for exchange of factors of production.

This interpretation draws from the perspective of Carrasco's regional studies in that the organization of empire is drawn along the same lines as that of the internal stratification of smaller, subordinate polities and independent states. It brings Carrasco's scholarship almost full circle back to a typological sort of comparative political theory quite similar to that Wittfogel's *Oriental Despotism* (1957) engendered, but richer in its culture-historical grounding and its connecting of imperial stratification to the organizing principles of smaller Mesoamerican and Andean polities.

New Directions in Ethnohistoric Research

As we consider features and findings of our contributors' scholarship that bring them nearly full circle back to comparison and generalization, we should avoid attributing to them a false unanimity of purpose. The ebb and flow probably represents a converging of a variety of scholarly currents. One is a dialectic in the analysis of empires, culture areas, or other large units; here initial emphasis on their great traditions, centers, institutions, or dynasties gives way to a concern for variation and process seen from below and within. This, in turn, enables more sophisticated reconsideration of the whole. Studies of late imperial China, for example, have undergone such a transformation (cf. Wakeman and Grant 1975) and are at a stage that bears comparison with the volume at hand.

At the same time, general disciplinary currents also flow in. "New Social History" has certainly contributed to the turn toward more systematic study of the experiences of hinterland peoples. In yet another vein, the writers are deeply interested in how ethnic local and regional leaders articulated the complex organization of Mesoamerican and Andean society. They draw on a powerful stream of anthropological thinking about politics that includes Fortes and Evans-Pritchard's (1940) discussion of politics in stateless societies, Swartz *et al.*'s (1966) examination of followers and of how leadership works in local arenas, and Barth's (1959) and Gluckman's (1965) examinations of the dynamics of ethnic and tribal politics within regions and states.

One current in which this book's scholarship participates is an increasing specification of ethnohistoric analysis. Much earlier research focussed on central institutions and personages of the indigenous and colonial state. Now tribute lists, *visita* reports on the goods and services local peoples rendered to their overlords, and archival documentation of the litigation involving Indians of a particular province turn our gaze upon the sub-imperial mechanisms for rule within the Andean and Central Mesoamerican civilizations. In numerous instances we regard how things work in particular contexts rather than by grand design. Yet this particularizing comes from several analytical strategies that begin to generalize in more sophisticated ways—ways that ethnohistorians share with their counterparts in the study of more readily interpretable historical societies of Europe and the Americas.

For instance, we know that regions varied in geography, economy, and in other ways affecting their cultural history. Historical studies of colonial Latin America have already demonstrated that economic and social institutions and processes varied significantly by region in a manner at least suggesting continuities within regions from one era to the next. Where once the colonial economic history of Mesoamerica was interpreted as that of New Spain writ large, now we explore how regions fared differently because of distinct geography, heritage, and placement in the colonial economy. Taylor's *Landlord and Peasant in Colonial Oaxaca* (1972) and MacLeod's *Spanish Central America* (1973), for example, have demonstrated convincingly that not all the features and phases of the evolution of "the great hacienda" can be extrapolated beyond the northern New Spain on which Chevalier based the construct. Altman and Lockhart's *Provinces of Early Mexico* (1976) has taken the logical next step of sorting out the shared and distinguishing characteristics of such regions and the colonial-era provinces to which they gave rise.

Extrapolating this strategy back to the analysis of the indigenous civilizations, our contributors are penetrating behind the facade of homogeneity imparted by Inca and Aztec hegemony. Thus John Murra, Catherine Julien, Nathan Wachtel, and Franklin Pease considerably advance our understanding of Andean civilization by examining the Huallaga, Lupaca, Chimor, Cochabamba, and other Andean regions in terms of how they shared or differed in their heritages, in the articulation of their populations in the Inca state, and in their experience of the transformation of indigenous empire into Spanish colonial hegemony.

Contextualizing also refines and sometimes reformulates our understanding of any society's institutions and principles of organization. We are able to focus on how prescription and practice, jural rules and behavior, and ideology and pragmatic politics actually relate to one another. In all too many instances our ideas about how these societies functioned and how they were governed under imperial or colonial rule overemphasize the power and effectiveness of state institutions. This is understandable, for the more readily available chronicles and accounts of officials and elites affiliated with their centers of political power naturally give greatest emphasis to these state institutions.

Our examination of colonial-era legal institutions and how Indians used them illustrates this particularly well. Woodrow Borah, explaining how the crown came to formulate a separate jurisdiction for Indian legal business by the end of the sixteenth century, acknowledges various bodies of Latin Christian law as the source of the principles justifying successive policies. But he emphasizes that litigation itself—the strategies Indians employed in the courts, the issues they disputed, the remedies they sought, and the sheer volume of litigation—was most definitively shaping the succession of judicial procedures that determined the substance of Indian law.

Similarly, Steve Stern finds the ultimate meaning for Indians of colonial judicial institutions in the pragmatic politics of their litigating. He focusses on how Indians of colonial Huamanga, Peru used the courts extensively to blunt the exploitive levying of their labor for mining. As Spanish provincials competed with one another for local Indian labor and tribute and with regional administrators, who were siphoning off Indian labor for mining, Indians could always find a patron willing to help them litigate to lower their levies for mining or to alter local labor and tribute obligations to mutual advantage. However, by so participating in the competitive politics of litigation, and by foregoing more radical resistance, Indians effectively consented in the long run to a system of "justice" that oppressed Indians as a class. Both studies emphasize not so much how imperial institutions compelled constituents as how the practical politics of constituents' engaging the state gave shape and meaning to its institutions.

Finally, ethnohistory and the closely allied New Social History both orient us toward the hinterland domains and heretofore little-used source materials to enliven our grasp of historical societies with the voices and vision of their diverse constituencies. One advantage of this strategy is that it seeks the authentic terms with which to view these civilizations. For example, in the primordial titles that seventeenth- and eighteenth-century Nahuatl villagers composed for their lands, James Lockhart uncovers an extraordinarily vivid expression of autochthonous corporate identity. He relates this identity to the integrity, even under colonial rule, of the *altlepetl*, or city-state, as a fundamental unit of Nahuatl social organization. This integrity is evident even though the city-state is not commonly thought to have lasted much beyond the first century of colonial rule.

Another advantage is that, when it reveals discrepancies between the perspectives of the less powerful and those that governed them, this strategy calls into question conclusions based on one-sided accounts of the latter group, which were more accessible to earlier scholarship. Jorge Klor de Alva, for example, discovers in *confesionarios*, and other materials churchmen devised for evangelizing, a much greater resistance to Christianity on the part of colonial Nahuatl Indians than that which the friars were willing to acknowledge. This leads him to reconsider Ricard's (1966) long-accepted thesis of spiritual conquest, which drew heavily from the views of the evangelizers.

Seeking evidence on which to base these strategies, ethnohistorians have had to search not only for appropriate sources but also for new ways of interpreting the native concepts and categories they embody. Mesoamericanists have the advantage of native-language wills, petitions, records of litigation, deeds of property, and other documents that Indians of the colonial era transcribed in a Latinate script in the conduct of their affairs. More than illuminating their ostensible subject matter, these records document how Indians conceptualized their world and offer the potential for examining the processes fostering continuity or change in native ideas. Frances Karttunen seizes the opportunity in these documents for linguistic analysis of processes of contact and mutual influence of Spanish and Indian culture in central Mexico. Nahuatl language reflects this influence in a systematic change, first in lexicon and phonology, and finally in grammar and syntax.

Keeping records through knotted-string *khipu* and symbolic schemata other than writing, Andean civilization did not develop a comparable genre of native-language writing in the colonial era. So Andeanists face the greater challenge of having to sort out the indigenous perspectives from the Spanish language and concepts of early colonial documentation. This requires attending to the kinds of sources most likely to embody the desired perspective in unbiased form.

For example, seeking to study the articulation of ethnic groups within the Inca state, John Murra sets aside the native accounts and Spanish chronicles, on which most Inca studies have been based, because of the biases of the Cuzco-centered perspectives of their authors. In their place he studies early colonial *visitas*. Spanish administrators apparently assembled these surveys by recording the responses of local leaders and their *khipu* keepers' responses to specific questions about tribute and labor obligations. Murra's insight is that the sequences of information recorded in the *visitas* approximates the sequential reading of the *khipu*, and this perspective enables him to unravel the ethnocategories of *khipu* organization in the order of their relative importance for pre-Hispanic tribute: laboring on state lands, herding the Incas' camelids, weaving specialized textiles, and gathering forest and lake products. Rendering these ethnocategories intelligible through careful interpreting of the *visita* texts, Murra's contribution exemplifies the sophistication ethnohistorians must bring to the weighing of their evidence.

New Generalization about Mesoamerican and Andean Empire

Studying Mesoamerican and Andean civilization in these ways has led to interesting conclusions about their organization and development. The focus on sub-imperial life, for instance, has made clear that the underlying and characteristic organization of both civilizations was at this level rather than at that of the relatively short-lived empires. Furthermore, the specification of analysis makes apparent that organization at the sub-imperial level lasted well into an era of colonial rule founded upon it. Both findings raise interesting questions regarding the workings and evolution of supremacy in these civilizations, be it indigenous or Spanish-colonial.

Sub-Imperial Continuities

The organizational units that emerge as fundamental and enduring in the core regions of both civilizations are the same as those Pedro Carrasco posits as underlying Andean and Mesoamerican stratification. For Carrasco, these units politically organize production relations; a ruling estate receives as labor or tribute the surplus of a class of producers. Minimally, the units thus have rulers and ruled. Further subdivisions may crosscut them, but usually such subdivisions are made within a unifying symmetrical framework through which tribute or labor obligations rotate temporally. Characteristically, they have stable, exactly defined boundaries. A center predominates over outlying settlements, although these need not all be territorially contiguous. Members distinguish themselves ethnically. We may refer to them as city-states or kingdoms, but by this we do not intend to invoke European models for their organization.

Recognition of these units as fundamental has been growing in the ethnohistorical literature for some time. Gibson, for example, equated the basic entity for early colonial rule of Aztecs, *cabecera* towns with *sujeto* outliers, with jurisdiction of pre-imperial or sub-imperial *tlato-que* rulers. His *Aztecs under Spanish Rule* (1964) massively demon-strated that most major institutions for colonial rule of Indians repeat-edly grafted onto or grew out of existing indigenous organization at this level of city-state rather than out of any other hierarchical level of Aztec organization.

Andeanists have been correlating ethnic populations' exploitation of widely separated ecological niches with age-old Andean organiza-tion of units of similar scope. John Murra (1972), for example, elabo-rated on the idea of the "vertical archipelago" as the characteristic mechanism whereby polities with a seat of substantial settlement at one altitude colonized noncontiguous niches from three to ten days' march up or down the Andean slopes to control the diverse production essential to their redistributive economies. Against the hypothesis that peace under Inca hegemony had made possible the development of such networks, he argued that the vertical archipelago was a pre-impe-rial and probably ancient organizing principle of Andean political econ-omies, and he documented several instances of ethnic kingdoms whose archipelago organization lasted well into the colonial era.

Our contributors substantiate the theory that the specific units of this kind evident in the early colonial era indeed were fundamental, age-old, and enduring in the core areas of these civilizations. In the case of central Mesoamerica, for example, Edward Calnek and James Lockhart trace their continuity over six centuries bracketing the Span-ish conquest. Calnek reviews recently completed settlement archaeol-ogy of central Mexico, which is establishing the prevalence and chron-ological depth of autonomous city-states. He concludes that political centers with established territorial bounds began to proliferate in the central Valley of Mexico from the thirteenth century onward and were perpetuated as building blocks in the coalitions and larger con-federacies, such as the Aztec Triple Alliance, which later came to the fore. As late as the eighteenth century, the integrity of these city-states echoes in the vivid consciousness of autochthonous identity that James Lockhart discloses in the language of primordial titles of towns of that period.

Comparable conclusions are drawn regarding analogous units of Andean organization. Franklin Pease examined the pre-Inca, pre-impe-rial organization of ethnic kingdoms in the Andes in relation to the articulation of ethnic groups under Inca rule. Although forceful colo-nizing and resettlement by the Inca sometimes transformed them, the integrity of these kingdoms generally outlasted Inca supremacy as their populations reconstituted their organization in the early colonial era. Furthermore, in their reaffirmation of territorial claims on far-flung and ecologically diverse colonies, some of these ethnic kingdoms suggest to Pease support for the hypothesis that their archipelago organization was no offshoot of a generalized *Pax Incaica* but rather considerably more ancient. As for the colonial era, the policies of Spanish governance that Karen Spalding characterizes as preserving indigenous structures of production to provision Andean colonial society with essential goods and labor were of use to Indian society. Such Indian organization was thus enabled to continue and in some measure to follow its own internal dynamics while adjusting its relationship to the larger economy and society of the colonial state.

The second general conclusion from studying Mesoamerican and Andean civilizations with increased specificity is that the Spanish conquest broke them off as civilizations far less definitively than had been assumed. Rather than coming to an end with conquest, the civilizations continued to organize indigenous life and livelihood well into, and in some respects beyond, the colonial era. Such reconsideration of the temporal frame most appropriate for these civilizations obviously follows in part from seeing pre-imperial and sub-imperial city-states and kingdoms endure in and under colonial rule.

Growing recognition of other lasting characteristics of indigenous civilization also lends weight to the argument for periodization that spans the conquest rather than being punctuated by it. The uniformity of changes in colonial Nahuatl through central Mexico, which Frances Karttunen describes, suggests a sphere of indigenous communication whose integrity was not undermined by Spanish conquest; indeed, in some measure it was even buttressed by legal institutions nurturing a new genre of Nahuatl literacy. The persistence of Andean systems of classification and cosmology hint of complex and sophisticated systems of thought that outlived conquest. Nathan Wachtel shows how these systems patterned indigenous colonization of the Cochabamba Valley in Inca and colonial eras, and Tom Zuidema relates these systems to lasting Andean schemata for scheduling agriculture.

Just when the period of indigenous civilizations should be thought to end is clearly a problem open to further study. Lockhart and Karttunen's contributions, however, point to continuities late into the eighteenth century in central Mexico. John Rowe's multifaceted investigation of colonial-era indigenous consciousness of having been part of the Inca state (1951, 1976, and Chapter 4 in this volume), suggests significant Andean continuities up to the catastropic effort, in 1780, of thousands of Indians to restore Tawantinsuyu.

Polities under the Sway of Empire

These conclusions regarding continuities in indigenous civilization, particularly at the sub-imperial level, serve as one point of departure for exploring Inca, Aztec, and Spanish colonial supremacy. We should consider how constituencies could sustain the sway of empire and what such continuity implies for peoples subject to colonialism. At the same time, we should attend to the larger political-economic fields of the native empires. From the perspective of pre-imperial and sub-imperial polities seen as stratified, both the Aztecs and Inca appear less innovative of power and state organization. Now we must examine them afresh by considering how they succeeded in drawing constituencies into their orb. We can then compare the larger Inca and Aztec systems with respect to their evolution.

Our studies afford two different ways of accounting for sub-imperial continuity under the sway of empire. On the one hand, supremacy did not have the power to alter some characteristics of regionally organized polities. On the other hand, continuities reflect organization out of which supremacies could grow and upon which they could build. The two explanations bring empire and subordinate polity closer to one another in the power and organization we now attribute to them.

Just as in other systems of regionally organized agrarian society, the enduring of sub-imperial life in Mesoamerica and the Andes stemmed to some degree from adaptations to the constraints and potentials of geography that supremacy did not have the power to alter quickly. Cycles of imperial ascendance and decline in China, for example, did not modify the hierarchically nested regional ground plan of Chinese society. In this plan the physiographic constraints on transport and trade served to orient districts of agrarian villages toward standard market towns. G. William Skinner (1971) argues that these districts continued fundamentally to organize regional kinship, marriage, politics, and religion even as they entered into empire in its ascendance or retrenched in its decline. We have to undertake regional systems analysis to decide whether Mesoamerican and Andean sub-imperial life had a basis in the organizing of natural regions comparable to that of the Chinese standard marketing district. Yet even without such analysis, we begin to connect the sub-imperial staying power of these civilizations to the degree of development of their regional foundations. In the Andes, as Franklin Pease observes, core *altiplano* kingdoms highly integrated as vertical archipelagos (such as the Lupaca) withstood Inca supremacy much less altered than did less-integrated frontier polities on the tropical forest slopes (such as the Chachapoyas). Thus the ability to endure supremacy unaltered varied to some degree with the polity's level and extent of naturally based integration.

The manner in which supremacy evolved also gave rise to continuity in sub-imperial life. It is now fully evident that the Aztec Triple Alliance and Tawantinsuyu did not develop from relatively primitive polities, as some writers (e.g., Eisenstadt 1963:11) have assumed. Rather, both grew out of ethnic kingdoms of the same kind they subsumed, and many of our contributors believe that both built supremacy by enlarging and extending previously evolved principles of sub-imperial organization.

Pedro Carrasco, for example, argues that the so-called evolution of Aztecs from tribe to empire was nothing of the kind, for it involved no fundamental changes in the estate-stratified political economy of central Mexico. Long before Aztec ascendance, overlordships exacted labor service and tribute from constituencies on the same principles already obligating commoners within them to serve and tribute their direct lords. Direct lords maintained a high degree of autonomy in local rule. Confederation and conquest could alter the alignments of political integration without modifying the stratification fundamental to them. Carrasco believes that Aztec hegemony did not change stratification fundamentally. For example, the Aztecs experimented only rudimentarily with administrative mechanisms beyond the scope of earlier overlordships such as provincial tribute depositories, garrisons, and the relocating of conquered groups. Otherwise polity and economy remained fused, and the state continued undifferentiated from the dominant estate. Thus Aztec supremacy entailed little sub-imperial change.

Analogously, the Inca enlarged and extended warehousing, colonizing, and other institutions already evident in pre-imperial rule, often leaving sub-imperial life internally intact. Murra and Pease discuss ethnic kingdoms, ruled indirectly by the Inca entirely through ethnic leadership. These populaces labored for the state by continuing the exploiting of diverse econiches already inherent in their vertical archipelago organization, and their internal affairs appear to have been altered little in other respects.

State supremacy also stood to gain from preserving significant aspects of sub-imperial life, particularly structures of production, as a foundation for activities in the imperial arena. This was the case both before and after Spanish conquest. Karen Spalding examines what

Spanish colonial society had to gain from a policy preserving the ethnic polities from which the Inca had drawn so much surplus as self-sustaining, semiautonomous Indian republics. She argues that the pre-capitalist economy of colonial Peru, oriented primarily to the export of silver, would have stagnated utterly had not the state actively intervened to guarantee both supply and demand for goods circulating in the market. In the last analysis, all this dynamism stemmed from surplus stripped from Indian republics by various levies. The tribute Indians paid in specie sustained native governing officials as well as the clergy and crown officials administering them and also provided steady income for *encomenderos*. Tribute goods auctioned by the state to colonial vendors guaranteed a steady supply of circulating market commodities. Levies of Indian labor sustained mining for export. The policies sustaining the Indian republics preserved the structures for producing these forms of surplus.

For those interested in the impact of European colonialism and capitalism on Third World peoples, these studies of sub-imperial continuity and of the forces engendering it will afford a rare view of how a particular articulation within the capitalist world system emerged as a product of history. More than 25 years ago Eric Wolf (1955, 1957) sought to explain how the closed-corporate articulation of the Indian community under capitalism in Latin America grew out of conquest and the subsequent dualizing of the colonial economy into an entrepreneurial sector and a peasant sector upon which entrepreneurs drew as a reserve for labor. Forced to subsist on limited and territorially segregated lands, Indians elaborated upon corporate control of land, ritual to ensure redistribution of surplus, and ethnic identity. These constituted cultural barriers for Indians to prevent their loss of one another's labor through emigration and to defend their situation in a dualized capitalist society. Now we are able to relate many elements of this articulation—corporate identity, labor-intensive production, redistribution, and significant rights in people rather than goods—back to different modes of production and articulation within the indigenous civilizations in a manner that helps trace forward a particular transition to capitalism.

Empire Building

When we shift our analysis to the development of indigenous empires, we also have to consider how they changed the political environment of sub-imperial constituencies they formed around. Lasting hegemonies do not merely grow out of or build upon constituencies without forestalling sub-imperial realignments that bring down the hegemonic house of cards.

What was the nature of the power with which the Inca and Aztec held their sway? Our sub-imperial emphasis particularly elucidates this power in terms of what Etzioni calls compliance, that is, "the relationship consisting of the power employed by superiors to control subordinates and the orientation of subordinates to this power" (1961:xv). More specifically, this refers to the alienation or commitment with which subordinates respond to the three types of power—coercive, remunerative, and normative—that superiors can employ. Primarily by exploring how sub-imperial constituencies articulated with empire, we examine these relationships between rulers and the ruled under Inca and Aztec hegemony. What we see in the development of both empires is a temporal shift from coercive, to remunerative, and finally to normative relationships. This is coupled with another change that is more apparent under the Inca. The situation in which constituents are endorsing sub-imperial leaders from below gives way to that in which the state is coopting and authorizing them from above.

An older emphasis on the militarism of these New World empires bears reexamination with respect to the role of coercion in empire building. Inca militarism is a case in point. Interpreting the Inca system of roads and way stations in terms of the deploying and provisioning of troops, many writers (e.g., Gorenstein 1966) conclude that military force was the key instrument of Inca political centralization. But coercion alienates those it controls, and it may not have figured so prominently in sustained articulation of the Inca state.

Craig Morris, for example, has begun to reinterpret the functions of the centers the Inca built along state roadways. His excavations at Huanuco Pampa, one of the largest, call into question the coercive function of these sites. Huanuco Pampa lacks fortifications and facilities to garrison troops. Only one small structure appears specialized enough to have housed state-level elite, suggesting no plethora of administrators. Instead, the excavations show the site served for storing supplies and brewing *chicha*, which was a prestation Andean sub-imperial leaders gave their followers in return for *mit'a* labor. Morris suggests the Inca had to establish these centers to co-opt regional leaders and help them administer their subjects for the state through state-supported public hospitality rather than through force. These findings emphasize the remunerative, as opposed to the coercive, power of the state. Inca hegemony undoubtedly arose through conquest or coercive threat, but once formed, its power over subjects, as Morris points out, was in no sense automatic or absolute. Their commitment had constantly to be earned.

Remunerative power figured importantly as an alternative to coercion in both empires. Although coercion played a role in the initial exacting of tribute or (in the case of the Inca) alienating of land for the state, both systems rewarded constituents committed to regular tribute both materially, and by according them substantial autonomy over their internal affairs. The Inca seem to have gone farther than the Aztec Triple Alliance in generating and using state economic resources as material reward. John Murra's earlier work (1955, 1960, 1962) has emphasized how the Inca redistributed food, cloth, weapons, and other products of labor service to constituents and retainers as state reward or generosity. In this volume Nathan Wachtel gives a sense of the scale and scope of such redistribution. He describes how Huayna Capac (ruling ca. 1493–1525) colonized the entire Cochabamba Valley as a state enterprise to legitimate and reward ethnic leaders from every quarter of the Inca realm. Fourteen thousand ethnic *mitima* permanent colonists and periodic *mit'a* corvees were brought in from other areas and put to work to produce goods from specific tracts for these leaders. But according a measure of political autonomy from above was probably equally important a reward for constituencies regularly fulfilling their tribute obligations. As Murra's discussion of *mit'a* obligations shows, great indirectness of Inca rule through state-authorized ethnic leaders accompanied the most elaborate differentiating of the services their subjects willingly performed for the state.

The identification of normative or ideological means of securing constituents' loyalties further displaces coercion from the central role it had assumed in older conceptions of these empires. John Rowe explores how initially coercive policies, devised by the Inca to undercut the potential for revolt, probably unified the empire more comprehensively by conferring honor and status on sub-imperial elites. For example, the Inca first required provincial nobility to send their children to Cuzco for education so as to hold these families' loyalties hostage, but those so educated formed future generations of provincial leaders whose identities had taken shape around the ideology of the state. Statuses initially created to expropriate labor for the state came also to undercut traditional provincial loyalties and to enhance bonds to the state. Thus *yanaconas,* raised in the personal retinues of the Inca ruler or Inca governors, often gained further honor through administrative positions reserved for those with strong bonds to the central government. When the Inca selected daughters of nobility from one region to

give as brides to honor men of other regions, they engendered a cosmopolitan, trans-regional association with the state in the nobility they
authorized to undertake provincial rule.

Under the Inca, compliance appears to have increasingly shifted
through time from coercive to remunerative and finally to normative
integration. This trend makes sense for an imperial system that was
expanding militarily while striving to overcome alienation in its hinterlands and to generate full commitment at its core.

Aztec supremacy also appears to have emerged by engendering
commitment through remunerative and then increasingly normative
rewards, especially for close associates of ruling dynasties. J. Rounds
focusses on Aztec leadership and the problems it encountered as elites
competed for the new resources flowing into the political arena from
Tenochca ascendancy in the Valley of Mexico. He interprets changes
in Aztec succession as strategic solutions for the centrifugal strains
among those elite who could claim close ties to leaders through kinship and strategic marriage and thus could compete for resources. As
resources grew in magnitude, leaders shared key offices, controlling
them among collateral lines of the ruling dynasty and diffusing the
remunerative power of the ruler. At the same time, the ritual and
sacred trappings of the ruler's position grew in emphasis, seemingly to
heighten his normative power.

Material and moral rewards were not the only means for gaining
and holding sway over sub-imperial constituencies. Under the Inca, at
least, state administration altered the position of sub-imperial elites to
the advantage of imperial integration by narrowing elites' independent
authority as leaders while fitting them into a broader administrative
hierarchy. Catherine Julien explores how Inca decimal administration
shifted the position of the leaders of the kingdom of Lupaca in these
ways. Decimal administration, attributed by later Inca to the reigns of
Pachakuti (up to ca. 1471) and his son Thupa 'Inka (ca. 1471–93),
assigned citizens' labor obligations to the Inca state. It aggregated them
into units of 10, 50, 100, 1000, 5000, and 10,000, and established a
corresponding hierarchy of officials to administer their labor. The decimal system was the ultimate device for converting leadership endowed
or delegated from below into leadership authorized from above.

In setting up decimal administration, Julien argues, the Inca
curbed the delegated power of local elites not only by replacing those
with disloyal tendencies, but also by reducing their discretionary control over citizens' labor, making many citizens' assignments permanent through the generations. At the same time, elites from a kingdom
such as Lupaca received positions as decimal officers over their own

constituencies or further up in the hierarchy. Obligating even decimal officers to participate in public works, albeit in inverse proportion to their rank, and symbolizing their relative status in the imperial hierarchy in other ways, the system effaced heterogenous regional variations in local leaders' claimed positions and linked them into an emerging imperial class system.

The issue of political evolution is worth examining in light of what we have learned about these dynamics of Inca and Aztec empire building. Did either development bring about fundamental and lasting change?

I have already alluded to Pedro Carrasco's theory that Aztec ascendance involved no fundamental changes in the principles of central-Mexican stratification. He characterizes the normative and remunerative processes of marital alliance and strategic manipulating of dynastic succession similarly as part of a previously evolved repertory of strategies enabling one central Mexican hegemony to displace another. Carrasco acknowledges that the Inca achieved far greater political centralization than the Aztecs; yet he argues that the Inca, like the Aztecs, did not fundamentally alter the type of stratification in which the economically powerful coincided with a ruling estate legitimated by descent in, or affinity to, a leading dynasty. Here Carrasco echoes Wittfogel's conclusion that hydraulic civilizations, among which he included the Andean and Mesoamerican, "in contrast to the stratified agrarian societies of Medieval Europe, . . . failed of their own inner forces to evolve beyond their general pattern" of social stratification (Wittfogel 1955:43). Neither ascendance brought about changes in class relations to the means of production, upon which Carrasco hinges his typology and his conclusion that the Inca and Aztec were fundamentally similar.

The question of evolution, by definition, has to be framed with respect to the long-term trajectory of political development. Would the Inca or Aztec hegemonies, but for the Spanish, not have succumbed to centrifugal strains tending to segment empires back down to a level of lower, sub-imperial integration? Or was the rapidity of conquest itself a consequence of structural weakness? Could either empire have sustained hegemony long enough to alter the foundations of its respective civilization? We have seen reason to attribute to the Inca a greater development of political centralization. But our fresh sub-imperial perspective should give pause to the guess that the Inca could succeed where the Aztec Triple Alliance would fail, for the perspective reveals how developed and enduring those sub-imperial foundations were.

Acknowledgments

This introduction draws liberally from comments and suggestions from several contributors, especially James Lockhart, Pedro Carrasco, John Elliott, John Murra, John Rowe, and Karen Spalding. Jane Collier, Don Donham, Nancy Donham, and Renato Rosaldo also will recognize their influence on it. These various points of view have not always been possible to reconcile, and I accept responsibility for the interpretation I have laid upon them.

References

Altman, Ida, and James Lockhart, (editors)
    1976   *Provinces of early Mexico: variants of Spanish American regional evolution.* UCLA Latin American Center Publications. Los Angeles: University of California Press.
Barth, Fredrik
    1959   *Political leadership among Swat Pathans.* London School of Economics Monographs on Social Anthropology No. 19. London: University of London, The Athlone Press.
Baudin, Louis
    1928   *L'empire socialiste des Inka.* Paris: Institut d' Ethnologie.
Calnek, Edward
    1978   El sistema de mercado de Tenochtitlán. In *Economía política e ideología in el México prehispánico,* edited by P. Carrasco and J. Broda. Mexico City: Instituto Nacional de Antropología e Historia. Pp. 95–112.
Carrasco, Pedro
    1963a   Los caciques chichimecas de Tulancingo. *Estudios de Cultura Nahuatl* **4:**85–91.
    1963b   Las tierras de dos indios nobles de Tepeaca en el siglo XVI. *Tlalocan* **4**(2):97–119.
    1966   Documentos sobre el rango de tecuhtli entre los nahuas tramontanos. *Tlalocan* **5:**133–160.
    1969a   Mas documentos sobre Tepeaca. *Tlalocan* **6**(1):1–37.
    1969b   Nuevos datos sobre los nonalco de habla mexicana en el Reino Tarasco. *Estudios de Cultura Náhuatl* **8:**215–221.
    1970   Carta al rey sobre Cholula. *Tlalocan* **6**(2):176–192.
    1976   Estratificación social indígena en Morelos durante el siglo XVI. In *Estratificación social en la Mesoamérica prehispánica,* edited by P. Carrasco, J. Broda, et al. Mexico City: Instituto Nacional de Antropología e Historia.
    1977   Los señores de Xochimilco en 1548. *Tlalocan* **7:**229–265.
    1980   Markets and merchants in the Aztec economy. *Journal of the Steward Anthropological Society* **11**(2):249–269.
Carrasco, Pedro, Johanna Broda, et al.
    1976   *Estratificación social en la Mesoamérica prehispánica.* Mexico City: Instituto Nacional de Antropología e Historia.
Carrasco, Pedro, and Johanna Broda (editors)
    1978   *Economía política e ideología en el México prehispánico.* Mexico City: Instituto Nacional de Antropología e Historia.

Choy, Emilio
  1960   Sistema social incaico. *Idea, Artes y Letras* (Lima), abril–junio, pp. 10–12.
Eisenstadt, S. N.
  1963   *The political system of empires.* New York: The Free Press.
Etzioni, Amatai
  1961   *A comparative analysis of complex organizations: on power, involvement, and their correlates.* New York: The Free Press.
Fortes, Meyer, and E. E. Evans-Pritchard (editors)
  1940   *African political systems.* London: Oxford University Press.
Gibson, Charles
  1964   *The Aztecs under Spanish rule: a history of the Indians of the Valley of Mexico, 1519–1810.* Stanford: Stanford University Press.
Gluckman, Max
  1965   *Politics law and ritual in tribal society.* Chicago: Aldine.
Gorenstein, Shirley
  1966   The differential development of New World empires. *Revista Mexicana de Estudios Antropológicos* **20**:41–67.
Lockhart, James
  1972   The social history of colonial Spanish America: evolution and potential. *Latin American Research Review* **7**(1):6–46.
MacLeod, Murdo
  1973   *Spanish Central America: a socioeconomic history, 1520–1720.* Berkeley: University of California Press.
Murra, John
  1955   *The economic organization of the Inca State.* Ph.D. Dissertation, Department of Anthropology, University of Chicago.
  1960   Rite and crop in the Inca State. In *Culture in history: essays in honor of Paul Radin,* edited by S. Diamond. New York: Published for Brandeis University by Columbia University Press.
  1962   Cloth and its functions in the Inca state. *American Anthropologist* **64**(4):710–728.
  1970   Current research and prospects in Andean ethnohistory. *Latin American Research Review* **5**(1):3–36.
  1972   El 'control vertical' de un máximo de pisos ecológicos en la economía de las sociedades andinas. In *Documentos para la historia y etnología de Huánuco y la selva central.* Huánuco: Universidad Nacional Hermilio Valdizán, **2**:427–76.
Olivera, Mercedes
  1978   *Pillis y Macehuales: las formaciones y los modos de producción de Tecali del siglo XII al XVI.* Mexico City: Ediciones de la Casa Chata.
Reyes Garcia, Luis
  1977   *Cuauhtinchan del Siglo XII al XVI: Formación social y desarrollo histórico de un señorio prehispánico.* Wiesbaden: Franz Steiner.
Ricard, Robert
  1966   *The spiritual conquest of Mexico: an essay on the apostolate and the evangelizing methods of the mendicant orders in New Spain, 1523–1572.* Translated by Lesley Byrd Simpson. Berkeley: University of California Press.
Rowe, John Howland
  1951   Colonial portraits of Inca nobles. *The civilizations of ancient America,* edited by S. Tax. Chicago: University of Chicago Press. Pp. 258–268.
  1976   El movimiento nacional Inca del siglo XVIII. In *Tupac Amaru II—1780,* edited

by Alberto Flores Galindo. Lima: Retablo de Papel. Pp. 11–66. (First published in *Revista Universitaria* (Cuzco) No. 7, 1954.)

Skinner, G. William
  1971 Chinese peasants and the closed community: an open and shut case. *Comparative Studies in Society and History* **13**(3):270–281.

Spalding, Karen
  1972 The colonial Indian: past and future research perspectives. *Latin American Research Review* **7**(1):47–76.

Swartz, Mark J., Victor W. Turner, and Arthur Tuden
  1966 *Political anthropology.* Chicago: Aldine.

Taylor, William Burley
  1972 *Landlord and peasant in colonial Oaxaca.* Stanford: Stanford University Press.

Wakeman, Frederic, Jr., and Carolyn Grant
  1975 *Conflict and control in Late Imperial China.* Berkeley: University of California Press.

Wittfogel, Karl A.
  1955 Developmental aspects of hidraulic societies. In *Irrigation Civilizations: A Comparative Study* by Julian Steward *et al.* Social Science Monographs I. Washington, D.C.: Pan American Union.
  1957 *Oriental despotism: a comparative study of total power.* New Haven: Yale University Press.

Wolf, Eric R.
  1955 Types of Latin American peasantry: a preliminary discussion. *American Anthropologist* **57**:452–471.
  1957 Closed corporate peasant communities in Mesoamerica and central Java. *Southwestern Journal of Anthropology* **13**:1–18.

PART I

A Comparative Model

1

The Political Economy
of the Aztec and Inca States

Pedro Carrasco

Editors' Introduction

In providing an overview Pedro Carrasco stresses the similarities in the political economy of the Aztec and Inca states at the time of Spanish conquest. In both cases, the state intervened in the economy and exacted tribute, usually in labor rather than kind. Both states grew up within broadly tropical zones where altitude brought major ecological variations. Diverse and relatively autonomous ethnic groups often inhabited different ecological niches and became interdependent through exchanging resources. This model of state organization views the well-known differences between the two states more as matters of degree and emphasis than substance.

This chapter compares the political economies of the Aztec and Inca civilizations. There is sufficient similarity between the two to justify placing both systems within one broad type of economic organization; an understanding of this similarity then makes possible a better assessment of the differences between the two.

Comparisons between the Mesoamerican and Andean civilizations have been common in the past. Some of these comparisons have been of a historical or diffusionist type, as in the discussions about possible connections between Mesoamerica and the coasts of northern Peru and of Ecuador. Others have been of a typological kind, more in the social science tradition, as for example, Katz's book on ancient American civilizations (1974), or Wittfogel's analysis of both Meso-american and Andean societies within his hydraulic society model (1957). This chapter follows in the latter tradition and considers only the political economy of the Aztec and Inca empires; it does not explore questions of their developmental backgrounds as might be inferred from an archaeological record spanning many centuries, or their possible historical connections.[1]

Assuming for each of the two areas a more or less stable structure at the time of the conquest, I examine the interconnections of the various aspects of society. Therefore, I do not stress evolutionary processes. This is not because of a lack of interest in social change; it simply means that I have chosen as my research strategy to start by analyzing how Mesoamerican and Andean societies worked at the periods best documented in our sources, that is, during the Aztec and Inca empires.[2]

Comparisons of the Aztec and Inca systems have often stressed their differences in order to define the individuality of each case. This chapter emphasizes their similarities. The shared features that make up a common type of economic organization are first formulated and the points of contrast are later discussed in terms of this common system.

My interpretation of both the Inca and Aztec economic organizations being of a common type depends to a large extent on my theoretical basis. I hold that production is the key area in the organization of any economy and that the understanding of any economic system and the establishment of any typology has to take as its central point the analysis of production. In the process of production converge, first, the material factors of production, that is, the natural resources exploited and the tools employed; second, the relations of production, that is, the social relations that occur in the process of production; and third, the property system, in other words, the rights that men have over material goods. In this way, the analysis of production compels us from the start to examine ecology, technology, and social structure as well as the relations among them. It is thus a key to all basic social processes.

Economic Organization

The basic and most significant characteristic of the Aztec and Inca economies is that they were politically organized economies; that is, the economic process was embedded in the political institutions of a stratified society. The common system can be briefly defined as follows.

The basic subsistence technique is intensive agriculture on permanent fields relying exclusively on human energy with the use of simple tools. The basic factors of production, land and labor, are controlled by the political organization. Two major categories of land exist. One is in the possession of the peasants, who produce for their own support as household units with supplementary help from labor exchange and cooperation at the community level. These peasant producers are always subject to the rendering of labor services and in some places also of tribute in kind. The peasant household, therefore, is one of the major units of production in these societies. The other type of land is held by institutions or members of the ruling level and is worked with the labor services of peasants. It is thus the basis for other production units; these are managed by institutions or members of the upper social level who use public lands and the labor services of the commoners assigned to them. The labor for units larger than the household is always provided as politically required services from determined status groups. Craft production takes place along similar lines either in household units or under the management of upper level institutions based on public resources and the labor services required from artisans.

Circulation takes place primarily in accord with administrative decisions, and wealth is distributed on the basis of status. In the case of the ruling estate, income is received primarily in the form of products from public lands and shares from other forms of revenue. The market mechanism exists to fill the gaps left by the politically defined distribution. It is of secondary importance because it does not enter into the process of production; land and labor are not handled as commodities.

The surplus appropriated by the ruling estate is used in maintaining its members and their privileged status, in the support of public works for the common good (such as irrigation works), and in ostentation (much of it in religious ceremony).

Let us examine these various features in more detail.

As in all archaic civilizations, intensive agriculture was the material basis of Mesoamerican and Andean societies. Generally, intensive methods of cultivation with high levels of productivity permit a more complex division of labor and the existence of a numerous population. Intensive cultivation also results in permanent utilization of the soil and in forms of ownership and control of the land that will direct part of what is produced to persons other than the cultivator himself.

A variety of techniques were used in both Mesoamerica and the

Andes, according to the nature of the lands and of the plants under cultivation: irrigation, fertilization, and modifications of the natural configuration of the land (by such means as terraces and raised or sunken fields). These techniques make cultivated land itself partly a product of human effort.

Agriculture was carried on with only rudimentary tools, and an intensive investment of labor was of greater importance than the complexity of the tools employed. The number of cultigens was very high and provided both food and raw materials for crafts. Given the great environmental variety in these two areas of civilization, almost all the plants that had been domesticated in the Americas could be cultivated in both areas.

In contrast with the great number of cultigens, very few domestic animals were kept, and their use was less varied and more restricted geographically than in Old World civilizations. In any case, with the exception of the partial use of llama manure as fertilizer, domestic animals were not integrated into the agricultural technology.

Industry was at a technical level similar to that of agriculture. The most highly developed were characterized by intensive and highly skilled human effort using simple tools. The slight utilitarian use of metal and the absence of the wheel and of work animals make clear the technical limitations of both industry and agriculture.

A characteristic of both centers of civilization in the New World was large-scale construction using great masses of workers. This is seen most memorably in the monumental architecture of public buildings such as temples, palaces, and storehouses; other examples include fortresses, roads, irrigation systems, dikes, and terracing that utilized and conserved hilly terrain. All such works constitute either the infrastructure necessary for the production and circulation of goods that are fundamental to the society, or else the means of demonstrating and maintaining the power of the rulers.

In spite of important differences, Mesoamerica and the Andean region present similar environmental factors: Both lie within the tropics and are crossed by high mountain ranges. This means in both cases that the land is divided into a great number of clearly separated natural regions that present different ecological conditions and resources.

The environmental diversity was related to the ethnic multiplicity and regionalism that were characteristic of both areas. From an economic point of view the diversity of resources in contiguous zones encouraged relations of interdependence among the inhabitants of different econiches. This was achieved through a variety of procedures. At times a given social unit utilized different environments directly; in other cases, different social groups exploited different environmental resources and were connected through systems of exchange based either on political relations or on commerce.

For the conservation and transmission of information certain techniques, such as the Inca *quipus* and the Mesoamerican pictographs, were used. These served as mnemonic aids and permitted the recording of numerical data necessary for the management of the economy. However, neither area had a true writing system, that is, a means of reproducing oral texts in their entirety. Only when Maya inscriptions have been completely deciphered will we know to what extent there may have been an exception in their case.

In both Mesoamerica and the Andes the sixteenth-century writers tell us that peasants were jacks-of-all-trades who could take care of all the basic necessities of their households, in agriculture as well as in craft production. Members of the family group constructed the simple peasant house and wove cloth for the family's clothes. To a large extent, therefore, the peasant household was organized as a self-sufficient unit. Some of the artisans who produced for the use of others were only part-time specialists, who also cultivated some land for their own subsistence. Thus, like the farmers, they were producing both for their own needs and also for local exchange; in addition, they either paid tribute or gave labor services in their specialized activities. The more intensive specialization was associated with the highly skilled crafts of artisans working for the upper level of society. In this case their products would be luxury objects for the rulers or buildings and ceremonial objects for state activities.

The cultivation of lands assigned to members and institutions of the ruling class and the construction of public works were effected through the personal services exacted from the mass of peasants. There are two basic elements in this system: First, the workers rendered their services during limited periods of time; second, because of the lack of draft animals and machinery a great number of workers were needed to accumulate sufficient work energy. These two elements were especially true in construction works, which is where the simple cooperation of great masses of workers was most used. Therefore, a form of labor organization prevailed similar to a military organization. It was based on the classification of the whole population in units arranged according to the numbering system of each region (vigesimal in Mesoamerica, decimal in the Andes), the age of the workers, and their territorial or social unit. Teams were formed to work in community projects, in production for their chiefs, and in public works according to the principle labeled in Spanish *rueda y tanda* ("turn and team"). Each team of workers discharged its obligations in turn, thus sharing the work load evenly among the available workers and at the same time maintaining a steady labor supply. This system was related to well-developed time counts in terms of which the work periods due from each group or individual were specified.

Social Stratification

The social division of labor in these two societies also included a distinction between those occupied in the different lines of material production and those who, supported by the former, were devoted to managerial and other nonproductive activities; in other words, these were stratified societies. As in other early civilizations, stratification was of the *estate* type. By this I mean a system in which there are politically defined social categories whose members have particular sets of rights and obligations in economic, political, and other social fields. Thus, in Aztec and Inca societies members of each estate had different property rights, tribute obligations, sumptuary rules, political rights, etc. However, the classification of every individual within an estate system did not eliminate social mobility. Within each estate there were distinctions as to the distribution of economic resources or political functions not strictly ascribed by estate rules. Also, social mobility could take the form of moving from one estate to another with the accompanying loss or acquisition of the rights and obligations pertaining to one or another estate.

This estate system was the basis in these societies of a power structure that controlled the distribution of land and labor and that also defined and regulated the production units.

In both civilizations social stratification was characterized by the existence of two major estates. The mass of the population were the commoners, organized in local communities that had the use of certain lands for their own sustenance but with the obligation of rendering personal services or tribute. Commoners participated in local government at the community level but not, as a rule, in the higher levels of wider political entities.

The dominant or ruling estate consisted of a hereditary nobility whose members had rights to the tribute and personal services rendered by the commoners. They also enjoyed privileges within the political organization, in effect constituting the personnel of government in all the higher administrative, military, and religious levels.

In both the areas we are comparing, one also finds intermediate social strata whose estate position was less precisely defined. Members of such strata might belong to lower levels of the noble estate, or they might be individuals or groups chosen from among the common people; sometimes they had a particular ethnic affiliation. They carried out functions pertaining to the organization of the state or were included in the households of the members of the ruling estate. They included the artisans who specialized in the production of luxury goods, the merchants, and lower level officers of the military and governmental organizations.

On another social level in both regions were certain menial groups; they were in a position inferior to that of the average common people because they were subject to a greater economic dependency. They included farmhands on state lands and those who worked as porters, servants, or clowns in state palaces or for members of the dominant estate. In some cases their position has been compared to serfdom or slavery. To a more limited extent individuals of this menial or semislave level may have also been in the service of commoners, but these are fewer in number and are incorporated into the households of their masters.

Corporate Groups

The existence of corporate groups with important economic functions was basic in these societies; they appeared within both social levels, the nobility and the commoners. They may also have been internally differentiated within each of the two ranks. These corporate groups were usually labeled *calpulli* in Mexico and *ayllu* in the Andes. Much has been speculated about the meaning of these terms from the point of view of kinship. I would emphasize, however, that descent simply regulated the composition and the recruitment process of the corporate groups. What matters most in an analysis of economic and political structure are the activities of such groups. They were corporate segments within a given political unit that functioned collectively as holders of a corporate title to land, in the setting up of cooperative work teams, in their collective responsibility for the prestation of labor services or tribute, and in the division of labor in productive, administrative, or ceremonial activities.

The different corporate groups were coordinated into larger social and political units by a division of labor that included either specialization in different activities or the procedure of taking turns in order to provide the same activity at different time periods. This latter procedure required the existence of numerical schemes for the coordination of human groups and time periods. Such schemes were an important characteristic of these societies, and were also related to natural forces, world directions, or calendrical periods.

In some way, these corporate groups were bound together by concepts of common descent; whether such concepts had to do with ethnic origin or a particular type of kinship is in this discussion of secondary importance. At any rate, there are differences as to the extent to which terms such as *ayllu* and *calpulli* refer directly to kinship. The term *ayllu* is clearly applied in old sources to a kin group; *calpulli* is used primarily for a social subdivision, although the idea of common origin of its members may also be present. The main point, however, is that these terms were applied to social subdivisions of various kinds, such as small rural communities or the wards or quarters into which cities were divided. Kinship rules were not necessarily uniform within the large areas and the many ethnic groups included in the Aztec and Inca empires.

Ethnicity and kinship are both of considerable importance in the definition of the estates and corporate groups that make up the system of social stratification in our two areas. Almost all regional political units—the dependent kingdoms (*tlatocayotl*) in Mexico or the provinces (*waman*) of the Inca empire—were pluriethnic societies, and the different ethnic units occupied somewhat different positions in the stratification scale. In the case of the wider political units, the ruling estate and the royal dynasty were clearly identified with a given ethnic element. This was the case of the Inca in Peru or of the Mexica and various Chichimeca ruling lineages in Mexico, which were superimposed on other ethnic groups. In these large polities, too, certain ethnic groups specialized in particular activities—such as various crafts, trade, or military service—that placed them on the intermediate levels of the social scale. Other ethnic groups were almost exclusively at the peasant level.

The ruling estate coincided almost entirely with the lineage of the ruler or with a series of noble lineages, that is, the ruling estate was organized into corporate groups defined on the principle of descent. Kinship, therefore, played a part in defining estate membership and in the transmission of offices, titles of nobility, and wealth.

The royal lineages of the Inca (*panaca*) and the palaces or chiefly houses (*tecpan, teccalli*) of Mexico are comparable corporate lineages that make up the composition of the upper levels of society. Differences in rank within the royal lineages and within the upper levels of society were also connected with the kinship principle because they were defined in terms of the different ranks of the royal wives or on the basis of relative distance from the direct line of the ruling sovereign.

All this shows that it is not possible to think that social stratification and the state arose in these societies through the growth of a civil type of organization based solely on property relations, moving away from a kinship based or gentile organization. In the native civilizations of the New World, as in some societies in Asia and Africa, the very principle of kinship provides the framework for the ascription of individuals to the different statuses in the stratification system, and kinship acts as an integrating factor in the definition of the corporate groups that make up the stratification structure.

Production Units

The approach favored here, which places emphasis on the organization of production, requires a detailed discussion of the social units in which production took place or that were expressly set up to engage in production. Present information on this subject is somewhat deficient, but the major points are clear. The commoner household was a basic production unit in cultivation and crafts. The working unit was the family; this unit could include other members of the household such as servants and, through labor exchange, members of other similar households in the community. The commoner household had an obligation to provide labor services that were used in joint enterprises at the community level or for the public works of the state.

The utilization of these labor services was related to the land system that assigned special plots to members of the ruling estate, officials, temples, and the ruler. Thus, production units of another type were organized for the cultivation of such lands. These units were under the management of stewards or petty officials. Corvée also supplied the labor for public projects such as water works, temples, palaces, roads, and terracing. Work teams were formed on the basis of the numerical organization of the population and the principle, described earlier, of *rueda y tanda*. Stewards in their official capacity arranged the drafting of the corvée workers, supplied them with tools and food, and directed the technical side of the work. Goods from the storehouses under their management could be used to reward the workers. Skilled artisans worked in temples and palaces for the production of goods delivered to their superiors. Among them were the women engaged in the production of high quality textiles (*aclla* in Peru, royal women in Mexico) and the craftsmen in Montezuma's palace.

An important feature of these societies was that the same organization for communal labor could be used for the labor exchange among households in the community, for communal work in the general interest of the local community, and for the corvées that would cultivate the public fields assigned to the ruler or build the public works demanded by the state.

I suggest, therefore, that an examination of production units reveals two basic levels: household production for the workers' support and reproduction, and publicly run enterprises on the public lands with the labor demanded from commoner householders. It reveals the close relationship between both levels because of the universal demands of labor services from commoner householders, and because the same principles of cooperation and labor draft organization were used both for the commoners' mutual labor exchanges and cooperation, and for the state's public works.

Distribution

The economy of these civilizations was basically a natural economy (i.e., almost all transactions were carried out in kind with those goods that would directly satisfy specified needs). They were thus economies in which production was aimed at use—whether the producers were producing for their own consumption, for that of their superiors, or for the expenses of collective activities of the local community or the state. In comparison, especially in the Andean region, the marketplace and money had limited importance. In Mesoamerica various goods, in addition to their value for use, were also employed as means of payment and served to effect transactions in frequent and well-attended markets. Nevertheless, mercantile activity had not entered into the organization of production; furthermore, the maintenance of the ruling class and the state through the revenue system was based on payments in labor and kind. In both civilizations, therefore, an economy controlled by the political structure predominated.

Thus, the accumulation of the economic surplus was brought about by the commoners' prestations and the appropriation by the state of the product of state enterprises. As is generally the case, a system of revenues levied in kind or labor implied that different social groups and even different communities or provinces contributed goods or services of different sorts according to the occupation of each group and the resources of each region.

The economic surplus was used for the maintenance of the dominant estate and for public works or other expenses of general interest. Part of this surplus went directly to individuals of the ruling estate or to institutions such as temples that had been endowed with goods-producing resources (i.e., lands and commoners whose surplus they extracted directly). Another part was accumulated in the sovereign's storehouses to be used as gifts to members and institutions of the ruling estate or for the support of those working on public projects. Public works carried on with this corvée labor included projects such as irrigation, terracing, and road building, which created and maintained the economic infrastructure. Another very considerable part of public works was the monumental architecture of temples, in which the economic, political, and religious power of the dominant estate took visible and lasting form. In times of necessity such as war or famine, the accumulated goods could also be used for the maintenance of the population.

Finally, part of the surplus was those luxury goods reserved for the dominant estate or for ceremonial use in religious festivals. Ceremonial expenses were considerable; celebrations were occasions for the distribution of goods such as clothing and jewels to the participants, for the consumption of great quantities of foodstuffs, and even for the destruction through sacrifice of goods and resources that represented part of the economic surplus.

Political System

Since we are dealing with politically directed economies, it is essential to assess similarities and differences on the basis of the respective political systems of the two areas.

As regards political organization, Mesoamerica and the Andean zone presented a clearly defined contrast at the time of the conquest. The Incas had unified all the areas of high culture in one centralized state; the whole civilized world known to Andean man had entered into a common political unit. In Mesoamerica different political units of a comparable level of civilization and with common cultural antecedents coexisted. The so-called Aztec empire consisted of what might be called a confederation of three political entities that were at least theoretically equal, and the greater part of the conquered territories had been integrated into the empire only in regard to tribute payments. The degree of political centralization was therefore much less than in the Andean world. In spite of this difference, however, there were important resemblances between the two regions in their forms of political organization.

In Mesoamerica, as in the Andes, the dominant estate coincided with the personnel of government. There was no distinction between an economically dominant class and those who governed. This identity of the economically powerful with the governing personnel is only one aspect of what has been called "primitive fusion," characteristic of primitive societies and archaic civilizations. To use a different terminology, there is no distinction between state and society, or indeed between private and public life. In these types of societies, activities that would be specialized functions of separate institutions in more complex societies occur in combined form within multifunctional institutions. In the civilized societies of Mesoamerica and the Andes economic, political, military, and ceremonial activities were closely integrated both as to institutions and personnel. The economy was directed by the state; economic relations in the production and distribution of goods were based on political relations of subjection and control. An essential part of the economic surplus was used for public works and the ceremonial expenses of political and religious institutions. Militarism was closely connected with religion; warriors and young men about to begin their military careers were the main participants in major rites and ceremonial observances of the yearly cycle. High-ranking government officers performed duties that were not only civil but military and religious as well.

Levels of politico-territorial integration also show fundamental similarities in Mesoamerican and Andean civilizations. In both areas the political entities of greatest size, which we call "empires," were constituted on the basis of a whole series of local units; each one had its own ethnic composition and particular internal organization based on the existence of peasant communities. When examined separately, these regional units reveal organizational traits similar to what has been described as characteristics of the chiefdom (cacicazgo) level. The local ruler had ethnic and sometimes kinship ties with his subjects; between him and them there were also economic relations based on reciprocity and redistribution that supported the common interests of the entire group. All this created feelings of community solidarity in opposition to other regions that constituted similar units. In the marginal areas of the empires, on the frontier or in the interior, there were minor political entities of this type similar to the chiefdoms of the circum-caribbean zone in their degree of social complexity. In the periods of political disintegration, which seem to have alternated with those of imperial integration, the number of political units of the chiefdom type would presumably increase.

Therefore the social transformation of the original Inca and Mexica (and Chichimeca) groups, which has often been described as an evolution from "tribe" to "empire," has to be seen in light of the fact that the wider political structures coexisted with their component regional units as well as with their marginal neighbors, whose organization was close to that of the chiefdom level of integration.

The distinction between the ruling estate and the commoners is most clearly seen when considering the empire as a whole. The chiefs of the various regions, related through descent or affinity to the imperial lineage, formed the upper social level of the whole empire. Within each regional unit, the ruling element consisted of the chief together with his relatives and attendants; local government was based on the functions that these persons assumed in the administration of the economy and the political organization. The household or palace of the chief was the central point of local public administration. Political unification came about when one or several of these regional units, previously independent, managed to acquire control over a great number of other regions. The resultant empire then accumulated its economic surplus from all of them, and the members of the dominant estate of the conquering region made up the highest level of the imperial government as a whole. Regional governments in subject areas were kept to the extent that the previously existing political entities became regional administrative units, and the native chiefs of each region continued to hold authority in local affairs. No matter how centralized an empire might appear to be, the survival of these local ethnic and political units was always evident; it is on the basis of these units that the empire had taken shape through processes of confederation and conquest. Furthermore, given the lack of physical and economic mobility (the lack both of efficient means of transportation and of a generalized use of money), the geographic extent of the empires compelled the formation of politico-territorial subdivisions with a considerable degree of autonomy.

The central government of these empires, then, was in effect similar to that of a single territory placed over all the others that it had conquered. The administration of the empire was closely related to the household of the ruler, for the highest imperial officials were chosen from among the ruler's closest relations. Local chiefs, by being kept in place as local governors, came to form part of the imperial administration. They became related through marriage with the imperial dynasty, and the chiefs or their sons attended the capital for certain ceremonial occasions. The heirs to local chieftainships went to the capital to be educated. Thus, they became culturally assimilated to the ruling group, while at the same time they served as hostages in case of conflict. On the other hand, provincial administration did not remain entirely in the hands of the local chiefs. In the various conquered regions, the central power established governmental mechanisms that it controlled directly. This is most highly developed in the Inca empire, but it is also found in a rudimentary form in the Aztec. Certain officials were placed above the local chiefs, on either a permanent or temporary basis, as tribute collectors and visiting judges or inspectors. Garrisons, tribute depositories, or rest houses were controlled directly from the center.

Conquered groups were moved from one part of the empire to another, and colonies of the dominant ethnic group were established in strategic points. Rebellion was thus made more difficult. Ethnic groups were scattered about the country, located far from the area they knew best, and mixed in with other ethnic groups with whom they had no ties of solidarity. Furthermore, these movements of population created governmental organs controlled directly by the central power. This was especially true if the people thus moved were colonies of the dominant ethnic group or of selected ethnic groups with specialized functions such as military responsibilities or the collection and storing of goods intended for the central power.

The means of increasing and maintaining the extension of the empire was always war and militarily imposed control. Occasionally booty may have been the principal object of a campaign, but there was always something more at stake than immediate plunder. A system of controls was set up that permitted the regular extraction of the economic surplus of conquered regions through the payment of tribute and labor services.

Points of Contrast

By recognizing that this general type of political economy was common to both the Aztec and Inca systems, we can better evaluate the peculiarities of each of these societies.

A number of contrasts between the Inca and Aztec economies are well known. The Andes offer a greater range of altitudes with very different environments under human exploitation; there was a high altitude area of tuber cultivation and domestication of auchenids, entirely absent in Mesoamerica. In the Andean area there was also much more use of metals for tools than was the case in Mesoamerica. The Inca empire had united into a single political unit all the civilized areas of the Andes, while Mesoamerica remained politically divided. Furthermore, the Inca political organization was more centralized and closely integrated than the Aztec empire. Consequently, there was

greater state control of the economy among the Inca. The state intervened more in the area of production. There were general renderings of
prestations in labor for publicly run units of production. Greater importance was laid on state redistribution and reciprocal exchanges in
the process of circulation. Because of the political fragmentation of the
Mesoamerican area, even such a powerful state as the Aztec empire did
not achieve a similar degree of centralization. Tribute in kind coexisted with prestations in labor, and the lack of extensive public works
in the conquered territories emphasizes the predatory side of the tribute levies in subject areas. Besides the politically controlled or regulated distribution of wealth, a system of markets flourished both in
internal and external trade.

These and other differences have long been pointed out. It has not
been the purpose of this paper to ignore or deny them, but I think that,
for the most part, they represent differences in the relative importance
in one or the other area of features that are actually present in both.

In the Andean area recent studies have pointed out the importance
of regional organizations, the existence of markets, and the distinction
between the personal estates of the Inca emperor and the state lands.
This has modified the picture often presented in the past of the Inca
economy and political organization as a monolithic structure. In the
Mesoamerican area the political character of the economy, especially
in regard to the importance of labor dues and utilitarian public works,
demands more emphasis than it has often received. It must also be
stressed that the market mechanism did not enter into the process of
production and that it was, in addition, subject to political controls.
The lands of the nobility that have sometimes been considered private
property were actually personal holdings of individuals from whom
public services were expected.

The differences between the political economies of our two areas
can therefore be expressed as variations of degree in terms of the
strength of organizational patterns present in both areas, primarily
degrees of economic and political centralization.

The greater political centralization of the Inca empire developed
with the conquest and incorporation of practically all the high culture
areas of South America. The Inca polity thus constituted a universal
empire. To this fact is related the empire's greater regimentation of
production and the standardization of revenue payments in the form of
labor services, the greater extent of public works to develop the productive capacity of areas incorporated into the empire, the greater concentration of the economic surplus in state storehouses, the system of

roads for its transportation, and the distribution by the state-run re-distribution mechanism (with the consequent lesser importance of commerce).

In contrast, Mesoamerica had not achieved total political integration. In this area a system of coexisting political units prevailed, which had developed stable patterns of interstate relations. In the political sphere these included regular embassies, invitations to ceremonial events, and rules about the proper conduct of warfare. In the economic sphere there were exchanges of presents among rulers, and professional merchants were given access to foreign territories where they participated in the activities of the marketplace in addition to effecting exchanges between the rulers. The importance of both interior and exterior trade in Mesoamerica lies in the fact that it constituted a supplementary means for the circulation of goods in an economy that the state had not entirely regimented through the mechanisms of tribute and redistribution.

The greater importance of trade in the northern end of the Inca empire, the area of late expansion, and the importance of traders in the Chincha coastal kingdom, which had a great pre-Inca tradition, suggest that the Inca state economy had developed from a previous situation in which commerce might have been more significant, as in the case of Mesoamerica. The possibility that a total conquest of Mesoamerica by the Aztecs could have led to an economy more like that of the Inca is a point that has been suggested by some scholars. However, at the time of the Spanish Conquest the Aztecs were still very far from having achieved such a result, and there is no clear evidence that it was heading in that direction.

I basically agree with Wittfogel's characterization of the distinction between Aztec and Inca economies, both of which he places in his hydraulic typology. In the simple type of the Inca there is state control of agriculture, craft production, and trade; in the semicomplex type of the Aztec there is state control of agriculture but some degree of independence in craft production and trade. However, the labor-intensive agricultural technology and the prevalence of prestations in labor for the cultivation of public lands and for public works define a particular level of technical and social complexity present in both areas. Furthermore, the limitations of mobility imposed by difficulties in transportation and the lack of a general mercantilization of the economy result in a situation in which even the most centralized polities have to endow their dependents not just with goods but with sources of production; in other words, there is of necessity a large measure of political and economic decentralization. This is one reason for the importance of sub-imperial regional units that are common to both empires. I would also stress the fact that the Mesoamerican market system, because of the existence of political controls such as price setting, can be better understood in connection with Polanyi's concepts of reciprocity and redistribution rather than in terms of the usual models of the free market. This brings the Aztec economy closer to the Inca type than would otherwise be the case.

Total control of the economy versus complete freedom of action, especially in fields such as craft production and trade, should be seen as polar types on a continuum, which can be used to analyze different modalities within various levels of technological and economic complexity. I am inclined to give greater importance to these levels than to the presence or absence of free craft production and trade.

The contrasts between Aztec and Inca, therefore, should not be seen as defining different major types of political economy. Rather, they characterize varieties within a basically similar developmental level, which is best defined in terms of the technology and the organization of production.

Notes

[1] My views about the Aztec economy are presented in more detail in Carrasco (1978). As regards the Inca economy, I have relied primarily on Hartmann (1968), Murra (1956, 1975), Rostworowski de Diez Canseco (1977), and Rowe (1946).

[2] I think that the native historical traditions of these areas can be best evaluated on the basis of an understanding of the societies that produced such traditions. However, especially in the case of Mesoamerica, I don't go so far as to doubt entirely the validity of traditional history (cf. Zuidema 1965).

Past studies, especially in the case of Mesoamerica, have assumed a model derived from Morgan's and Bandelier's early formulations that postulate a transition "from tribe to empire," that is, from a first stage based on communal, kinship-based institutions to a second one in which private property, social classes, and the state developed. Sometimes data referring to the contact period have been arbitrarily interpreted as applying to either the early or the late stage (Katz 1974:138ff.). I do not favor this procedure. As regards Mesoamerica, I think that the social changes reported in historical traditions represent cyclical or minor variations within a long-lasting social type (Carrasco 1971:371–374; cf. Bray 1977).

References

Bray, Warwick
    1977   Civilizing the Aztecs. In *The evolution of social systems*, edited by J. Friedman and M. J. Rowlands. London: Duckworth. Pp. 373–398.

Carrasco, Pedro
1971 Social organization of ancient Mexico. In *Handbook of Middle American Indians* (Vol. 10), edited by R. Wauchope. Austin: University of Texas Press. Pp. 349–375.
1978 La economía del México prehispánico. In *Economía política e ideología en el México prehispánico*, edited by Pedro Carrasco and Johanna Broda. México: Imagen. Pp. 13–76.
Hartmann, Roswith
1968 *Maerkte im alten Peru.* Bonn.
Katz, Friedrich
1974 *The ancient American civilizations.* New York: Praeger.
Murra, John
1956 The economic organization of the Inca state. Ph.D. dissertation, Department of Anthropology, University of Chicago.
1975 *Formaciones económicas y políticas del mundo andino.* Lima: Instituto de Estudios Peruanos.
Rostworowski de Diez Canseco, María
1977 *Etnía y sociedad: Costa Peruana prehispánica.* Lima: Instituto de Estudios Peruanos.
Rowe, John H.
1946 Inca culture at the time of the Spanish conquest. In *Handbook of South American Indians* (Vol. 2). Washington, D.C.: Smithsonian Institution. Pp. 183–230.
Wittfogel, Karl August
1957 *Oriental despotism.* New Haven, Connecticut: Yale University Press.
Zuidema, Reiner Tom
1965 Review of *Empire of the Inca*, by B. C. Brundage. *American Anthropologist* **67:**176–177.

PART II

Aztec State Formation

Patterns of Empire Formation in the Valley of Mexico, Late Postclassic Period, 1200–1521

Edward E. Calnek

Editors' Introduction

Edward Calnek argues that the Valley of Mexico showed surprisingly sparse settlement in the twelfth century. Up to this juncture Calnek (not unlike Murra) interprets states as forming on the basis of economic exchange arising from demographic growth within ecological constraints.

In central Mexico's next stage of development the cultural heritage of earlier states, particularly the ideology of dynasties ruled by divine right, now patterns the interchanges between polities. Some conquered others, claiming overlordship on the basis of Toltec ancestry. Rivalries for overlordship ensued with interdynastic marriages legitimating alliances. Extensive overlordships such as the Aztec Triple Alliance emerged without a large state bureaucracy because subordinated groups were allowed local rule. Their leaders were co-opted by material and ritual ties to imperial centers, and their nobility were obligated by kin alliances stemming from dynastic intermarriages. Under these conditions threats of force could convert bilateral treaties of exchange into exactions of tribute. Aztec administration did develop primarily in Tenochtitlan to manage tributes.

Introduction

The process of state and empire formation, which culminated in the rise of the Aztecs as a dominant power in northern Mesoamerica,

THE INCA AND AZTEC
STATES, 1400–1800

commenced with the founding of several dozen new city-states in the Valley of Mexico during the thirteenth century. This large-scale colonization occurred gradually over several decades, but it marked the beginning of a major transformation in the already ancient sequence of Mesoamerican cultural development.

Throughout the classic and early postclassic periods (A.D. 1–1200) no more than two or three major regional centers were simultaneously active in central Mexico. Teotihuacan was the dominant center until its collapse in about A.D. 750 (Millon 1973: Fig. 12; 1982). The flourishing of Cholula and Xochicalco—both smaller but highly urbanized centers—overlapped the end of this period. From the early tenth century until the end of the twelfth century, most of the high *altiplano* region was controlled by Tula and Cholula. Apart from these centers, it is difficult to identify settlements of intermediate rank with populations larger than about 2000–4000 inhabitants. Most rural populations instead were organized into small villages with a few hundred inhabitants, or in widely dispersed individual homesteads (Parsons 1974; Sanders *et al.* 1979).

This unusual pattern survived until the fall of Tula, after which refugee peoples from the north and west moved rapidly into central Mexico, absorbing or sweeping aside remnants of earlier populations, and laying a basis for the city-state system that was to emerge shortly thereafter. In the Valley of Mexico, more than 50 minuscule polities, each with territories of about 100–150 km^2, had been formed by the end of the thirteenth century (Gibson 1964:34; Sanders and Price 1968:151–152). A few more—including the Aztec capital, Tenochtitlan, and its sister-city, Tlatelolco—were founded in the mid-fourteenth century. However small in size, these were at least semiautonomous and self-governing communities, each with its own politico-religious center and recognized frontiers. Most remained intact not only until the time of the Spanish conquest in 1521, but throughout much of the colonial period.

Whereas earlier types of political organization may have inhibited rural demographic growth, the new pattern of dispersed political authority appears to have had the opposite result. By the late fifteenth century there were at least a dozen cities with populations larger than 10,000 in the Valley of Mexico alone, including Tenochtitlan with a population probably greater than 150,000 (Calnek 1976:288; Parsons 1974:101). Although no single city, possibly excepting Tenochtitlan, was as large as Teotihuacan at its height, the total number of city-dwellers was several times greater. Agricultural settlements were individually larger and more densely clustered than at any previous time.

Agricultural production, which also reached a peak of intensification, included widespread construction of irrigation systems, reclamation of swamplands for *chinampa* cultivation, and extensive terracing of mountain slopes and the higher piedmont zones (Armillas 1971; Parsons 1974:98–101).

Major political and demographic centers were growing up in full sight of each other. Thus Texcoco, Huexotla, and Coatlichan—all city-states of the first rank before the era of Tenochtitlan's ascendancy—were originally spaced at distances of about 2 km along the eastern shore of Lake Texcoco. At the time of the conquest they are said to have formed a zone of nearly continuous settlement extending for 5 km or more (Cook and Simpson 1948:34–46; Torquemada 1723 [Vol. I]:304). Tenochtitlan and Tlatelolco, both island-cities, were by the time of the conquest separated only by the width of a single canal. Both were approximately 6 km by causeway from Tlacopan on the mainland. Azcapotzalco was a kilometer or so further north.

This cheek-by-jowl distribution of primary political units, together with their exceptionally small size, necessarily influenced the external relations and internal development of each of the separate city-states. No individual polity remotely approached economic self-sufficiency, nor does this seem to have been particularly desired. Basic resources such as obsidian, salt, adobe, timber, building stone, firewood, and some agricultural crops could not be found easily within the narrowly circumscribed territorial frontiers of individual states. In earlier times, such strongly centralized states as those based on Teotihuacan or Tula could have easily extracted needed resources from their own widely deployed rural satellites. The only option for independent polities of the thirteenth century was exchange.

References to periodic markets in fact appear in very early historical records and become more frequent in later times (e.g., Durán 1967 [Vol. II]:49; Tezozomoc 1944:16–17). The critical role of trade is well illustrated by instances when potential military adversaries continued to visit each other's markets until an actual battlefield confrontation was imminent. When women from Tenochtitlan were finally turned out of the market at Coyoacan, preparations for active warfare were well advanced on both sides (Durán 1967 [Vol. II]:86–87; Tezozomoc 1944:44–45). Normal trade relations were generally resumed as soon as hostilities had ended.

The great cities of the classic and early postclassic periods were sufficiently distant from each other that their internal political development could be largely self-contained and self-generated. This was hardly possible under the conditions just described. From the beginning of the thirteenth century until the era of complete Aztec ascendancy, the real question was, Which of the several originally distinct political and cultural systems brought into the valley by the ethnically diverse founding populations would eventually predominate? In the remainder of this chapter, I briefly outline the main stages in the process of regional political development within which the solution to this and similar questions must be sought.

Early Development of the City-State System

The extreme fragmentation of politico-territorial units in the Valley of Mexico during the late postclassic period (1200–1520) can be traced to separate but related sets of events. First, within the Valley of Mexico, the collapse of Teotihuacan in about A.D. 750 was followed by the formation of numerous small rural settlements, which changed only slightly in the course of the next 5 centuries (Parsons 1974). Toward the end of the twelfth century, according to early historical references, these were further decimated by war, famine, and epidemic, so that the valley was an all but empty arena so far as its human population was concerned (see Calnek 1973; Guzman 1938; Ixtlilxochitl 1952 [Vol. II]:35–37; Torquemada 1723 [Vol. I]:40ff.).

Second, during the middle decades of the twelfth century, agricultural settlements in the northern frontier region of Mesoamerica were gradually abandoned, possibly because of prolonged drought, and their populations were reorganized into small mobile bands that began to move south in search of new lands (Adams 1977:241; Kelley 1971). At the same time, the still poorly understood Toltec empire centered in Tula declined in influence. In about 1168 or somewhat later, Tula itself was abandoned (Davies 1977:413; Jimenez Moreno 1954-1955: 224–225). The situation was further complicated by a southward movement of hunter–gatherer nomads—the so-called wild chichimecs—who had previously ranged over arid lands still further north (Davies 1980:42ff.).

When groups from each of these regions first began to move into the valley, abundant empty lands were open to occupancy. Groups from Tula, together with previously sedentary farmers from the north and west, quickly occupied the agriculturally rich lands in the south and west. Chichimec nomads meanwhile occupied land in the north and east. The historical records available for this era describe case after case in which small bands peacefully occupied suitable areas, constructed politico-religious centers, and began to cultivate the surrounding lands (see Chimalpahin 1965; Ixtlilxochitl 1952; Torquemada 1723 [Vol. I]). The only case where there was significant military resistance was in the southeast, where the founders of Amecameca forcibly dislodged an earlier population of Xochtecas, Olmecas, Quiyahuiztecas, and Cocoltecas (Chimalpahin 1965:77).

In some cases, several distinct bands came together in a loosely federated state, as at Chalco Tlalmanalco, where at least six were involved (Chimalpahin 1965:164–165). Latecomers, on the other hand, were often forced to disperse, or to settle as client peoples on land controlled by other groups. The Aztecs, for example, settled briefly in several localities before dividing into a main group, which founded Tenochtitlan and Tlatelolco, and several others which settled in Chalco, Colhuacan, Texcoco, and Azcapotzalco (Chimalpahin 1965:56, 58–59, 61; Ixtlilxochitl 1952 [Vol. II]:74).

The process of resettling vacant lands seems to have proceeded slowly. Although reliable population data are lacking, the very small territories claimed by individual city-states, as discussed earlier, suggest that founding populations were not larger than a few thousand individuals. The same conclusion is implied by the infrequency of genuinely severe military conflicts until the middle decades of the fourteenth century. The depredations of a marauding Nonoalca band led by Timal in the late thirteenth or early fourteenth century ended when this feared leader died in battle (Berlin 1948:35–36). Soon thereafter, the Aztecs were attacked and partly dispersed by a coalition of neighbors while encamped at Chapultepec. The opposing coalition disbanded once its immediate goal had been realized (Berlin 1948:36–37; Chimalpahin 1965:58ff.).

If currently accepted chronologies are even approximately correct, the first serious attempts at empire formation within the valley did not begin until a century and a half after the fall of Tula. This may have been the time required for even partial demographic recovery after the extremely sharp reductions in regional population said to have occurred in the turbulent years just before and after the collapse of the Toltec empire. It is significant that the Aztecs could still find unoccupied land for the founding of Tenochtitlan and Tlatelolco—albeit only by settling in swamplands rejected as unsuitable by others—as late as 1325 or even 1345. If this view is correct, the lack of intense warfare must be attributed less to any particular pacifism on the part of the new city-states than to a quite reasonable preoccupation with community building, land reclamation, and population growth until the point that military conquest could be profitable and not merely exciting.

In any case, this era of relative quiescence allowed the evolution of a highly complex pattern of city-state organization that was to dominate later political development until the Spanish conquest. All of the major politico-religious centers were established and their territorial frontiers defined during this period. When wars of conquest began on a large scale later in the fourteenth century, the ideological basis for perpetuating individual city-states as semiautonomous units within more inclusive types of regional organization was so firmly entrenched that it was not again seriously challenged.

The Formation of Dynastic Groups

The process of state formation in the late postclassic period was so intimately connected with the rise of hereditary dynastic groups that both must be discussed together under this heading. The city-states formed in the thirteenth century originally differed widely in the types of internal organization represented, but by the fifteenth century most were ruled by aristocratic lineages of Toltec descent and organized on closely similar principles of government.

The specific manner in which early patterns of authority (which differed from region to region within the valley) that were developed to cope with the need for mobility and military protection under the chaotic conditions prevailing in the twelfth and early thirteenth centuries gave way to more uniform types of authoritarian rule, depended on the cultural status and ethnic affiliations of immigrant bands. As noted earlier, these can be placed in three main categories: (*a*) refugees from Tula; (*b*) displaced farmers from the Mesoamerican frontier; and (*c*) Chichimec nomads. Each of these could be further subdivided, but for the present only a few of their more salient characteristics need be noted.

Toltec refugees introduced a highly evolved model of governmental organization and an ideology of elite rule, which were later adopted, albeit with important modifications, by other city-states throughout the valley. Both rested on the principle that only those individuals descended from ancient dynasties of royal status were qualified to supply incumbents for the office of *tlatoani* ("He who speaks," or the ruler) and other titled positions of the highest rank.

Sullivan (n.d.) has particularly stressed the religious basis of kingship, noting that "the *tlatoani* ruled by divine right . . . he was the surrogate of the deity and ruled in his name . . . [he] spoke for the deity, that is, gave orders for the deity; and in the name of the deity, punished those who did not obey." Here Sullivan is describing the Aztec *tlatoani* just before the conquest, but the root concept derives from Tula and, possibly before that, from Teotihuacan.

The Toltec system was transferred more or less intact to Colhuacan, Xico, Tlalmanalco, and other settlements in the southern part of the valley (Jimenez Moreno 1954–1955). Although centralized authority must have been seriously weakened after the fall of Tula, it was easily reconstituted when stable social and economic conditions had been restored. The formerly paramount dynasty at Tula continued its rule at Colhuacan; others claiming Toltec affiliations may, like the Nonoalca Teotlixca Tlacochcalca, have claimed no more than that their kings had been confirmed in office at Tula itself (Chimalpahin 1965:130–131). The chief distinction between the earlier and later systems is that the Colhua rulers, while still more prestigious than the other monarchs, could no longer command their erstwhile inferiors with any expectation of obedience.

Elsewhere, when the colonization process was well advanced, local leaders were ranked according to whether or not their ancestors were of royal status; those descended from the rulers of Tula had the greatest prestige. However, lacking these genealogical connections, powerful rulers could demand women of royal rank as wives and as the mothers of a new generation of recognized *pipiltin*, who were entirely legitimate candidates for the throne. When *tlatocamecayotl* ("The lineage of rulers") was introduced by a woman, only her own offspring and descendants were so recognized. By defining the concept of nobility in these terms, and since several generations were needed to produce a significantly large number of qualified adult members of any local dynastic group, the practical consequences of this purely ideological factor were fundamentally important with respect to political growth patterns (Calnek 1974:200–204 discusses this factor in connection with the early rise of the Aztec state).

In later times, the *pipiltin* held a nearly complete monopoly of the highest offices in each city-state, displacing all competing elites of nonroyal status. It was not so much a question of whether Toltec principles of rulership would be adopted, but when and under what conditions. Chichimec nomads, for example, self-consciously combined these with their own system of hereditary leadership soon after adopting a settled agricultural life (Offner 1979). Among groups that had been sedentary cultivators before migrating to the Valley of Mexico, slightly different patterns of acceptance, which I shall describe shortly, were also available. The Aztecs of Tenochtitlan (but not Tlatelolco) were unique in resisting neo-Toltec ideologies of legitimate rule until as late as 1426, when they too were forced to capitulate to regional trends.

The case of the Chichimec nomads exemplifies the ease with which a genuinely preclass social system could be transformed into strongly authoritarian government based on hereditary class distinctions. When these nomads arrived in the Valley of Mexico, hereditary band leaders were already recognized. There may have been a single paramount chief, such as the celebrated Xolotl Tecuanitzin, with some authority over all groups. The Texcocan histories state that Xolotl placed individual band chiefs in control of large territories, while reserving Tenayuca and Texcoco for himself and his descendants. As the shift from hunting and gathering to agriculture was accomplished, these families retained their positions as leaders, intermarried among themselves, and because they commanded strong military contingents, easily obtained wives of royal rank from the south (Calnek 1973; Ixtlilxochitl 1952 [Vol. II]:37ff.; Offner 1979; Torquemada 1723 [Vol. I]:38ff.).

Quinatzin of Texcoco went further, bringing in a woman of royal rank to educate his son, Techotlallatzin, in the Nahuatl language, courtly etiquette, and the wearing of elaborately stylized Toltec dress and personal ornamentation (Chimalpahin 1965:74; Ixtlilxochitl 1952 [Vol. II]:73). This self-conscious adaptation of new social and political institutions was accompanied by the acceptance of Toltec religious ideologies involving divine kingship and elite rule. A highly detailed recent study of this process by Offner (1979:153ff.) has shown, however, that these were by no means blindly copied by the newly formed Chichimec dynasties, but were frequently revised and reinterpreted in the light of Chichimec culture and local needs.

The important point is that these and similar changes were accomplished throughout the zones held by Chichimec bands without significant resistance, except from recalcitrantly nomadic groups later driven north out of the valley (Ixtlilxochitl 1952 [Vol. II]:51–52; Torquemada 1723 [Vol. I]:65–66). With few exceptions, the dynasties founded by band chieftains in the thirteenth century survived until the time of the conquest and, in some instances, until well into the colonial era (Gibson 1964).

Previously sedentary peoples from the frontier region pose more difficult problems of interpretation, since their cultural status and antecedents are not yet well understood. Whether these were recently acculturated Chichimec nomads barely familiar with agriculture and the "arts of civilization," as so frequently claimed, is at least very difficult to prove.

The conventional interpretation is summed up in Bray's character-ization of the Aztecs (1977), who appear to have been typical of the frontier peoples: a "half civilized" group, who "must be classed among those Chichimec tribes which had lived in the marginal lands on the fringe of civilization, and had picked up farming and some useful arts from their more advanced neighbors, as opposed to the 'Teochichime-ca', the 'extreme' or 'true' Chichimecs of the Mexican annals, who remained hunters and gatherers." If this were true of the Aztecs, it would have been equally true for the Tepaneca and many other groups who claimed precisely the same historical background.

Against the view that these were recently acculturated nomads, archaeological evidence discussed by Kelley (1971) indicates that the north frontier region of Durango-Zacatecas was colonized by north-ward moving farmers beginning in Teotihuacan times, about A.D. 300 and again in the early Toltec period after A.D. 900. Chichimec nomads formerly in this semiarid region must have been pressed steadily northward, after which they would have been held in check by the many fortified hilltop settlements described in the cited archaeological report by Kelley.

The Aztecs themselves described their ancient homeland in Aztlan as a well-settled town or large village with temples and houses. They emphasized that new communities of the same type were con-structed several times along their later migration route. Their cultural inventory from the beginning of their migrations included ritual books, seeds for staple crops, a typically Mesoamerican pantheon, and a well-established division into *calpullis*—none of which characterized nomadic Chichimec bands (Castillo 1980:81ff.; *Codex Aubin* 1963; Durán 1967 [Vol. II]:26–30; Tezozomoc 1944:7–9; 1949:13–27). In Du-rán's words (1967 [Vol. II]:26), "They were bellicose, animated and would undertake great deeds without fear, they were political and cultivated people" (*"eran belicosos, animosos y emprendian sin temor grandes hazanas y hechos, eran gente politica y cortesana"*). In short, it is reasonable to state that we deal with frontier peoples, less sophis-ticated than the city-dwellers of Tula, but otherwise typically Meso-american with respect to basic culture, religion, and social organiza-tion.

The earliest chronicles state no more than that Aztlan was aban-doned because of political conflict, overpopulation, or insufficient land—all reasonable consequences of the drought conditions prevail-ing from about 1150–1300 as noted earlier.

Like many other Mesoamerican peoples, the Aztecs recognized a type of theocratic leadership. Commands and decisions throughout the migration period were imputed to the god Huitzilopochtli, who spoke to his priests (*teomama*, or "god bearers") in dreams, or possibly oracular trance states (see, e.g., Castillo 1980:83ff.; Tezozomoc 1949:12, 19–20, 29, 32). Leadership positions, in addition to the four *teomama*, included seven *calpulli* leaders with priestly functions, and in later times, thirteen important personages identified only as elders (*huehuetque*). These positions appear to have been transmitted from father to son or grandson, so that political leadership was to some extent already in the hands of hereditary elites. Once in the Valley of Mexico, a ruler of nonroyal status or war leader (*cuauhtlatoani*, or "eagle ruler") was elected (see early chapters in works cited by Duran, Tezozomoc, and Castillo).

The Aztec system is frequently described as a *preclass, traditional*, or even *egalitarian* system (e.g., Katz 1966; Kirchoff 1954 - 1955; Monzon 1949; Rounds 1979; and Carrasco 1971:349–350 provides a convenient summary of the main points raised in this debate). However, these terms seriously misrepresent the historical significance of early Aztec social organization. Chimalpahin (1965:75) more accurately refers to their status as commoners (*macehualtin*) before leaving Aztlan; in the Valley of Mexico the fact that their traditional leaders lacked royal pedigrees made them unfit to rule in the eyes of the neo-Toltec dynasties already in power among the neighboring city-states. So far as these were concerned, the Aztecs and other similarly organized bands were not precisely preclass societies, but they were certain *one-class* societies within the established system of class stratification.

In most cases, this redefinition of legitimate authority was simply accepted by newly arrived immigrant bands. If they were militarily powerful, their rulers, like those of the Chichimec nomads, intermarried with royalty. If less powerful or willing to acquiesce in their lower standing, the already established neo-Toltec dynasties were asked to provide a younger son of royal rank who could legitimately hold the office of *tlatoani* (Chimalpahin 1965). Again, the adoption of Toltec ideologies and governmental institutions was accomplished rapidly and without serious internal dissent. Indeed, many peoples, impressed with the enormous prestige of Tula, appear to have welcomed the establishment of kingship, perhaps because they did not fully understand the long-term characteristics of class rule.

The Aztecs differed from others primarily in their stubborn refusal to accept externally imposed definitions of their own social and political status until compelled to do so late in the fourteenth century. The *teomama* and other traditional leaders remained in complete control of whatever government may have existed from the founding of Ten-ochtitlan until 1367 or 1376, when it was decided that the seating of Acamapichtli, son of an Aztec warrior and Colhua princess, as *tlatoani* would improve their position vis-à-vis neighboring city-states (Tezozo-moc 1949:80–81). Although Acamapichtli's sons and grandsons appear to have collaborated closely with traditional leaders until 1426, they were evidently not permitted to make or execute important decisions without first obtaining the consent of a strong popular assembly in which traditional leaders retained a dominant voice. In 1426, on the eve of the Tenochcan uprising against Azcapotzalco, the recently formed dynastic group seized control of the state apparatus, forced traditional leaders to accept an inferior status, and soon commenced their own highly successful career of imperialist expansion (see Durán 1967 [Vol. II]:75ff.; Tezozomoc 1944:29ff.).

Precisely how this victory over the last bastion of traditionalist resistance to neo-Toltec ideologies was achieved cannot now be deter-mined with any certainty. The fourth *tlatoani*, Itzcoatl (1426–1440), destroyed or rewrote earlier historical manuscripts on the ground that "government will be defamed" (Sahagún 1961:191). Since there is a marked hiatus in the Tenochcan chronicles that describe the period between the founding of Tenochtitlan (c. 1325?) and the accession of Acamapichtli (c. 1367 or 1376), and since there are only a few carefully selected references to events thereafter until the 1420s, it is possible that Itzcoatl wished to expunge knowledge of the period when tradi-tional leaders rather than the *pipiltin* still controlled the Tenochcan state. Precisely how the system of government was organized before 1426 cannot be determined now on empirical grounds, nor can earlier patterns of internal stratification be accurately described given the lack of pertinent documentary information.

Whatever occurred at Tenochtitlan, the question of who would rule was finally and irreversibly settled in favor of hereditary elites of Toltec descent. An ideology of class rule derived from the same back-ground was now firmly entrenched throughout the Valley of Mexico. It differed from the earlier system primarily in that there was no single paramount dynasty but rather a congeries of autonomous or semi-autonomous polities, each governed by men with precisely the same genealogical credentials.

Equally important, all local dynasties accepted the principle that none could be permanently dissolved without violating the religious principles underlying the system as a whole. Because interdynastic marriages were frequent, multiple ties of kinship crosscut political divisions. This created a network of relationships between *pipiltin* that was to be of vital importance in the forming of military coalitions, and in determining later patterns of relationship between imperial centers and subject states.

As discussed elsewhere (Calnek 1978), even when local *tlatoanis* were executed or forced into exile, every effort was made to retain and eventually restore local dynastic groups within a generation or two, and to strengthen the class position of local *pipiltin* as against that of the common people. It was, however, possible to force individual dynasties, whatever their rulers' pedigrees, into a subordinate status vis-a-vis a powerful imperialist center. We must now consider the nature of the political systems that were devised to achieve this result.

Empire Formation

The era of relatively peaceful colonization and population growth came to an end in the middle decades of the fourteenth century. A Chichimec dynasty at Xaltocan may have commenced a series of conquests toward the north early in the century, but exact dates cannot be provided until calendrical dates can be more reliably correlated to those of the European system. Jimenez Moreno (1954–1955) has briefly described the early expansion of several other city-states—including Xico, Cuauhtitlan, Coatlichan, and Colhuacan—but their *empires* were so minuscule and short-lived that they hardly merit this name.

Sometime just before or after 1350, however, interstate rivalries began to assume a greater intensity. The Texcocan histories include confused but vivid accounts of a bitterly contested struggle for supremacy among the northern Chichimec dynasties; the Tepanecs of Azcapotzalco rapidly joined this struggle (Ixtlilxochitl 1952; Offner 1979; Torquemada 1723 [Vol. I]). At issue, according to these sources, was the right to claim the title of *Chichimeca Tecuhtli,* or "Lord of the Chichimecs," which involved paramount rule over all of the newly formed Chichimec kingdoms. Ixtlilxochitl of Texcoco asserted that this was strictly hereditary within the line descended from Xolotl. Whatever the merits of this claim, Xolotl's descendants were soon opposed by the rising power of Azcapotzalco. Here the famous Tezozomoc slowly pieced together a powerful combination of coalition partners and subject states, as much by shrewdly contrived royal marriages and political manipulations as by outright conquests.

Tenochtitlan and Tlatelolco, for example, were relatively unimportant subjects of Azcapotzalco until the last years of the fourteenth century, after which both began to receive important privileges in return for military support. Tlatelolco received one of Tezozomoc's sons as its own ruler (Berlin 1948:45–48); Acamapichtli's son, Huitzilihuitl (c. 1391–1415), married one of his daughters (Durán 1967 [Vol. II]:63–65). The two cities thereafter grew rapidly in wealth and population, and their rulters were given important responsibilities in the administration of states conquered on behalf of Azcapotzalco (Chimalpahin 1965:185ff.). After the Tepanec's conquest of Texcoco in 1418, both received a share in the lands and tributes from that region (Ixtlilxochitl 1952 [Vol. II]:99).

The prolonged conflict between Azcapotzalco and Texcoco provides a particularly clear example of the Machiavellian political strategies pursued by Tezozomoc. If Ixtlilxochitl's account (1952 [Vol. II]:81ff.) of the rivalry between these two city-states is even approximately correct, Texcoco was the more powerful at the end of the fourteenth century, when they forced the Tepanecs to the point of total surrender. Tezozomoc nonetheless negotiated a partial capitulation by acknowledging the superior rank of the Texcocan ruler, while retaining for himself *de facto* control over previously won territories. During the next two decades, he successfully won over Chichimec states formerly allied with Texcoco, using interdynastic marriages to form new coalitions and what amounted to outright bribery of local elites. In 1418, the Texcocan ruler, Ixtlilxochitl, went onto the battlefield with an army so inferior that he himself is said to have regarded defeat as inevitable (Ixtlilxochitl 1952 [Vol. II]:95).

During the same period, Tepanec conquests had been undertaken far to the north and west of the Valley of Mexico (Barlow 1949:33). Despite its still makeshift organizational character, it was by this time a major conquest· empire. Tezozomoc's capital city had become "the largest and most populous in the land" ("*la mayor y mas populosa de la tierra*")(Durán 1967 [Vol. II]:101).

But the Tepanec hegemony was short-lived. Immediately after the death of Tezozomoc in 1426 or 1427, a fratricidal dispute over the royal succession forced both Tenochtitlan and Tlatelolco into rebellion (Durán 1967 [Vol. II]:71ff.; Tezozomoc 1944:24ff.). Nezahualcoyotl, dispossessed heir to Texcoco, had meanwhile recruited a large military force from Huexotzinco, located east of the valley (Ixtlilxochitl 1952 [Vol. II]:147ff.). Many of Azcapotzalco's erstwhile subjects and coalition partners either remained neutral or provided covert economic support to the rebels (Durán 1967 [Vol. II]:72).

Azcapotzalco fell and its empire was dismembered in 1428. Soon thereafter, the Tenochcan dynasty consummated its internal victory by ousting traditional leaders from all positions of genuine power in the state apparatus, while pointedly ignoring their claims to a share in the spoils of conquest (Durán 1967 [Vol. II]:83). Together with the force commanded by Nezahualcoyotl, the Aztecs then attacked and conquered "the rest of the most important cities of the Tepanec domain, such as Tenayuca, Tepanoaya, Toltitlan, Cuauhtitlan, Xaltocan, Huitzilopochco and Colhuacan" ("*las demas ciudades mas principales del reino de los tepanecas, como fueron Tenayocan, Tepanoaya, Toltitlan, Quauhtitlan, Xaltocan, Huitzilopochco y Colhuacan*") (Ixtlilxochitl 1952 [Vol. II]:151). By the early 1430s, Coyoacan, Xochimilco, and Cuitlahuac had also been subdued (Durán 1967 [Vol. II]:85–123; Tezozomoc 1944:43–73).

During the 1430s a new coalition between Tenochtitlan, Texcoco, and Tlacopan—the famous Triple Alliance—was formed, and soon began to send its armies far outside the Valley of Mexico (the powerful Chalcan confederacy within the valley was not, however, fully subdued until 1465). By the early sixteenth century, the Triple Alliance controlled a territory of approximately 200,000 km², and a total population that numbered in the several millions (Armillas 1964).

Aztec supremacy within the Triple Alliance was strongly asserted only from about 1504 until the Spanish conquest. In 1504, Moctezuma Xocoyotzin (1502–1520) seized land in Chalco previously held by Texcoco; in 1506 he forced the Texcocans to elect his sister's son, Cacamatzin, as successor to the recently deceased Nezahualpilli (Ixtlilxochitl 1952 [Vol. II]:325, 329–333). But these were primarily symbolic acts, which demonstrated that Tenochtitlan was first among equals within the Triple Alliance but did not otherwise modify the formal character of the coalition.

Organization of Empires

The pattern of empire formation described to this point involved the subordination but not absorption of conquered city-states, which normally retained a great deal of autonomy in the conduct of purely internal affairs. The rights and obligations of defeated states were outlined in bilateral treaty agreements, frequently negotiated on the field of battle. These included a specification of the tributes to be paid to the victor and the obligation to provide manpower and material resources on demand for later military campaigns or large-scale construction projects (Calnek 1978; Gibson 1956).

The most important characteristic of this system was that local rulers retained control over their own manpower and material resources, organizing the collection of tributes and functioning temporarily as an administrative staff when summoned to perform labor services at or on behalf of an imperial center. Similarly, military contingents recruited from subject states fought under their own leaders, who therefore occupied all but the highest positions in the military chain of command.

These policies greatly reduced the need for creating any form of overarching bureaucratic administration, but at the same time limited the extent to which centralized authority could act outside the immediate territorial limits of the dominant city-state. The most remarkable characteristic of this system is that the imperial centers did not at any time seriously attempt to simplify their organizational problems by abolishing and annexing the petty, often minuscule, city-states that fell to their armies. On the contrary, local rulers were deposed or executed only if there was a serious threat of future rebellion. Frequently, local dynastic groups were protected and even strengthened by interdynastic marriages, so long as they remained loyal and subservient to the empire. In cases when a military governor (*cuauhtlatoani*) was imposed, he was likely, as in the case of Tlatelolco after that city's conquest in 1473, to be a lower ranking member of the local nobility (Berlin 1948:59ff.; Sahagún 1959:2). If a royal prince was sent out from the capital to govern, as often happened, he was usually a kinsman of his new subjects through a maternal connection formed by an earlier marriage (see, e.g., Chimalpahin 1965:204).

Under these circumstances, any successful imperialist center rapidly found that it was strongly outnumbered by its own subjects, who could be controlled only so long as subject rulers remained loyal. Instead of overt coercion (although the threat of force was always present), the historical records emphasize attempts at conciliation, including the waiving of tributes and the awarding of shares in the spoils of future conquests to peoples who had been only recently conquered. Thus, the ruler of Xochimilco was invited to participate in Tenochcan councils-of-state early in the period of imperialist expansion (Durán 1967[Vol. II]:114), and heavy tributes imposed after the defeat of Chalco were not collected in full until about 1510 (Anunciación 1953). The same policy was followed after the defeat of Tlatelolco slightly less than a decade later (Tezozomoc 1944:197–201, 463–464).

The Triple Alliance did not, however, adopt an attitude of complete *laissez faire* toward their subjects. Local rulers were expected to spend several months in each year at the imperial capitals; their sons may have remained there to be educated and to serve as hostages for the good behavior of their fathers. The images of local deities, which could also be taken as hostages, were housed in a temple within the ceremonial precinct constructed by Moctezuma Xocoyotzin (Chimalpahin 1965:217; Lopez de Gomara 1943; Tezozomoc 1944: 454).

Although not even the most powerful emperors directly challenged the quasi-sacred relationship held to exist between local dynasties and their own peoples, the persons of individual rulers were by no means inviolable. Tzotzomatzin, ruler of Coyoacan, was executed by order of Ahuitzotl of Tenochtitlan (1486–1502) for criticizing the technical feasibility of a proposed construction project (Durán 1967 [Vol. II]:371–372).

An important consequence of the frequent interdynastic marriages, which began as early as the thirteenth century, was that *pipiltin* everywhere in the Valley of Mexico were soon closely linked to each other by ties of kinship. When the ruler of a subject state arrived at the court of Moctezuma, he might well be greeted as an uncle, cousin, nephew, or grandparent, rather than as an inconsequential lord representing an equally insignificant polity. It is by no means certain that local dynastic groups, however much they complained about Aztec oppression, would have seriously risked their own positions in the hope of at some time gaining the upper hand themselves. Even among the lower ranks of the *pipiltin*, as I suggest elsewhere, "the right to share in tribute redistributions and other benefits [of the imperial system] created a vested interest which transcended local boundaries and hinged instead on the perpetuation of the imperialist *status quo*" (Calnek 1978:467).

The Tribute System

The strongest evidence for the creation of a professional administrative staff subservient to the supreme ruler exists in connection with the tribute system. Major construction projects and corvée labor, so far as can be determined, played no significant role in this process, since as noted earlier, work groups were supervised by local authorities.

The greatest proliferation of purely technical administrative positions concerned with tribute collections occurred at Tenochtitlan. As the empire began to expand at an accelerated rate in the last years of the fifteenth century, an army of hierarchically organized tribute collectors was recruited from the ranks of the *pipiltin* to supervise the flow of goods from the imperial provinces (Barlow 1949; Sahagún 1954:44). Although tribute deliveries were technically under the jurisdiction of local rulers, after the mid-fifteenth century it was the practice to assign stewards (*calpixque*) to subject provinces. These *calpixque* informed local rulers when tributes were due and were on hand at central collection points to supervise actual deliveries.

As the number of Tenochtitlan's subjects increased, the empire was divided into 38 large tributary provinces, each under the authority of a high steward (*hueicalpixqui*), who supervised the activities of lower ranking *calpixque*. At the imperial capital, the tributes from each province were received in separate warehouses by a steward responsible for ensuring that deliveries agreed with pictorial records of tributes owed, and for balancing accounts of goods on hand against those redistributed at the ruler's command. The system as a whole was coordinated by a single official holding the title of *petlacalcatl* (Sahagún 1954:44).

It is possible that the technical efficiency of this hierarchically organized system might have stimulated a new approach to the consolidating of Tenochtitlan's recently won empire. It should be recalled that the period of imperialist expansion began only with the conquest of Azcapotzalco in 1428 and effectively came to an end at the time of the Spanish invasion in 1519—a period of only 91 years.

Summary

Widespread population movements and the twelfth century collapse of the Toltec empire opened the way for the creation of new patterns of settlement, governmental organization, and demographic growth throughout central Mexico. In the Valley of Mexico, numerous small autonomous city-states were quickly formed by militaristic bands of diverse cultural origins. After a prolonged period of growth and consolidation, during which most groups accepted Toltec political and religious ideologies, these began to compete among themselves for regional hegemony. Once established under the aegis of a Triple Alliance of Tenochtitlan, Texcoco, and Tlacopan in the mid-fifteenth century, a series of external conquests were launched. These were still continuing when Cortes landed at Veracruz in 1519.

The system of government adopted throughout the Valley of Mexico was based on the acceptance of hereditary elites claiming Toltec descent as a permanent ruling class. Political relationships between city-states, whether involving coalitions or conquest empires, were negotiated between these groups. It was assumed that local dynasties would remain in power even if conquered in war. In most cases, the loyalty of subject states was sought through indirect means, such as interdynastic marriages, although force was applied when required. There was no significant development of bureaucratic administration at the regional level, apart from the special case represented by the tribute system as described in the preceding section. The discussion of empire formation presented in this paper differs from conventional interpretations of the rise of the Aztec empire primarily in that greater emphasis is placed on the early development of the city-state system. Unfortunately, little attention has thus far been given to events in the Valley of Mexico between the fall of Tula and the rise of Tenochtitlan. It may, therefore, be necessary to revise this account in important respects in the light of future studies of this critically important era.

References

Adams, R. E. W.
  1977   *Prehistoric Mesoamerica.* Boston: Little Brown.
Armillas, Pedro
  1964   Northern Mesoamerica. In *Prehistoric man in the New World.* Chicago: University of Chicago Press.
  1971   Gardens on swamps. *Science* **174:**653–661.
Barlow, R. H.
  1949   *The extent of the Empire of the Culhua Mexica.* (Ibero-Americana, Vol. 28). Berkeley: University of California.
Berlin, H.
  1948   *Anales de Tlatelolco: Unos annales historicos de la nacion mexicana y Codice de Tlatelolco.* (Fuentes para la Historia de Mexico, 2.) Mexico: Antigua Libreria Robredo.
Bray, W.
  1977   Civilizing the Aztecs. In *The evolution of social systems,* edited by J. Friedman and M. J. Rowlands. London: Duckworth. Pp. 373–398.
Calnek, Edward E.
  1973   The historical validity of the Codex Xolotl. *American Antiquity* **38**(4):423–427.
  1974   The Sahagún texts as a source of sociological information. In *Sixteenth century Mexico: The work of Sahagún,* edited by M. S. Edmunson. Santa Fe, New Mexico: School of American Research. Pp. 189–204.
  1976   The internal structure of Tenochtitlan. In *The Valley of Mexico,* edited by E. R. Wolf. Albuquerque: University of New Mexico Press. Pp. 287–302.
  1978   The city-state in the Basin of Mexico: Late Pre-Hispanic period. In *Urbanization in the Americas from its beginnings to the present,* edited by R. P. Schaedel, J. E. Hardoy, and N. Scott Kinzer. Mouton: The Hague.
Carrasco, P.
  1971   Social organization of ancient Mexico. In *Handbook of Middle American Indians* (Vol. 10), edited by R. Wauchope. Austin: University of Texas Press. Pp. 349–375.

Castillo, Cristobal del
  1908   *Fragmentos sobre la obra general sobre historia de los Mexicanos.* Florence: S. Landi.
Chimalpahin Cuauhtlehuanitzin, Don Francisco de San Anton Munon
  1965   *Relaciones originales de Chalco Amaquemecan.* Paleografiadas y traducidas del Nahuatl con una introduccion por S. Rendon. Mexico: Fondo de Cultura Economica.
Codex Aubin
  1963   *Historia de la nacion Mexicana.* Reproduccion a todo color del Codice de 1576 (Codice Aubin), Version paleografica y traduccion directa del Nahuatl por el Doctor Charles E. Dibble (Coleccion Chimalistac, 16). Madrid: Ediciones Jose Porrua Turanzas.
Cook, S. F., and L. B. Simpson
  1948   *The population of Central Mexico in the sixteenth century* (Iberoamericana 31). Berkeley and Los Angeles: The University of California Press.
Davies, N.
  1977   *The Toltecs, until the fall of Tula.* Norman: University of Oklahoma Press.
  1980   *The Toltec heritage from the fall of Tula to the rise of Tenochtitlan.* Norman: University of Oklahoma Press.
Durán, Fray Diego
  1967   In *Historia de las Indias de Nueva España e Islas de la Tierra Firme,* edited by A. M. Garibay K., Mexico: Editorial Porrúa.
Gibson, C.
  1956   Llamamiento general, Repartimiento, and the Empire of Acolhuacan. *Hispanic American Historical Review* **36:**1–27.
  1964   *The Aztecs under Spanish rule.* Stanford, California: Stanford University Press.
Guzman, Eulalia
  1938   Un manuscrito de la coleccion Boturini que trata de los antiguos Senores de Teotihuacan. *Ethnos* (Stockholm) 3(4–5):89–103.
Ixtlilxochitl, Fernando de Alva
  1952   *Obras historicas de Don Fernando de Alva Ixtlilxochitl* (2 vols.), publicadas y anotadas por Alfredo Chavero. Mexico: Editora Nacional.
Jimenez Moreno, W.
  1954–1955   Sintesis de la historia precolonial del Valle de Mexico. *Revista Mexicana de Estudios Antropologicos* **14:**219–36.
Katz, F.
  1966   *Situacion social e economica de los aztecas durante los siglos XV y XVI.* Mexico: Universidad Nacional Autonoma de Mexico.
Kelley, J. C.
  1971   Archaeology of the Northern Frontier: Zacatecas and Durango. In *Handbook of Middle America Indians* (Vol. 11), edited by R. Wauchope. Austin: University of Texas Press. Pp. 768–801.
Kirchoff, P.
  1954–1955   Land tenure in ancient Mexico. *Revista Mexicana de Estudios Antropologicos* **14:**351–361.
Lopez de Gomara, Francisco
  1943   *Historia de la conquista de Mexico.* Mexico: Joaquin Ramirez Cabanas.
Millon, R.
  1973   *Urbanization at Teotihuacan, Mexico* (Vol. 1, Part 1). Austin: University of Texas Press.

1982   Teotihuacan: City, state, and civilization. *Handbook of middle American Indians* (Vol. 1, Supplement), edited by J. A. Sabloff. Austin: University of Texas Press (to be published).

Molina, Alonso de
1966   *Vocabulario nahuatl-castellano, castellano-nahuatl.* Mexico: Ediciones Colofon, S.A.

Monzon, A.
1949   El Calpulli en la organizacion social de los tenochca. *Publicaciones del Instituto de Historia* (Ser. 1, No. 14). Mexico: Universidad Nacional Autonoma de Mexico.

Offner, J. A.
1979   Law and politics in Aztec Texcoco. Unpublished Ph.D. dissertation, Department of Anthropology, Yale University, New Haven, Connecticut.

Parsons, J. R.
1974   The development of a prehistoric complex society: a regional perspective from the Valley of Mexico. *Journal of Field Archaeology* 1:81–108.

Rounds, J.
1979   Lineage, class and power in the Aztec state. *American Ethnologist* 6(1):73–86.

Sahagún, Fray Bernardino de
1954   *Florentine codex, Book 8: kings and lords,* translated by A. J. O. Anderson and C. E. Dibble. Monographs of the School of American Research, No. 14, Pt. 9. Santa Fe, New Mexico: School of American Research and University of Utah.
1959   *Florentine codex, Book 9: the merchants,* translated by C. E. Dibble and A. J. O. Anderson. Monographs of the School of American Research, No. 14, Pt. 10. Santa Fe, New Mexico: School of American Research and University of Utah.

Sanders, W. T., and B. J. Price
1968   *Mesoamerica: the evolution of a civilization.* New York: Random House.

Sanders, W. T., J. R. Parsons, and R. S. Santley
1979   *The basin of Mexico: ecological processes in the evolution of a civilization.* New York: Academic Press.

Sullivan, Thelma D.
1978   Tlatoani and Tlatocayotl in the Sahagún manuscripts. Paper presented at the annual meeting of the Society for American Archaeology, Tucson, Arizona.

Tezozomoc, Fernando Alvarado
1944   *Cronica Mexicana.* Mexico: Editorial Leyenda.
1949   *Cronica Mexicayotl.* Traduccion directa del nahuatl por Adrian Leon (Ser. 1a, No. 10). Mexico: Universidad Nacional Autonoma de Mexico, Instituto de Historia.

Torquemada, Fray Juan de
1723   *Primera (Segunda, Tercera) parte de los veinte i un libros rituales i monarchia indiana* (3 vols.). Madrid.

3

Dynastic Succession and the Centralization of Power in Tenochtitlan

J. Rounds

Editors' Introduction

J. Rounds asks how Tenochtitlan evolved from a polity lacking central authority into a state with power seemingly concentrated in a dynastic ruler. Tenochtitlan began with power allocated to leaders by followers. In 1372 the Tenochca leaders invited the Toltec bloodline of Culhuacan to establish a Tenochca dynasty to strengthen their military defense. Dynastic leaders eventually parlayed this goal into substantial control of internal relations as well, seemingly delegating power down from newly emerging central authority. This shifting from allocated power to delegated power was facilitated by new resources flowing into the political arena from Tenochca ascendancy into the Valley of Mexico. As resources grew in magnitude, leaders shared key offices controlling resources among collateral lines of the ruling dynasty, diffusing the power of the ruler even as the ritual and sacred trappings of his position seemed to heighten his absolute power.

Rounds suggests that strategic management of the resources of the state determined the development of the polity.

Two of my colleagues have noted that the political structure of Aztec Tenochtitlan developed in the context of a regional political system based upon the divinely sanctioned rule of the descendants of

63

THE INCA AND AZTEC STATES, 1400–1800

the kings of the ancient Toltec empire. Pedro Carrasco (Chapter 1) has concentrated on reconstruction of this regional political system as it existed at the time of European contact, noting that the Tenochca political structure of that period was representative of the type general throughout the Valley of Mexico, and was linked to other localities through the kin ties of the regional ruling class. Edward E. Calnek (Chapter 2) has more explicitly raised the historical question of the process by which the Tenochca power system came to reflect this general model. He notes that the Aztecs were exceptionally resistant, holding to their earlier political system long after most other localities had adopted the Toltec elite. However, in light of the recognized deficiencies and distortions in the primary sources for Aztec ethnohistory, Calnek expresses pessimism about the possibility of understanding the processes through which this transformation finally took place, and he demurs from further consideration of the problem.

I am more sanguine in this matter. Comparative studies of state formation and local politics produced by social anthropologists have given us theoretical tools capable of overcoming some of the deficiencies in the data. Theory is, of course, no substitute for good historical data. The body of literature on the Aztecs is littered with theoretical schemes proposed in blatant disregard for historical facts. Theory can never tell us what did happen where data are absent. However, theory grounded in empirical studies of better documented polities passing through similar phases of development can improve our recognition of distortions and fabrications in the chronicles, and it can suggest the meaning or significance of obscure events. Where explanations of Aztec politics are consistent with the data (or provide clear reasons for selecting among conflicting data) and make sense in terms of general theory, they should be more reliable than explanations lacking such a comparative base. Thus, more theoretically informed approaches than have typified past Aztec studies can—when employed with proper caution and respect for data—help us retrieve the maximum information from our problematic sources.

In this chapter, in light of recent theoretical treatments of dynastic succession in early states, I interpret aspects of the process by which the Tenochca political system moved toward the regionally dominant model. The fundamental process at issue is movement from a relatively dispersed structure of power to a relatively centralized one. The "black box" view of the process—which assumes it is sufficient to state simply that the Tenochca "adopted" the Toltec system, treating the process of adoption as nonproblematic—tends to understand power in the Aztec city as concentrated in the person of the *tlatoani*, since strong centralization is usually held to have been characteristic of the common Toltec system the Tenochca are said to have emulated.[1] The process analysis advocated here treats centralization in this situation as inherently problematic and suggests a more complex distribution of power even by the period of first European contact. The adoption of the Toltec dynasty in Tenochtitlan was not an imposition of structure upon a previously unstructured situation. An entrenched elite already existed in the semiindependent *calpulli* that formed the organizational units of the prestate polity. Though these traditional elite arranged the foundation of the Toltec dynasty of the city, they probably did not intend thereby to relinquish all of their privileges and power in favor of the new ruler and to relapse into commoner status. Comparison with better documented cases of state formation suggests instead that we should expect to find the traditional elite implementing strategies to maximize their own share of power in the new system, or to trade power for guaranteed supplies of other resources. At the same time, the elite of the new central dynasty would pursue strategies promoting stronger centralization of power in their own hands. Thus, rather than the foreign political structure being adopted intact and completely displacing the traditional power structure, the process may actually have been one of interaction between competing elites, which produced a hybrid political structure reflecting the interests of both.

In an earlier article (Rounds 1979) I showed that there is considerable evidence that such a process did take place in Tenochtitlan. This chapter extends this argument through examination of significant changes in the patterns of succession to the offices of *tlatoani* and *cihuacoatl*, the two highest positions in the state. In anthropology's first extensive theoretical treatment of dynastic succession, Jack Goody came to the conclusion that "succession systems can be linked to changes in the economic and military potential" of a government—in other words, to the power it derives from its control of "human, economic and military resources" (1966:42). Succession practices, Goody was able to demonstrate, reveal much about the power structure of a society, both because they focus attention on the means by which power is accumulated and invested in individuals and because they deal with periods of crisis in the power system, that is, discontinuities that pose great dangers to the stability of the society. This chapter argues that changes in the succession practices of Tenochtitlan were closely associated with changes in the power relationships between the dispersed traditional elite and the centralized dynastic elite.

Tenochca political evolution may be broadly conceived as moving through three distinct phases: predynastic, early dynastic, and late dynastic. The predynastic phase extended from the formation of the city in 1325 or 1345–1372. During this period the city was apparently ruled by a council of the leaders of the various *calpulli*, each of which remained largely self-governing. There was no developed central authority.

The early dynastic phase began with the seating of the first *tlatoani* in 1372 and extended through the reigns of his first two successors. Acamapichtli, the founder of the dynasty, was invited to the throne by the *calpulli* elite, apparently in response to two forces. First, the highly charged military pressures of the valley necessitated more centralized leadership, at least in external relations. Second, a widespread ideology made the legitimacy of a polity dependent upon the Toltec blood of its ruler; this dictated the choice of a man with Acamapichtli's distinguished ancestry. During the early dynastic phase the *calpulli* elite retained the upper hand in the domestic power structure; the activities of the *tlatoque* were confined to public works, religious functions, and external relations.[2]

The late dynastic phase opened with the accession of Itzcoatl, the fourth *tlatoani*, in 1426. This phase was marked by a rapid advance of centralization under a succession of progressively more powerful rulers. Shortly after taking office, Itzcoatl led the alliance with neighboring cities that toppled the Tepanec empire, to which the Aztecs had been subordinated since the founding of Tenochtitlan. The Tenochca fell heir to the bulk of the tribute empire of the vanquished Tepanecs, and this sudden influx of vast new wealth for the first time gave the *tlatoque* a source of power independent of the traditional political structure.

This wealth was used by the *tlatoque* as a tool in their drive toward greater centralization of the internal power structure. The rigid class stratification that was constructed in Tenochtitlan was fueled by the economic differentiation resulting from the astute distribution of the incoming wealth. The class stratification was further buttressed by a series of symbolic and legal innovations aimed at making clearly visible distinctions between the strata, as well as formalizing cross-strata interactions. This process created a cohesive ruling class, whose members identified their self-interests as resting in solidarity with the throne rather than with the older local power structures. The *calpulli* leaders were included in this royal "corporate group."[3] The advantages in wealth and sumptuary privileges they gained thereby compensated for the inevitable separation from their traditional power base in the *calpulli.*

Construction of the corporate ruling group was thus the basic strategem responsible for the increased centralization of internal power during the late dynastic phase, as the new wealth of the empire tipped the balance of power from the traditional to the dynastic leadership. Nevertheless, it must be noted that this strategem for subversion of the old structure involved concentration of power in a distinctive ruling class (into which the traditional leaders were co-opted), rather than in the individual holder of the office of *tlatoani.* We find this fact reflected in the related changes in the pattern of dynastic succession.

At the beginning of the late dynastic phase the Tenochca moved from a pattern of filial succession to a rule of fraternal succession, stressing (as I argue in a moment) the corporate nature of the dynasty in which real and potential participation in the exercise of power was relatively widely dispersed. The uncertainty of the rule of succession, which allowed for a selection among a number of eligible candidates, further stressed this doctrine. At the same time, the dangers of the interregnum between the death of one ruler and the seating of the next, an inevitable problem of uncertain systems of succession, was answered by another common pattern: A "stand-in" held temporary power during the interregnum but was excluded from eligibility for the succession himself. However, within this public doctrine of widely dispersed potential eligibility for supreme power the *tlatoque* were able to develop considerable control over real access to the succession.

Fraternal Succession and the Corporate Dynasty

Dynastic succession in Tenochtitlan differed in a significant way from the pattern most common among its neighbors in the Valley of Mexico, and this deviation was clearly related to the start of the late dynastic period and the changing distribution of power in the emerging state. In his important early chronicle Alonso de Zorita (1891:79–82) says that the usual rule of succession in the valley was from father to son; daughters were ineligible to succeed. Among the eligible sons, the one most competent to rule would be chosen. A ruler without a competent son or son's son might be followed by his daughter's son. If no qualified sons or grandsons existed, the deceased ruler's brother might ascend the throne. Zorita goes on to say that, in contrast to this most common practice of filial succession, in Tenochtitlan brothers were preferred to sons as successors. The Aztecs believed, he notes, that "being sons of one father, they (the royal brothers) should be equals."

On this point the two principal exemplars of the regional system from which the Tenochca political system is thought to be drawn, Azcapotzalco and Culhuacan, offer contrasting patterns. In Azcapotzalco the throne passed from father to son (Ixtlilxochitl 1891–1892[Vol. I]:129, 189), while in Culhuacan fraternal succession was favored.[4] An examination of the genealogy of the Tenochca dynasty (Figure 3.1) shows that Zorita is correct for the late dynastic period in characterizing the Aztec system as fraternal, but that the first three *tlatoque* were related filially.[5] Thus, at the ascension of Itzcoatl the Aztecs appear to have switched from a filial to a fraternal mode of succession.

The significance of the timing of this change is apparent, since Itzcoatl was the *tlatoani* who led the Aztecs in the rebellion against the Tepanec empire, and who thus started the late dynastic phase in Tenochca political development. Most accounts in the early chronicles of the ascension of Itzcoatl, who led the rebellion shortly after taking office, state that his predecessor, Chimalpopoca, was murdered by agents of Maxtla, the Tepanec ruler of Azcapotzalco. Maxtla had only

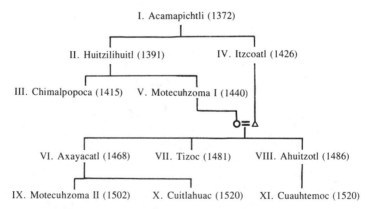

Figure 3.1   The dynasty of Mexico-Tenochtitlan (1372–1521). (Dates indicate ascension to the throne.)

shortly before usurped the throne of that city, wresting power from his half brother Tayauh. The latter was the designated heir of their recently deceased father, Tezozomoc, who had built the Tepanec empire over a remarkable 60-year reign. Chimalpopoca, himself a grandson of Tezozomoc (through his mother) and a loyal tributary of the aged king, had followed his grandfather's wishes and supported Tayauh against the usurper Maxtla. According to the majority of the chronicles, this ill-fated alliance cost both men their lives at the hands of Maxtla's assassins. This murder then helped touch off the rebellion in which the Aztecs and their allies crushed the power of Azcapotzalco and began their own imperial career. These unusual circumstances may have dictated the need to select the older and more experienced Itzcoatl to guide the dangerous times ahead.

However, a variant of this story derived from Chimalpahin (*Anales Mexicanos* 1903:49–50) suggests a different interpretation. This version clearly implicates Itzcoatl in the death of his nephew. Chimalpopoca's seeming capitulation after receiving threats from Maxtla angered the faction led by Itzcoatl and Motecuhzoma I, who favored war. Itzcoatl arranged with the friendly ruler of a neighboring Tepanec city to send two men to garrote Chimalpopoca. Itzcoatl then joined in taking revenge against the killers, pretending not to be involved. His election to the throne of his victim immediately followed this initiative in silencing the "dove" faction.

Nigel Davies (1974:61) argues that this is the more credible of the two versions, pointing out that Maxtla was surely acquainted with the personalities of the two men. Thus, he would have been unlikely to do away with the relatively subservient Chimalpopoca only to allow his belligerent uncle to ascend the throne. Rather, this seems to have been a case of internal politics, that is, a usurpation based on support of the military leadership for rebellion against the Tepanec domination. Some evidence suggests that the Aztec histories were rewritten shortly after the Tepanec war to reflect new official ideology. Itzcoatl may have taken this opportunity to blame the death of his nephew on Maxtla. This revisionist history would then have found its way into the majority of the chronicles we use today.

Southwold (1966:91) has pointed out that successful usurpers are usually individuals with some real eligibility to succeed. If a strict rule of filial succession had been in use at the time of Chimalpopoca's death, clearly his uncle Itzcoatl would have been an inappropriate successor, and his acquisition of the office would have been of problematic legitimacy. Actually there is no direct evidence that such a rule did exist at the time—beyond the fact that the first three *tlatoque* were related as father, son, and grandson. Such statistical normality does not prove the existence of a jural norm, and it is altogether possible that whatever general rule then governed the definition of eligible candidates for the succession specified nothing more than the best qualified near kinsman of the deceased *tlatoani*.

Nevertheless, after the ascension of Itzcoatl, the rule cited by Zorita favoring fraternal succession evidently replaced whatever had preceded it, and it is this fact that must be examined. The simplest explanation would be that the old Culhuaque principle of fraternal succession was reasserted as a post-hoc legitimation for Itzcoatl's usurpation of the throne. Since, according to Chimalpahin, the conspirators in the assassination of Chimalpopoca were Itzcoatl and Motecuhzoma I, both of whom were brothers of previous *tlatoque*, there was an obvious advantage in disavowing the filial mode of succession practiced in Azcapotzalco and asserting the fraternal principle of Culhuacan, which now became an ally in the rebellion against the former city. However, whatever the original impulse for the change, there is also a systemic reason why fraternal succession may have proven advantageous at this juncture in Aztec history: It was well suited to the basic tactic in political centralization, that is, development of the expanded, corporate ruling-class.

The Aztec system was what Goody (1966:24–29) characterizes as "uncertain" succession (i.e., the rules designated a pool of eligibles rather than a specific individual, and the successor was selected from among this group). Goody (1966:26) argues that uncertain succession is related closely to "corporate" dynasties, which are kin groups marked by a "plurality of 'royals' who regard the crown as in some sense a common property even though it has to be held by one member at a time". These "royals," all technically eligible for the throne, are not automatically excluded from it by any abstract rule of succession. Rather, the emphasis is placed on achievement of power through individual merit and service in the name of the dynasty as a whole.

This sense of corporateness strengthens the polity by spreading loyalty to the kingship among a larger group that feels some personal stake in the throne. Through their part in choosing the successor, the members of the corporate dynasty participate indirectly in the kingship, and the necessity of building support forces a candidate to acknowledge the power of others and to offer suitable avenues for its exercise in his administration. The "participation in the crown" of members of the dynasty thus consists of more than the chance each has of eventually obtaining the supreme office himself; it includes an important role in the complex power structure that makes the kingship viable. Ultimately, the corporate dynasty is a special type of power system in which power is considerably diffused throughout the group, and the power of the kingship is itself dependent on an extensive network of alliances.

Fraternal succession is particularly expressive of this principle: It emphasizes the corporateness of the ruling group by spreading direct participation in the kingship through several members of each generation, while avoiding diffusing real eligibility so widely as to make consensus on the successor too difficult to achieve. Borrowing a phrase from Radcliffe-Brown, Goody(1966:28) says that one underlying principle is "the equivalence of siblings," which is reminiscent of the Aztec dictum that "being sons of one father they should be equals." Beyond the ideological principle, since each brother has some hope to succeed to the supreme office legitimately, his interest presumably lies in strengthening, rather than subverting, the political system. Intrigue tends to be focused on rivals for the succession, rather than on the incumbent, thus lending some greater stability to the supreme office.

In sum, uncertain fraternal succession provides for mobilizing wide political support for both the throne and its incumbent, starting with those brothers directly eligible for the succession and then moving outward through their networks of allies, clients, and followers. I described earlier how the *tlatoque* were pursuing their goal of increased political centralization through the formation of a clearly defined ruling class, a corporate group that included the traditional *calpulli* leaders as well as the members of the central line of the dynasty. Thus, whereas Goody's analysis was limited to a group relatively narrowly defined by close kinship, in the Aztec case it appears that the *tlatoque* were using an expansion of the corporate principle beyond this narrow group to bring other key figures in the existing power structure into a close identification with the ruling dynasty.[6]

Identification of the structural consequences of a practice does not constitute an explanation of its origins. There were no teleological forces at work that somehow caused advantageous political forms to emerge. I assume that there were clear advantages visible to the actors involved in establishing the new pattern. Although these actors would not have analyzed the advantages in quite the same way as the modern anthropologist, the advantages would have been sufficient to produce the decisions that led to the emphasis on fraternal succession. Apparently, the need for a rapid expansion of internal alliances during this crucial phase in Tenochca political development led the dynasty to adopt this particular method of simultaneously sharing and centralizing power. In the short run, at least, there was no "invisible hand" at work here—only the familiar give-and-take of practical politics.

As I have argued, this process of the expanding coalition did not stop with the "royal brothers." The deliberate expansion of class consciousness that was producing the corporate ruling class must be interpreted in this light. Calnek (1974a:202–203) has pointed out that by the time of the Tepanec war the legitimate direct descendants of Acamapichtli would still have constituted a rather small group. It would hardly have been large enough to provide a sufficient power base to support central control of the rapidly expanding empire and increasingly complex internal polity, and it was certainly not large enough to staff an entirely new administrative structure for the city. As one provision for broadening the ruling group, Motecuhzoma I issued a decree that sons of noblemen by slaves and servants, formerly designated bastards, would henceforth be considered legitimate so long as they proved their mettle in the wars that were then consolidating and expanding the empire (Durán 1951 [Vol. I]:241–242). The *calpulli* leaders, however, were the major pivotal figures in this strategy, since they brought with them the traditional control of the masses. This left the *tlatoani* free to deal with the more pressing issues of power posed by the growing empire and the impact of tribute wealth on his own high-ranking subordinates.

Thus far, I have emphasized one side of the process: the expansion of the corporate ruling group through uncertain and fraternal succession and the mechanisms that maximize the size of the cooperating group within each generation by maximizing the number of persons with a direct or indirect stake in the throne (see Burling 1974:50 for a general discussion of some important aspects of this argument). The expansion of the ruling class by broadening the definition of legitimacy and including the *calpulli* leaders was an extension of this same political principle. Nevertheless, since my thesis is that the direction of Aztec political evolution was toward greater centralization of power, how was this seeming diffusion of power related to the process of centralization?

Examining African political systems in which relatively decentralized polities were associated with strong ritual kingship, Max Gluckman argues that "the very deficiency in the internal integration of the state's components seems here to heighten the kingship's symbolic and ritual value, as unifying its disparate sections. Hence trespasses on the symbolic and ritual insignia and exclusive privileges of the king and his kingship are grave offenses" (1972:60). During this crucial period of Aztec political evolution strong symbolic differentiation of ranks was established by decrees such as the famous law code of Motecuhzoma I (Durán 1951 [Vol. I]:214–217), which placed great emphasis on the ritual and symbolic privileges of the *tlatoani*. The symbolic legitimation of the rulership was developing on both secular and religious fronts simultaneously (cf. Broda 1976; Webster 1976) and served to express the doctrine of centralization.

Nevertheless, Gluckman's formulation of the problem seems too limited to the symbolic aspects of the process. Some greater attention to the more concrete political processes involved seems justified, at least in the Aztec case.

Goody (1966:27–28) has shown that uncertainty, besides protecting the kingship itself, helps to protect the incumbent by providing him with a means of playing off his potential heirs against one another, and thus distracting their plotting from his own person. However, Goody has neglected the other side of this coin. At the same time that uncertainty protects the throne, it also threatens it by increasing the valuation placed upon it. The ultimate fear of the early king is not so much usurpation of his office as fragmentation of his realm. Undifferentiated units, which constitute subordinate centers of power, may find the rewards of participation in the larger polity too slight to justify continuation, and the power of the king may be too weak to prevent their separation. A multitude of strategems may be employed by the king to avert this possibility, but among the most important is increasing the benefits to which the leaders of the sub-units of the political structure gain access by their participation in the kingdom. Uncertainty in the succession accomplishes this, when widely enough defined, by granting the possibility of participation in the kingship to a number of pretenders and to the larger number of their powerful political allies. This stimulates intrigue within the system by making the throne the ultimate focus of all ambition. It thus acts as a countermeasure to the threat of fragmentation in a political system composed of similar units and, thereby, serves a key purpose of the incumbent.

In the Aztec case we see a ruler attempting to integrate and centralize a somewhat fragmented political system by raising key figures into positions of either real or symbolic power. The prestige of the throne supports the prestige of the subordinate nobles, and the treasury of the *tlatoani* finances their sumptuous life-styles. The *tlatoque* were trading power against political cooperation, which under the circumstances was perhaps the only condition in which centralization could be advanced. Thus, political centralization in Tenochtitlan was based upon the continuing success of the *tlatoque* in supplying inducements to the lesser powers sufficient to guarantee identification of their own interests with those of the throne. This is certainly a very different thing from possessing sufficient unchallenged power to enforce one's will down the system, a power attributed to Motecuhzoma II by the Spaniards, who mistook the symbolic trappings of absolutism for the real thing.

Like all early political systems, this one was fraught with dangerous sources of instability, many of which were revealed under the pressure of the Spanish invasion. One theoretical issue, which was raised by Robbins Burling and which concerns the dangers associated with fraternal succession, must be explored briefly before turning to the process of succession. Burling (1974:50–51) argues that fraternal succession is rare throughout the world because it is inherently unstable, always likely to give "some members of the system both the motives and the means for subverting the rules." This instability manifests itself primarily when a string of brothers is exhausted and the succession must fall to the next generation. How, Burling asks, can intense rivalry be avoided among the large number of sons in the second generation and among the geometrically larger numbers in the third and fourth generations?

Burling's analysis seems to be based upon an assumption of unilineal descent in the ruling group, but the ambilateral tendency of Aztec kin reckoning (i.e., the tendency to stress descent in either the male or female line, depending upon which offered the greater advantage in the particular situation) offered at least a temporary solution to this problem. Carrasco (1971:370) has noted the frequent occurrence of close patrilineal marriages among the dynasty. He argues that this is related to fraternal succession because it is a way of keeping the branch of the inner dynasty, which has been bypassed on the male side, involved in the succession through its females. The most dramatic case is the marriage of the daughter of Motecuhzoma I with the son of Itzcoatl, which produced three *tlatoque*. There were, however, many others. When Motecuhzoma II succeeded his father's brother, Ahuitzotl, he married Ahuitzotl's daughter, thus ensuring that that branch would not thereafter be too far removed from the succession to hold a stake in it. Similarly, Ahuitzotl's son, Cuauhtemoc, married a daughter of his father's brother's son, Motecuhzoma II. As Carrasco points out, such marriages were far less common among those Meso-american dynasties favoring filial succession. The marriage pattern is thus one more demonstration of the relationship of the principle of fraternal succession to the expanding mobilization of political support for the throne.

Selection of the Successor

In a system of uncertain succession some mechanism must exist for choosing among the eligible candidates. Sahagún asserts that in Tenochtitlan the selection was made at a large meeting attended by all the nobles, who "cast votes for all the princes who were sons of lords" (1954:61–62). This doctrine of open election among the nobility, including the *calpulli* leaders, was a powerful support for the ideology of the corporate ruling class, symbolizing the participation of all in the throne. At the same time (as Goody 1966:28 has pointed out) it also symbolizes the limitations on the power of the ruler. Besides forcing the ambitious candidate to form political alliances that bind his later actions, the doctrine of election usually contains at least some covert suggestion that those who give may take away—a lesson seemingly learned by Motecuhzoma II at the very end of his life. In this, as in its other facets, there were deep contradictions in the dynasty's strategy for centralizing power. Their resolution of this problem seems to have been to combine the ideology of open dynastic election with a procedure that was, in reality, much more closely controlled.

The accounts of the elections given in Durán and Tezozomoc are filled with speeches stressing the openness of the process. In one case (Tezozomoc 1878:572) a speaker lists as eligible candidates 20 sons of the three previous rulers. However, it is difficult to discern in these descriptions any honest portrayal of the decision-making process. A single name is usually advanced by a major dignitary and seems never to be refused. Debate appears rarely. This agrees with Motolinía's rather cynical summation of the process:

If it could be called an election, it was among the sons and brothers of the deceased ruler, and although for this election many great and minor lords gathered, there were no votes nor election by balloting, but already they had all looked to whom the kingdom belonged, and if in him there were no faults that would render him incapable, and if there were diverse opinions, the elections depended on the ruler who had the right of confirmation, who was already well resolved and informed of to whom the lordship belonged, and without contradiction that was accepted by all (1971:338).

I interpret this to mean not that the rules of succession were so precise as to designate an exact heir, but only that by the time of the "election" the choice had already been agreed upon by the real powers of the realm. The gathering would then have been a formality symbolizing the doctrine of openness, but actually serving only to acclaim a choice already made "in the back room." In Sally Falk Moore's phrase, the public meeting would then have produced a "simulation of unanimity" (Moore 1977).

Who, then, made the choice? The members of the Council of Four, which I will discuss in a moment, are often referred to as "electors." Also mentioned in this context are the *cihuacoatl* and the kings of the two other cities of the Triple Alliance, Tetzcoco and Tlacopan. Zorita (1891:80) states that the ruler of Tenochtitlan would be selected by the lords of that city and confirmed in office by the rulers of Tetzcoco and Tlacopan; new rulers of these two cities would be confirmed by the Tenochca king. In one case, Motecuhzoma II was able to use this power of confirmation to force an unpopular selection on Tetzcoco, thereby causing a rebellion still active when Cortés arrived on the scene (Ixtlilxochitl 1891–1892 [Vol. I];331–332).

In the quotation earlier Motolinía referred to "the ruler who had the right of confirmation" as the ultimate authority in a disputed succession. Unfortunately, neither in Motolinía's statement nor in the derivative version in Las Casas (1967 [Vol. II];409) is it clear to whom this refers.[7] Although the chronicles of Durán and Tezozomoc show that the Tetzcocan and Tlacopan rulers were regularly present at the elections, often making elaborate speeches, it seems doubtful that they could enforce their own choice on the Tenochca. Possibly they operated in league with the most powerful figures in the internal politics of Tenochtitlan in order to arrive at a suitable candidate whom all could endorse in the more public meeting.

Presumably these most powerful figures in internal politics were the *cihuacoatl* and the members of the Council of Four. This council consisted of the four closest advisors of the *tlatoani* (other than the *cihuacoatl,* who will be discussed in the next section), including the two highest military officers, the *tlacateccatl* and the *tlacochcalcatl.*[8] Apparently, these four individuals, who were invariably close relatives of the *tlatoani,* were appointed by him. Durán (1951 [Vol. I]; 102–103) claims that the new *tlatoani* had to be selected from among the members of the Council of Four. Although this does not seem to be stated elsewhere (except in a few manuscripts derived from the same source used by Durán), a review of the chronicles shows that, beginning with Chimalpopoca, every one of the later *tlatoque* held one of the two military offices of the council prior to ascension to the throne.[9] Whether or not Durán was correct about the jural rule, .the reality of the statistical norm will suffice for the present argument.

Aside from the oft-demonstrated value of military command in obtaining high office, this pattern is significant in that it establishes one means of the dynasty's control over the succession. Since the *tlatoani* selected the council (or perhaps nominated the council for the acclamation of the nobility), he was in effect able to narrow the field to two candidates. Because these candidates held the reins of the Aztec military force, they could not easily be dislodged from their advantageous access to the succession. Furthermore, since the military was organized through *calpulli*-based units under the direct command of the lesser nobility, their command afforded the *tlacateccatl* and *tlacochcalcatl* excellent opportunities to build rapport and personal loyalties among that essential constituency. At the same time, the uncertainty of the succession remained, especially in the original choice of the Council of Four members, so the doctrine of open succession and the encouragement of merit could be maintained. Furthermore, neither position clearly held the inside track for promotion. Although various passages hint that the *tlacateccatl* was the higher position, many of the *tlatoque* entered supreme power directly from the post of *tlacochcalcatl.* (In some cases the chronicles are ambiguous or in disagreement about which post a *tlatoani* formerly held.) Many persons who are listed as holding one of these posts never ascended the throne; moreover, the positions were sufficiently insecure that in one case Motecuhzoma I had the *tlacateccatl* (his brother Zaca) executed for what seems a trivial offense (*Crónica Mexicayotl* 1949:132–133). Thus, although membership in the Council was a necessary step toward the throne, the hopeful candidate had still to prove his military prowess in the post and consolidate sufficient support among the powerful nobles to advance ahead of his rival commander.

It is notable that the Council of Four, like the emphasis on fraternal succession, seems to have first gained prominence in the context of the Tepanec war and the beginnings of the Aztec empire. Davies (1974:43) believes that the emergence of the Council of Four dates from the reign of Itzcoatl, thus placing this institution in the context of the whole complex of innovations tending toward centralization at the beginning of the late dynastic period. At the same time that they fostered the ideology of an enlarged, corporate ruling-class by redefining legitimacy and co-opting the *calpulli* leaders, the *tlatoque* moved to maintain close limitations on real accessibility to the succession.

The Role of the Stand-in in the Maintenance of Continuity

The advantages gained from a system of uncertain succession are paid for by the dangers of the interregnum, the period when the continuity of power lapses while the throne sits vacant. In the internal polity, rivalries formerly repressed to avoid seeming to threaten the incumbent break to the surface and may lead to violent confrontation. The longer a decision is deferred, the more difficult a final resolution becomes. Additional competing interests arise and organize themselves into coalitions backing rival candidates. The more problematic the succession, the greater the chance that lingering hostilities will undermine the authority of the newly seated ruler.

In external relations, rival powers may look to the lapse of leadership as an opportunity to test their strength against a divided enemy, and tributaries may see a chance to rebel. Under the system of imperial administration adopted by the Aztecs, any prolonged lapse of power in Tenochtitlan could have resulted in a rapid dissolution of the empire. In fact, it was common for at least one major tributary to rebel during an interregnum, and by the time of the late *tlatoque* a field campaign against recalcitrant territories had become a standard part of the process of coronation.

The Tenochca, who were obviously sensitive to the need to contain the rivalries of the candidates, achieved this in part by proscribing too blatant campaigning. Motolinía (1971:338) states that a likely heir to the throne who advertised his ambition by soliciting support or demonstrating vanity would be denied office by the electors. Sahagún (1954:62) adds that noblemen who thought they might be selected would hide themselves during the meeting to avoid being chosen for such an arduous responsibility. Motecuhzoma II is said to have been found sweeping out the temple when messengers arrived to inform him of his selection.

It is typical of the lack of serious attention to Aztec power systems that these claims have often been taken at face value by modern writers, who have reported them as accurate descriptions of behavior rather than as jural rules. It seems safe to surmise that Aztec candidates were as ambitious and manipulative as their counterparts in other societies, and that this ostensible humility was simply a device for exercising the rivalry for the supreme office in a manner least destructive to the continued unity of the state and empire.

Nevertheless, such rules concerning competition for the throne clearly would have been inadequate by themselves for ensuring a relatively smooth passage of power. Some institutionalized means for maintaining the continuity of power was necessary. In addressing this problem, the Aztecs followed a common pattern by using a stand-in, a role described by Jack Goody (1966:10–12) in his study of royal succession. (For earlier relevant discussions, see Fortes 1962:69–71 and Richards 1961:140–141.) The stand-in is a person or group who serves as a temporary deputy during an interregnum. He or she sometimes has few duties but often has full administrative control, including an important role in the selection and installation of the new ruler. In ancient Norman society the stand-in was an officer called the "Justicias" (Goody 1966:29); examples abound in Africa, including the Maigira of Kogu (Cohen 1977), the Ngabe of the Kamba (Abrahams 1966:131), the Katikkiro of the Baganda (Southwold 1966:84), and the "first circumcised prince" of the Swazi (Burling 1974:23).

In Tenochtitlan the role of the stand-in was provided by the office of *cihuacoatl*, which after the defeat of Azcapotzalco rapidly became the second most powerful in Tenochca society. The title is the name of a goddess who was the patron deity of Culhuacan (*Historia de los Mexicanos por sus Pinturas* 1891:247) and probably was originally her chief priest. In the role of priest the *cihuacoatl* appeared in many other cities of the valley, but nowhere else with the importance that he assumed in Tenochtitlan.

In the Aztec capital itself the office of *cihuacoatl* had apparently existed at least since the founding of the dynasty. However, Torquemada (1969 [Vol. I]:104) states that at the time of Huitzilihuitl (the second *tlatoani*) the *tlacochcalcatl* was the second most powerful post of the land.[10] It was not until Tlacaelel assumed the title under his brother, Motecuhzoma I, that the post of *cihuacoatl* rose to its full power. The emergence of the powerful *cihuacoatl* thus coincided with the period of formation of strong class stratification, the establishment of the Council of Four, and the pattern of fraternal succession. It was another element in the evolving power complex pushing toward more centralized control.

The *cihuacoatl* is described in various chronicles as a kind of viceroy or prime minister of the *tlatoani*, who headed the legal system of the state and performed various military, religious, and administrative duties. None of the sources gives a really clear picture of how the office functioned.[11] However, the duties significant to the present question are quite clear in the chronicles. When the *tlatoani* was absent from Tenochtitlan, on military campaigns or for other reasons, the *cihuacoatl* acted in his stead. Furthermore, when the *tlatoani* died, it was the *cihuacoatl* who ruled during the interregnum, and who called and presided at the meeting at which the new *tlatoani* was selected (Durán 1951 [Vol. I]:254–255,411; Tezozomoc 1878:456 - 457,568 - 569).

However, another aspect of the role of the stand-in raises an important question about the *cihuacoatl*. Goody (1966:10–11) points out that the role of the stand-in, by definition, is temporary. The role cannot confer such power that the stand-in is tempted to refuse to relinquish his position once the rightful successor is chosen. The standard tactic, according to Goody, is to have the stand-in position be filled by an individual who is technically ineligible for the throne, thus ensuring that he make no reasonable claim to legitimacy should he usurp permanent power.

Although we can clearly see that the Aztec *cihuacoatl* filled the stand-in function, we cannot so easily see what prevented him from using his post as a stepping-stone to the supreme office. He was a permanent official with enormous responsibility and power; he must certainly have been capable of organizing the personal support necessary to retain power. He was, furthermore, of excellent blood.

Figure 3.2 shows the genealogy of the four holders of the title during its period of ascendancy. During this time the office passed in a dynastic fashion similar to that of *tlatoani*, though the primary sources indicate that the *cihuacoatl* was an appointee of the *tlatoani*. The important point is that the founder of this line, Tlacaelel, was of the most royal blood. He was the son of a *tlatoani* and the brother of two

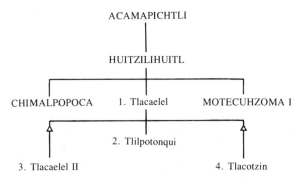

Figure 3.2   Genealogy of the holders of the title *cihuacoatl* of Tenochtitlan. (Holders of the title *cihuacoatl* are numbered in order of incumbency. Reigning *tlatoque* are in capitals.)

others. Under a rule of fraternal succession he logically should have succeeded Motecuhzoma I. He did not, however, and none of his descendants who followed him as *cihuacoatl* ever became *tlatoani* either.[12] Why this was the case is uncertain, but a speculative answer can be advanced.

According to Durán (1951 [Vol. I]:254–255), following the death of his brother Motecuhzoma I, Tlacaelel called together the nobles to select the new *tlatoani.* After a speech in which he noted that "all my brothers are dead and only I remain," Tlacaelel was offered the throne by the assembled nobles. However, he refused in an elaborate speech in which he asked, "What greater power could I have than I have now and have had?" In Tezozomoc's account of this event (1878:372–373), Tlacaelel states that it is more fitting that he and his sons be the second person to the ruler in order to guide, advise, and counsel him. This proposal was accepted, and it apparently established the principle that the title would thereafter remain in Tlacaelel's lineage.

There is, of course, reason to be suspicious of these accounts, and this case definitely calls for some reading between the lines.[13] Tlacaelel does appear to have been the logical successor, and it is hard to accept the explanation that he voluntarily refused the crown simply because he already had too much power. I would speculate that he was squeezed out of the succession by a coalition of the families of his two predecessors, Motecuhzoma I and Itzcoatl. Although Motecuhzoma had at least three legitimate sons, two of whom had served as *tlacatec-catl* and *tlacochcalcatl* (*Anales de Cuauhtitlan* 1945:51), the succession jumped an entire generation, settling on a group of brothers who were the offspring of a son of Itzcoatl and a daughter of Motecuhzoma (see Figure 3.1). The most likely explanation for this irregular pattern is that a compromise between two powerful branches of the royal family was effected to join them in office rather than pit them as rivals.

Tlacaelel would then appear as the loser in the internal politics of the dynasty, but the price of his cooperation is suggested by an African comparison. In examining the choice of the stand-in among the Pabir of Kobu, Cohen's informants claimed that the post "should go to a former King's daughter whose brothers represent a lineage segment that is likely to be, or already is, in danger of being de-royalized by the succession. Again they stress the idea that this *Magira*-ship is therefore a compensation or consolation for the loss that is coming, or has already come, to this particular segment of the royal lineage" (1977:20).

The ascension of Axayacatl virtually ensured that no sons of Tlacaelel would ever reach the throne, even though they remained theoretically eligible. Their line was separating from the mainstream of the succession and was thus being "de-royalized" in Cohen's sense of no longer being serious candidates. However, a substantial consolation prize was indeed proffered, making the office of *cihuacoatl* hereditary in Tlacaelel's line. Considering the power of the post, this must have been a reasonably attractive alternative for Tlacaelel; under a system of fraternal succession, it is impossible for all the sons of all the brothers who reign in one generation to have their own chance at the throne, and it is possible that if Tlacaelel had become *tlatoani* his lineage might have lost out completely in the next generation. By accepting a hereditary right to the office of *cihuacoatl* in lieu of the throne, his lineage was thus more secure in their continuing claim to high power than even those who remained in competition for the supreme office. A sticky dynastic dilemma appears to have been solved to the satisfaction of all.[14]

The *cihuacoatl*, then, was discouraged from using his enormous authority to usurp the throne by the value of retaining his lineage control over the number-two office, and by the acknowledged lack of sufficiently royal blood in Tlacaelel's descendants to claim true legitimacy. Of course, usurpers have been known to assert even more tenuous claims to a throne, and as Goody (1966:44) has aptly noted, concentration on the marital arrangements of a dynasty at the expense of its martial organization gives a distorted picture of the way things really work. The final answer to why the *cihuacoatl* did not usurp the throne does seem to lie in the military system. Although Tlacaelel began his career as a field officer in the Tepanec war, thereafter his military duties seem to have been limited to strategic planning with the *tlatoani* and Council of Four. Actual field command of Aztec military power lay with the *tlatoani* and with the *tlacateccatl* and *tlacochcalcatl*, the real candidates in the succession. The holders of the military power were thus precisely those men who stood to lose the most should the *cihuacoatl* attempt to mount a coup. The powerful stand-in role of the *cihuacoatl* was to their advantage, since it guaranteed an orderly succession and ensured the house could be kept in order while the *tlatoani* was absent building his empire; a *cihuacoatl* who challenged these legitimate successors would have in effect challenged the Aztec military machine. The balance of power favored the *tlatoani* and the legitimate line of succession.

Summary and Conclusions

When viewed not as a set of static rules but as an historical progression of political events, the patterns of Aztec dynastic succession reveal much about the process of political centralization in the emerging state. Succession was initially conducted as a de facto filial system with heavy stress on legitimacy of the bloodline. Under the exigencies of the rebellion against the Tepanecs and subsequent events, the succession rapidly changed into a fraternal system in which somewhat questionable blood might be purified by military success. The necessity of mobilizing a broadened base of political support for the throne favored the uncertain fraternal system with its sense of corporate sharing of the royal power. The stress on military prowess helped ensure the imperial growth and increasing tribute essential in demonstrating to the lower nobility the material advantages of loyalty to the throne. The lowered threshold of legitimacy increased the group available for military and administrative leadership. The rise of the powerful office of *cihuacoatl*, with its associated lineage, both protected against internal fragmentation of the dynasty and provided a means of protecting the succession against usurpation. From the clash of competing political interests a new structure of power was emerging that cannot be adequately characterized as the simple "adoption" of a system common among the city's neighbors. Rather, the search for legitimacy through acquisition of a Toltec elite (and the resulting kinship ties to the regional ruling elite), so important to external politics, interacted with the equally important internal realities of the preexistent power structure to produce a unique variant on the common theme.

Acknowledgments

This paper has benefited greatly from extensive advice by H. B. Nicholson and from critiques of earlier drafts by David W. Caddis, Edward E. Calnek, Pedro Carrasco, Walter Goldschmidt, Bruce Kapferer, Sally Falk Moore, and the editors of the present volume.

Notes

[1]It should be acknowledged that the claimed absolutism of the *tlatoani* receives considerable support in the primary sources, which abound in statements like the following: "All persons from the highest to the lowest were servants of the supreme ruler . . . whose they all were, and no one had jurisdiction except solely the supreme ruler" (Anonymous 1940:147–148). The frequency of such passages probably stems from two factors. In the preconquest polity the stress on the claimed absolutism of the *tlatoani* reflected the ideological component of the dynasty's political strategy and the ostentatious trappings of power affected by those whose authority in actuality remains insecure (Webster 1976). In the postconquest period, when the bulk of the sources were written, the need for the elite to justify their authority under the Spanish doctrine of "natural lordship" (Chamberlain 1939) would have produced the same effect. Sally Falk Moore, in her study of the Incas (1958:90), indicates that the Spaniards found it advantageous to accept and perpetuate similar claims by the Andean elite, and her arguments doubtless apply with equal force to the Aztec case. Thus, as with so much in the primary sources, the claimed absolutism of the *tlatoani* must be interpreted in light of the motives of the authors.

[2]After publishing an extended version of this argument concerning the continued dominance of the traditional leadership during the early dynastic period (Rounds 1979), I discovered that Calnek had made a similar analysis in an unpublished paper delivered orally several years earlier (Calnek 1974b).

[3]I am here following the description of the structure and dynamics of corporate groups proposed by Smith (1974).

[4]In Culhuacan "if the ruler had legitimate brothers, even though he had sons his brothers would succeed first, and afterward the sons of the oldest brother, the one that reigned first; but the sons of the second and third brothers could not succeed" (*Relación de la Genealogía* 1891:270). Note that Goody (1966:36) postulates such a system as a hypothetical possibility that is unknown (and unlikely) empirically. Unfortunately, the data are insufficient to tell how the Culhuaque system functioned in practice.

[5]Ixtlilxochitl (1891–1892 [Vol. II]:449) and various other sources claim that Chimalpopoca was actually the brother of Huitzilihuitl and Itzcoatl, but other sources, generally better informed on genealogical matters, are unanimous in describing him as the son of Huitzilihuitl. This is accepted by most modern authorities, in part because of

the historical evidence that Chimalpopoca was a grandson of Tezozomoc of Azcapotzalco through a daughter married to Huitzilihuitl. Ixtlilxochitl's version may be a belated attempt to make the genealogy conform to the principle of fraternal succession.

[6]Recruitment to the ruling class was, however, still accomplished through the kinship idiom, since the claim of the *calpulli* leaders to membership was based on their descent on one side of the cognatic kin reckoning from Acamapichtli, the first *tlatoani* (Rounds 1979). Carrasco (see Chapter 1 in this volume) has argued that it is meaningless to suggest that Tenochca society moved from a lineage-based to a class-based system during this period, given that the ruling class was itself based on lineage recruitment and that elites existed prior to the seating of the dynasty. This viewpoint overemphasizes the significance of the continuities in idiom and ignores the real differences emerging at the beginning of the late dynastic period. As Smith (1974:139) notes, it is not the presence of inequality itself (which in some form and degree is a social universal) "but the modes of its institutionalization, its bases and forms, [that] are the relevant materials for identifying and analyzing stratification systems." The host of legal and symbolic innovations that defined and hardened class lines during this period stand in strong contrast to the ranking within the *calpulli* that earlier produced elites without creating classes. Vertical divisions of the society into separate *calpulli* (each with its own internal ranking) were being superseded by horizontal division of the society into classes that crosscut the *calpulli* structure. The ambilaterality of Aztec kinship reckoning thus facilitated recruitment of a class legitimated in the traditional lineage idiom while including within its bounds those who also held top rank in the *calpulli*. This class stood at the point of intersection between two structural principles and thus of competing structures of power and social control. Kinship-based recruitment into the ruling class was, in short, structurally equivalent as a principle to kin-based recruitment to the *calpulli*, but was very different from the latter in its implications for the power structure of the polity.

[7]Motolinía's Spanish is confusing and seemingly self-contradictory on this point. To facilitate the reader's own interpretation, I offer here the original passage that is translated in the body of the paper.

De manera que si elección se puede llamar, era entre los hijos o hermanos del señor difunto, y aunque para aquella elección se ayuntaban muchos principales e otros menos principales, no tenían voces ni se hacía elección por escrutinio, mas ya tenían todos mirado aquel que (el) señorío le pertenecía, y en él no habiendo falta por do fuese incapaz, y si había diversos pareceres, dependía la elección del señor cuya era la confirmación, el cual estaba ya bien resuelto e informado de lo que al señorío pertenecía, y sin contradicción aquel tal era acebtado por todos.

[8]H. B. Nicholson (personal communication) is skeptical of the existence of the Council of Four and suggests that *tlacateccatl* and *tlacochcalcatl* were generic terms for a class of officers, rather than designating unique high officials. I suspect that there were indeed multiple holders of the title, but that each such title was geographically linked. Thus, Cuauhtemoc is described as having been the "the *tlacateccatl* of Tlatelolco." This would have provided for internal ranking of the holders of the title; the individuals claimed in the Chronicle X sources to constitute the Council of Four would be the *tlacateccatl* and *tlacochcalcatl* of all of Tenochtitlan, or, for that matter, of all the empire. Assuming that, as argued later, all *tlatoque* after Chimalpopoca had held one of these two highest offices before becoming *tlatoani*, whether or not the Council of Four was formally recognized as an entity really has no bearing on my subsequent argument.

[9]My sources for this statement are: Chimalpopoca, *Anales de Cuauhtitlan* 1945:35; Itzcoatl, *Crónica Mexicayotl* 1949:98; Motecuhzoma I, Durán 1951 [Vol. I]:124; Ax-

ayacatl, Torquemada 1969 [Vol. I]:172; Tizoc, Torquemada 1969 [Vol. I]:172; Ahuitzotl, Mendieta 1870:151; Motecuhzoma II, Mendieta 1870:151–152, Tezozomoc 1878:573; Cuitlahuac, Torquemada 1969 [Vol. I]:208; Cuauhtemoc, McAfee and Barlow 1945:39.

[10]Torquemada's use of the titles *tlacateccatl* and *tlacochcalcatl* is confused, and he usually employs only the Spanish term *Capitan-general*. In this passage it is possible that he actually meant the *tlacateccatl* rather than the *tlacochcalcatl*.

[11]VanZantwijk (1962:133–134) says that the *tlatoani* controlled external state policy while the *cihuacoatl* managed internal administration, but this theory is not well documented in the primary sources.

[12]Actually, Tlacotzin, the last *cihuacoatl*, was elevated to *tlatoani* in 1525 by Cortés, after the Spaniards had executed Cuauhtemoc. This was clearly outside the native tradition.

[13]The most complete sources on the career of the *cihuacoatl* are the "Chronicle X" group of related manuscripts, all apparently derived from a common lost original (*Codex Ramírez* 1944; Durán 1951; Tezozomoc 1878). However, as Nicholson suggested some years ago (1964:1409), internal evidence—especially the really extraordinary stress placed on the activities of the *cihuacoatl* at the constant expense of the *tlatoani*—suggests that the anonymous author of the lost original may have been a descendant of Tlacaelel, who had a stake in gilding the importance of his distinguished ancestors. The *cihuacoatl* is, in fact, rarely mentioned in other sources; were it not for the important role played by the last *cihuacoatl* in the resistance to the Spanish conquest, we might have no other confirmation of the importance of this office. With this in mind, a skeptical approach must be taken in interpreting the accounts given in the "Chronicle X" sources.

[14]Twice thereafter Tlacaelel was again offered the throne and again refused (Tezozomoc 1878:437,456–457). However, these accounts have a ritualistic quality that suggests they were intended to reinforce the principle that the *cihuacoatl* would never seek nor usurp the throne, while giving recognition to his high status and power.

References

Abrahams, R. G.
    1966   Succession to the chiefship in northern Unyamwezi. In *Succession to high office*, edited by Jack Goody. Cambridge Papers in Social Anthropology, No. 4. London and New York: Cambridge University Press. Pp. 127–141.

Anales de Cuauhtitlan
    1945   *Códice Chimalpopoca: Anales de Cuauhtitlan y Leyenda de los Soles*. Publicaciones del Instituto de Historia, No. 1. Mexico: Imprenta Universitaria.

Anales Mexicanos
    1903   Anales Mexicanos (México-Azcapotzalco) 1426–1589. *Anales del Museo Nacional de Mexico* 7:49–74.

Anonymous
    1940   Relación anónima, describiendo la división que tenían los indios en sus tierras en tiempo de Moctezuma y el orden que tenían en la sucesión de las mismas. In *Epistolario de Nueva España 1505–1818* (Vol. 14), edited by Francisco del Paso y Troncoso. Mexico: Antigua Librería Robredo de José Porrúa e Hijos. Pp. 145–148.

Broda, Johanna
1976   Los estamentos en el ceremonial mexica. In *Estratificación social en la Meso-américa prehispánica*, edited by Pedro Carrasco and Johanna Broda. Mexico: Instituto Nacional de Antropología e Historia. Pp. 37–66.
Burling, Robbins
1974   *The passage of power: studies in political succession.* New York: Academic Press.
Calnek, Edward E.
1974a   The Sahagún texts as a source of sociological information. In *Sixteenth-century Mexico: The work of Sahagún,* edited by Munro S. Edmunson. Albuquerque: University of New Mexico Press. Pp. 189–204.
1974b   The rise of the monarchy in Tenochtitlan. Paper read at the 41st International Congress of Americanists, Mexico City, September 1974.
Carrasco, Pedro
1971   Social organization of ancient Mexico. In *Handbook of Middle American Indians* (Vol. 10, Part 1), edited by Robert Wauchope. Austin: University of Texas Press. Pp. 349–375.
Chamberlain, R. S.
1939   The concept of the *Señor Natural* as revealed by Castilian law and administrative documents. *Hispanic American Historical Review* **19**:130–137.
Codex Ramírez
1944   *Códice Ramírez: Relación del origen de los Indios que habitan esta Nueva España, según sus historias.* Mexico: Editorial Leyenda.
Cohen, Ronald
1977   Oedipus Rex and Regina: the Queen Mother in Africa. *Africa* **47**:14–30.
Crónica Mexicayotl
1949   *Crónica Mexicayotl.* Publicaciones del Instituto de Historia, No. 10. Mexico: Imprenta Universitaria.
Davies, Nigel
1974   *The Aztecs: a history.* New York: Putnam's.
Durán, Fray Diego
1951   *Historia de las Indias de Nueva-España y Islas de Tierra Firme.* Mexico: Editoria Nacional.
Fortes, Meyer
1962   Ritual and office in tribal society. In *Essays on the ritual of social relations,* edited by Max Gluckman. Manchester: University of Manchester Press. Pp. 53–88.
Gluckman, Max
1972   *The ideas in Barotse jurisprudence* (revised edition). Manchester: University of Manchester Press.
Goody, Jack
1966   Introduction. In *Succession to high office,* edited by Jack Goody. Cambridge Papers in Social Anthropology, No. 4. London and New York Cambridge University Press. Pp. 1–56.
Historia de los Mexicanos por sus Pinturas
Historia de los Mexicanos por sus Pinturas. In *Nueva colección de documentos para la historia de México* (Vol. 3), edited by Joaquín García Icazbalceta. Mexico: Francisco Díaz de León. Pp. 228–262.
Ixtlilxochitl, Don Fernando de Alva
1891–1892   *Obras históricas.* Mexico: Oficina Tip. de las Secretaría de Fomento.

Las Casas, Fray Bartolomé de
1967   *Apologética historia sumaria.* Mexico: Instituto de Investigaciones Históricas, Universidad Nacional Autónoma de México.
McAfee, Byron, and Robert H. Barlow (editors)
1945   Anales de la conquista de Tlatelolco en 1473 y en 1521. In *Tlatelolco a Través
de los Tiempos V.* (Sobretiro del No. 3, Vol. IV), edited by B. McAfee and R. H.
Barlow. Mexico: Imprenta Aldina. Pp. 32–44.
Mendieta, Fray Jerónimo de
1870   *Historia eclesiástica Indiana.* Mexico: Francisco Díaz de León.
Moore, Sally Falk
1958   *Power and property in Inca Peru.* Morningside Heights, New York: Columbia
University Press.
1977   Political meetings and the simulation of unanimity: Kilimanjaro in 1973. In
Secular ritual, edited by S. F. Moore and B. Myerhoff. Amsterdam: Van Gor-
cum. Pp. 151–172.
Motolinía, Fray Toribio de Benavente o
1971   *Memoriales o Libro de las Cosas de la Nueva España y de los Naturales de
Ella.* Mexico: Universidad Nacional Autónoma de México.
Nicholson, H. B.
1964   Review of The Aztecs: the history of the Indies of New Spain. (Fray Diego
Durán). *American Anthropologist* **66:**1408–1410.
Relación de la Genealogía
1891   Relación de la genealogía y linaje de los Señores . . . de la Nueva España. In
Nueva colección de documentos para la historia de México (Vol. 3), edited by
Joaquín García Icazbalceta. Mexico: Francisco Díaz de León. Pp. 263–281.
Richards, A. I.
1961   African kings and their royal relatives. *Journal of the Royal Anthropological
Institute* **91:**135–150.
Rounds, J.
1979   Lineage, class and power in the Aztec state. *American Ethnologist* **6:**73–86.
Sahagún, Fray Bernardino de
1954   *Florentine codex: general history of the things of New Spain* (Book 8), edited
and translated by Charles E. Dibble and Arthur J. O. Anderson. Monographs of
the School of American Research, No. 14, Part X. Santa Fe, New Mexico:
School of American Research.
Smith, M. G.
1974   *Corporations and society.* London: Duckworth.
Southwold, Martin
1966   Succession to the throne of Buganda. In *Succession to high office,* edited by
Jack Goody. Cambridge Papers in Social Anthropology, No. 4. London and
New York: Cambridge University Press. Pp. 82–126.
Tezozomoc, Hernando Alvarado
1878   *Crónica Mexicana.* Mexico: Ireneo Paz.
Torquemada, Fray Juan de
1969   *Monarquía Indiana.* Mexico: Porrúa.
Webster, David L.
1976   On theocracies. *American Anthropologist* **78:**812–828.

Zantwijk, Rodolfo van
1962   La Paz Azteca, ordenación del mundo por los Mexicas. *Estudios de Cultura Nahuatl* **3**:101–135.
Zorita, Alonso de
1891   Breve y sumaria relación de los señores, maneras y diferencias que había de ellos en la Nueva España. In *Nueva colección de documentos para la historia de México* (Vol. 3), edited by Joaquín García Icazbalceta. Mexico: Francisco Díaz de León. Pp. 71–227.

PART III

Inca State Administration and Colonization

4

Inca Policies and Institutions Relating to the Cultural Unification of the Empire

John Howland Rowe

Editors' Introduction

John Rowe shows how Inca policies devised to prevent revolt unified the state more comprehensively than the architects of those policies realized. *Yanacona, camayo,* and *Mitima* statuses, which were all initially created to expropriate labor for the state, eventually undercut traditional provincial loyalty. *Yanaconas* raised in the personal retinues of the Inca ruler or Inca governors often gained further honors through administrative positions reserved for the state's most loyal subjects. *Camayos* could perform skilled labor for the state as they did before the Inca conquest, but now their hereditary status led them to identify closely with the state, whatever their place of residence. *Mitima* relocation exclusively undercut provincial loyalties. In these, and other ways, the Inca transformed organized government of the provinces and spread their ideology of supremacy.

Introduction

In 1532, at the time of the Spanish invasion, the Incas of Cuzco controlled an empire extending over 32° of latitude on the west coast of South America. The first significant Inca conquests had taken place

THE INCA AND AZTEC
STATES, 1400–1800

less than a century earlier, and the greater part of the area under Inca control had been acquired within the previous 60–70 years. In consequence, there had not been enough time for much cultural unification to take place, or for a sense of common identity to develop among the peoples subject to the Incas. The situation was further complicated by the outbreak of a fratricidal civil war among the Incas themselves at the very time the Spanish arrived. The combination of surviving traditional divisions and the Inca civil war helped to make possible first the Spanish conquest itself and then the consolidation of Spanish power. Once the invaders felt secure, however, they had no interest in perpetuating native factions or local differences. The Spanish regime came increasingly to treat the native population as an undifferentiated labor force, thus creating new pressures both for cultural unification and for the development of a sense of common identity.

The Incas contributed more to the unification process than this brief summary of events suggests. The Spanish colonial regime incorporated in modified form many Inca institutions that the new masters of the country found convenient, especially ones relating to the use of native labor. Furthermore, when circumstances led the native peoples to undertake any joint action in opposition to Spanish decisions, the Inca Empire provided them with a symbol of common identity. There had been earlier empires in the Andean area, but they were completely prehistoric. In the absence of any native system of writing, the very existence of such empires had been forgotten; even the ruined buildings they had left were explained by myth. Native unity, in consequence, could be conceived only in Inca terms.

In the perspective of later developments, then, the policies and institutions adopted by the Incas that might have promoted or impeded the cultural unification of their empire have a certain importance. This importance is not dependent on Inca intentions. We need not be very concerned over the degree to which the Incas tried deliberately to encourage cultural unification. Probably all imperial regimes consider some cultural unification administratively convenient, and a case can be made that the Incas shared this common view, particularly with regard to language. Some Inca policies, however, seem to have been designed to perpetuate local differences. My impression from much reading of sixteenth-century sources is that cultural unification was probably not a primary goal of the Inca government. I am inclined to agree with Bernabé Cobo, who said of the Incas in 1653, "The whole foundation of their policy of government rested on means designed to keep their people subject and deprive them of the zeal to revolt against them" (Cobo Lib. 13, Cap I; 1890–1895, Vol. III:302).[1]

In this study I propose to look first at the Inca policies and institutions that should have promoted cultural unification, comment more briefly on the conditions that tended to perpetuate local differences, and conclude with some discussion of the consequences that followed these antecedents after the Spanish took control.

Education and Language

The Incas required provincial nobles to maintain a residence in Cuzco and to spend 4 months a year there. Maintaining a residence in the capital involved settling some retainers nearby who could provide service for it (Ruiz de Arce 1933:268; Sancho de la Hoz Cap. XVI; 1938:176). The nobles also had to send their sons and other relatives (presumably possible heirs, such as brothers) to the court to learn the Inca language and all that was expected of them by the ruler (Segovia 1943:33). Boys were sent to Cuzco at the age of 14 or 15 years (Bandera 1881:101). Cieza de León, writing in 1550–1553, said that the noble boys stayed in Cuzco continuously until their court education was complete but would then return home, as it were making room for others (Cieza de León, Señorío Cap. XIV; 1967:44). Informants replying to a legal inquiry made by Viceroy Francisco de Toledo in 1571 said that provincial nobles, at least the most important ones, were obliged to keep their eldest son in residence at court constantly and to maintain also a representative competent to inform the ruler about the affairs of their territory (Levillier 1940:132, cf. also p. 157). Cieza's account is not necessarily in contradiction of the 1571 testimony, as there may have been two requirements: one regarding education, applying to a larger number of young men, and another involving heirs as hostages for the loyalty of the more important native nobles.

Later writers, Murúa and Valera, speak of the instruction at court as a formal school (Murúa, Historia del origen Lib. 3, Cap. IV; 1946: 169–170; Historia general Lib. 2, Cap. 12; 1962–1964, Vol. II:60–62; Valera, in Garcilaso de la Vega Lib. 4, Cap. XIX; 1945, Vol. I:214 and Lib. 6, Cap. XXXV; 1945, Vol. II:81). Murúa gives an outline of the curriculum and says that the whole course took 4 years. Although there is. nothing in Murúa's more detailed account that conflicts with the testimony of earlier writers, the idea of a curriculum organized by years is a little too reminiscent of European educational planning to be convincing.

One of the principal objects of the court education program was, of course, to ensure that at least second-generation provincial nobles were fluent in the Inca language. We have numerous statements that the Inca rulers ordered that all their subjects learn "the general language" (Atienza Cap. III; 1931:26; Cieza de León, Señorío Cap. XXIV; 1967:84; Gutiérrez de Santa Clara Lib. 3, Cap. LXI; 1950:527; Sarmiento de Gamboa Cap. 39; 1947:198, for example). A program of local schools would have been necessary to make such an order effective; the only reference I have found to the existence of such schools is in Gutiérrez de Santa Clara (as cited). Damián de la Bandera probably described the effective practice when he said that "all the caciques and chief persons of the whole kingdom who held any office or position in the state were obliged to know the general language in order to be able to give whatever information was necessary to their superiors" (Córdoba Mexía 1925:278).

For the court education program to be intelligible, the reader needs to be aware that it was Inca policy to confirm the native nobility in its authority where such a nobility already existed, and to create one where it did not (see section entitled Policies Perpetuating Local Differences). The power of the native nobility was limited by the appointment of Inca governors who were the immediate representatives of the Inca ruler and who had ultimate authority in their jurisdictions.

Polo de Ondegardo (1940:194–195) commented that if a provincial noble had several sons, and one of them had been educated at the Inca court, that particular son had to succeed to his father's post when his father died.

Yanaconas, Camayos, and Mitimas

The three terms—*yanacona, camayo* (or *camayoc*) and *mitima*—refer to three different kinds of male status, not three contrasting categories of men. *Yanacona* designated a man as having a particular kind of civic status, which will be explained in due course; *camayo* indicated that he had a specialized occupation; and *mitima* marked him as someone who was not residing in his place of ethnic origin. In the Inca state, it was possible for a man to have all three of these statuses, a combination of two, or just one. An analogy may help to clarify the situation. In the United States the same person may be a civil service employee, a librarian, and an immigrant. Which status or statuses are mentioned may depend on the context of discourse. In the Inca case our information is frequently drawn from Spanish documents relating to a colonial problem in which certain pre-Spanish institutions need to be explained as they relate to the antecedents of the problem at issue.

Rarely is a complete explanation called for or furnished. If the problem is one of land or jurisdiction, it may be important to emphasize that the man involved or his father was a *mitima*. If the problem is one of supply, his occupation may be important. The fact that we are generally dealing with incomplete information creates difficulties in interpretation. For example, it is possible that all *yanaconas* also had some occupation title, but it is also possible that some did not. For the present, it is best to leave the problem as a subject for further research.

The reason for singling out these three kinds of status for special discussion here is that they represent major ways in which the Inca state interfered with men's traditional loyalties. Taken together, men in these three statuses formed a group that contrasted with the farmers, who lived on lands in the traditional territory of their ancestors, possessed sufficient craft skills to take care of their own needs, and were subject to levies by the central government for military service or unskilled labor. Such farmers called themselves *hatun runa* ('big man') and were called by the yanaconas *suyu runa* ('district man'). The *suyu runas* represented local traditions and loyalties; the *yanaconas*, *camayos*, and *mitimas* were identified in various ways with the interests of the Inca government.

It is a mistake to see the difference as one of degree of servility. No one was "free" in the Inca state. No man could choose his place of residence, occupation, or civil status; theoretically, at any rate, he could not choose his wife. Women's choices were similarly restricted. The important difference was not more or less freedom but more or less access to honor and privilege. The source of honor and privilege was the Inca government; the more closely a person was identified with the government, the greater was his or her chance of attaining the rewards available in the system.

Yanaconas

There has been much confusion in the literature regarding the category of *yanacona* in pre-Spanish society, a confusion to which I have myself contributed (Rowe 1946:238). This is not the place to attempt a solution to all problems relating to *yanaconas*. Here we are interested in what effect the institution might have had on cultural unification. This limitation means that we are concerned with *yanaconas* attached to the Inca rulers or officials of the central government and not with those, fewer in number, who were attached to *curacas*, the provincial nobility (for the latter, the reader is referred to Murra, 1966, 1975:225–242).

In my earlier discussion I translated *yanacona* by the English word *servant*. This translation is seriously misleading. The commonest Spanish translation of *yanacona* is *criado*. This word does mean "servant" in modern Spanish, and the modern Spanish meaning was the basis of my choice of a word in English. However, the fact that *criado* is the past participle of the verb *criar*, 'to raise or bring up,' should have alerted me to the likelihood that the word once had a different meaning, and so should the contexts in which the word is used in sixteenth-century documents.

A great deal of the technical terminology of mediaeval Spanish was still in use in the sixteenth century, and the traditional social relationships of Spanish feudalism had not been forgotten. In his great etymological dictionary Corominas (1954, Vol. 1:941), cites the twelfth-century *Poem of the Cid* for *criado* with the meaning of "*vasallo educado en casa de su señor.*" The reference is to a list of seven of the Cid's most distinguished followers, one of whom was "*Muño Gustioz,—que so criado fo*" (Cid 1946:100). Muño Gustioz was indeed brought up in the Cid's household and later became his wife's brother-in-law. He clearly owed the Cid service in a feudal sense, but he equally clearly was not a "servant" in the modern sense.

In the thirteenth and fourteenth centuries *criado* was used also with the meaning of *hijo* or *discípulo*. This usage is clearly related to the meaning of the verb from which *criado* is derived. Corominas's earliest documentation for the modern meaning of *sirviente* is 1330. Usage in the sixteenth-century literature on Peru suggests that all three meanings of *criado* were current. In social and political contexts it usually implied some kind of service, but that service might be honorable and fully compatible with high social status.

A factor complicating our efforts to understand what it meant to be a *yanacona* before the Spanish invasion is that the Spanish invaders inherited the institution. In the chaotic situation that developed following the arrival of the Spanish, many Incas and former Inca subjects sought protection by attaching themselves to individual Spaniards and were treated as servants, regardless of what their former status had been. Others were probably pressed into personal service. All such dependents were called *yanaconas;* the term was intelligible to the native population, and the Spanish found it a convenient euphemism for something close to slavery. There was a natural tendency to interpret the pre-Spanish institution in terms of the colonial one.

The necessity of reconsidering the status of *yanaconas* before the Spanish invasion was brought home to me when, after reading some modern statements about *yanaconas*, I went back and read what Fernando de Santillán had to say on the subject. Santillán, writing in 1563, compiled information to answer a royal inquiry of 10 years earlier on Inca government and taxation. The inquiry had been addressed to the *Audiencia* of Lima, of which Santillán was a member, and his answer was based on reports solicited from persons considered to be experts, such as the Dominican Fray Cristóbal de Castro; Santillán did not cite his sources, and I cannot identify the one who supplied his information on *yanaconas*.

Santillán wrote:

> The Inca [ruler] took from each valley or province the number of yanaconas he wanted and assigned them to himself. These were chosen from the best people, most of them sons of curacas and people of strength and good disposition. As his 'criados' he made them exempt from the authority of the curacas, who had no responsibility for them; rather, the Inca governor kept them occupied in affairs relating to his service. Some [the ruler] took to Cuzco and retained in his own service, and these he sometimes made curacas in their provinces. Others he assigned to the houses of the dead rulers" (Santillán Par. 36; 1879:39).

The testimony of witnesses in the legal inquiry made in 1571 by Viceroy Toledo supports Santillán's picture of the relatively high status of at least some royal *yanaconas*. Don Juan Cusipoma said that he was one of the *"orejones criados del ynga"* and that his parents had been *criados* of Guayna Capac. It is not clear from the published text what Don Juan's specific duties were (Levillier 1940:105). The *orejones* constituted the Inca elite class; if some of them were *criados* of the ruler, he was indeed taking his *yanaconas* from the "best" people.

Another interesting witness is Don Juan Puyquin, *curaca* of four towns near Cuzco. He testified that his father, Poyquin [sic], was a native of a town named Pia, "in the direction of Quito," and had been taken as a young boy by Topa Inga when he conquered the area. Topa Inga "had killed all the rest because they resisted him" but spared Poyquin because he was so young and made him his *criado*. When the Incas established their government, they appointed as *curacas* "the persons they wished and who seemed to them to have the abilities that were required to govern, even though they were their 'criados,' and so the father of this witness, who, as he has said, was a 'criado' of the said Topa Inga . . . was appointed curaca in this area" (Levillier 1940: 55–57).

For reasons not relevant to this inquiry, we happen to have especially detailed information on the *yanaconas* of Guayna Capac, who lived in the valley of Yucay, near Cuzco, and took care of his estates there. These *yanaconas* comprised the inhabitants of four villages native to the area, probably around 400 men and their families, and 2000 *mitimas*, 1000 levied from Chinchaysuyu and the other 1000 from Collasuyu (Villanueva Urteaga 1971:94, 98, 136, 139). A number of these *yanaconas* testified in Toledo's inquiry of 1571. One was Don Alonso Condor, who identified himself as a native of Soras (there were Soras in both Chinchaysuyu and Collasuyu, and this witness did not specify which Soras he meant). He said that his father had been brought to Yucay and made *curaca* of Pomaguanca (a *yanacona ayllu*). Don Alonso had been a page of Guayna Capac. His father, who died when Guayna Capac was in Quito, had commended Don Alonso to the ruler's care. Guayna Capac made Don Alonso *curaca* in Yucay and rewarded his elder brother for good service by making him a *curaca* in Tomebamba (modern Cuenca, Ecuador) (Levillier 1940:108).

These examples should suffice to establish the accuracy of Santillán's description of the *yanaconas* as personal retainers who performed honorable service and might be rewarded with responsible administrative posts. Of course, the great majority of *yanaconas* performed routine tasks not very different from those of the *suyu runas*. Many of the *yanaconas* at Yucay, for example, cultivated the fields belonging to Guayna Capac's personal estate. Others served as his domestic servants, but there is no reason to think that domestic service for the Inca ruler was considered less honorable than domestic service for European kings.

The fact that *yanaconas* might be recruited as war captives is well documented but evidently not significant in determining subsequent status. We noted the case of Poyquin, who was taken as a war captive and later made a *curaca*.

The status of *yanacona* was inherited. It will be remembered that Don Juan Cusipoma, one of Toledo's witnesses in 1571, identified himself as one of the *"orejones criados del ynga"* and said that his parents had been *criados* of Guayna Capac. Another witness in the same inquiry was Gómez Condori, a native of Collaguas living in Chinchaypuquio, near Cuzco. He said that his father had been brought from Collaguas to be a *criado* of Amaro Topa Inga, Topa Inga's brother, and that he had subsequently served Guayna Capac. When Condori's father died, "they took this witness to serve the said Guayna Capac" (Levillier 1940:113–114). The office of *curaca* was also hereditary; when *yanaconas* who received appointments as *curacas* (such as Poyquin) died, the office was passed on in the usual way. Juan Puyquin succeeded his father as *curaca*.

Yanaconas not only might be appointed *curacas* of *yanaconas*, as happened in the case of Don Alonso Condor's father; they could also be appointed *curacas* of *suyu runas*. To cite a documented example, Guayna Capac deposed the *curaca* of the *hunu* (10,000, the largest decimal unit in the Inca administrative system) of Cochabamba and Leimebamba in Chachapoyas, and, according to testimony taken in 1572, "he gave the said lordship . . . to an Indian who was serving him as a yanacona who was named Chuquimis; it was given him in remuneration of the services he had rendered, and because, in a war the said Guainacaba [i.e., Guayna Capac] had waged in which he had been wounded in a foot, he [i.e., Chuquimis] sucked the blood from the wound" (Espinoza Soriano 1969:294).

Santillán made a distinction between *yanaconas* who were personal retainers of the Inca ruler and ones who served Inca provincial governors. The distinction may be clarified by the contrast made in a legal inquiry in Yucay in 1573 between the private estates of individual Inca rulers and property belonging to or administered by the Inca government in the abstract (Rostworowski de Diez Canseco 1970:159, 258–259). If Inca governors were responsible for the administration of government lands as well as provincial political affairs, they would need relatively large staffs.

Temples also had *yanaconas* attached to them. According to Betanzos, [Pachacuti] Inca Yupanqui assigned 200 *yanaconas* to cultivate the lands he had set aside for the support of the Temple of the Sun in Cuzco (Betanzos Cap. XI; 1880:66).

A witness in the Yucay inquiry of 1573 spoke of certain men who called themselves *apo yanaconas* because they took care of the body of Guayna Capac "and made offerings to him according to their ancient rite" (Villanueva Urteaga 1971:135). '*Apu* in Inca means a great lord and is used in this context as a royal title of Guayna Capac.[2]

It is very difficult to estimate what proportion of the population of the Inca realm served in the capacity of *yanaconas* of Inca rulers or of the Inca government. There is, in fact, only one document that provides some kind of quantification, and that is the *visita* of Chupachos (Huánuco) of 1549. In a list of services provided "to the Inga" four entries can be interpreted as representing *yanaconas* assigned to the service of individual Inca rulers in Cuzco (Helmer 1957:40–41). These entires are: (*a*) "for yanaconas of Guaynacaba [i.e., Guayna Capac], 150 Indians continually"; (*b*) "for the care of the body of Topa Inga Yupangue after [he was] dead, 150 Indians continually"; (*c*) "for the care of his arms, 10 yanaconas"; and (*d*) "for the care of the body of Guaynacaba after [he was] dead, 20 Indians." The total number of adult men involved is 230, or 5.6% of the 4108 listed.

The *yanaconas* furnished by the Chupachos were not subject to the authority of their home *curacas* for the purpose of fulfilling other kinds of labor obligations, but they were obviously carried on the home accounts.

Yanacona service drained off some of the most competent and best qualified people from the provinces into a special force in which men from many different provinces might work side by side, and their service to the Inca ruler was the one thing they had in common. It also provided some opportunities for promotion to positions of responsibility that might be in a province other than that which the *yanacona* regarded as his native one.

Camayos

Camayos, according to a witness who testified in the Yucay inquiry of 1573, "means 'oficiales' [men having a trade or craft] or [men] who were in charge of jobs to be done" (Villanueva Urteaga 1971:136). Lists of *camayo* occupations are given by Falcón (1867:466–468; better text in Rostworowski de Diez Canseco 1976:334–336, 1977:248–250) and Murúa (Historia del origen Lib. 3, Cap. LXVII; 1946:332–334). The two lists are partly parallel and should be used together; Murúa's gives somewhat more explanation of the Inca terms. There are also several lists of occupations in Guaman Poma (especially 1936:191 [193]–192 [194] and 338 [340]).

Falcón gives separate lists for the coast and the sierra, and Rostworowski has discussed the differences in practice in the two areas. On the coast, for example, craft specialists had no farmland and obtained whatever they needed by trading the goods they produced. *Camayos* in the sierra were given land and farmed it for their subsistence in addition to carrying on their specialized activities (Rostworowski de Diez Canseco 1976:323–324, 1977:231). In the sierra *camayos* were apparently also given clothing from the royal stores of garments made by *camayo* weavers (Santillán Par. 51; 1879:45).

Like *yanaconas*, *camayos* were expected to work full-time for the ruler or the royal governor. That meant that they were not subject to the general labor levy or military service, unless, of course, they were professional soldiers. Their status and specialty were hereditary. Thus, whether or not they were also called *yanaconas, camayos* had closely similar civil status. Craftsmen, however, probably had fewer opportunities for personal advancement than those *yanaconas* who were personal attendants of the ruler.

Some *camayos* worked in their own country. According to Martín Carcay, one of the Chupacho witnesses in the *visita* of Huánuco in

1562, the weavers whose profession it was to weave fine cloth did so *en su tierra* (Ortiz de Zúñiga 1967:239). The same witness went on to say, however, that the *oficiales* "settled and took up residence where the Inca [ruler] ordered them and did not return again to their own countries and remained as mitimas where they were put" (Ortiz de Zúñiga 1967:240). Unfortunately, none of the Huánuco documents gives a clear accounting of the numbers of *camayos* moved and where they were settled. Murra's essay on ethnological data in the *visitas* of Huánuco brings together a number of examples from which I get the impression that the *camayos* were generally settled in groups or *pueblos* by occupation (Murra 1967). Clearly, as Murra suggested, the location of some of these settlements, such as those of herders or *coca camayos*, was related to an economy of verticality. Other *camayo* settlements were related to Inca administrative centers, and, according to the *visita* of Chupachos of 1549, a considerable number of *camayos* were settled in Cuzco (Helmer 1957:40).

Probably the best documented example of a settlement of *camayos* related to an Inca administrative center is provided by the potters from the coast who settled near Cajamarca by Topa Inga (Espinoza Soriano 1970). This settlement consisted of a *pachaca* (a unit of 100 men) of potters from Collique, near Chiclayo. Potters appear as *sañu camayoc* in Falcón's list of *camayo* occupations. The members of this settlement are also referred to as *mitimas* and *yanaconas* (*yanayacos* is the common form in the Cajamarca documents). They had been given lands, which they cultivated for their support, and were issued clothing by the government. This is the sierra pattern rather than the coast pattern. These *camayos* made pottery only for the Inca ruler and were attached to the service of the Inca governor (*tocricoc*); they were not subject to any of the Cajamarca *curacas* (Espinoza Soriano 1970:10–16; the documents are late, and there is some confusion regarding the status of *tocricoc*).

The Chupacho *camayos* settled in Cuzco are listed in two groups of 400 men each. The first group was there "to make walls," an occupation listed as *pirca camayoc* by Falcón. The second group was sent to Cuzco to cultivate fields "so the people could eat and make their camarico" (Helmer 1957:40). Since *camayos* normally cultivated lands for themselves in the sierra, the builders were presumably self-supporting, and the men of the second group may represent the support settlement for the residence or residences maintained in Cuzco by the Chupacho nobles (see earlier section on Education and Language). *Camarico* means a more or less obligatory gift and may include offerings in this case. Farmers are not included in Falcón's list of *camayo* occupation, but the appropriate term, *chacara camayo* (i.e., *chacra camayoc*) does appear elsewhere, as we shall see.

A very different case on which we have some information is that of the settlement of 1000 *coca camayos* from Cayambi (northern Ecuador) at Matibamba on the tropical lowland edge of Angaraes (Espinoza Soriano 1974). The production of coca leaf was something of a specialty in the home country of the Cayambis (Paz Ponce de León 1897:117), and coca was a royal monopoly under the Incas. The Matibamba area had a suitable climate and apparently no significant human occupation when the Cayambis were settled there by Guayna Capac; the land had to be cleared for cultivation. As usual in the sierra, the *coca camayos* were given land to cultivate for their own support. This settlement seems to have been part of an Inca program of development of the lands along the edge of the tropical forest.

At least some of the *yanaconas* who worked on Guayna Capac's estate in Yucay were also *camayos*. Two *criados* of Guayna Capac from Yucay who testified for Toledo in 1571 identified themselves as such. One was Martín Capta, a native of the town of Cache, who said he was a *cachi camayo*, "which means salt maker" (Levillier 1940: 108). There are salt works within the limits of Guayna Capac's estate that are still being exploited. It is quite possible that this witness was a *yanacona* but not a *mitima*; four of the five *ayllus* of the town of Cache were made up of natives of Yucay (Villanueva Urteaga 1971:16, 59–67). The other witness said he was a *chacara camayo*, a farmer (Levillier 1940:109). Farmers must have made up a large proportion of the *yanaconas* on Guayna Capac's estate. In an inquiry made there in 1551, the witnesses were asked whether the men who cultivated the lands of the Inca ruler or the Sun cultivated any of these lands for themselves. They replied that these men had their own lands to support them, and that all the produce of the ruler's lands was for him and was taken to Cuzco or wherever else he ordered (Villanueva Urteaga 1971:42–43).

There is some evidence suggesting that there were large numbers of *camayos* serving the central government who were settled near Cuzco. One of Toledo's witnesses in 1571, Don Diego Roco of the town of Marco (Inka *Markhu*, on the plain of Anta) testified that his father had been *curaca* of a *hunu* (the Inca term for a unit of 10,000 men), which he kept busy maintaining causeways, river channels, and bridges for Guayna Capac (Levillier 1940:151). These men are not specifically called *camayos*, nor do our lists of *camayo* occupations include a term obviously appropriate to the work they did. This *hunu* may have been unique, however, in that it included all the specialists needed by the empire for this particular kind of work. It seems likely that these specialists worked for the central government rather than the personal estate of Guayna Capac, since the estate would not need anything like 10,000 specialists for the kind of work these men did.

An Inca garrison settlement in the Huánuco area consisted of men who called themselves *pucara camayos, pukara* being the Inca word for fort (Ortiz de Zúñiga 1972:177). This settlement consisted of 200 Incas from Cuzco and Quichuas (probably, judging from the partial totals, 200 of each, but the testimony is not entirely clear). They had been sent to the area by Topa Inga to garrison three forts, the stated purpose of which was to keep the Chupachos from revolting. For each fort the settlement provided 20 men, doing 1-year tours of guard duty. While on guard duty in the forts, the men had no other obligations than to make their own weapons. The settlement also provided a bridge guard to control unauthorized travel. The settlement had lands, including one maize field that was cultivated for the government; the rest provided subsistence for the settlers. Presumably, the men who were not on guard duty cultivated the fields of those who were, as well as their own (Ortiz de Zúñiga 1972:25, 27, 34, 177, 179, 187, 195, 197, 227). Garrisons of this type are mentioned in Murúa's list of *camayos*, but they are simply called *mitimas* (Murúa, Historia del origen Lib. 3, Cap. LXVII; 1946:333–334). The Chupachos had to provide 200 men for guard duty in Chachapoyas and 200 in Quito, according to the *visita* of 1549 (Helmer 1957:40).

It seems clear that very large numbers of *camayos* were resettled away from their original homes for a variety of different purposes relating to the service of the central government and present and past rulers. The *camayo* program is interesting from a number of different points of view. What interests us here is that one of its effects would have been to weaken the local loyalties of some *camayos* and create bonds to the Inca state.

Mitimas

We have seen that some *mitimas* were *camayos, yanaconas,* or both and served the Inca ruler directly. There were two other kinds of *mitimas,* however. One kind consisted of *mitimas* who were incorporated into the regular administrative organization of the provinces. There were *mitimas* of this kind in all parts of Inca territory, and it is probably to them that most general accounts of the Inca institution of *mitimas* refer. The second kind of *mitimas* remaining to be discussed consisted of colonists sent by the sierra *naciones* of Collasuyu to grow crops at lower elevations. These colonists remained under the jurisdiction of the *curacas* of the districts from which they came.

So many recent studies of specific groups of *mitimas* refer to settlements of *camayos* that I found it unexpectedly difficult to document the existence of *mitimas* who were incorporated into the regular provincial administration. The clearest evidence for the contrast is provided by a *visita* of Cajamarca dating from 1540 (Espinoza Soriano 1967). In this *visita*, the *curacas* of Cajamarca testified that there were six *parcialidades* of natives subject to them in the land of Cajamarca and one *parcialidad* of *mitimas*. In other documents, these *parcialidades* are identified as *guarangas*. The division of the *guarangas* of Cajamarca into Hanansaya and Hurinsaya is not given in this *visita* but appears in a *visita* of 1642 as follows:

	Hanansaya	Hurinsaya
Mitimas	Guzmango	Bambamarca
	Chuquimango	Caxamarca
	Chondal	Pomamarca

The *visita* of 1540 lists four groups of *mitimas*, which appear as four *pachacas* in the *visita* of 1642 (Visita of 1642, ms.). In view of the agreement between these two *visitas* a century apart, I am somewhat puzzled by Espinoza Soriano's statement that there were actually more than 15 groups of *mitimas* incorporated in the administrative structure of Cajamarca (Espinoza Soriano 1967:19–20). Whatever the numbers, however, the important point is that the 1540 *visita* distinguishes the *mitimas* who were incorporated into the provincial organization from other *mitimas*, some from the sierra and some from the coast, who had their own officers and served the Inca ruler directly. The potters from Collique, whom we discussed under the heading of *camayos*, belonged to the latter group.

In the land of Cajamarca probably more *mitimas* were serving the Inca government directly than were subject to the local administration. Since the 1540 *visita* does not give a breakdown of this *mitima* population, this comment is based on the number of different *mitima* groups listed. There may very well have been proportionately more *mitimas* subject to local administration in other areas; Cajamarca was probably exceptional because it was an important collecting point for goods supplied to the Inca government (Cieza de León, Crónica Cap. LXXV; 1922:251; Señorío Cap. XX; 1967:65).

The colonists sent out from the sierra districts of Collasuyu to grow crops in the lowlands require only passing reference here, since they have little or nothing to do with Inca policies relating to unification. Polo de Ondegardo (1940:177–178) claimed credit for having been the first to recognize the special character of these colonies and to call their existence to the attention of the Spanish government. It is very likely that the system of maintaining special colonies at lower elevations was established by local initiative well before the Inca conquest. The Incas continued it, however, and may have expanded it.

As I pointed out in my 1946 treatment of the subject of population movement under the Incas, there were some areas or provinces in which the proportion of *mitimas* was very high. I cited in particular Angaraes and Yamparaes, using the numbers of towns established in the colonial period as a basis for estimating the proportion of *mitimas* to natives (Rowe 1946:270). At the time there was no other basis on which an estimate could be made. Subsequently, Espinoza Soriano has published population figures for Angaraes in 1571 (1974:12). In 1571, a third of the population listed for Angaraes consisted of descendants of *mitimas*. Espinoza names three groups of *mitimas* that are omitted from the population totals; one of them is the settlement of Cayambi *coca camayos* we have already discussed. If these groups had been included, the proportion of *mitimas* might have been greater. However, we have no way of knowing whether or not all the native Angaraes were counted. Perhaps a more significant reason for suggesting that the proportion of *mitimas* was higher before the Spanish conquest is that some *mitimas* returned to the lands of their ancestors in the confusion attending that conquest. It is probably safe to estimate the *mitimas* in Angaraes in the time of Guayna Capac at between a third and a half of the total population. For Yamparaes I have no new figures; the native population was reduced in three towns in the colonial period and the *mitimas* in four (Calancha Lib. II, Cap. XL; 1638:519. The figure of five *mitima* towns I gave in 1946 is in error). An impressionistic estimate is that the proportion of *mitimas* in the population of different provinces varied between about 10% and about 80%.

Chosen Women

Just as the Inca rulers selected young men for service as *yanaconas*, so they selected young women for service as *acllas*, or 'chosen women' (Inca *'aklla*). The women were selected for beauty and included daughters of the highest nobility. A summary of the classes into which the chosen women were divided and the ways in which they were used by the government is given in my 1946 account of Inca culture (p. 269), and I need add only that much more detail on them is available. The list of references I provided is far from complete.

What is of interest for present purposes is that some chosen women were given by the Inca ruler as brides to men whom he wished to honor. Santillán says: "He gave some of them as wives to those he wished to favor, something he always did with those who were his 'criados' and yanaconas, even though they had other wives. Without obtaining their consent or that of their parents, he distributed them to each as he pleased, even though the men to whom he gave them were not natives of their provinces but of others very different in climate and in distance" (Santillán Par. 34; 1879:37–38). Polo de Ondegardo (1940:139) has a similar account of the distribution of chosen women as brides but does not specifically mention the *yanaconas*. Santillán's account emphasizes what is implicit in many others: The chosen women given as brides were selected without reference to their place of origin or that of the man to whom they were given. If *yanaconas* were indeed particularly likely to be honored with brides given by the ruler, *yanacona* families were likely to have a particularly cosmopolitan character.

Religion

The Incas had a state religion that they imposed on their subjects. It involved worship of a hierarchy of nature deities culminating in a creator god. The Creator was followed in importance by the Sun, who was supposed to be the ancestor of the royal house; the Thunder; and the Earth Mother. Some writers include the Moon, a female deity, in this top group; others do not. The Moon was supposed to be the wife of the Sun, and her phases provided a popular calendar for regulating everyday affairs. There is some evidence that the nature deities of the Inca pantheon were already widely worshiped in the Andean area before the rise of Inca power, although their relative importance was not a matter of general agreement.

At each provincial capital the Incas also set up an elaborate system of local shrines modeled on the system of Cuzco (Polo de Ondegardo, Errores Cap. XV; 1585, F. 16; 1872:64–65; 1940:154). The local shrines at Cuzco that were recognized by the state included a number that were traditionally identified with peoples in the vicinity of Cuzco whom the Incas had conquered, such as the Ayarmacas, and it is likely that existing local shrines were accepted in a similar fashion at the provincial capitals.

Since the Incas believed that almost everything had some supernatural power, it was natural for them to accept the deities and sacred objects of the people they conquered, insofar as the native cults did not conflict with Inca religious values. When a new province was conquered, its chief deity or sacred object was taken to Cuzco and installed there either in the Temple of the Sun or in a special shrine maintained by priests and attendants furnished by the province in question (Polo de Ondegardo, Errores Cap. XV; 1585, F. 16; 1872:17–18; 1940: 183–184). The provincial cult objects were of course held as hostages for the loyalty of their people, but they were treated with honor as long as their people did not revolt. According to another account, the people of each province brought one of their deities or sacred objects to Cuzco every year at the time of the Zithuwa festival; it remained in Cuzco for 1 year and was then replaced by another, the previous one being returned to its home shrine (Molina 1943:46). Probably what we have here are references to two separate arrangements: one involving the permanent removal to Cuzco of the principal deity or sacred object of each province, and the other concerning annual visits by lesser objects of worship, which acquired honor and recognition by their stay at the Inca capital.

A number of major oracles in the Inca realm enjoyed considerable political power in the regions they served at the time of the Inca conquest. Two of these, Pachacamac on the coast and Titicaca in the sierra, received special recognition by the Inca government. The details of the arrangements made about Pachacamec are not clear. In the case of Titicaca, the shrine was incorporated into the Inca creation myth, and Topa Inga established a large settlement of *mitimas* there under the governorship of a grandson of Viracocha Inga. The *mitimas* were drawn from all over the realm, from 42 *naciones*, according to Ramos Gavilán, who provided a list (Ramos Gavilán Lib. 1, Cap. XII; 1976:43). A temple of the Inca state religion was established near the traditional native shrine. There were 2000 *mitimas* in the Inca settlement, and they were "reserved from all tribute and served only to maintain the temples clean and in good repair" (Cobo Lib. 13, Cap. XVIII; 1890–1895, Vol. IV:60). I infer from this wording that the *mitimas* at Titicaca had a status like that of *yanaconas*, whether or not they were so called (see also on this settlement Espinoza Soriano 1972a).

Another religious institution that may have had some unifying effect was the *capacocha*, an especially elaborate form of human sacrifice described in general terms by Molina (1943:69–77). Selected boys and girls of about 10 years of age were brought from the provinces to Cuzco for a special ceremony and then distributed for sacrifice to the major shrines of the realm. We have specific information on some details of this institution for Recuay in the province of Huaylas (Hernández Príncipe 1923). As late as 1622 the names of the *capacochas* furnished by Recuay were remembered by their *ayllus*, and the tombs of the ones who were returned to Recuay for sacrifice were known and revered. The places to which the others were sent were also remembered. The *capacocha* sacrifices thus provided another kind of network holding the great Inca realm together.

Policies Perpetuating Local Differences

As noted in the introduction, there were some Inca policies that seem designed to perpetuate local differences and traditional loyalties as well as ones that might have worked to promote cultural unification. Some brief comments on these other Inca policies are now in order.

When the Incas conquered a kingdom ruled by a native dynasty, they usually kept the ruling family in office. The ruling family and its subordinate officials were fitted into the Inca decimal hierarchy, the higher ranks of which were hereditary. Where there was no existing organized government, the Incas created one by appointing the prestige chiefs who were willing to serve them to the appropriate hereditary office. There is direct native testimony that the Incas applied the policy of creating an organized government to the Guancas in central Peru (Levillier 1940:19–20; compare Vega 1881:24). In drawing provincial boundaries, the Incas seem to have tried to respect existing ethnic units (*naciones*), although small groups were combined for administrative convenience, as in Collaguas (Ulloa Mogollón 1885:42–43). Very large states, such as the Kingdom of Chimor, were broken up (Rowe 1948:45). The subdivisions of the kingdom were respected, however, and their governing families continued in office.

Mitima settlements, both those incorporated in the provincial organization and those that remained outside it, were made in ethnically homogeneous blocks—perhaps of 100, 200, or 1000 married men with their families, all from the same *nación*—and these blocks maintained their separate identity wherever they settled. *Mitimas* were handled in this way for security reasons, and the settlers were supposed to keep the natives loyal, even when the reason for their resettlement was distrust of their own loyalty. Naturally, the natives tended to regard the *mitimas* as spies for the government. It was not an arrangement likely to produce any immediate melting-pot effect.

The Incas insisted that all their subjects maintain their traditional costumes, especially head ornaments. This policy was another security measure, and there were severe penalties for changing costume (Córdoba Mexía 1925:276).

Consequences

The formation of the Inca Empire and the policies and institutions by which it was governed were effectively the work of only three successive rulers: Pachacuti (also called Inga Yupangui), Topa Inga, and Guayna Capac. Writing in 1550–1553, Cieza de León remarked, "The realm is full of Indians who knew Topa Inga Yupangue and followed him in the wars, and they heard from their parents what Inga Yupangue did in the time of his reign" (Cieza de León, Señorío Cap. IX; 1967:27; spelling of names according to the Crónica). Even if the Incas had put more emphasis on cultural unification, there had clearly not been time enough for their institutions to achieve any very profound effect in this direction. Use of the "general language" had, however, become sufficiently widespread so that the Spanish were able to use it as a lingua franca in dealing with the native population.

The Spanish invaders started fighting among themselves even before Inca resistance to them was broken. The result was some 20 years of intermittent chaos, which some of Toledo's native informants referred to as "la behetría de los españoles," that is, a time when men could, within certain limits, choose their own masters (Levillier 1940:150, 159). The Inca central administration was swept away, leaving its camayos and yanaconas masterless and without protection. These camayos and yanaconas tended to attach themselves to Spanish patrons or to curacas who were able and willing to use their services. Some remained on their land allotments; some went "home" to their ancestral territory, where there was likely to be land available to them on account of the catastrophic population loss that was taking place.

Meanwhile, Cari, the lord of Chucuito, a powerful curaca in the Lake Titicaca basin, proclaimed himself son of the Sun (an Inca royal title) and attacked his neighbors (Sitio del Cuzco 1934:121). On the coast, the people of Ica decided that they were free and proceeded to eliminate all Inca influence from their pottery style (Menzel 1976:243). The Cañares, on the other hand, became fanatical adherents of the Spanish, as, to a lesser extent, did some other peoples resentful of Inca rule.

With the supervision of the Inca governors removed, the power of the *curacas* was held in check only by their responsibility to provide tribute and service to their Spanish *encomenderos* and sometimes other Spanish officials (for details and references, see Rowe 1957). The more powerful *curacas* took advantage of the situation to .assume as many of the royal prerogatives of Inca rulers as they could (Polo de Ondegardo 1940:144, 1872:89, 163). It looked for a while as if the regional loyalties would triumph and any hope of a greater unity be buried.

Some *curacas* invented glorious pasts for their people by projecting the sixteenth-century situation back to the time of the Inca conquest. If the Guancas did not do this kind of inventing on their own initiative, it is being done for them in our day; Espinoza Soriano has published a claim, unsupported by references, that the Guancas had hereditary kings before the Inca conquest (Espinoza Soriano 1972b:38).

The Incas, meanwhile, still had an independent government in exile with its headquarters at Vilcabamba. From 1558 to 1571 this government was headed by a very able man, Titu Cusi Yupanqui. Titu Cusi kept up elaborate diplomatic negotiations with the Spanish authorities, while he tried to organize a religious revival and a general revolt. Enough time had passed since the Spanish invasion so that much of the bitterness of the anti-Inca reaction had evaporated. Spanish rule was considerably more oppressive than Inca rule had been, and supporting a *curaca* in each *encomienda* who wanted to act the part of a king was a heavy load to bear on top of meeting the demands of the *encomenderos*. The *curacas* themselves were disillusioned; they did not relish being treated as lackeys and tax collectors when they considered themselves hereditary lords of large districts. The further the Inca regime faded into memory, the more desirable it became. Titu Cusi found a lot of people interested in his message.

On March 6, 1565, Governor Lope García de Castro wrote to the king of Spain that he feared a native rising. He had received a report that the Guancas of the valley of Jauja, who had dinstinguished themselves by loyal service to the Spanish crown, had been secretly manufacturing 3000 pikes. It is evident from Governor Castro's correspondence over the next 7 months that he had discovered that the plot was general and had traced it to Titu Cusi. His answer to it was to appoint a *corregidor de indios* in each province to provide the kind of control over the *curacas* that the Inca governors had exercised and make the natives pay for this measure as a punishment (Levillier, 1921–1926, Vol. III:59–60, 70–71, 80–83).

The religious revival is described in some detail by Cristóbal de Molina. It was called the *taqui oncoy* (Inca *taki 'onqoy*, 'dance sickness'), and it was not stamped out by the Spanish religious authorities until 7 years after it was first discovered (i.e., until the Inca government in exile was destroyed in 1572). It extended through the territories of Chuquisaca, La Paz, Arequipa, Cuzco, Guamanga, and Lima. The doctrine preached by the leaders of this movement involved a rising of the native deities against the Christian God, which would make possible a military victory on the human level (Molina 1943:78–82. On the movement of 1565, compare Hemming 1970: 305–307, 310, and references on pp. 592–593).

The Inca-inspired movement of 1565 and the appointment of the Spanish *corregidores de indios* marked the beginning of the end of the regionalism of the *curacas*. Governor Castro was succeeded by Viceroy Francisco de Toledo, who organized a tough, uniform Spanish administration. The last spokesman for the old order of the early colonial *curacas* was Felipe Guaman Poma de Ayala, a survivor of the Toledo era whose monumental plea for a return of authority and privilege to the *curacas* was finished in 1615 (Guaman Poma 1936).

Guaman Poma was in part protesting the new order imposed by Castro and Toledo, which in effect put the *curacas* back into about the same position in the administration they had occupied under the Incas. The native population was increasingly treated as a common labor pool; only the Cañares retained any special privileges as a reward for their fanatical loyalty to the Spanish cause. This situation created new pressures for cultural unity, which in some respects were felt through what had survived of Inca institutions.

Use of the Inca "general language" was so convenient that this language was widely adopted both by secular administrators and Spanish priests assigned to teach Christianity to the natives. It was even introduced by the Spanish in areas where the Incas had never ruled, such as Sibundoy in southern Colombia and Santiago del Estero in Argentina. Spanish was used chiefly in areas such as the coast where population loss had been particularly devastating.

Further displacement of population had occurred in the wars following the Spanish invasion, and Toledo generally settled people where he found them, whether they were *mitimas* or war refugees. The Spanish had developed a program of forced labor at inadequate pay, which was a distortion of the labor levies to which the *suyu runas* were subject under Inca rule. In Inca practice, members of each *pachaca* subject to the levies assumed this service by turns (Inca *mit'a*), and the Spanish program of forced labor, which was assessed in the same way, came to be called *mita* in consequence. Toledo systematized *mita* service in such a way that it became one of the most oppressive aspects of the Spanish regime in Peru. Efforts to escape the *mita* and other exactions led many native tribute payers to abandon their lands and look for work in another province, where they were counted as *forasteros*, not subject to the same exactions as the *originarios*. In the seventeenth and eighteenth centuries, this movement took place on a large scale, producing further significant mixture of population and consequent weakening of traditional local loyalties (Rowe 1957:esp. pp. 175, 180).

Native religion was driven underground by Spanish persecution, and this process also had a unifying effect. The Spanish were fairly successful in destroying the shrines that had great regional importance, or replacing them with Christian ones, as they replaced Titicaca by Copacabana. What was left of native religion was essentially a core of ideas and rituals which was in large part much older than the Incas, but which they had respected and incorporated in their own practice.

With growing resentment of Spanish oppression and the decline of old local loyalties, the Inca tradition emerged as the obvious symbol shared by the native peoples, which marked their common difference from the Spanish and represented their opposition to foreign domination. Ironically, it was Spanish policies as much as Inca ones that gave the former subjects of the realm a sense of Inca national identity and a degree of cultural unification in the native tradition that we are only just beginning to appreciate.

Acknowledgment

This study owes much to the intellectual stimulation I have derived from discussions of Inca historical problems with Catherine J. Julien. Her own research on Inca administration in the provinces has helped to maintain my interest in the subject. She called attention, when necessary, to serious weaknesses in my arguments and raised problems relating to *camayos* and *mitimas*, which forced me to do more research on these institutions. The solutions presented here are mine, and I take full responsibility for them; but if the problems had not been recognized, the solutions would never have been sought.

Notes

[1]For published sixteenth and seventeenth century works that are divided into chapters or numbered paragraphs, a system of double citation is used. It permits readers who only have access to a different edition than the one cited to locate the passage in question.

[2]In this discussion, Inca words are usually given their most common sixteenth-century Spanish spellings. When a spelling in Inca orthography is given, it is designated as Inca. The Inca orthography used is the one approved by the III Congreso Indigenista Interamericano (La Paz 1954).

References

Atienza, Lope de
1931   Compendio historial del estado de los indios del Perú [1572–1575] (La religión del imperio de los Incas, por J. Jijón y Caamaño, Apendices, Vol. I). Quito: Escuela Tipográfica Salesiana.
Bandera, Damián de la
1881   Relación general de la disposición y calidad de la provincia de Guamanga, llamada San Joan de la Frontera, y de la vivienda, y costumbres de los naturales della.—año de 1557. In Relaciones Geográficas de Indias. Perú [edited by Marcos Jiménez de la Espada], Vol. I:96–104. Madrid: Ministerio de Fomento.
Betanzos, Juan de
1880   Suma y narración de los Incas [1551]. Publícala Marcos Jiménez de la Espada. Biblioteca Hispano-Ultramarina, Vol. V, second paging. Madrid: Imprenta de Manuel G. Hernández.
Calancha, Antonio de la
1638   Coronica moralizada del Orden de San Avgvstin en el Perv, con svcesos egenplares en esta monarqvia. Barcelona: Pedro Lacavalleria.
Cid
1946   Poema de mio Cid. Texto primitivo establecido por Ramón Menéndez Pidal; transcripción moderna versificada de Luis Garnier; prólogo de Dámaso Alonso (Colección Crisol, No. 96). Madrid: M. Aguilar, Editor.
Cieza de León, Pedro de
1922   La crónica del Perú [1550] (Los Grandes Viajes Clásicos, [No. 24]). Madrid: Calpe.
1967   El señorío de los Incas (2.a parte de la Crónica del Perú) [1553]. (Fuentes e Investigaciones para la Historia del Perú, Serie: Textos Básicos, No. 1). Lima: Instituto de Estudios Peruanos.
Cobo, Bernabé
1890–1895   Historia del Nuevo Mundo [1653], publicada por primera vez con notas y otras ilustraciones de D. Marcos Jiménez de la Espada (4 vols.). Sevilla: Sociedad de Bibliófilos Andaluces.
Córdoba Mexía, Pedro de
1925   Información hecha en el Cuzco, por orden del Rey y encargo del Virrey Martín Enríquez acerca de las costumbres que tenían los Incas del Perú, antes de la conquista española, en la manera de administrar justicia civil y criminal [1582]. In Levillier 1921–1926, Vol. IX:268–288.
Corominas, Juan
1954   Diccionario crítico etimológico de la lengua castellana. (Biblioteca Románica Hispánica, V. Diccionarios Etimológicos) (4 vols.). Madrid: Editorial Gredos.
Espinoza Soriano, Waldemar
1967   El primer informe etnológico sobre Cajamarca. Año de 1540. Revista Peruana de Cultura, 11–12 (enero-junio):5–41. Lima.
1969   Los Señoríos étnicos de Chachapoyas y la alianza hispano-chacha. Visitas, informaciones y memoriales inéditos de 1572–1574. Revista Histórica, Vol. XXX (1967):224–332. Lima.
1970   Los mitmas yungas de Collique en Cajamarca, siglos XV, XVI, y XVII. Revista del Museo Nacional, Vol. XXXVI (1969–1970):9–57. Lima.
1972a   Copacabana del Collao; un documento de 1548 para la etnohistoria andina. Bulletin de l'Institut Français d'Etudes Andines I (1):1–16. Lima.
1972b   Los Huancas, aliados de la conquista. Tres informaciones inéditas sobre la

participación indígena en la conquista del Perú, 1558–1560–1561. *Universidad Nacional del Centro del Perú. Anales Científicos* 1 (1971):5–407. Huancayo.

1974   La coca de los mitmas cayampis en el reino de Ancara. Siglo XVI. *Universidad Nacional del Centro del Perú. Anales Científicos* 2 (1973):5–67. Huancayo.

Falcón, Francisco
1867   Representación hecha por el Licenciado Falcón en Concilio Provincial, sobre los daños y molestias que se hacen á los indios [1567]. *Colección de Documentos Inéditos, relativos al Descubrimiento, Conquista y Organización de las Antiguas Posesiones Españolas de América y Oceanía . . .* por D. Luis Torres de Mendoza, Vol. VII:451–495. Madrid: Imprenta de Frías y Compañía.

Garcilaso de la Vega, "El Inca"
1945   *Comentarios reales de los Incas* [1609]. Edición al cuidado de Angel Rosenblat (second edition, 2 vols.). Buenos Aires: Emecé Editores S.A.

Guaman Poma, Felipe
1936   *Nueva corónica y buen gobierno (codex péruvien illustré)* [1615] (Université de Paris. Travaux et Mémoires de l'Institut d'Ethnologie XXIII). Paris.

Gutiérrez de Santa Clara, Pedro
1905   *Historia de las guerras civiles del Perú (1544–1548) y de otros sucesos de las Indias. Tomo tercero* [part on the Incas written 1546–48] (Colección de Libros y Documentos referentes a la Historia de América, Vol. IV). Madrid: Librería General de Victoriano Suárez.

Helmer, Marie
1957   "La visitación de los yndio chupachos" inka et encomendero 1549. *Travaux de l'Institut Français d'Etudes Andines*, Vol. V (1955–1956):3–50. Paris— Lima.

Hemming, John
1970   *The conquest of the Incas.* New York: Harcourt Brace Jovanovich, Inc.

Hernández Príncipe, Rodrigo
1923   Mitología andina [1621–1622]. Nota final por Carlos A. Romero. *Inca* I (1, enero-marzo):25–78. Lima.

Levillier, Roberto
1921–1926   *Gobernantes del Perú. Cartas y papeles, siglo XVI. Documentos del Archivo de Indias* (Colección de Publicaciones Históricas de la Biblioteca del Congreso Argentino) (14 vols.). Madrid.

1940   *Don Francisco de Toledo, supremo organizador del Perú; su vida, su obra (1515–1582). Tomo II, Sus informaciones sobre los Incas (1570–1572).* Buenos Aires: Espasa-Calpe, S.A.

Menzel, Dorothy
1976   *Pottery style and society in ancient Peru. Art as a mirror of history in the Ica Valley, 1350–1570.* Berkeley, Los Angeles, London: University of California Press.

Molina, Cristóbal de
1943   Relación de las fábulas y ritos de los Incas [1575]. *Los Pequeños Grandes Libros de Historia Americana*, serie I. Vol. IV, second paging. Lima: Lib. e Imp. D. Miranda.

Murra, John Victor
1966   New data on retainer and servile populations in Tawantinsuyu. *XXXVI Congreso Internacional de Americanistas, España, 1964. Actas y Memorias*, Vol. 2:35–45. Sevilla.

1967   La visita de los Chupachu como fuente etnológica. In Ortiz de Zúñiga 1967:381–496.

1975   *Formaciones económicas y políticas del mundo andino* (Historia Andina 3). Lima: Instituto de Estudios Peruanos.

Murúa, Martín de

1946   *Historia del origen y genealogía real de los reyes incas del Perú* [c. 1605]. Introducción, notas y arreglo por Constantino Bayle (Biblioteca "Missionalia Hispanica", Vol. II). Madrid: Instituto Santo Toribio de Mogrovejo.

1962–1964   *Historia general del Perú* [1611–1615]. Introducción y notas de Manuel Ballesteros-Gaibrois (Colección Joyas Bibliográficas; Bibliotheca Americana Vetus, I, II). Madrid: Instituto Gonzalo Fernández de Oviedo.

Ortiz de Zúñiga, Iñigo

1967   *Visita de la provincia de León de Huánuco en 1562. Tomo I. Visita de los cuatro waranqa de los Chupachu.* Edición a cargo de John V. Murra (Documentos para la Historia y Etnología de Huánuco y la Selva Central, Vol. I). Huánuco: Universidad Nacional Hermilio Valdizán, Facultad de Letras y Educación.

1972   *Visita de la provincia de León de Huánuco en 1562. Tomo II. Visita de los Yacha y mitmaqkuna cuzqueños encomendados en Juan Sánchez Falcón.* Edición a cargo de John V. Murra (Documentos para la Historia y Etnología de Huánuco y la Selva Central, Vol. II). Huánuco: Universidad Nacional Hermilio Valdizán, Facultad de Letras y Educación.

Paz Ponce de León, Sancho de

1897   Relación y descripción de los pueblos del partido de Otavalo—1582. In *Relaciones Geográficas de Indias. Peru* [edited by Marcos Jiménez de la Espada], Vol. II:105–120. Madrid: Ministerio de Fomento.

Polo de Ondegardo, Juan

1585   Los errores y svpersticiones de los indios sacadas del tratado y aueriguación que hizo el Licenciado Polo [1559]. In *Confessionario para los cvras de indios.* Instrucion contra las cerimonias, y ritos que usan los indios conforme al tiempo de su infidelidad, Ff.7–16. Lima: Antonio Ricardo.

1872   Relación de los fundamentos acerca del notable daño que resulta de no guardar á los indios sus fueros.—junio 26 de 1571. *Colección de Documentos Inéditos, relativos al Descubrimiento, Conquista y Organización de las Antiguas Posesiones Españolas de América y Oceanía . . . por D. Luis Torres de Mendoza,* Vol. XVII:5–177. Madrid: Imprenta del Hospicio.

1940   Informe del Licenciado Juan Polo de Ondegardo al Licenciado Briviesca de Muñatones sobre la perpetuidad de las encomiendas en el Perú [1561]. *Revista Histórica,* Vol. XIII:125–196. Lima.

Ramos Gavilán, Alonso

1976   *Historia de Nuestra Señora de Copacabana.* Segunda edición completa, según la impresión príncipe de 1621 (Publicaciones Culturales: Cámara Nacional de Comercio, Cámara Nacional de Industrias). La Paz: Academia Boliviana de Historia.

Rostworowski de Diez Canseco, María

1970   El Repartimiento de Doña Beatriz Coya, en el valle de Yucay. *Historia y Cultura* 4:153–267. Lima.

1976   Pescadores, artesanos y mercaderes costeños en el Perú prehispánico. *Revista del Museo Nacional,* Vol. LXI (1975):311–349. Lima.

1977   *Etnía y sociedad; costa peruana prehispánica* (Historia Andina 4). Lima: Instituto de Estudios Peruanos.

Rowe, John Howland
   1946   Inca culture at the time of the Spanish conquest. *Handbook of South American Indians* (Bureau of American Ethnology, Bulletin 143), Vol. 2:183–330. Washington.
   1948   The Kingdom of Chimor. *Acta Americana,* VI, (1–2, enero-junio):26–59. Mexico.
   1957   The Incas under Spanish colonial institutions. *Hispanic American Historical Review* XXXVII (2, May):155–199. Durham.
Ruiz de Arce, Juan
   1933   Relación de los servicios en Indias de don Juan Ruiz de Arce, conquistador del Perú [1543]. *Boletín de la Academia de la Historia* CII (cuaderno II, abril-junio):327–384. Madrid.
Sancho de la Hoz, Pedro
   1938   Relación para S. M. de lo sucedido en la conquista y pacificación de estas provincias de la Nueva Castilla y de la calidad de la tierra [1534]. *Biblioteca de Cultura Peruana,* serie 1, No. 2:117–185. Paris: Desclée, De Brouwer.
Santillán, Fernando de
   1879   Relación del origen, descendencia, política y gobierno de los Incas [1563]. In *Tres relaciones de antigüedades peruanas* [edited by Marcos Jiménez de la Espada], Pp. 1–133. Madrid: Ministerio de Fomento.
Sarmiento de Gamboa, Pedro
   1947   *Historia de los Incas* [1572] (Biblioteca Emecé de Obras Universales, No. 85). Third edition. Buenos Aires: Emecé Editores.
Segovia, Bartolomé de
   1943   Relación de muchas cosas acaecidas en el Perú [1553]. *Los Pequeños Grandes Libros de Historia Americana,* serie I, Vol. IV, first paging. Lima: Lib. e Imp. D. Miranda.
Sitio del Cuzco
   1934   Relación del sitio del Cusco [sic] y principio de las guerras civiles del Perú hasta la muerte de Diego de Almagro, 1535–1539 [1539]. *Colección de Libros y Documentos referentes a la Historia del Perú,* serie 2, Vol. X:1–133. Lima.
Ulloa Mogollón, Juan de
   1885   Relación de la provincia de los Collaguas para la discrepción de las Yndias que Su Magestad manda hacer [1586]. In *Relaciones Geográficas de Indias. Perú* [edited by Marcos Jiménez de la Espada], Vol. II:38–50. Madrid: Ministerio de Fomento.
Vega, Andrés de
   1881   La descripción que se hizo en la provincia de Xauxa por la instrución de S. M. que a la dicha provincia se invio de molde [1582]. In *Relaciones Geográficas de Indias. Perú* [edited by Marcos Jiménez de la Espada], Vol. I:79–95. Madrid: Ministerio de Fomento.
Villanueva Urteaga, Horacio
   1971   Documentos sobre Yucay en el siglo XVI. *Revista del Archivo Histórico del Cuzco* 13 (1970):1–148. Cuzco.
Visita of 1642
   ms.   *Bisita del obraxe desta villa y autos que se an echo en birtud della.* Juez Don evjenio de Segura, escribano Joseph luiz de Arana. Caxamarca, 1642. 20ff. (transcript by J. H. Rowe; present location of original not known).

5

Inca Decimal Administration in the Lake Titicaca Region

Catherine J. Julien

Editors' Introduction

Catherine Julien argues that the Inca curbed the power of local elites both by reducing their discretionary control over citizens' labor and by replacing possible dissidents. Since even decimal officials were obligated to participate in public works, albeit in inverse proportion to their rank, their relative status was symbolized in other ways. The hierarchical system effaced heterogeneous regional variations in local leaders' claim to positions and paved the way for an imperial class system. Julien thus emphasizes how decimal administration would have rationalized state control, even in provinces from which populations were not removed by *mitima* assignments to other locations.

Although Julien's evidentiary base differs little from that of Pease and Murra, as will be seen, her analysis differs markedly. Whereas Murra discounts decimal administration because of its scant mention in the *visitas*, Julien stresses indirect evidence for decimal groupings. Whereas Murra emphasizes the ways in which provincial productive activities continued unchanged and whereas Pease sees only a limited surplus flowing to the Incas, Julien points to the state's permanent expropriation of substantial proportions of provincial labor.

Inca use of a decimal system of administration was reported to be general throughout the empire, and yet little specific information

THE INCA AND AZTEC
STATES, 1400–1800

about its application can be found in documentary sources.[1] It functioned primarily as a means of distributing the labor obligataion imposed by the Inca government on the provinces. The labor assessed might result in the production of goods, but the demand was for labor. The decimal administration was basically a labor recruitment organization.

Decimal administration is described in general accounts of Inca administration, but references to it seem to be much rarer in the more specific administrative records kept by the Spanish colonial government. These administrative records have been appreciated in recent years as a source of information about those aspects of local organization that were not imposed by the Incas (Murra 1968: 115). However, administrative records often contain direct testimony about the Inca administration by people who were adults at the time of the Spanish invasion in 1532. The Spanish government was interested in inquiring into aspects of Inca administration, especially during the years from 1559 to 1586, and often asked for information about it.[2] Sometimes these inquiries elicited direct information about the decimal administration (Ortíz de Zúñiga 1967: 29). Even when they did not, it is often possible to detect traces of the decimal organization in the accounts given.

A case in point is the documentation published for the Lupaca province, located on the southwest side of Lake Titicaca. In recent years a body of administrative records concerning this province has been published. A *visita*, or administrative survey, of the Lupaca province in 1567 provides particular detail about the Lupacas unavailable for most other parts of the Inca empire (Diez de San Miguel 1964). At first glance the Lupaca province appears not to have been organized along decimal lines, and it seems, therefore, to constitute an exception to the general accounts. On closer examination a number of features of decimal organization are evident.

Since traces of decimal administration can be detected in the documentation for the Lupacas, other features of the tribute system may also be found. Details of the Lupaca tribute obligation are contained in several interviews with local authorities, or *kurakas*. The *kurakas* listed specific labor services their people were expected to provide to the Incas. These lists resemble an Inca labor assignment recorded for the Huánuco province in the north-central highlands. Thus, it appears that two widely separated provinces were under a similar labor assignment. Furthermore, the labor assignments imposed on these two provinces are consistent with information contained in the general accounts about the labor obligation imposed by the Incas.

Since local people staffed the decimal administration, the Lupaca case provides a concrete example of the role given to local people in the Inca government. Recruitment was the administrative area defined for them. In this area the Inca government would have had the most need of local authority in order to execute its demands. At the same time the power held by local elites was problematic because they were often behind attempted rebellions. One way of limiting local authority was to remove tributaries from the recruitment pool by assigning them to perform services for the government on a permanent basis. In the Huánuco province fully half of the tributaries were permanently assigned, and it can be expected that a similar proportion of tributaries was withdrawn in other provinces.

The origins of decimal administration in the Andes are obscure. The Incas may have adopted it for their purposes as early as the reign of Pachakuti (1438–1471).[3] Subsequent emperors may also have modified the decimal administration in concept or in application. An obvious time for input from later rulers was when new territories were annexed to the empire during their reign; the Lupaca example is probably a reflection of a specific epoch in the evolution of Inca administration.

Since the Lupaca materials were collected after the effective dismantling of the Inca provincial administration, they also serve to document what happened when Inca rule came to an end. The *kurakas* interviewed by Garci Diez in 1567 were descended from officers of *kuraka* rank in the Inca administration. At some time following the Spanish conquest in 1532, these *kurakas* assumed control of tributaries who had been outside of their control during the later Inca empire and so emerged victorious among the possible contenders for direct authority over the people of the Lupaca province in the absence of the Inca government.

The Inca Tribute System and the Role of Decimal Administration

An overview of the Inca tribute system and the role of decimal administration within it can be reconstructed from general accounts of Inca administration.

The Inca government extracted goods and services from provinces organized for the payment of tribute. Major expropriations of land and movable property were effected at the time a new territory was annexed, and further expropriations may have occurred at later dates. The ongoing administration of the provinces, however, functioned without any expropriation of land or movable property (Polo de Ondegardo 1917:51; 1940:133; Cobo Lib. 12, Cap. XXVII; 1964, Vol. 92:120). Labor was the principal contribution exacted, even if the labor resulted in the production of goods (Falcón 1867:461, 471–472; Guaman Poma 1936:338; Polo de Ondegardo 1916:66–67, 88; 1940:136–137, 165).

The Inca provincial administration was intended to oversee the payment of labor service owed to the empire by those provinces incorporated within the tribute system. In each province the administration was centralized under the control of a provincial governor, chosen from among the Cuzco nobility (Cobo Lib. 12, Cap. XXV; 1964, Vol. 92:114; Bandera 1881:99; Guaman Poma 1936:184, 346–347; Pizarro 1968:498–499; Santillán 1968:382–383). This governor had a number of lieutenants, called *michoc*, who aided in civil administration (Bandera 1881:100). Accountants, or *khipukamayoq*, who kept knot records (*khipu*) provided additional administrative support (Guaman Poma 1936:348–349; Diez de San Miguel 1964:117; Cieza de León, Señorío Cap. XX; 1967:67).

Because labor was the principal exaction of the government, one of the chief tasks of the provincial administration was labor recruitment. Some of the goods and services could be more efficiently extracted if those assigned to generate them did so on a permanent basis. A growing body of evidence documents the existence of specific groups who were under permanent assignment (Espinoza Soriano 1970:11–16; 1974; Villanueva Urteaga 1971:94, 98, 136, 139). Labor was also recruited on a temporary basis.

Permanent versus temporary assignment was the major subdivision of the Inca tribute system. Since each tributary was assigned to perform only one kind of labor service (Bandera 1968:509; Santillán 1968:398, 418), those who were not permanently assigned formed a general pool of tributaries subject to recruitment either for temporary projects or for permanent assignment.

Those tributaries who were permanently assigned were still accounted with their province of origin, but for all practical purposes they were no longer subject to its recruitment organization. A labor assignment that accounts for the labor services owed by all the tributaries of the Huánuco province in the north-central highlands has been published (Helmer 1957:40–41). This document indicates that each province was under some kind of standing labor assignment. Moreover, since all tributaries are covered in the labor assignment, it accounts for both permanent and temporary labor services.

In other important regards, those who were permanently assigned were in a class apart from the other tributaries of their province. They were frequently relocated, sometimes outside their province of origin (Guaman Poma 1936:191, 195, 338; Cobo Lib. 12, Cap. XXVII; 1964, Vol. 92:119; Cieza de León, Señorío Cap. XXII; 1967:75; Ortíz de Zúñiga 1967:238–240; Pizarro 1968:507; Santillán 1968:398). They were not supported by the government but had access to plots of land for their subsistence needs, at least in the highlands (Guaman Poma 1936:195; Ortíz de Zúñiga 1967:239–240; Espinoza Soriano 1970:12; 1973:270, 284; Rostworowski de Diez Canseco 1975:323–324). Their responsibility was to produce goods, given the raw materials, or provide a service on a regular basis (Ortia de Zúñiga 1967:29).

Tributaries who were permanently assigned passed their assignment on to their descendants. If their line was extinguished, they were replaced by other tributaries from their province of origin (Ortíz de Zúñiga 1967:239–240; Diez de San Miguel 1964:106–107). It was for this reason that they continued to be accounted with other tributaries in their home province. In other ways they formed a separate entity more closely allied with the Inca government (Chapter 4, pp. 96–107; Julien 1978:52–53, 57, 68).

Both the tributaries in the general pool and those permanently assigned were organized into decimal units. The decimal units are listed in a number of general accounts of Inca administration. The lists vary in minor details, but a standard list of units can be reconstructed (Table 5.1) (Falcón 1867:463–464; Polo de Ondegardo 1917:51; Cobo Lib. 12, Cap. XXV; 1964, Vol. 92: 114; Bandera 1968:505; Santillán 1968:382).[4]

Each decimal unit was composed of a number of tributary households. A tributary household usually included a married couple, but female households with grown children may also have been counted

TABLE 5.1
Decimal Units from 10 to 10,000

Unit name	Number of tributaries
Hunu	10,000
Piska waranqa	5,000
Waranqa	1,000
Piska pachaka	500
Pachaka	100
Piska chunka	50
Chunka	10
—	5

(Cobo Lib. 12, Cap. XXVII; 1964, Vol. 92:119; Santillán 1968:383–384, 401, 420). The number of tributaries in each unit probably did not match the number implied by its name, but adjustments were made to keep the numbers relatively close (Castro and Ortega Morejón 1974: 98; Santillán 1968:385). Periodic updating of the census, recorded on *khipus*, kept the situation from getting out of hand (Cobo Lib. 12, Cap. XXIV; 1964, Vol. 92:112; Castro and Ortega Morejón 1974:98).

At the head of each decimal unit was an officer, and these officers stood in a hierarchical relationship to one another (Cobo Lib. 12, Cap. XXXIII; 1964, Vol. 92:132; Castro and Ortega Morejón 1974:96). There may have been a single officer for each decimal unit in the hierarchy, but some evidence suggests that one of each group of ten decimal officers served as head of the other nine. For example, one of the ten *pachaka* officers served as a *waranqu* officer as well (Santillán 1968: 382; Castro and Ortega Morejón 1974:94); the *chunka* officer was said to have been in charge of nine, not ten, tributaries, as the officer was counted in the total (Cobo Lib. 12, Cap. XXV; 1964, Vol. 92:114).

Decimal offices were usually held by local people, and it was probably in the decimal administration that provincials were best represented in the Inca government. Some provincials held more important positions in the government, such as captain general in the army or councilor representing one of the four quarter divisions on the imperial council in Cuzco (Guaman Poma 1936:183–184; Cobo Lib. 12, Cap. XXV; 1964, Vol. 92:114). These individuals probably spent most of their time accompanying the *Inka* or his delegates in Cuzco or on special projects elsewhere in the empire, and may have had little to do with the day-to-day operation of provincial government. Some were called *'apu*, a term denoting extremely high status in the Inca hierarchy (Falcón 1867:463; Guaman Poma 1936:330–341; González Holguín 1952:51). This term may have indicated some kind of special rank; it was also applied to individuals with Inca royal blood, some of whom were close relatives of the emperor. The rank of *'apu* appears to have been held by provincials who occupied higher positions than decimal office.

Decimal officers were organized into a numerical order by the size of the decimal units under them, but there is some evidence that they were divided into an upper and lower rank (Falcón 1867:463–464; Bandera 1881:99; Guaman Poma 1936:182, 198, 330, 336; Cobo Lib. 12, Cap. XXV; 1964, Vol. 92:114; Cap. XXVII; 1964, Vol. 92:119). The definition of these ranks, however, is not consistent. For example, the term *kuraka* appears to apply to the upper rank of decimal officers from the *hunu* down to the *pisqa pachaka*, though some sources include the *pachaka* in this rank. The only early writer to supply a name for the lower rank of decimal officers was Guaman Poma, an early seventeenth-century writer whose information cannot always be trusted. Guaman Poma called the *chunka* and the officer who headed a unit of five by the term *camachicoc* (1936:189, 330).

Regardless of the naming problem, it is still possible to distinguish two generalized ranks of decimal officers on the basis of other evidence. At certain times, for example, during succession to office or participation in the general agricultural labor levies, differences between the two groups are manifested.

Succession to office differed for the different decimal officers. Inheritance of office was characteristic only of offices in the *kuraka* rank. Officers of *kuraka* rank inherited their positions (Ortíz de Zúñiga 1967:25) but were said to have been initially chosen from locally powerful individuals at the time the Incas conquered a region (Falcón 1867:463; Cabello Valboa Pt. 3, Cap. 9; 1951:348; Cobo Lib. 12, Cap. XXV; 1964, Vol. 92:115). *Pachaka* officers may have inherited their positions like officers of *kuraka* rank, but Falcón, who had particularly detailed information on the tribute system, observed that the *pachaka* officers were appointed by the *waranqa* officer and that the appointment was for one lifetime. The officeholder could be removed only for some serious offense (Falcón 1867:463–464). The lower officers were appointed by *kuraka* officers, and these people could be thrown out of office on lesser pretexts (Falcón 1867:463–464; Cobo Lib. 12, Cap. XXV; 1964, Vol. 92:114–115). *Hunu* officers may have been set apart from the rest. Falcón suggests that the *hunu* officers were like the councilors of the four quarters; that is, their descendants did not automatically inherit their positions but had to have demonstrated that they were deserving of office (1867:463–464). Since the *Inka* had absolute authority and could remove people from inherited positions, Falcón's statement may simply mean that closer scrutiny was given to *hunu* succession.

The difference in status between ranks was also demonstrated at the beginning of work on general agricultural projects. Everyone, even the *Inka* himself, participated. The highest ranking individuals began the project and participated briefly; the amount of time decreased with increasing rank. All holders of *kuraka* rank retired to other festivities before long, leaving the *pachaka* officers to work alongside the common tributaries (Falcón 1867:469–470; cf. Polo de Ondegardo 1940: 138).

Both the *hunu* and *pachaka* officers were set apart somewhat from other officers of *kuraka* rank, perhaps because these officers occupied transition points between the three ranks mentioned previously. This kind of rank hierarchy and the ladderlike numerical hierarchy implicit in the concept of decimal administration may have been modified somewhat in their application to tributaries who were permanently assigned. These decimal units may have been directly subject, for all practical purposes, to the authority of the Inca governor in the province where they found themselves (Espinoza Soriano 1970:16). The qualifications for permanent office also may not have been the same as for officers who headed units of tributaries in the temporary pool. Guaman Poma (1936:330) notes that these officers were descended not from the local elites but from people of more common origin.

Decimal administration had some immediate administrative benefits and some far-reaching consequences. By creating standardized units of population, it increased the responsiveness of the provincial administration to Inca recruitment demands and facilitated an equitable distribution of the labor obligation (Polo de Ondegardo 1917:74; Cobo Lib. 12, Cap. XXXIII; 1964, Vol. 92:132; Ortíz de Zúñiga 1972: 55). An important result of decimal administration was the achievement of a numerical equivalence between local leaders from all parts of the empire (Cobo Lib. 12, Cap. XXV; 1964, Vol. 92:114). Reducing the heterogeneous political organization of the area conquered by the Incas to a single hierarchical system paved the way for the institution of an imperial class system and a common identity among members of the elite. The formal inheritance of government office and the rank associated with it standardized the numbers of the hereditary provincial elite recognized by the Inca government within a given unit of population. The system may also have prescribed certain obligations, as well as privileges, common to all officers in charge of the same size decimal unit (Guaman Poma 1936:189; Cobo Lib. 12, Cap. XXVII; 1964, Vol. 92:119–120; Cieza de León, Señorío Cap. XVIII; 1967:64).

Decimal administration was widespread at the time of the Spanish invasion, but information about its application to specific provinces is quite scarce. There are few references to decimal administration for any part of the southern quarter of the Inca empire. For Sipe Sipe, in central Bolivia, a published fragment of the *visita* of Toledo mentions the organization of that area in *pachakas* (Romero 1924:215). For Chuquiabo (now La Paz), there is also a reference to *pachakas* (Jiménez de la Espada 1881–1897, Vol. II:72).[5] The indirect information contained in the Chucuito *visita* is all the more important considering the scarcity of information on the subject for this part of the empire.

The Lupaca Case

The Chucuito *visita* makes almost no reference to decimal units. In fact, they are mentioned only as part of a question and a response to it that is framed in the same terms as the question (Diez de San Miguel 1964:14–15, 27). Indirect information about decimal administration, however, is abundant in the *visita*.

The chief source of information about decimal administration in the Lupaca province is a knot record, or *khipu*, said to be the last Inca census of the province (Diez de San Miguel 1964:64–66). The *khipu* census makes use of a series of political divisions still in existence in 1567 and, therefore, establishes their antiquity (Table 5.2). The tributary counts themselves suggest that these political divisions were organized along decimal lines, but before turning to the *khipu* census, I

TABLE 5.2
Categories of the Last Inca Census of Chucuito

	Aymara	Uru	Other	Total
Lupaca Province				
Hanansaya of Chucuito	1,233	500		1,733
Hurinsaya of Chucuito	1,384	347		1,731
Hanansaya of Acora	1,221	440		1,661
Hurinsaya of Acora	1,207	378		1,585
Hanansaya/Hurinsaya of Ilave	1,470	1,070		2,540
Hanansaya/Chanbilla of Juli	1,438	158	153	1,749
Hurinsaya of Juli	1,804	256		2,060
Hanansaya of Pomata	1,663	110	20	1,793
Hurinsaya of Pomata	1,341	183		1,524
Hanansaya/Hurinsaya of Yunguyo	1,039	381		1,420
Hanansaya of Zepita	1,112	186		1,298
Hurinsaya of Zepita	866	120		986
Colony in Pacific coastal valley				
Hanansaya/Hurinsaya of Sama			200	200
Totals	15,778	4,129	373	20,280
Total Hanansaya[a]				10,214
Total Hurinsaya[a]				9,866

[a]The totals for Ilave and Yunguyo were halved to approximate *saya* division totals.

shall outline the political organization of the Lupaca province from evidence in the *visita*.

The Lupaca province was organized around seven towns and their districts.[6] Each town was divided into two parts, or *sayas*, called Hanansaya and Hurinsaya. One town, Juli, was further subdivided, but since the subdivisions were affiliated with either Hanansaya or Hurinsaya, a division in two parts was preserved. Cuzco was also divided into Hanansaya and Hurinsaya, and there, each was a separate district (Sarmiento de Gamboa Cap. 37; 1906:75–77; Cap. 40; 1906:81–83; Cobo Lib. 12, Cap. XXIV; 1964, Vol. 92:112). The Lupaca towns may also have been divided into districts in this way. In Chucuito, the only town for which information is available about the surrounding territory subject to it, it appears that the Hanansaya and Hurinsaya division extended beyond the urban center but that there may have been overlap between the two divisions (Diez de San Miguel 1964:14, 27).

Saya division lines also served to unify the political divisions of the Lupaca province. Two *kurakas* headed the major *sayas* of Chucuito, and each was also the head of the respective *saya* division of the entire Lupaca province. Thus, Martín Qari, head of Hanansaya of Chucuito town, was also head of Hanansaya of the province, and Martín Kusi headed Hurinsaya for both the town and the province (Diez de San Miguel 1964:14, 27, 37).

These two men had copies of the *khipu* census in their possession. One of these *khipus*, brought forward by a *khipukamayoq* subject to Qari, was read into the record of the *visita* (Diez de San Miguel 1964).

> Don Martín Cari, principal *kuraka* of Hanansaya, appeared and brought with him some woolen cordage with knots in it that he said was the *khipu* which accounted the number of tributaries there had been in Chucuito province in Inca times and that it was the last one to be made in Inca times [p. 64].
>
> [The *kurakas* of Hanansaya of Chucuito] said that the number of indians accounted by the *khipu* presented by don Martín Qari is correct. Francisco Salisaya declared that he is *khipukamayoq* and accountant, and that he had had the *khipu* in his possession and had given it to don Martín Qari [pp. 84–85; author's translation].[7]

The *khipu* census accounted the tributary population of the entire Lupaca province. Thirteen entries were listed, each representing either a *saya* division of one of the Lupaca towns or an entire town. The census entries of Qari's *khipu* are duplicated in Table 5.2 in the same order as they were given in the *visita*. Totals (in the far right column and at the bottom of the other columns) are supplied for the purposes of analysis but were not recorded in the *khipu*.

A second *khipu*, in the possession of Martín Kusi, was produced to corroborate Qari's (Diez de San Miguel 1964:75). When consulted, it was found to be identical to Qari's *khipu* in every entry except one. An entry of 22 Canas, presumably a colony from Canas province nearer to Cuzco, was reported for Hanasaya of Pomata instead of the 20 Canas reported by Qari (see "Other" column for Hanansaya of Pomata, Table 5.2). The *khipu* produced by Kusi differed, therefore, by only two tributaries. Kusi also came forward with a *khipukamayoq*, Lope Martín Ninara, who was responsible for keeping the census document (Diez de San Miguel 1964:74).

The tributary counts contained in the *khipu* census provide key information for arguing that the Lupaca province was organized into decimal units. The first observation to be made about the tributary counts is that they total 20,280 tributaries, or approximately two *hunu*.[8]

Since an internal breakdown into Hanansaya and Hurinsaya is reported for all but two of the Lupaca towns in the province proper, it is also possible to estimate the number of tributaries in each of the provincial *sayas*. A total of 10,214 tributaries can be estimated for Hanansaya, and a total of 9,866 for Hurinsaya (see Table 5.2). Each provincial *saya* contained approximately a *hunu* of tributaries.

When this information is viewed in light of the provincial organization outlined earlier, it is evident that Qari and Kusi, in addition to being heads of the provincial *saya* divisions, were also *hunu* officers. Using other evidence provided in the text of the *visita*, one can trace the position of head of the provincial *saya* division back to the time of the later Inca empire (Diez de San Miguel 1964:22, 34) and argue that *hunu* office and provincial *saya* division office were held by the same person at that time.

That Qari and Kusi had provincial census records in their possession also suggests they were the descendants of important officers during the later Inca empire. It was probably owing to their descent from former *hunu* officers that they retained the census *khipus*.

In addition to *hunu* units, the tributary counts reveal the existence of other decimal units. Qari and Kusi each had 17 Chucuito *ayllus* in his command (see Table 5.3). Since the *khipu* census recorded just over 1700 tributaries for each of the two *saya* divisions of Chucuito, there is every indication that the *ayllus* of Chucuito were also *pachakas* (units of 100). Moreover, Qari and Kusi detailed several categories of *ayllus*, each one approximating a decimal unit. Each commanded 10 *ayllus* of tributaries classified as Aymara, 5 of Uru, and 1 each of potters and silversmiths. Although neither *kuraka* made a direct statement, they were in effect saying that in their command was a *waranqa* of tribu-

TABLE 5.3
Ayllus Subject to Qari and Kusi

| | Number of Ayllus | | | | | Number of Tributaries | |
| | | | | | | Actual total | Ideal total |
	Aymara	Uru	Potters	Silversmiths	Total		
Qari (Hanansaya of Chucuito)	10	5	1	1	17	1733	1700
Kusi (Hurinsaya of Chucuito)	10	5	1	1	17	1731	1700

taries classified as Aymara, a *piska pachaka* of Uru, and a *pachaka* each of potters and silversmiths. In the *khipu* census the specialized tributaries in Chucuito were probably accounted with the tributaries classified as Aymara (see Table 5.2).

If Chucuito was organized along decimal lines, it is likely that the other Lupaca towns were too. Documenting this organization is more difficult, though, because less information was provided about them.[9] Nonetheless, it is possible to infer decimal organization when information from the *khipu* census and from interviews with *kurakas* in the other towns is considered in light of the Chucuito organization.

The only other town besides Chucuito for which the number of *ayllus* was reported by *saya* division is Acora. There a group of *kurakas* reported 11 *ayllus* for Hanansaya and 9 for Hurinsaya (Diez de San Miguel 1964:89–97). How these *ayllus* were classified was not reported, but at one point in the interview the presence of *ayllus* of potters and silversmiths was noted (Diez de San Miguel 1964:98). Since *ayllus* of people classified as Aymara and Uru were accounted for in the *khipu* census, Acora appears to have had a composition similar in nature to that of Chucuito. Acora had a similar number of tributaries as well (see Table 5.2). A reconstruction of decimal units for Acora based on the Chucuito model can be hypothesized (see Table 5.4). The reconstruction assumes a symmetry between Hanansaya and Hurinsaya, and 10 *pachakas* of Aymara tributaries have been reconstructed instead of 11 and 9, the number of *ayllus* mentioned in the Chucuito *visita*. The absolute symmetry of the Chucuito organization may not have been followed in Acora, but the passage of time may account for the difference.

As indicated by the number of people in each *khipu* entry (see Table 5.2), it is apparent that the political divisions of Acora could be expected to be the most similar to those of Chucuito. The entries for

TABLE 5.4
Reconstruction of Acora Ayllus

	Number of Ayllus					Number of Tributaries	
	Aymara	Uru	Potters	Silversmiths	Total	Actual total	Ideal total
Cauana[a]							
(Hanansaya of Acora)	10	4	1	1	16	1661	1600
Cachi[a]							
(Hurinsaya of Acora)	10	4	1	1	16	1585	1600

[a]Names of the *kurakas* in 1567.

the other towns are less similar. Still, one feature common to all the political divisions represented in the *khipu* census is a roughly similar number of tributaries classified as Aymara. Except for Hurinsaya of Zepita, the number of tributaries classified as Aymara exceeds 1000, and in only two cases does it exceed 1500. Moreover, the number of Aymara tributaries varies far less than the total tributary count for each political division.

The similarity in the number of Aymara tributaries is suggestive, but the real evidence for the significance of the Aymara group is provided by the lumping of Hanansaya and Hurinsaya in some cases but not in others. Both Ilave and Yunguyo were accounted by a single entry instead of two, one for each *saya* division, as was usually the case (see Table 5.2). Although in the case of Yunguyo the small number of people would seem to be a sufficient reason for lumping the two *sayas* together, in the case of Ilave the combined population was larger than the population of Zepita, which was accounted with entries for each *saya* division. The large number of tributaries classified as Uru in Ilave seems not to have influenced the accounting. It appears that the real basis of each political division was a *waranqa* of Aymara tributaries.

Another piece of evidence supports the idea that a *waranqa* was the focus of each political division. Accompanying the hierarchy of decimal units was a hierarchy of decimal officers, and the groups of *kurakas* interviewed in the *visita* suggest a remnant of this hierarchy (see Table 5.5). Only the *kurakas* of Acora, Chucuito, and Juli were interviewed. However, because these three towns contained 6 of the 12 political divisions of the Lupaca province proper, they may provide an adequate basis for generalization. In Chucuito and Acora a principal *kuraka* and 7 to 12 subordinates were interviewed (Diez de San Miguel 1964:79–80, 84, 89, 96, 114, 119). The rough correspondence between these numbers and the number of *waranqa* and *pachaka* officers required to staff a *waranqa* suggests that these *kurakas* were descended from the officers who staffed the *waranqa* of Aymara tributaries in the time of the *khipu* census. Because of the time elapsed since the end of the Inca empire, no exact correspondence should be expected; however, if these people owed their positions to an Inca antecedent, then this kind of correspondence is not surprising. If *waranqa* office was the highest office in the *saya* division of each town, then Qari and Kusi were probably descended from the *waranqa* officers of Chucuito town. When questioned in the *visita*, they generally framed their answers only in terms of their responsibilities in Chucuito itself, referring all questions about the other towns to parallel authorities there (see note 9). Since Qari and Kusi appear to have occupied the positions of former *hunu* officers, it is not surprising that they should have been *waranqa* officers as well, as such a possibility was suggested in the general accounts (see p. 124). So far only the similarities between Chucuito and the other political divisions have been examined. The one obvious exception to the Chucuito model is Juli. Several features of the Juli organization stand out. One is that one or both of the major *saya* divisions were further subdivided. Juli is the only Lupaca town for

TABLE 5.5
Kurakas Interviewed in the Chucuito Visita (1567)

Hanansaya of Chucuito	1 principal *kuraka* (Qari)
	10 subordinate *kurakas*
Hurinsaya of Chucuito	1 principal *kuraka* (Kusi)
	7 subordinate *kurakas*
Hanansaya of Acora	1 principal *kuraka* (Cauana)
	12 subordinate *kurakas*
Hurinsaya of Acora	1 principal *kuraka* (Cachi)
	9 subordinate *kurakas*
Hanansaya/Chanbilla of Juli	2 principal *kurakas* (Paca, Nina Chanbilla)
	13 subordinate *kurakas*
Hurinsaya of Juli	2 principal *kurakas*[a] (Calisaya, Chui)
	9 subordinate *kurakas*
Ayanca of Juli	2 principal *kurakas* (Tira, Vicsa)
	7 subordinate *kurakas*
	2 *marcacamayos*[b]

[a]Only one principal *kuraka* was listed at the beginning of the interview (Diez de San Miguel 1964; 119), but it is clear from the text that there were two (p. 121).

[b]One of the witnesses interviewed in the *visita* said that *marcacamayos* were in charge of calling people in for labor on public works projects; they were also said to be responsible for provisioning *tambos* (Diez de San Miguel 1964; 158, 165).

which there is any evidence for further subdivision. Hurinsaya was divided into two parts labeled Hurinsaya and Ayanca in the *visita* text (see Table 5.5); curously enough, however, Ayanca was not mentioned in the *khipu* census (see Table 5.2). In the *khipu* census Hanansaya appears to have been divided in two parts, labeled Hanansaya and Chanbilla. The existence of Chanbilla can be detected from the *visita* text, but it was not identified as a separate entity as Ayanca was. In Juli either Hanansaya, Hurinsaya, or both were divided into two parts. Juli is also unique among the Lupaca towns in that six principal *kurakas* were interviewed, two for each of the three groups mentioned in the *visita*. The Juli example does not lend itself to explanation following the Chucuito model as easily as Acora did.

Decimal Administration in the Lupaca Province

Now that the Lupaca case has been considered it is possible to temper the picture of decimal administration presented in the general accounts.

Due to the heterogeneous nature of political organization in the Andes at the time of the Inca conquest, it could be hypothesized that local conditions would necessitate modifications in the application of decimal administration. In the Lupaca case certain local conditions were respected.

One local condition was organization around a number of prominent urban centers. Other students of Inca administration have commented on the planning and founding of towns by the Incas for use as administrative centers, particularly along the royal roads (Morris 1973:134, 138). The Lupaca towns may have been reorganized by the Incas, but it is precisely for the Lupaca province that we have a reference to pre-Inca urbanism. Before the Inca conquest of the area, either during or before the reign of Wiraqocha 'Inka, one of the Qaris made a name for himself by founding towns along the southwest shore of Lake Titicaca, in Lupaca territory. Cieza de León records the names of the towns he founded, including Ilave, Juli, Zepita, Pomata, and Chucuito (Señorío Cap. IV; 1967:7; Cap. XLI; 1967:139–140).

The application of decimal units suggests that the decimal system was applied to a preexisting urbanism. Twelve political divisions, based on the Lupaca towns and their subdivisions, were created from a total tributary population of 20,000. By comparison the application of decimal administration to the Huánuco province does not suggest a similar respect for preexisting nuclei of population. Each of 40 *pachakas* there was a discrete unit (Ortíz de Zúñiga 1967:22,24).

Another local condition respected by decimal administration was the division of Lupaca territory into Hanansaya and Hurinsaya. Some early writers have maintained that the Incas were responsible for division in halves, but *saya* division may well have been native to the Lake Titicaca area (Molina 1916:38–40; Cobo Lib. 12, Cap. XXIV; 1964, Vol. 92:112; Santillán 1968:382, 400; Castro and Ortega Morejón 1974:94). The fact that the Incas worked around the Lupaca towns, and that *saya* division was basic to their organization, suggests that *saya* division was at home in the area. It certainly was found throughout the south-central Andes at the time of the conquest, and it persists to this day in the region south of Cuzco (Gorbak *et al.* 1962; Cordero *et al.* 1971; Albó *et al.* 1972; Šolč 1975; Martínez 1976; Platt 1976).

Attention to a particular segment of the population, in this case to the group of tributaries classified as Aymara, was also a response to local conditions. The two largest groups of tributaries in the *khipu* census were labeled Aymara and Uru. It is difficult to ascertain what these terms meant when used in some of the sixteenth-century and early seventeenth-century sources, owing to a confusion over the complicated overlapping of cultural features in the area—including language, ethnicity, occupation, and wealth (Julien 1978:40–49). In the context of the *khipu* census the two terms referred to two major tribute groups, and wealth was probably the key difference between the tributaries classified as Aymara and those classified as Uru under both the Inca and Spanish administrations.[10] The two terms served to classify the population, without regard for language or other cultural features, in the Toledo tax assessment of 1571–1573. In that assessment tributaries classified as Uru were customarily taxed at half the rate of people classified as Aymara (Toledo 1975).

Differences in the organization of Lupaca towns and the districts around them also altered the application of decimal administration. Here the differences between the Chucuito and Juli divisions are an example. Such differences cannot be interpreted at present, but they indicate possible differences in pre-Inca organization.

Although local conditions influenced the application of decimal administration, some of the features outlined in the general accounts are confirmed by the Lupaca case. For instance, 1 officer in a group of 10 served to head a unit composed of all 10. As mentioned earlier, Qari and Kusi probably served as both *hunu* and *waranqa* officers. Also, the impression given by the general accounts that the *hunu, waranqa,* and *pachaka* officers were more important to the functioning of decimal administration than the other officers seems to be borne out by the Lupaca case (Santillan 1968:403).

The Lupaca documents also support the contention in the general accounts that prominent local people figured in the decimal administration. Martín Qari, head of Hanansaya of Chucuito and the entire province, was the grandson of 'Apu Qari, an important figure at the time of the Spanish conquest and shortly thereafter (Cabello Valboa Pt. 3, Cap. 21; 1951:368; Cobo Lib. 12, Cap. XVII; 1964, Vol. 92:91). Even before the Inca conquest of the area, during the reign of Wiraqocha 'Inka (ending in 1438), a Qari was an important figure. In later times the office was passed down in the Qari family, though not in a direct line from father to son.[11]

One feature of the Lupaca case seems to negate the impression left by the general accounts. From the general accounts it would seem that the decimal hierarchy had a straightforward, top-down chain of command (Cobo Lib. 12, Cap. XXXIII; 1964, Vol. 92:132). The organization might be diagrammed as a pyramid with the *hunu* officer at the apex. In the Lupaca case recruitment activity was probably focused at the level of the 12 political divisions. The recruitment role of the *saya* division heads for the entire province is not clear because *saya* division was disregarded in several of the political divisions. The *hunu* officers may have had only a symbolic role in recruitment, but they would still have been entitled to more wives, retainers, and other privileges of rank (Falcón 1867:469; Guaman Poma 1936:189; Cobo Lib. 12, Cap. XXVII; 1964, Vol. 92:120; Cap. XXX; 1964, Vol. 92:126; Cap. XXXIV; 1964, Vol. 92:133).

The Labor Assignment of the Lupaca Province

If the Lupaca province was organized along decimal lines, other aspects of the tribute system may be found. A feature basic to the tribute system was the assignment of different kinds of labor service. The Huánuco labor assignment, referred to earlier, provides an index of goods and services required from that province. Information contained in the 1567 *visita* of Chucuito indicates that the Lupaca province was under a labor assignment like the Huánuco case. For purposes of comparison the Huánuco labor assignment will be briefly reviewed.

The Huánuco labor assignment was recorded in a 1549 *visita* of that province (Helmer 1957:40–41; Mori and Malpartida 1967:290–304). Additional information about labor assignment, including a direct statement about the proportion of people tied up in permanent assignments, was collected in 1562 (Ortíz de Zúñiga 1967, 1972). This labor assignment is a fascinating document. It was very likely recorded on a *khipu* that was read into the record of the *visita,* just as the last Inca census of the Lupaca province was read into the Chucuito *visita* (see Chapter 9, this volume). Unlike the presentation of the *khipu* census, no duplicate *khipu* was brought forward to corroborate the labor assignment. Acceptance of this document depends largely on a belief in the accuracy of Inca record keeping, because it is unlikely that the *khipu* was falsified.[12]

The Huánuco labor assignment is reproduced in Table 5.6 in the order in which it was recorded in the *visita.* The number of tributaries in each entry is also given exactly as in the *visita.* For the purposes of analysis a total number of tributaries (4108) was calculated. The Huánuco tributaries were organized into 4 *waranqas* and 40 *pachakas,* so the percentages of tributaries involved in each assignment were calculated from an ideal total of 4000. This total was used because it seems the quotas were based on an ideal number. For example, the number of tributaries assigned to weave *qompi* cloth was 400, or 4% of the total tributaries in 4 *waranqa.*

An indication of the extent of permanent assignment in the Huánuco province is not contained in the labor assignment, but it was provided by a witness in the 1562 *visita.* The witness was Martín Carcay, the *kuraka* of Uchec, whose statement is important enough to be cited in full. After listing a number of services provided to the Inca government by his *pachaka,* he said

> Each pachaka gave 49 tributaries for all of these services. Throughout the year, nothing else was required of them. These people were assigned permanently and their children succeeded them, no matter how many children they had. If they died without leaving descendents, others were assigned in their place. They gave an additional tributary to make grindstones, so that from a *pachaka* of 100 tributaries, 50 were assigned to perform all such services. The other 50 who remained worked in the fields of the Inka, went to war, and carried burdens for the army, and did anything else the *Inka* ordered them to do. The tributaries who were assigned to perform services [on a permanent basis] were settled where the *Inka* sent them and never returned to their own lands, remaining as *mitimas* in the place where they were settled. The 50 tributaries who remained divided up the agricultural labor and other tasks they were assigned among themselves. Many times those who went to war or carried burdens for the army died and did not return, so that fewer people remained. All of what he has said he [Carcay] remembers having seen, because he was a boy at the time of the Inca empire [Ortiz de Zúñiga 1967:239–240; author's translation].[13]

In one brief paragraph Martín Carcay managed to say more about how the Incas distributed the labor obligation than perhaps anyone else. Carcay spoke for more than just his *pachaka* and implied that in Huánuco half the tributary population was under permanent assignment.

In order to interpret the labor assignment in light of Carcay's statement and in light of other evidence for determining whether an assign-

TABLE 5.6
Huánuco Labor Assignment

Category	Assignment	Total	Percentage of 4000
I	Gold miners	120	3
	Silver miners	60	1.5
II	Masons in Cuzco	400	10
	Cultivators of Inca lands in Cuzco	400	10
III	Retainers (*yanacona*) of Wayna Qhapaq	150	3.75
	Guards for the body of Thupa 'Inka	150	3.75
	Guards (*yanacona*) for the weapons of Thupa 'Inka	10	.25
IV	Garrison of the Chachapoyas	200	5
	Garrison of Quito	200	5
III	Guard for the body of Wayna Qhapaq	20	.5
V	Feather workers	120	3
	Honey gatherers	60	1.5
	Weavers of *qompi* cloth	400	10
	Dye makers	40	11
	Herders of Inca herds	240	6
	Guard for corn fields in the valley, transport to Cuzco	40	1
	Cultivators of *ají* fields in the valley, transport to Cuzco	40	1
	Salt miners (variable assignment)	60/50/40	1.5/1.25/1
	Cultivators of coca, transport to Cuzco and Huánuco	60	1.5
	Hunters to go on royal deer hunts	40	1
	Sole preparers [for shoes], transport to Cuzco and other centers	40	1
	Carpenters, transport to Cuzco	40	1
	Potters, transport to Huánuco	40	1
VI	Guard for the *tambo* at Huánuco	68	1.7
	Carriers from *tambo* at Pumpu, and from Hatuncancha to *tambo*	80	2
	Guard for the women of the Inka	40	1
VII	Soldiers and carriers	500	12.5
	Cultivators of Inca lands, others who remained in the valley	500	12.5
	Totals	4108	100

TABLE 5.7
Outline of the Huánuco Labor Assignment

Category	Description	Percentage of 4000
I	Mining service	4.5
II	Unspecialized services in Cuzco	20
III	*Yanacona* service	8.25
IV	Frontier garrison service	10
V	Specialized services	30.25
VI	Guard and carrier service	4.7
VII	Unspecialized services (including military service and general agricultural service)	25

ment might be permanent or not, the Huánuco labor assignment has been broken down into several categories of service (see Tables 5.6 and 5.7). Both general agricultural and military service were probably assigned on a temporary basis (see Carcay's statement and Falcón 1867: 469–470). Many of the specialized services and *yanacona* service were permanent assignments. Frontier garrison service was also permanently assigned (Ortíz de Zúñiga 1972: 25–27, 34). If the categorization indicated by the order of the list can be followed, then categories III–V probably represent permanent assignments, while categories I, II, VI, and VII probably represent more temporary assignments.

Services other than those listed in the Huánuco labor assignment may have been required in other provinces (Cobo Lib. 12, Cap. XXXIII; 1964, Vol. 92:132–133), but evidence indicates that certain services were required everywhere. Lists of permanently assigned services were included in two of the general accounts (Falcón 1867:466–468; Morúa Lib. 3, Cap. LXVII; 1946:332–334). In each case two slightly different lists were given, one for highland provinces and one for coastal. The Huánuco labor assignment does not include all of the assignments on the list for highland provinces, but it includes many of them. With certain notable exceptions it appears that the Inca government assigned a similar range of labor services in each province.[14]

No quantified list of assignments was included in the Chucuito *visita*. Answers to a question about tribute paid the Inca government indicate that the province was under a labor assignment similar to the Huánuco one. From seven interviews, two with principal *kurakas* and five with groups of *kurakas* from the *saya* divisions of several Lupaca towns, a list of services provided to the Inca government can be compiled (Table 5.8) (Diez de San Miguel 1964:39, 80–81, 85, 92–93, 99,

TABLE 5.8
Labor Obligation of the Lupaca Province

	Vilcacutipa	Hanansaya, Chucuito	Hurinsaya, Chucuito	Hanansaya, Acora	Hurinsaya, Acora	Hanansaya, Juli	Cutinbo
Gold miners	X		X	X	X	X	X
Silver miners	X		X	X	X	X	X
Lead miners							X
Copper miners							X
People to build houses, walls							X
People to build houses in Cuzco	X	X	X	X		X	
People to cultivate fields in Cuzco				X			
Men and women in the *Inka*'s service	X	X	X	X			X
Men and women in the *Inka*'s service, specifically *yanacona*					X		
People who made clothing			X		X		X
People who made *qompi* cloth	X			X		X	
People who made *'awasqa* cloth	X			X		X	
Feather workers	X		X	X			X
People who made sandals	X		X	X		X	
People who made headbands				X		X	
People who made slings				X			
Salt miners	X						
People who made a varnish (*llimpi*)				X			X
People who made copper bars for the *Inka*'s house				X			X
People who made copper axes							
People who made *bolas* for hunting						X	
People who made *charki*				X			X
People who contributed ducks							X

(continued)

TABLE 5.8 (*Continued*)

	Vilcacutipa	Hanansaya, Chucuito	Hurinsaya, Chucuito	Hanansaya, Acora	Hurinsaya, Acora	Hanansaya, Juli	Cutimbo
People who contributed fresh fish	X	X	X	X			
People who transported fresh fish to Cuzco	X		X	X			
People who contributed dried fish	X	X	X				
People who contributed fish							X
People who contributed partridges							X
People who contributed *chuño*		X	X	X			
People who transported *chuño* to Cuzco				X			
People who contributed *kañawa*	X		X				X
People who contributed *quinoa*	X		X				
People who contributed other foods				X			
People who transported other foods to Cuzco				X			
People who contributed fungus			X				
People who contributed *cohucho*			X				
People who contributed coastal maize			X				
People who contributed wool from the community herds							
People who cultivated unspecified fields		X		X	X	X	X
People who transported the product of these fields to Cuzco	X		X	X			
Soldiers	X	X	X	X	X	X	X
Post runners (*chaski*)		X				X	
Children for sacrifice	X			X		X	
People for sacrifice	X	X	X	X			X
Daughters of *kurakas* for concubines				X		X	
Women to serve the state cults						X	X
Women	X		X	X		X	
Livestock	X		X	X		X	X
Mitimas		X	X			X	X

106–107, 116–117). These services are listed in roughly the same order as the services included in the Huánuco labor assignment (see Tables 5.6 and 5.7).

Since the verbal description of the services varies a bit, it is often hard to equate the description given by one *kuraka* or group of *kurakas* with that of another. For that reason, the list is probably too long, and it may contain services performed by people who were not properly speaking "tributaries." Another problem with the Chucuito list is that the same service may be listed twice because it was described in two different ways. For example, those interviewed appear either to have said they paid tribute in "clothing" or to have mentioned one of the two kinds of cloth they produced for the government. However, this apparent duplication might be correct. There is some evidence that, in addition to the two kinds of textiles woven by tributaries on a permanent basis (*'awasqa* and *qompi*) (Falcón 1867:466–468; Morúa Lib. 3, Cap. LXVII; 1946, 332–334), there may have been a general exaction of finished textiles (Cobo Lib, 12, Cap. XXIX; 1964, Vol. 92:123; Santillán 1968:402, 421; Castro and Ortega Morejón 1974:102). A third problem with the Chucuito list is that it is impossible to separate labor on specific cultivated crops from general agricultural service; this distinction was made in the Huánuco labor assignment. The list in Table 5.8 preserves the description of each service as it was reported; thus, there may be some crossover between these two kinds of agricultural service.

Following the categorization suggested for the Huánuco labor assignment (Table 5.7), only two groups appear to have been left out of the reconstructed Lupaca assignment. One is guard and carrier service (Group VI at 4.7% of the Huánuco total), and the other is service in frontier garrisons (Group IV at 10% of the Huánuco total). These kinds of service may have been subsumed under other entries in Table 5.8 or, alternatively, may not have been required of the Lupaca population.

Although the two lists are not identical, the similarity between them is unmistakable. It suggests that the Lupaca province was under a labor obligation similar to the one imposed in Huánuco.[15] Such a similarity agrees with the impression given in the standard sixteenth-century written sources that the Incas intended to impose a uniform and equitable administration.

The Role of Local Power under Centralized Authority

A large body of sixteenth-century written material consists of administrative records with a regional or local focus. Such records provide new and important information about local organization after the end of centralized administrative control from Cuzco. They are also a source of indirect information about the Inca provincial administration, since the local elites who participated in Inca government continued to serve as intermediaries after the Spanish invasion. To the extent that this elite group remained intact, the outline of the local decimal hierarchy is probably visible.

From a study of the role of local elites in administering the tribute system under the Inca regime, structural limits to their authority can be detected. One means of limiting their authority was to confine it to recruiting labor from a general pool of tributaries. A second limit was achieved by reducing the number of tributaries in the general pool. A major means of accomplishing the latter was to assign tributaries to perform services on a permanent basis. Those tributaries who were permanently assigned served the Inca government directly and were more closely identified with it. Since rank and privilege were said to have been based on the size of the tributary population represented by decimal office, position in the prestige hierarchy was preserved while the authority exercised by local elites was reduced.

In the Lupaca province the structure of the recruitment organization can be detected. A standing labor assignment like one imposed on the Huánuco province in the north-central highlands is also evident, even from the meager information provided in the Lupaca source materials on this subject. Although regional differences should not be minimized, one can still reasonably suggest that the proportion of tributaries tied up by permanent assignment in the Lupaca province may have approximated the proportion permanently assigned in the Huánuco provinces; thus, as in Huánuco, half of the tributaries may have been removed from the temporary pool in this way. Like the Huánuco labor assignment, which encompassed all of the tributaries, including both temporary and permanent assignment, the *khipu* census accounted for all of the tributary population in that province. The features of provincial administration that served to limit the authority of local elites are evident in the Lupaca documentation.

The Lupaca source material also serves to document the very different position of the same elite group in 1567. Administrative records are very valuable for the information they contain about the transition from Inca to Spanish control. In the Chucuito *visita* there is no evidence that an Inca governor or members of his staff were present in the Lupaca province, and clearly the *kurakas*, in the absence of the Inca provincial government, were the power to be reckoned with by the Spanish administration. At some point during the 35 years between the conquest and the time of the *visita,* the *kurakas* assumed a position of authority over the entire tributary population and so were able to respond to demands for goods and services as intermediaries of the new Spanish regime.

This outcome was not the only possible one, and the success of the *kurakas* may not have been ensured until about 1550. Both Polo de Ondegardo and Cieza de León describe this transitional period.

Polo gives a periodization for the early years following the Spanish invasion. The first period covers the years from the invasion to the time of Francisco Pizarro's distribution of *encomienda* rights (1532–1540). The second period extends through the period of conflict following the establishment of the Audiencia of Lima (1544–1548) and ends when the Audiencia became firmly established. Polo describes another two periods covering the time from 1549 to 1561, but his remarks about these two periods are not relevant here (Polo de Ondegardo 1940:155). According to Polo, before the assignment of *encomienda* rights the Spaniards acted like military commanders and pillaged the countryside to supply their needs (Polo de Ondegardo 1940:155–156). The granting of *encomienda* rights limited these activites, and only *encomenderos* had the right to demand goods and services from the native population. A few *encomenderos* were assigned grants in areas near Spanish cities, but most had to gather armed men and journey to the place where the people named in their grant lived. Once there, they took what they could find and returned to the Spanish city of their own residence. The *encomendero* had to divide up the booty amongst his men, and so such expeditions were similar to the *entradas* later conducted on the frontiers of the Inca empire.

Polo notes that only during the second period, and most specifically during the time of unrest between 1544–1549, did the *encomenderos* begin consolidating their hold on the native population. In particular, he credits the consolidation to the realization, by the people of the provinces, that they could throw off Inca rule and rid themselves of the Inca governors by accepting this new relationship with the Spanish *encomendero.*[16]

Since Polo was speaking in general of a phenomenon that probably did not occur at the same time all over the former Inca empire, his chronology may not serve equally well everywhere. Still, in some parts of the empire at least, the Inca governors maintained their hold on the provinces for 10–15 years after the Spanish usurped control of the Inca empire by capturing the emperor.

Polo was not the only Spaniard to document the continued authority of the Inca governors. Cieza de León remarked that many of the

Inca governors retained control of the province they were assigned under the Inca empire and that he had met several who were still in power (Señorío Cap. XX; 1967:67). One individual he met was Chiriguana, said to be governor of the Lupaca province (Señorío Cap. IV; 1967:7). Cieza met these individuals in 1549, when he·traveled through the highlands.

Some of the Inca governors were so entrenched in power that they were able to pass their positions on to their sons, though the position of governor had not been inherited under the Incas (Señorío Cap. XX; 1967:67). Cieza's statement makes it apparent that the governors were no longer behaving like governors, but like emperors in their own right. It is clear, too, from his description of many ruined Inca administrative centers that the provincial administration subject to these governors did not survive intact through this period.[17]

The Chucuito *visita* of 1567 was clearly conducted some years after the position of the *kurakas* as sole agents for the native population had been secured. The *kurakas* and their relationship to the Lupaca population were a major focus of inquiry in the *visita*. Because the *kurakas* were descended from decimal officers in the Inca administration, the Chucuito *visita* quite naturally is a source of information about it.

Notes

[1]The present paper is an offshoot of research that went into a doctoral dissertation on another Inca province in the Lake Titicaca region (Julien 1978). This research benefited at all stages from the counsel of John H. Rowe. Discussions with him about the nature of Inca administration served to refine my thinking on a number of matters. He also offered a number of useful suggestions for revision of this manuscript. John Hyslop graciously read the manuscript in its final stages and offered several constructive comments.

[2]Questionnaires, issued by the crown and the viceroyalty, were often directed toward obtaining information about the Inca tribute system and other matters. A particularly important example of the questionnaires used by the administration is the questionnaire of Gante (1559), which was answered by Polo de Ondegardo, among others (1940). It consisted of 14 questions, 6 of which inquired specifically into Inca administrative practices. It was also used in the *visita* of Huánuco (Ortíz de Zúñiga 1967) in tandem with a set of questions issued by the viceroyalty (pp. 12–19). A questionnaire was also administered during the *visita* of Chucuito (Diez de San Miguel 1964: 8–10); it included a question on the Inca tribute system.

[3]The dates for Pachakuti's rule, given earlier, as well as dates for other reigns given in the text, are reasonable estimates for the length of the later emperor's reigns as published by Rowe (1945:277).

[4]The army was also organized along decimal lines (Garcilaso de la Vega Lib. 2, Cap. XIV; 1959, Vol. I:169; Cieza de León, Señorío Cap. XXIII; 1967:80). The organization of

the army is not a separate issue from the organization of the tribute system, as army service was part of the labor obligation (Helmer 1957:41; Cobo Lib. 12, Cap. XXXIII; 1964, Vol. 92:131). Specific information from the *visitas* of Huánuco and Chucuito suggest that whole decimal units were assigned to military service (Helmer 1957:41; Diez de San Miguel 1964:106).

[5]The source published by Jiménez de la Espada equates *pachaka* with *hilacata*, an Aymara term for a political office. Bertonio glosses *hilacata* as: "Hilacata: Principal del ayllo" (1879 [Vol. 2]:133). Cobo uses the terms *hilacata* and *pachaka* in such a way as to suggest that a *hilacata* represented fewer people than a *pachaka* officer, and he does not suggest any decimal meaning for the term (Cobo Lib. 12, Cap. XXVII; 1964, Vol. 92:119; Lib. 12, Cap. XXVIII, 1964, Vol. 92:121).

[6]For ease of reference "town" will be used to refer to the basic political subdivision of the Lupaca province. Except where particular reference is made to an urban center, "town" should be understood as "town and district subject to it." The spatial organization of each town and surrounding district is a problem which has yet to be unravelled; precision in the discussion of these political and territorial divisions is therefore difficult.

[7]The Spanish texts are as follows:

pareció don Martín Cari cacique principal de la parcialidad de Anansaya y trujo consigo unos hilos de lana con unos nudos en ellos que dijo ser el quipo y cuenta de los indios tributarios que en el tiempo del ynga había en esta provincia de Chucuito y que el dicho es el útimo [sic] que se hizo en tiempo del ynga.

dijeron [the kurakas of Anansaya of Chucuito] que había los indios que parecen por el quipo que tiene dado don Martín Cari cacique principal el cual dicho quipo dijeron que era cierto y verdadero y el dicho don Francisco Salisaya declaró que él es quipocamayo y contador y tenía en su poder el dicho quipo que dio el dicho don Martín Cari.

[8]When the 200 tributaries from the Sama valley (a coastal valley some distance from the Lupaca province proper) are excluded from the total, the remaining number of tributaries (20,080) even more closely approximates two *hunu*. These people may have been drawn from both *sayas* and sent to the Sama area to cultivate or gather materials not available in their high-altitude home province. The reason for the separate accounting of this colony is not clear, since there were other colonies in other areas. At least two kinds of colonies existed: those subject to particular *kurakas* and those producing for the province in general (Documentos sobre Chucuito 1970:25, 45). Differences in accounting may well reflect the differences between types of colonies.

[9]Particular attention was devoted in the *visita* to the town of Chucuito. Diez de San Miguel recognized Qari and Kusi as heads of the entire Lupaca province and consequently directed a disproportionate amount of time to interviewing them and collecting information about them. Qari and Kusi answered many of the inquiries put to them in their capacity as *saya* division heads of Chucuito town, referring questions about other towns to their counterparts there (Diez de San Miguel 1964: 14–15, 27). Unfortunately, Diez de San Miguel did not ask for parallel information in the other towns.

[10]Julien (1978:45–47). From the Toledo tax assessment and elsewhere, it is clear that only people classified as Aymara could be counted on to have access to land and animal wealth (Diez de San Miguel 1964: 14, 59, 92, 112, 140, 196; Toledo 1975), the basis of material well-being among the people of the Lake Titicaca region. A group of people classified as Uru requested Toledo to tax them like the tributaries classified as Aymara, because they had access to animals. This motion on their part may indicate that, had they been dealing with an Inca administration, they might have expected a

reclassification. Requesting assignment to a higher tax bracket requires some kind of an explanation.

[11]Martín Qari was the grandson of 'Apu Qari (Diez de San Miguel 1964:107). 'Apu Qari was still alive at the time of the Spanish conquest (Sitio del Cuzco 1934:121; Murra 1978:418–419) and lived until at least 1535. At some time before 1540, he was succeeded by Qari 'Apasa who held the position until some time before 1549 (Cieza de León, Crónica Cap. CIV; 1924:298–300; Barriga 1939–1955, Vol. 11:17–20). There is some evidence that Martín Qari did not succeed directly from Qari 'Apasa, but that one or more members of his family occupied the position at some time between 1549 and 1567. Pedro Cutinbo testified in 1567 that he was 44 years old and had governed Hanansaya of the Lupaca province for 16 years (Diez de San Miguel 1964:36–37). If his statement is correct, he would have governed almost the entire period from 1549 to 1567. Cutinbo was a member of the Qari family, perhaps an uncle of Martín Qari, because some of the retainers given to the Qari family by the town of Juli served him (p. 22). Another member of the Qari family also enjoyed the services of retainers from Juli; his name was don Bernaldino Qari (pp. 22, 201). If these retainers were attached to the succession, don Bernaldino Qari may have also governed Hanansaya of the Lupaca province at some point.

[12]Falsification is not likely even though the document concerns tribute. It is not likely for two reasons. First, the obligations accounted by the *khipu* were to be paid in labor, and so it is impossible to under- or overrepresent the amount of tribute owed. It would only be possible to increase of decrease the obligation by falsifying the number of tributaries in Huánuco. The number accounted by the labor assignment, 4108, accords very well with the total of four *waranqa* (4000) said to have been the count of the tributary population under the Inca empire. Second, the proportion of the tributary population performing each service would have been irrelevant to the Spanish administration, as would, to some extent, the kinds of services performed. The Spanish administration, even at the time of Toledo when Inca administrative practices were occasionally imitated, was not trying to duplicate the output of the Inca tribute system. If anything, the document is proof that everyone of tributary status owed some kind of labor service to the Inca government. Some minor errors in transcription are the most likely inaccuracies in the Huánuco labor assignment.

[13]The text in Spanish is as follows:

Dijo que cada pachaca daban cuarenta y nueve indios para todas estas cosas dichas que en todo el año no entendían en otra cosa y estos eran para siempre y sus hijos que tenían sucedían en lo mismo aunque fuesen multiplicando muchos y si morían sin dejar hijos ponían otros en su lugar y estos daban un indio más para hacer piedras de moler por manera que de una pachaca que son cien indios daban cincuenta para todos oficios y los otros cincuenta que quedaban trabajaban en las chacaras del ynga e iban a la guerra y con cargas y hacían todas otras cosas que el ynga les mandaba y no volvían más a sus tierras y quedaban como mitimaes de donde se ponían de asiento y los cincuenta indios de la pachaca que quedaban repartían entre sí los trabajos de chacaras y tributos que daban al dicho ynga y muchas veces morían los que enviaban a la guerra y con cargas y no volvían más y quedeban menos y que esto todo dicho tiene se acuerda este principal de haberlo visto así en tiempo del ynga que era muchacho.

[14]A notable exception is the Charcas province. *Kurakas* interviewed there in 1582 said that their tribute obligation consisted entirely of military service (Espinoza Soriano 1969:24).

[15]Very little information about the number of tributaries assigned to different kinds of labor service is contained in the Chucuito *visita* (but see Vilcacutipa's testimony; Diez de San Miguel 1964:106). In a nearby area, near Huancané at the north end of Lake Titicaca, a *pachaka* of tributaries was assigned to produce pottery, while a *waranqa* was under assignment to produce *qompi* cloth (Murra 1978:418). The proportion between potters and *qompi* producers (1:10) is exactly the same as was found between these two labor services in Huánuco (see Table 5.6). The tributaries assigned to produce pottery and *qompi* cloth in Huancané lived in a mixed community composed of people from a number of towns in the area. The dispute that generated the information about the two labor services makes it clear that the origins of these people were in question. Depending on who was testifying, the people were either from towns in the Qolla province of 'Umasuyu, district of Cuzco, or from that province *and* the Qolla province of 'Umasuyu, district of La Paz (Julien 1978:Map. 2; Murra 1978:419–420). Occupationally specialized communities composed of tributaries from several parts of a province were found in Huánuco (Helmer, 1957:27–38; Julien 1978 [Note 30]:249), and so there is another parallel between the Huánuco province and a Lake Titicaca region province. Mixed communities of people from various parts of the Lupaca province were mentioned in the Chucuito *visita,* but their connection with labor services was not established (Diez de San Miguel 1964:89).

[16]Polo de Ondegardo (1940:155–157). The Spanish text is as follows:

En esta misma hera vino otro tienpo y pasó en medio del alçamiento de la tierra [1543–1549], y vinieron en conosçimiento de los repartimientos y los yndios de sus amos y a entender que podían exentarse de la jursidièión [sic] y dominio del ynga y echar los governadores, y acudieron a seruir a sus encomenderos.

[17]Because of the resistance of the Inca governors to the conquest and its threat to their authority, some aspects of Inca provincial administration may have survived for some time. Local people may have even contributed to these survivals. In Jauja, for example, tributaries continued to fulfill their labor obligations, deposit the product of their labor in the storehouses and make the appropriate sacrifices to the state cults. The people there thought they would eventually be called to account by the Inca government (Cobo Lib. 12, Cap. XXX; 1964, Vol. 92:126). This effort met with Spanish approval because, for example, it allowed Pedro de la Gasca to support a loyalist army in Jauja for seven months out of the Jauja storehouses (Cobo Lib. 12, Cap. XXX; 1964, Vol. 92:126). An Inca governor continued in power in Huánuco for some years after the Spanish conquest, at least until 1542 (Hemming 1970:249), and so it may be no coincidence that the 1549 *visita* of Huánuco contains so much detailed information about Inca provincial administration.

References

Albó, Javier, y equipo de CIPCA
  1972   Dinámica en la estructura inter-comunitaria de Jesús de Machaca. *America Indigena* **32**(3):773–816. Mexico.
Bandera, Damian de la
  1881   Relación general de la disposición y calidad de la provincia de Guamanga, llamada San Joan de la Frontera, y de la vivienda, y costumbres de los naturales

della.—año de 1557. *Relaciones Geográficas de Indias. Perú* [edited by Marcos Jiménez de la Espada], Vol. I:96–104. Madrid: Ministerio de Fomento.

1968   Relación del origen é gobierno que los Ingas tuvieron [1557]. *Biblioteca Peruana* (Serie 1, Vol. 3). Lima: Editores Técnicos Asociados. Pp. 493–510.

Barriga, Victor M.

1939–1955   *Documentos para la historia de Arequipa* (11 vols.). Arequipa: Biblioteca Arequipa, Editorial La Colmena.

Bertonio, P. Ludovico

1879   *Vocabulario de la lengua aymara compuesto por el Ludovico Bertonio* [1612], publicado de nuevo por Julio Platzmann, edición facsimilaria (2 vols.). Leipzig: B. G. Teubner.

Cabello Valboa, Miguel

1951   *Miscelánea antárctica, una historia del Perú antiguo* [1586]. Lima: Universidad Nacional Mayor de San Marcos, Facultad de Letras, Instituto de Etnología.

Castro, Cristóbal de, and Diego Ortega Morejón

1974   La relación de Chincha (1558). [Edited by Juan Carlos Crespo]. *Historia y Cultura* **8**:91–104. Lima: Museo Nacional de Historia.

Cieza de León, Pedro de

1924   La crónica general del Perú [1550]. Anotada y concordada con las crónicas de Indias, por Horacio H. Urteaga. *Colección Urteaga, Historiadores clásicos del Perú*, Vol. 7. Lima: Librería y Imprenta Gil.

1967   *El señorío de los Incas (2.a parte de la Crónica del Perú)* [1553]. (Fuentes e Investigaciones para la Historia del Perú, Serie: Textos Básicos, No. 1). Lima: Instituto de Estudios Peruanos.

Cobo, Bernabé

1964   Historia del nuevo mundo [1653]. Estudio preliminar y edición del P. Francisco Mateos de la misma compañía. *Biblioteca de Autores Españoles desde la formación del lenguaje hasta nuestros dias (continuación)*, Vol. 91–92. Madrid: Ediciones Atlas.

Cordero, Ariel, Rosa Maria de Casani, Vilma Valencia, and Felix Casani

1971   *Hatunqolla*. Puno: Centro de Estudios y Reflexiones del Altiplano.

Diez de San Miguel, Garci

1964   Visita hecha a la provincia de Chucuito por Garci Diez de San Miguel en el año 1567. Versión paleográfica de la visita y una biografía del visitador por Waldemar Espinoza Soriano. *Documentos Regionales para la Etnología y Etnohistoria Andinas*, Vol. I. Lima: Casa de la Cultura.

Documentos sobre Chucuito

1970   Documentos sobre Chucuito. *Historia y Cultura* **4**:5–48. Lima: Museo Nacional de Historia.

Espinoza Soriano, Waldemar

1969   El memorial de charcas; "crónica" inédita de 1582. *Cantuta* **4**:117–152. Huancayo: Universidad Nacional de Educación.

1970   Los mitmas yungas de Collique en Cajamarca, siglos XV, XVI, y XVII. *Revista del Museo Nacional*, Vol. XXXVI (1969–1970):9–57. Lima.

1974   La coca de los mitmas cayampis en el reino de Ancara. Siglo XVI. *Universidad Nacional del Centro del Perú. Anales Científicos* **2**(1973):5–67. Huancayo.

Falcón, Francisco

1867   Representación hecha por el Licenciado Falcón en Concilio Provincial, sobre los daños y molestias que se hacen a los indios [1567]. *Colección de Documentos Inéditos, relativos al Descubrimiento, Conquista y Organización de las Antiguas Posesiones Españolas de América y Oceanía* . . . por D. Luis Torres de Mendoza, Vol. VII:451–495. Madrid: Imprenta de Frías y Compañía.

Garcilaso de la Vega, "El Inca"
1959   *Comentarios reales de los Incas* [1609] (3 vols.). Estudio preliminar y notas de José Durand. Lima: Universidad Nacional Mayor de San Marcos, Patronato del Libro Universitario.

González Holguín, Diego
1952   *Vocabulario de la lengua general de todo el Peru llamada Qquicchua, o del Inca* [1608]. Nueva edición, con un prólogo de Raúl Porras Barrenechea. Lima: Imprenta Santa María.

Gorbak, Celina, Mirtha Lischetti, and Carmen Muñoz
1962   Batallas rituales del Chiaraje y Tocto de la Provincia de Kanas (Cuzco-Perú). *Revista del Museo Nacional*, Vol. XXXI:245–304. Lima.

Guaman Poma, Felipe
1936   *Nueva corónica y buen gobierno (cqdex péruvien ilustré)* [1615]. (Université de Paris. Travaux et Mémoires de l'Institut d'Ethnologie XXIII). Paris.

Helmer, Marie
1957   "La visitación de los yndios chupachos" inka et encomendero 1549. *Travaux de l'Institut Français d'Etudes Andines*, Vol. V (1955–1956):3–50. Paris–Lima.

Hemming, John
1970   *The conquest of the Incas.* New York: Harcourt Brace Jovanovich, Inc.

Jiménez de la Espada, Marcos
1881–1897 *Relaciones Geográficas de Indias. Perú* (4 vols.). Madrid: Ministerio de Fomento.

Julien, Catherine Jean
1978   Inca administration in the Titicaca Basin as reflected at the provincial capital of Hatunqolla. Ph.D. thesis, Department of Anthropology, University of California, Berkeley.

Martínez, Gabriel
1976   El sistema de los uywiris en Isluga. *Homenaje al R. P. Gustavo Le Paige*, pp. 255–327. Antofagasta: Universidad del Norte.

Molina, Cristóbal de
1916   Relación de las fábulas y ritos de los incas [c. 1575]. *Colección de Libros y Documentos referentes a la Historia del Perú*, anotaciones y concordancias de los textos por Horacio H. Urteaga, [serie 1] Vol. I:1–103. Lima: Imprenta y Librería Sanmartí y Ca.

Mori, Juan de, and Hernando Alonso Malpartida
1967   La visitación de los pueblos de indios [1549]. Ortíz de Zúñiga, Iñigo, *Visita de la provincia de León de Huánuco en 1562. Tomo I. Visita de los cuatro waranqa de los Chupachu.* Edición a cargo de John V. Murra (Documentos para la Historia y Etnología de Huánuco y la Selva Central, Vol. I). Huánuco: Universidad Nacional Hermilio Valdizán, Facultad de Letras y Educación.

Morris, Craig
1973   Establecimientos estatales en el Tawantinsuyu: una estrategía de urbanismo obligado. *Revista del Museo Nacional:* Vol. XXXIX: 127–139. Lima.

Morúa, Martín de
1946   *Historia del origen y geneología real de los reyes incas del Perú* [c. 1605].
        Introducción, notas y arreglo por Constantino Bayle. (Biblioteca "Missionalia
        Hispánica", Vol. II). Madrid: Instituto Santo Toribio de Mogrovejo.
Murra, John Victor
1968   An Aymara kingdom in 1567. *Ethnohistory,* Vol. XV:115–151. Seattle.
1978   Los olleros del Inka: hacia una historia y arqueología del Qollasuyu. *Historia,
        Problema y Promesa; homenaje a Jorge Basadre,* pp. 415–423. Lima: Pon-
        tificia Universidad Católica del Perú.
Ortíz de Zúñiga, Iñigo
1967   *Visita de la provincia de León de Huánuco en 1562. Tomo I. Visita de los
        cuatro waranqa de los Chupachu.* Edición a cargo de John V. Murra (Docu-
        mentos para la Historia y Etnología de Huánuco y la Selva Central, Vol. I).
        Huánuco: Universidad Nacional Hermilio Valdizán, Facultad de Letras y
        Educación.
1972   *Visita de la provincia de León de Huánuco en 1562. Tomo II. Visita de los
        Yacha y Mitmaqkuna cuzqueños encomendados en Juan Sánchez Falcón.*
        Edición a cargo de John V. Murra (Documentos para la Histona y Etnología de
        Huánuco y la Selva Central, Vol. II). Huánuco: Universidad Nacional Her-
        milio Valdizán, Facultad de Letras y Educación.
Pizarro, Pedro
1968   Relación del descubrimiento y conquista de los reinos del Perú . . . [1571].
        Biblioteca Peruana, serie 1, Vol. 1: 441–586. Lima.
Platt, Tristán
1976   Espejos y maíz: temas de la estructura simbólica andina. *Cuadernos de Inves-
        tigaciones CIPCA* No. 10.
Polo de Ondegardo, Juan
1916   Relación de los fundamentos acerca del notable daño que resulta de no guardar
        á los indios sus fueros. Junio 26 de 1571. *Colección de Libros y Documentos
        referentes a la Historia del Perú,* notas biográficas y concordancias de los
        textos por Horacio H. Urteaga, Vol. III:45–188. Lima: Imprenta y Librería
        Sanmartí y Ca.
1917   Del linage de los Ingas y como conquistaron [1571]. *Colección de Libros y
        Documentos referentes a la Historia del Perú,* notas biográficas y concordan-
        cias de los textos por Horacio H. Urteaga, Vol. IV:45–94. Lima: Imprenta y
        Librería Sanmartí y Ca.
1940   Informe del Licenciado Juan Polo de Ondegardo al Licenciado Briviesca de
        Muñatones sobre la perpetuidad de las encomiendas en el Perú [1561]. *Revista
        Histórica,* Vol. XIII:125–196. Lima.
Romero, Carlos A.
1924   Libro de la visita general del Virrey Toledo, 1570–1575. *Revista Histórica,*
        Vol. VII (entrega II):115–216. Lima.
Rostworowski de Diez Canseco, María
1975   Pescadores, artesanos y mercaderes costeños en el Perú prehispánico. *Revista
        del Museo Nacional,* Vol. XLI:311–349. Lima.
Rowe, John Howland
1945   Absolute chronology in the Andean Area. *American Antiquity* **10**(3):265–284.
        Menasha.
Santillán, Fernando de
1968   Relación del origen, descendencia, política y gobierno de los incas [1563].
        Biblioteca Peruana, serie 1, Vol. III:377–463. Lima.

Sarmiento de Gamboa, Pedro
1906   Geschichte des Inkareiches von Pedro Sarmiento de Gamboa [1572]. Herausgegeben von Richard Pietschmann. *Abhandlungen der Koeniglichen Gesellschaft der Wissenschaften zu Goettingen, Philologisch-Historische Klasse*, Neue Folge, Vol. VI(4). Berlin.

Sitio del Cuzco
1934   Relación del sitio del Cusco [sic] y principio de las guerras civiles del Perú hasta la muerte de Diego de Almagro, 1535–1539 [1539]. *Colección de Libros y Documentos referentes a la Historia del Perú*, anotaciones y concordancias con las crónicas de indias por Horacio H. Urteaga, serie 2, Vol. X:1–133. Lima.

Šolč, Václav
1975   Casa aymara en Enquelga. *Annals of the Naprstek Museum* **8**:111–146. Prague.

Toledo, Francisco de
1975   *Tasa de la visita general de Francisco de Toledo* [1571–1573]. Introducción y versión paleográfica de Noble David Cook. Lima: Universidad Nacional Mayor de San Marcos, Seminario de Historia Rural Andina.

Villanueva Urteaga, Horacio
1971   Documentos sobre Yucay en el siglo XVI. *Revista del Archivo Histórico del Cuzco* **13** (1970):1–148. Cuzco.

6

The Infrastructure of Inka Control
in the Peruvian Central Highlands

Craig Morris

Editors' Introduction

Craig Morris uses archaelogocal materials from two centers (Huánu-co Pampa and the *tampu* of Tunsukancha) along Inca state roads to depict the political administration of empire in 1532. The recent evidence that Morris cites indicates that such centers provided a place for leaders to give their followers feasts accompanied with heavy drinking and much political-religious ceremony. This argument points to the fragility of administrative mechanisms, which more nearly resembled village rituals of solidarity than the full-time bureaucracies and standing armies too easily suggested, at least to the modern mind, by the elaborate state roadways, edifices, and stored goods constructed and accumulated by the Inkas.

The consolidation and maintenance of a state as large and diverse as that of the Inka would prove a difficult challenge even with a modern technology of transportation and communication. The Inka achievement, which lacked even wheeled vehicles and the animals to pull them, has drawn substantial comment and admiration, beginning with the publication of the "chronicles" of several writers soon after the Spanish invasion. The early writers documented a fabulous system of roads, lodgings, and supply depots that supported royal travel.

THE INCA AND AZTEC
STATES, 1400–1800

For it was their custom, when they traveled anywhere in this great realm, to go with great pomp and be served with great luxury, as was their custom. It is said that, except when it was necessary for their service, they did not travel more than four leagues a day. And so that there would be sufficient provisions for their people, at the end of each four leagues there were lodgings and storehouses with a great abundance of the things that could be had in this land; and even if it was uninhabited there had to be these lodgings and storehouses (Cieza de Leon 1550/1962:430).

It has long been assumed that this logistics network lay at the heart of the Inka strategy to rule such a vast territory. Unfortunately, the system of roads and, particularly, the centers they connected for the most part did not survive the Spanish invasion in a functioning state. By the time of Cieza, whose observations are probably the most perceptive, the system was already in ruin. He says of Vilcas Waman:

What there is to see of this are the foundations of the buildings and the walls and enclosures of the adoratorios, and the said stones, and the temple with its steps—although destroyed and full of weeds—and the storehouses demolished; finally, it was what is not, and by what it is we judge what it was. (Cieza de Leon 1550/1962:435–436)

The administrative records, such as the *visitas* of Garci Diez de San Miguel (1567/1964) and Iñigo Ortiz de Zúñiga (1562/1967, 1972), which have provided more direct access to native Andean institutions are of even later dates and deal largely with the various local political and ethnic units. The insights they provide into the functioning of the infrastructural system are largely incidental.

Given this dearth of reliable observation, interpretation of the infrastructural network and the administrative system it apparently supported has followed the tendency begun by the early Spanish writers and has reconstructed a system with basically European utilitarian principles. The network has been seen as a system for facilitating and managing the movement of people and goods about the realm and as an extension of the state bureauracy and decision-making mechanism into the provinces. Prominent among their inhabitants were the soldiers and bureaucrats who secured and administered the local regions for the Inka. My own discussions of some of the centers in the system (e.g., Morris 1972) have recognized many of the peculiarities of their populations and relationships to preexisting settlements, but they have also emphasized the importance of the centers in supporting military operations and a state bureaucracy.

The material remains of the roads and building complexes that constituted the network are in many cases remarkably intact. The obvious strategy should be to link the study of the material record to the information in the written sources. The careful coordination of the two independent sources should help overcome the limitations inherent in the fragmentary historical data. Research begun by John V. Murra in Huánuco in 1963 used this approach; our recent research on the Inka center at Huánuco Pampa has continued it.

From the outset we have concentrated on two somewhat different aspects of what seems the logical role of hinterland centers. On the one hand, we wanted to see what kinds of strictly infrastructural functions they discharged. What was the nature of the transportation, communication, and supply network that backed up state operations in executing the aims of Cuzco? On the other hand, we wanted to see how these centers acted as intermediaries between Cuzco and the diverse peoples they had conquered. Were the larger nodes in the network in a sense provincial capitals with resident authorities and the bureaucratic apparatus to make and carry out decisions that substantially affected the local populace? Was their role vis-à-vis the populace a more limited one of simply helping to reinforce and control a perexisting authority structure in a system of indirect rule?

The outlines now emerging for the Peruvian central highlands clearly substantiate the existence of a sophisticated transportation, communication, and supply system. It easily matches in extent and technological sophistication what we would expect from the sixteenth-century observers. Yet the activities that appear to have been taking place in the centers we have studied do not support the notion of an infrastructural system devoted mainly to an army and a bureaucracy as the primary agents of government. The emphasis was rather on rituals and ceremony in a variety of contexts, and the infrastructural system seems to have been more geared to supply these ceremonial activities than to armies and bureaucrats.

The functions of linkage between the state and the local populace seem also to have relied heavily on the ceremonial aspects of the larger centers. They provided the settings in which large numbers of people were brought together in elaborate rites of legitimation. The distribution (by the state) and consumption of food and other classes of goods were critical aspects of such rites. An integral part of the activities of these centers was thus the supply, processing, and, in some cases, the manufacture of such goods. Seen in light of this evidence, the "administrative" functions of the larger provincial centers are lodged mainly in traditional reciprocities. I believe the tentative results of our research presented here suggest that we need to put more emphasis on clarifying these traditional reciprocities as they were employed by the state. Although communication and supply are critical, they are, after all, only support operations that give us a very indirect view of the principles through which the Inka governed.

Communication, Administration, and the Supply of the State Operations

A state cannot endure unless it has effective means of collecting information, communicating it to those who make decisions, and communicating the decisions in turn to those who must implement them. In the absence of a rapid communication technology, the movement of information must depend on the transportation system and its ability to move people with messages. This is made more reliable through the use of a notation device, such as the *khipu* in the Inka case.

Communication was a special challenge for the Inka because of the extent and severity of the terrain they controlled. The systems of roads they established in solution to communications and logistics problems is by now legendary, although they are only now receiving real scientific study as a result of John Hyslop's ongoing work. Hyslop's (personal communication 1982) evaluation of his results to date on the road network suggests that at least 30,000 km of roads were in use. The system of relay-runners carrying messages and probably *khipu* and other small objects has been described many times. It has been estimated (Rowe 1946:231) that the average speed of the runners was 240 km a day.

As important as the roads themselves were, I prefer to stress the significance of the centers placed along them. The maintenance and protection of the people and animals who moved products and information and provided services was essential. Although the construction of levees, bridges, and stepped or graded inclines made travel easier, the provision of food and shelter made it possible. Besides providing food and shelter, the centers also monitored and supervised the flow of goods, services, and information and served as collection and distribution points for all of these in relation to adjacent hinterland areas.

In the Peruvian central highlands the centers along the road network appear to fall into two major classes: (a) relatively small sites that served as simple way stations in the transportation and communication network, and (b) larger "administrative" centers that encompassed a wider range of functions. The distinction between the two classes of centers should not be taken as too rigid, however, since at least one site surveyed (Tarma) appears to have been intermediate in both size and functional range. We have examined one example of each kind of center rather closely: the large center at Huánuco Pampa (Morris 1976, 1980; Morris and Thompson 1970) and the *tampu* of Tunsukancha (Morris 1966), some 20 km to the south. The same variety of Late Inka style ceramics were found in the two sites. Other large Inka centers surveyed, such as Pum Pu and Jauja, have different interpretations and imitations of the Cuzco shapes and motifs. This pattern in the ceramics suggests that Tunsukancha received its pottery from the same sources as Huánuco Pampa, and it may be that the larger center held administrative control over the smaller one in this case.

In terms of the present discussion, three characteristics of Tunsukancha are of primary importance. On its eastern periphery were 24 storehouses with an estimated volume of slightly less than 400 m³, which was, by Inka standards, a modest storage facility. Around its plaza were grouped three long buildings of the type frequently called *kallanka*. Such buildings are thought to have provided temporary housing for transients (Gasparini and Margolies 1977:208–209; Morris 1966:103). The buildings in question provided about 1770 m² of floor space.

Other features of the site include a compound that archaeologists might characterize as an "elite residential facility," a small religious structure, and a group of small houses probably for service personnel. Excavations in parts of the residential facility revealed only small quantities of refuse, not the amounts of material that would suggest intensive use. Perhaps the buildings were some sort of official residences that were used only sporadically. The excavations at Tunsukancha were limited, but nothing was found to suggest that the site was anything more than a way station providing supplies, lodgings, and a small offering place for travelers.

Huánuco Pampa supported a far wider range of activities, its role transcending that of a supply depot. Some general interpretations of the site have been offered previously (Morris 1976, 1980; Morris and Thompson 1970; Murra and Morris 1976). Analyses of the data are not complete, and we expect further work to identify many additional activities. The progress to date already shows the center to have been of enormous complexity. It brought together the people who provided a large number of state services and furnished the facilities for their support. In terms of complexity Huánuco Pampa was similar to a city, but its standardized architecture and pottery show that it was built and furnished by the state. It was, thus, part of the elaborately planned governmental infrastructure.

The evidence on support of communication and transportation at

Huánuco Pampa is similar in kind to that from Tunsukancha: Large buildings were placed around the center's central plaza (Figure 6.1) to house transients, and storehouses were built to feed them. The amounts of space involved, however, are very different. If we assume that all of the structures around the plaza served as housing for transients, about 5500 m² were available. The granaries at Huánuco Pampa had a maximum volume of about 39,700 m³. If completely filled with food, this volume could have held over a million bushels. Because of the methods and containers of storage, the actual volume of food must have been smaller, but the amount was nonetheless enormous.

It is interesting to compare the estimates for transient housing and food storage in the two centers. Huánuco Pampa provided somewhat more than four times as much space for transient housing. The ratio of food storage capacity, however, is almost 100:1. We would expect that a larger, more important center would have a greater need for transient housing. Besides the usual long-distance travelers along the roads, people from the surrounding hinterland would have numerous reasons for visiting Huánuco Pampa. The high storage ratio between the two centers, of course, indicates something more than just supplying a larger volume of transients. A much larger resident service population was present and apparently supplied from state stores. I have suggested elsewhere (Morris 1981) that the differences between the capacities of the two storage facilities transcended what we would expect on the basis of overall housing in the two sites. I believe the differences in capacities and other evidence suggest that Huánuco Pampa was concerned with long-term storage to absorb the burden of seasonal and annual variation in the availability of food for state purposes, while Tunsukancha's stores were devoted to rather immediate supply considerations related to support of transportation (Morris 1981).

The use of military force or the threat of its use is inevitable in political expansions on the scale of that of the Inka, and there is little doubt that the army played a critical role. There is also little doubt that the administrative and logistics centers along the roads that connected them served essential military functions. Although our evidence from the frontiers of Inka expansion is not very good, at least in the north the road system and regional administrative centers (e.g., Quito) were established rather quickly near the front lines. Both supplies and supervision from the highest levels were readily available.

Unfortunately, the search for direct evidence of military operations and activities at Huánuco Pampa has been disappointing. There are numerous suggestions of barrack-style living in the center, but the artifacts that would tie these to military activities have been few and

0   100 200
      meters

Figure 6.1 Preliminary architectural plan of Huanuco Pampa.

far between. Weapons are not ordinary artifacts; in a society as highly organized as that of the Inka they would probably not have been used and disposed of casually. Weapons broken beyond further use would probably have been abandoned in the field. We also must remember that Huánuco was in a region of strong resistance to the Spanish invasion, and the brief Spanish occupation at Huánuco Pampa perhaps could not have afforded to leave weapons lying about. Any arms not taken by the natives who left Huánuco Pampa may have been confiscated by the Spanish and kept under their tight control. The patterns of artifact spread and disposition, which the archaeologist is dependent on in studies such as ours, may not accurately reflect the use of the center by the Inka.

Besides the impact of events in the early colonial period, we also have to consider possible alterations of the military role of logistics and administrative centers as the frontier moved outward, leaving such centers to cope more specifically with intermediate support and supply operations. This might well mean an emphasis on backup logistics and the supply of troops in transit rather than on actual combat. The evidence does lend itself to this interpretation, but we would, nevertheless, expect some preparation for a rapid response to rebellion in the surrounding region and for the protection of the city itself.

One aspect of the archaeological record not subject to easy rearrangement in the years of turmoil following 1532 is architecture. Huánuco Pampa and its sister centers in the Peruvian central highlands are notable for their lack of defensive architecture. A compound with a tall wall in an outlier to the north of Huánuco Pampa may have been a small fortress. It is located on the edge of the pampa on which the site is built and overlooks the valley of the Orqumayu River, now called Vizcarra. Except for this possible fortification, the site seems almost to flaunt its exposed position, advising that its strength and security did not depend on a defensive posture.

From eyewitness accounts of the events at Cajamarca, we know that the Inka army on the move made extensive use of tents and in that case was actually lodged outside the town (Jerez 1534/1917:47, 53). I have seen no mention of large groups of armed soldiers in the town itself. These circumstances may have been conditioned in part by the special situation of Cajamarca, where the Inka was temporarily installed at the baths. But they may also suggest such Inka towns were not regularly filled with soldiers. Besides the problems resulting from our lack of evidence so far of armaments in significant numbers, our difficulties in studying military operations archaeologically may in part result from a European bias, which has trained us to look for something like the quarters for garrisons of troops in a standing army. There is no evidence that such was the Inka model. Rowe has pointed out that all able-bodied taxpayers were liable for military service, that there was no standing army aside from the ruler's bodyguards, and that much of the fighting force was made up of men recruited for the regular labor tax (Rowe 1946:278).

Although this situation may have been in the process of being altered by the deployment of ethnic groups such as the Cañari for military purposes in the final years of the empire, in 1532 there is no reason to expect rigid distinctions between military and nonmilitary personnel. A range of housing facilities was probably provided for various groups of people; when the need arose, appropriate available groups would have been pressed into service. If no appropriate men were available in residence, they would have had to be recruited. It does not now look as if we will be able to identify the warehouses of weapons that might have been supplied to such a group, at least not at Huánuco. But further study may identify residences of some of those groups that were available, as well as some of those that were not.

In summation, the evidence of military operations at Huánuco Pampa is minimal. It may be, for the reasons just outlined, that the archaeological evidence for military activities has been obscured. However, I believe the best interpretation of our data is that the army played only a secondary role in the functioning of major centers along the road system. The smaller centers, such as Tunsukancha, simply did not offer the facilities for anything but a minor supply role for troops on the move. Perhaps the Spanish perception of the military role of the centers was somewhat exaggerated by their own military concerns and the fact that the brief glimpse they had of the system came in the immediate aftermath of a civil war. A sophisticated system of military logistics was probably in place in the provinces, but, at least once a frontier situation had been transcended, its emphasis appears to have been on readily available food supplies and housing facilities rather than on combat forces on constant alert.

Administrative activities are extremely difficult to identify archaeologically since most of them are not accompanied by concentrations of durable artifacts as are production, storage, and domestic activities. Although architecture may be suggestive of how space is used, corroborative evidence is required from written sources or associated artifacts. It is clear from the written record that bureaucratic activities such as collecting information and recording it on *khipu* must have been carried out at centers like Huánuco Pampa. Unfortunately, the *khiphu* is a perishable artifact, and we are frequently reduced to arguing that buildings and sectors of the center were devoted to administration on the basis of their architectural characteristics combined with a lack of positive evidence for alternative uses.

In identifying administration, we are faced once again with the problems that administrative duties were probably not rigidly separated from other activities. Indeed, they were probably associated with activities and spaces that were primarily "residential" or "ceremonial." Any real statement on administration will thus have to wait until such activities can be studied. What we can state now is that major blocks of space were not given over to purely bureaucratic and administrative operations. There are small clusters of buildings that we believe to have housed record-keeping and supervisory duties related to specific activities. The primary example of this is the building group below the storehouses in the southern part of the site (Figure 6.1). It contained a group of large, long buildings, which were almost certainly devoted to storage processing and record keeping, and a series of residences, which perhaps housed the people responsible for the operations. There are also structures that probably housed checking and recording procedures near the entrances to other compounds that served a variety of functions. The compound where spinning and weaving was carried out is a case in point (Morris 1974).

Our European vision of a provincial capital sees a center capable of considerable independence on certain local matters. Information was collected for the central government, and that government's decisions were carried out; however, in addition, decisions were made on a whole range of local matters, thereby decreasing the administrative load in the main capital. In a relatively loosely structured state such as Tawantinsuyu, which had to cope with problems of great distance, the need for a considerable measure of regional autonomy would seem great.

Although we must bear in mind the archaeological comlexities mentioned, the fact that we have not been able to pinpoint a concentrated bureaucratic and administrative core at Huánuco Pampa (largely because most building groups appear to have served other functions) raises some important questions about its role in provincial administration. First, except for purely record-keeping matters, administration per se was probably not strongly differentiated as a separate activity. It was rather part and parcel of the ceremonial and hospitality functions that I will discuss in a moment. Second, an elaborate decision-making structure may simply not have been present in Huánuco Pampa. The material evidence suggests that such centers were extensions of Cuzco; they facilitated communications, supported numerous aspects of state policy, and in a sense represented the capital. The emphasis was on helping centralize the state administration rather than on setting up regional capitals with significant autonomy.

The study of residential patterns based on domestic artifacts now in progress should clarify some of these issues by providing additional information on possible administrative personnel. On the basis of architecture alone, only one residential compound stands out from the rest. That is the group of buildings just west of the great trapezoidal enclosure in the eastern sector of the site (Figure 6.2). Its dressed stone masonry and associated bath, as well as its prominent position in the site plan, signal its extraordinary nature. Unfortunately, the structures of this compound had been cleared to a level well below their floors by nonprofessional excavators prior to our project, so we will never know what kinds of artifacts were associated with them. Cieza de Leon (1550/1962:220) and other chroniclers tell us that the Inka maintained a palace in Huánuco and other provincial capitals. If there was a "palace," this compound seems to be the most likely candidate. No other buildings of residential dimension even approach such a high degree of architectural elaboration. Although there are gradations in the quality of both residential architecture and ceramics elsewhere in the site, there is no other building, or group of buildings, that stands out from the rest as the elite residential compound.

Does this mean that the role of any permanent person in charge of the center was played down? Our data do not yet allow us to go that far, but my interpretation of the architectural evidence does imply that only one residential enclave was clearly elevated above the rest. If it was reserved for the use of the Inka, it must customarily have stood empty. If further analysis confirms this absence of residences at a very high level of luxury, we have further indications of a deemphasis of permanent and important authority figures in the center. The emphasis may have been on facilities for the Inka himself, so that his presence was symbolized in the architecture even though he was rarely in residence. If some other high-level authority figure was maintained in the center, his visibility would appear to have been played down. As in the case of resident armed garrisons, the concentration of administrative authority in the centers could have been a decentralizing force in the state. The whole question of provincial governors and their relation to centers like Huánuco Pampa requires additional research both in archaeology and in the historical sources.

Obviously many local matters were dealt with locally. It would simply not be possible to centralize day-to-day operations for the whole state in Cuzco. How much of the local administrative operation

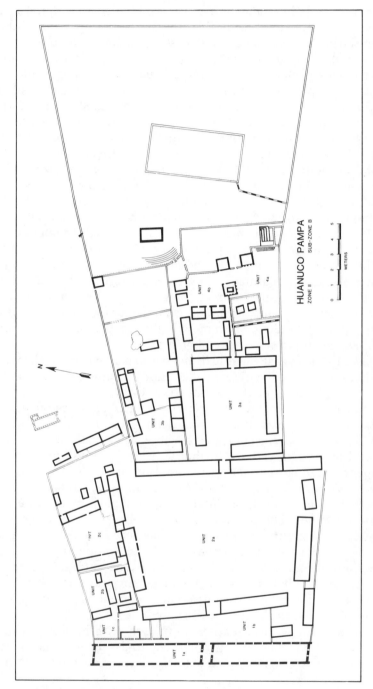

HUÁNUCO PAMPA
ZONE II   SUB-ZONE B

0 1 2 3 4 5
METERS

Figure 6.2   Area of fine architecture in the eastern sector of Huánuco Pampa.

was directly in the hands of the state—and therefore presumably located at Huánuco Pampa—and how much of it was in the hands of local ethnic leaders residing in settlements that predated the Inka expansion? My present impression for Huánuco favors the alternative of heavy stress on indirect rule. Of course, the state frequently altered existing leadership patterns, by replacing uncooperative leaders and breaking up or combining certain groups, but I doubt that critical functions involving the direct government of local groups were removed to state-built centers. As I have pointed out previously (Morris 1972), these centers along the roads appear intrusive in the local settlement pattern. They give the impression that the state was still almost a separate structure that had extended its chain of centers into foreign territory. Groups such as the Chupaychu and Yacha were still viable entities. Their leaders exercised local control, acting under orders from the state on certain matters. The role of the state regional centers in the hierarchy requires continuing clarification. But it does not appear to me to be a simple intermediate administrative tier with a sizable bureaucracy charged with managing the region and reporting to Cuzco.

The Link between State and Region

If Huánuco Pampa was neither an omnipresent military garrison nor a specifically administrative center in the sense of providing a substantial and permanent bureaucratic and formal decision-making apparatus, what was its role in enabling the state to control local ethnic groups? How did it mediate between the seat of ultimate authority in Cuzco and the people it ruled in the countryside? How did it differ from the much smaller *tampu* centers that seem to have been little more than way stations for certain categories of travelers?

Although the material record cannot give us full answers to these questions, one set of data from Huánuco Pampa suggests the general direction in which the answers may lie. In the eastern sector, adjacent to the residential compound that may have housed the ruler himself, are a series of 12 long rectangular buildings grouped around two spacious plazas (Figure 6.2). Virtually everyone who has studied or visited the site has singled out this group of structures because of its centrality to the site's overall plan (e.g., Harth-Terré 1964). Prior to excavation we tended to view these plazas as stately halls housing administrative bureaucratic activities. Excavations supervised by Pat H. Stein in the buildings of the area put any idea of solemn bureaucratic halls immediately to rest. She found a whole complex of culinary pottery, food remains, cooking areas, and literally tons of large jars thought to be primarily associated with *chicha* (Stein 1975).

The role of *chicha* in Inka religion and ceremony has been noted by many scholars (Murra 1960; Rowe 1946:292), and I have recently made some observations on its large-scale production at Huánuco Pampa and its overall importance in Inka political and economic growth (Morris 1978). One of the most complete pictures of the political importance of *chicha* has been brought together by Maria Rostworowski de Diez Canseco (1977:240–244) for the Peruvian north coast. The north-coast leaders operated what appeared to the Spanish to be "taverns" in which great drinking bouts took place. When a local chief traveled, people came to drink at his expense each time his litter rested. In addition to brewers, there were numerous bearers to carry the drink in generous quantities; this created a great retinue that accompanied the leaders. The Spanish mounted a campaign to stamp out what they considered excessive drinking, frequently carried out in the contexts of what to them were pagan rituals (Rostworowski de Diez Canseco 1977:241; Rowe 1946:292).

Rostoworowki's analysis demonstrates that political power and the economic rights associated with it were closely related to these ceremonies involving drink. Though probably they were at least nominally religious, they were a way of establishing and maintaining a relationship between the leaders and the led. They were the chiefly generosity that could bring together political loyalty and the labor to till fields and build cities. If our preliminary interpretations are correct, the elaborate space provided along with the thousands of jars of beer represents one of the principal investments made by the Inka state at Huánuco Pampa. In terms of state-local relationships this may even have been the key function, and many of the other spaces and activities in the center served to support it. An elaborate setting had been constructed for the ceremonies that forged a relationship between the Inka and those whose service was important to him.

The role of public hospitality as a source of authority is well documented in other societies. Barth's analysis of Swat Pathans is instructive:

> It might seem . . . that gifts and hospitality would be less important than bribes and payments in supporting claims to authority. As a matter of fact, the reverse is true. Bribes and payments create relationships which render them onerous and hazardous. Gifts and hospitality on the other hand, are of prime importance in the building up of a political following [Barth 1959:77].

In the Swat Pathan case, according to Barth, this "prime importance" stems largely from the magnitude of the goods redistributed; that is, the recipients actually become dependent on them. "A continuous flow of gifts creates needs and fosters dependence, and the threat of its being cut off becomes a powerful disciplinary device" (Barth 1959:79). But quantity is not the only factor: "The scene of most gift-giving and hospitality is the men's house. Here the efficacy of the gifts is enhanced by their transfer; the chief's character as a lavish giver becomes known to outsiders, who are thus attracted to visit his men's house" (Barth 1959:80).

Lacking the kinds of real ethnographic data available to Barth, we are still in no position to measure the extent of the "generosity" of the redistributive Inka state that Murra (1955/1979:Chapter 6) first outlined more than 2 decades ago. State storage centers clearly held enormous wealth, and the relatively permanent state service personnel in places like Huánuco Pampa had probably become dependent on that wealth by 1532. The critical question, however, is how dependant the smaller political and economic units—the people who lived in the towns and villages—had become on state goods. The state's power would be greatly enhanced if it were able to exercise direct control over local economies. The quantitative information necessary to answer that critical question is not in hand. The data available give the impression, however, that while the reciprocal economy may have been moving toward increasing state control, in 1532 that control was likely limited to certain sumptuary goods (Morris 1974, 1978; Murra 1964). These goods, such as cloth, were fundamental in the state's relationship with local leaders.

The state's involvement in the redistribution of food was probably limited to feast occasions and the support of labor service. Although the actual quantities of food were comparatively large, support was in most cases only temporary and involved a relatively small segment of the population. The main beneficiaries, again, were local leaders. A role for the state storehouses in times of famine cannot be ruled out, but local economic units seem to have remained basically self-sufficient in subsistence goods, at least in the Peruvian central highlands. The state's economic role was in support of state services and the redistribution of goods identified with the redistribution of prestige and power. In the region of Huánuco for which we have data, this redistribution appears to have been channeled through existing local political structures. In a sense it was a classic case of indirect control.

The place of such centers as Huánuco Pampa in this scheme of reciprocally based indirect political and economic control was that they provided a ceremonial context and even a structure of physical layout (Morris n.d.), which was designed to articulate various local units in their relationships to each other and their relationships to the

Inka. Although most of the units were pre-Inka, the larger forms of organization were new. The central and dynamic aspect of the "administrative" centers was, therefore, that they used reciprocity and related Andean economic and political traditions to make legitimate (and often to create) the large-scale organizational units essential to such a large state. Thus, they were true administrative centers, but the form of administration and linkage between units was fundamentally different from the bureaucratic norms we tend to associate with "regional capitals."

Concluding Comment

It is symptomatic of our difficulties in devising an adequate conceptual framework for the Inka that the data and interpretations presented in the two sections of this paper seem somehow contradictory. The evidence of planning on a grand scale that produced the roads, communication system, and masses of stored goods does not quite fit with administrative practices that depended heavily on feasting and politico-religious ceremony to hinge the state to the groups it ruled. We tend to associate sophistication in planning and engineering with secular states staffed with permanent, sizable bureaucracies. In Tawantinsuyu the sophistication, planning, and even the bureaucratic activities were integrated into the state through a series of institutions we usually associate with smaller scales of organization.

Part of the contradictions stems from the fact that the Inka state was changing rapidly. This rapid change may account not only for our difficulties of interpretation but also for what appears to be an emerging disparity between the archaeological record and part of the information we encounter in the historical sources. As Julien demonstrates in Chapter 5, there is ample written evidence for a relatively fixed and orderly decimal hierarchy of administrators, particularly in relation to taxation. Although a rich ceremonial life is documented by the early writers, it is not given the central position in power and administration that I tend to assign it from the archaeology.

The difference between these two emphases is, of course, in part the difference between two radically different kinds of material. Bureaucratic positions cannot easily be seen in the material record, nor can the written sources fully reflect a system already in disarray and only vaguely understood by its chroniclers. Additionally, one would expect decimal administrators to be more dispersed throughout the units for which they were responsible and only the few at appropriate upper levels to be resident in a regional center. I suspect, though, that the disparity is partly the result of the rapidly changing times and discrepancies between the plans and ideals of the Inka rulers—the decimal system of administration was supposedly the invention of Pachakuti—and the realities of older Andean traditions on which the growth and control of the empire were still based.

The directions of native development were forever altered by the events of 1532, and we are left mainly to speculate about the processes that may have been changing Andean statecraft at that time. The Andean tradition to which the Inka were heir had evolved complex social, political, and economic institutions that effectively managed and coordinated the resources of varied ecologies and created large stored surpluses to safeguard the governing infrastructure that held the system together. Much of the energy of the system was devoted to "investments," such as terracing and other land habilitation projects, or to storage; this enabled it to sustain the economic growth necessary to finance political ambitions and maintain an increasingly large elite. However, the information presented here suggests that, at least in part of the empire, enormous resources were being put into the infrastructural and ceremonial apparatus, which was mainly concerned with the perpetuation and growth of power itself. The emphasis was on distribution and consumption, not production.

The necessity of creating and maintaining upper-level management functions in such a system is apparent. The questions have to do with the costs of maintaining the management apparatus. Limits may be set because the costs outstrip the advantages gained from the coordination of ever greater ranges of resources. On the one hand, there is the much belabored tendency of stratified societies to devote a seriously disproportionate part of total production to the support of its managerial elite. On the other hand, there are what we might call the "redistributive costs" of constantly earning power in a system where roles and statuses are not well defined. In the Inka case I would guess these latter costs were particularly heavy and that—if we could have a clear view of the dynamics of the last years of Inka rule—we would see an attempt on the part of the state to turn a system based on multiple sets of reciprocal relationships between multiple and varying tiers of leaders below the state level into a better defined, more permanent, and neatly ordered hierarchy with power flowing from the top.

At this point we do not understand enough of the variables in Andean political and economic development to pursue these matters further. But I believe we can conclude from the new archaeological information that the most critical functions of administrative centers such as Huánuco Pampa, and perhaps the infrastructural system as a whole, were to provide the facilities and goods through which authority could be earned.

Acknowledgment

Archaeological research at Huánuco Pampa is financed by grants GS28815 and BNS-7825109 from the National Science Foundation and was authorized by the Peruvian government (Resoluciones Supremas, nos. 015 and 1030, 1972 and 31-74-ED).

References

Barth, Fredrik
  1959   *Political leadership among Swat Pathans.* London and New York: Oxford University Press (Athlone).
Cieza de Leon, Pedro de
  1962   *La Crónica del Peru* [1550]. Madrid: Espasa-Calpe.
D iez de San Miguel, Garci
  1964   *Visita hecha de la provincia de chucuito por Garci Diez de San Miguel en el año 1567.* Lima: Ediciones en la Casa de la Cultura del Perú.
Gasparini, Graziano, and Luise Margolies
  1977   *Arquitectura Inka.* Caracas: Facultad de Arquitectura y Urbanismo, Universidad Central de Venezuela, Centro de Investigaciones Historicas y Esteticas.
Harth-Terre, Emilio
  1964   El pueblo de Huanuco Viejo. *Arquitecto Peruano* **320**(21):1–20.
Jerez, Francisco de
  1917   Verdadera relacion de la conquista del Peru [1534]. In *Coleccion de libros y documentos referentes a la historia del Peru* (Vol. 5), edited by H. H. Urteaga. Lima: Imprenta Sanmarti.
Morris, Craig
  1966   El tampu real de Tunsucancha. In *Cuadernos de investigacion* (Antropologia 1). Huánuco, Peru: Universidad Nacional Hermilio Valdizan. Pp. 95–107.
  1972   State settlements in Tawantisuyu: a strategy of compulsory urbanism. In *Contemporary archaeology: a guide to theory and contributions,* edited by M. P. Leone. Carbondale: Southern Illinois University Press. Pp. 393–401.
  1974   Reconstructing patterns of non-agricultural production in the Inca economy: archaeology and ethnohistory in institutional analysis. In *The reconstruction of complex societies,* edited by C. Morre. Philadelphia: American Schools of Oriental Research. Pp. 49–60.
  1976   Master design of the Inca. *Natural History* **85**(10):58–67.
  1978   The archaeological study of Andean exchange systems. In *Social archaeology: beyond subsistence and dating,* edited by C. Redman, M. J. Berman, E. V. Curtin, W. T. Langhorne, Jr., N. M. Versaggi, and J. C. Wagner. New York: Academic Press. Pp. 315–327.
  1980   Huánuco Pampa: nuevas evidencias sobre urbanismo Inca. *Revista del Museo Nacional* (Lima) **44**:139–152.

1981   Technología y organizacion Inca del almacenamiento de vivres en la sierra. In *Runakuna Kawsayninkupaq Rurasqankunaga: tecnología del mundo Andino*, edited by H. Lechtman and A. M. Soldi. Mexico: Instituto de Investigaciones Antropologicas, Universidad Nacional Autonoma de Mexico. Pp. 327–375.

n.d.   Architecture and the structure of space at Huanuco Pampa. Unpublished manuscript.

Morris, Craig, and Donald E. Thompson
1970   Huánuco Viejo: an Inca administrative center. *American Antiquity* **35**(3):344–362.

Murra, John V.
1960   Rite and crop in the Inca state. In *Culture in history*, edited by S. Dimond. New York: Columbia University Press.

1962   Cloth and its functions in the Inca state. *American Anthropologist* **64**:710–728.

1980   The economic organization of the Inca state [1955]. Supplement No. 1 to Research in Economic Anthropology. Greenwich, Connecticut: JAI Press.

Murra, John V., and Craig Morris
1976   Dynastic oral tradition, administrative records and archaeology in the Andes. *World Archaeology* **7** (3): 259–279.

Ortiz de Zúñiga, Iñigo
1967   *Visita de la provincia de León de Huánuco en 1562* (Vol. 1). Edición a cargo de John V. Murra. Huánuco, Peru: Universidad Nacional Hermilio Valdizán.

1972   *Visita de la provincia de León de Huánuco en 1562* (Vol. 2). Edición a cargo de John V. Murra. Huánuco, Peru: Universidad Nacional Hermilio Valdizán.

Rostworowski de Diez Canseco, María
1977   *Etnía y sociedad.* Lima: Instituto de Estudios Peruanos.

Rowe, John H.
1946   Inca culture at the time of the Spanish conquest. In *Handbook of South American Indians* (Vol. 2), edited by J. H. Steward. Washington, D.C.: Smithsonian Institution. Pp. 183–330.

Stein, Pat H.
1975   The Inca's hospitality: food processing and distribution at Huánuco viejo. Paper read at Annual Meeting, Society of American Archaeology, Dallas.

7

The Formation of Tawantinsuyu: Mechanisms of Colonization and Relationship with Ethnic Groups

Franklin Pease G.Y.

Editors' Introduction

Franklin Pease analyzes how Andean regions varying in the complexity of their ethnic integration fared when the Inca imposed colonization and other policies of supremacy. In some regions multiethnic kingdoms that had practiced colonization on their own endured Inca rule without much internal change. The ethnically stratified *altiplano* kingdom of Lupaqa, for example, colonized territories as distant as the Pacific coast long before the Inca advent. According to Pease, Lupaqa's internal organization changed little even after the Inca resettled some of its *altiplano* populations and began to exact tribute. At the other extreme, the independent communities of the Chachapoyas region at the tropical forest fringes of Inca expansion, for example, resembled stateless societies until the Inca imposed *yana* retainers as *curacas* having administrative authority and control at the local level.

Pease concludes that the monolithic character of Inca state control suggested by the Cuzco-centered view of the chroniclers was a misrepresentation of the substantial regional diversity in multiethnic stratification and in level and quality of articulation to the state.

During the last 35 years researchers have discovered new perspectives for understanding the Andean state of Tawantinsuyu. It began,

THE INCA AND AZTEC
STATES, 1400–1800

perhaps, in 1946 with John H. Rowe's study–synthesis, which has become a classic. Other contributions that date back to this time include (a) the progressive revelation of the multiethnic reality that Tawantinsuyu almost managed to hide, (b) more complete information about some of these ethnic groups through documentation and archaeological work (i.e., Huánuco or Chucuito) which made it possible to contrast them with Tawantinsuyu (see Morris 1972, 1973; Morris and Santillana 1978; Murra 1968, 1972, 1975), and (c) confirmation that not only classic chronicles but also numerous administrative and judicial documents could be used as sources in researching Tawantinsuyu.

Despite these new sources of information, conflicting interpretations of the economic articulation of power and the use of resources have arisen: (a) Murra's hypothesis of multiple ecological control, (b) Rostworowski's explanation of the differentiation of the coast as a separate economic universe, and (c) presence of a mercantile relationship between ethnic groups that are almost conceived of as feudal entities presented by Rostworoski, Schaedel, Hartmann, and Espinoza.[1] These are the best descriptions we have of a very imprecise Incan mosaic.

There is agreement that the centralized powers of Cuzco made it important in redistribution of resources. However, although there are many examples, we can say little with certainty, except that the level and extent of this redistribution took on a new dimension during the Tawantinsuyu, in the storage and importance of resources, and in the expansion of the mechanisms for obtaining resources. We know little of how the Cuzco state really exercised its control. Some researchers have written a great deal about Inca domination and about Cuzco as an invader in the Andes, which naturally helped the Spanish in 1533 to gain support and acceptance (Espinoza Soriano 1971, 1974). This reopens the discussion about Tawantinsuyu's real control over ethnic groups and about the conditions that governed the attainment of that control, that is, the mechanics of the Inca conquest.

However, this last point instills in us some doubt about the nature of the information offered us by classic chronicle sources and brings us directly to a first question: What do we really know about the beginnings of Tawantinsuyu's eminence over the ethnic units, over various groupings of ethnicities, and over an individually considered ethnicity? This presents great problems, as evidenced also in other fields considered at the symposium organized by the Wenner-Gren Foundation in 1967 (Barth 1976). The initial summary of this meeting was a useful statement of the question, and it recognized the extreme difficulty of clearly delimiting ethnicity and its identifying mechanisms. If we admit that the articulation of the diverse ethnic groups will demand that "their interdependence will be limited even though they may live in the same region" (Barth 1976:23), then we accept as a theoretical statement the proposal made in the Andean example in reference to the colonies peripheral to the principal nucleus of population (Murra 1964, 1972, 1975) or even in reference to specific nuclei where an apparent or real multiethnicity was found (Pease 1977a). Barth continues, "The articulation will tend to be concentrated principally in the commerce which may be practiced in a ceremonial or ritual sector" (Barth 1976:23). If in place of *commerce* we say *interchange*, we can speak of *reciprocity* (see Alberti and Mayer 1974; Murra 1975; Polanyi *et al.* 1957), thus making the sentences valid for the Andean area. That confronts us with the Andean documentation that affirms the existence of uniethnic and/or multiethnic nuclei (Pease 1977a). We still do not know the rules of uniting for these groups, nor is it easy to situate them in a diachronic context without more archaeological research on historically determined ethnic groups, assuming that both the composition of these groups and the space they occupy are variable in time.

We could outline various levels of *multiethnicity:*

1. In the example of the Lupaqa nucleus (Diez de San Miguel 1567/1964; Murra 1964, 1975), does the fact that Lupaqa head towns or principal towns have other population (Uru Chinchaysuyu) incorporated in them indicate a level of multiethnicity?

2. In the example of Lake Titicaca considered as a "macronucleus," if we speak of *Lake kingdoms,* what sense does Sarmiento de Gamboa's statement (1572/1947:191) proposing a maximum dimension for the *Collas* region of expansion make? Here it still would not be clear, on the level of documentation, which of the three "kingdoms" would be the nucleus of a Lake Titicaca macrosystem.

3. Another example would be that of Collaguas, where there could be a lengthy discussion of whether or not the nucleus includes Collaguas and Cabana, distinguished from each other in the sixteenth century by their language (Aymara and Quechua, respectively) and also on a Spanish administrative level (in what refers to the *encomiendas,* not in what refers to *corregimiento*).

This would lead us to assume a level of analysis in which the image of "nucleus" in each of the known examples could turn out to be different, at least in its components, depending on the level or scope of the system of overall adaptation.[2] On the other hand, some doubt exists as to whether the ethinic groups proposed by the classic Andean chronicles are really so, or whether it is actually a matter of identities "fabricated" during the colonial process.[3]

Another type of problem is certainly related to the presence of a ruling power unit, as in the example of Tawantinsuyu, the only Andean state it is possible to study on the basis of more than archaeological testimony. Here we should remember Fuenzalida's annotation to Murra's suggestions about the "vertical control of a maximum number of ecological levels in Andean societies." Fuenzalida referred to this as the "umbrella" function. In this case Tawantinsuyu itself would have provided this function in order to establish a *pax incaica* in which relationships between different ethnic groups could be possible in terms that would not necessarily include violence (Murra 1975:110). However, since the Lupaqa's ecological control on the coast, which occasioned Fuenzalida's commentary, can be dated back much earlier than the Tawantinsuyu, the previously mentioned "umbrella" is unnecessary as a precondition of ecological control (Hyslop and Mujica Barreda 1974; Lumbreras 1974; Trimborn *et al.* 1975). Murra himself has suggested that in his example, specifically in the information of Garci Diez de San Miguel about the Lupaqa, the relationships between the groups that lived together in a marginal colony could easily be the consequence of a conflictive or conflict-inclined equilibrium.

Patterns of Migration

Despite these possibilities, evidently not all the relationships between different ethnic groups and not all the forms of ecological control were equally affected by this state pattern during the time of Tawantinsuyu's ascendency. The first three of the following examples refer to patterns of migration (*mitmaqkuna*) transplanted by the Inca state or by ethnic units. The difference between these patterns—as well as the Spanish imposition of tolerance for the finalization or maintenance of the state of things or even for the reestablishment of previous situations—may offer a way to examine the extent to which Tawantinsuyu modified relationships that existed prior to it.

> Quando don Francisco Pizarro llegó al Cuzco vino (al pueblo de Moho, en la actual prouincia de Huancané, Puno) un cacique principal de la prouincia de Chucuito que se llama Care ya muy viejo y gouernador desta prouincia y llegó al pueblo de Millirea y les dijo a los yndios mitimaes que allí estauan: hermanos *ya no es tiempo del ynga agora y os podéis boluer a vuestra tierra cada uno* y assí saue este

testigo que se fueron muchos que no quedaron hasta trienta dellos no más y que después se fuéron los que quedaron.

When don Francisco Pizarro arrived in Cuzco there came (to the town of Moho, in what is now the province of Huancané, Puno) one of the principal chiefs of the province of Chucuito, named Care, now very old and governor of this province and he arrived in the town of Millirea and he told the Indian *mitimaes* who were there: brothers *it is no longer the time of the Inca and each of you can go back to his own land* and thus this witness knows that many left, that only thirty of them remained and that afterward those who remained left [Archivo Nacional de Bolivia, Sucre, EC-1611, No. 2, ff. 33v/34r].

This example, like others, clearly indicates that these people were ruled by state-determined patterns of migration, that is, they were *mitmaqkuna* of the Inca. Others, however, were not placed by the Inca. The men of Chucuito who worked in the coastal colonies of Sama, Moquegua, or Inchura were dependent on the Lupaqa *curacas*. They remained in these colonies until the time of the modifications produced by the successive *encomiendas* and by the Toledan *reducciones* that restricted travel (access to resources) to great distances. Years later these people made legal protest against the marginality to which they were condemned; apparently, the first legal claim in a case of this sort was that of those same inhabitants of Chucuito, who requested the return to them of the *pobladores* in Sama, Inchura, and Moquegua (that is, that they should be permitted to reestablish and maintain the connection and the access to resources in these lowlands) as Polo de Ondegardo indicated.

Al tiempo que la primera vez se visitó la tierra para repartirla, estos yndios que se hallaron en algunos valles, como está hecha rrelacion, que estaban puestos para el efecto susodicho, contáronlos e rrepartieronlos con los del mismo valle, de manera que los sacaron de las subjecion de los principales, e los repartieron sin ellos e les dieron diferentes encomenderos. No trato yo aquí si se pudiera hazer mejor de otra manera de la que se hiço, porque está ya hecho e no tiene rremedio; pero la duda es agora que acaece los caciques destos yndios llevárselos a sus tierras e despues pretender tener derecho a las chácaras o suyos que sembrauan para el ynga . . . e ansí gouernando estos rreynos el Marqués de Cañete, se trató esta materia, y hallando verdadera esta ynformación que yo le hice . . . se hizo desta manera: que a la prouincia de Chucuito se le volvieron los yndios y las tierras que tenyan en la costa en el tiemp del ynga donde cogían sus comidas, y a Juan de Sanjuan, vecino de Ariquipa, en quien estauan encomendados, se le dieron otros que vacaron en aquella ciudad, e ansí quedó aquella prouincia rremediada; e lo mismo se avía de hacer en todas las demás si fuera posible.

At the time the land was first visited in order to divide it up, these Indians who could be found in some of the valleys, as has been described, who were placed for the mentioned effect, were counted and divided with those from that valley, in such a way that they were taken out of subjection to the *principales*, and they were divided without them or they were given different *encomenderos*. I do not deal here with whether it could have been done better in some other way, because it is done and over with; but now there is some doubt about it because the chiefs of these Indians are taking them to their lands and then claiming to have right to the fields that they used to plant for the Inca . . . and the Marqués of Cañete was governing these realms and this matter was dealt with, and finding this information which I provided to be true . . . it was done in the following way: to the province of Chucuito were returned the Indians and the lands that they had on the coast at the time of the Inca, and to Juan de Sanjuan of Arequipa, to whom they were *encomendados*, others were given who came from that city, and thus that province was resolved; and the same things would be done in all the others if it were possible [Polo de Ondegardo 1571/1916:79–81; again in 1917:72–73].

This situation could be prior to the description by Licenciado Polo, since in the "Renta que repartió el Presidente (La Gasca) entre los que ayudaron que pacificar el Perú" (1549) it is stated: "*A los Yndios de Chucuito [darles, devolverles] los mitimaes que tenía San Juan que fueron de los dichos Yndios*" ["To the Indians of Chucuito shall be given, returned the *mitimaes* which San Juan had, which belonged to those Indians"] (Loredo 1958:359).[4] On the other hand, the "first visit" Polo de Ondegardo refers to could not be the one ordered during Francisco Pizarro's life (1540), but rather must be the one in 1549 and La Gasca's distribution; in this case, the information has to do with the first *cédulas* of *encomienda* between Pizarro and La Gasca. If the La Gasca information is clear, it is possible that Polo de Ondegardo confused the case with another similar one, which took place in 1557, during D. Andrés Hurtado de Mendoza's government. Then in response to the same *curacas* of Chucuito return was made of the towns of

> Auca, con el principal nombrado Aura con cincuenta yndios naturales del cacique Cariapasa, y otro pueblo que se dice Incchenchura[5] con un principal que se dice Canche natural del cacique Cariapasa con noventa y quatro yndios con los demás que hubieren multiplicado, que son naturales del dicho repartimiento y están encomendados en Lucas Martínez Vegazo.

> Auca, with the *principal* named Aura with fifty Indians originally of the *cacique* Cariapasa, and another town called Incchenchura with a *principal* called Canche originally of the *cacique* Cariapasa with ninety-four Indians with the others who may have multiplied, who are originally from the mentioned *repartimiento* and are *encomendados* to Lucas Martínez Vegazo [Barriga 1939–1955 (vol. III):229–300; Los Reyes 20 February 1557].

These towns had been given to Lucas Martínez by Francisco Pizarro in 1540 (Barrisa 1939–1955:vol. III:18). Moreover, the connection of the coastal zones with the colonial province of Chucuito was maintained, as is continually indicated by the notarial protocols of Moquegua, for example, at least well into the seventeenth century. In 1661 the Count of Alba de Liste issued a new provision in which the inhabitants of Sama connected to Chucuito continued to be considered as *mitimaes* of that province. The provision indicated that they should pay up to 87% of the *tasa,* or the part of this that was imposed in corn (155 *fanegas*), for the *"communidad de la dicha prouincia de Chucuito"* (Archive of the Museo Nacional de Historia, Lima; Document No. 58, of the section corresponding to Arequipa: 61–176). Thus, these *mitimaes* remained in the place where they were found at the time of the invasion, and the traditional *abastecimiento* of corn, *ají,* etc., which came from the coastal valleys and was sent to the Lupaqa zone, continued at least until the second half of the seventeenth century. (Like other similar situations, this *abastecimiento* still continues today; see Flores Ochoa, 1973.)

In the previously mentioned 1661 text, privileges that came from the "time of the Inka" were only cited in a way that equated this time with everything in the past. Here we see the necessity of stating an objective of this research: The people sent as *mitmaqkuna* of the Inka would be rapidly returned to their places of origin, while the other people sent by the ethnic groups would remain in the productive colonies.[6] One might think that this is one of the best differentiations between the different classes of *mitmaqkuna,* and it suggests that more extensive research in this area might better define the changes that the Tawantinsuyu did or did not cause in various ethnic groups; this could provide a way to study the relationships between Tawantinsuyu and the ethnic groups that preceded it and survived it. In the known cases of control exercised by the ethnic groups the management of the "islands," or colonies, seems to have required more permanent people (see note 8) than in the cases where the control was exercised by the Tawantinsuyu. (In Cochabamba people were moved from distant groups to work the corn; in Collagua contemporary oral versions recall how the Inca took many people to sow and harvest the corn of Cabanaconde. However, these larger numbers of workers can only have been for the times of sowing and harvesting, not on a permanent basis.)

One case, considered as *mitmaqkuna* of the Inca, might be discussed as an example. Among those cases mentioned by Wachtel are found the Ycayungas of Sipe Sipe (in Cochabamba), who found themselves separated from their place of origin (Ica and Chincha, on the central coast of Peru) and who, in the time of Huayna Cápac, were moved many hundreds of kilometers away. *"Las tierras de ycayun-*

ga . . . las an poseido sembrado y cultivado los yndios yca yungas plateros de sipe sipe porque este testigo oyo dezir que se las auia dado el ynga . . . que serbían al ynga mascara hijo de guayna capa . . . que eran mitimaes de Chincha." ["The lands of Ycayunga . . . have been owned, sowed and cultivated by the Ycayunga Platero Indians of Sipe Sipe because this witness heard it said that the Inca had given them . . . to serve the Inca Mascara son of Guayana Capa . . . that they were *mitimaes* of Chincha"] (National Archives of Bolivia, Sucre, EC 1584, No. 72, f. 23, cited by Wachtel 1976:113, No. 89). They are here mentioned as *mitmaqkuna* of the Inca. However, if they were placed by the Inca, why were they not withdrawn or restored (or did not restore themselves) to their place of origin, in order to be made legal tributaries, as they originally were? What caused them to remain in Sipe Sipe until after Toledo and the *reducciones* in the region? How long did they remain?

This reminds us of one of the most serious problems with information provided by documention in general: The Spanish who were asking the questions in the written accounts insisted a great deal on the "time of the Inca." Both in substance and on the level of translation this could easily have caused considerable confusion. Interethnic relationships remained forever restricted to the temporal informative plane of the Cuzqueño state, a situation that originated in the identification of the past with the "time of the Inca."[7] This aspect of the information creates an uncertainty that apparently can be resolved only through information that does not come only from the classic chronicles but from judicial or notarial documentation referring concretely to the *curacazgos*. In this latter documentation we find examples in which the location of people in a certain place—an "island" or a peripheral colony, as in the case of Cochabamba and many others—is not the result of the managerial activity of the state, but of the ethnic administration or even of the *ayllu*, insofar as this can be defined. Relevant to this, Murra has described (1975:Chapter 3) the management of the "islands" or colonies of the Lupaqa of Chucuito or the Chupaychu of Huánuco[8]; it is as yet unspecified how many gradations or levels of management were possible, on the level of the *ayllu*, *parcialidad*, ethnic group, and the Tawantinsuyu, and it will be necessary to consider what happens on each of these levels after the Spanish invasion.

We can also examine how these groups retained control of their respective colonies after the disappearance of the Tawantinsuyu; the previously mentioned examples are good evidence of this, since legal claims, whether favorably resolved or not, are a form of manifesting and maintaining the law (see Warman 1976). At the very least this retention was effective as long as the Spanish crown was incapable of definitively imposing the system of *reducciones*. We do not really know how it was exercised or maintained afterward; in order to find out about this, we would have to extend our information and the discussion about the *reducciones* and their consequences. Related to this, it would also be interesting to extend research to include the study of the gradual transformation of the systems of ecological control under regimes that restricted or excluded interchange; perhaps the Collaguas can, in the future, provide better evidence of this.

The "island" colonies are also places of interethnic confrontation, about which we know practically nothing. This is true despite the fact that many colonial conflicts, judicially registered, must have originated in these situations of control "shared" by the Tawantinsuyu and different ethnic groups or by various different groups. It is harder to understand the example of the productive colonies of the Lupaqa in the eastern regions of the Bolivian *altiplano*—Cochabamba, for instance. Although it is fragmentary, some documentation that has been published (Morales 1977) and discussed by Wachtel in this present book indicates how it was possible to superimpose the information and to assume within Tawantinsuyu colonization models, which were presented as such to the colonial functionaries. These were forms of control that the Lupaqa represented as theirs in the 1567 visit. When Western property ownership was introduced on an agrarian level in the Andes, what could occur but an indefinable conflict in a situation like this? Even bearing in mind that there is evidence of coexistence in the productive or "island" colonies, the parish books can throw new light on the situation; for example, between 1685 and 1714 in the case of Ichuña, in the Moquegua mountains, marriages were registered of people coming from Yanque, Cabana, and Tisco (Collaguas); from Chucuito, Pomata, Zepita, Ilave, Hatuncolla urinsaya, Hutun Cabana, Nuestra Señora de Copacabana, Moho, and Macha (lacustrian zone); Chuquiabo, Laracaja (Charcas). The dates would make one think of "foreigners," but archaeological evidence indicates ancient and multiple occupation.[9]

Consent and Redistribution

Maurice Godelier has called attention to the contrasting terms of *violence* and *consent*, suggesting that

All power of domination is indissolubly composed of two elements which, in combination, give it its strength: violence and consent. At the risk of shocking some, I shall advance the idea that, of the two components of power, the strongest force is not the violence of the rulers but the consent of the ruled to their domination. I do not wish to be misunderstood here. I am well aware of all the differences that exist between enforced consent, passive acceptance, cautious support and shared conviction. I am quite conscious of the fact that in any society, even a classless one, there is never complete consent to the social order, even of a passive kind, among all individuals and groups. And even when active, consent is not free from reservations and contradictions. The reason for this lies beyond thought, in the fact that in every society, including the most primitive and egalitarian, there are common or particular interests which come into conflict and are reconciled daily. Otherwise there would be no such thing as history. But although it is enormously important, both for the evolution of a society and for the individual or collective destiny of its members, whether the ruled feel a profound conviction of the legitimacy of their system, mitigated support for it, reluctant acceptance of it, latent opposition to it, or finally declared hostility towards it, we are still dealing here with the different possible forms of a major historical force for the conservation or transformation of societies—the force of ideas, of ideologies, a force which springs not only from their content but from the way in which they are *shared* [Godelier 1978:93].

In the lines that follow this passage Godelier seeks the conditions that made participation in what he calls "consent" possible in various examples, generally African. For instance, he points out the need of the dominated to seek interpretations of the world that legitimize in their eyes their own situation of domination. A reading of Godelier, therefore, suggests new possibilities of analysis. We might apply his idea to a rereading of the classic chronicles and of the documentation that refers to the growth of the Tawantinsuyu and to the relationship of the Tawantinsuyu with the ethnic groups that it subdued during the course of its development. The first question would be about the levels of relationship between the Tawantinsuyu and the ethnic groups. This requires a new look at what the classic chronicles say about the form of Cuzqueño expansion (not about its motives, certainly), and a comparison of this information with other more local or regional data. In general terms we could form an opinion about the lack, or partial lack, of consent to the Inca presence. Both the classic chronicles and the regional documentation suggest various levels of conflict, but not necessarily a generalized opposition as one would gather from descriptions by some authors (Espinoza Soriano 1974). However, bearing in mind the variants that Godelier himself ascribes to consent, I would suggest a level of stable relationship that made Tawantinsuyu's predominance possible.

The first point mentioned refers to the image which we are given, on one hand, by the group of classic chroniclers and, on the other hand, by regional documentation, of a very varied nature. With respect to the former we could agree about the generalization of two retrospective utopias: On one hand, there is the well-known image popularized by Garcilaso de la Vega, who described a state that was certainly very powerful, but also benevolent and paternal, simultaneously capable of guaranteeing a social peace that some called socialism and of brutally repressing the opposition to that paradisiacal society. Here the conquests were almost triumphal processions, war was not excluded because that would eliminate the princes' right to heroism, and great value was placed on alliances of the ethnic groups (the *curacazgos*) with the Tawantinsuyu. On the other hand, a second form of utopia, normally attributed to the chroniclers called Toledan, pictured the opposite image: This is an equally powerful state, but ferociously incapable of any benevolence. It dominated the whole Andean region with a political apparatus that was as solid as it was "illegitimate" or "usurping." In this latter image the conquests were rapid and established a kind of uniformity through terror; although the alliances remained, what took precedence was certainly the imposition that included recognition of the capacity of the Cuzqueño state to administer efficiently the Andean economy on a level superior to the communal or ethnic.

In addition to this image substantially based on the chroniclers, other possibilities have been proposed that are closer to the second utopian vision: Given the existence of Tawantinsuyu as a dominating state, it was feasible and even logical that the populations subject to this "imperialist state" would rise up against it and that, at the moment of the Spanish invasion, they would definitely and decisively support the invader against Cuzco.[10] A relationship could be established between the criterion that governed the Toledan vision and the preceding suggestion; both are based on the existence of a state not only powerful but "illegal" and "usurping," a violent dominator of the Andean ethnic groups. This criterion was established in the sixteenth century to make the Spanish invasion morally justifiable and acceptable, since it destroyed a power structure—and even an *Inka*—that was illegitimate and restored to the native population of the Andes their right and capacity to receive a new dominating regime.

Rolena Adorno has pointed out the value of Guaman Poma's account in which he describes how Tawantinsuyu was turned over "voluntarily" to the King of Spain, who in this way reaffirmed his condition as "legal" heir of the Incas. Thus, there is no conquest trauma, since Tawantinsuyu offers itself up (through Huáscar) to the Spanish crown, conferring upon the crown a *de jure* situation different from that of the Incas. The Incas were internal invaders in the text of the same chronicler, who deplored the destruction of the society previous to the Incas, but who accepted them insofar as he could establish a relationship with the governors of Cuzco as a "grandson" of Túpac Inca Yupanqui (Adorno 1978; Guaman Poma de Ayala 1615/1936:81, 376[378]). This attitude and opinion of the chronicler may have reflected his interest in maintaining his dual relationship—as an ideal mediator?—with the Andes and with Spain, situated among the descendants of the Incas and the Spanish crown that succeeded them in their power with paradoxical legitimacy.

However, we should not forget that today's criticism of the classic chronicles does not eliminate them as sources of information about Tawantinsuyu, but rather demands the contrasting of their information with that of the *visitas* and other administrative documentation. Likewise, users of these later sources, which are colder and less personally involved than the chronicles, cannot ignore that (a) administrative documentation is also immersed in a similar ideological context, which accepts the official image in order to justify the conquest in a polemic with the diffusion of Las Casas's theses, and that (b) much of this documentation is also dominated by the desire to fit Andean reality into European categories. This latter characteristic may be noticed, for example, in the European categorization applied to the decisions about the *curacazgos'* succession rights and in the clear intention of the Toledan visits to tranform the ethnic leaders into functionaries of the crown, that is, simple mediators between the people and the colonial authority and direct executors of the politics of the authority (see Ramírez Zegarra 1575).

Three Examples of Tawantinsuyu

Thus, one must limit, insofar as possible, the weight of this ideological context of the sixteenth century and of the present without forgetting it. Using this strongly ideologized documentation, one must try to arrive at a more prosaic image that will allow us to better understand the mechanics of expansion and, above all, the methods of control employed by the Tawantinsuyu in the Andean region. Here I must refer to a previous paper, where I suggested differences between the Incan colonization of various Andean regions (Pease 1978:chapter 1).

The following discussion examines three different examples:

1. The first example is the *altiplano* realms, which bordered on Lake Titicaca and which have been studied especially by Murra. Here the presence of Tawantinsuyu was early, and apparently did not substantially modify the organization for access to resources. The general lines of that organization may be found from before the Tawantinsuyu

(Lumbreras 1974) until after it. This has been substantiated by the visits made by the Spanish administration in the sixteenth century (Diez de San Miguel 1567/1964: Gutiérrez Flores and Ramírez Zegarra 1574; Ramírez Zegarra 1575/1787). At this point I should mention a distinction between the political power and the economic politics of Tawantinsuyu, which will be described in more detail farther on.

2. The second example is Chimor, a kingdom of the north coast, where the Tawantinsuyu took over after a bloody war. Here the local organization survived only weakly, afflicted not only by rigid state control but also by a demographic crisis. In this case, too, there is archaeological evidence of a high degree of political and economic organization prior to the Incas.

3. The third example is the region of Chachapoyas on the edge of the jungle in what is now northeastern Peru. Here the Incan presence was of shorter duration than in the other two places, and apparently no political organization existed here that was as clearly definable as in the two other situations. The documentation about this area is primarily Spanish, and very little is known about the region before the expansion of Tawantinsuyu; thus, it is a different kind of example.

Altiplano

The *altiplano* realms, exemplified basically by the Lupaqa, for whom we have extensive documentation about colonial life and Spanish information about prior times (cf. Murra 1975, especially Chapter 7, and Pease 1978:Chapter 2), represent a first example of colonization and level of consent. Here we have two types of evidence: First, Hyslop and Mujica have called attention to the fact that the Tawantinsuyu obliged the inhabitants of the Lupaqa area to abandon their hillside establishments and *pukara* and to establish themselves in the places that the Spanish found to be *cabeceras*, or principal towns, of the Lupaqa (Chucuito, Acora, Juli, Ilave, Pomata, Yunguyu, Zepita); this was recorded by Garci Diez de San Miguel in 1567. Moreover, Julien (1978) has described how the place traditionally known as Hatuncolla, to the north of Lake Titicaca, was occupied only by the Incas. A second type of evidence would allow us to say that Tawantinsuyu did not change the Lupaqa's traditional means of obtaining resources, either on the southern coast or in the lowlands situated to the east of the *altiplano* (see Murra 1964 and 1975 for a description of these means). In any case, the Tawantinsuyu superimposed its economic system on that of the Lupaqa and obtained its resources above and beyond the needs of the Lupaqa population.

These two attitudes of the Cuzqueño state suggest that in the Lupaqa case there was a distinction between political and economic domination. The first would require reprogramming the patterns of settlement, and the forced abandonment of the old higher places may be due to this. The second attitude assumed simply a resource-securing system that functioned on top of the Lupaqa system.[11] In fact, the example of Cochabamba, studied by Wachtel in Chapter 8, allows us to see how the Tawantinsuyu organized large groups of people of the *altiplano* and moved them toward the indicated region. However, that same document does not contradict the statements of the Lupaqa, made in 1567 and 1574–1575, about their continuous control of productive cornfields in the same Cochabamba zone. Instead it allows us to differentiate between the lands "distributed by the Inka" and those of the Lupaqa.[12]

In this context I would point out the level of consent as described by Godelier. Only in a situation where the Tawantinsuyu has "respected" local organization to a high degree would it be possible for this organization to be maintained after the disappearance of the Cuzqueño state. If the *visitas* after that of Diez de San Miguel, such as the Toledan visits and other cited documents, can provide us with such clear evidence of the management of the "islands" situated to the east and west of the *altiplano* many years after the disappearance of the Tawantinsuyu, it is apparent that the superimposition of the state upon the structure of Lupaqa power did not destroy this power but rather allowed it to survive. This would mean a high level of consent, and in addition, it would seem to carry with it a special degree of redistribution on a state level. We have already seen how access to state resources in the region indicated not only access to storage facilities so conspicuous in other places, but also access to the distribution of the herds of the Inka or of the Sun, as for ritual use. This may have been a way of explaining, within reciprocity, new obligations to the state, perhaps to justify a certain type of *yana* (Murra 1975:136). Perhaps, too, the possible distributions of the Inka's herds were the highest level of "institutionalized generosity." The Lupaqa, and the lacustrian kingdoms in general, could have developed an adaptability to imposed state structures, which could well have helped them to undergo the Spanish invasion better than others (at least initially).

Chimor

The Chimor would be a different kind of example. We know about the area's agricultural, urban, and hydraulic development, which could compete with the most developed areas of the Andes. However, the

Tawantinsuyu seems to have conducted itself in this region in the most drastic manner: Emphasis has long been placed on the rapid depopulation of the area, evident after the Spanish invasion but begun before this, according to some authors. It has also been suggested that shortly after the arrival of the Spanish, some of the most important canals ceased to function. The classic chronicles, in general, as well as accounts that are more specifically about that particular area, call attention to the violence of the conflict between the Tawantinsuyu and the Chimor. Rowe (1948/1970) has reviewed the matter and indicated the principal sources.[13] Once the Chimor had been dominated by Tawantinsuyu, the exercise of the new power may be seen in the presence of many specialized *mitmaqkuna* (gold and silversmiths) in many different places in the Andes (see Crespo 1975; Pease 1978:104–105; Rostworowski 1962:158, 1976:107; Zárate 1555/1944:46).[14]

Evidently in this case, unlike the Lupaqa example, there was not the "active consent" that greatly facilitated the redistribution that the state undertook in the lake zone. We do not find evidence of anything similar in the Chimor. At almost the same time as Garci Diez de San Miguel visited Chucuito, Gonzalez de Cuenca (1566) traveled in the lands of the old Chimor kingdom. He did not, however, provide the information that the former did about the relationships between the visited region and the Tawantinsuyu. A previous visit (Gama 1540/1975) and another later one (Roldán 1568/1975) also did not leave any testimony about this matter. Did the rapid demographic shrinkage diminish the administrative interests of the sixteenth century Spaniard? It would be worth a careful review of what happened in another order of activity. Other documents like the judicial ones do refer to this situation and to the heritage of the *curacas* and give us testimony of memories and information about times prior to the Spanish invasion. However, this leads us again to the problem of the value of documentation that is fabricated as proof of rights being claimed within very different circumstances. In fact, the opposite thing could have happened, and Tawantinsuyu could have intervened more (and destroyed more) in the local economy and organization. It has even been suggested that the prohibition of bearing arms in the zone and the fact of "not giving soldiers in tribute" during the Tawantinsuyu were a consequence of the sturdy resistance of the Chimor population to the Cuzqueño state. We could add another serious consequence to this: Tribute seems to have been more severe in this region than in others (see Rostoworoski de Diez Canseco 1976:107).[15] This could have caused the *yungas* to support the Spanish against Cuzco.

Thus, we are left with an impression that is curiously opposed to Cieza de León's view of another case: the marginality of the population of today's Colombia, and its rebellion against the conquest for a state or state apparatus. It has been suggested many times that the "most civilized" zones offered the least resistance to the Spanish invasion and, inversely, that the least civilized offered a more active opposition. This example would indicate the opposite: Chimor, with a high degree of urban development, was apparently more opposed than the Wanka to Cuzco. I have mentioned the Wanka here particularly because of the suggestion that their resistence and permanent opposition to Tawantinsuyu were such that they were led rapidly to an alliance with the Spanish (Espinoza Soriano 1971, 1974).[16]

Chachapoyas

A last, totally dissimilar example would be that of the Chachapoyas. Here the published documentation (Espinoza Soriano 1966) provides a different view. At the time of the Spanish invasion the Tawantinsuyu had been in this region for a shorter time than it had been in the lacustrian areas and in the central and northern coastal areas. Chachapoyas suggests a marginal situation, perhaps of larger dimension than other places indicated by archaeologists on the edge of the jungle to the east of the Andes (Bonavía 1968a,b, 1970, 1972; Bonavía and Ravines 1967, 1968). These latter areas would certainly include the Bolivian area, with places of Inca settlement on the edge of the jungle.[17] An interesting aspect of the Chachapoyas documentation is the *curacas'* greater dependence on the *Inka*. They unquestioningly accepted the notion that it was the Inka Túpac Yupanqui who had installed them.[18] The successive *curacas* not only maintained their predominance but also intervened actively in regional extensions of the conflict between Cuzco and Tumipampa (Espinoza Soriano 1966:290–301, 312 and following, e.g.). The fact that the *curaca* was a *yana* of the Inka gives us a clear situation that should not be confused with simple customary formulae about slavery. The *yana* or *yanacona* is doubtlessly a multivalent formula; however, it clearly identifies a type of dependence—not necessarily *our* image of dependence—about which we really know very little, since the presence of the colonial *yanacona* openly predominated in the documentation.[19] Were the *curacas* who were installed by the Inka always, in some form, *yanas*? (Platt has pointed out that the translation of *yan* is "help." Compare this with *yanapay*, which means "to help" [1976:27].)

There are some important differences between this example and others:

    1. the peculiar situation of the *curacas* as *yanas*

2. the lack of documentation about tribute (at least until now), which would allow us to compare more clearly what the Chachapoyas gave the Inka with what they later gave to their colonial *encomenderos*
3. the little information we have had so far about the region, in archaeological terms
4. the point already made that known colonial documentation does not speak of a dual situation.[20] But this would require extensive discussion.

The problem in this case, as in the two earlier examples, is to determine the level of consent. One researcher has stated that before the Tawantinsuyu the region lacked a political structure more defined than *ayllu, pueblo,* or a group of these. "Among the chachas each ayllu and pueblo—or group of ayllus or of pueblos—lived independently from the others. Each ayllu evolved freely in its pueblo and in its marca or parcialidad. . . . The curacas of ayllus were not subject to anyone" (Espinoza Soriano 1966:233). Although they had "a uniform culture and spoke the same language [and] had the same god. . . . Nevertheless they never constituted a unified state" (Espinoza Soriano 1966:235). This could be stated with near certainty about any place in the Andean area; however, this type of statement assumes a search for a "political order" of a Western sort, which the Spanish did not find in the same manner everywhere. This recalls once again the old suggestion by Fortes and Evans-Pritchard that it is possible to analyze a political system in which there does not exist—apparently at least—a central organ of government and in which authority is expressed through the structured entirety of "independent" but interrelated authorities (Fortes and Evans-Pritchard 1967:5 ff).

Thus, although no determined order would have been the same throughout the whole Andean area, documentation easily conveys the impression that the Tawantinsuyu produced this order for the first time and eliminated local chaos. Is the presence of a system of *ayllus, pachacas,* and *guarangas,* instead of the *mitades* traditionally known in the south, a result of the Tawantinsuyu's different attitude or different activity in the Chachapoyas region (and in the North Andean area in general)? Thus, is every system of ethnic unity a product of the Tawantinsuyu? Or are we falling again into the problem of identifying, through documentation, ethnic groups where they do not exist? On the contrary, apparently we cannot accept a "static" image of ethnic groups, although documentation suggests this to us. We must overcome the temptation to consider the ethnic groups as static "parcels" that, although modified by the Tawantinsuyu, later reverted to their exact previous situation. For this reason we must try to see what modifications could have been incorporated into the various ethnicities by Cuzco, and which of these were assimilated sufficiently to endure after the Spanish invasion. This requires greater precision with the instruments of analysis, which is beyond this present text.

In conclusion, we might say that the various forms (limits and extent) of explicit consent (Lupaqa, Chimor, Chachapoyas) could have produced different models of Incan colonization, which need to be studied archaeologically (as in the first and last examples). We still have questions about the colonial Spanish establishment and its relationship with the results of the Incan colonization. Using both examples, the expansion of Cuzco and the Spanish invasion, we may be able to profile an Andean pattern of consent and pattern of relationship with large-scale power. However, we are also aware that some of the most important things in this area of Andean research are the restatement and refinement of the categories we are accustomed to using, effective examination of the contents of each one of these, and definition of the upper and lower limits of ethnic combining. Is Lupaqa the lower limit in the Lake Titacaca group? Does the Lake group form part of a larger macrosystem, as yet undefined? What were the conditions and duration of a Lake-region macrosystem? What differences are there in the organization of the Chachapoyas before and after the Tawantinsuyu? We must recognize the difficulties of speaking of interethnic interrelationships in research conditions such as have been described.

Finally we mention a last reflection about the real political structure that made up the Tawantinsuyu. It would be possible to have the impression, which has grown stronger in recent years, that the Tawantinsuyu is more a complicated and extensive network of relationships than it is the apparently monolithic and showy apparatus of power that the chroniclers described in the sixteenth century. The description of these relationships, which can reveal macrosystems of interchange greater than we are accustomed to handling, may well provide better understanding of the relationships of the Tawantinsuyu with the Andean ethnic groups.

(Translated by Mary G. Berg)

Notes

[1]Rostworowski and Hartmann added a new dimension to an often proposed hypothesis, which suggests the presence of mercantile relationships. They thus interpreted the chroniclers' statements about bartering or interchanges in small or large quantities at small or great distances. Rostworowski also called attention to the difference that exists

between coastal and mountain organizations, indicating that in the former the market would function fully whereas in the mountains a form of interchange would be accepted that would be more in accord with Murra's suggestions (Rostworowski de Diez Canseco 1977:16–17; see Hartmann 1971). This could be related to other studies that mentioned possible monetary systems, that is, copper axes (Holm 1966–1967). A more recent discussion, which includes a description that is closer to feudalism, may be seen in Schaedel 1977/1978 and in Espinoza Soriano 1978a:329–356.

[2]Since 1964, Murra has called attention to the need to consider problems of this sort, when he compared the management of different ecologies in a small group (Chupaychu) to a larger one (Lupaqa); see Murra 1975:Chapter 3 *passim*.

[3]Bringing the discussion up to the present, Ossio asks if it is important whether present boundaries of Andean "communities" were established by the Spanish or by the Incas (1978:8); this exemplifies present interest in the problem. The discussion is important because it would relate to the situation in which resources were obtained, to original boundaries of the resources, to the ethnic situation, to the diminutions attributed to the *reducciones*, and to the successive composition of landholdings, etc. It is certainly very different to speak of "communities" than of ethnic groups, but it reflects the same problem (see Arguedas 1968; Fuenzalida Vollmar 1970; Matos Mar 1976).

An additional point would refer to the simultaneous control of a single territory: "Given the simultaneous control which various lacustrian ethnic groups exercised on the coast, there is no reason to assume that differences of cultural content necessarily represent different eras. It would not surprise me if we were to find unstratified settlements with different antecedents in the same valley. They would be simply peripheral colonies established 'on the plains' by nuclei which were contemporary of each other, but different in their culture" (Murra 1975:76). See also the archaeological works cited there by Murra, and Trimborn's annotations (1973a,b; Trimborn *et al.* 1975), which describe the migrations to Sama of "Aymara groups which came from the western bank of Titicaca" (Trimborn *et al.* 1975:57). That would archaeologically confirm Murra's initial suggestion that "the populators of the 'islands' controlled by Chucuito were mountain people. By 1964 we already suspected that many if not all of them were mountain people" (1975:206–207, No. 16). Rómulo Cúneo Vidal had said this many years before.

On the other hand, the verified fact that "vertical" ecological control is earlier than the Tawantinsuyu makes it evident that Fuenzalida's suggestion could be valid only in the cases in which Tawantinsuyu itself obtained its own resources, on top of the resource system of ethnic groups. The protective "umbrella" could thus reduce the conflict in favor of the state's interest. In addition to insisting here on the antiquity of vertical control, we must call attention to the fact that we really do not know how relationships meshed on the peripheral "islands," where various groups functioned. The case of Cochabamba shows us what apparently occurred under the Tawantinsuyu, but we cannot be too sure that the documental descriptions about the *Inka* and the distribution of lands to *mitmaqkana* of different ethnicities are a way of "legalizing," under a state blanket, old practices used by previous ethnic groups, who were reorganized by the state when it added the necessity of obtaining state resources. Without denying the evidence of Cuzqueño manipulation in this area, we must reiterate that the Lupaqa, for example, seem to maintain their production on the margin of Cuzco's. However these may be different lands and people than those mentioned in the 1556 document.

[4]It is also indicated here that what Alonso de Cáceres left was given then to Juan de San Juan; thus, the the *canónigo* Martínez's statement is incomplete when he speaks of him (San Juan) as an *encomendero* only in Ocoña and Cayma (Martínez 1936:177).

[5]Incchenchura or Inchura is the town of San Benito de Tarata in the present depart-

ment of Tacna ("Los yndios mitimaes de Chucuito. Prouisión que el virrey Conde de Alba le despachó del tributo que an de pagar en cada un año los que residen en el pueblo y valle de Zama, términos de la ciudad de Arica", Arica, 14-III-1661). Manuscript, Archivo del Museo Nacional de Historia, Relación correspondiente a Arequipa, No. 58).

[6]*Mitmaqkuna* were the men moved by the state to work in regions a distance from their place of origin; some were also sent by ethnic groups. *Mittani* were the ones who fulfilled a *mitta*, or particular job; they represented energy lent to the state or local authority. Apparently, the difference between *mitmaqkuna* and *mittani* could be in their permanence—stable in the former, temporary in the latter.

[7]The legal case in colonial times between two *curacas* has been mentioned. One wanted to legalize the primacy he claimed in his statement to have held since *"tiempo inmemorial"*; the other litigant stated *"que era de poca importancia que don Rodrigo Guamarico fuese señor de Chimbo desde tiempo inmemorial, por 'tiempo inmemorial' debería entenderse aquel de los gobernantes Inca"* (Ossio 1976–1977:201; legal case between Lorenzo Guamarico, *curaca* of Chimbo, and Santiago, *curaca* of Cusibamba. Archivo General de Indias, Sevilla, Escribanía de Cámara, Audiencia de Quito, Leg. 669, R° 1, 1565).

[8]Here it is worth mentioning how control of the "islands" was maintained in the Toledan epoch, though it may have been under the guise of what the Spanish often understood as "commerce," in order to accuse the *curacas* of employing Andean labor to enrich themselves (in the European manner) by its use. See the statement of Rodrigo Halanoca, *principal* of Hanansaya of Acora, who said that *"algunas veces le a alquilado su curaca para Potosí y Arequipa"* (Ramírez Zegarra 1575:11v); this relates to movements understood as "commercial." A year before, the Toledan *visitadores* had verified the maintenance of control over the coastal colonies and those situated to the east of the *altiplano* (Gutiérrez Flores and Ramírez Zegarra 1574:19r, for example), indicating that *"los yndios mitimaes del balle de Moquegua son trescientos y quatro . . . (los) mitimaes del balle de Larecaxa son setenta y dos yndios."* These statistics also allow us to see that the numbers given by Garci Diez's informants a few years before were clearly moderate (see the table published by Murra (1975:212–213)); although we do not really know which people are referred to by Alonso de Buitrago, Garci Diez's informant, when he stated the *"en Sama y Moquegua le parece que habrá novecientos yndios tributarios"* (Diez de San Miguel 1567/1964:54), since he does not distinguish the Lupaqa from the populators of the area.

[9]Archive of the Parish of San Pedro, Tacna. Book of Marriages of Ichuña, beginning 23-VII-1685, ending 14-VIII-1714. Ichuña has lithic dating (Menguin and Schoeder 1957; Ravines 1972). It formed part of Ubinas until its separation in 1795; during the eighteenth century it had *"un trapiche de moles metales de plata"* (Bueno 1774–1778/1951:90; Valdivia 1847:160; see also Alvarez y Jiménez 1790–1793/1946 [Vol. II]:*passim*). Another question would be about the real difference (or similarity) between some types of colonial "foreigners" and those who were previously *mitmaqkuna* or *mittani*. It is not clear that those called "foreigners" always correspond to the Spanish notion. As a parallel example we can recall the "traders" dedicated to a restricted interchange, as stable interlocutors, in a type of enterprise identifiable with ecological control, complementary or substitutive.

[10]This image was suggested by Espinoza Soriano (1966, 1971, 1974). Apparently the published documentation can lead us to such a conclusion, but in many cases documents were prepared in order to obtain privileges from the colonial system. One would need to examine each case to determine the real influence of this attitude and of this intention, since the account of an attitude or of a group of "historical events" does not

necessarily mean the same thing in Andean and in European thought even in the same century. As an example of this we may see the difference between the history of the Inca conquests presented by the chroniclers as such, and the account of a ritual of conquest, extracted from the same sources, in two different readings of the classic chronicles (Pease 1978: 108–114). We should, therefore, retain some prudent doubt about hypotheses of a frontal opposition to the Tawatinsuyu on the part of ethnic groups, which have not been well defined. This should remain true at least until a critical analysis of the documentation has been made and until we know whether the motivations that sustained the *reclamos*, the declarations or the attitudes of generalized confrontation with Cuzco, are derived from the colonial context, or if they are a real reflection of the situation prior to the Spanish invasion.

[11]As a reminder that during the colonial period there was a consequence relative to this attitude, we can look at the abundant information of the Toledan visits. This distinguishes clearly between the tributary regime, which required the presence of patterns of the *reducción* settlement type, and the commercial regime, which functioned on the margin of the first. The notarial protocols of Moquegua, at least between 1587 and 1601, registered the double jurisdiction over the valley. One came from the province of Chucuito, whose *curacas* contracted extensively during the early colonial period, and another came from Arequipa, where the system of *encomiendas* was closely tied to the valley of Moquegua (see Protocolos de Diego Dávila, 1587–1595, 1596–1600, 1601; Archivo Notarial de D. Víctor Cutipé, Moquegua). See also the examples mentioned in the first part of this essay of the return of people and land to the populators of Chucuito.

[12]In 1556 it was stated specifically: *"El segundo [suyu, correspondía] a yndios lupacas de chucuito que venian al beneficio del dho suyo de sus tierras los quales al tiempo que los españoles entraron en este valle se fueron a su tierra"* (Repartimiento de tierras . . . , in Morales 1977:21). The Toledan *visitadores* registered the problem clearly in another sense. Initially, Ramírez Zegarra told of it, for example, in Larecaja and Chicanoma (1575:34r). The final *tasa* of the viceroy indicated *"lo que auían de pagar en particular cada yndio de los susodichos [de la prouincia de Chucuito] assí los que estaba mandado que fuesen a la villa imperial de Potosí a la labor de las minas e yngenios de aquel asiento como los que avían de rresidir y rresidían en la dicha prouincia y en los valles subjetos della de Cama, Moquegua, Larecaxa, Xicanoma y otras partes donde estauan yndios de la dicha prouincia"* (Toledo 1570–1575/1924:235, see also 239v, 242v).

[13]However, Rowe himself then (1948) extended the decay of Chimú culture back to the first half of the seventeenth century, basing this on the effects of the eradication of the "idolatries" (Rowe 1948:349). This is no doubt independent of the demographic crisis or the politics that were prior to the eradication of the idolatries. It leads us to the interesting problem of the continuity of cultural patterns: "We can be sure that the Indians of the North Coast changed the pattern of their aboriginal culture with some Spanish adornments . . . a long time after 1600" (Rowe 1948).

[14]Apart from this, the presence of the Tawantinsuyu also brought a great increase in the production of bronze, which may be seen in the existence of entire objects of this metal in refuse deposits.

[15]It is worth adding that the published visits about the coast agree that no coastal group gave soldiers as tribute (see Carvajal and Rodríguez de Huelva 1549/1977).

[16]The studies by Espinoza Soriano do not refer to the Chimor, but rather to the Jauja region; nevertheless, his argument is pertinent.

[17]Various studies have again brought up the link between the mountains and the jungle, especially in the Cuzco zone (Camino 1977; Lyon 1978).

[18]The original lawsuit refers not so much to this as to the matter of new successive formulae in a process of juridical acculturation.

[19]Certainly, the figure of the colonial *yanacona* has served as a point of departure for the categorization of its pre-Hispanic antecedent, conferring upon it the contours of slavery that accompany it in the literature. In fact, there are examples of colonial *yanaconas* who were slaves before obtaining the status of *yanaconas*, at least in the sixteenth century. On March 30, 1591, Juan de Jáuregui, resident of the town of Oropesa, sold to Diego Inga, resident of Juli, a woman *"de nación Chiriguana nombrada Yamonda de hedad de diez y ocho años . . . la qual se uende por esclaua perpetua . . . y la otra [mujer, que vende él mismo] . . . es de nacion chane nombrada Yndupa de hedad de vente años . . . la qual* uendo por esclaua por diez años y estos cumplidos queda por yanacona perpetua *como se declara en las dichas prouisiones."* (Archivo Notarial de D. Víctor Cortipé, Moquezua, Protocolo de Diego Dávila 1587–1595:ff. 100 ss.).

[20]If there was no dual division between the Chachapoyas (Espinoza Soriano 1966:232–233), then why is there a struggle between two competitive authorities as it would seem in the same documentation? It is possible to discuss the absence of the duality, but then we would need to answer a different question: Why does the Hanan-urin formula seem to predominate in the southern region, while in the northern region, including Chachapoyas, Allaucaichoc predominates? It is more interesting to see the complementarity than the opposition, which in the Aymara zone is seen in Uma-Urco. What we do not see in the published Chachapoyas documentation is the institutionality that would guarantee the power structure. This does not necessarily mean that it does not exist. Actually, the fact that as a consequence of the colonial *repartimientos,* each of these circumscriptions would come to be governed by a *curaca,* independently of the others, leaves us with the possibility of a previous political structure (see Espinoza Soriano 1966:272–273; Ravines 1973).

References

Adorno, Rolena
1978   Las otras fuentes de Guaman Poma: sus lecturas castellanas, in *Histórica* (Lima) **2** (2):37–159.
Alberti, Giorgio, and Enrique Mayer
1974   *Reciprocidad e intercambio en los Andes peruanos.* Lima: Instituto de Estudios Peruanos.
Alvarez y Jiménez, Antonio
1946   Relaciones de la visita del Intendente [1790–1793.] in *Memorias para la historia de Arequipa, 1790–1793,* edited by Victor M. Barriga. Arequipa: Establecimientos Gráficos la Colmena.
Arguedas, José María
1968   *Las comunidades de España y del Perú.* Lima: Universidad Nacional Mayor de San Marcos.
Barriga, Víctor M.
1939–   *Documentos para la historia de Arequipa* (3 vols.), Arequipa: Biblioteca Are-
1945   quipa, Editorial La Colmena.
1946   *Memorias para la historia de Arequipa, 1790–1793.* Arequipa: Establecimientos Gráficos La Colmena.
Barth, Frederik
1976   *Los grupos étnicos y sus fronteras.* México: Fondo de Cultura Económica.

Bonavía, Duccio
1968a Núcleos de población en la ceja de selva de Ayacucho (Perú) *Actas y Memorias, XXVII Congreso Internacional de Americanistas.* Vol. I: 75–83.
1968b *Las ruinas de Abiseo.* Lima: Universidad Peruana de Ciencias y Tecnología.
1970 Investigaciones arqueológicas en el Mantaro medio. *Revista del Museo Nacional* (Lima) **35:** 211–294.
1972 Factores ecológicos que han intervenido en la transformación urbana a través de los últimos siglos de la época precolombina. *Actas y Memorias, XXXIX Congreso Internacional de Americanistas,* Vol. II: 79–97.

Bonavía, Duccio, and Rogger Ravines
1967 Las fronteras ecológicas de la civilización andina. *Amaru* No. 2: 61–69.
1968 Villas del horizonte tardío en la ceja de selva del Perú: algunas consideraciones. *Actas y Memorias, XXVII Congreso International de Americanistas* Vol. I: 153–158.

Bueno, Cosme
1951 *Geografía del Perú virreinal* (siglo XVIII) [1774–1778]. Lima: Universidad de San Marcos.

Camino, Alejandro
1977 Trueque, correrías e intercambio entre los quechuas andinos y los Piro y Machiguenga de la montaña peruana. *Amazonía Peruana* (Lima) **1** (2): 123–142.

Carbajal, Garci Manuel, and Hernán Rodríguez de Huelva
1977 Visitación de los indios de Carmona cuyos son los de Atico y Caravelí [1549]. *Revista del Archivo General de la Nación* (Lima) **4–5:** 55–80.

Crespo, Juan Carlos
1975 Chincha y el mundo andino: la relación de Cristóbal de Castro y Diego Ortega Morejón. Unpublished thesis, Universidad Católica del Perú.

Diez de San Miguel, Garci
1964 *Visita hecha a la provincia de Chucuito* [1567]. Lima: Casa de la Cultura del Perú.

Espinoza Soriano, Waldemar
1966 Los señoríos étnicos de Chachapoyas y la alianza hispano-chacha. *Revista Histórica* (Lima) **30:** 224–283.
1971 Los Huancas aliados de la conquista. Tres informaciones inéditas sobre la participación indígena en la conquista del Perú. *Anales Científicos de la Universidad Nacional del Centro del Perú* **1:** 9–407.
1974 *La destrucción del imperio de los Incas: La rivalidad política y señorial de los curacazgos andinos.* Lima: Retablo de Papel.
1975 El valle de Jayanca y el reino de los Mochica. *Boletín del Instituto Francés de Estudios Andinos* (Lima) **4** (3–4): 243–274.
1978a Dos casos de señorialismo feudal en el imperio Inca. In *Los modos de producción en el imperio de los Incas.* Lima: Editorial Mantaro.
1978b (editor) *Los modos de producción en el imperio de los Incas.* Lima: Editorial Mantaro.

Flores Ochoa, Jorge
1973 El reino lupaqa y el actual control vertical de la ecologia. *Historia y Cultura* **6:** 195–202.

Fortes, Meyer, and E. E. Evans-Pritchard
1967 *African politcal systems.* London: Oxford University Press.

Fuenzalida Vollmar, Fernando
1970   La matriz colonial de las comunidades indígenas del Perú: una hipótesis de trabajo. *Revista del Museo Nacional* (Lima) **35**: 92–123.

Galdos Rodríguez, Guillermo
1977   Visita a Atico y Caravelí. *Revista del Archivo General de la Nación* (Lima) **4–5**: 55–80.

Gama, Sebastián de la
1975   Visita hecha al valle de Jayanca [1540]. In *Boletín del Instituto Francés de Estudios Andinos* (Lima) **4** (3–4): 243–274.

Godelier, Maurice
1978   Infrastructures, societies and history. *New Left Review* **112**:84–96.

Guaman Poma de Ayala, Felipe
1936   *El primer neuva corónica y buen gobierno* (edition facsimilar). Paris: Institut d'Ethnologie.

Gutiérrez Flores, Frey Pedro, and Juan Ramírez Zegarra
1574   *Visita y Tasa hecha de orden y por comisión del virrey del Perú don Francisco de Toledo de los Indios de la Provincia de Chucuito que eran del patrimonio real.* Manuscript in Archivo General de Indias (Sevilla), Contaduría No. 1787.

Hartmann, Roswith
1971   Mercados y ferias prehispánicas en el área andina. *Boletín de la Academia Nacional de la Historia* **54** (118).

Holm, Olav
1966–   Money axes from Ecuador. *Folk (Quito)* **8–9**: 135–143.
1967

Hyslop, John
1976   An archaeological investigation of the Lupaca kingdom and its origins. Unpublished Ph.D. Thesis, Columbia University, New York.

Hyslop, John, and Elías Mujica Barreda
1974   El estado del núcleo de un reino altiplánico según la técnica arqueológica. Paper presented at II Congreso del Hombre y la Cultura Andina, Trujillo, Perú.

Julien, Catherine J.
1978   Inca administration in the Titacaca Basins reflected at the provincial capital of Hatunqolla. Unpublished Ph.D. dissertation, University of California, Berkeley.

Loredo, Rafael
1958   *Los repartos.* Lima: Imprerta Miranda.

Lumbreras, Luis G.
1974   Los reinos post-Tiwanaku en el área altiplánica. *Revista del Museo Nacional* **40**: 55–86.

Lyon, Patricia J.
1978   The attackers or the attacked: The invention of 'hostile savages' in the valleys of Paucartambo, Cuzco, Perú. Paper presented at the International Colloquium of the Defense of the Latin American Indian Cultures at its Present Projections, Notre Dame, Indiana.

Martínez, Santiago
1936   *Los fundadores de Arequipa.* Arequipa: Tipografía La Luz.

Matos Mar, José
1976   *Hacienda, comunidad y campesinado en el Perú* (Perú Problema No. 3). Lima: Instituto de Estudios Peruanos.

Menguin, O. F. A., and Gerhard Schoeder
1957   Un yacimiento de Ichuña (Departamento de Puno, Perú) y las industrias pre-

cerámicas de los Andes Centrales y Septentrionales. *Acta Prehistorica* (Buenos Aires) **1.**

Morales, Adolfo de
  1977   Repartimiento de tierras por el Inca Huayna Cápac (Testimonio de un documento de 1556). Cochabamba: Universidad Mayor de San Simón, Departamento de Arqueología.

Morris, Craig
  1972   El almacenamiento en dos aldeas Chupaychu. (*in* Ortiz de Zúñiga 1972).
  1973   Establecimientos estatales en el Tawantinsuyu: una estrategia de urbanismo obligado. *Revista del Museo Nacional* (Lima) **39:** 127–142.

Morris, Craig, and Idilio Santillana
  1978   Perspectiva arqueológica en la economía incaica. *Histórica* (Lima) **2**(1):63–82.

Murra, John V.
  1964   Una apreciación etnológica de la visita. In *Visita hecha a la provincia de Chucuito* [1567]. Lima: Casa de la Cultura del Perú.
  1968   An Aymara Kingdom in 1567. *Ethnohistory* **15**(2):115–151.
  1972   El control vertical de un máximo de pisos ecológicos en las sociedades andinas. (*in* Ortiz de Zúñiga 1972)
  1975   *Formaciones económicas y políticas del mundo andino.* Lima: Instituto de Estudios Peruanos.

Ortiz de Zúñiga, Iñiqo
  1972   *Visita de la provincia de Leon de Huanuco* [1562]. Huanuco: Universidad Hermilio Valdizan.

Ossio, Juan M.
  1976–   Guaman Poma y la historiografía indianista de los siglos XVI y XVII. *Historia*
  1977   *y Cultura* (Lima) **10:** 181–206.
  1978   Relaciones interétnicas y verticalidad en los Andes. *Debates en Antropología* (Lima) **2:**1–24.

Pease G. Y., Franklin
  1977a   Collaguas: una etnía del siglo XVI. Problemas iniciales. In *Collaguas* (vol. I), edited by F. Pease. Lima: Pontificia Universidad Católica del Perú-Fondo Editorial.
  1977b   (editor) *Collaguas* (Vol. I). Lima: Pontificia Universidad Católica del Perú-Fondo Editorial.
  1978   *Del Tawantinsuyu a la historia del Perú.* Lima: Instituto de Estudios Peruanos.

Platt, Tristan
  1976   Espejos y maíz: temas de la estructura simbólica andina. La Paz: Cuadernos de Investigación CIPCA No. 10.

Polanyi, Karl, Conrad M. Arensberg, and Harry W. Pearson (editors)
  1957   *Trade and market in the early empires.* Glencoe, Illinois: Free Press.

Polo de Ondegardo, Juan
  1916   Relación de los fundamentos acerca del notable daño que resulta de no guardar a los indios sus fueros [1571]. *Colección de Libros y Documentos referentes a la Historia del Perú* (Serie 1, Vol. 3, reissued in Vol 4, Serie 2 under the title *Del linaje de los incas y como conquistaron*).

Ramírez Zegarra, Juan
  1757   Información que hizo . . . corregidor de la provincia de Chucuito. Manuscript in Archivo General de Indias (Sevilla) Contaduría No. 1787.

Ravines, Rogger
  1970   (editor) *100 años de arqueología en el Perú.* Lima: Instituto de Estudios Peruanos.

Ravines, Rogger (*continued*)
1972   Secuencia y cambios en los artefactos líticos del Sur del Perú. *Revista del Museo Nacional* (Lima) **38:** 133–184.
1973   Los caciques de Pausamarca: algo más sobre las etnías de Chachapoyas. *Historia y Cultura* (Lima) **6:** 217–248.
Roldán, Juan
1977   Visita del pueblo de Ferreñafe de la encomyenda de Melchior de Hosorno vecino de la ciudad de Truxillo [1568]. *Historia y Cultura* (Lima) **9:** 155–178.
Romero, Carlos A. (editor)
1924   Libro general de la visita del virrey don Francisco de Toledo. *Revista Histórica* (Lima) **7:** 113–216.
Rostworowski de Diez Canseco, María
1962   Nuevos datos sobre tenecia de tierras en el Incario. *Revista del Museo Nacional* (Lima) **31:** 130–164.
1977   *Etnía y sociedad: costa peruana prehispánica.* Lima: Instituto de Estudios Peruanos.
Rowe, John H.
1963   Inca culture at the time of the Spanish conquest [1946]. In *Handbook of South American Indians* (Vol. 2). Washington: Smithsonian Institution.
1970   El reino de Chimor [1948]. In *100 años de arqueología en el Perú*, edited by Rogger Ravines. Lima: Instituto de Estudios Peruanos.
Sarmiento de Gamboa, Pedro
1947   *Segunda parte de la Historia General llamada Indica* [1572]. Buenos Aires: Emece Editores.
Schaedel, Richard P.
1978   Formation of the Inca State. *3rd Congreso Peruano del Hombre y la Cultura Andina* 1977, Vol. 1.
Toledo, Francisco de
1924   Libro general de la visita. *Revista Histórica* (Lima) **7:** 113–216.
Trimborn, Hermann
1973a   Neuvas fechas radiocarbónicas para algunos monumentos y sitios prehispánicos de la costa peruana. *Atti, XL Congreso Internazionale degli Americanistici*, Vol. 1: 313–315.
1973b   Investigaciones arqueológicas en el Departamento de Tacna (Perú). *Atti, XL Congreso Internazionale degli Americanisti* Vol. 1: 333–335.
Trimborn, Hermann, Otto Kleemann, Karl J. Narr, and Wolfang Wurster
1975   *Investigaciones arqueológicas en los valles de Caplina y Sama (Dep. Tacna, Perú).* (Studia Instituti Antropos 25) Estella Navarra, Editorial Verbo Divino.
Valdivia, Juan Gualberto
1847   *Fracmentos para la historia de Arequipa.* Arequipa: Imprenta Mariano M. Madueño y Compañía.
Wachtel, Nathan
1976   *La visión de los vencidos. Los indios del Perú frente a la conquista española (1530–1570)* [1971]. Madrid: Alianza-Universidad.
Zárate, Agustín de
1944   *Historia del descubrimiento y conquista del Perú* [1555]. Edición a cargo de J. Kermenic, prólogo de Raúl Porras Barrenechea. Lima: Imp. Miranda.
Zevallos Quiñones, Jorge
1975   La visita del pueblo de Ferreñafe (Lambayeque) en 1568. *Historia y Cultura* (Lima) **9:** 155–178.

The *Mitimas* of the Cochabamba Valley:
The Colonization Policy of Huayna Capac

Nathan Wachtel

Editors' Introduction

In the valley of Cochabamba, Huayna Capac organized a big "state archipelago" dedicated to the massive production of maize, essentially for the aliementation of the army. The Inca expelled the majority of the autochthonous inhabitants (Cota Cotas, Chuis, and Sipe Sipes) and distributed the land of the valley. Its exploitation was effected by laborers recruited from a very extensive area, from Cuzco to Chile. Among these workers (estimated at 14,000) two categories were distinguished: (a) permanent *mitimaes* who surveyed the granaries, and (b) *mittayoc* who were annually renewed and who did the difficult work. The Indians established in the valley were grouped together according to their ethnic origin and with their own *caciques*, but all were placed under the superior authority of two Inca governors. In the last part of the chapter the author enlarges upon his perspective by making a comparison between Cochabamba and the valleys of Yucay and Abancay.

The institution of the *mitimas* appears to be one of the original features of the Andean world. Nothing is known about its origins, but the archaeological data available now indicate that it is quite old, going back at least to the Tiawanaku era.[1] It is known that this institution enabled ethnic groups and *señorios* of varying sizes (at different levels of political authority) to gain control over areas ecologically different

THE INCA AND AZTEC
STATES, 1400–1800

from their own by sending "settlers" and thereby acquiring complementary resources. Subsequently, the Inca state adopted this institution and used it, on a hitherto unknown scale to further its economic or military aims.[2] The problem of the *mitimas* is closely related to questions concerning the evolution of the *Tawantinsuyu* on the eve of the European invasion.

In recent years our documentation concerning the *mitimas* has been considerably enriched, thanks notably to the research of Waldemar Espinoza.[3] As the examples accumulate, one realizes that situations varied from case to case, and one becomes increasingly aware of the extreme diversity of the Andean world. In this chapter, therefore, I make use of two complementary kinds of approach: On the one hand, I present a monographic study of the *mitimas* of the Cochabamba Valley, and on the other hand, I use the comparative method in order to place my findings in a larger context, namely, the colonization policy of Huayna Capac.

The classical sources already mentioned the presence of many *mitimas* in the Cochabamba Valley. In fact, Sarmiento de Gamboa attributed their relocation to a decision made by Huayna Capac at the time of his voyage to Chile: *"Fué al valle de Cochabamba y hizo alli cabezera de provincia de mitimas de todas partes, porque los naturales eran poco y habia aparejo para todo, en que la tierra es fertil."*[4] Indeed, one finds traces of this undertaking in the rich documentation left by the colonial administration, which I recently discovered in the Historical Archives of Cochabamba. These are two enormous bundles containing the papers relating to a lawsuit that took place during the years 1560–1570 between the valley's *encomenderos* (Rodrigo de Orellana and the famous Polo de Ondegardo) and the Caranga, Quillaca, and Sora Indians.[5] Following my stay at Cochabamba, the director of the archives, M. Adolfo de Morales, published some excerpts of these documents, but the texts are incomplete and hastily put together.[6] I am preparing a more complete edition, whose first findings are presented here.

The lawsuit arose from the fact that, following the creation of the *encomiendas*, the *mitimas* of the valley were separated from their native groups, so that they were claimed both by the *encomenderos* and by their *curaca* in the highlands. One of the most important documents is an *Interrogatorio*, dated 1560 and written by Polo himself (this as yet unpublished text appears in Appendix 2). It is rather intriguing to observe that, in defending his own interests, Polo used arguments that were exactly the opposite of those he had advanced when defending the interests of the crown. Recall that he prided himself on having been one of the first Europeans to have understood the Andean system of vertical complementarity and to have helped the Lupaqa of Lake Titicaca to retrieve their *mitimas* of Sama and Moquegua on the Pacific coast after they had been adjudicated as an *encomienda* to Juan de San Juan.[7] In 1560 he adduced this very case, though in the opposite sense, when he demanded that the *mitimas* of Cochabamba be separated from their native groups in order to remain in his own *encomienda!* Question 14 (of the *Interrogatorio*) is explicit on this point:

Yten si sauen etc. que despues que su Magestad hizo el repartimiento en este rreyno rrepartio ansi mismo [353 v] todos los mitimaes tierras y charracas en el mismo lugar tonde los hallo y que las tierras que beneficiauan se quedaron para los dhos yndios y sus encomenderos lo qual fue universal en todo este rreyno y ansi los yndios carangas se quedaron sin las tierras y mitimaes en la costa y lo mismo los de chucuito.[8]

Who, then, were the *mitimas* of Cochabamba? How were the lands of the valley distributed? Who received its products? An analysis of the minutes of the proceedings (along with other documents) brings to light a hitherto unsuspected situation: apparently the colonization of the Cochabamba Valley was an undertaking of exceptional scope.

The Origin of the *Mitimas* of Cochabamba

Huayna Capac's father, Tupac Yupanqui, conquered the Cochabamba Valley, populated at the time by three indigenous groups: the Sipe Sipe, the Cota, and the Chui.[9] Under his rule, colonization entered its first phase. He transferred a certain number of Cota and Chui to Pocona and Mizque, where he assigned land to them in order to guard the border against the Chiriguano.[10] In addition, in the Cochabamba Valley itself, he claimed for himself *ciertas chacaras,* those of Cala Cala (today located in the outskirts of the town), which he had cultivated by *algunos indios desta provincia.*[11] In other words, we find in Tupac Yupanqui's policy the two aspects that have always been recognized as the main characteristics of the *mitimas*. Those who were sent to Pocona carried out a military function, and those who were brought to Cala Cala had an economic function. The thing that characterized Tupa Yupanqui's operation was that it was still relatively limited in scope, and its military aspect was more important than its economic aspect.[12]

One wonders whether all the Cota and all the Chui were deported at the time of Tupac Yupanqui. The document does not say so explicitly, and the testimonies unanimously insist that a new era began with his successor. We are told that Huayna Capac carried out the distribution of all the lands in the valley, to which he brought 14,000 Indians *de muchas naçiones*.[13] This enormous number (if it is correct) represents a new order of magnitude and amounts to a true mutation:

> Preguntado que pues dicen que topa yupangui padre del dho guayna capa vino a estos ualles y señalo tierra para si en cala cala que como no hizo partiçion de las tierras que despues rrepartio el dho guayna capa su hijo—dixeron quel dho topa ynga yupangui no era yacha que quiere decir en nuestra lengua que no sauia ni entendia cossas de sementeras e que solamente señalo para si en cala cala un pedaço de tierra e que el dho guayna capa hera hombre que governaua mucho e hizo hazer muchas sementeras e conquisto muchas tierras.[14]

The witnesses thus contrasted the reign of Huayna Capac with that of Tupac Yupanqui. What is meant by the term *yacha?* The old dictionaries fully confirm the explanation given by the informants. Bertonio, for example, says: *"Yacha: vocablo corrupto de la lengua quichua, por dezir yachakh. Sabio, ladino, entendido."*[15] Holguin translates *Yachani* precisely as *saber* and adds *"yachachic: el maestro."*[16] Tupac Yupanqui, then, "did not know," at least in economic matters. But the conquering Inca was succeeded by an Inca administrator, so that henceforth the economic function of the *mitimas* took precedence over their military function.

From which ethnic groups (*naçiones*) did Huayna Capac take his contingents of *mitimas?* In order to reconstitute the general picture of the valley, we must assemble all kinds of different fragments, always situated in a particular context. In the *Interrogatorio* Polo distinguished two different groups of *mitimas*, corresponding to the two *encomenderos* to whom they had been entrusted. Rodrigo de Orellana had received tribute *"de los indios mitimaes quillacas y los mitimaes carangas y los mitimaes chilques y chiles y collas de asangaro,"* all of whom were under the command of the *cacique* don Hernando Cuyo;[17] while Pedro de Ondegardo had as his *encomendados "los indios uros y soras mitimaes del repartimiento de Paria"* and *"los indios caracaras chichas y charcas y amparaes,"* all of whom were under the command of the *caciques* don Geronimo Cuyo and don Diego Tanquire.[18]

One should not be surprised to see contingents coming from regions as distant as the Chilque (near Cuzco) or Chicha territory (near Potosi); Polo also mentions "Chiles" Indians.[19] There are other examples of *mitimas* who had been sent from equally far away: In the Abancay Valley, studied by Waldemar Espinoza, the *mitimas* were from the Pacific coast and even from Quito.[20] Thus, the *mitimas* often crossed vast distances and came literally from the length and breadth of the entire *Tawantinsuyu*.

Here one question arises: Did some of the cited groups control land, if not in the Cochabamba Valley, then at least in the adjacent area? This problem concerns the groups living closest to the valley, the Sora, and possibly also the Charca, Caraca, Caranga, and Quillaca. The territory of the Sora extended east from Lake Paria to Arque and maybe (perhaps intermittently) as far as Capinota.[21] We do not have the data for the other ethnic groups, but we have seen that the Caranga were oriented toward the Pacific coast, where they owned enclaves.[22] It is probable that they (like the Quillaca, Charca, and Caracara) had access to the Cochabamba Valley only thanks to the intervention of the Inca. At least this is suggested by a well-known document, the *Memorial de Characas*, which corroborates and confirms the information furnished by the minutes of the lawsuit. The group of *curaca* who presented this petition in 1582 pointed out that *"el inga Topa Inga Yupangui y su hijo Guayna Caba nos repartieron tierras en el valle de Cochabamba a todas las naciones de Charcas, Caracaras, Soras, Quillacas y Carangas para que en ella sembrasemos y cultivasemos e senalando y amojonando a cada nacion por si."*[23] The Spanish court confirmed the Sora's, Quillaca's, and Caranga's right to certain lands they held in Cochabamba,[24] which is why the authors of the *Memorial* demanded a similar confirmation for the Charca and the Caracara, each of whom had received from the Inca four *suyos* and *urcos*.[25] (I shall return presently to the meaning of these terms.)

Other documents also help to complete Polo's list. The registers of Francisco Gallegos attest that some *yndios de condesuyu*—and their origin is not stated more precisely—had received the lands of Guayruro and Condebamba in the valley.[26] In an earlier study I have drawn attention to a document found in the Archives of Sucre, which seems to belong to the same set of court records as Polo's *Interrogatorio*. In this case the litigation was between Juan Duran and the "Ycallungas" Indians of Sipe Sipe.[27] We learn that the same Huayna Capac had brought in *plateros* originally from Ica (on the Pacific coast, hence their name *yungas*) from Chinchasuyu. Again, these people had crossed the entire Andes at their widest point. Why were they deported so far? Here, too, we do not have the details, but we know from other indications that these artisans of the coast had furnished many *mitimas*, notably to the Cuzco region.[28] In the case of Cochabamba they were also given lands for their subsistence in accordance with the model obtaining in the Sierra.

Another remarkable point deserves to be stressed, namely, the presence of the Uru of Paria (i.e., Lake Poopo) at Cochabamba. There is a well-known stereotype, bequeathed by the chroniclers of the six-teenth century and repeated by travelers and ethnologists, which de-picts the Uru as "barbarian" Indians, living exclusively on fishing, hunting (of waterfowl), and gathering. I have treated the Uru problem in another study.[29] Suffice it to say here that the report of Garci Diez de San Miguel's "inspection tour" of Chucuito in 1567 already makes us suspect a rather more complex situation, and that the report of Pedro Gutierrez Flores in 1574 assimilated a certain number of Uru with the Aymara because they too owned a great deal of land and large herds.[30] Now we learn from the Archives of Cochabamba that the Uru of Paria ("reduced" in the early years of the colonial period at Cha-llacollo, near Lake Poopo) not only owned land, like other ethnic groups, but this land was located some 100 km from the lake, precisely in the Cochabamba Valley. Furthermore, another document (an *amo-jonamiento* dated 1593, which I found in the judicial archives of Poopo) describes holdings in the vicinity of Charamoco in the southern part of the valley.[31] The total holdings amounted to a considerable area: according to a later evaluation, 30 *fanegas* of irrigated maize land, 60 *fanegas* of unirrigated maize land, and pastureland extending over an area 1½ leagues (7.5 km) long and 1 league (5 km) wide.[32] It should be noted that until the end of the sixteenth century the Uru of Cha-llacollo and those of Charamoco formed a single *repartimiento*, even though they did not live in a contiguous area. Obviously, this is an-other instance of the Andean model of the "archipelago," in which a central nucleus located on the high plateau reaches out to peripheral establishments. But we are here in the presence of an unheard of case: an Uru "archipelago"!

How did it come into being? Probably it was established through the distribution made by Huayna Capac, who recognized the Uru of Paria as agriculturalists suitable for his service and therefore integrated them into a vast "archipelago" belonging to the state. In the docu-ments of Poopo as well as in those of Cochabamba one finds the same place names, Poto Poto and Yllaurco, given to two *suyos* assigned to the Uru by the Inca.[33] Was this also the case for the lands of Cha-ramoco? Did the Uru hold them before Huayna Capac made his dis-tribution? If this were the case, they would be an ethnic "archipelago" similar to those that had been constituted by other groups of the *al-tiplano*. Or did the Uru acquire them later, taking advantage of the upheavals caused by the Spanish invasion to extend the central nu-cleus assigned to them by Huayna Capac? For the moment there are no data that would permit us to decide this question.

The Land Distribution of Huayna Capac

The Cochabamba Valley extends from east to west and then dips southward. It presents an asymmetrical shape, since its northern rim descends gradually, while in the south the Rocha River runs along a steep mountain range. The documents pertaining to the lawsuit furnish detailed information only for the western part of the valley (including the sector located in the "dip"). Having been written on behalf of the Caranga and Quillaca Indians, they describe only the lands to which these Indians laid claim and say very little about the central and eastern parts (containing, on the one hand, the pasturelands of the Inca and, on the other hand, plots assigned to other groups such as the Charca, Caracara, and Chicha).[34]

Let us therefore begin by examining the modalities of distribution in the western sector. The document enumerates five *chacaras:* Yllaurco, Colchacollo, Anocaraire, Coachaca, and Viloma. A sixth one, that of Poto Poto, is mentioned as bordering on Yllaurco to the east. The context clearly indicates that the "fields" are described in an order running from the northeast to the southwest, from Quillacollo to Sipe Sipe, so that it is possible to locate them on the map with a certain precision. Indeed today one can easily find the field names or the *haciendas* Viloma, Coachaca, and Anocaire, located east of Vinto.[35]

To evaluate the size of these fields one must understand the meaning of the previously mentioned terms *suyos* and *urcos*, which in their context appear to be synonymous.[36] However, a simple translation ("plots") may not be adequate, for we know that the Andean categories were always rich in multiple connotations. Turning to the old dictionaries, we find that Diego Gonzales Holguin gives the following explanations:

Suyu: lo que cabe de parte de trabajo a cada un suyo o persona; provincia
Suyu suyu: ropa listeada vareteada menudo
Suyu suyurana, o suyuchasca: los puestos en su lugar o por sus suyos
Suyuni: dividir tierras chacáras, obras, dar partes del trabajo[37]

Bertonio has the following entries:

Suyu: la parte que alguno, o muchos toman de alguna obra para trabajar, como de
    Iglesia, Chacara, Edificios, etc.
Suyuiranacasitha: trabajar la parte que le cabe
Suyusitha: repartir entre si la parte que les cabe del trabajo
Suyuni: uno que tiene ya la parte que ha de trabajar[38]

In addition to the idea of "share of work," I shall retain the notion of "band" or "stripe" decorating a piece of cloth, which suggests a narrow, long shape.[39] In his *Parecer*, Francisco de Saavedra Ulloa furnishes information about measures and also describes such a shape: "*Y cada urco tenia quarenta e quatro braças en ancho y en largo de una cordillera a otra conforme a la disposicion del dho ualle.*"[40] In other words, these "plots" were indeed long and narrow strips running crosswise through the valley (from north to south or northwest to southeast) from end to end. All these strips were of equal width (44 *brazadas*) but unequal length (2–4, even 5 km), depending on the conformation of the valley. Given the asymmetrical shape of the valley, one can state quite precisely that the *suyos* stretched from the northern *cordillera* to the Rocha River itself (see Figure 8.1). This description is confirmed in the judicial document from Poopo by the claims of the Uru of Charamoco: "*El un suyo llamado poto poto y el otro yllaurco que corren desdel rrio grande de cochabamba hasta llegar a las faldas de la cordillera del propio balle por sus lindes y acequias que corren del alto alto [sic] auajo.*[41]

Another striking coincidence must also be mentioned here: This mode of land distribution corresponds exactly to the practice of the Uru of Chipaya today. I have described this practice elsewhere.[42] Each year the *alcaldes* of each moiety mark off a certain number of plots (called *tsvis*) to be assigned to members of their community. These plots, which run vertically through the arable terrain, are of equal width (3–5 *brazadas*) but of varying length (500 m–1 km) due to the irregular relief of the territory. Crops are planted on land that is first inundated in order to wash the salt content out of the soil and then drained. Depending on the size of this terrain, the *alcalde* executes a variable number of *vueltas* and follows a predetermined order in distributing the plots, lineage by lineage, in accordance with strict rules. Within each lineage the heads of the different nuclear families receive an equal number of plots; these plots are also always served in the same sequence, which is determined by the ties of kinship among them.

It is remarkable indeed that Huayna Capac's land distribution in the Cochabamba Valley seems to have been subject to an equally fixed order. The five *chacaras* of Yllaurco, Colchacollo, Anocairaire, Coachaca, and Viloma numbered respectively 13, 16, 5, 20, and 23 *suyos*, or altogether 77 *suyos*. This means that these fields extended from east to west over 3388 *brazadas*, or abour 5.4 km. This is approximately the distance between Quillacolla and the River Viloma (see Figure 8.1). One also realizes that in the sector as a whole the same

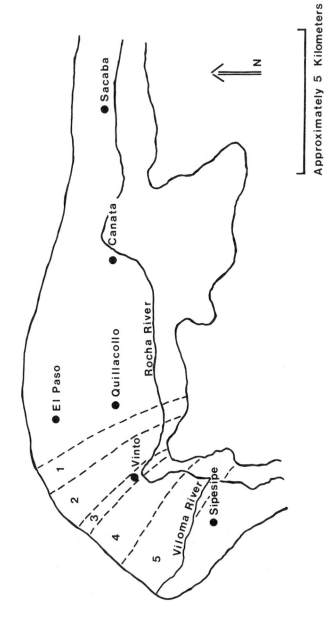

Figure 8.1 Cochabamba Valley and the divisions made by Huayna Capac: (1) Yllaurco lands, (2) Colchacollo lands, (3) Anocaraire lands, (4) Coachaca lands, and (5) Viloma lands.

TABLE 8.1
Distribution of *Suyos* by Ethnic Group

Ethnic groups	Subgroups	*Suyos* at Yllaurco	*Suyos* at Calchacollo[a]	*Suyos* at Anocaraire[b]	*Suyos* at Coachaca	*Suyos* at Viloma	Total
Soras	Soras of Sipe Sipe	1	½ + ½		4	⅔	
	Casayas of Paria	½	½		} 6	} ⅓	
	Soras of Paria	½	½				30⅔
	Soras of Tapacari	1	½ + ½	2	6	⅓	+ 2
	Soras of Caracollo	1	½ + ½		4	⅓	
	Urus of Paria	1	—				
			(+ ½)[a]				+ ½
Quillacas	Aracapis	1	½			⅓ + 2	
	Quillacas	1	½	1		⅓ + 2	15⅓
	Uruquillas and Aullagas	1	½			⅓ + 2	+ 1
	Asanaques	1	½			⅓ + 2	
			(+ ¼)[b]				+ ¼

Carangas	Andamarca and Urinoca	1	½		2⅓	
	Samancha	1	½		2	14⅓
	Chuquicota	1	½	1	2	+ 2
	Totora	1	½	1	2	
			(+ ¼)[a]			+ ¼
Collas	Calapanca		½ + ½		⅓	
	Chucuyto		½ + ½		⅓	
	Callapa		½ + ½		⅓	
	Chuquicacha		½ + ½		⅓	9⅔
	Tiaguanaco		½ + ½		⅓	+ 1
	Caquiaviri		½ + ½			
	Urcosuyos				1	
	Umasuyos				1	
			(½ + ½)[a]			
Total of *Suyos*						77

[a]At Cochacollo two half-*suyos* were directly given to the Indians of the upper moiety, and two more [half-*suyos*] to those of the lower moiety. How the *suyos* were distributed among the ethnic groups is not indicated. On the basis of their distribution, I have assumed that ½ + ½ *suyos* went to the Colla, ½ to the Sora, ¼ to the Caranga, and ¼ to the Quillaca.

[b]The *Suyos* of Anocaraire were assigned to *caciques*.

ethnic groups (or political units) are again located side by side, namely, the Sora, the Caranga, the Quillaca, and the "Colla." Nor is this all. The distribution of the *suyos* enables us to reconstitute, within each of these major units, a certain number of subdivisions usually mentioned in the same order. To be sure, it is sometimes difficult to identify the level of these subdivisions, but at least it is clear that we are dealing with a genuinely Andean classification rather than with subdivisions more or less arbitrarily imposed by the Spaniards when they divided the *encomiendas* among themselves. What, then, was this organization?

We know that the structure of the Andean chiefdoms was a pyramid-shaped agglomeration of groups within groups, which often brought together different groups in a kind of "federation." This was true in the case of the "Sora," who in addition to the Sora proper (subdivided in turn into Indians of Paria, Sipe Sipe, Tapacari, and Caracolla) also included the Casaya and the Uru of Paria.[43] It was also true for the "Quillaca," who in addition to the Quillaca proper included the Anasaque, the Aullaga, the Uruquilla (no doubt including some Uru also), as well as the Aracapi from the Puna region south of Potosí. The chiefdom of the Caranga appears to have been ethnically more homogeneous, but it too can be divided into four subgroups: the Andamarca and Urinoca, the Samancha (no doubt a moiety of the Corque), the Chuquicota, and the Totora. As for the Colla, they raise a more complex problem. The text enumerates *mitimas* from Calapanca, Chucuito, Callapa, Chuquicache, Tiaguanaco, and Caquiaviri and also mentions "Urquosuyos" and "Omasuyos."[44] Does this mean that all these "Colla" subgroups formerly belonged to one major political unit? Before the Inca conquest, they had constituted at least three distinct units: those of the Paucarolla, the Lupaqa, and the Pacaje. But one also notes that all of their component groups do not seem to have sent *mitimas* to Cochabamba. That is why among the Lupaqa only the Indians of Chucuito are mentioned, and not the subjects of the other lords of the western shore of the lake (those of Acora, Hilave, Juli, etc.).

Appendix 1 presents a complete list of the *suyos* for the sector of the valley that is known in detail, and of the groups to which these *suyos* were attributed. I have listed them in the order in which they are cited, from east to west. By gathering together this information for each of the groups concerned, we can study them quantitatively. A summary of these findings is presented in Table 8.1.

Table 8.1 indicates that the Sora obtained the largest number of *suyos* (30⅔ + 2 + ½)—as many as the Quillaca (15⅓ + 1 + ¼) and the Caranga (14⅓ + 2 + ¼) together—while the Colla (9⅔ + 1) received only a very small part.[45] Is this predominant position of the Sora due to the fact that their territory was located immediately next to the Cochabamba Valley, while that of the Colla was farther away? In view of these quantitative data, the researcher must particularly regret the lack of detailed information concerning the other part of the valley, from Poto Poto to Sacaba, the area occupied by Charca, Torpa, Caracara, Chui, and Inca Indians.[46]

Let us now take a closer look at the Colchacollo *chacara*, which presents some striking particularities. Located in an area where the valley is 3–4 km wide, it consisted of 16 *suyos*. It had been divided into two halves: one of them in the higher area, running from the *cordillera* halfway down the slope; the other in the lower area, from the middle of the slope down to the river. Moreover, an additional division was made within the first one, so that the end result was a division into four parts:

> La qual dha characa partio por medio el dho ynga atravesando la por medio y la hizo quatro quartos. . . . Con el qual dho suyo haze fin la media chacarra de colchacollo por la parte de arriba hacia la cordillera y sierra de los moxos y luego entra la otra media que alinda toda ella con el rrio por la parte de abaxo.[47]

The description of the half-*suyos* obtained in this manner is so precise that one can reconstitute their exact disposition within the "field" (Figure 8.2). The text clearly indicates that the first half-*suyo*, assigned to the Colla of Calapanca, extended downward to the half-*suyo* assigned to the *mitimas* of Aracapi (*"y comienza el primero questa alinde del otro medio questa escripto ques de los collas capahanca que se llama el suyo de aracapi yndios de puna"*).[48] It thus becomes clear that each ethnic group was installed in its own particular quarter, which, in turn, constituted a subset. The first quarter (northeast) was alloted to the Colla; the second (northwest) to the Sora; the third (southeast) to the Quillaca and Caranga (who were usually associated); and the fourth (southwest) again to the Colla. A summary of Figure 8.2 thus yields the following schema:

	NW	Sora	Colla	NE
			Quillaca	
	SW	Colla	Caranga	SE

Did this disposition result from the application of the principle of dual division, which, as we know, was one of the fundamental rules governing the organization of the Andean societies? The regular succession of subgroups, always in the same order, suggests that the general configuration was governed by an underlying logic. Since the docu-

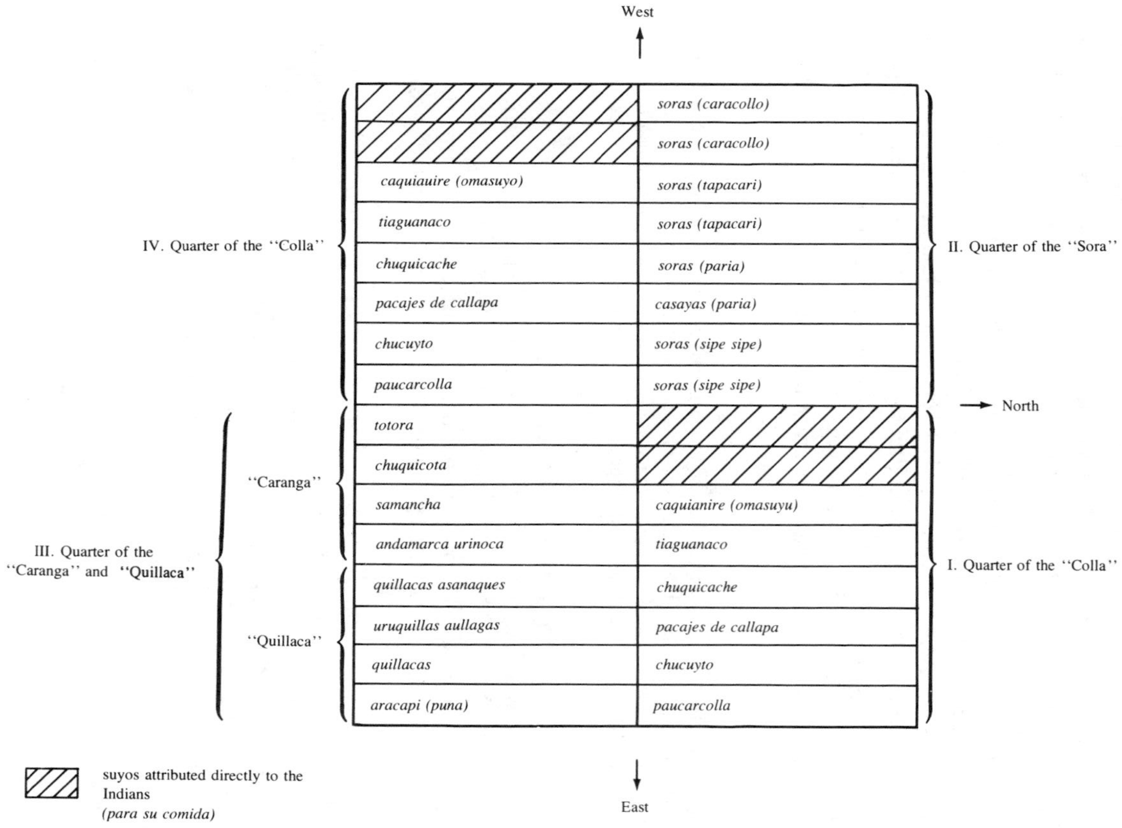

West ←

soras (caracollo)
soras (caracollo)
soras (tapacari)
soras (tapacari)
soras (paria)
casayas (paria)
soras (sipe sipe)
soras (sipe sipe)

II. Quarter of the "Sora"

↑ North

caquiauire (omasuyo)
tiaguanaco
chuquicache
pacajes de callapa
chucuyto
paucarcolla
totora
chuquicota
samancha
andamarca urinoca
quillacas asanaques
uruquillas aullagas
quillacas
aracapi (puna)

caquianire (omasuyo)
tiaguanaco
chuquicache
pacajes de callapa
chucuyto
paucarcolla

I. Quarter of the "Colla"

East →

IV. Quarter of the "Colla"

"Caranga"

"Quillaca"

III. Quarter of the "Caranga" and "Quillaca"

suyos attributed directly to the Indians (para su comida)

Figure 8.2   Chacara of Colchacollo: disposition of suyos.

ment gives us no more than a list of *suyos*, it is difficult to go further than that. Yet the fact that it explicitly mentions the term *quarter* is significant in itself. It may not be by coincidence that the Colchacolla *chacara* consisted of 16 *suyos*; this number allowed for additional divisions within each of the quarters (consisting of 8 half-*suyos*). Indeed new four-part subdivisions were made within these quarters:

1. In the northwest quarter, alloted to the Sora, the *suyos* were distributed two by two; hence we find four sectors assigned, respectively, to Indians from Sipe Sipe, Paria, Tapacari, and Caracollo.

2. In the southeast quarter the first four *suyos* were assigned to the Caranga, and the next four to the Quillaca.

3. In the northeast and southwest quarters the schema is not quite as clearly visible, but here too one discerns the presence of four different ethnic groups: the Paucarolla, the Lupaqa, the Pacaje, and the Omasuyo. (In the next section I shall return to the two *suyos* that were, in two cases, assigned to Indians "for their own subsistence.")

These observations seem indeed to confirm the contention that the schema of dual and four-part division, which theoretically (from the Inca point of view) informed the organization of the *Tawantin-suyu*, also ruled the distribution of land made by Huayna Capac in the Cochabamba Valley.

The Organization of Work and the Distribution of Produce

How did the contingents sent by so many different ethnic groups cultivate the land once it was distributed in this manner? As we have seen, Francisco de Saavedra-Ulloa in his *Parecer* cited a figure; but were all of the 14,000 Indians he mentioned actually *mitimas*? In point of fact, he did make a fundamental distinction: "*Y algunos eran perpetuos y otros venian de sus tierras al beneficio de las chacaras del dicho ynga.*"[49] This passage indicates that some Indians permanently lived in the valley; whereas others came for a special purpose and later returned to their homes. Only the first of these categories conforms to the notion of *mitima*; the second one implies temporary and rotating labor services, namely, services performed under the terms of the *mit'a*. In fact, the Indians who traveled back and forth were replaced every year: "*Preguntado que donde venian los yndios que beneffiçiauan estas chacaras . . . suyos della dixeron que en sus tierras y de alli venian a lo beneffiçiar por sus mitas e que auia algunos mitimaes.*"[50]

Assuming that there was a total of 14,000 workers, what were the respective proportions of these two categories of workers? Did all the groups, even those living farthest away, furnish both permanent *mitimas* and Indians taking turns in performing the *mit'a*? How were these workers chosen, and how were they replaced? For the moment it is not possible to answer these questions. But at least we do have some information concerning the organization of work. It appears that the *mitimas* were given specific supervisory tasks (notably the maintenance of the granaries), while the *mittayoc* performed the ongoing work, such as sowing and harvesting. Here is what was said by one of the witnesses cited by Polo, the Sora Indian Juan Anton Churma: "*Y los yndios que alli residian eran guardas de las piruas del maiz que se cogia en los dhos suyos del ynga y que para el sembrar y coger y beneficiar venian muchos yndios de tapacari a hazello y beneficiado se boluian a sus casas y quedaban las guardas de las piruas.*"[51]

All the witnesses stressed the fact that the lands of Cochabamba belonged to the Inca; all the maize raised there was stored in his granaries (*pirua*), then collected at the *tambo* of Paria, and from there transported to Cuzco.[52] These transports, at least as far as Paria, were handled by the Sipe Sipe herdsmen (*llamacamayos*) who, as we know from other sources, were in charge of tending the Inca's herds.[53] The execution of these operations was the responsibility of the ethnic lords, but the overall planning and direction came from two governors called in from Cuzco. Another witness, Pedro Mamani (also a Sora Indian), even tells us the names of these "captains": "*Para . . . tener cargo dello y de governar este valle de cochabamba estavan en el dos yngas capitanes del ynga que se llamauan tupa el uno y el otro curimayo y que estos tenian cargo de mandar a todos los yndios del valle y hazer senbrar y linpiar y coger la comida y llevalla al cuzco.*"[54]

Who consumed the maize that had been stored and then transported in this manner? All the witnesses concur in their answers. It was for the Inca, and more precisely for his army: "*Que el maiz que se senbraua en los dhos suyos que asi se rrepartieron hera para todas las naçiones de yndios que andauan en la guerra con el dho ynga guayna capa.*"[55] The status of the *suyos* of Cochabamba thus became clear. When it is said that they "belong to the Inca," this means that they were part of the state domain, not that they belonged to the Inca personally. This distinction between the person of the sovereign and the bureaucratic or military machinery of the state (proposed by John V. Murra as early as 1956 and largely confirmed since then) bespeaks the changes that took place in the organization of the *Tawantinsuyu* during the last decade before the European invasion. Indeed, the informants do not say explicitly that Tupac Uypanqui's lands at Cala Cala were his personal property. But it is quite certain that in the reign of Huayna Capac a vast network of state management developed on a hitherto unknown scale.

The contrast between these two kinds of landownership is reinforced by the unquestioned presence in the Cochabamba Valley of nonstate-owned fields, which were also worked by *mitimas*. These were the *chacaras* of Guayruro and Condebamba, which were cultivated, as we saw earlier, by "Conde Indians of Condesuyo"; we are also told that these lands had been given by Huayna Capac to one of his sons.[56] This, then, was property of the "private" type, similar to property that is known to us from other examples, notably in the Yucay Valley.[57] But in comparison with the total amount of state-owned *suyos* at Cochabamba, these personally owned "fields" seem to have occupied only a small part of the area.

Yet one fundamental problem remained to be solved. A way had to be found to provide for the subsistence of the 14,000 workers, whether *mitimas* or *mittayoc*, who worked for the state. They constituted a huge mass of people (which became even larger if the *mittayoc* brought their wives). We know that the Indians who came to the valley brought no food with them. This fact fits in with the traditional descriptions that make the point that all the subjects who worked the Inca's land were given food and drink on behalf of the Inca himself, as a testimony to his "generosity": *"De la comida que coxian de las characas del ynga no les era permitido y de sus tierras no lo trayan ni podian traer."*[58]

There were several ways of providing for the subsistence of the workers. In the example of Colchacollo, we have seen that certain *suyos* were not subject to the general rule and were assigned directly to the Indians themselves (*"para los indios que cultivaban, con que se sustentasen," "a los indios para su comida."*)[58,59] This land consisted of four half-*suyos* located in each half of the field or, to be more precise, in the two quarters assigned to the Colla (cf. Figure 8.2). How was this land used? Did the Colla use all of it for themselves, or did they share it with the Sora in the upper section and the Caranga and Quillaca in the lower half? The second hypothesis seems to be the most likely one.[59]

However, if Colchacollo included some *suyos* reserved for the use of the workers, this was not the case in three other *characas*. None of the *suyos* of Yllaurco, Coachaca, and Viloma, which together amounted to 61 *suyos*, is described as being used by the Indians themselves. On the other hand, the entire field of Anocaraire—to be sure the smallest one of the lot (*"pedaço de tierra que tiene 5* suyos")—was alloted to different *caciques:* (a) Guarache, *"cacique de los quillacas"*; (b) Achacapa, *"cacique de los carangas de chuquicota"*; (c) Vilca, *"cacique de totora carangas"*; (d) Machacata, *"cacique principal de tapacari"*; (e) Condo, *"cacique principal de tapacari."* Nonetheless, the informants state that these were "whole" *suyos,* not *suyos* divided into two parts. They were cultivated, we are told, by Indians who worked on the Inca's land, and the products were redistributed to them by the *caciques,*[61] who thus practiced "generosity" on their own level. Yet one notes that not every *cacique* had the use of a *suyo.* There is no mention of the Colla lords, nor of the Quillaca, Caranga, or Sora *caciques.* Was Guarache the principal *curaca* of all the Quillaca? The context does indeed suggest this (*"de quien suçeden los guaraches de los dhos quillacas que agora ay"*).[62] Why was there only one *curaca* for the Quillaca, who had a complex "confederation," but two for the Caranga and the Sora? Here again, more detailed data concerning the principle of dual division in the organization of Andean society are simply not available.

By adding up the plots used by the workers, either directly or indirectly (i.e., through the intermediary of their *caciques*), one arrives at the figure of 7 out of 77 *suyos,* that is, less than 10% of the cultivated area.[63] Was this enough? One would also have to know about the quality and the productivity of these plots; however, since they were interspersed among the Inca's *suyos,* one can assume that they were not appreciably different.

If the area reserved for the subsistence of the Indians seems relatively small, one must take into account that the people had other resources as well. The informants indicate that the Indians also cultivated the upper and lower margins of the Inca's *suyos* for their own use: *"Preguntado que los dhos yndios donde hazian chacaras para comer dixeron que en los altos y baxos de las dhas chacarras."*[64] Given the disposition of the *suyos,* which ran crosswise through the valley (on the northern rim, by reason of the asymmetry), these were indeed the edges located on the upper slopes (in the north-northwest) and near the river (in the southeast). Here again, it is interesting to compare this practice with the customs of the present-day Chipaya, who every year designate a certain number (about a half-dozen) of *camayos* and charge them with watching over the fields and carrying out the requisite fertility rites. Significantly, these *camayos* not only receive extra plots, they are also entitled to use "everything that protrudes," that is, the *sobras* that are not included in the distributed plots and are located at the edges of the cultivated territory.[65]

Following the tortuous path taken by the lengthy testimonies given in the course of the court proceedings, one comes upon one significant detail that throws light on certain aspects of the distribution of maize by the Inca. Responding to Polo de Ondegardo's question 3, the witness Pedro Guanca, *"yndio sora de sipe sipe,"* having confirmed *"quel mais que della se cogia lo lleuaban los dhos yndios al cuzco para el ynga e que el que quedaua era e lo guardauan para el ynga,"* immediately adds: *"y los mas rruyn dello apartauan para haçer açua y comer la gente que beneficiaua las dhas chacarras."*[66] Thus, even the nonmilitary Indians, the *mitimas* and the *mittayoc* of the Cochabamba Valley, benefited from the Inca's granaries. These benefits did have certain limits, as suggested by this rather amusing note: they were given only the poorest grade of maize. Nonetheless, the Inca's "generosity" was extended to all of his subjects, and an allusion to *chicha* ("beer") indicates that in Cochabamba as elsewhere the workers adhered to certain ceremonial forms in carrying out their work.

Conclusions: Comparative Perspectives

The principal features of Huayna Capa's colonization policy in the Cochabamba Valley can be outlined as follows:

1. He set up a vast state-owned "archipelago" for the purpose of large-scale maize production, essentially for the use of the army. The work was performed by a multiethnic labor force recruited from a very large area (ranging from the Cuzco region to Chili). Among these workers, three categories can be distinguished.
   a. Certain aborigines were permitted to remain in place (the Sipe Sipe who tended the herds "belonging to the Inca").
   b. Permanent *mitimas* were specifically charged with maintaining the granaries.
   c. *Mittayoc* rotated on a yearly basis and performed the heavy work. The Indians who were brought to the valley stayed together in accordance with their ethnic origins and kept their own *caciques;* but all were placed under the authority of two Inca governors.
2. Sustenance for the workers was provided by the products of different plots of land.
   a. Certain *suyos* were directly alloted to them (although this total surface seems to have been relatively small).

b. Other *suyos* were assigned to their *caciques.*

c. They also benefited from some of the Inca's land (either by cultivating its marginal areas or by receiving some of the maize gathered in the granaries).

3. Finally, there were certain special situations in the valley.

    a. The Icallunga were *mitimas* who, although they had been assigned land like other ethnic groups, performed specialized work as *plateros.*

    b. There are also traces of "private" property rights over certain plots; Tupac Yupanqui may have personally owned the plots of Cala Cala, and one of Huayna Capac's sons certainly owned lands at Guayruro and Condebamba (where "Conde" *mitimas* were established).

The time has come to compare these findings with what we know about the colonization of other zones of the *Tawantinsuyu.* The similarity that immediately strikes the observer is with the neighboring region of Yamparaes, whose location (in relation to the Inca empire) and geographical conditions were analogous to those of the Cochabamba Valley. Many *mitimas* were transferred there as well,[67] and I suspect that the vast archipelago set up by Huayna Capac comprised both of these regions. Unfortunately, the data for Yamparaes are still meager indeed. I shall, therefore, turn to two other examples, namely, the Abancay and Yucay regions, for which we have relatively good documentation. A comparison of these regions with the Cochabamba Valley enables us to bring out the characteristic features of Huayna Capac's policy.[67bis]

In all three of these cases we are dealing with valleys whose warm climate was favorable to the cultivation of maize. It should be kept in mind that maize was not only a major food staple but also an important component in ritual.[68] It should also be noted that at Yucay and Abancay agricultural production was more diversified, since *aji* ("chili peppers"), coca, *yucas* ("sweet manioc"), cotton, etc. were also raised there.[69] Yet settlements of multiethnic *mitimas* are found in all three of these valleys. The Inca's intervention at the time of Tupac Yupanqui is attested in all three areas,[70] but Huayna Capac so greatly expanded his predecessor's policy that it became qualitatively different. The indigenous populations of the three valleys were expelled in part or *in toto* and settled in other regions, sometimes as *mitimas.*[71] Thus, it appears that nothing was left of the indigenous population of Abancay; at Cochabamba only the Sipe Sipe (a tiny minority) remained; at Yucay the *naturales* represented about half of the population (divided into three *pueblos:* the Chauca, Paca, and Cachi *pueblos*).[72] As for the *mitimas*, in all three cases they came from neighboring zones as well as from very far away. Among the fifteen groups that have been identified at Abancay, the Aymara of Cotarma or the Haquira Yarahuara lived nearby; the Huancavilca, the Tallanes, and the Mochica came from as far away as Guyaquil, Piura, and Trujillo.[73] At Yucay the *mitimas* consisted not only of Chumbivilca and Aymara, but also of Colla, Yunga, and Cañari Indians; as we know, this last group came from the present-day Ecuador.[74]

Yet in considering the order of magnitude of these transfers, one does find a marked contrast between Cochabamba, on the one hand, and Abancay and Yucay, on the other. The former case involved some 14,000 Indians (even though not all of them were *mitimas* in the proper sense); the latter involved 1,000 to 2,000 heads of families.[75] The colonization of the Cochabamba Valley thus emerges as an undertaking of unprecedented scope.

Moreover, Cochabamba was the only area to which *mittayoc* came in such large numbers and where, thanks to the rotation of these *mittayoc*, the *mitimas* and their native groups maintained close ties. The problem of providing food for the workers also assumed different scope in these three areas. On this point, the comparison brings to light an important difference. At Abancay and Yucay the *mitimas* had received individual plots, called *tupus*, which were assigned to each head of a family. There is an abundance of testimonies to this effect. We hear, for example, that at Abancay, *"los yndios yungas que se ponian por mitimas en el dho valle de Abancay y otras partes no les dauan mas de un topo de tierra para comer, y esto por su uida."*[76] At Yucay every head of a family had the use of a piece of land equaling, on the average, one or two *tupus* (Pedro Gutierrez Flores was to make a census of these lands in 1572).[77] By contrast, as we have seen, the labor force of Cochabamba could only use collective *suyos* (or, at best, land alloted to certain *caciques*). Nowhere in the two huge bundles of documents pertaining to the lawsuit do we find the trace of an individual *tupu.*

Yet from a different point of view, another distinction must be made between Cochabamba and Abancay, on the one hand, and Yucay, on the other. Both at Abancay and at Cochabamba the land cultivated by the *mitimas* was state owned, and its products were destined essentially for the army (and one is struck to find that in these two cases the texts use almost identical words).[78] In the Yucay Valley, by contrast, Huayna Capac owned land outright as personal property (*"como el dho valle era casa de Guayna Capac. . . ," "en tiempo de Guayna Capac ynga este valle de yucay fué como rrecamara suya."*[79] The status of these lands was therefore explicitly defined by contrasting it with the state-owned lands: *"distintos y apartados de la Corona y Reynos de los yngas; y asi sucedian en ellos, como cosa apartada."*[80] Other great lords, such as Mama Anahuarque, also owned *chacaras* at Yucay as "private" property.[81] It is true that such lands also existed at Cochabamba (as we have seen it); however, they represented only a tiny fraction of the total area. Conversely, the entire Yucay Valley seems to have been subject to personal property rights.

It is, therefore, no coincidence that the *mitimas* of Yucay exhibited another peculiarity that is not found elsewhere. In addition to being called *mitimas*, they were also referred to as *yanaconas*. Why? What does this term mean in this context? Neither the *mitimas* of Cochabamba nor those of Abancay were referred to in this manner. Yet at Yucay the term *yana* was applied indiscriminately both to the *naturales* of the valley and to the *mitimas* from other places:

> Todos los yndios del dicho valle se llamauan del ynga y que eran dos parcialidades la una de mitimaes que quiere dezir yndios aduenediços e la otra parte de naturales e todos servian el ynga e a sus hijos e mugeres e parientes e les benefiçiauan la chacaras que tenian e le seruian todos de yanaconas como yndios que los tenia el dicho ynga ocupados en el servicio de su casa.[82] Y estar todos ellos en titulo y voz de yanaconas . . . que quiere dezir en lengua española criados de su servicio y casi todos los yndios del dho valle mitimas y naturales eran yanaconas del ynga.[83]

Service to the state was thus not sufficient to define the category of *yana.* If all of the Indians of the Yucay Valley were designated by this term, it was because they were part of Huayna Capac's "household" and attached to him by ties of personal dependence. This is the reason why they were no longer under the jurisdiction of any of the "four provinces" and do not appear in the *khipu,* the census of the Inca's tributaries. In short, they were definitively cut off from their ethnic groups.[83bis]

The strength of the ties between the *mitimas* and their native groups thus varied greatly, and in this spectrum Cochabamba and Yucay occupied the opposite poles. In the first case these ties remained very strong, since they were kept up by the comings and goings of the *mittayoc;* in the second case they were completely severed. Midway between these two poles, Abancay represented an intermediary situation (despite the absence of *mittayoc*). Indeed, we can test the strength of these ties by examining what happened in the three valleys at the time of the Spanish invasion. At Cochabamba and Abancay many *mitimas* fled and returned to their native ethnic groups (although in both cases enough of them remained to give rise to the lawsuit to which we

TABLE 8.2
Three Models of Colonization

	Cochabamba	Abancay	Yucay
Presence of *mitimas*	+	+	+
State-owned land (+)			
"Private" land (−)	+	+	−
Distribution of *tupu*	−	+	+
Presence of *mittayoc*	+	−	−
Presence of *yana*	−	−	+
Ties with native ethnic group	+	(+) (−)	−

owe our information).[84] At Yucay, by contrast, no mention is made of the departure of any of the *mitimas;* even under Spanish rule all of them seem to have stayed on in the valley (and we know from other sources that many Cañari continued to live in Cuzco). At Cochabamba one other phenomenon also indicates the permanent nature of the ties between the *mitimas* and their native ethnic groups. Even under the colonial regime the Indians of the highlands (the Caranga, Quillaca, Sora, and the Uru of Paria) laid claim to their possessions in the valley in order to preserve their ethnic "archipelagos." This did not happen at Abancay, where the litigation was between the Spanish *hacendados* and the resident *mitimas,* not their faraway *caciques.* The different situations obtaining in these three valleys thus reflect three distinct types of evolution. The principal findings of our comparative study are summed up in Table 8.2.

The two principal criteria of differentiation were, ultimately, the status (state-owned or private) of the land cultivated by the *mitimas* and the strength of the ties with the native ethnic group. But all of these situations were complex and changeable, and shifts in direction could occur at any time. Can it be assumed that if the Spanish invasion had not interrupted the evolution of the *Tawantinsuyu,* a gradual changeover from the Cochabamba to the Yucay type would have taken place? To make this assumption, one would have to know more about the circumstances associated with the privatization of certain lands and the creation of interpersonal ties. The fact is, however, that the sheer scope of the labor-services performed in the Cochabamba Valley testifies to the development of a realm of state management that functioned by a logic of its own and had nothing to do with either ethnic particularities or ties of personal dependence.

One concluding remark: The figure of 14,000 *mitimas* and *mit-*

tayoc in the Cochabamba Valley—whether it is correct or not—strikes me as significant indeed, for it suggests one last correspondence. Is it a coincidence that under the Spanish rule Francisco de Toledo called for a work force of 13,500 (later 14,200) *mitayos* for the mines of Potosi? It is a fact that in organizing the colonial system, the viceroy made use of a preexisting Andean institution, the *mit'a*. One wonders whether he modeled his plan, down to the details, on the colonization of the Cochabamba Valley in the days of Huayna Capac. The connection between one form of labor-service and the next may well have been established by none other than Polo de Ondegardo, who was intimately acquainted with the indigenous world and also played a prominent role both in the lawsuit of Cochabamba and in the colonial administration. Since in both cases the imposition of labor-services by the state was involved, this is an outstanding example showing the continuity of certain Andean institutions from the *Tawantinsuyu* to the *Virreynato*. Only the context changed, for the notion of "wealth" had shifted from Cochabamba to Potosi, from the production of maize to the mining of silver.

Translated by Elborg Forster

Notes

[1]See, for example, the article by Lautaro Núñez, "L'evolution millénaire d'une vallée: peuplement et ressources à Tarapacá," in the special issue "Anthropologie historique des sociétés andines" of *Annales, E.S.C.* (September–December 1978):906–920.

[2]Cf. John V. Murra, "El control vertical de un maximo de pisos ecologicos en la economia de las sociedades andinas," (1972), republished in *Formaçiones economicas y politicas del mundo andino*, Lima, Instituto de Estudios Peruanos (19), 1975, pp. 59–115.

[3]Cf. Waldemar Espinoza Soriano, "Los mitmas yungas de Collique en Cajamarca, siglos XV, XVI y XVII," *Revista del Museo Nacional* 36 (1969–1970):9–57; "Colonias de mitmas multiples en Abancay, siglos XV y XVI: una informacion inédita de 1575 para la etnohistoria andina," *Revista del Museo Nacional* 39 (1973):225–299; "Los mitmas huayacuntu en Quito o guarniciones para la represion armada: siglos XV y XVI," *Revista del Museo Nacional* 41 (1975).

[4]P. Sarmiento de Gamboa, *Historia Índica* [1572] (Buenos Aires, 1942), p. 124.

[5]*Archives Historiques de Cochabamba* (hereafter cited as AHC), AR 1540 and AR 1570 (this last *legajo* is not paginated). The oldest document, the "repartimiento de Huayna Capac," dates from 1556; the other documents were produced between 1560 and 1570.

[6]Adolfo de Morales, *Repartimiento de tierras por el Inca Huayna Capac* [1556], (Cochabamba, Museo Arqueologico, Universidad de San Simon, 1977).

[7]J. Polo de Ondegardo, *Los errores y supersticiones de los yndios . . .*[1554], Coleccion de libros y documentos referentes a la Historia del Peru, series 1a, [1554], vol. 3, (Lima, 1916), p. 81:

"e ansi gobernando estos rreynos el Marques de Cañete, se trató esta materia, y hallando verdadera esta ynformacion que yo hiçe, queriendola sauer de my, y el remedio que podia tener, se hizo desta manera: que a la provincia de Chucuyto se le volvieron los yndios y las tierras que tenyan en la costa en el tyempo del ynga donde cogían sus comydas, y a Juan de Sanjuan, vezino de Ariquipa, en quien estaban encomendados, se le dieron otros que vacaron en aquella çiudad, e ansi quedó aquella provincia rremediada." Cf. also *Del linaje de los Incas* [1567], Coleccion de libros y documentos referentes a la Historia del Peru, series 1a, vol. 4 (Lima, 1916), p. 73.

[8]AHC, AR 1540, f.353r–353v.

[9]AHC, AR 1570, *Parecer* by Francisco de Saavedra Ulloa: "*por las dha ynformaçion paresce que topa ynga conquisto el dho valle y a los yndios naturales que en ella hallo que eran cotas e chuis e sipi sipis los sscaco de su natural y a los cotas y chuis los passo a pocona y mizque.*"

[10]AHC, AR 1570, *Repartimiento: "les mando que dexasen este valle e se pasasen a la frontera de los yndios chiriguanaes."*

[11]AHC, AR 1570, *Parecer* by Francisco de Saavedra Ulloa: "*y a los dhos de sipe sipe les señalo en el dho ualle tierras e metio algunos yndios desta provincia para que le benefiçiasen çiertas chacaras.*"

[12]On this point, see also Waldemar Espinoza Soriano, "Los mitmas yungas de Collique," (cited in note 3).

[13]AHC, AR 1570, *Parecer* by Francisco de Saavedra Ulloa: "*y despues guayna capa hizo rrepartimiento general de todas las tierras del dho ualle para ssi y metio en benefiçio de las dhas sus chacaras catorze mill yndios de muchas naçiones.*"

[14]AHC, AR 1570, *Repartimiento.*

[15]Ludovico Bertonio, *Vocabulario de la lengua aymara* [1612] (La Paz, 1952), p. 390.

[16]Diego Gonzalez Holguin, *Vocabulario de la lengua general de todo el Peru* [1608] (Lima, 1952).

[17]AHC, AR 1540, f. 352r.

[18]AHC, AR 1540, f. 352r–352v.

[19]AHC, AR 1540, f. 351v.

[20]Waldemar Espinoza Soriano, "Colonias de mitmas multiples en Abancay" (cited in note 3), p. 232ff.

[21]Cf. the document I cite in Notes 31, 32, and 33, which I found in the *Archives of the tribunal of Poopo, Expediente* no. 10, f. 1415: "*Amojonamiento entre los yndios soras y los yndios huros de charamoco.*"

[22]Cf. question no. 14 of Polo's *Interrogatorio,* cited in the text and Note 8.

[23]Waldemar Espinoza Soriano, "El Memorial de Charcas: 'Crónica' inédita de 1582," *Canuta: Revista de la Universidad nacional de educacion* (Chosica, 1969), p. 21.

[24]*Ibid.*

[25]*Ibid.: "que se nos dé posesion de las dichas nuestras tierras del Valle de Cochabamba que son cuatro* suyos *y urcos cada uno con sus zanjas de la nacion de los Charcas y otros matro* suyos *y urcos de la nacion de los Caracaras.*"

[26]José Macedonio Urquidi, *El origen de la noble Villa de Oropesa: La Fundacion de Cochabamba,* Editorial Canelas, S. A. (Cochabamba, 1971), pp. 491–494.

[27]*National Archives of Bolivia* (Sucre), EC no. 72: "*Juicio en grado de apelacion ante la Real Audiencia de la Plata seguido entre Don Juan Duran y los caciques de Sipe Sipe en Cochabamba sobre las tierras de Ycallungas,*" [1584], ff. 80, cited in Nathan Wachtel, "La réciprocité et l'Etat Inca: de Karl Polanyi à John V. Murra," *Annales, E.S.C.* (November–December 1974): 1346–1357.

[28]Cf. Maria Rostworowski de Diez Canseco, "Pescadores, artesanos y mercaderes costenos en el Peru prehispanico," *Revista del Museo Nacional* 41 (1975): 312–349.

[29]Nathan Wachtel, "Hommes d'eau. Le problème uru (XVIe–XVIIe siècle)," *Annales, E.S.C.* (September–December 1978) (special issue devoted to "Anthropologie historique des sociétés andines"): 1127–115.

[30]*Visita hecha a la provincia de Chucuito por Garci Diez de San Miguel* (1567), Casa de la cultura del Perú (Lima, 1964); *Archivo General de Indias* (Seville), Contaduria, no. 1887.

[31]*Archives of the Tribunal of Poopo, Expediente* no. 10.

[32]*Ibid.*, f. 147v–148r.

[33]*Ibid.*, f. 150r: *y ansi mismo tenemos dos suyos en el valle de cochabamba questaran quatro leguas y media de charamoco el un suyo llamado potopoto y el otro yllaurco.*"

[34]AHC, AR 1570, *Repartimiento: "que por no auer en ella suyos dados e rrepartidos a los dhos yndios carangas no se declara aqui."*

[35]The map published by Adolfo Morales (reference in note 6) seems to me to be wrong. Since the *chacaras* are described from east to west, running toward Sipe Sipe, *Yllaurco* is the "field" located on the eastern, not the western extremity!

[36]Waldemar Espinoza Soriano, "El Memorial de Charcas," p. 25.

[37]Diego Gonzalez Holguin, *Vocabulario*, p. 333. In addition, *Urco* designates *"el cerro," "el macho de los animales"* (p. 357). Despite the equivalence suggested in the *Memorial de Charcas*, the relationship between *suyo* and *urco* remains obscure. On this point, cf. the study by Thérèse Bouyse-Cassagne, "L'espace aymara: urco et uma," *Annales, E.S.C.* (September–December 1978): 1057–1080.

[38]Ludovico Bertonio, *Vocabulario*, p. 332.

[39]On the relationship between the notion of "stripe" (decoration of a piece of cloth) and that of a field of a long, narrow shape, cf. Veronica Cereceda, "Sémiologie des tissus andins," *Annales, E.S.C.* (September–December 1978): 1017–1035.

[40]AHC, AR 1570, *Parecer.*

[41]*Archives of the Tribunal of Poopo, Expediente* no. 10, f. 150r.

[42]Nathan Wachtel, "Le système d'irrigation des Chipayas," in *Anthropologie des populations andines* (Paris: INSERM 1976), pp. 87–116.

[43]The Uru formed the majority of this group (representing 2/3 of the population), but it is difficult to define their status. Cf. the *Tasa de la visita general de Francisco de Toledo*, Noble David Cook, ed. (Lima, 1975) Universidad Nacional Mayor de San Marcos, p. 15: in the 1574 *repartimiento* for the Sora and the Casaya, 3,801 tributaries were listed, 1243 of them Aymara and 2558 Uru. Cf. also Nathan Wachtel, "Hommes d'eau."

[44]AHC, AR 1570, *Repartimiento.*

[45]For each of the ethnic groups, the first figure designates the number of *suyos* cultivated for the state, the second the number of *suyos* assigned to the caciques, and the third the number of *suyos* assigned to the Indians directly for their subsistence. In this last category it was not altogether clear how the plots of the Colchacollo "field" were distributed among the "Colla," the "Sora," the "Quillaca," and the "Caranga"; I have therefore adopted the pattern that seemed most likely to me, given the disposition of the *suyos.*

[46]AHC, AR 1570, *Repartimiento: "e que lo demas que senalo desde la dha hacara poto hasta canata y ualle de sacagua, no la sauen que los charcas e torpas y caracaras e yngas y chuys daran la rrazon dello."*

[47]*Ibid.*

[48]*Ibid.*

[49]AHC, AR 1570, *Parecer.*

[50]AHC, AR 1570, *Repartimiento.*

[51]AHC, AR 1540, f. 404v.

[52]AHC, AR 1570, *Repartimiento: "dixeron que todo la que sembraban en esta dicha chacara poto poto e yllaurco y colchacollo y coachaca y esta de Viloma loco grande lleuaban al tambo de paria y de alli al cuzco en ganados del ynga."*

[53]AHC, AR 1540, cf. the witness Pedro Anzules Palentaya, *"principal de los yndios chichas encomendados en el licenciado polo": "e que los dhos yndios de sipe sipe eran ganaderos del ganado del ynga."*

[54]AHC, AR 1540, f. 414v.

[55]AHC, AR 1570, *Repartimiento.*

[56]Urqidi, *El origen,* p. 495.

[57]Cf. Maria Rostworowski de Diez Canseco, "El repartimiento de doña Beatriz Coya, en el valle de Yucay," *Historia y Cultura* (1970): 158; Horacio Villanueva Urteaga, "Documento sobre Yucay en el siglo XVI," *Revista del Archivo Historico del Cuzco* (1970): 14, 36, etc.; Nathan Wachtel, *La vision des vaincus* (Paris, 1971), p. 169.

[57]bis. AHC, AR 1570, *Parecer* by Diego Nuñez Bazan.

[58]AHC, AR 1570, *Repartimiento.*

[59]This is the hypothesis I have adopted in drawing up Table 8.1.

[60]AHC, AR 1570, *Repartimiento.*

[61]*Ibid.: "los dhos capitanes mandavan sembrasen para los dhos caciques e yndios."*

[62]*Ibid.*

[63]This area would be even smaller if the Anocaraire field contained only three *suyos.* Cf. the arguments on this point presented by the other informants at the end of the *Repartimiento.*

[64]AHC, AR 1570, *Repartimiento.*

[65]Cf. Nathan Wachtel, "Le système d'irrigation des Chipayas."

[66]AHC, AR 1570, f. 359r.

[67]John Howland Rowe, "Inca Culture at the Time of the Spanish Conquest," *Handbook of South American Indians,* vol. 2 (Washington, 1946), p. 270.

[67]bis. Cf. Waldemar Espinoza Soriano, "Colonias de mitmas multiples en Abancay," (cited in note 3); Maria Rostworowski de Diez Canseco, "el repartimiento de dona Beatriz Coya," (cited in note 57); Wachtel, *La vision des vaincus,* pp. 168–176, 188–192, 202–208.

[68]Cf. John V. Murra, "Maiz, tuberculos y ritas agricolas (1960), reprinted in *Formaçiones* (cited in note 2).

[69]Espinoza Soriano, "Colonias de mitmas," pp. 230–231; Rostworowski, "Repartimiento de doña Beatriz," p. 159.

[70]At Abancay the colonization of the valley by *mitimas* even seems to have been in full swing as early as under the reign of Tupac Yupanqui.

[71]Espinoza Soriano "Colonias de mitmas," pp. 230, 236.

[72]Horacio Villanueva Urtega, "Documento sobre Yucay," (cited in note 57), p. 139.

[73]Espinoza Soriano, "Colonias de mitmas multiples," pp. 232 ff.

[74]*Historical Archives of Cuzco, Genealogia de Sayri Tupac,* libro 2, f. 416r. It is remarkable that in the three valleys we are comparing here, the *mitimas* always remained grouped together according to their origins; in fact they gave their name to the land they occupied: at Yucay, for example, *"dicen que cada anden de ellos tenia su nombre que no se acuerda de ellos y que de ciertas provincias venian cada uno a sembrar su anden y conforme a la provincia que lo sembraba se llamaba el anden,"* (Historical Archives of Cuzco, *Genealogia de Sayri Tupac,* libro 3, indice 5, f. 29r., cited in Wachtel, *La vision des vaincus,* p. 170.

[75]Cf. Espinoza Soriano, "Colonias de mitmas multiples," p. 233–234; for Yucay: "*el dicho Guayna Capac en su vida habia puesto en el dicho valle dos mil indios, mil de Chinchaisuyo y mil de Collasuyo.*" (Historical Archives of Cuzco, *Genealogia de Sayri Tupac*, libro 2, f. 174v–175r.)

[76]Espinoza Soriano, "Colonias de mitmas multiples," p. 284.

[77]Wachtel, *La vision des vaincus*, pp. 174ff.

[78]For example, for Abancay: "*el dicho Guayna Capa invio un indio llamado Sacapacha para que llevase todo el algodon y aji y otras cosas que se habian cogido y estauan en deposito* para el sustento de la guerra *que tenia entonces.*" (Espinoza Soriano, "Colonias de mitmas multiples," p. 287; emphasis added.)

[79]Wachtel, *La vision des vaincus*, p. 169.

[80]Rostworowski, "Repartimiento de doña Beatriz," p. 252–253.

[81]Wachtel, *La vision des vaincus*, p. 169.

[82]Historical Archives of Cuzco, *Genealogia de Sayri Tupac*, libro 2, indice 4, f. 102v. (cited in Wachtel, *La vision des vaincus*, p. 170–171).

[83]*Ibid.*, libro 2, indice 4, f.97.

[83]bis. Cf. Wachtel, *La vision des vaincus*, pp. 168–169.

[84]AHC, AR 1570, *Parecer*; cf. also Espinoza Soriano, "Colonias de mitmas multiples," p. 251.

Appendix 1:   List of Suyos Assigned by Huayna Capac

I. Chacara Yllaurco

("Soras")

1. soras de sipe sipe
2. soras aj Casaya de Paria
3. "todo el repartimiento de tapacari"
4. "répartimiento de caracollo"
5. uros de paria

("Quillacas")

6. "aracapi que son yndios del repartimiento de puna"
7. "quillacas de Juan Guarache"
8. uruquillas aullagas
9. "asanaques que son del repartimiento de quillacas"

("Carangas")

10. "andamarca en los carangas y urinoca"
11. "samancha carangas de colquemarca"
12. carangas de chuquicota
13. totora carangas

II. Chacara Colchacollo

A. Upper Half

1. "collas llamados calapanca . . . de paucarcolla"
2. lupacas de chucuyto

3. pacajes de callapa
4. poco poco collas de chuquicache

("Collas") 5. collas de tiaguanaco
6. collas de caquiauire en omasuyu
7.⎫
  ⎬ "para los yndios que benefiçiauan . . . con que se
8.⎭ sustentasen"

9. soras de sipe sipe
10. soras de sipe sipe
11. casayas de paria
12. soras de paria

("Soras") 13. "parcialidad llamada chio . . . soras de tapacari"
14. "parcialidad de malconaca . . . soras de tapacari"
15. "parcialidad de machacauana de caracollo yndios soras"
16. "parcialidad de araycabana del dho caracollo"

B. Lower Half

1. aracapi de puna
2. quillacas

("Quillacas") 3. "uruquillas de aullaga"
4. quillacas asanaques

5. carangas de andamarca urinoca
6. samancha carangas

("Carangas") 7. carangas de chuquicota
8. carangas de totora

9. "collas capahanco de paucarcolla"
10. collas lupacas de chucuyto
11. pacajes de callapa
12. "collas de poco de chiquicache"

("Collas") 13. "collas de pucarani tiaguanaco"
14. collas de caquiauire
15.⎤ "donde hazian sus sementeras los yndios que los
16.⎦ beneffiçianan para su comida"

III. Chacara Anocaraire

"para los dhos caciques" :

1. guarache, cacique de los quillacas
2. achacapa, cacique de los carangas de chuquicota
3. vilca, cacique de los carangas de totora

4. hachacata, cacique de tapacari
5. condo, cacique de tapacari

IV. Chacara Coachaca*

1. "a paria"
2. "a tapacari"

3.⎫
4.⎬"a yndios de sipe sipe"
5.⎪
6.⎭

7.⎫
8.⎬"a yndios del rrepartimiento de paria"
9.
("Soras")   10.
11.⎭

12.⎫
13.⎬"ayllos de tapacari"
14.⎪
15.⎪
16.⎭

17.⎫"a yndios de caracollo"
18.⎪
19.⎬
20.⎭

V. Chacara Viloma

"cinco suyos atrabesados en tres partes" :
a) "primera parte de abaxo"

1. aracapi
2. quillacas
("Quillacas")   3. aullagas
4. asanacas
5. andamarca carangas

b) "la otra segunda parte . . . de en medio" :

1. caracollo soras
2. paria

---

*From a different document, located in the *legajo* AR (1540) f 22v–26v (which allows completion of the list of AR 1570).

("Soras")   3. tapacari
      4. sipe sipe
      5. sipe sipe

      c) "la otra tercera parte . . . por la falda de la sierra ques lo mas alto" :

      1. collas de paucarolla
      2. collas de chucuyto
      3. pacajas de callapa
("Collas")   4. collas de poco poco de chiquicache
      5. collas de tiaguanaco e pucarani
      6. "urcosuyo collas"
      7. "los de omasuyo"

      8. carangas de totora
      9. chuquicota
("Carangas") 10. colquemarca
      11. andamarca y urinoca

      12. asanaques de quillacas
      13. uruquillas
("Quillacas") 14. quillacas (de guarache)
      15. "aracapi que es puna"

      16. totora carangas
      17. chuquicota
("Carangas") 18. colquemarca
      19. andemarca e urinoca

      20. asanacas de quillacas
      21. aullagas
("Quillacas") 22. quillacas
      23. aracapi

Appendix 2: Interrogatorio de J. Polo de Ondegardo (Archives Historiques de Cochabamba)

AR 1540

[Pleito Sipe Sipe.] [1560]

[351r°] Por las preguntas siguientes sean preguntados los testigos que fueren presentados por parte de don Hernando Cuyo e don Diego Tanquire e don Geronimo Cuyo caciques del ualle de Cochabamba y de el licenciado Polo e Rodrigo de Orellana sus encomenderos en el pleito que tratan con los caciques de Paria sobre las tierras.

1. Primeramente sean preguntados si conocen a los dichos don Hernando Cuyo y don Diego Tanquire e don Geronimo Cuyo caçiques del valle de Cochabamba y a el liçenciado Polo y a Rodrigo de Orellana sus encomenderos y si tienen notiçia de las tierras del asyento de Potopoto y de la chacara llamada Yllaurco y la chacara de Colchacollo y la chacara que llaman Anocarayre y la chacara que llaman Uillauma y las demas.

2. Yten si sauen etc. que del dicho ualle de Cochabamba son caçiques principales del don Geronimo Cuyo y don Diego Tanquire y don Hernando Cuyo caçiques de la encomienda del licenciado Polo y de Rodrigo de Orellana y que todas las dichas chacaras de Potopoto e Yllaurco y de Colchacollo y de Anocarayre y de Uillaoma y todas las demas que coxen y siembran los yndios mitimaes puestos por el ynga en el dicho ualle de Cochabamba son del dicho ualle y estan en los terminos y districtto e tierra de los dichos caciques.

[351v°] 3. Ytten si sauen etc. que al tiempo que el ynga señalo las dichas chacaras las tomo y adjudico para sy propio y para que lo que dellas se coxiese comiese el y su gente de guerra lleuandoselo a la ciudad del Cuzco en sus ganados sin que las personas que benefiçiaban el dicho mayz se pudiesen aprouechar dello en ninguna manera lo qual se hazia ansy en todas las chacaras que el ynga tenia propias suyas para el dicho effecto.

4. Yten si sauen etc. que en las dichas chacaras que el ynga señalo para si y tomo a los dichos yndios de Cochabamba puso en ellas mitimaes para que las sembrasen benefiçiasen y coxiesen de la prouincia de Paria ansy Soras como Uros y de la prouincia de los Quillacas y de la prouincia de los Chichas y de la prouincia de los Carangas y de la prouincia de Chile y de la prouincia de los Chilques que es junto al Cuzco y de otras muchas para que entendiesen en el dicho benefiçio y coxiesen la comida para el dicho ynga digan lo que saben.

5. Yten si sauen etc. que al tiempo que los españoles entraron en estos rreynos y los pusieron debaxo del amparo y dominio de Su Magestad los dichos yndios mitimaes questauan en el dicho ualle de Cochabamba para beneficiar las dichas tierras y sementeras del ynga fueron encomendados con sus chacarras [352r°] e tierras en Rodrigo de Orellana y en Juan de Caravajal a quien suçedio Camargo y ultimamente el liçenciado Polo digan lo que sauen.

6. Yten si sauen etc. que por virtud de la dicha encomienda todos los dichos mitimaes quedaron debajo de la subjeçion de los caçiques de

Cochabamba y antes de la tasa y despues de la tasa contribuyen e pagan su tassa con los dichos caciques y siembran para su tributo las tierras que antes estauan señaladas por el ynga digan lo que sauen.

7. Yten si sauen etc. que debaxo de la encomienda del dicho Rodrigo de Orellana estan los yndios mitimaes Quillacas y los mitimaes Carangas y los mitimaes Chilques y Chiles y Collas de Asangaro los quales tienen pueblos en el dicho ualle de Cochabamba y estan en las mismas tierras que se benefiçiauan para el ynga y acuden con sus tributos al dicho don Hernando Cuyo e a Rodrigo de Orellana su encomendero.

8. Yten si sauen etc. que los yndios Uros y Soras mitimaes del rrepartimiento de Paria questaban en Hayata y al presente estan fuera de algunos que [352vº] se an juntado y los que estauan en Cota y en otros poblezuelos Soras y Uros todos son y an sydo sujetos al caçique don Geronimo Cuyo y don Diego Tanquire despues de la dicha encomienda y siempre an tributado con ellos e ayudadoles a pagar su tassa a Juan de Caruajal y a Camargo y al liçenciado Polo sus en comenderos digan lo que sauen.

9. Yten si sauen etc. que los yndios Caracotas Chichas y Charcas y Amparayes questauan mitimaes en Cochabamba para el benefiçio de las dichas chacarras del Ynga todos ansimismo fueron encomendados al dicho Juan de Caravajal y sirvieron al dicho Alonso de Camargo y siruen y an servido al liçenciado Polo deuaxo de la subjeçion del dicho Geronimo Cuyo e don Diego Tanquire caçiques del dicho valle de Cochabamba sin auer cosa en contrario.

10. Yten si sauen etc. que despues de las dichas encomiendas nunca los yndios Carangas Carangas [sic] ni Quillacas ni Chichas ni Yamparayes Soras ni Uros an enbiado a sembrar al dicho ualle de Cochabamba ni tomado ni aprovechadose de las tierras quel dicho ynga señalo para si sino tan solamente los mitimaes questaban en el dicho ualle dandoles tributos [353rº] a los dichos caciques y contribuyendo con ellos con su tasa.

11. Yten si sauen etc. que dende tres o quatro años a esta parte despues que Juan Gºs fue a visitar por comision de Antonio de Hozmayo estando el licençiado Polo ausente en servicio de su Magestad por corregidor en la ciudad del Cuzco algunos yndios Uros del repartimiento de Paria se a entrado y hecho sus casas en el dicho pueblo de Hayata y enpeçado a sembrar algunas tierras digan lo que saben.

12. Yten si sauen etc. que si algun yndio Uro de Paria antes de la dicha visita querian sembrar y sembrauan en el dicho ualle pagaua a los dichos yndios de Cochabamba tributo y les ayudaba con sus personas digan lo que saben.

13. Yten si sauen etc. que el dicho licençiado Polo tiene su chacarra y sementera en el asiento y chacarra de Potopoto y la siembra y coxe de doze años a esta parte sin contradicion de persona alguna y un pedaço de la dicha chacarra siembran los caciques de la dicha su encomienda y otros yndios della para pagar su tasa digan lo que sauen.

14. Yten si sauen etc. que despues que Su Magestad hizo el rrepartimiento en este rreyno rrepartio ansimismo [353v°] todos los mitimaes tierras y chacarras en el mismo lugar donde los hallo y que las tierras que benefiçiauan se quedaron para los dichos yndios y sus encomenderos lo qual fue universal en todo este rreyno y ansi los yndios Carangas se quedaron sin las tierras y mitimaes en la costa y lo mismo los de Chucuito y todos los demas los quales fueron repartidos a la ciudad de Arequipa y despues si traen comida de los dichos ualles de mitimaes es comprandola por sus dineros y rrescate digan lo que sauen.

15. Yten si saben etc. quel pueblo de Totora que esta junto a los Andes esta poblado de mitimaes Charcas del ualle de Cochabamba questauan alli puestos para beneficio de chacarras del ynga que auia tomado para si e por virtud de la encomienda que se hizo por Su Magestad se encomendaron con sus tierras y chacarras a don Gomez de Lima y a Luis Perdomo y agora los posee Antonio Aluarez y Su Magestad sin que los yndios de Cochabamba gozan dellos ni de las dichas chacarras y ansi se haze en todos los demas deste rreyno donde acaeçio lo susodicho digan lo que sauen.

16. Yten si sauen etc. que los yndios Soras de Paria tienen y poseen en su tierra muchas chacarras de maiz y todas las que el ynga tenia señaladas en ellas de donde an pagado y pagan sus tributos en los ualles de Çicaya Capinota y Charamoco y Cuchira y otros munchos ualles donde comodamente siembran y coxen para sus comidas y tributos.

[354r°] 17. Yten si sauen etc. que en todos estos rreynos dondequiera que ay yndios Uros nunca el ynga les rrepartio ni dio tierras de mayz para ellos mismos digan lo que sauen.

18. Yten si sauen etc. que al tiempo que el dicho Juan G°s visito el dicho ualle tubo atado y mandado pringar al caçique principal del rrepartimiento del licenciado Polo que se llama don Geronimo Cuyo y a otros digan lo que sauen.

19. Yten si sauen etc. que todo lo susodicho es publico y notorio el licenciado Polo el liçenciado Pedro de Herrera Francisco Muñoz.

[359r°] T° Pedro Guanca yndio Sora de Sipesipe testigo presentado por parte de los dichos don Hernando Cuyo e don Diego Tanquire. 70 años.

3. Dixo que porque al tiempo que el dicho ynga rrepartio este ualle lo rrepartieron por su mandato dos yngas sus capitanes e gobernadores que se llamaban el uno Uchimayta y el otro Guacamayta y este testigo

los conocio y se hallo presente en este ualle quando lo rrepartieron por mandado de Guayna Capa y que los dichos gobernadores vido este testigo que las dichas tierras y chacarras de Potopoto e Yllaurco y Colchacollo e Anocarayre e Vilomo las tomaron e [359v°] repartieron para el mismo ynga y pusieron en ellas mitimaes yndios por el dicho ynga Guaina Capa para que labrasen las dichas tierras y las senbrasen para el ynga y ansi vido este testigo que los dichos yndios las senbrauan para el dicho ynga y uido quel maiz que della se cogia lo lleuaban los dichos yndios al Cuzco para el ynga e que el que quedaua era e lo guardauan para la gente de guerra del ynga y lo mas rruyn dello apartauan para hacer acua y comer la gente que beneficiaua las dichas chacarras y ansi vido este testigo que todo aquello que se cogia en las dichas chacarras era para el ynga y las tierras eran suyas y por esto la sabe.

4. Dixo que sabe e vido este testigo como el ynga puso yndios mitimaes en las dichas chacarras y tierras para que la beneficiasen y labrasen para el propio ynga e que los yndios que puso eran Soras de Paria y Huros de Challacollo y Quillacas y Carangas y Chichas y de Chile y Chilques y Collas y Charcas de Caracara y otros yndios de otras naçiones para el benefiçio de las dichas tierras y esto sabe y vido de lo en la pregunta contenido.

6. Dixo que sabe e uido este testigo que los dichos yndios mitimaes quedaron sujetos a los caciques de Cochabamba que se llamauan el uno Alaaui y el otro Uasi y que don Diego Tanquire es hijo de Alaaui e que sabe e uido este testigo que los dichos yndios contribuyan y pagan su tasa [360r°] con los caciques de Cochabamba y que los dichos yndios acudian a los dichos caciques y los caciques a sus encomenderos y que an senbrado y sienbran en las dichas tierras para pagar sus tributos como la pregunta dice y esto sabe della.

7. Dixo que sabe este testigo que los yndios mitimaes en la pregunta conthenidos son de la encomienda de Rodrigo de Orellana e que los Chiles y Chilques estan en Taquina y los Collas en Viloma y los Carangas en Cholla y en Colchacollo y los Quillacas estan con los dichos Carangas en Cholla y en Colchacollo y todos tienen sus pueblos en este ualle en los dichos suyos y tierras que se beneficiauan para el ynga y que a uisto y uee este testigo que acuden con sus tributos a don Hernando Cuyo y a Rodrigo de Orellana su encomendero y esto sabe dello.

8. A la octaua pregunta dixo que lo que della sabe es que los yndios Uros y Soras mitimaes de Paria de Ayata y de Cota y otros poblesuelos de Soras y Uros deste ualle los que estauan y agora estan ecepto algunos yndios que dellos de poco aca se an juntado en los dichos pueblos todos an sydo y son subjetos a don Diego Tanquire y a don Geronimo Cuyo caçiques de Cochabamba de la encomienda del licençiado Polo despues

que el dicho repartimiento se encomendo y que siempre los a oydo decir este testigo que tributaron a Juan de Caruajal y a Camargo y esto les a oydo dezir este testigo a los mismos yndios de Ayata y de Cota Soras y Uros y esto sabe della.

[360v°]   10. Dixo que porque despues que este ualle se rrepartio a los cristianos y los yndios siruen a los cristianos nunca mas desde entonçes a esta parte jamas a uisto este testigo que ningunos de los yndios en la pregunta conthenidos ayan uenido ni an uenydo a beneficiar las dichas tierras de las dichas chacaras del ynga ni las an beneficiado ni senbrado sino tan solamente los yndios mitimaes deste dicho ualle los quales an tributado y an sido sujetos a los caçiques de Cochabamba y por esto la sabe.

11. Dixo que porque de tres a quatro años a esta parte poco mas o menos a uisto este testigo que algunos yndios Uros del rrepartimiento de Paria de Challacollo se an uenido y entrado en el pueblo de Ayata e alli an hecho sus casas y an senbrado algunas tierras y que en este tiempo a estado ausente el dicho licenciado Polo que dezian questaua en el Cuzco por justicia y por esto la sabe.

12. Dixo que lo que della sabe es que en el tiempo que la pregunta dice uido este testigo que algunos yndios Uros de Challacollo uenian y senbrauan en Cochabamba y que porque los dejasen senbrar ayudauan a senbrar y linpiar sus chacarras a los yndios cuyas eran las tierras y trayan yerua y leña y paja para los encomenderos de los dichos yndios de Cochabamba quando los caçiques de Cochabamba los mandauan y esto hazian y en esto ayudauan y no en otra cosa y esto sabe della.

[361r°]   14. Dixo que lo que della sabe es que este testigo a uisto que los yndios desta tierra ansi como estauan en las tierras donde estauan fueron encomendados a los cristianos y ansi los tales yndios se quedaron con las tierras donde estauan quando los encomendaron y que si algunos yndios bienen a Cochabamba Carangas o Quillacas o de las naciones de los mitimaes questan en este ualle que lleuan sus comidas compradas por sus rrescates o dineros y este sabe della.

16. Dixo que sabe e a uisto este testigo que los yndios de Paria an senbrado y sienbran en Sycaya y en Capinota y en Charamoco las quales tierras sabe e uido este testigo que el ynga se la dio a los dichos yndios Soras y Uros de Paria para que senbrasen para si propios porque no tenyan tierras en la puna para sembrar mayz e que de las sementeras de las dichas tierras de Sicaya y Capinota y Charamoco y Cuchira se sustentan y pagan y an pagado sus tributos y que las dichas tierras les bastan a los dichos yndios para su sustento y para su tasa y esto sabe della.

17. Dixo que porque [361v°] este uido que nunca el ynga jamas dio

ni rrepartio tierras para maiz a ningunos yndios Uros porque no sauian beneficiar las chacarras de maiz y porque eran haraganes y no sabian andar sino en las lagunas y si acaso algun maiz sembraban en estando en choclo o maçorca se lo comian en una noche y se yban a las lagunas donde biuian y ansi no les dio tierras de maiz ningunas el ynga para ellos propios y esto uido este testigo y por esto la sabe.

9

The *Mit'a* Obligations of Ethnic Groups to the Inka State

John V. Murra

Editors' Introduction

John Murra argues that the Inka state exacted prestations in energy, not "tribute" in kind. He also claims that Tawantinsuyu's impact on the local ethnic level has been overstressed. Many ethnic groups endured without much change at the local productive level; after articulation into the Inka state, indirect rule was the norm in politics and administration. Murra draws on the evidence of *khipu* (knotted strings recording administrative obligations), submitted as testimony by the native lords as part of sixteenth-century litigation in the colonial courts.

We still cannot infer whether the state appropriated ethnic lands only at the moment of incorporation or later as well, but subsistence and herding activities changed little on territories left in ethnic hands. Local polities undertook some new activities, notably road building, military duties far from home and weaving vast quantities of cloth for state purposes. Otherwise, most farming and craftwork continued to exploit the diverse econiches they had controlled before articulation.

The categories of state-imposed decimal administration appear only sporadically in the *khipu* records, particularly as one moves toward the *altiplano,* in the south. Murra refers to them as part of a bookkeeping vocabulary, rather than as indicating administrative reorganization of ethnic polities. He regards this stress on the local, ethnic level as a corrective to Cusco-centered interpretations of Tawantinsuyu, which tend to exaggerate the nature of the changes imposed during the Inka period.

THE INCA AND AZTEC
STATES, 1400–1800

The articulation of scores of ethnic groups, large and small, into the Inka state is poorly understood. We know that most of them continued to be administered by their *señores naturales*, who tended to be confirmed in their jobs by Cusco—if not the very pair in power before Cusco rule, then some of their kinsmen who turned out to be more "loyal." Although in some cases, particularly on the coast, Cusco did bring in completely new people to rule an ethnic group, as alleged by Viceroy Toledo, most of the evidence available today argues that the Inka preferred to freeze succession to ethnic leadership within narrower, kin-based limits than had prevailed earlier.

The major changes that followed incorporation into Tawantinsuyu had more to do with economics than with politics. In each ethnic territory the Inka carved out estates that henceforth produced food, cotton, maize, or wool for the crown, the several state cults, and the royal lineages; the local group thus lost the productivity of the alienated acreage. Sometimes, as Wachtel documents in Chapter 8, the total population of an exceptionally productive area could be deported and their irrigated maize-lands taken over for state purposes.

Alienation of ethnic holdings was not the only way of acquiring productive capacity. New terracing, expansion of the irrigation network, and enlarged herding facilities could occur as a consequence of the state's ability to mobilize larger work forces and feed them for longer periods. The relative proportion of alienated versus created state acreage in 1520 is still not known, but my guess is that in the highlands and away from the immediate circum-Cusco area, most of the state's productive lands had once been in the ethnic domain.

The presence of such state fields, dispersed throughout every ethnic territory, was one form of articulation and a daily reminder of Cusco's might. Even where there was no Inka administrator, the link was continually reiterated since these holdings had to be worked by the local ethnic group in whose territories they had been installed.

Located in all altitudes and latitudes, the state acreage is an aspect of the salient feature of the Andean and Inka systems to create the authority's revenues: There was no tribute in kind. Once the original alienation had been enforced, the household and the ethnic polity are said to have owed nothing from their own larder. Even when the year's harvest had been a disaster in any given locale the state expected to make up its losses to drought, hail, or frost from complementary production on its holdings elsewhere, *salpicados* said the awed Europeans, "sprinkled" over thousands of miles. This is probably the most notable difference from Mesoamerican political economy.

There were some exceptions to the rule of "no tribute in kind." Things gathered, creatures hunted, and items otherwise "raw" (those neither cultivated nor manufactured by human labor) were owed in kind: the feathers of many birds needed for military clothing, honey from the eastern lowlands, the eggs of wild ducks that nest on the islands of Lake Titicaca, both saltwater and freshwater fish. This "raw" ethnocategory deserves further study (see Note 14), but given its marginality in Andean subsistence and economics, its existence does not effect our characterization of the state revenue system.

Elsewhere I have tried to figure out the proportion of effort owed by the peasantry to the superordinate authority when compared to the energy that could be retained for one's subsistence and ceremonial needs.[1] No decision on the allotment of energies in pre-European times can be reached in 1980.

In recent years I have chosen a different approach to the articulation of ethnic groups within Tawantinsuyu. Instead of concentrating on the study of the "chronicles," with their Cusco-centric bias, I have stressed local, provincial, and ethnic sources, few of which had been available in 1955. These sources have many advantages: Among them is the fact that some reach into earlier stages of the European colonial regime, when numerous informants were still alive who had functioned as adults in the Andes before 1532.

La Visita General of 1549

One such primary source was the general inspection of 1549, ordered by "pacifier" La Gasca: 72 teams were sent throughout the realm to evaluate population figures and the other resources. The operation was coordinated by a knowledgeable trio of Dominican friars. Until very recently only one of these 72 reports was available: the one compiled about the ethnic groups inhabiting the Pillkumayu (now the Huallaga) Valley, a region where European penetration had been delayed for years by Inka-led resistance.[2] Eventually, in 1542, 10 years after the disaster at Caxamarca, the invaders and their Wanka allies broke through; the surviving resistors were distributed among several *encomenderos.*

Only 7 years later came the order from Lima to conduct the first *visita general.* The inspectors found they could gather the information required in a few short weeks; some never bothered to go into the countryside. They consulted the local lords and their *khipu-kamayuq,* who had continued knotting down the demographic and other quantitative data through almost a decade of armed resistance plus 7 years of colonial rule. Fortunately for us, who still cannot read the ethnocategories recorded on a *khipu,*[3] the questionnaires sent from Lima included queries about past as well as current conditions. Here I will comment only on the ethnic group-to-state articulation that they suggest: So far the 1549 answers are unique in their details.[4]

The first question asked by the inspectors dealt with a European obsession, and I assume here that the answer recorded reaches us torn from its knotted, Andean context: It inquires about silver and gold. We can only guess where the mining cord really belonged among the ethnocategories.[5] We can postpone examining the veracity and the implications of this first answer, but we should note that the respondents did phrase it in the decimal vocabulary encouraged by the Inka administration.

Chupaychu

The Chupaychu, the main ethnic group in the Huallaga Valley, were deemed to have been four-*waranqa* strong (roughly 4000 households) before the invasion. We need not take these figures literally, to notice that two of the four *waranqa* dwelt west of the river.[6] Upon archaelogical study we have discovered that one of the remaining two *waranqa* on the right bank, east of the Huallaga, have left behind quite distinct architectural and other material remains.[7] This confirms historical references that claim that in order to complete the 4000, the Cusco state had had to detach several hundred households from a neighboring, upriver polity, the Yacha.[8] The decimal enumeration required considerable administrative tinkering, if not vivisection, to fit ethnic realities.

The 4000 Chupaychu were alleged to have contributed three women and three men for each "hundred" households to wash gold; this would mean a total of 240 men and women, assuming there were actually 10 hundreds to each *waranqa*. Half as many pairs were reported to have minded silver in what today is the Cerro de Pasco region.

I now return to the information recorded in the rest of the *khipu*. Although the knotted strings transcribed into the 1549 protocol are most likely an incomplete record and although some of the items have been listed by the European scribe out of their Andean order, certain clusters do emerge and they deserve scrutiny.[9]

[Cord 1] They were asked what services did [the Chupaychu] give to the Inca in Cuzco *a la continua*

and they said that 400 Indian men and women remained in Cuzco *a la continua* to build walls and if one died they gave another.

On the precedent of the answer about the miners, mentioned previously, I assume that the 400 were two pairs of 100. Four hundred, particularly if they were couples, would be 10% of the total Chupaychu adult population—a very high percentage, even if we do not take these figures literally and concentrate on the proportions.[10]

A la continua in the question needs interpretation. I read it to mean some kind of "full time," but not for life. If the latter were the case, the masons would no longer be enumerated with the ethnic group of their origin. I suggest that they were *mit'ayuq* who rotated annually, not *yana*.[11]

[Cord 2] They also gave 400 Indians to plant the fields in Cuzco so people could eat y hacer su camarico.

Again, I assume these are 200 pairs. In passing, Cord 2 also explains what was meant by *camarico* in pre-European times: work performed by the household and ethnic community on behalf of those away— herding, digging for salt, or growing coca leaf. At the state level, by extension, *camarico* also meant planting on behalf of those on military and other duties. In post-European times, the term was extended again and distorted to cover such new chores as growing food for the resident friar or for the family of the potter required by his *encomendero* to learn making roof tiles in the city. I interpret Cord 2 to mean that these 200 pairs grew food for the 200 engaged in masonry in Cord 1 as well as for themselves. This reading assumes that Tawantinsuyu, the Inka state, preferred to have those working for it feed themselves—as indicated also in the Cochabamba state maize plantations, discussed in Chapter 8 by Nathan Wachtel.[12]

[Cord 3] They also gave 150 Indians *a la continua* as *yana* of Guayna Capac.

[Cord 4] 150 more to guard the body of Topa Ynga Yupanqui after he died, *a la continua*

The only reason I separate these two cords from cords 5–8, which follow, is that *a la continua* reappears in the answers, as written down by the European scribe. Otherwise my guess would be that Cords 3 through 8 form a single macrocategory.

[Cord 5] 10 *yana* more to guard his weapons[13]

[Cord 6] 200 Indians more to guard the Chachapoya

[Cord 7] 200 Indians more to guard Quito

[Cord 8] 20 Indians more for the guard of the body of Guana Cava after his death

Cords 3–8 deal with prestations to the persons and mummies of the last two pre-European kings; Cord 8 may have been an afterthought or simply recorded out of order. Cords 4 through 8 have in common *la guarda*, a translation of the informant's efforts to convey something that grouped into a single ethnocategory soldiering and service to the person of the king. All we know of the interpreter is that he was one *"Diego indio ladino que entiende nuestro romance castellano y la lengua de los dichos indios."* We should recall that the Quechua spoken in the Huallaga Valley is, and probably was then, not mutually intelligible with the Cusco variety.

[Cord 9] 120 Indians more to make feathers

[Cord 10] 60 more to extract honey

These cords refer to wild, uncultivated products, usually gathered by young, unmarried men.[14]

[Cord 11] 400 Indians to weave fine cloth

[Cord 12] 40 Indians to make more dyes and colors

Since Cords 1 through 8 record prestation far from home on state business, while 9 and 10 deal with gathering by youths in the local lowlands, Cords 11 and 12 are the first of the knot-strings to record energy expenditures at home. This premier position of cloth in the hierarchy of Andean goods as reckoned by the state can also be read on the *khipu* submitted by the Wanka lords during their litigation against the Spanish crown in the Audiencia of Los Reyes in 1560.[15] See also Cord 27 later in this discussion.

[Cord 13] 240 Indians to guard the sheep [camelids]

[Cord 14] 40 Indians to guard the fields which they had throughout this valley; the maize grown was mostly taken to Cuzco and the rest to the warehouses [at Huanuco Pampa].

[Cord 15] 40 additional Indians to plant hot peppers which were taken to Cuzco

I group these three cords together since they all refer to "guarding" agricultural and pastoral resources of the state, located in Chupaychu and Yacha home territories. On the Wanka *khipu*, food also followed immediately after the strings listing cloth, but there the camelids were enumerated earlier. The animals were grouped with human beings, in a macrocategory of "living creatures," knotted at the head of the *khipu*.[16]

[Cord 16] and they also gave 60 Indians and sometimes 45 to make salt

[Cord 17] 60 Indians to make [raise] the coca leaf which they took to Cuzco and to the warehouses of Huanuco [Pampa] and sometimes they hauled 200 sacks and at others 40

[Cord 18] 40 Indians to accompany the Inca in person to hunt deer

I hesitate in grouping these three cords together. I am guided in doing so by the peripheral location of the resources enumerated: The salt mines of Yanacachi are high above the Pillkumayu Valley and so are the deer; coca leaf grows far below in the hot country. But the deer do not fit since they are a "raw," uncultivated good, similar to those on Cords 9 and 10. An alternative would be to group the beaters with the skilled folk on the cords immediately below.

[Cord 19] and 40 Indians more to make soles and they took them to Cuzco and to the storehouses[17]

[Cord 20] 40 more carpenters [woodworkers] to make plates and bowls and other things for the Inca and they took them to Cuzco

[Cord 21] 40 more potters to make pots and they took them to Huanuco [Pampa]

Here, as in all other cases where the number of *mit'ayuq* is given as a function of the decimal accounting, what matters is the proportion, one household per "hundred." This would add up to three artisans from each *pachaka*, and if we include the beaters, Cord 18, then four.

[Cord 22] and 68 more Indians to guard the *tampu* at Huanuco

[Cord 23] 80 more to carry loads from the *tampu* to Pumpu [some five to six days' march] and from Sutun Cancha to Tambo [one day's, coming back]

[Cord 24] 40 more Indians to guard the women of the Inca

[Cord 25] 500 to go with the person of the Inca to war, to carry him to hammocks, and they went to Quito and to other places

All these activities are either performed or initiated at the administrative center of Huanuco Pampa, which was also used as a *tampu* way station. It is located almost two days' walk west of the Huallaga.[18]

[Cord 26] 500 more Indians, to plant and [do] other things without leaving their territory

I have noted that this cord, like Cord 14, dealt with agriculture in the home valley, though each of them deals with a distinct set of obligations to Tawantinsuyu. The 500 households of Cord 26 owed relatively short periods of seasonal (*mit'a*) work; the 40 knotted on Cord 14 were said to be "guarding." This I gloss as "were responsible" for the state acreage. Like the artisans of Cords 19–21, they had been contributed by their *pachaka*. Although they probably also followed a rotational cycle, their duties are likely to have been more committing; they may have directed the work of the 500. The listing of this mass activity at the very end of the *khipu* raises questions. It may be listed here because it was the most generalized of duties, involving least absence from home and least responsibility.

The account ends with a general comment, probably in response to European questioning: "All of which they gave and were used to give the Inca and no other things whatever and if they did make woolen things, [the fiber] was issued by the Incas and then they wove it." Since weaving had already been dealt with on Cord 11, I think this final comment was not a twenty-seventh cord but a transitional observation to what followed, that is, a record of what the Chupaychu now owed their *encomendero*. The main burden now was textiles, a commodity easily convertible in both the European and the Andean economies.[19]

Reviewing the preceding 26 cords, we find that Chupaychu articulation to Cusco was pervasive and continuous. Some have tried to deal with the figures arithmetically, adding the numbers of "Indians" contributed.[20] This is not my aim since the numbers are not comparable: They reflect differences in the skill of craftsmen, length of service, managerial responsibilities, age and social status of the *mit'ayuq*, and prestations at distant Cusco or places nearby.

I do find suggestive the order and clustering of ethnocategories and the proportions of total population. The use of the decimal terminology used for bookkeeping is rare in our sources, though casual references are frequent. The multiples of four (the number of the subdivisions, *waranqa*-strength, of the Chupaychu), used to calculate the proportions of how many *mit'ayuq* were owed, are unique to my knowledge in the Inka corpus.

The next step would be to compare the Chupaychu account with *khipu* recording the "services" owed by other ethnic groups. Recent research indicates that some polities incorporated by Tawantinsuyu were excused from some or most of the tasks listed on the preceding cords. Their lords proudly proclaimed that they did no farming, herding, "hill-moving," porterage, or entertaining at court because of their military skill and long service in the wars of the distant north (where the Chupaychu also fought—Cords 6, 7, and 25).[21]

In contrast, other ethnic groups from the coast were excluded from participation in war—either for insufficient political loyalty or out of considerations of altitude.[22] The unusually heavy tasks owed by the Chupaychu so far from their homes must be seen in this diversified ethnic context. As long as *khipu* records remain so scarce among our sources, it will be difficult to determine how accurate or how representative the Chupaychu claims were, or how reliable the translator and the scribe.

Whatever their reasons in 1549 to exaggerate the heaviness of their burdens, there is no reason to assume that what the clerk recorded was a complete account of every kind of *mit'a* owed. An understandable omission so soon after the "pacification" is that there is no mention in the record of the state shrine at Huanacauri, located by the Inka in Chupaychu territory.[23] Thirteen years later, by which time the bulk of the population had been baptized, several of the same witnesses who had testified in 1549 appeared again before an inspector, who had been sent from Lima to conduct a house-by-house inquiry. Interviewed in 1562, the lords stated routinely that indeed, in heathen times, the Inka shrine had had its own fields, producing maize and coca leaf. These had been cultivated by villagers sent in rotation from the same Chupaychu settlements listed in 1549. One of the witnesses also mentioned full-time custodians, the women of the shrine, *mamakuna*, "*mugeres que la guardavan.*" Although the Europeans who looted and vandalized the Inka shrine were supposed to have "freed" these guards, 30 years later one old woman and her 50-year-old son were still reported at the site, "since Inka times."

Another task that remained unlisted on the *khipu* read into the record of 1549 was road building. In the 1562 inspection don Diego Xagua reported that they had built and maintained their share of the royal highway (two days' walk to the west and were also responsible for the section of the road that led to the Huanacauri temple—it ran through their valley.[24] The same lord reported the unique detail that the shrine had no herds of its own: When sacrificial animals were needed, they were supposed to be drawn from the herds of Cord 13.[25]

Finally, one should mention, if only in passing, the absence from the 1549 *khipu* of any mention of the staple, highland tubers, which we know were grown above the Huallaga Valley floor. They may well have been included on Cord 26.

The most impressive feature of this early record is the clarity with which it confirms the principle of "no tribute in kind" owed the Inka state. If we compare this with what the Chupaychu owed their *encomendero*, we see that only 7 years after the European occupation of Huanuco virtually all entries on the colonial *khipu* dealt not with time or energy but with commodities: cloth, food, wax, and imported hens. Only in the thirteenth position on the colonial list do we find a statement about a prestation in energy. By then, the *encomendero*, one Gomez Arias de Avila, had accepted the notion that if he wanted finished textiles, he was to provide the wool, like the Inka before him.

Canta

Since so few transcripts of the many *khipu* the inspectors had been ordered to record in 1549 are available to date, I thought I would consider here some of the others that have turned up.[26] The first is a much briefer list, part of a perfunctory inquiry. Many more ethnocategories are omitted by the witnesses, the inspectors, or both. It is likely that this transcript from Canta reflects different obligations to Cusco; it is also possible that the Atawillu, whose nucleus was Canta, were reacting to the fact that the 1535–1549 period had been much harder on them since they lived so much closer to Lima.[27] Everywhere in this country the inspectors report almost as many still thatched but empty houses as were then occupied.

The first question, inevitably, dealt again with precious metals,[28] which the Canta lords answered without giving either the number of miners in Inka times or the proportion they represented of the seven Atawillu *parcialidades*, so no comparison is possible with the Huánuco answers.[29] The lords of Canta confirmed that the whole production was turned over to *"los mayordomos que alli tenia puestos el ynga."*

Once past the miners, the list of what they owed each year is stated in European commodity phrasing, not as time devoted to Cusco:

[Cord 1] 100 sheep [camelids]
[Cord 2] 50 woolen garments, for women and men

This reproduces the sequence of the Wanka *khipu* of 1560, mentioned earlier, where camelid herding and weaving follow each other, both early in the knot record.

[Cord 3] 10 large sacks of coca leaf
[Cord 4] 10 large sacks of hot peppers

As in the case of the Chupaychu, (their Cords 17 and 15), these *yunga* crops are recorded after weaving and herding. Although the Canta were a highland group, their territories also extended into the middle Chillón Valley to gain access to warmer lands where coca leaf, fruit, and cotton could be cultivated. Some of these settlements were multiethnic.[30]

[Cord 5] 100 pairs of *oxota* ["sandals"] of *cabuya* fiber

This corresponds to Cord 19 of the Huánuco list and Cord 16 on the Wanka record. In both of these accounts, sandals are knotted on after cloth and before food production.

[Cord 6] 50 loads of *charqui*
[Cord 7] 100 *pocchas* of maize and all this they sent to Cuzco[31]

As in the Huánuco case, work that produced good and services for Cusco is recorded separately, and prior to the energy expended at the regional installations of the state.

[Cord 8] and they also gave 50 Indians for war and they went with him [the Inka]
[Cord 9] 100 Indians as bearers

These correspond to the macrocategory of Cords 22–25 of the Chupaychu *khipu*, so the approximate sequence is respected. No indication is given as to which administrative center is involved.[32]

[Cord 10] ten women and ten men, their brothers, for *sus* yanaconas[33]

The fact that the women are listed first may imply that they were "chosen" (*aqlla*); in that case their "brothers" would be the equivalents of the "guards" on Cord 24, listed for Huanuco Pampa. In some ways, this last cord from Canta is the most interesting one since it can also be read that the *yana* were pairs, not couples.

This is a disappointingly short list. Although question 8 of La Gasca's inquiry had asked for "what things and tribute they were used to giving the ynga and the other lords they may have had,"[34] the Canta list omits the whole first group of cords (Chupaychu 1–8), those dealing with duties in and for Cusco and the crown. It is, of course, possible that the Canta owed fewer and different duties from those of the polities in the Huallaga Valley. We know that the Inka had favored their neighbors', the Yauyu's, claims to hegemony in this region, against the Canta.[35] A village-by-village reinspection, which was ordered 4 years later in 1553, offered no further clues to Cusco-Canta relations but stressed the terrible depopulation.

However, there is one dimension of the Canta inspection that may turn out to be a major contribution to Inka economics: the willingness of those from Canta to give details about state lands and herds in their territories.

Elsewhere, queries about such crown holdings are turned away or answered in Andean manpower terms (see Cords 14 and 26, the Chupaychu *khipu*). In Canta the 1553 inspectors asked the surviving lords about Inka acreage and were told that locally there were "19 fields of potatoes and *caby*[36] planted . . . about one and a half fanegas and in the said fields they now plant the tribute . . . and they also declared a fanega and a half of maize." Elsewhere in the region, at Racas, they admitted the Inka alienation of two more fields of potatoes, "up to one *mati* [calabash] of seed and two fields of maize, up to another *mati* worth of seed."[37] The informants stress the small size of the state's acreage, knowing that the Europeans saw themselves as the heirs to Inka royal lands and those of the solar cult. Beyond such maneuvering in self-defense, the answer opens the possibility that the acreage alienated by Cusco need not have been extensive in every region.

Caraveli

The hope of unraveling the rights in land of the state and the royal lineages in the many conquered "provinces" is fed by the fact that such fields lead all answers on the third and last *khipu* from 1549. This time the witnesses came from Caraveli, which is located on the western slope some 200 km north of Arequipa and well to the south of any of the information quoted earlier. This ethnic group, which included the coastal settlement of Atico, was part of the Kuntisuyu quarter of the Inka state.[38] The questions and answers were again quite perfunctory since the questionnaire was administered in Arequipa, not in the field. None of the information is stated in the decimal vocabulary.

[Cord 1] They had the custom to plant the fields of ynga in their own country and [also] maize and one year they carried 100 loads to Cuzco and in another 50 and the rest they kept in storage until he sent for it, when they delivered it.

As on the Chupaychu *khipu*, the witnesses are stating the prestation in terms of labor owed, not tribute in grain. As will be seen later in Cord 3, the interviewers will insist and eventually manage to get the answer they wanted—tribute in kind.

[Cord 2] and the ynga sent them wool and they wove *cumbi* cloth for him and they took it wherever he ordered

Qunpi textiles were a high quality cloth, woven by specialized craftspeople. Confirming what we saw for the Chupaychu and the Canta, the authority must supply the fiber. Although at Xauxa and Canta the weaving and herding cords were hung close together, there is not mention of camelids at Caraveli.

[Cord 3] and they gave tribute to the ynga of all the things which they planted and harvested in their territories and they took it to him, wherever he was

I doubt if this statement corresponds to a cord on the Caraveli *khipu*. It uses the last words of the previous cord and hangs a general obligation on it, which would validate "tribute."

[Cord 4] and from Guanca Velicas [in what today is Ecuador] they brought them some colored shells called *mollo*, out of which they carved figurines of men and women and also beads and usually they kept 50 Indians in Cuzco for this work[39]

If the artisans weaving the *qunpi* remained at home, the carvers were sent to the capital; no previous list of artists or craftspeople known from Inka studies mentions these Kuntisuyu specialists. *Mullu* shells usually appear in ritual contexts, so the carvers doing their work in Cusco are a new dimension in the articulation of the ethnic group and the state.

Xagua's Testimony of 1562

The results of this 1549 harvest are still thin, but it does get us beyond the classical chronicles. As more of the 72 protocols of the 1549 inspection are located, we can expect additional detail since La Gasca's query about what local polities owed Tawantinsuyu was in all the questionnaires issued to the *visitadores*.

There is no reason to limit this study to the earliest instrument. Although there is no *visita general* for the 1550s, several published local inquiries (Damián de la Bandera in 1557; Castro and Ortega Morejón in 1558) indicate that valuable new information can still be expected on the topic of state-ethnic group relations from informants who were already adults in 1532. Several of the Chupaychu and Yacha lords testifying in 1562 were in this age group.

One survivor in the Huallaga Valley was Xagua, mentioned earlier as having been stationed in Cusco at the time of the European invasion. By 1562 he was "don Diego," and he testified in some detail about events he claimed to have witnessed. Since he had also been present at the inquiry in 1549, we can assume that he was aware of the discrepancies between what had been recorded on that *khipu* and his own testimony in 1562.

Xagua's testimony was that of a high-status man. What he recalls in 1562 has to do with others like himself, who had served the Inka king in person, not some faceless state. When he returned to Chupaychu country, he brought with him four *yana* retainers, whom he describes as *"orejones,"* southerners of high status, conceivably royals. It is unclear if he had received these four as a crown grant before 1532 or if he took advantage of disturbed conditions after that date to staff his compound. The Europeans were not the only ones to expand the *yana* category way beyond its pre-1532 proportion in the population.

Although there is no evidence that Xagua was reading from a *khipu*, which was done in 1549, he was also careful to distinguish between the *mit'ayuq* sent to the capital and those households doing their share in the home valley. The latter, he said, "gave" maize to be stored at Huañuco Pampa, the regional administrative center. Carrying it on "their backs" took them 7 days (counting, Andean style, the duration of the round trip). Xagua is more affirmative about just the things the 1549 *khipu* left vague: "The maize was harvested in this valley on the lands of the ynga which they [the Chupaychu] worked and from their own acreage they gave nothing." More than once Xagua insisted on this distinction. He also stressed coca leaf, "which they harvested in the Anti and it took them 9 days to put it into the warehouses of Huanuco [Pampa]." This is equivalent to Cord 17, cited earlier.

The Anti made him think of the wooden dishes (*mati de palo*) also placed in storage, and "salt and hot peppers and sandals and feathers from the Anti which they stored in the said Huanuco Pampa and the very good ones they took to Cuzco." (Cords 16, 15, 19, and 9, in that order, of the 1549 *khipu*). Earlier he had referred to *qunpi* cloth,

half of which went to the said Huanuco Pampa and the other half to Cuzco . . . and they also took out silver to send the ynga, from the town of the Yaros who now belong to don Antonio de Garay[40] and everything they dug up they gave the said ynga without keeping anything for themselves;

and they also extracted gold from the river of Ninamarca which is in the territory of these Indians, and in Tomarica, which also belongs to them, and everything taken out was also carried to Cuzco. . . . not daring to keep anything, given the serious punishment.

Were Xagua using a *khipu*, this would locate the miners somewhere among the artisans (Cords 19–21, *khipu* of 1549), a notion strengthened by the next and last group among those who fulfilled their *mita'a* without leaving the Huallaga Valley, that is, those making the ropes used in hunting. This may reenforce the perception of the beaters (Cord 18, 1549) as a kind of artisan.

At this point in his testimony Xagua reverted to those "serving" in Cusco, who according to him made weapons and *"camisas de plumas para la guerra"* and did not have to do anything else—a group of soldiers whose equivalent on the 1549 *khipu* may have been the 10 *yana* of Cord 5, who "guarded his weapons."

Then came the herders of the state (Cord 13) and others of the Sun;[41] the women selected for the state and for service to the solar cult—some of these were sent to Huanuco Pampa and the others to Cusco:[42] "and these had to be beautiful and of these the king awarded some as wives to those who seemed to lack them."

After the *aqlla* women, Xagua shifted back to artisans: potters for Huanuco Pampa (Cord 21, 1549 *khipu*). Among those located at Cusco, there were makers of litters for the Inka, "since they were masters at this," an item close to Xagua's priorities and his claims of proximity to the kings, a matter that had been ignored on the 1549 list. Finally, fish from highland lakes, which was dried and sent to the state warehouses.

He then concluded with a general statement:

> "All worked in the fields of the ynga and they hauled the maize they harvested and this was the rule also followed with coca leaf, gold and silver. . . . The said ynga did not set a fixed amount . . . beyond setting aside the lands on which they planted and it was he who fixed the number of those mining . . . and there were lords who directed those who worked."

A comparison of the two accounts, 13 years apart, confirms the absence of tribute and clarifies some of what was read into the record of 1549. It leaves one major discrepancy: what of the 400 (or even 800) Chupaychu households reported building and farming in Cusco? There is no trace of them in Xagua's survey. I have stated earlier my uneasiness about such a large proportion of able-bodied women and men working so far from home. As further sections of the 1549 inquiry come to light, we may be able to confirm or reject such proportions.[44]

La Visita General of 1571

Nothing as early and detailed as the Huánuco inspection is available to us in 1982 from other parts of the Andes. There are however two later sources, from 1567 and 1571, which may not be too late. Few informants who had been participant and well-informed adults in 1532 were still alive, but some had survived and could continue an oral tradition.

I shall begin with an account from an area close to Canta and also to the Quiwi gardens in the *chawpi yunga* above Lima, known to us in some detail from the litigation record indexed as *Justicia* 413.[45] The Guancayo, Macas, and Guarauni formed a small ethnic enclave occasionally mentioned in accounts of Lima's hinterland, but marginal to the 1549 inspection. They do, however, emerge as one of the polities whose account of what they owed the Inka state was recorded during the second great *visita general*, the one ordered by Viceroy Toledo in 1571.[46]

Toledo's questionnaire included a query about "tribute" owed "to the said ynga and the Sun and to the women of the ynga and in what items and what quantities and what services by the Indians."

So far as I am aware this inquiry is independent of the 1549 one, and there is no evidence that the interviewer had before him the answers given more than 20 years earlier.[47] Each set of answers continues to raise new issues, yet the grouping and ordering of topics is roughly similar and there is a suggestive overlap.

Although the 1571 protocol of the Guancayo inspection still uses a decimal framework, elsewhere by that date the European inspectors have managed to impose the "tribute in kind" vocabulary on their informants. According to the witnesses, each of the nine units of "one hundred" households is alleged to have "given":

[Cord 1] five large baskets of coca leaf [commodity which was knotted on Cord 3 of their neighbors from Quiwi]

[Cord 2] 26 *pilas*[48] of cotton clothing, half for men and the other half for women

[Cord 3] 2 pieças de *cumbi galanas*

All these are products easily convertible on the European market since the city of Lima was nearby.

[Cord 4] 3 hanegas of maize and

[Cord 5] 4 large baskets of hot peppers

As we saw on the previous *khipu*, listing textiles before food is routine. Coca leaf may well have belonged to this group, as it does on pages 242–43, but was probably pushed to the head of the list because of its convertibility.

[Cord 6] 20 pairs of sandals

[Cord 7] 10 boxes of small dried birds made into *charqui*

[Cord 8] 5 small reed boxes of coca leaf . . . for the ynga

[Cord 9] 2 small boxes of dried crayfish for ynga

[Cord 10] 3 small boxes of dried guabas and

[Cord 11] 10 pairs of wooden *rodejones* for the members of the royal lineages and

[Cord 12] 1 elegant blanket of cotton to be used as a hammock . . .

Most of the items are coastal products, probably grown on state lands; only the crayfish seem to be "raw."[49] The elegant blanket may be an afterthought and belongs with Cords 2 and 3.

Like the Canta and Caraveli lists, this may seem too skimpy when compared with the first Chupaychu *khipu*. Still, it does have its unique features: Whereas the earlier knot records evaded mentioning the *mit'a* prestations owed the solar and other cults, the 1571 account reports a *huertecilla* planted to coca leaf, which was offered to the Sun while the leaf was still green. In passing, we note that this report has the advantage of reverting to an Andean statement of obligation: The solar cult had its patch, and the harvest was burned for its benefit. The Guancayo account is also a contribution to the debate about the comparative size of state and cult holdings: Although most European sources ignored the issue, Polo de Ondegardo compared their respective warehouses and concluded that the Sun's acreage was much smaller.

Martinez Rengifo's informants proceed to answer the question about the support provided to the king's women, presumably those residing in the region: Each of the nine "hundred households" turned in 10 *poccha* of maize, which is 4 more than the same informants claimed they owed the royal warehouses. The ladies also received an equal amount of beans, 10 pots large and small, and 5 loads of cotton they were expected to spin. I cannot tell if the *khipu* recording these obligations is a continuation of the previous one, or if it is a separate account. I note that it lists food before textiles.

After the cotton, one expects to hear about wool, since the very next cord read into the record talks about the 300 head of camelids that all the Guancayo and their neighbors "guarded" on the king's behalf. But all we hear is that the royal women ate the meat. This makes the informant think of food, and he records that they also received pumpkins, manioc, and hot peppers.

At this point, possibly in response to the question about "services," the custodian of the *khipu* returned to what I take to be the main account:

[Cord 13] the whole *repartimiento* gave three brave men, sons of the three lords, for the ynga's service.

[Cord 14] another three to guard the said women

[Cord 15] and from the said *repartimiento* 10 good-looking women chosen to be the king's *mamakuna*[50]

Two Lupaqa Testimonies

The last account in this series is not strictly comparable since it deals with a much larger ethnic group, a rival of the Inka for Andean hegemony a few generations earlier. It also was located in a very different environment from all previously mentioned *khipu:* the *altiplano* of Lake Titicaca. Despite these differences, I could not forego its use since the series available to us in 1982 is so short.

Several Lupaqa informants provide testimony of interest in this context, but I will refer only to two: Cutinbo and Vilca Cutipa. In 1567, the first was the senior upper-moiety lord, a man who earlier had ruled both halves during 16 crucial years. Although he was already a young adult at the European invasion, he now spoke Spanish and could sign his name; he may even have been literate. The second was the senior lord of one of the seven "provinces" of the Lupaqa polity. He claimed to have fought in the northern campaigns of the Inka and was now a centenarian.

Cutinbo

Cutinbo reported that "at times" they gave Cusco 3,000 men for war; for the fighting around Tumbes they had "given" 2,000. In a civil war between two Inka "brothers" the Lupaqa had sent 10,000, and only 7,000 had come back. Even though the "last Inka *khipu*" listed 20,000 Lupaqa households, the proportions quoted are very high. I will stress here the "3,000 men" statement and consider it the first cord, since it came in response to the questionnaire administered by Garci Diez de San Miguel, a formal occasion. When Vilca Cutipa was asked the same question, he assessed the obligation at 6,000, which could be the same proportion if the army was made up of both genders.[51]

[Cord 2] At other times they gave him all the Indians he demanded, to make walls and houses.

Construction work in Cusco was listed first on the Chupaychu *khipu*. Other Aymara-speaking groups, who claim to owe no duties beyond military service, specify that they were exempt from "making walls."[52]

[Cord 3] and for his service

I assume that "all the Inka demanded" in the preceding would also apply to this cord. We may want to come back to these "services."

[Cord 4] and sons to be sacrificed and virgins to serve him and the Sun and Moon and Thunder.

These may well be more than one cord. Like other post-1549 informants, Cutinbo was willing to talk about heathen practices since he had been baptized and was known to get along with the Dominican friars settled among the "Emperor's Yndians," as the Lupaqa were called.

[Cord 5] and clothing
[Cord 6] and they worked for him many fields

Where the first four cords referred to duties owed away from the lake, Cords 5 and 6 deal with local prestations.

[Cord 7] and they gave him gold and silver and the gold came from Chuquiago and the silver from the mines at Porco . . . and lead . . . a red varnish called *llimpi* and copper

This list may also refer to more than one cord. Note that here again mining is listed after weaving and agriculture.

[Cord 8] and feathers . . . and many partridges and *charqui* and ducks from the Lake and fish from it reached Cuzco which is 60 leagues [300 km] away in two days

I have grouped together all these items in the order in which they were strung by Cutinbo; they seem to form a "raw" macrocategory. In the text the feathers are separated from the partridges by an aside: "Whatever he asked for, they gave him, he being their lord." One can interpret this aside as referring specifically to the "raw" commodities for which there was no set proportion or a quota for energy expenditure.

[Cord 9] The very first quinoa to ripen was taken by 100 men who carried it, singing, from here to Cuzco.

"Gifts" of this kind are frequently listed in a ritual context by the European eyewitnesses describing the Inka. Cutinbo is one of our best informants.[53]

[Cord 10] and they gave him a large amount of clothing to be sacrificed to the Gods

The separate listing of this clothing from the textiles on Cord 5 may be an afterthought elicited by the ritual context, but I am quite prepared to believe that these two kinds were enumerated in different categories of Inka bookkeeping.[54]

[Cord 11] and they gave him sheep [camelids] for the ceremonies . . . of the ynga . . . when they pierced their ears and the first time they cut their hair

Vilca Cutipa

The list of the centenarian, Vilca Cutipa, is similar, and I will not reproduce it in detail. Like Cutinbo, he listed the soldiers first, followed by precious metals. Then follow men and women "for service"; he specified that sometimes they gave 100 and at others 200; also builders and clothes. In an aside, missing in the other account, the old gentleman reminds us that those who worked for the Inka were fed "meat and maize and cornbeer[55] . . . and he treated them very well." Such institutionalized hospitality is claimed from hearsay by many European chroniclers; it is useful to have it confirmed by a participant.

Vilca Cutipa then reported men for sacrifices and "daughters of the lords" for concubines, before getting to the fields of potatoes and kinoa that they worked for the Inka. He also listed the state's herds, which had escaped Cutinbo's notice or more likely his scribe's. Then followed the fish—both fresh, hauled "with much diligence", and dried.

Vilca Cutipa also states that, apart from the youths meant for sacrifice and other religious purposes, mitmaq colonists were also given when requested. He adds the crucial detail that "if some of these died, they gave them others." Since Lupaqa mitmaqkuna were shipped off as far as Jauja, Quito, Yucay, Cochabamba, and even Chile, this was a heavy burden.

Qunpi cloth is again listed separately from clothing, late in the khipu, and it was woven by specialists; "and everything else asked for they gave, even salt and feathers and all this . . . they gave as a province, allotted by ayllos."[56]

Summary and Conclusion

A comparison of the obligations owed by the conquered polities to Tawantinsuyu, reveals no major deviation from what has become familiar: The chief source of state revenues was the *mit'a,* an energy expenditure by the many ethnic groups on alienated state lands. The *mit'a* included herding Cusco's camelids, weaving the many kinds of cloth, and gathering the "raw" products of forests and lakes.[57]

The series being so short, the new data do not solve the questions about proportion of total land alienated following incorporation into the Inka state. For example, we cannot confirm or deny any known quota for land alienated, as suggested by Castro and Ortega Morejón. Nor do we know if this initial alienation could be followed by later ones; the litigation recorded in *Justicia* 413 says this could happen. The holdings of "rebels" could and were confiscated.[58]

This survey has stressed the persistence of many ethnic groups and their "indirect" rule by Tawantinsuyu. Traditionally, and also at the Stanford gathering recorded in this book, this articulation has been seen from a Cusco-centric point of view since that is what the Europeans' chroniclers' informants have provided. A first breakthrough came with Marcos Jiménez de la Espada's efforts: He published Salcamayhua's Andean version and also the *Relaciones Geográficas.* Additional incentive for changing our approach became available in 1920 when Domingo Angulo began to print in installments the 1562 inspection of the Chupaychu, filled out in 1955 by Marie Helmer. Since then it has been easier to see Tawantinsuyu from the inside.

It is likely to become a productive point of view, generating curiosity about additional local resources and more *khipu* records. It may also provide additional information about the profound changes the Inka state underwent as it stretched to incorporate ethnic polities from Mendoza to Carchi. Some of these changes are familiar;[59] others were freshly analyzed at this gathering. What some would fashionably call a new mode of production could well have been emerging in the final decades of Inka rule. One of the major ways the ethnologist can contribute to its study is to focus the attention on the component ethnic groups and their fate before 1532.

Notes

[1]Murra [1955], 1980.

[2]Marie Helmer [1955], 1967. One of the earliest settlers in the region, Juan Sanchez Falcon, testified that he had taken part in the capture of Illa Thupa, leader of the resistance (Archivo General de Indias, LIMA 254).

[3]In one case we do find the quantitative information grouped into Andean categories: W. Espinoza has published records of litigation initiated by the Wanka against the European authorities. Their brief includes the sworn transcription of a *khipu* admitted in

evidence to support their claims against their former European allies (1971–1972). I have commented on these ethnocategories in an article honoring Gonzalo Aguirre Beltrán (1974; reproduced in Murra 1975).

[4]In the last few years some additional fragments of this inspection have come to light—see Rostworowski 1975, 1978; Galdós 1977.

[5]See below, testimony of don Diego Xagua, lord of all the Chupaychu after 1560.

[6]Gordon Hadden has studied the ethnographic equivalences of the decimal system (in Ortiz [1562], 1967:pp. 371–380). He showed that the "hundred households" who in theory formed a *pachaka*, corresponded to five identifiable, neighboring hamlets, all belonging to one ethnic group. How fragile this decimal overlay was can be deduced from the protocol of the 1562 inspection of the very same region: Only 13 years after the first, virtually all references to the *waranqa*-level of organization have disappeared.

[7]D. E. Thompson, in Ortiz [1562], 1967:pp. 357–362.

[8]See the testimony of Xulca Condor, lord of the Queros, who stated, "*que en tiempo del ynga Guayna Capa eran de la guaranga que se decia los yachas que eran mil yndios y despues Guascar ynga los dividio y junto estas tres pachacas con los chupachos.*" (Ortiz [1562], 1967:pp. 41 and 191).

[9]The transcription used here follows without altering the order of the 1549 testimony, as recorded by the scribe. The clustering and the numbers assigned to the cords are my own.

[10]In a seminar that analyzed this *khipu* in the spring of 1976, at the Ecole des Hautes Etudes en Sciences Sociales, Paris, don Guillermo Lohmann Villena indicated his skepticism about these figures. If many other ethnic groups sent similar proportions of their population to Cusco, there would literally have been no place for them to stand.

[11]*Yana* were not absent from the Chupaychu countryside. In 1549 Xagua was not yet the don Diego he would become by 1562, but already he reported that he had four *yndios orejones* he had brought back from Cusco, where the invasion of 1532 had found him.

[12]It is probable that Cords 1 and 2 formed a single macrocategory. See Murra 1975, article 9.

[13]As before, I assume that those enumerated on Cord 5 (as well as those on Cord 3) were not *yana* at all. The Europeans had an interest in creating more *yana* than had ever existed before 1532. See Murra 1975:article 8.

[14]See Murra 1975:p. 251.

[15]The Wanka *khipu* deserves much closer examination than it has received to date. It was first observed in use by Cieza de León in 1547; 13 years later it was read into the record at Lima. It eventually found its way to the Peninsula, on appeal to the *Consejo de Indias*. The ethnocategories used by both state and ethnic *khipu* custodians for their records were not random: "*Las cosas ivan puestas por su orden enpeçando de las de mas calidad i procediendo hasta los menos.*" (Calancha [1639], Bk. I, ch. xiv; p. 90).

[16]Murra 1975, cuadro IV, facing p. 252.

[17]For storage at the administrative centers, see Morris 1967; 1978.

[18]In Huánuco (1963–1966) we followed the Inka road both north and south of Huánuco Pampa. See Morris 1966. The Institute of Andean Research has sponsored a long-range study of the Inka highway system, conducted by Dr. John Hyslop. He surveyed the whole distance between Pumpu and Huanuco Pampa, mentioned by the *khipu.*

[19]In Ortiz [1562], 1967:p. 307–308.

[20]Helmer 1955; Mendizábal 1966.

[21]Espinoza Soriano 1969; Murra 1978.

[22]Rostworowski 1977.

[23]This state shrine was located during fieldwork in the Huánuco region in 1963–1965. Unfortunately, the permit to excavate this provincial manifestation of the state religion was not utilized.

[24]Ortiz [1562], 1967:p. 27.

[25]Ortiz [1562], 1967:p. 30. See also Murra 1960.

[26]One is the inspection of the Atawillu, known also as "those of Canta," an ethnic group who formed Francisco Pizarro's own *encomienda* in the *cordillera* above Lima.

Two other inspection reports from the same period are reproduced in the *Anales Científicos* of the Universidad del Centro, no. 4, 1975. One of them was located by María Rostworowski, the other by Waldemar Espinoza. Mrs. Rostworowski was also kind enough to allow the use of the Canta *khipu* before it was published.

[27]The Atawillu were, like the Wanka, some of the earliest allies of the Europeans. Both their numbers and their resources were badly depleted in the physical construction of Lima and in supplying the new capital.

[28]The questionnaire used in 1549 has been reproduced by Waldemar Espinoza 1975:pp. 52–57.

[29]The Canta inquiry does not use the decimal vocabulary so we cannot be sure that *parcialidades* refers to *pachaka*, but from the detailed description of settlements and houses I am inclined to accept this gloss.

[30]All this is based on material from AGI, *Justicia* 413, which I was able to consult courtesy of María Rostworowski. See her 1972, 1977, and 1978 work. See also Murra 1975, article 3.

[31]The *poccha* was a measure equivalent to half of a *fanega*. See Gonzalez Holguin [1608], 1952:p. 291; Rostworowski 1962:p. 106.

[32]It was probably Pumpu, near today's Cerro de Pasco.

[33]It is uncertain if *sus* referred to the women's kin or "his," meaning the Inka's.

[34]Espinoza 1975:p. 55.

[35]Rostworowski 1972.

[36]"Kaui"—*el caui, ocas pasadas al sol* (Gonzalez Holguin [1608], 1952:p. 139.

[37]Measuring the size of a field by the amount of seed it would take to plant it, is reported both from the peninsula and the Andes.

[38]Galdós Rodríguez 1977.

[39]*Mullu* are *Spondylus* mollusks that live in the warm waters of the Gulf of Guayas and near the island of La Plata. They were the object of major coastal traffic. See Rostworowski 1970 and 1977; Murra [1971], 1975, article 10; Paulsen 1974; Marcos and Norton 1979.

[40]The Yarush lived in what today is the mining country near Cerro de Pasco. For ethnohistorical detail, see Espinoza 1975.

[41]Earlier I quote the same Xagua claiming that the Huanacauri shrine had no herds of its own—see note 25.

[42]These women were not listed on the 1549 *khipu*, although Cord 24 enumerated their "guards." I interpret this as part of reluctance to speak of religious matters soon after the European victory.

[43]The translation by the Greek interpreter is recorded as "*habian de ser hermosas y que de estas daba el ynga por mujeres a los yndios que a el le parecia que no las tenia.*"

[44]In note 13, I indicated my belief that those serving in Cusco were not *yana*. I continue to feel that way about the masons and cultivators, but Xagua's testimony makes one rethink the claim on Cord 5 that some of those in Cusco had been permanently removed from Chupaychu jurisdiction.

[45]This record of litigation filed in the Archivo de Indias, in Seville, has been copied at least twice—by María Rostworowski and Pierre Duviols.

[46]Waldemar Espinoza (1963) published the text of this *visita* by Juan Martinez Rengifo.

[47]In some inspections, for example Diego Alvarez's *visita* of the Chupaychu [1557], the inspector did have before him earlier protocols.

[48]Waldemar Espinoza suggests that this be read *pieças*.

[49]See Murra 1975, article 9.

[50]Another reading of this account would place the Sun cord and the eight strings referring to items given the king's women as part of the main record. Note that these women and their guards appear at the end of the *khipu*, just as they did on the one from Canta.

[51]For more on the army, see Murra 1978.

[52]Espinoza Soriano 1969.

[53]See his discussion comparing the Andean and the European ways of calculating populations, in Diez de San Miguel [1567], 1964:p. 170.

[54]Murra 1962.

[55]In context, all these were sumptuary foods.

[56]Diez de San Miguel [1567], 1964:p.

[57]See chapters V and VI of Murra [1955], 1980.

[58]Murra 1978.

[59]Murra [1955], 1980:ch. VIII.

References

Alvarez, Licenciado Diego
  1557   *Visita* of the Chupaychu. Unpublished manuscript used by Iñigo Ortiz [1562].
Calancha, Antonio de
  1639   *Coronica moralizada del orden de San Agustin en el Peru.* Barcelona.
Diez de San Miguel, Garci
  [1567], 1964   *Visita hecha a la provincia de Chucuito.* Lima: Casa de la Cultura del Perú.
Espinoza Soriano, Waldemar
  1963   La guaranga y la reducción de Huancayo. *Revista del Museo Nacional* (Lima) **32**:8–80.
  1969   El "memorial" de Charcas [1582]. *Cantuta* (revista de la Universidad Nacional de Educación, Chosica, Perú).
  1971–1972   Los huancas aliados de la conquista. *Anales Científicos* (Universidad del Centro, Huancayo) no. 1:9–407.
  1975   Ichoc–Huanuco y el señorío del curaca Huanca en el reino de Huanuco. *Anales Científicos* (Universidad del Centro, Huancayo) no. 4:7–70.
Galdós Rodríguez, Guillermo
  [1549], 1977   "Visita a Atico y Caraveli. *Revista del Archivo General de la Nación* (Lima) nos. 4–5.
Gonzalez Holguin, Diego
  [1549], 1952   *Vocabulario de la lengua general de todo el Peru.* Universidad de San Marcos, Lima.

Hadden, Gordon J.
1967   Un ensayo de demografía histórica y etnológica en Huánuco. In *Visita de la provincia de León de Huánuco* by Iñigo Ortiz de Zúñiga [1562]. Huánuco. Pp. 369–380.
Helmer, Marie
1955   La visitación de los indios Chupachos: Inka et encomendero, 1549, *Travaux*, Institut Français d'Etudes Andines, Paris–Lima. (Reproduced in *Visita de la provincia de León de Huánuco* by Iñigo Ortiz de Zúñiga [1562], 1967.)
Marcos, Jorge, and Presley Norton
1979   Excavations at La Plata island, Ecuador. Paper read at the XLIII International Congress of Americanists, Vancouver, British Columbia.
Mendizábal, Emilio
1966   Continuidad cultural y textilería andina. Unpublished thesis, Universidad de San Marcos, Lima.
Morris, Craig
1966   El tampu real de Tunsucancha. In *Cuadernos de investigación* (Vol. I). Universidad de Huánuco.
1967   *Storage in Tawantinsuyu.* Unpublished thesis, Department of Anthropology, University of Chicago.
1978   L'étude archéologique de l'échange dans les Andes. *Annales (ESC)* (Paris) **33** (5–6).
Murra, John V.
[1955], 1980   *The economic organization of the Inka state.* Greenwich, Conneticut: JAI Press.
1962   Cloth and its functions in the Inca state. *American Anthropologist* **64:** 710 - 728.
1974   Las etno-categorías de un khipu estatal. In volume honoring Gonzalo Aguirre Beltrán, published by the Instituto Indigenista Interamericano, México. (Reproduced in Murra 1975.)
1975   *Formaciones económicas y políticas en el mundo andino.* Instituto de Estudios Peruanos, Lima.
1978   La guerre et les rébellions dans l'expansion de l'état inka. *Annales (ESC)* (Paris) **33** (5–6).
Ortiz de Zúñiga, Iñigo
[1562], 1967, 1972   *Visita de la provincia de León de Huánuco.* (2 vols.). Huánuco.
Paulsen, A. C.
1974   "The thorny oyster and the voice of God: Spondylus and Strombus in Andean prehistory," *American Antiquity* **39:**597–607.
Rostworowski, María
1970   Mercaderes del valle de Chincha en época prehispánica: un documento y unos comentarios. *Revista Española de Antropología Americana* (Madrid) **5:**135–178.
1972   Etnías Guancayo en el valle de Chillón. *Revista del Museo Nacional* (Lima) **38:**250–314.
1975a   Pescadores, artesanos y mercaderes costeños en el Perú prehispánico. *Revista del Museo Nacional* (Lima) **41:**311–349.
1975b   La "visita" a Chinchaycocha. *Anales Científicos (Universidad Nacional del Centro, Huancayo)* **4:**73–88.
1977   *Etnía y sociedad: costa peruana prehispánica.* Instituto de Estudios Peruanos, Lima.

1978 *Señoríos indígenas de Lima y Canta.* Instituto de Estudios Peruanos, Lima.
Wachtel, Nathan
1981 Les *mitimas* de la vallée de Cochabamba. La politique de colonisation de Huayna Capac. *Journal de la Société des Américanistes* **66:**297–324. (Spanish version of same in *Historia Boliviana,* no. 1, Cochabamba).

PART IV

The Imposition of
Spanish Governance

 **10**

The Spanish and Indian Law: New Spain*

Woodrow Borah

Editors' Introduction

Woodrow Borah shows how litigation both shaped colonial policy toward Indians and changed Indian customs in ways not envisioned by policy. The various bodies of law developed by sixteenth-century Latin Christianity—Christian law, natural law, and law pertaining to other peoples known as *Ius Gentium*—did not in themselves establish policies for Spanish colonial rule. Borah describes how the crown steered policy between economic expediency and political pressures brought by colonial settlers and administrators. Although it began rather modestly to spread Christianity, implant settled town life, and harness Indian labor, Spanish crown policy unintentionally brought deeper changes in Indian life in the long run because the legal principles of appeal and accountability opened the use of colonial courts to Indians.

Quickly mastering Spanish legal procedures, Indians flooded the courts with litigation invoking Spanish concepts of property, succession, and inheritance, thereby altering major domains of Indian customary law. In response the viceroyalty simplified judicial remedies available to Indians, and by the end of the sixteenth century these procedural changes produced a separate jurisdiction for Indian legal business that codified the

*Both this chapter and a paper presented at the Las Casas Colloquium at the University of Notre Dame, October 1978, are derived from material gathered for a book on the General Indian Court of colonial Mexico to be published by the University of California Press.

THE INCA AND AZTEC
STATES, 1400–1800

emerging conception of Indians as *miserables*, "the wretched of the earth."

The Spanish conquest of what is now Mexico (and indeed of all regions of America that the movement reached) posed problems for Renaissance Europe for which it was not fully prepared. During the sixteenth century, a much clearer conception of the issues and theories for dealing with problems of colonialization evolved (Ayala 1945:302–321; García Gallo 1957–1958:613–680; Höffner 1957:3–84; Pérez de Tudela Bueso 1960–1961:140–151; Rumeu de Armas 1967:61–103) in a process that continues to the present. This chapter examines the conflict in the sixteenth century between the retention or destruction of native institutions and law and the imposition of European institutions and law.

Latin Christianity had reached a consensus at the end of the fifteenth century and the beginning of the sixteenth century on the general categories and applicability of law. Christian theory, derived from Roman theory and augmented by numerous glossators and theologians, held that there was *Ius Naturale*, binding upon all people. Furthermore, there was *Ius Gentium*, a common content of law and custom, that could be found in the practices of all peoples. Commentators differed upon the boundaries of these two categories, so that *Ius Naturale* tended to be enlarged by inclusion of much of *Ius Gentium*. Beyond these two basic categories lay a variety of human observance, all of it licit so long as it did not conflict with the previous two. Conversion to Christianity added further limitations (García Gallo 1955:135–512; Sánchez Gallego 1932–1933:41–51). In instances of individual conversion, the convert was bound to forsake the non-Christian law he had observed previously and adhere to the law of the Christian community he entered (Kirchner 1954:7–11; Wittram 1954:27). In instances of mass conversion, the converts might continue to observe their native law insofar as it was not contrary to what was regarded as *Ius Naturale, Ius Gentium,* and Christian requirements.[1] Polygyny, for example, is contrary neither to *Ius Naturale* nor *Ius Gentium* but is offensive to Christian precept. Differing forms of inheritance theoretically are in harmony with all categories, although attorneys in practice might persuade tribunals otherwise.

For dealing with the Indians of America, three schools of thought emerged among the Spaniards of the sixteenth century. Led eloquently by Francisco de Vitoria, one school held that the Indians, having developed their own society, were entitled to their own institutions and law. Should they come under the rule of a foreign sovereign, the sovereign was bound to uphold and defend existing institutions and laws and the rights of existing nobles and chiefs since he served as the native prince. The most that might be conceded in the way of imposed change was the minimum necessary for the extirpation of idolatry and the introduction of Christianity (Ballesteros 1945:618–621; León Romano 1553/1933:556–562; Vitoria 1539/1967:2–134). A second school, typified perhaps most expressively by Jerónimo de Mendieta, preached the idea of the two republics. Spaniards and Indians constituted two distinct commonwealths, each entitled to its own institutions and law. The Spainards were so corrupt and given to vice that the Indians should be kept as isolated as possible. Although their institutions and law should be modified to conform to Christianity and to ensure proper governance, the Indians should retain as much as possible of the old or be moved to a new that would be different from the world of the Spaniards (Mörner 1970:17–51; Phelan 1970:41–91; Ricard 1933:66–68; Zorita 1942:39–54).

A third view, held by crown jurists and most of the colonists, advanced the idea of one republic: The Indians should be assimilated as rapidly as possible into the European system and be moved thus to Castilian institutions and law. Although the adherents of this view never developed a rhetoric as eloquent as that of the first two views, the position had very real strength; in it lay obvious immediate economic utility to the crown and to the settlers. The crown jurists who held this view (Góngora 1951:210–211, 215–216) manned the courts and much of administration in the colony; they were also a major component of the royal bureaucracy in Spain. Agreement by the colonists may be seen, for instance, in the decision of the municipal council of Mexico City on December 16, 1552 that Indians might slaughter pigs freely and sell the meat in the city *"atento que los yndios son libres basallos de su magestad e que toda la republica es una."* (Mexico City 1884–1916 [Vol. 6]:79).

Official royal policy steered an ambiguous course among these schools. The position of the school of Francisco de Vitoria was strong medicine for a regime founded upon conquest, but the crown did enjoin its governors to preserve Indian organization and custom so long as they were not contrary to reason or Christian precept. In the first comprehensive regulations for the guidance of provincial governors in New Spain, issued in 1530, the crown expressly commanded continued observance of good Indian usages and customs. These regulations were to remain in force pending a report and review of Indian town polity for the purpose of deciding what to allow and what to delete (Puga

1563/1945:54ff.). Further, the crown was pledged to respect the rights of Indian rulers, nobility, and commoners; the rulers were no longer sovereign but were still entitled to respect and revenue; all ranks were entitled to security of possessions and good treatment.[2] On the other hand, the crown tried for some decades to keep Indians as separate as possible from Spaniards and Europeanized elements in the population and moved to settle the Indians in proper polity in new towns (Encinas 1596/1945 [Vol. 4]:247–252; Mörner 1970).

The difficulty of detecting clear lines in royal policy arises largely because there were few explicit formulations of it. The crown proceeded by decisions on specific cases and problems as they arose, the decisions setting a precedent for the future and for other regions of America (García Gallo 1964 [Vol. 1] :103). Also, royal policy itself changed; the crown found itself bound by theological and legal formulations that it was loath to transgress directly yet caught in issues not easily handled unless these formulations were transgressed or evaded. Moreover, it was beset by pressures to which it had to pay attention. The conquerors and settlers, who constituted the militia that had brought New Spain to the crown of Castile and kept the colony in submission, produced one of the major pressures. They had their own ideas and desires in dealing with the Indians. When in the matter of the New Laws the crown chose to flout their interests too directly and grievously, it learned a lesson that inhibited further drastic experiment for over two centuries.

Changes Brought to Indian Society by Spanish Rule

Whatever the theory or rhetorical justification, the imposition of Spanish rule meant sweeping change for the natives because the Castilian crown and its European subjects were responding to a series of imperatives that accompanied the imposition of an alien sovereignty, an alien religion, and an alien upper class. It was unthinkable that the crown permit continued practice of idolatry and human sacrifice or continued functioning of the old heathen religious hierarchies, which were deeply imbedded in the heathen political and social systems. The new monarch and his agents were bound to substitute the Christian religion and to establish a Christian hierarchy and religious territorial administration on the Latin model of the Western world. That meant not merely the profound wrench of substitution of one pervasive cement of native life for another of considerably different nature and the virtual obliteration of the culture-carrying stratum of native society, but also a new set of rules and tribunals controlling observance, belief, and family relations. The new Church's control of belief brought into play the episcopal Inquisition and, as a logical consequence, the burning at the stake of the *cacique* of Texcoco in 1539. However, that severity in a newly converted population led to revulsion and a royal order that the Indians not be subject to the jurisdiction of the Inquisition (Greenleaf 1963:68–75; Medina 1914 [Vol. 1] :140–186). Nevertheless, they remained subject to the ordinary episcopal courts for their expressions and lapses of belief (Greenleaf 1963:74–75, 1965 - 1966:138–166). Church jurisdiction over validity of marriage, including bigamy and forbidden degrees of real and fictive relationships, meant power to determine legitimacy and the right to inherit.

It was further unthinkable that the Castilian crown and its governors not replace the old native political superstructures and their administrative hierarchies. Thus, the imperial political structures of Tenochtitlan and its allies in the Triple Alliance, the Zapotec kingdoms, and the Tarascan state disappeared. In general, in all Indian towns the old native ruling dynasties and the Indian nobility were reorganized into *caciques* and *principales.* The *caciques* were forbidden to use the title *señor natural*, which was now reserved for the king; they were permitted to retain lands clearly in their patrimony and were assigned a moderate revenue from their former subjects (Encinas 1596/1945 [Vol. 4] 291; Gibson 1952:89–123, 1964; Spores 1967).

From the first, as is evident in the royal instructions to Diego Velázquez and to Hernán Cortés, the Crown enjoined that the Indians be settled in proper polity (Encinas 1596/1945 [Vol. 4] 247–252; Mörner 1970; passim). In practice, proper polity turned out to be a European-style town that was laid out in checkerboard fashion in accordance with the best European ideas of planning. Streets met at right angles, and church and administrative buildings were grouped around a central square. The town officials were a governor, a council, and lesser officials—again in European style that rendered the old native administrative hierarchies obsolete. The first instances of such towns may well have been the new settlements of Indian allies close to Spanish, such as San Martín Mexicapan and Santo Tomás Xochimilco near Huaxyacac for Mexican and Tlaxcaltecan Indians. These two towns had a Spanish-style government (Chance 1978:32) but may not have had the checkerboard layout. As far as we now know, the full model appeared in 1526 when the Franciscans founded the Indian town of San Francisco Acámbaro in Michoacán. The *Audiencia* confirmed the elections of officials and conferred the staves of office. In 1530 the crown instructed the *Audiencia* to appoint Indian *regidores* in Mexico City as well as in Indian towns and to use Indians as *alguaciles* for investigations. The intent was clear. Despite some difficulties in implementation, Indian government in New Spain was remade in a Spanish image, town by town, between 1530 and 1564. For a time the Indians tried to combine the old native hierarchy and the new Spanish one, but by the middle of the century, the new Spanish forms prevailed (Chevalier 1944:352–386; Encinas 1596/1945 [Vol. 4] 336; Gibson 1955:581–607, 1964:166–219). Their victory was greatly aided by a sweeping policy of relocating the Indian populations, who had been living until then in dispersed *rancherías* or on hilltops for defense, to valley settlements that were laid out in the new manner (Gerhard 1972, 1976 - 1977: 347 - 395; Miranda 1962:186–190).

The Spanish program for the reorganization of Indian society thus meant very considerable change even in the terms in which the crown and the clergy conceived of it—that is, as a relatively moderate program designed to implant Christianity, to harness the Indians to the service of the Spanish, and to cement Spanish rule beyond the possibility of reversing the conquest. But the changes, once initiated, set in process a revolution in native society that went far beyond what the royal bureaucracy and the clergy had contemplated. We can see now that the Spanish conquest called into question the relationships that had been firmly imposed during previous centuries. Occupation of land by one town rather than by a neighboring town or the dependence of a village upon a town could now be challenged by appeal to the Spanish. The reorganization of native society led to a bitter fight within it to obtain the most favored position; the circumstances challenged previous relationships and placed a premium upon Spanish favor (Miranda 1965:59–61, 71–72; Zorita 1942). Moreover, without malice but also without genuine understanding, the Spanish imposed a number of their own conceptions such as proper polity, the nature of ownership and use of land, the nature of slavery, and proper administration and relief within it.

Land Ownership

Proper polity and the far-reaching changes brought by imposing it have been sketched already. Differences in conceptions of land ownership and use also brought substantial change. For the Indians, land was essentially a means of production held by the community or clan and allocated to support certain offices or functions. Tenure fundamentally was conditional and subject to requirements of use. Indian conceptions of the nature of land holding most closely approximated those of the feudal linkage of land tenure to service or office. It is unlikely that aboriginal Indian society had any conception of land ownership in the sense of Roman law. According to that tradition, a man could be master of land that was his to allow to remain idle, destroy, or till as he chose; this was subject only to the right of the sovereign to tax or take for public use on due compensation. The Spanish, however, not only imposed the conception of land ownership embodied in the Roman or civil law but further declared that all land not actually occupied by Indians or used by them was vacant and so royal domain available for grant or purchase. For the Spanish, land was not merely a means of production. Ownership of stretches of it far larger than the owner could make use of directly or through tenants was a visible sign of prestige in the community and one of the few safe forms of investment. The result was a vast series of conflicts between Spanish and natives and far-reaching readjustments within the Indian towns as the more powerful and more alert members strove to assert and extend ownership in Spanish fashion usually at the expense of the peasantry and of other members of the preconquest upper class (Chevalier 1952:176–194; Esquivel Obregón 1937–1948 [Vol. 1] 369–374, 431, [Vol. 3] 173–218; Miranda 1965:69–72; Parry 1948:59).

Slavery

Similarly, slavery was another illustration of the way in which an almost unwitting imposition of a Spanish conception brought sweeping change, so that a fairly benign native institution became a harsh and destructive form of exploitation. Slavery existed widely among the preconquest Indians of northern Mesoamerica. It seems, in general, to have been a rather mild arrangement, which entitled the owner of the slave to service for life but left the slave very substantial rights. For example, a slave could have property and even own slaves himself. The only truly harsh aspect of aboriginal slavery was the selection of some slaves for fattening, sacrifice, and human consumption; however, this affected only a very small percentage of Indian slaves. Under Spanish law, on the other hand, slaves had far fewer rights. Civilly dead, they were chattels who might be worked like domestic animals, transported, and sold like any other form of merchandise. The Spanish equation of slavery under Indian custom with slavery under Castilian and civil law meant that Indian slaves could be subjected to merciless exploitation. Enterprising Spanish acquired Indian slaves by purchase, levy on tributary villages, or straight kidnapping, and worked them to death in mines or shipped them for sale to new and very different climates, where they soon died. Though this use of slaves was shortsighted, it was, for example, profitable enough to bring about the destruction of the Indian population in the Pánuco region. Until the danger was averted by royal legislation, the slave trade threatened to repeat the experience of the Antilles on the mainland. Finally put into effect in the 1550s, the legislation abolished Indian slavery save for fairly rare exceptions (Quiroga, July 24, 1535, in Colección 1864–1884 [Vol. 10] 370–372; Simpson 1940:3–14).

Administration and Appeal

One of the most important Spanish conceptions that affected Indian institutions and law was that of appeal against the acts of judicial and administrative officials; indeed any person, however high his status so long as he was not the monarch himself, could be brought into court. It is unlikely that preconquest Indian society had this concept, except in highly restricted and attenuated form. For the Spanish, on the other hand, the idea of appeal and accountability was part of the very fabric of the state. From the beginning of orderly royal administration under the Second *Audiencia*, the Indians of New Spain found that they could haul any official into court and challenge his decisions, that any grant of land could be disputed, that boundaries and political arrangements could be challenged, and that any private person or corporate entity could be held to redress for damage done or be forestalled through petition for an order of *amparo*. They found very quickly, furthermore, that any decision once rendered could be appealed up the long line of reviews provided by Castilian law. The conquerors thus placed a potent weapon at the disposal of the conquered, one that might be used against them as well as the subjected (Bishops of New Spain, 1565, in Colección 1864–1884 [Vol. 13] 288–289; Esquivel Obregón 1937–1948 [Vol. 1] 430–431; Mendieta, January 1, 1562 and October 8, 1565, in García Icazbalceta 1886–1892 [Vol. 1] 15–29, 43–50; Montúfar, May 15, 1556 in Paso y Troncoso 1939–1942 [Vol. 8] 85–87; Zorita 1942: 42–46). Fear of direct, extralegal reprisal and the reluctance of Spanish judges and officials to rule against fellow Spaniards undoubtedly limited its use against the whites, especially those of superior status, but the Indians made very great use of their right.

As early as 1531 the Second *Audiencia* reported to the crown that Indian cases, civil and criminal, were occupying a great deal of its time. Although the *Audiencia* tried to deal with the civil cases by as abbreviated a process as possible, the defeated parties promptly appealed, even to Spain; in criminal cases, long delays and lack of proper counsel prevented hearings and executions of decisions. The remedy of the *Audiencia* was to order that Indians not be charged fees because of their poverty. Nothing, however, could stop the flood of litigation, which the Spanish found astonishing in a people apparently so docile. To conduct suits, delegations of Indians, including bearers to carry supplies and women to prepare food, made their way to local capitals and on to Mexico City, where they remained for long periods. Expenses of the delegations and their accompanying servants, plus all the fees and gifts needed, were borne by the towns, usually through special assessments on the tributaries. The litigation favored the clever and the unscrupulous. Former rulers survived, if at all, as native bosses, and the more enterprising among their former subjects could aspire to replace them. Among the Spaniards, virtually the entire legal and notarial professions, which derived their sustenance from honoraria and fees, showed little objection to the rain of silver (Second *Audiencia*, August 14, 1531 and February 9, 1533, in Colección 1864–1884 [Vol. 41] 42 and Paso y Troncoso 1939–1942 [Vol. 3] 27–32 respectively; Henry Hawks in Hakluyt 1903–1905 [Vol. 9] 394; Vera Cruz, March 7, 1560, and Bustamante and Vera Cruz, July 26, 1561, in Vera Cruz 1968–1972 [Vol. 5] 167–169 and 177–187 respectively; Gante, February 15, 1552, in Spain, Ministerio de Fomento 1877:97–98; Zorita 1942:52–54).

The flood of native litigation brought about substantial replacement of native usages, despite formal recognition by the crown of their validity to the extent that they did not conflict with natural law, reason, or Christian doctrine (Clause 25 of the New Laws, 1542, in Colección 1864–1884 [Vol. 14] 376–460; Encinas 1596–1945 [Vol. 2] 166–167). Even though few records have been found thus far and most proceedings may never have been committed to written record, it seems likely that local custom would continue to be important at the lowest levels of native litigation and justice. The Indian *alcaldes* would be better versed in it than in Spanish law and would rely upon what they knew. Moreover, the community itself would insist upon its own custom. But at any point at which the dispute involved other communities or was carried before higher authority—especially when it came before a Spanish provinical justice, the *Audiencia*, viceroy, or the Council of the Indies—the situation changed; the higher the level, the more nearly was it reversed. Despite all prohibitions and limitations, the Indians resorted to *letrados*, solicitors, and other agents versed in Spanish procedures. They had to present the types of petition and testimony that Spanish law prescribed and that the Spanish authorities could understand. They had to pay fees and make gifts. Inevitably, the losing party appealed, and one party or the other based his claim upon Spanish practice and law. Equally inevitably in the long series of claims and counterlcaims, the Spanish authorities found themselves relying upon Spanish procedure and law rather than upon a strange native custom that could not be clearly ascertained because of widely conflicting testimony. In the end the native usage was likely to be held contrary to reason or Christian doctrine (Clause 14, Ordinances for Council of the Indies, 1571, in Colección 1864–1884 [Vol. 14] 415; García Gallo 1951–1952:613–618).

Indian Cases

We may classify the Indian cases that flooded the Spanish courts and the audience chambers of administrators into two primary categories: Church and royal. Church cases, which might involve civil litigation or criminal offenses under ecclesiastical law, covered such matters as tithes, marriage, and orthodoxy of belief and practice. All fell within the jurisdiction of Church tribunals, who functioned under Church rules of procedure and Canon Law, in a gradation of levels of jurisdiction beginning with the parish and extending through the diocese. There was even a theoretical but rarely used right of appeal to the Rota in Rome. Judges, lawyers, notaries, and secretaries qualified under Canon Law and held Church appointments. Recourse to the royal jurisdiction was possible through *recurso de fuerza*, the allegation that the Church jurisdiction was being exercised to abridge rights guaranteed by royal law. As far as one may judge from the little work done on such cases, the basic problems of Indian adaptation turned out to be much the same as in royal cases, so that in the end considerable adjustment to Indian needs and circumstances had to be made (García Gallo 1964 [Vol. 1] 85–86, 101; Greenleaf 1965–1966: 138–166; Maldonado 1954:281–290; Montúfar, September 18, 1555, in Paso y Troncoso 1939–1942 [Vol. 8] 42–45).

Royal cases fell into three basic groups: civil, criminal, and administrative—each with somewhat different law and procedure. Since the categories of cases within each group are vast and since our time and space are limited here, our examination must proceed by selection of illustrative categories.

Civil Cases

For civil cases a good illustration of the fate of Indian custom under Spanish rule is inheritance among the former rulers and their descendants, that is, the *tlatoque* reduced to *caciques*. Aboriginal custom in succession varied from region to region and even within regions but was seldom strictly patrilineal. In the Valley of Mexico inheritance more frequently moved through brothers before entering the next generation; an element of election existed among a group of potential heirs. In the Mixteca Alta eligibility for inheritance required descent from a ruler on both sides; for some towns, in default of a properly qualified person, inheritance returned to the original line of Tilantongo from which so many ruling houses sprang. Although these customs differed from Spanish law, nothing in them is contrary to natural law or Christian doctrine. Nevertheless, as disputes over succession were brought to Spanish judges for decision, the judges began to apply Spanish ideas of rights in inheritance, holding that the *cacicazgo* must go to the oldest son or, in default of a son, to the nearest heir by Spanish rule. Indian custom was refused validity as contrary to reason. One of the more interesting cases concerned the failure of qualified heirs eithin the direct line of the ruling house of Teposcolula. When one claimant advanced the pleas that the right of succession reverted to the parent house of Tilantongo in accordance with Mixtec custom, a claim that would seem to accord with Mixtec tradition, the Spanish judges dismissed it as contrary to reason. Inevitably, the proper heirs under Spanish ideas always could secure validation of their claims by recourse to a Spanish court. Indian custom, where contrary, gave way by the later sixteenth century to succession to *cacicazgos* through primogeniture on the Spanish model; possessions moved *en bloc* in a form of entail (Gibson 1952:74–75, 1955:587; Llaguno 1585/1962:152–153; Spores 1967:131–154).

Another important imposition of Spanish conceptions involved the right of pasture regardless of ownership of land, an issue that came into being with the introduction of livestock. Under Spanish custom, once crops were harvested, the stubble became common pasture that might be grazed by any livestock, however the peasants and towns objected. That kind of invasion would have given rise to much dispute in any case, but it was greatly intensified by the fact that much of the livestock wandered loose the year around and was rounded up only for branding and slaughter. Inevitably, Spanish livestock invaded Indian *milpas* even before the crop was lifted. Without fencing and guards, nearly feral animals could not be kept from the *milpas*, which were the best source of fodder available. In such instances of trespass and damage, Spanish law made available two avenues of redress: administrative complaint and civil suit. Both were used extensively by the Indians with varying success, but the right to graze on stubble without regard to land title remained (Chevalier 1952:102–114; Montemayor y

Córdova de Cuenca 1678 [Part 3] 17v–40r; Recopilación 1681/1943: IV:XVII:v–vii).

Criminal Cases

Our second group of cases within royal jurisdiction is criminal. The crown had planned from the beginning to take jurisdiction in this area. The crown's long-term policy in Spain, as in America, was to bring to royal judges all cases punishable by death or mutilation. Judgment or review in such cases was expressly reserved to the *Audiencia*. Royal judges thus found themselves forced to deal with a large number of Indian offenses against Indian custom. They had to decide whether to honor the custom or disallow it as contrary to reason or Christian practice. Many criminal offenses occurred as infractions of laws and ordinances that were new to the Indians or involved actions that under Indian custom were not considered improper. Many others occurred in the general weakening of Indian structures after the conquest and the development of the usual behavior of a subject race. However virtuous and well-behaved the Indians may have been in their relations with each other and the state power before the conquest, they astonished their conquerors by their proneness to theft, assault, homicide, rape, riot, drunkenness, and a host of other transgressions, most of which called for infliction of the more gory penalties of Spanish law.

The attempts of the crown and its officials to deal with the problem took a number of forms. One was to declare that verbal insults and blows delivered by the hand without any weapon should be considered matters for reprimand rather than trial and punishment (Puga 1563/1945: 56f). Another was to commute the more severe penalties such as death and mutilation. In 1531 Vasco de Quiroga urged that service in the mines be the substitute (Quiroga, August 14, 1531, in Colección 1864–1884 [Vol. 13] 425–426). With royal consent the *Audiencia* adopted a policy during the 1530s of branding and selling as slaves Indians convicted of crimes that otherwise would have been punished by mutilation, torture, service in the galleys, or death. This solution became impossible in the 1540s when the New Laws abolished Indian slavery. The *Audiencia* again laid the problem before the crown for decision, pointing out that the full rigor of the laws could not be enforced against the Indians, who were weak people and committed many crimes. When the crown persisted in demanding the full application of Spanish law (Prince Philip, October 28, 1548, in Konetzke 1953–1962 [Vol. 1] 248–249; Puga 1563/1945:121r), the *Audiencia* argued in 1553 that if the crimes of Indians were to be so punished the butchery of men in Mexico City would be greater than the slaughter of animals for food. In 1555 the crown gave way, although it did pay respect to the New Laws by stipulating that no Indian might be condemned to life service (Puga 1563/1945:155v–156r). Thereafter, sale of service became standard throughout New Spain as punishment for serious offenses by Indians (Borah and Cook 1958:38–46). The practice also provided a profitable source of labor for the Spanish community.

Administrative Cases

Our third major group of Indian cases falling within royal jurisdiction were those calling for administrative decision and remedy. Very often they involved a series of proceedings that at viceregal level were not easily distinguishable from judicial process, except that the final order was issued as an administrative decree. The number of administrative cases was enormous, perhaps exceeding all other kinds. Under administration fell grants of land and protests against them, protests against abuses by officials of Indian government as well as Spanish government, petitions for release from government restrictions (i.e., permission for an Indian to bear arms or ride a horse), most actions arising in *visitas* and *residencias,* and the issuance of the colonial version of the present-day writ of *amparo* (Archivo General de la Nación, Mexico City, ramos of Mercedes and Indios). The viceroys very soon found themselves devoting a considerable part of each week to hearing Indian petitions and ordering investigations (Mendoza, 1551, in Colección 1864–1886 [Vol. 6] 489, 490, 498–499, 504–505; Velasco, February 7, 1554, in Cuevas 1914:211–212). Provincial administrators must have been equally burdened, even if it was very often their own actions or failure to act that led to recourse to the viceroy.

The total amount of business represented by Indian cases of all kinds clearly was enormous and left untouched few of the more important aspects of Indian life. Further, the mass of Indian litigation and petitions served to nullify the recognition of Indian custom by the crown. Despite continuing injunctions validating Indian usage, Spanish procedure and law became the basis for handling Indian suits and complaints in royal courts and administration (Mendieta in García Icazbalceta 1886–1892: Vols. 1–5; Zorita 1942). Inevitably the European mode moved downward into native society, displacing the older native ways.

Proposals for Reform

The cautious validation of native custom, abortive though it proved to be, emobided a sincere desire on the part of the crown and at least some of its officials to ease the burden of the conquest upon the Indians and make their transition to Christianity and European polity as painless as possible. The same desire gave rise to a series of proposals that, although coupled in the beginning with injunctions to preserve native custom, in the end worked more effectively for adjustment within the new. These proposals basically involved simplification of procedures, avoidance of costs, and provision of special legal assistance. The three headings are hardly mutually exclusive, but they do point to the main directions.

Simplification of Procedures

Spanish legal proceedings were complicated and, in fact, represented a reduction to nonviolent dispute of the pageantry of a tourney. Presentation of complaint and answer, the gathering of testimony and counter-testimony, arguments by counsel, and the decision took months and years. After the hearing in first instance, the case could be appealed if the money value of the property or act in dispute was sufficiently high. If the value was higher still, the case might be appealed a second time. Appellate hearings invariably took years, especially if the case had to be carried to the Council of the Indies. The proceedings were slowed down yet further by the need to communicate by annual sailings of fleets.

The proposals of royal officials for simplifying procedures were not entirely altruistic; they found that the mass of Indian cases clogged royal courts and administrative offices. The difficulty may be illustrated by appeals in criminal cases at the time of the Second *Audiencia*. Under Spanish law, appeals from sentences of death or mutilation by the *Audiencia* might be made to the Council of the Indies in Spain. Once notice of intention to appeal was given, execution of the sentence was suspended until the appeal could be made and an order rejecting it be received from the Council. The Indians very quickly discovered this feature of Spanish law, so that those sentenced to torture, mutilation, or death promptly announced intention to appeal. Letting the case rest, they were then content to remain in prison and to take advantage of any opportunity for escape. Legally there could be no denial of the right to appeal by reason of failure to carry it forward since virtually all of the Indians affected were paupers. Nor was the crown in those years prepared to pay the costs of transmission to Spain and counsel for a hearing before the Council of the Indies. The *Audiencia*, which relied upon public execution to reinforce respect for the laws, was scandalized at the number of Indians in its jails under suspended sentence. Its concern was heightened by the fact that in civil suits the same device of appeal was used to delay execution of judgment for years. In 1533 it asked the crown for a decision (*Audiencia* of Mexico, February 9, 1533, in Paso y Troncoso 1939–1942 [Vol. 3] 27–28). The following year a royal order abrogated the right of appeal to the Council of the Indies by Indians in criminal cases. Instead the *Audiencia* was to hear appeals from sentences of death, mutilation, or torture (Puga 1563/1945:93v–94r).

Perhaps the basic element in most proposals for simplifying legal procedures was increasing the discretionary power of the judge and dispensing with requirements for written documents. In handling minor offences, which were legion among the Indians, the *Audiencia* of Mexico early adopted the policy of having one judge, instead of the two required by Castilian law, make the weekly visit to each of the two Indian jails in the vicinity of the capital. The cases were dispatched on the basis of such testimony as there was, oral or written. Very often the only written document in the trial was the record of judgment. Such summary procedure had the additional advantage of avoiding assessment of the Indians for costs. The procedure was approved by the crown in 1570 (Encinas 1596/1945 [Vol. 2] 67) and presumably furnished a model for proceedings by provincial justices.

For civil suits between Indians, the crown in 1530 ordered that they be decided orally without recourse to documents or judicial procedures (Puga 1563/1945:55v–56v). The earliest substantial observance of the royal will in this regard by a court in New Spain was in the hearings on petitions for freedom of Indians held as slaves. Vasco de Quiroga, sitting as delegate of the *Audiencia* for all such cases, summoned four of the highest of the old native judges to explain Indian custom in each case, heard the case as informally as possible, and rendered judgment (Quiroga, July 24, 1535, in Colección 1864–1884 [Vol. 10] 349). The injunction to use summary procedures in Indian suits was repeated in the New Laws and in a series of subsequent orders and enactments (Colección 1864–1886 [Vol. 14] 385–386; Encinas 1596/1945 [Vol. 2] 166–167). The intention was to do away entirely with judicial process with its complicated and expensive procedures, substituting for it an informal hearing with as little use of witnesses and written documents as possible. By the middle of the sixteenth century, a further incentive for reform was the knowledge that the Indians were committing perjury on a grand scale and that subornation of witnesses was so invariable that it could not be punished (Bishops of New Spain, 1565, in Colección 1864–1884 [Vol. 13] 288–289; Mendoza, in Colección 1864–1884 [Vol. 6] 489, 490,

498–499, 504–505; Escobar, in Colección 1864–1884 [Vol. 11] 199;
Mendieta, January 1, 1562, in García Icazbalceta 1886–1892 [Vol. 1]
19].

All proposals proved difficult, if not impossible, to implement.
The bulk of Indian civil suits concerned towns and nobles, who were
entitled to and insisted upon full judicial process. Further, ascertaining
the facts of any dispute was very difficult and, if the Indians came from
any distance, virtually impossible without formal and costly investigation by special agents (Encinas 1596/1945 [Vol. 2] 367). Under continued pressure from the crown, the Audiencia did attempt in 1570 -
1572 to reduce the complexities of judicial process for Indians. The
number of witnesses permitted each party and those de officio was
reduced to five. Only one submission of probanzas was to be permitted
in any suit and none on appeal. Appeals were limited to a single review. Moreover, the Audiencia forbade use of such pleas as nullity and
restitution that created subsuits within suits (Autos, May 19, 1572 and
June 20, 1570, in Archivo General de la Nación, Mexico City, ramo of
Reales Cédulas, Duplicados 1982 [Vol. 27] 382v–383r, 475v). These
provisions represented a very substantial curtailment of procedure. It
is unlikely, however, that they were successful in speeding up the
hearing of Indian suits over the opposition of notaries, lawyers, judges,
and other professional men who had a direct interest in prolonged
litigation. The Indians themselves resisted; upon any decision they
were unwilling to accept, they promptly raised the issues again in new
cases (Mendoza, 1551, in Colección 1864–1884 [Vol. 6] 489, 490,
498–499, 504–505).

Avoidance of Costs

The matter of costs was central in the problem of Indian suits and
petitions. On the one hand, the Spanish social and political structure
was far more dependent than ours on fees. The proportion of the Spanish community that made its living from fees was a relatively large and
very important segment (Parry 1953:1–5). On the other hand, legal
costs were a heavy burden upon the Indian peasants, for the nobles
were able to shift the load and enrich themselves as well as Spanish
and mestizo agents at law and in fact (Escobar, in Colección 1864 -
1884 [Vol. 11] 199; Mendieta, January 1, 1562 and February 20, 1591, in
García Icazbalceta 1886–1892 [Vol. 1] 18 and [Vol. 5] 109–111 respectively). The crown and viceregal government tried to solve this problem in two ways. In the first place, they tried to restrict the levy upon

the commoners of the Indian towns by requiring viceregal permission, a series of measures that seems to have met with indifferent success (Archivo General de la Nación, Mexico City, ramo of Mercedes). In the second place, they tried to set schedules of fees that were lower for Indians than for Spaniards and to excuse the poorest Indians from any fees at all, as was done for indigent Spaniards. Protests by officials who received their compensation from fees led the *Audiencia* to hold that, despite the terms of a royal order to the contrary, Indians were to be charged at triple the rate customary in Spain unless they had taken oath as paupers. Eventually, the *Audiencia* decided that the maximum amount of wealth that an Indian might have and still qualify as a pauper should also be triple the amount set for Spain, and this effectively returned some of the intended protection.

The problem of fees also extended to securing administrative papers and ran into the same kind of obstacles. In the end the powerful fraternity of notaries and secretaries prevented any significant reduction and probably managed to charge more than the legal schedules. Disputes between the judicial and administrative hierarchies over jurisdiction also forced the Indians to take out double sets of documents for assurance and pay double fees (Encinas 1596/1945 [Vol. 2] 315–318 and [Vol. 4] 275–276; Audiencia of Mexico, February 9, 1533, in Paso y Troncoso 1939–1942 [Vol. 3] 32; Puga 1563/1945:128v–129v; Velasco I and Audiencia of Mexico, February 26, 1552 and Gante, February 15, 1552, in Spain; Ministerio 1877:277–278 and 97–98 respectively; Velasco II, Correspondencia MS: 6v–7v, 16r–16v, and 22v–23r); Zorita 1909:404–405.

Provision of Special Legal Assistance

Provision of special legal assistance without costs for poor Indians theoretically was possible through the *abogado de pobres*, a special attorney for the poor, an office that became customary at higher levels of jurisdiction and in larger Spanish cities by the sixteenth century (Novísima recopilación 1805–1829 [Vol. V, Part I] xxix, [Vol. V, Part V] x). It might have taken on the function of representing Indians, but the *abogados de pobres* in New Spain seem to have confined their efforts to non-Indians (Velasco II, Correspondencia: 189v–190r; Archivo General de la Nación, Mexico City, ramo of Mercedes 1982 [Vol. 1] 3v). A possible substitute lay in the office of *protector de indios*, which existed at various times in New Spain. In the later 1520s, when it was first held by Zumárraga, it had a potential of providing legal representation for the Indians, or even of taking jurisdiction over their cases as happened in Central America, but Zumárraga was soon restricted to punishing minor offences against Indians and citing perpetrators of major offences before the Spanish courts (Bayle 1945:59–82). Protectors were appointed too sporadically for any significant effect.

A third possibility of providing special legal assistance for Indians in their encounters with Spanish law and Spanish administration lay in the provision of special officials specifically charged with that function. The first such appointment came in 1550 in connection with the royal program for freeing Indian slaves. The crown ordered the *Audiencia* of Mexico to appoint a *procurador general de los indios,* to serve as attorney before the *Audiencia* for Indians whose claims to freedom were disputed. His salary was paid from royal revenues, and the Indians were to be charged no fees. Unfortunately, the appointment was a temporary one, limited to the specific purpose of freeing Indian slaves (Encinas 1596/1945 [Vol. 4] 375–377). But, in the general reforming impulse arising from the New Laws, the crown asked the *Audiencia* in 1551 to report on the advisability of appointing a special salaried defender who would bring Indian suits before the *Audiencia* and so both remedy Indian ignorance of Spanish law and spare them exploitation by *letrados* (Puga 1563/1945:125r–125v). Measures taken fell far short of the idea, for the function of defender was entrusted to the fiscal of the *Audiencia,* who was to act only for Indians qualifying as paupers (Puga 1563/1945:150v–151r). The general ordinances for *audiencias* of 1563 made the *fiscal* of each *audiencia* protector of the Indians in his district but with no more power than previous protectors had had (Encinas 1596/1945 [Vol. 2] 269).

One defect was remedied in 1575 by a further royal order that the *fiscales* of all *audiencias* in the Indies act as attorneys for Indians in criminal as well as civil cases (Encinas 1596/1945 [Vol. 2] 269). All of this legislation had the basic defect that it entrusted a heavy load of additional business to already busy officials, whose careers depended upon the discharge of their other functions. Moreover, the provisions applied only to cases coming before the *Audiencia* and left untouched the far greater mass of business before provinical courts and administrative officials as well as complaints by Indians against Spaniards (i.e., cases in which the Indians were plaintiffs). Much of the effect of this inadequate provision was further undone in 1573 when the crown conferred upon the ordinary judges of the Spanish towns jurisdiction in first instance in the smaller civil suits of Indians against Spaniards (Fonseca and Urrutia 1845–1853 [Vol. 1] 536–537).

Reforms

The greatest possibility of approaching an adequate solution lay in the creation of a special jurisdiction for Indian legal business—whether civil, criminal, or administrative—with greatly simplified procedures and its own salaried staff forbidden to charge fees. Development of as much of this solution as was eventually adopted took almost exactly six decades from the coming of the Second *Audiencia* and seven from the fall of Tenochtitlan. The beginnings may be found in the exercise of administrative powers and the reserve judicial powers of the crown by Antonio de Mendoza. He set aside certain days of the week for hearing Indian petitions, complaints, and whatever business natives chose to bring before him. He heard them in person, made the necessary investigations, and either sent the matter to the proper agency for summary hearing and decision—particularly if the decision must be judicial—or issued the order himself. He rapidly found that a substantial part of his time went on Indian business, but considered his intervention in resolving grievances so important that he continued the practice throughout the fifteen years of his administration and recommended continuation of it to his successor, Luis de Velasco I (Mendoza, 1551, in Colección 1864–1884 [Vol. 6] 489–490, 498–499, 504–505). During the 13 years of the Velasco administration, essentially the same system continued (Velasco, February 7, 1554, in Cuevas 1914:211–213; Sarabia Viejo 1978:25–26). The system provided a sympathetic hearing for Indian cases with summary proceeding that waived much of the formalities and requirements of Spanish law. Although it did not eliminate fees entirely, it reduced them substantially.

Operation of this system stimulated strong opposition from the *Audiencia*, which held that much of the business handled as administrative was really judicial and should have come before it. Involved also was the rivalry of the two sets of notaries, secretaries, and other officials in the viceregal secretariat and the *Audiencia*, both avid for business and accompanying fees. Further, the protection afforded the Indians by use of administrative process in cases of seizure of land and goods, invasion by livestock, and extortion by Spaniards (in private and public function) evoked widespread opposition among the Europeans in the provinces as well as in Mexico City.

Upon the sudden death of Velasco in 1564 and the ensuing interim administration of the *Audiencia*, the latter was able to redress the balance in accordance with its own wishes. During the next years of a weak viceregal administration and the upheaval of the so-called Conspiracy of the Second Marqués, it was impossible to restore the system of Mendoza and Velasco. Upon the restoration of a strong viceregal administration in 1567, with the coming of Enríquez, such restoration might have been possible but too much ground had been lost (Royal cédula, December 10, 1566, in Archivo General de la Nación, Mexico City, ramo de Reales Cédulas, Duplicados 1982 [Vol. 48] 328; Velasco, February 7, 1554, in Cuevas 1914:211–213; Mendieta, January 1, 1562, in García Icazbalceta 1886–1892 [Vol. 1] 15–23). Meanwhile, the numbers of Indians visibly melted away, while the Spanish population with its need for them increased. At the same time, the decay of Indian institutions and custom and the imposition of Spanish institutions and law upon the Indians flowed as an inexorable tide.

The move for reform came in the administration of Luis de Velasco II, backed by a by then sympathetic Philip II (Velasco II, Correspondencia; Solórzano Pereira 1647/1930 [Vol. 1] 417–429; Recopilación 1681/1945:VI:X:xxi). Under urging from the viceroy, the monarch ordered the creation of a new unified judicial jurisdiction for Indian cases, civil and criminal, in which the Indians were defendants. The viceroy was to function as judge in first instance, although he was to act on the advice of a legal assessor. Administrative complaints and remedies continued to lie within the viceroy's jurisdiction as before, and so could be united with the new judicial jurisdiction. Complaints, hearings, and decisions were to be by summary process and largely oral. In practice, one leaf or paper embodied complaint and decision; the decision alone was entered in the records of the viceregal secretariat. The truly revolutionary decision was to place all officials and secretarial personnel involved in the cases, from assessor to doorman, on a salary paid from a fund raised by a new levy of one-half real annually on every Indian tributary in the *Audiencia* of Mexico. For all Indians except *caciques*, nobles, and towns, who might continue to use ordinary Spanish process, all fees and charges, even the cost of paper, were to be eliminated. Finally, the Indians *en masse* were declared *miserables*, and so, whether poor or rich, entitled to the special protections and assistance that had grown up during the more than two millennia of legal development in the Mediterranean and Christian Europe.

The new jurisdiction did not cover cases in which Indians sued Spaniards, for the old medieval legal maxim of *actor sequitur forum rei* continued to govern, nor did it apply to Indian needs at provincial and town jurisdictions, although cases might be removed from those to viceregal hearing on simple appearance of the Indian with his complaint. Presumably the new universal status of *miserables* with its multiple legal privileges would cover judicial cases in which Indians sued Spaniards and their needs at lower jurisdictions provided that the officials and secretaries complied with the rules. Nevertheless, the new jurisdiction and the universalized conception, whatever their shortcomings, represented the culmination of Spanish reflection and enactment on the need to ease Indian transition to Spanish institutions and laws. Established as a functioning entity between 1591 and 1593, the new jurisdiction lasted until 1821. The conception of the Indians as "the wretched of the earth" remains with us, in one form or another, to this day.

Notes

[1]As in the conversion of the Germanic peoples after the *Völkerwanderungen.*
[2]The pledge was inherent in the recognition of the crown that the Indians were its vassals, a proposition that began with Isabel I. The functioning of the concept is apparent in the innumerable orders and regulations in the *ramos* of Mercedes and Indios in the Archivo General de la Nación, Mexico City.

References

Archivo General de la Nación, Mexico City
      Ramos of Indios; Mercedes; Reales Cédulas, Duplicados.
Ayala, Francisco Javier de
   1945   El descubrimento de América y la evolución de las ideas políticas (Ensayo de interpretación). *Arbor* 3(8):304–321.
Ballesteros, Pío
   1945   Los indios y sus litigios según la recopilación de 1680. *Revista de Indias* 6:607–633.
Bayle, Constantino
   1945   El protector de indios. *Anuario de Estudios Americanos* 2:1–180.
Borah, Woodrow, and Sherburne F. Cook
   1958   Price trends of some basic commodities in central Mexico, 1531–1570. In *Ibero-Americana* (Vol. 40). Berkeley and Los Angeles: University of California Press.
Chance, John K.
   1978   *Race and class in colonial Oaxaca.* Stanford, California: Stanford University Press.
Chevalier, François
   1944   Les municipalités indiennes en Nouvelle Espagne, 1520–1620. *Anuario de Historia del Derecho Espanol* 15:352–386.
   1952   *La formation des grands domains au Mexique. Terre et société aux XVIe-XVIIe siècles.* Paris: Université de Paris, Institut d'Ethnologie.
Colección de documentos inéditos relativos al descubrimiento, conquista y organización de Indias.

1864–1884   42 vols. Madrid: Imprenta de Manuel B. de Quirós and others.

Cuevas, Mariano
1914   *Documentos inéditos del siglo XVI para la historia de México.* Mexico City: Museo Nacional de Arqueología, Historia y Etnología.

Encinas, Diego de
1945   *Cedulario indiano recopilado por* [1596]. (4 vols.). Madrid: Ediciones Cultura Hispánica.

Esquivel Obregón, Toribio
1937–1948   *Apuntes para la historia del derecho en México* (4 vols.). Mexico City: Editorial Polis.

Fonseca, Fabián de, and Carlos de Urrutia
1845–1853   *Historia general de real hacienda* (6 vols.). Mexico City: Imprenta de V. G. Torres.

García Gallo, Alfonso
1951–1952   La ley como fuente del derecho en Indias en el siglo XVI. *Anuario de Historia del Derecho Espanol* **21–22**:607–730.
1955   El derecho común ante el nuevo mundo. *Revista de Estudios Politicos* **80**:133–152.
1957–1958   Las bulas de Alegandro VI y el ordenamiento jurídico de la expansión portuguesa y castellana en Africa e Indias. *Anuario de Historia del Derecho Espanol* **27–28**:461–829.
1964   *Manual de historia del derecho español* (2nd revised edition, 2 vols.) Madrid: Alfonso García Gallo.

García Icazbalceta, Joaquín
1886–1892   *Nueva colección de documentos para la historia de México.* (5 vols.). Mexico City: Andrade y Morales, sucesores.

Gerhard, Peter
1972   *A guide to the historical geography of New Spain.* London and New York: Cambridge University Press.
1976–1977   Congregaciones de indios en la Neuva España antes de 1970. *Historia Mexicana* **26**:347–395.

Gibson, Charles
1952   *Tlaxcala in the sixteenth century.* New Haven, Connecticut: Yale University Press.
1955   The transformation of the Indian community in New Spain 1500–1810. *Cahiers d'Histoire Mondiale* **2**:581–607.
1964   *The Aztecs under Spanish rule: a history of the Indians of the Valley of Mexico, 1519–1810.* Stanford, California: Stanford University Press.

Góngora, Mario
1951   *El estado en el derecho indiano: epoca de fundación 1492–1570.* Santiago de Chile: Universidad de Chile, Instituto de Investigaciones Histórico-Culturales.

Greenleaf, Richard E.
1963   *Zumárraga and the Mexican Inquisition, 1536–1543.* Washington, D.C.: Academy of American Franciscan History.
1965–1966   The Inquisition and the Indians of New Spain: a study in jurisdictional confusion. *The Americas* **22**:138–166.

Hakluyt, Richard
1903–1905   *The principal navigations, voyages, traffiques and discoveries of the English nation* (12 vols.). Glasgow: J. MacLehose and Sons.

Höffner, Joseph
1957   *La ética colonial española del Siglo de Oro: Christianismo y dignidad humana.* Madrid: Ediciones Cultura Hispánica.
Kirchner, Walther
1954   *The rise of the Baltic question.* Newark: University of Delaware Press.
Konetzke, Richard
1953–1962   *Colección de documentos para la formación social de Hispano-América 1493–1810* (3 vols.), Madrid: Consejo Superior de Investigaciones Científicas, Instituto Jaime Balmes.
León Romano, Luis de
1933   Letter to the Emperor. In *Miscelânea de estudos en honra de D. Carolina Michaëlis de Vasconcellos* [1553], edited by Robert Ricard. Coimbra: Imprensa da Universidade.
Llaguno, José A.
1963   *La personalidad jurídica del indio y el III Concilio Provincial Mexicano* [1585]. Mexico City: Editorial Porrúa.
Maldonado, José
1954   Los recursos de fuerza en España. Un intento para suprimirlos en el siglo XIX. *Anuario de Historia del Derecho Espanol* **24**:281–380.
Medina, José Toribio
1914   *La primitiva inquisición americana (1493–1569): estudio histórico* (2 vols.). Santiago de Chile: Imprenta Elzeviriana.
Mexico City
1884–1916   *Actas de cabildo* (54 vols.). Mexico City: Various publishers.
Miranda, José
1962   La *pax hispanica* y los desplazamientos de los pueblos indígenas. *Cuadernos Americanos* November-December 1962:186–190.
1965   In Alfonso Caso, Silvio Zavala, and José Miranda, etc. Métodos y resultados de la política indigenista en México. *Memorias del Instituto Nacional Indigenista* **6**.
Montemayor y Córdova de Cuenca, Juan Francisco
1678   *Svmarios de las cedvlas, ordenes y provisiones reales* (3 parts in 1 vol.). Mexico City: Imprenta de la Viuda de B. Calderón.
Mörner, Magnus
1970   *La corona española y los foráneos en los pueblos de indios de América.* Stockholm: Almqvist and Wiksell.
Novísima recopilación de las leyes de España
1805–1829   6 vols. Madrid: Various publishers.
Parry, John Horace
1948   *The audiencia of New Galicia in the sixteenth century: a study in Spanish colonial government.* London and New York: Cambridge University Press.
1953   The sale of public office in the Spanish Indies under the Hapsburgs. *Ibero-Americana* (Vol. 37). Berkeley and Los Angeles: University of California Press.
Paso y Troncoso, Francisco del
1939–1942   *Epistolario de Nueva España, 1505–1818* (16 vols.). Mexico City: Antigua Libería Robredo.
Pérez de Tudela Bueso, Juan
1960–1961   Ideas jurídicas y realizaciones políticas en la historia indiana. *Anuario de la Asociación "Francisco de Vitoria"* **12**:137–171.

Phelan, John Leddy
1970   *The millennial kingdom of the Franciscans in the New World* (2nd revised edition). Berkeley and Los Angeles: University of California Press.
Puga, Vasco de
1945   *Provisiones, cédulas, instrucciones para el gobierno de la Nueva España* [1563]. Madrid: Ediciones Cultura Hispánica.
Recopilación de leyes de los reynos de las Indias [1681]
1942   3 vols. Madrid: Consejo de la Hispanidad.
Ricard, Robert
1933   *La "conquête spirituelle" du Mexique. Essai sur l'apostolat et les méthodes missionaires des ordres mendiants en Nouvelle-Espagne de 1523–24 à 1572.* Paris: Université de Paris, Institut d'Ethnologie.
Rumeu de Armas, Antonio
1967   Los problemas derivados de contactos de razas en los albores del Renacimiento. *Cuadernos de Historia, Anexos de la Revista Hispania* 1:61–103.
Sánchez Gallego, Laureano
1932–1933   Luis de Molina, internacionalista. *Anuario de la "Asociación Francisco de Vitoria"* 5:41–69.
Sarabia Viejo, María Justina
1978   *Don Luis de Velasco, virrey de Nueva España, 1550–1564.* Sevilla: Escuela de Estudios Hispano-Americanos.
Simpson, Lesley Byrd
1940   *The emancipation of the Indian slaves and the besettlement of the Freedmen 1548–1553.* Berkeley and Los Angeles: University of California Press.
Solórzano Pereira, Juan de
1930   *Política indiana* [1647] (5 vols.). Madrid and Buenos Aires: Compañía Ibero-Americana de Publicaciones.
Spain, Ministerio de Fomento
1877   *Cartas de indias.* Madrid: Imprenta de Manuel G. Hernández.
Spores, R. E.
1967   *The Mixtec kings and their people.* Norman: University of Oklahoma Press.
Velasco, Luis de
1590–1600   Correspondencia . . . con Felipe II y Felipe III, acerca de la administración de los virreinatos de Nueva España y del Perú. MS 3636 295 ff, Biblioteca Nacional, Madrid.
Vera Cruz, Fray Alonso de la
1968–1972   *The writings of . . . the original texts with English translations* (5 vols.). Edited by Ernest J. Burrus, S. J. Rome: Istituto Storico della Società di Gesù.
Vitoria, Fray Francisco de
1967   *Relectio de indis o libertad de los indios.* Madrid: Consejo Superior de Investigaciones Científicas.
Wittram, Reinhard
1954   *Baltische Geschichte: Die Ostseeland, Livland, Estland, Kurland, 1180 - 1918.* Munich: Wissenschaftliche Buchgesellschaft.
Zorita, Alonso de
1909   *Historia de la Nueva España . . . tomo primero.* Madrid: V. Suárez.
1942   *Breve y sumaria relación de los señores de la Nueva España.* Mexico City: Universidad Nacional Autónoma de México.

The Social Significance of Judicial Institutions in an Exploitative Society: Huamanga, Peru, 1570–1640*

Steve J. Stern

Editors' Introduction

Whereas Borah stressed the Spanish legal system's role in eroding Indians' customary lifeways, Stern emphasizes its role in further subjecting them to colonial rule. Looking closely at the local situation in colonial Huamanga, Stern shows that in the short run Indians used judicial politics to lessen the exploitation of their labor. They played state bureaucrats concerned with the supraregional distribution of *mita* labor for mining, against colonials who had more regionally concentrated interests in labor for *obrajes,* and *hacendados* and *encomenderos* who had yet narrower interests in local labor and tribute. Yet, in the long run, indigenous litigation weakened capacities for independent resistance by fostering rivalry and conflict among Indians, and by integrating native society more tightly into the Hispanic power structure.

One of the hot issues in colonial Latin American history has been what Lewis Hanke calls the Spanish "struggle for justice." Hanke and others before and after him reacted against the Black Legend, which

---

*Much of the material in this chapter appears in Chapter 5 of *Peru's Indian Peoples and the Challenge of Spanish Conquest: Huamanga to 1640,* published by the University of Wisconsin Press © 1982.

THE INCA AND AZTEC
STATES, 1400–1800

viewed brutality and exploitation as the enduring legacy of Iberian imperialism. By emphasizing the ineffectiveness of Spanish juridical institutions as enforcers of paternalistic laws, the Black Legend tradition negated their historical significance. The notorious "I obey but do not fulfill" formula, used repeatedly to thwart metropolitan intentions, symbolized the gap between law and reality that reduced justice to a mere formality or legal charade. The revisers of the Black Legend tradition stressed that Spanish conquest indeed generated a serious and bitter struggle for social justice by priests and others who worked on behalf of the Indians and hoped to "civilize" them. The enlightened side of the colonial venture, they argued, revealed just as much about the nature of Iberian imperialism as the exploitative side, and even produced benefits for the natives against formidable odds.[1]

Historians extended the debate to include the now famous controversy comparing Iberian and Anglo-American slavery. Frank Tannenbaum's seminal study analyzed Iberian law and religious traditions, and their "softening" effect on racial relations. The legacy of Iberian slavery, compared with its harsh northern counterpart, was a more humane moral and social milieu, which paved the way for easygoing relations after emancipation. The opponents of such a view countered in the tradition of the Black Legend debate by documenting a brutal reality that rendered favorable legal or moral traditions inconsequential.[2]

The debate, as traditionally defined, has grown stagnant. On the one side, scholars discover genuine efforts, including court proceedings, on behalf of the exploited, which seem to balance or vindicate the Iberian legacy. On the other side, historians offer evidence of brutal exploitation and greedy disregard of legal or moral constraint. But the accumulation of evidence and arguments for one side or the other does not advance a more comprehensive understanding of the contradictory aspects of Iberian colonialism. In my own research on sixteenth- and seventeenth-century Huamanga, I found the usual story of socioeconomic interests that cast aside the Indians' rights. But I also found numerous examples of a more or less working system of justice that the natives learned to use, with surprising success, on their own behalf. In short, I found data that could be used to fuel both sides of the debate, but without resolving very much, or explaining possible relationships between contradictory patterns. I began to think that, rather than tally points on the traditional balance sheet, we need to redefine the terms of the discussion. By focusing much more closely on the social significance of juridical institutions in the daily lives of natives and colonials, we could perhaps better evaluate the place of "justice" in the colonization of the Americas.

In particular, such a focus would better equip us to consider two issues left aside by the conventional terms of debate. First, we could look directly at the natives' own initiative when pressing for their juridical rights. The traditional debate encourages us to assume that those rights were in reality nonexistent, or that they amounted to something because of heroic efforts by paternalist defenders. Either way, the discussion tends to relegate the natives to a passive role sharply at odds with their aggressive use of Spanish juridical institutions. Second, we could consider the social functions of a system of justice from the point of view of the colonials. The traditional debate revolves around an attempt to assess the relative merit or ignominy of Spaniards as a colonizing people. It encourages us to think simply of the split between the interests of economic exploitation, on the one hand, and those of religious salvation or justice, on the other. But such a split constituted only one aspect of a broader, more complex relationship between the quest for profit and the pursuit of justice. Indeed, as an institutional force in local and regional life, the colonial system of justice often served to bind the natives to a power structure that always exploited them, and that used legal or moral authority as instruments of extraction.

What follows, then, is an attempt to redefine issues by analyzing the social significance of juridical institutions, both as an instrument of colonial rule and exploitation, and as a tool available to the natives in their struggle against oppression. The data are drawn from the region controlled by the colonial city of Huamanga (today Ayacucho). Huamanga's hinterland corresponded roughly to the contemporary Departments of Ayacucho and Huancavelica in south-central Peru, and included the strategic mercury mining center of Huancavelica. The region gained mature shape as an enduring social structure during the period under consideration, 1570–1640. These were decades of reorganization according to the design of the great Viceroy Francisco de Toledo, and response by natives and colonials to the Toledan institutions. As we shall see, the successful consolidation of brutally exploitative relations in Huamanga was not symptomatic of an ineffective or unworthy system of justice. But the establishment of a working system of justice, which sometimes ruled on behalf of the natives to the detriment of their exploiters, did not vindicate or somehow balance the colonial legacy. Rather, colonial justice played a crucial—perhaps indispensable—part in the subjugation of the natives to an exploitative society that lasted for centuries. Far from vindicating an exploitative experience, "justice" rooted it into the fabric of colonial Andean society.

Toledo's Reforms: A "Mixed Blessing" for Colonizers

As he strode past the soft white stone of Our Lady of Mercy, Huamanga's oldest monastery, Don Miguel de Bendezú seethed with anger. A refined young aristocrat, Don Miguel had recently come into possession of a modest family *encomienda*. Ever since, the deceitful Indians, led by the *kuraka* Don Pedro Astocuri, had taken unfair advantage of the Spanish laws. In 1622, when Don Miguel was still a legal minor, the natives managed to get a *revisita*, or reinspection, which bypassed the customary citation of interested parties. By pushing through their claim that nearly 200 tributaries had died or fled, they lowered the annual tribute assessment by some 700 pesos (of 12.5 reales each). Now, just 2 years later, Don Pedro and his people were at it again. This time, Don Miguel had been cited to respond to their petition for a new count of the tributary population. As he made his way toward the plaza to declare his answer before a notary, the exasperated young patrician determined not to fall prey again to the "ignorance and malice" of Don Pedro and his followers. He would appeal to the royal court in Lima to cancel the *revisita*. Another inspection, he explained desperately, would bring "the complete ruin of the said *repartimiento*, because the said *cacique*, to avoid paying tributes and complying with the Huancavelica mitas, will send off the Indians. They will order them to hide and claim them for dead or escaped, as is their custom."[3] As the more experienced citizens of Huamanga might have told him, Don Miguel would have to master the formal and informal rules of the legal game quickly, if he wanted to protect his income. By learning how to assert some legal rights of their own, the natives, source of so much wealth, had also become a source of great trouble.

For Don Miguel and others like him, the political revitalization of Peru brought mixed blessings. On the one hand, Viceroy Toledo's regime (1569–1581) established reigns of power effective enough to fashion and plenish an unparalleled economic boom. A rationalized system of tributes and *mitas* (rotating labor drafts drawn from reorganized Indian villages) supplied Huamanga's leading citizens with generous incomes and allotments of cheap labor. Mining production skyrocketed, and the commercial economy prospered. On the other hand,

Toledo's reforms tied elites to a colonial state that defined legitimate and illegitimate rules of exploitation, and whose judges and bureaucrats would decide upon their implementation. Spanish legal philosophy associated sovereignty with the idea of jurisdiction, which was conceived as responsibility for reconciling life on earth with the principles of a higher, divinely ordained law. The state was fundamentally a dispenser of justice, and its officials were invariable known as "judges" or the like.[4] The great burst of legislation and political reform in the 1570s gave new life to this tradition. The reforms included detailed statements of the natives' legal rights and procedures for claiming them. In addition, the state's administrative network included bureaucrats like the "protectors of Indians," whose stature, money-making possibilities, and power depended upon their potential as formidable legal defenders of the natives. In short, the juridical institutions that sponsored the extractions of a colonial ruling-class also gave the natives an opening by which to constrict exploitation. As long as some bureaucrats or colonial powers found it in their interest, in some cases, to back an assertion of the natives' legal rights, the Indians could find ways to impede, obstruct, or subvert extraction.

Making the most of the opportunity, the native entangled exploitative practices in juridical labyrinths whose final outcomes were often uncertain. In the end, the Indians' struggle for Spanish justice weakened their capacity to mount a radical challenge to the colonial structure, and thereby contributed to the dominance of a colonial elite. Along the way, however, resistance within Spanish juridical frameworks locked the colonials in a social war that hammered away at specific privileges and left the ultimate victors with a good many bruises and headaches.

Indian Legal Battles

From early on, the natives earned a reputation as litigious peoples. By the 1550s, they had flooded the viceregal court, or *audiencia,* in Lima with petitions and suits—the majority of them between native communities, *ayllus,* or ethnic groups. In the 1570s, Viceroy Toledo hoped that local reorganization might streamline the litigation and avoid overtaxing the Lima jurists.[5] In practice, however, the consolidation of a harsh exploitative system administered through a set of justices and legal guidelines did little to discourage litigation. Instead, the natives learned how to press aggressively for the "rights" allowed them. By the 1600s, they had developed legal forms of struggle into a major strategy for protecting individual, *ayllu,* and community interests.

Even at a time of demographic decline, some of the conflicts with colonials concerned land. Spaniards and other proprietors coveted areas whose ecology, fertility, or location promised high rewards for commercial agriculture. Despite the absence of generalized land pressure (until the eighteenth century),[6] competition in the prized zones sparked fierce conflicts. Spaniards enjoyed the advantages of a legal system that enhanced their claim on lands. The *composiciones de tierras* permitted Crown inspectors to award a community's "unused" or surplus lands to petitioners.[7] Since Andean agricultural technology depended on a rotation system that let many lands lie fallow, the *composiciones* of the 1590s, 1620s, and 1630s offered land-grabbers an opportunity to claim essential community lands that lay unworked in any given year.[8] Communities that spent money and energy to contest the legality of Spanish or even *mestizo* claims faced great risks. Spanish law officially devalued the credibility of native witnesses,[9] and colonials enjoyed more resources to spend on litigation and bribes. The judges shared social affinities and sympathies with Hispanic claimants. Even if a judge ruled on behalf of the natives, the *corregidor* or his lieutenant might neglect enforcement. With the balance of forces tipped against them and their funds eaten up, the natives sometimes withdrew the suits.[10]

Yet despite the disadvantages of law, economics, social prejudice, and modest political clout, Indians won important local victories. In Socos, near Huamanga, a literate Indian woman fought skillfully to fend off the incursions of a local landowner on several prized hectares. When, in the 1590s, Don Cristóbal de Serpa tried to claim vast tracts of valuable lands just south of the Río Pampas, the community of Tiquihua won a decree by the viceroy in Lima that kept Serpa out. Even when natives could not carry through a struggle to a final victory, their litigation might prove costly and disruptive to a colonial entrepreneur. One family, eager to invest funds to improve lands in the prosperous Huatata Valley near Huamanga, paid its *encomienda* Indians 500 pesos (of 8 reales each) to withdraw their lawsuit.[11]

The legal battles from which the natives simply refused to withdraw concerned labor rather than land. Though the colonials accumulated a good share of valuable land, the most threatening feature of the Toledan system was the *mita.* The labor drafts drained away energy, threatened health, and undermined local demography and reciprocity relations.[12] By the 1590s, communities were waging an aggressive campaign to protect themselves from "excessive" demands that violated official guidelines. *Kurakas* from Huanta and Vilcashuamán empowered the solicitor of suits at the Lima *audiencia* "to present certain provisions that we have won . . . about the *mita* of Indians which we have to [send to] Huancavelica."[13] The Tanquihuas Indians cut in half the contingent of 120 natives they had sent to their *encomendero's obraje*.[14] Since the *mita* legally drafted up to one-seventh of the tributary population (able-bodied males, 18–50 years old), a *repartimiento* with declining population could seek a *revisita* to revise their *mita* quota downward. With the ascent of the sympathetic Viceroy Luis de Velasco, a major reinspection effort got under way around 1600. At least 10, and probably more, of Huamanga's 23 "core" *repartimientos* lowered their tribute and *mita* assessments.[15]

The Indians threw their most dogged, stubborn efforts into resistance against the *mita*. The *kuraka* of one *ayllu* sued for at least 3 years to avoid turning over just one native for a *mita de plaza* in Huancavelica.[16] Much of the energy colonials had to expend to drive the natives to comply with the hated and feared labor drafts involved drawn-out legal battles. In Andahuaylas, for example, *kurakas* tried to back their unwillingness to fulfill a *mita* order with a legal ruse that disrupted the draft. Ordered in October 1606 to turn over an allotment of 15 *mitayos* for 2 years to the Jesuits in Huamanga, the Chanca *kurakas* replied with a statement opposing the draft. Their *repartimiento* legally owed no more than 429.5 natives (one-seventh a tributary population of 3000). Since, by the *kurakas'* count, they had already turned over 462 natives, the chiefs appealed the order. But their count included 112 functionaries of Indian municipal and church government. Legally, the municipal officials and lay assistants enjoyed individual exemption from *mita* service, but communities held no right to count this "reserved" group among its quota of natives fulfilling *mita* duties authorized by the state. Like other groups, the Chancas tried to stretch the legal exemptions into a means of reducing the communities' total *mita* liabilities[17] (to 317.5 natives, from 429.5). The Jesuits' priest-lawyer contested the legality of their count, and in December he won an order to force compliance. Still, the *kurakas* proved obstinate. In April 1607, they claimed that the enforcement order issued by the royal *audiencia* in Lima was illegal! After all, they argued, it forced the Indians to send more than the one-seventh quota to *mita* service. For months, the Chancas simply reappealed unfavorable decisions with legal arguments of their own until—in October—the *corregidor* threw the *kurakas* in jail. Even then the chiefs held out. Only after the *corregidor* approved the Jesuits' request to seize the *kurakas'* property and keep them in jail indefinitely did the chiefs submit. Finally, from the jail of Andahuaylas, they dispatched 15 *mitayos* off to Huamanga, "without prejudicing our right and what we seek to plead before Your Excellency." The *kurakas'* recalcitrance had held up the *mita* order for a full year.[18]

In their search for legal techniques to erode or disrupt forced labor, the Indians sometimes uses shrewd tactics. From the 1580s, the Tanquihuas Indians had gained considerable experience in a protracted struggle with Hernán and, later, Diego Guillén de Mendoza over *mitayos* and other natives working on the family's *obraje-hacienda* complex. In 1615, the group failed to send some 20 peasants to Huancavelica for the September–October *mita*. At a time of year when *ayllus* had to prepare and plant fields for Guillén as well as themselves, they probably could not spare any hands. When a judge commissioned at Huancavelica arrived later to investigate, the Tanquihuas blamed the incident on "the many Indians that their *encomendero* Don Diego Guillén de Mendoza has working." The tactic worked brilliantly, for it shifted the focus of the investigation to the *hacienda* complex and its impact on the Huancavelica *mita*. In the end, the legal actions inspired by the miners' complaint cost Diego Guillén over 600 pesos.[19]

The Indians' inferior social, legal, political, and economic status, of course, threw up great obstacles to juridical success and reduced some "victories" to insignificance. The *residencias*, judicial reviews taken by incoming officials of the conduct and accounts of outgoing functionaries, theoretically offered a forum for redress against abuses. But even when the natives could break through the notorious tendency of incoming and outgoing *corregidores* to collude in the *residencia*, their "victory" often amounted to very little. Many penalties and fines were owed to the Crown courts rather than to the natives. Even worse, the long process of appeal gave the functionary time to mobilize well-placed friends on his behalf. In more than one case, officials initially sentenced to stiff penalties managed to reverse or lighten the results.[20] Similar politics clouded the "justice" of other proceedings as well. When, around 1600, the Indians sued for an investigation of labor practices at the *obraje* of Chincheros, the findings condemned the powerful Oré family to the tune of thousands of pesos. The natives' triumph gave them a legal excuse to abandon the workshop, but on appeal the victory proved elusive. The family reduced the penalty to a mere 100 pesos and mobilized the bureaucracy to force the Indians to return to work.[21]

Still, the well-known corruptions, abuses, and collusions that made a mockery of Indian "rights" did not constitute the whole story. Indeed, the first *obraje* built by the Oré family had been shut down when an investigation supported complaints that the workers could not collect wages. When Jerónimo de Oré built a new *obraje* in 1584, he made sure, said the Indians later, to pay the workers well at the start.[22] As we have seen, the natives fended off some incursions on lands, won revised *mita* quotas in accordance with population decline, and constructed legal arguments against specific cases of forced labor. Even when legal claims failed to prevent abuse or extraction, the nuisances held up the colonials, carved out a bit of breathing space to plant crops, or earned the Indians payoffs to withdraw their suits. The Indians succeeded enough to make legal action a viable form of struggle, but we may ask why, in a society set up to exploit the native peasantry, such redresses were possible.

The Opportunity: Cleavages within the Colonial Elite

The exploitative system consolidated under Toledo functioned not as a monolithic bloc of power but as an alliance of various local, regional, and supraregional elite networks. Though the overall structure transformed native Andean peoples into "Indians" available for colonial appropriation, the elite networks were beset by sufficient internal contradictions to give the natives room to maneuver. In addition, Spanish colonial institutions gave law and, more generally, the juridical system central importance in the administration of rationalized extractive institutions such as tribute or *mita*. By mastering the art of defending themselves in alliance with appropriate bureaucrats or colonial powers, Indians—despite the general disadvantages that hampered litigation—improved their chances of winning specific victories.

Any figure who sought to carve out a local fiefdom of privilege and profit had reason to defend Indian clients against excessive greediness by a rival elite. Consider, for example, the *encomendero* who held lands near "his" Indian communities. Interested in tributes, fertile or well-placed lands, and native workers for his *hacienda*, an *encomendero-hacendado* frequently opposed competing landholders whose claims might undermine the self-sufficiency or productivity of his *encomienda* Indians. By assisting the natives against the usurpation of others, the *encomendero* also enhanced his capacity to demand favors from his clientele. Again and again, *encomenderos* supported the struggles of their Indians against land claims by other colonials or by rival natives.[23] Indeed, colonials caught in land fights tended to blame their troubles on European patrons rather than the natives themselves. As one besieged landowner, himself an *encomendero*, put it: "Doña Teresa de Castañeda, for her own ends, goes about settling two Indians of Luis Palomino her son [also a local *encomendero-hacendado*] in order to disturb and upset my peaceful, long-standing possession."[24] The elites of any given locale, of course, often worked out mutually beneficial relationships that allied them in the exploitation of the natives. Nevertheless, attempts by outsiders to establish themselves, or efforts by the established to expand their share of the spoils, sparked conflicts. As with the *encomenderos*, such conflicts provided the Indians with willing, if unreliable, defenders. In the mines of Huayllay, Spanish miners spoke with vehement outrage when accusing a priest-miner whose usurpations cut into their own privileges.[25]

More important, perhaps, than factional divisions within a local terrain were the endemic contradictions between local and supralocal interests. In a certain sense, all local lords shared with the natives an interest in subverting tribute and *mita* allotments to distant centers which undermined the local economy or drained away its surplus. All supralocal claimants, on the other hand, sought to squeeze out a maximum of goods, money tributes, and labor from distant hinterlands. The contradiction pitted local exploiters against outsiders. An *encomendero-hacendado*, joined by local *kurakas* and *corregidor* alike, denounced the destructive effect of the Huamanga *mita de plaza* on his *repartimiento*'s Indians and requested that the *mitayos* sent to Huamanga be assigned instead to his local *haciendas*.[26] Royal officials, city residents, and miners always suspected that local *corregidores, kurakas*, and priests conspired against formal *mita* and tribute institutions. By manipulating population counts, contending that it was unrealistic to expect complete *mita* contingents, and documenting that it was "impossible" to collect tributes from the impoverished natives, local officials extended their ability to command unofficial tributes, set up a textile business relying on labor-intensive putting-out systems, or organize a lucrative local commerce.[27] These extractive relationships, and the continuing vulnerability of poor Indians to *mita* drafts, differentiated the interests of local lords, Hispanic or Andean, from that of the poorer peasantry. Nevertheless, the elites' interest in maintaining viable local economies supported *ayllus* and communities in their most serious struggle—the attempt to minimize forced labor away from local homelands.

Compounding these contradictions was the resurgence of the Spanish colonial state, under Toledo, as a vital patron of exploitation. Law and juridical administration grew into a serious fact of life, an undeniable component of the field of forces confronted by colonials as well as Indians. (Compare the essays by Karen Spalding and Woodrow Borah in this collection.) The support natives enlisted from jurist-bureaucrats did not necessarily imply that administrators acted as disinterested executors of legal guidelines. Though some displayed a certain integrity or commitment to the legal rules of the game, the vast majority deserved their reputations for corrupt patronage and money making. More to the point than a disinterested sense of integrity was the way in which jurist-bureaucrats found it in their interest to support some of the natives' struggles. As we have seen, *corregidores* had good reason to support native sabotage of institutions that sapped the local economy. In cities such as Huamanga, Huancavelica, or Castrovirreyna, the "protector of natives" enjoyed social influence and attracted bribe offers by virtue of his capacity to represent the natives aggressively.[28] The eye on money making which rendered bureaucrats corruptible by Spanish clients also opened the door to bribery by the natives. The citizens of Huamanga appointed one of their own, Juan Nuñez de Sotomayor, to take legal action to correct the chronically incomplete *mita* contingents sent by the natives. To their chagrin, however, Sotomayor's loyalties faded before his private business interests. Traveling through the rural provinces, Sotomayor "converted the *mitas* into his benefit, and allowed that the [tributary counts] be lowered."[29]

By legal or illegal means, the natives gained access to a more or less working juridical system and, as much as they could, pressed it into their service. In the long run, all colonial elites shared a common general interest in exploiting the Indians through political coercion. This shared interest found a conscious expression in mutually beneficial alliances, marriage and kinship bonds, diversification of interests, and a disposition to accommodate one another rather than invite conflict.[30] Still, they were in the colonial world to make money, and their narrower interests as competing exploiters often clashed. For native Andean peoples, these contradictions, in conjunction with a juridical system susceptible to their claims, represented an opening to defend themselves on issues concerning labor, lands, and tributes. The Indians saw the opportunity, and they took it.

From Defense to Manipulation

As a result, legal tactics mushroomed into a major strategy of Indian life. By the 1580s, *kurakas* commonly gave Spaniards general powers of attorney to represent their legal interests.[31] At least one ethnic group institutionalized its legal activity. "Each new year," declared seven *kurakas* in 1597, "we are accustomed to naming solicitors to use our power in all our [legal] causes." With license from an *alcalde* and protector of natives in Huamanga, eight chiefs appointed three persons—two *kurakas* and a Spanish solicitor in Huamanga—to look after the group's legal interests.[32]

As the natives grew more adept at defending their rights, the distinction between defensive action against colonial disregard of legal guidelines, and more aggressive manipulation of the juridical system to sabotage the colonials, grew increasingly blurred. In particular, the legal correlation of tribute and *mita* burdens with the tributary counts (healthy males, 18–50 years old) of *repartimientos* lent *ayllus* and communities a potent tool with which to fight colonial extraction. By petitioning for *revisitas*, or reinspections, of their populations, native peoples lowered their legal tribute and *mita* quotas in accordance with real and pretended demographic declines. By the early seventeenth century, the *revisita* institution had become the battleground of a social war fought to control official population figures and tax liabilities. Rather than offer a reliable guide to the human resources available to native societies, the *revisitas* expressed the outcome of this ongoing struggle.

On the one side, *encomenderos*, miners, royal treasury officials, and others interested in maintaining current levels of tribute or *mita* labor hoped to either postpone the *revisitas* or to minimize their impact. In almost any legal proceeding, affected parties held the right to participate and defend their interests. In the *revisitas*, *encomenderos* received an official citation giving them notice of the coming recount, and they led the attempt to maintain the status quo. By appealing the legality or necessity of a *revisita* to the Lima *audiencia*, or objecting to the proposed judge, an *encomendero* or pensioner could postpone or slow down the process.[33] In the meantime, he (or occasionally, she) held right to the old tribute levels. Once a reinspection was under way, the opposed parties did whatever they could to have the claims of the natives thrown out. Asserting that *kurakas* hid tributaries and then pretended they had died or fled to unknown parts, *encomenderos* and like-minded judges demanded rigorous proof of the native contentions. If an alleged death did not appear in the local priest's "book of deaths," a judge often recorded the Indian as a living tributary unless proved otherwise.[34] In one inspection, even a priest's testimony that he had indeed buried the Indians did not suffice to reverse the practice![35] Similarly, *kurakas* had to offer proof that escaped natives had truly fled their community and eluded kinfolk's attempts to locate them.[36] In a *revisita*, Indians and *ayllus* always had to contend with colonial efforts to inflate or maintain the list of tributaries liable to taxes and *mita*. One *encomendero* got an inspector to reverse the exemption of local Inca descendants from normal tributary status.[37] By the conclusion of a *revisita*, colonial recipients might still enjoy tribute and *mita* rights based on census lists that included dead or long-gone males among the tributaries.

On the other side, the natives did all they could to use the *revisita* to lessen *ayllu* burdens. *Kurakas* mobilized the testimony of priests and Indians to certify deaths and flights and to explain the faultiness of parish mortality books; they had Spanish doctors confirm mercury sickness and endorse the removal of the ill from tributary rolls; they led inspectors on tours of crumbling, abandoned homes to prove that natives had fled the community.[38] Within several years of a completed *revisita*, they came back with evidence that tributes and *mita* assessments should be lowered further.[39] To the extent that native groups, in alliance with judges or priests or on their own, managed to include hidden tributaries among the dead or absent, they might even push through a reduction that exceeded true demographic declines. The powerful Hernando Palomino, whose Soras Indians pressed aggressively for reductions by the early 1600s, complained that local priests confirmed the "deaths" of hidden tributaries "in order to employ them in their trade and business and to satisfy the *caciques.*" The priests who certified 44 deaths between 1607 and 1609, Palomino observed pointedly, "did not say that they buried the natives." Instead, they went along with the natives' story on the strength of "having seen their wives dressed as widows."[40]

The day-to-day process of a *revisita* mirrored this tug of war. At the beginning of his tour and at each village to which he came, the judge normally included a standard warning in his announcement to the throng gathered at the plaza. "Those who may know that the *caciques* or other persons have Indians hidden should declare them. If they do so, they will be rewarded and likewise those uncooperative . . . will be punished."[41] The identity and political sympathies of a judge concerned the natives as much as it did the colonials. One ethnic group petitioned for appointment of their *corregidor* as judge of a *revisita*. Since the *corregidor* already received a salary, they argued, he could perform the *revisita* without subjecting the natives to the salary and costs of another official. Probably, the Indians also thought their *corregidor* held enough interest in local exploitative relationships to cooperate with their efforts to cut back tribute and *mita*. When the viceroy tried to sidestep possible collusion by appointing an independent judge, the natives' strenuous objections held up the *revisita* for 74 days.[42]

Once they began, the *revisitas* dragged out into painstaking expeditions—village by village, *ayllu* by *ayllu*, household by household—which recorded each individual, checked age and death classifications against parish records, demanded written proof for all contentions, and earned the judge a mounting daily salary.[43] The inspections took on a quality of hide-and-seek played with documents, witnesses, payoffs or political alliances, and elusive settlement patterns. The nucleated population clusters sponsored by Toledo had broken down sufficiently to allow *ayllus* and *kurakas* to settle natives "in hidden and remote parts" that escaped inspection. The possibility of native subterfuge, on the other hand, gave harsh judges a rationale to dismiss Indian claims as suspect. When two *kurakas,* supported by a "protector of the natives," organized written testimony to prove the death of a Lucanas tributary in Castrovirreyna, the judge declared "that it is not enough [to have] Indians testify . . . and not a Spaniard." Most Indians, he went on to observe, "do not hesitate to perjure themselves" in order to lessen their *ayllus'* tribute and *mita* rolls.[44]

The results of the recounts thus reflected the relative skills, advantages, and luck of the interested parties as much as they did demography. The Soras Indians, with 2441 tributaries in 1570–1575, managed to lower their count by a mere 46 tributaries around 1600 despite the major epidemic of the 1580s. Less than a decade later, despite the absence of major epidemics, they lowered the tributary count by an impressive 439 tributaries. Between 1600 and 1610, they had clearly learned how to use the *revisita* institution more effectively.[45] In a less fortunate case, the Chancas of Andahuaylas lowered their count by a large sum, only to find that a subsequent investigation of the *revisita's* accuracy wiped out most of the relief. The original *revisita* of 1604 revised the 1594 count by compiling figures of 1429 male deaths, 456 men who had passed 50 years of age, and 1117 new tributaries who had reach 18 years of age. The net decline was thus 768 tributaries (from a total of 3277 in 1594 to 2509 in 1604). The Andahuaylas *encomienda* had reverted to the Crown, which received substantial tributes from the Chancas by the 1600s. Crown officials objected to the credibility of the recount, claiming that the judge was too interested in personal profit to double-check alleged deaths or to include some 500 able-bodied young males in the count of new tributaries. By 1606, the accusations of fraud against the royal treasury led to the appointment of a special investigating judge, who held power to replace *kurakas* if necessary. Aided by "discord among the *caciques*," the new inspector claimed to discover an undercount of 641 tributaries, which raised the total to 3150 (a net decline of only 127 from the count in 1594).[46]

By the early seventeenth century, the Andean peoples of Huamanga had developed sufficient skills in local politics, juridical procedures, and subterfuge to lower the official tributary population by dramatic proportions. By 1630, *revisitas* had cut the regional count from about 22,000 in 1570–1575 to some 4,000. The drop cut gross tributes from over 85,000 pesos (of 12.5 reales each) to only 15,000 pesos and squeezed the once plentiful flow of over 3,000 *mitayos* to 600 or less. In the initial period of 1570–1600, *repartimientos* in Huamanga only managed to lower official counts to some 80% of the Toledan tributary population. But between 1600 and 1630, the evidence suggests growing native skill and experience. *Revisitas* proliferated until they reduced tributary counts to a mere 15–20% of the Toledan figures (see Figure 11.1).[47]

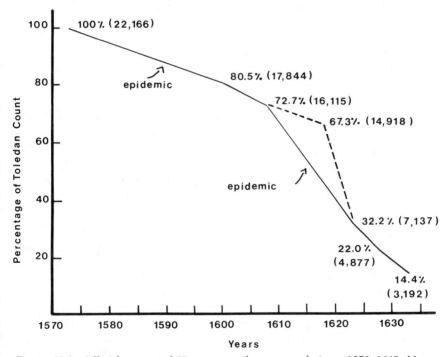

Figure 11.1 Official counts of Huamanga tributary populations, 1570–1640. Note: dashed line is curve based on counts for only two *repartimientos*, whose 1606–1610 percentage seemed abnormally high (17.3% higher) when compared with the regional count based on 12 *repartimientos*.

Moreover, by the 1620s many *revisita* figures may have underestimated the human energy available in local economies. Anyone familiar with Andean terrain and indigenous settlement patterns knows how easily a determined social group could hide a portion of its human, animal, or even agricultural resources from outsiders. An investigation of idolatry in the Huancavelica-Castrovirreyna district showed that ethnic groups concealed some of the newborn even from local parish records. Several major *huacas* (native gods) each enjoyed the services of 20 or 30 men and women reserved for the cults. To protect the servants from discovery and from *mita* labor in the mines, the Indians "would hide them when [they were] children and would not baptize them so that they would not appear in the priest's books."[48] The Bishop of Huamanga, who toured the region extensively during 1624–1625, noted that so many adult males had either died or fled to live in hidden places away from villages that "it is impossible that one could fulfill the *mita* of Huancavelica." Finding hidden natives was not easy, since "those who look for them do not want to find [the natives] but rather their money."[49]

In addition to this concealed population, communities built access to a significant group of able-bodied males legally exempt from its tributary count. Flight from home communities had created a sector of immigrant Indians known as *forasteros*, some of whom opted to live in rural community settings rather than attach themselves to European estates or enterprises, or live in cities or isolated *montaña* regions. These community *forasteros* often married native *ayllu* women and participated actively in local economic life.[50] Until the eighteenth century, however, they were legally exempted from the tribute-*mita* counts of their adopted communities. The bishop who toured Huamanga in 1624–1625 certainly exaggerated when he said that the total native population of rural parishes had remained fairly stable—if one included children, hidden people, and *forasteros* (of all kinds).[51] But a 1683 census of Chocorvos *ayllus* settled in Vilcashuamán confirmed that the community *forasteros* constituted an important, if hitherto unquantified, sector of seventeenth-century *ayllu* economies. Twenty-seven *forasteros* expanded the communities' population of able-bodied males aged 18–50 by 33.8%. All but one lived in one of the two towns inspected, where they raised the count by 54.2%.[52]

The sharp cutback in tribute and *mita* thus represented a considerable native achievement against formidable odds rather than an inescapable consequence of objective demographic trends. Even had the *revisita* figures reflected population losses accurately, demographic decline per se had not led automatically to commensurate reductions of tribute-*mita* levies. As we have seen, the rate and scale of reductions were the result of hard-fought juridical wars. Nor did demographic decline, by itself, necessarily undercut the objective capacity of communities to support tribute-*mita* levies based on higher tributary counts. The viability of alternative means of extracting large profits from native communities belies the assumption that *ayllus* simply could not have satisfied tribute-*mita* quotas in excess of the ratios (per male-headed household) established by Toledo. Indeed, Indian communities or individuals unwilling or unable to satisfy *mita* quotas in persons frequently paid money equivalents as an alternative, or hired other natives to replace *mitayos*. *Kurakas* who managed to accumulate monies paid tributes for men who had fled the community.[53] Finally, the effect of hidden Indians and *forasteros*, combined with the developing skills of native petitioners, meant that the official tributary counts, in at least some cases, seriously underestimated the total human network available to local societies. Andean communities, to be sure, suffered appalling losses to disease (epidemics in 1585–1588 and 1610–1615), abuse, and flight which high birth rates or in-migration could reverse only partially.[54] The net effect may have cut the region's ethnic populations by half or more between 1570 and 1630, from over 120,000 to a measure in the tens of thousands. But the dramatic drop in tributary counts to 15–20% was not a direct index of the decline in human resources or economic surplus available from native society. It measured instead the effects of the Indians' never-ending sabotage campaign against tribute and *mita*.

Effects of Judicial Politics: The Colonial Elite

During the early seventeenth century, the state's official extractive institutions (*mita*, tribute) rapidly lost credibility as adequate suppliers of labor and revenues to an expanding regional economy. The natives' campaign against exploitation did not subject Huamanga to a generalized crisis. Mercury production—a key measure of economic dynamism and markets—suffered occasional setbacks due to technical and labor problems and never recaptured the heady boom years of the 1580s and 1590s. Nevertheless, Huancavelica continued to compile a reasonably consistent record of prosperity (see Figure 11.2),[55] and colonial Huamanga escaped sharp economic decline until much later in the seventeenth and early eighteenth centuries. But the Indians' struggles generated a series of local or temporary crises that disrupted enterprise and incomes, shut down workshops, and pinched production with la-

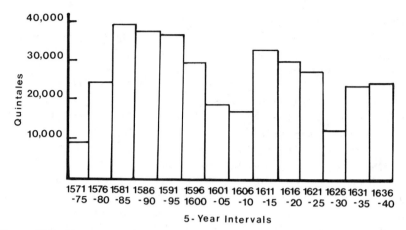

Figure 11.2 Mercury production registered at Huancavelica. Source: Guillermo Lohmann Villena, *Las minas de Huancavelica en los siglos XVI y XVII* (Seville, 1949), 452–454.

bor bottlenecks. Cheap *mita* labor grew scarce and unreliable. The natives' growing ability to evade or lower tribute-*mita* quotas and to entangle exploitative relations in legal battles gave the colonials strong incentive to find alternative sources of profit more independent of state authority or patrimony. Under pressure, colonial elites turned increasingly to more direct modes of exploiting Indian labor, based on economic dependencies and more "private" forms of political control, to shield their enterpises from vulnerability to legal action.[56]

For the colonials, then, the natives' juridical activity constituted far more than an occasional nuisance. The natives squeezed the legal flow of *mitayos* and tributes to painful levels, and perhaps worse, imposed crises and disruptions upon colonials who enjoyed nominally plentiful quotas of tribute or labor. As we saw earlier, litigation shut down the Oré family's *obraje* in 1584 and disrupted work at a second *obraje* in 1601. Enforcement of *mita* or tribute rights always ran up against peasant resistance and juridical tactics. In 1607, when the Soras still owed a large annual tribute, their *encomendero* complained that the Indians used a dispute over tributary counts as an excuse to cease payment on thousands of pesos.[57] Even after population decline and Indian petitions cut back the initial Toledan allotment of workers to the Cacamarca *obraje* in Vilcashuamán, the owner still held rights to 60 *mitayos*. But around 1610, his *encomienda* natives, embroiled in continual fights over labor practices and obligations, temporarily crippled production by getting the Lima *audiencia* to cancel the *mita* altogether! Later, the drafts were reinstalled, though *revisitas* reduced them to insignificance. In 1642, local natives won an order (subsequently reversed) to close the *obraje*. By this time, the new owner, like his predecessor, understood that only by cultivating direct relationships with a controlled clientele of dependent workers could he protect the enterprise from community litigation.[58]

Effects of Judicial Politics: Andean Society

The Indians' juridical strategy inflicted considerable hardships upon many colonials, but nevertheless brought unfortunate consequences to native Andean society. Given the bitter conflicts over lands, *kurakazgos* (chieftainships), and tribute-*mita* burdens that shaped *ayllu* and ethnic life, one could not expect that the natives would limit judicial politics to peasant actions against colonial exploitation. Andean litigants used their juridical rights and skills against one another—a practice that left native society divided and dependent upon colonial authorities to settle internal disputes. In addition, access to Spanish power and legal institutions encouraged a certain individualization, or privatization, of interest and perspective on the part of natives who acquired private land titles, secured legal exemptions from *mita* or tribute, mediated *ayllu* relationships with *corregidores* or other colonial powers, and the like. By reinforcing *ayllu* and ethnic strife and fostering class dynamics that tied privileged Indians to the colonial power structure, a working system of colonial justice weakened the capacity of native societies to unite around a more ambitious, radical assault upon the exploitative structure as a whole. A more fragmented strategy pursued more limited victories—that is, the particular causes of particular native groups or individuals. And the Indians grew increasingly dependent upon the legal institutions and favor of their exploiters to advance such causes, even when the disputes involved only Indians.

For many native groups, the most persistent land fights stemmed not from colonial incursions, but from rivalries with other *ayllus* and ethnic groups. Particularly in regions such as the Río Pampas or Huamanga-Huanta-Angaraes, a proliferation of interspersed ethnic groups generated centuries of conflict over lands and pastures. To settle such disputes until the next outbreak, local groups could resort to war, negotiation, or appeal to outside authority. Access to a legal system that presumed to resolve local disputes may actually have intensified conflict. A group too weak to win a violent battle, or to accept a *modus operandi* based on local power balances, could try to compensate by securing legal backing from a Spanish judge. But rival groups, particularly if they were stronger, could not very well renounce their own claims simply because their enemies held legal title to the prized resources. Ethnic disputes repeatedly flared up, and the group able to back up its claims with legal precedents always turned to colonial judges to help protect its local interests.[59]

Even within an ethnic group, access to colonial juridical institutions fostered conflicts that undermined internal authority and cohesion. Succession to major chieftainships had always constituted a difficult, thorny process in Andean societies. The potential heirs of a *kurakazgo*, or chieftainship, almost always included several rivals—sons, and even nephews or brothers of the incumbent chief.[60] Since a major *kuraka* was identified more closely with one of the several *ayllus* constituting a community or ethnic group, his practical authority and acceptance by all the *ayllus* in his domain depended upon his political skills and fulfillment of popular expectations.[61] The identities of major *kurakas* held crucial economic implications, since they supervised distribution of tribute and *mita* burdens among the various *ayllus*. The endemic rivalries between individual aspirants could spill into such social divisions, tearing apart a community or ethnic group. In more than one case, the ensuing civil war led to "many deaths and misfortunes" among warring "brothers."[62]

By offering defeated aspirants a tool with which to overturn the status quo, access to colonial judges kept disputes and local polarization alive, and left ethnic chiefs dependent upon Spanish power to back up their standing even with local kinfolk. Two Soras cousins revived a dispute between their fathers until the aggressive challenger displaced his cousin as *kuraka* in 1594. An Angaraes chief, Don Juan Llanto, complained that his nephew, a source of trouble since the 1570s, had curried "the favor . . . of the *corregidor* and notary." With their help, the upstart relative had gotten two chiefs replaced and threatened to do the same to his uncle. The resulting "rebellion over *cacicazgos*" sent Llanto to Huamanga in 1589 to commission a lawyer to present his case before the *audiencia* in Lima. In Huanta, a conflict over succession turned into such a bloody and costly affair that the three rivals, each apparently backed by a significant following, agreed to settle upon an uneasy truce in 1596. Litigation, they discovered, "has no end" and burdened the Hurin Acos *ayllus* with costly legal fees and trips to Lima.[63]

Spanish judicial authority developed into a major internal force used by Indians against their own authorities. By obtaining the favor of

Spanish judges, complained an embittered Lucanas native, a "tributary Indian pretending to be *kuraka* reserved all of his people from the mines and [*mita* labor] without consulting the *cacique* principal [chief *kuraka*]."[64] A sick peasant ordered by his *kurakas* to pay tribute and serve *mita* turned to the protector of Indians for an appeal to the *corregidor*, which undercut the chiefs' orders. When Don Bernabé Sussopaucar passed 50 years of age, he got the *corregidor* of Huanta to issue an order reserving him from tribute and *mita*. Still, his chiefs pressured the wealthy native, a minor lord himself and holder of private title to irrigated lands, to contribute to the *mita* burdens of the community. Don Bernabé responded by securing a viceregal provision threatening to remove the *kurakas* if they persisted. The Anta *ayllu* of Huamanguilla included wealthy descendants of the Incas who legally enjoyed exemption from *mita* and tribute. Higher *kurakas*, particularly those of more powerful *ayllus*, looked askance at the Incas' privileges and wealth. Even as an old man, an Inca descendant complained, "they force him to [serve] the said *mita* or to hire someone in his place." By winning a viceregal order, presenting it to the *corregidor*, and securing his public promise to enforce the order, the Inca descendants could defend their economic advantages.[65]

Indeed, Spanish legal authority encouraged Indians to develop individualized interests and privileges that shielded them from the lot assigned to the poorer peasantry. Legal immunity from *mita* or tribute enabled municipal and church functionaries, Inca descendants, and artisans to sidestep burdens that impoverished kinfolk.[66] Dependence upon colonial authorities to uphold a *kuraka*'s tenure, or to protect him from personal liability for the *mita* and tribute obligations of his *ayllus*, encouraged a native lord to work out private arrangements that accommodated the exploitative ventures of local functionaries. Such arrangements enabled the chief to avoid the physical abuse, jailings, and confiscations of wealth that befell *kurakas* of "delinquent" taxpayers; to secure needed help in his efforts to sabotage state-sponsored labor drafts and tributes; and to mediate native-white relationships that yielded profits to all the collaborating elites.[67] The periodic *composiciones de tierras* gave further incentive to a process of privatization that differentiated Indian elites from poorer kin. Legally, the judge of a *composición* could sell any community lands deemed "surplus" to petitioners for private title. But the *composiciones* also allowed wealthy Indians to purchase the auctioned lands, and *kurakas* to "privatize" their traditional land use rights. Huamanga's chiefs responded aggressively to the opportunity; one lord converted himself into a spectacularly large landowner by listing over 70 sites, totaling thousands of hectares, which "I have always possessed since my ancestors."[68] It is doubtful that a lord could truly emancipate *all* such resources, if he wished to maintain his local standing and mobilize labor to work the lands, from the traditional claims of *ayllu* society. But individual title allowed him to begin to superimpose private property rights on a traditionally *ayllu* domain. An Indian with individual title to lands could sell them as one's own, and protect landed wealth from the usurpations that threatened collective *ayllu* property. As one successful petition put it: "The said lands [are] not common but rather their own individual [property] from which [the petitioners] cannot be despoiled."[69]

The natives' very success at using Spanish juridical institutions created forces in everyday life and struggle that undermined organization of a wider, more unified, and independent movement on behalf of the peasantry. First, judicial politics reinforced costly internal divisions along *ayllu*, ethnic, and even class lines. Notarial accords among ethnically distinct chiefs testify that common subjection to *mita* and tribute spawned efforts to unite ethnically diverse groups with similar interests and complaints.[70] But as we have seen, in practice juridical tactics could also pit Indians against one another. Ethnic groups fought over lands, rival elites battled for recognition of *kurakazgos,* and individual natives searched for ways to accumulate and protect wealth and privileges. During a *revisita* of the Chancas, all *ayllus* shared an interest in corroborating claims of death, which would lower their collective tribute-*mita* quota. But a Spanish judge adept at polarizing the endemic bickering that plagued a ranked hierarchy of *ayllus* and *kurakas* discovered hundreds of "false" deaths.[71]

Second, a strategy of defense that depended upon colonial institutions to resist exploitation tied the natives more effectively than ever to Hispanic power. Indians who evaded or cut back *mita* burdens, protected landholdings, or enforced murky claims to *kuraka* status through the "grace" of powerful colonials used the rules, formal and informal, of Hispanic dominance to defend themselves. Those rules demanded acceptance of colonial relationships that ultimately impoverished the Andean peasantry. Indians who won limited but important victories by securing the favor of colonials and their institutions held a certain interest in avoiding wholesale challenges of authority that might invite punishment or revocation of their achievements. Moreover, judicial politics fostered loyalties among Indian elites and Hispanic patron-allies, which held dangerous implications for the peasantry. Over time, the means by which *ayllus* battled state-sponsored extractions encouraged alliances that assimilated native elites to the colonial power structure, substituted extralegal extractions in place of the old "legal" burdens, and differentiated the interests and perspectives of native elites—as an emerging class—from those of peasants.[72]

The juridical strategy developed by 1600 made good sense for its time—given the defeat of radical conspiracies and millenarian movements of the 1560s,[73] the decline of *ayllu* demography and wealth, a colonial power structure whose outposts extended throughout the countryside, and the possibility of genuine inroads against the Indians' most hated and feared burden, the colonial *mita*. Aggressive use of the colonial system of justice, complemented by "laziness,"[74] flight, and anonymous forms of sabotage (hidden populations, mysterious fires[75]) offered "realistic" means of resistance. By mastering the art of judicial politics, ethnic groups, *ayllus*, and even individuals won battles on pressing real-life issues such as *mita*, tribute, and land rights.

But on another level, the natives' achievement cost them a great deal. From the point of view of a society's ruling class, a system of justice functions successfully if it represents a pact on the part of social groups and individuals not to go to war over their differences, but rather to settle conflict within the framework of rules established by society's dominant forces. Turning established rules or institutions to one's favor does not, of course, by itself signify an unwillingness to use force or to organize more radical strategies. But to the extent that reliance on a juridical system becomes a dominant strategy of protection for an oppressed class or social group, it may undermine the possibility of organizing a more ambitious assault aimed at toppling the exploitative structure itself. When this happens, a functioning system of justice contributes to the hegemony of a ruling class. This was the case, in Huamanga at least, by the early seventeenth century. By then, subversive religious movements spoke not of eliminating Hispanic society or power, but simply of resisting cooperation with Spaniards "unless forced to."[76] The Indians' struggle for Spanish justice subjected a good many colonials to constraints and hardships and even forced some of them to search for alternative ways to extract labor and profits. What it could not do, however, was challenge colonialism itself. Spanish justice, in some instances and on some issues, favored the natives against their exploiters. But for that very reason, it set into motion relationships that sustained colonial power, weakened the peasantry's capacity for independent resistance, and contributed to the oppression of Andean peoples.[77]

Notes

Abbreviations used in notes:

AAA   Archivo Arzobispal de Ayacucho
ADA   Archivo Departamental de Ayacucho
AGI   Archivo General de Indias (Seville)
AGN   Archivo General de la Nación (Lima)
BNP   Biblioteca Nacional del Perú, Sala de Investigaciones (Lima)
HAHR   *Hispanic American Historical Review*
HC   Harkness Collection, Library of Congress (Washington, D.C.)
RGI   Marcos Jiménez de la Espada, ed., *Relaciones Geográficas de Indias—Perú,* vols. 1–2, reprinted in *Biblioteca de Autores Españoles,* vol. 183 (Madrid, 1965).
RPIA   Registro de Propiedad Inmueble de Ayacucho
YC   Latin American Collection, Sterling Library, Department of Manuscripts and Archives, Yale University (New Haven, Ct.)

[1]Lewis Hanke, *The Spanish Struggle for Justice in the Conquest of America* (Philadelphia, 1949). For a good introduction to the historical context of the revisionist trends, see Charles Gibson, "Writings on Colonial Mexico," *HAHR,* 55:2 (May, 1975), 293–295. For more recent studies of Spanish efforts on behalf of the oppressed, see Eugene H. Korth, *Spanish Policy in Colonial Chile: The Struggle for Social Justice, 1535–1700* (Stanford, 1968); Norman Arthur Meiklejohn, "The Observance of Negro Slave Legislation in Colonial Nueva Granada" (Ph.D. diss., Columbia University, 1968). Cf. Philip Wayne Powell, *Tree of Hate: Propaganda and Prejudices Affecting United States Relations with the Hispanic World* (New York, 1970), which includes a useful bibliography.
    One should note that long ago Mario Góngora pointed out that the "do not fulfill" formula had a juridical rationale entirely consistent with Spanish legal philosophy. *El estado en el derecho indiano. Epoca de fundación (1492–1570)* (Santiago de Chile, 1951), 283–284.
    [2]Frank Tannenbaum, *Slave and Citizen: The Negro in the Americas* (New York, 1946). The comparative literature on slavery is as voluminous as the corpus of work relevant to the Black Legend debate. For a good introduction to contrasting views, see Laura Foner and Eugene D. Genovese, eds., *Slavery in the New World: A Reader in Comparative History* (Englewood Cliffs, N.J., 1969).
    [3]AGN, Derecho Indígena, Leg.39, C.798, 1624, "Provisión . . . librada a Dn. Juan Ramirez Romero, Corregidor . . . de Vilcashuamán, para que visite," f.3r for quotations. La Merced, the church mentioned above, is on the street from the plaza to the house of a descendant of the family in contemporary Ayacucho.
    [4]Góngora, *El estado,* 29–35, 196, 308–309; John Leddy Phelan, *The Kingdom of Quito in the Seventeenth Century: Bureaucratic Politics in the Spanish Empire* (Madison, 1967), 38.
    [5]HC, Doc. 1012, 1556, Viceregal provision; Roberto Levillier, ed., *Gobernantes del Perú. Cartas y papeles, siglo XVI* (14 vols., Madrid, 1921–1926), VIII, 257–260, 263–272.
    [6]The investigations of Lorenzo Huertas Vallejos show that struggles over land held a prominent place in Ayacucho's eighteenth-century history, but not earlier.
    [7]On the *composiciones,* see John H. Rowe, "The Incas Under Spanish Colonial Institutions," *HAHR,* 37:2 (May, 1957), 181–182; Rolando Mellafe, "Frontera agraria: el

caso del virreinato peruano en el siglo XVI," in Alvaro Jara, ed., *Tierras nuevas* (Guanajuato, 1969), 36–40.

[8]The *composiciones* for lands without legal title always included statements testifying to their unused state, but for evidence that fallow lands were subject to usurpation even by other Indians, see AGN, Derecho Indígena, Leg. 6, C.107, 1642, "Autos seguidos por doña Catalina y doña Luisa Cucichimbo . . . de Socos," f.27v.

[9]Rowe, "The Incas," 191.

[10]See BNP, A393, 1594, "Expediente sobre la petición presentada por Domingo de Villamonte," ff.47v–48r; Z1067, 1685, "Título de la Hda. de Sillco y Guallacha," ff.237r–238v.

[11]AGN, Derecho Indígena, Leg.6, C.107, 1642, ff.5r–v, 10r–11v, 14r–v, 82r–v; RPIA, tomo 5, partida LXI, "Registro por la comunidad . . . de Tiquihua . . . 1906," 176; ADA, Protocolos, Navarrete 1615–1618/1627/1630, ff.712v–718r, 711v–712r, 720r–725v. Cf. BNP, Z1067, 1685, ff.205r–206r, 237r–238v, for another payoff to get Indian litigants to withdraw a suit.

[12]For a discussion of the *mita* and its impact on native societies, see my *Peru's Indian Peoples and the Challenge of Spanish Conquest: Huamanga to 1640* (Madison, 1982), 82, 84–89.

[13]ADA, Protocolos, Peña 1596, f.82r.

[14]AGN, Derecho Indígena, Leg.6, C.113, 1646, "Real provisión . . . a favor del tesorero D. Juan de la Maza," ff.1r–2v; BNP, B1370, 1625, "Despacho expedido . . . a pedimiento de Hernán Guillén de Mendoza," f.1r.

[15]See Appendix, "Official Counts of Huamanga Tributary Populations, 1570–1635"; BNP, A18, 1599, "Repartición de los indios de plaza." For evidence of even earlier inspections, see BNP, Z436, 1595, "Información de las haciendas y ganados y de los indios," f. 222r.

The 23 "core" *repartimientos* of the Huamanga region are listed in Noble David Cook, ed., *Tasa de la visita general de Francisco de Toledo (1570–1575)* (Lima, 1975), 260–280. The "core" districts exclude the Jauja *repartimientos* to the north, five small groups of ethnic *mitmaq* settled in the Chocorvos district, and several *repartimientos* on the peripheries of Huamanga. (*Ibid.*, 257–260, 282–284, 275–276, 280–282.)

[16]BNP, B934, 1616, "Expediente . . . presentada por el Cacique Principal . . . de Luricocha."

[17]See Pablo Macera, "Feudalismo colonial," in Macera, *Trabajos de historia* (4 vols., Lima, 1977), III, 170–171.

[18]BNP, B28, 1607, "Relación de la visita practicada al repartimiento . . . de Andahuaylas," *passim.*, f.6v for quote.

[19]BNP, Z313, 1616, "Causa de cuentas dada por Dn. Diego Guillén de Mendoza," ff.196r–206r; Z351, 1616, "Sobre la causa seguida . . . en nombre de Diego Guillén de Mendoza," f.661v.

[20]See AGI, VI, Lima 529A, "Residencia de Don Juan Manuel de Anaya," esp. ff.1332v, 1406v–1407r, and Anaya's comeback as royal treasurer in 1601, in ADA, Protocolos, Soria 1593/1601, f.105v; AGN, Juicios de Residencias, Leg.11, C.29, 1593, "Autos promovidos por Dn. Salvador Salas y de Valdéz, Corregidor . . . de Huamanga," f.350r–v; Leg.24, C.64, 1618, "Autos . . . a Dn. Cristóbal de Ulloa y Mercado . . . Corregidor . . . de CASTROVIRREYNA," ff.1r–2v, 193r–194v, 202r–203r.

[21]Miriam Salas de Coloma, *De los obrajes de Canaria y Chincheros a las comunidades indígenas de Vilcashuamán. Siglo XVI* (Lima, 1979), 163–169.

[22]BNP, B1485, 1600, "Para que el corregidor . . . de Vilcashuamán . . . hara averiguaciones," ff.62r, 247r, 49r.

[23]See BNP, Z1067, 1685, ff.206r–238v; A393, 1594, ff.36r–v, 47v–48v, 50r, 51v–52r; B1525, 1647, "Expediente . . . para que se restituya a los indios Chocorbos las tierras," ff.2r–3v; ADA, Corregimiento, Causas Ordinarias, Leg.1, C.2, 1599, Untitled document regarding lands of Cañares Indians, f.4r–v; [Leg.2], 1678, Untitled document regarding history of lands in Huanta, f.935r.

[24]BNP, Z304, 1591, "Escritura de venta de las tierras de Huancapuquio," ff.2v–3r.

[25]AAA, Siglo XVII, Estante 3, Exp.28, 1626, "Causa de captitulos Puestos . . . a El Padre Andres gomez de arsila."

[26]BNP, Z436, 1595, ff.222r–223r, 225v–227r, 229r–230v, 231r–v.

[27]For widespread suspicions and evidence that many were well-founded, see BNP, B57, 1616, "V.E. confirma . . . las provisiones . . . acerca de que la mita de Choclococha se entere"; B59, 1618, "Provisión . . . para que el corregidor de los Chocorvos envíe a . . . Huancavelica la cantidad de indios"; B1505, 1644, "Expediente . . . en nombre del Cap. Juan de Arriaga y de la Rosa, Corregidor de Lucanas," ff.24v–25r; Z37, 1640, "Instrucción que . . . ha de guardar y cumplir . . . en el juicio de residencia," ff.387v–389v, 398v–401r; A236, 1597, "En la residencia secreta . . . de Parinacochas," ff.51v–52r, 106r–110v; B1485, 1600, f.59v; AGN, Juicios de Residencias, Leg.23, C.62, 1617, "Autos que promovió . . . contra Dn. Perefan de Rivera," ff.66v–67r, 79v, 92v–93r, 124r, 142r–v, 144r–v, 145r–v, 171r–198v. The latter case documents favorable opinions of a Vilcashuamán *corregidor* by Indians whom he supposedly abused in a vain attempt to collect tributes, and the *encomenderos'* contention that the tribute collection attempts were perfunctory coverups of an unofficial extractive system managed by *corregidor* and *kurakas*.

[28]On the *protector de indios*, see Constantino Bayle, *El protector de indios* (Seville, 1945); Guillermo Lohmann Villena, *El corregidor de indios en el Perú bajo los Austrias* (Madrid, 1957), 333–334. On the profit-making possibilities of a protector, see AGI, VI, Lima 1189, "Sentencias contra Gregorio Fernández de Castro . . . 1647," charges against Alonso de Sotomayor.

[29]*Ibid.*, charges against Sotomayor.

[30]See Stern, *Peru's Indian Peoples*, 93–102.

[31]ADA, Protocolos, Cárdenas 1585, ff. 178v–180r; Soria 1589, ff.140r–141r, 207r–v, 208r–v, 269v–270v.

[32]ADA, Protocolos, Peña 1596, ff.237v–238v, 237v for quote.

[33]See AGN, Derecho Indígena, Leg.39, C.798, 1624, ff.2v–3v; Leg.24, C.686, 1601, "Auto original . . . para que termine la revisita de los indios . . . de ANANCHILQUES," f.1r–v.

[34]In particular, see the record in BNP, B1079, 1629, "Expediente . . . en nombre de . . . caciques de Huaros para que se envíe revisitadores," *passim*. Cf. AGN, Derecho Indígena, Leg. 4, C.73, 1622, "Autos . . . sobre acreditar el fallecimiento del indio tributario," esp.ff.311r, 316r; Leg.3., C.50, 1606, "Autos que siguió Agustín Arce de Quirós, Juez y escribano . . . de la revisita . . . de Andahuaylas," ff.88r, 106v.

[35]BNP, B1079, 1629, ff.86r–93r.

[36]*Ibid.*, ff.68r–80r.

[37]AGN, Derecho Indígena, Leg.6, C.109, 1643, "Autos que siguieron don Melchor y don Salvador Ataurimachi, indios principales . . . de Huamanguilla," f.5r.

[38]BNP, B856, 1616, "Memoria de los indios muertos . . . de los Andamarcas"; B876, 1629, "Revisita de los indios . . . de Aspite y Vilcanchos," f.13v; B1079, 1629, ff.68r–80r, 82r–85r, 86r–93r; B1159, 1629, "Sobre el empadronamiento de los indios tributarios . . . de Huancavelica," ff.7r–32v; B1505, 1644, ff.13v–17r; AGN, Derecho Indígena, Leg.4, C.73. 1622.

[39]AGN, Derecho Indígena, Leg.39, C.798, 1624, f.3r; BNP, B1505, 1644, ff.13v–17r; B1159, 1629, ff.3r–v, 4r.

[40]BNP, B1505, 1644, ff.24v–25r.

[41]BNP, B1079, 1629, f.10v.

[42]AGN, Derecho Indígena, Leg.3, C.50, 1606, ff.64r, 110v–111r.

[43]For a day-by-day account of a *revisita* that took nearly 5 months and produced a written record of 740 folio pages, see *Ibid.*, ff.101r–107v.

[44]AGN, Derecho Indígena, Leg.4, C.65, 1619, "Testimonio de . . . documentos relativos a la visita y reducción . . . en las doce provincias de Huamanga," f.2v; Leg.4, C.73, 1622, ff.311r, 316r.

[45]BNP, B1505, 1644, ff.24r–31r, esp. 26r–27v. Cf. the case of Lucanas Laramati in *Ibid.*, ff.13v–16r.

[46]See AGN, Derecho Indígena, Leg.3, C.50, 1606, ff.81r–v, 65r–66v, 86r–89r, 86v for quote.

[47]The figures cited (and the representation in Figure 11.1) are based on the recounts listed in the appendix at the end of these notes. The regional percentages and estimates assume that the *revisitas* found are fairly representative of the recounts in the region as a whole. They include 23 "core" *repartimientos* and data for Sancos. There was one major epidemic wave between 1570–1600, and another between 1600–1630. The percentage given for 1600 consolidates figures for 1596–1600 and 1601–1605, particularly since I have not been able to specify exactly which of these 5-year intervals is appropriate for some of the recounts.

[48]BNP, B54, 1609, "Letras annuas de este colegio [de Jesús] de Huamanga," Año 1613, f.21v. The idolatry investigation recorded in this document was transcribed, with some errors, as "Idolatrías de los indios Huachos y Yauyos," *Revista Histórica,* 6 (1918), 180–197.

[49]AGI, V, Lima 308, Report of the inspection by Bishop Verdugo, 1625, pp. 3, 9 (of microfilm copy).

[50]For evidence of the significance of *forasteros* in a *revisita* before 1650 (despite the group's unimportance for inspection purposes at the time), see AGN, Derecho Indígena, Leg.6, C.119, 1648, "Revisita y padrón . . . de SAN JUAN DE LOS SANCOS . . . de Lucanas," ff.109r, 111v, 113r, 114r, 116v. Cf. ADA, Cabildo, Causas Civiles, Leg.1, C.6, 1673, Untitled document concerning Huanta lands of Clemente de Chaves, f.5r; AGI, V, Lima 308, Description of the Bishopric of Huamanga, 1624–1625, notations for Tambo, Mayoc, Pampas, Huambalpa, Gerónimo; Report of the inspection by Bishop Verdugo, 2–3.

[51]*Ibid.*, 8.

[52]Lorenzo Huertas Vallejos *et al.*, *La revisita de los Chocorbos de 1683* (Ayacucho, 1976), 55, 61–70, 145, 150. These figures exclude *forasteros* attached to European lands, but include three adult sons of community *forasteros.* For background on the *forasteros* and data that support their statistical importance, see Nicolás Sánchez-Albornoz, *Indios y tributos en el Alto Perú* (Lima, 1978); Oscar Cornblit, "Society and Mass Rebellion in Eighteenth-Century Peru and Bolivia," in Raymond Carr, ed., *Latin American Affairs,* St. Anthony's Papers, No.22 (London, 1970), 24–27.

[53]See Luis J. Basto Girón, *Las mitas de Huamanga y Huancavelica* (Lima, 1954), 5–6, 10–11; AGI, V, Lima 308, Report of the inspection, 3; ADA, Protocolos, Palma 1609, ff.82v, 207v; AGN, Derecho Indígena, Leg.6, C.109, 1643, f.3r; BNP, B1079, 1629, ff.73v, 75r, 76v, 79r. Cf. Felipe Guamán Poma de Ayala (1615), *Nueva corónica y buen gobierno* (Paris, 1936), sketch on 531.

[54]For a discussion of birth rates and population fluctuations in preindustrial so-

cieties, see E. A. Wrigley, *Population and History* (New York, 1969), 62–106. For eighteenth-century evidence that an ethnic group could double a reduced population in 30 years, see Arthur Preston Whitaker, *The Huancavelica Mercury Mine. A Contribution to the History of the Bourbon Renaissance in the Spanish Empire* (Cambridge, 1941), 49.

[55]For the colonial history of Huancavelica, see Guillermo Lohmann Villena, *Las minas de Huancavelica en los siglos XVI y XVII* (Seville, 1949); D. A. Brading and Harry E. Cross, "Colonial Silver Mining: Mexico and Peru," *HAHR*, 52:4 (November, 1972), 545–579; Whitaker, *The Huancavelica Mercury Mine*; Gwendoline Ballantine Cobb, "Potosí and Huancavelica. Economic Bases of Peru, 1545 to 1640" (Ph.D. diss., Univ. of California, Berkeley, 1947).

[56]Lack of space prevents me from describing in detail the impact of the *mita*'s decline, colonial attempts to reverse its demise, and the transition—under pressure—to alternative labor arrangements. I presented an outline of this argument in "Luchas sociales y evolución de la explotación de mano de obra indígena en Huamanga colonial," *Ideología*, 5 (Ayacucho, 1977), 47–52. A more detailed discussion is in my *Peru's Indian Peoples*, 128–132, 140–148, 155–157, 191–193.

[57]BNP, B1505, 1644, f.24r.

[58]The data above can be gleaned from BNP, B1370, 1625, f.1r; Z313, 1616, ff.164v–165v; Z351, 1616, ff.662r–v, 663r, 668v; AGN, Derecho Indígena, Leg.6, C.113, 1646; BNP, B450, 1643, "Para que el corregidor . . . de Vilcasguamán guarde y execute la provisión," ff.2r–4r; B164, 1640, "Provisión . . . [para que] no impidan a los indios que voluntariamente quisieran trabajar."

[59]For a revealing set of documents on land histories of rival communities, see the community registries of lands in RPIA, tomo 5, partida VI, 18–21; tomo 8, partida XL, 132–134; tomo 10, partida CXXIII, 404–409; tomo 10, partida CXL, 468–469; tomo 13, partida LV, 328–334; tomo 14, partida VI, 39–60; tomo 21, partida XLVII, 457–469. Cf. AGN, Derecho Indígena, Leg.6, C.107, 1642, ff.16r–v, 32r; AGN, Tierras de Comunidades, Leg.3, C.19, 1806, "Autos que sigue el Común de Indios . . . de Chiara," ff.40r–43r, 46r–47v; ADA, Protocolos, Soria 1589, f.65v.

[60]See María Rostworowski de Diez Canseco, "Succession, Coöption to Kingship, and Royal Incest Among the Inca," *Southwestern Journal of Anthropology*, 16:4 (Winter, 1960), 417–427; Rostworowski, *Curacas y sucesiones, costa norte* (Lima, 1961); and the sources in notes 62–63 below.

[61]John V. Murra, *Formaciones económicas y políticas del mundo andino* (Lima, 1975), 193–223, esp. 221, 223; BNP, A387, 1594, "Expediente . . . presentada por Lázaro Yupa Inca Vacachi," f.2r; YC, Vol.5, "Libro común de sumas . . . 1572–1573," ff.62v, 63r (tribute payments by ayllu and ethnic lord).

[62]ADA, Protocolos, Peña 1596, f.137r. Cf. Soria 1589, f.67r.

[63]BNP, A371, 1594, "Don Pedro Quispillamoca, contra Dn. Pedro Vilcanacari . . . de los Soras"; ADA, Protocolos, Soria 1589, ff.67r–71r (67r for Llanto quotes); Peña 1596, f.137r. Cf. Cárdenas 1585, f.144v.

[64]Poma de Ayala (1615), *Nueva corónica*, 974. The example is from Sancos, south of the Río Pampas.

[65]See "Información presentada . . . en nombre de Juan Mocante," included in BNP, B856, 1616; AGN, Derecho Indígena, Leg.6, C.107, 1642, ff.8r–v, 16r–v, 27v–28r; Leg.6, C.109, 1643, ff.1r–4v, 3r for quote (cf. Leg.6, C.108, 1643, "Autos seguidos por Don Fernando y don Melchor Ataorimachi," f.1r).

[66]See Karen Spalding, *De indio a campesino. Cambios en la estructura social del Perú colonial* (Lima, 1974), 72–85, esp. 77, 82–83.

[67]See *Ibid.*, 77–79; and note 27 above.

[68]BNP, A387, 1594, f.2r–v, 2v for quote. The sites totaled some 1650 topos, an Andean measure that varied depending upon ecological conditions affecting productivity. One sale of 27 topos by the same chief was, according to Spanish measure, thirty fanegadas (nearly ninety hectares). At that rate, the chief's total holdings would have amounted to some 5000 hectares. *Ibid.*, f.4r–v. Cf. AGN, Derecho Indígena, Leg.6, C.107, 1642, ff.16v–20r, 25v, 27r–v.

[69]*Ibid.*, f.14r.

[70]ADA, Protocolos, Cárdenas 1585, ff.110r–112v; Soria 1598, ff.302r–303v.

[71]AGN, Derecho Indígena, Leg.3, C.50, 1606, ff.86v ("discord among the *caciques*"), 90v–91r (ranked hierarchy). Skilled investigators of seventeenth-century idolatry made use of the same technique. Pablo José de Arriaga (1621), *La extirpación de la idolatría en el Perú*, Horacio H. Urteaga, ed. (Lima, 1920), 133, 138.

[72]This process was partial and contradictory, in part because class and racial bonds sometimes worked at cross-purposes. But it was nonetheless very real and served to integrate native elites more effectively into the world of Hispanic power. See Stern, *Peru's Indian Peoples*, 158–183; cf. Spalding, *De indio a campesino*, 31–87, 147–193.

[73]See the articles by Luis Millones and Nathan Wachtel in Juan M. Ossio, ed., *Ideología mesiánica del mundo andino* (Lima, 1973), 85–142; cf. Stern, *Peru's Indian Peoples*, 51–79.

[74]See Pedro de Ribera y Antonio de Chaves y de Guevara (1586), "Relación . . . de Guamanga y sus términos," in *RGI*, 185–186 for a common characterization; BNP, Z1124, 1631, "Expediente . . . en nombre de los hijos . . . de Dña Bernardina de Romaní," ff.472r–485r for records of missed workdays at an *hacienda* "because there were no people"; Poma de Ayala (1615), *Nueva corónica*, 529–530, for a revealing anecdote about a timid Spaniard unable to get the Indians to serve him.

[75]BNP, B1441, 1634, "Expediente sobre el juicio de residencia . . . al Corregidor . . . de Andamarcas," ff.27v, 28v; Z1124, 1631, ff.481v, 518v, 543r. For an important treatment of anonymous or covert forms of protest as the normal outgrowth of an outwardly deferential society, see E. P. Thompson, "The Crime of Anonymity," in Douglas Hay *et al.*, *Albion's Fatal Tree: Crime and Society in Eighteenth-Century England* (New York, 1975), 255–308.

[76]BNP, B54, 1609, f.26r; Steve J. Stern, "Las ideologías nativistas, la aculturación y las clases sociales," *Churmichasun*, 4–5 (Huancayo, June, 1977), 26.

[77]Any understanding of legality and ethics as an instrument of the hegemony of a ruling class benefits from the pioneering work of Antonio Gramsci. See especially "State and Civil Society," in Gramsci, *Selections from the Prison Notebooks*, Quintin Hoare and Geoffrey Nowell Smith, eds. (New York, 1971), 206–276. It should be noted, however, that Gramsci developed the concept of hegemony with reference to modern capitalist societies. For important treatments of the social significance of "justice" or law in other kinds of societies, see Douglas Hay, "Property, Authority and the Criminal Law," in Hay *et al.*, *Albion's Fatal Tree*, 17–63; Eugene D. Genovese, *Roll, Jordan, Roll: The World the Slaves Made* (New York, 1974), 25–49.

Appendix: Official Counts of Huamanga Tributary Populations, 1570–1635

Table 11.1 compiles demographic data illustrated in Figure 11.1. The *repartimientos* listed correspond to the 23 "core" districts men-

TABLE 11.1
Official Counts of Huamanga's Tributary Populations, 1570–1635

Repartimiento	5-year interval								
	1570–1575	1596–1600	1601–1605	1606–1610	1611–1615	1616–1620	1621–1625	1626–1630	1631–1635
Soras	2441			1956					
Lucanas	2793	2395		1736			793	369	286[a]
Laramati								501	444
Lucanas Andamarcas	2065			1530					
Angaraes (2)[b]	1842			1288[c]					
Guayllay	662			707[c]					
Calamarca	117			89[c]					
Quiguares orejones	185			168		149			
Huaros	321			160[c]			118	98	
Guaytará	1073			771[c]					
Huachos	683			572		435			
Chocorvos									

Quinua	876	689				
Parija	1500	1431[c]				
Caviñas	102	91	71[c]			
Angaraes de Hontiveros	902	473[c]	473[c]			
Tayacaja	793	396[c]	396[c]			
Quichuas y Aymaraes	1964	1734		1303		552[d]
Tanquihuas	739	510			242	181
Totos	378	207			132[d]	64[d]
Papres	578	546	477			
Pacomarca	595	380				
Hanan Chilques	772	619				
Hurín Chilques	600	413				
Sancos	185				139	94

[a]Modified by correction in 1636, from 1635 count of 300.

[b]Total count for *two* Angaraes repartimientos.

[c]Best estimate of *revisita* date. When unable to specify the 5-year interval with certainty, I listed data in the two most likely intervals.

[d]Estimates based on averages of two counts.

tioned in note 15, *plus* Sancos, for which separate data were available. The figures are based on tributary counts, total *mita* quotas, and *revisita* date information drawn from the following sources: Cook, ed., *Tasa de la visita*, 260–275, 276–280; Antonio Vázquez de Espinosa (1629), *Compendio y descripción de las Indias Occidentales*, Charles Upson Clark, ed. (Washington, D.C., 1948), 653–655; BNP, B1505, 1644, ff.3v–5r, 10v–16r, 24r, 26r–30r; B1441, 1634, ff.34r–35r, 46r–47v; AGN, Derecho Indígena, Leg.4, C.62, 1616, "Padroncillo y Tasa . . . de los Quiguares orejones"; BNP, B1079, 1629, esp. ff.61r - 62r; AGN, Juicios de Residencias, Leg.24, C.65, 1618, f.295r and the "Testimonio de la retasa" directly following; BNP, A18, 1599, loose folio recording changes in total *mita* of various districts; B620, 1636, "Para que los indios . . . de Quinua cumplan con dar para . . . las minas . . . y otras mitas"; AGN, Juicios de Residencias, Leg.23, C.62, 1617, ff.30r–31r, 43v–44r, 56v–57v, 69v–70v, 82v–83v, 95v–96r, 105v–106r, 113v–114v, 126v–128r; BNP, B1159, 1629, ff.3r–5r.

12

Exploitation as an Economic System: The State and the Extraction of Surplus in Colonial Peru

Karen Spalding

Editors' Introduction

Karen Spalding shows that Peru's colonial state created a unified rather than a dual economy. Indians in this period never enjoyed existence as an autonomous peasant society. In particular, the state compelled Indians to orient their labor and production toward colonists' requirements by exacting tribute in kind and labor. At the same time, official policy attempted to maintain the integrity of indigenous communities, thus dampening the changes put into motion by levies exacted by the state. The model of the Peruvian economy at once breaks new ground and poses questions for further research.

For many years those of us who have sought to comprehend the mechanisms and the structure of the Spanish colonial system have often been reminded that the economy of Spanish Peru rested ultimately upon the backs of the Indian population, whose members supplied the motor power of the productive system of the colony. The almost total dependence of the viceroyalty of Peru upon the labor of the native Andean population was well known to contemporaries; we can hardly find a more graphic statement of the dependence of the colony upon Indian labor than the words of a Spanish observer at the beginning of the eighteenth century:

THE INCA AND AZTEC
STATES, 1400–1800

Leaving aside the principal populations of the seacoast, where many Negroes, mulattos, quadroons, and mestizos serve, in the whole viceroyalty the Indians are those who do the work. There is no market in the kingdom that is not constituted by Indians. In Lima, they are the fishermen who supply the great abundance of fish found in streets and plazas. They transport the foodstuffs to the cities, *villas*, and towns; they cultivate the fields, transport the wheat, the wine, the oil, the meat. They are the shepherds and guardians of the innumerable *estancias* in the kingdom; they scale the mountains to serve us; they penetrate the hot valleys for our comfort . . . the artisans of all kinds of mechanical professions are almost entirely Indians, and [Indians] dress us and provide us with what we need to maintain our decency. In Cuzco alone, the persons who perform all kinds of mechanical labor total more than 12,000, and almost all such professions are controlled by Indians. Who built the cities, *villas*, and towns of the *sierra* if not the Indians . . . who repairs the bridges and the roads, levels the mountains and opens the jungles?[1]

Although I have long been familiar with this quote, until recently I have failed to see in it anything but the admittedly valuable and graphic illustration of the economic burden for the native Andean population represented by the conquest and the subsequent erection of the colonial system. Like the author of my quote, I viewed such material with the eyes of a muckraker, joining in the denunciation of the excesses and the brutality of the colonial regime in Peru. Since the sixteenth century, outraged observers and writers have produced a body of literature describing the exploitation of the members of native Andean society that is unexcelled in its detail and its impact. But the regime we are denouncing is long gone; continued denunciation of a system that has passed away adds little to broader understanding, even if we are able to delineate the continued maintenance and reappearance of old forms of exploitation under new names in the present. The real value of taking a closer look at the specific forms of colonial exploitation in the Andean area lies in the help they may provide in understanding the mechanism of the economic system of colonial Latin America.

Socioeconomic Structure in Colonial Peru

In recent years much analytic effort has been spent to determine the specific character of the socioeconomic formation of the Spanish colonies in America. Some scholars have argued that the new societies founded by the Spaniards in the New World were essentially capitalist, the products of a world economy in a process of rapid transformation toward a fully developed capitalism. Others have pointed out that Spain in the sixteenth century was by no means a capitalist society.

They maintain that it was, in fact, rapidly "underdeveloped" in the centuries between the discovery and initial settlement of the Americas and the triumph of capitalism in Europe, never breaking the economic and social bonds that held back the full development of a capitalist economy in the countries outside of England.

Although I regard the socioeconomic formation of Peru from the sixteenth to the nineteenth century as essentially precapitalist, I suspect that we could argue over definitions for a long time without agreement. In order to solve these problems and, in the process, contribute to a broader understanding of the genesis of both capitalism and underdevelopment, we desperately need to move beyond assertion and theoretical argument, valuable as they may be, to a detailed look at the specific ways in which the colonial economy functioned. In this chapter I want only to suggest a few of the directions that I think will prove useful in building a model of the structure and the operation of the economic system of colonial Peru. Criticism, debate, and discussion may then lead to the creation of a model that will answer the basic questions about what kind of a system this was and what in it contributed both to the rise of capitalism in Europe and, more urgently for those of us directly concerned with Latin America, to the rise of what is today called "underdevelopment" in Latin America. I am confining my analysis and discussion to the core area of the viceroyalty of Peru, an area equivalent to the Inca empire destroyed by the invading Spaniards in the sixteenth century. In the case of other areas outside the Andes, particularly New Spain, the other major pole of the Spanish colonial system in the Americas, the specific character of the socioeconomic system emerging in that area was very different. It awaits a detailed study of the relation between the Spanish settlers and the administrative system introduced by Spain, on the one hand, and the structure of the Mesoamerican societies conquered by the Europeans, on the other.

First, I think that it is essential to discard many of the basic assumptions with which we have been operating to date. Many specialists in economic history have tended to follow the model proposed by W. A. Lewis and to define the colonial economic system as composed of two distinct sectors: (a) a modern, "progressive" sector actively involved in the production of commodities for market exchange, and (b) a "natural" or peasant sector intent upon producing goods for its own use. According to this theory, the "natural" or peasant sector supplies only labor to the progressive sector, participating in no other way in the local economy, whose dynamism is supplied by the modern sector.[2]

Now there are certain elements of the economic structure of colonial Peru that appear to fit this model quite well. The entire economy of the viceroyalty was divided into two distinct sectors, separated from one another by the entire corpus of colonial law and regulation. The Indians, who continued to function according to the mechanisms of traditional Andean society, provided the labor power that propelled the wheels of the enterprises owned and operated by members of European society. It would be convenient to follow the separation clearly delineated in colonial law and to treat the colonial economic system as two sectors, one of which was essentially self-sufficient and participated little except as a labor force in the production and distribution of the goods that issued from the other. Consciously or unconsciously, most of us who study the colonial world have done just that. We study the internal operation and transformation of the traditional Indian sector, converted into a peasantry by colonial law and regulation and the forces that impelled members of Indian society to provide labor to run the Spanish enterprises. Or, focusing upon the Spanish economy, we study the forces, means, and techniques of production characteristic of the *haciendas*, mines, and *obrajes* of the colonial world. In this latter case we often ask why those enterprises never became the leading edge of a process of economic expansion and growth leading to the full development of capitalism in Latin America.

Although some elements of the model of a dual sector economy are useful, I do not think that we will understand the mechanisms of the colonial economy or the blocks to the expansion and growth of the Spanish market-oriented sector unless we alter our perspective to look at the colonial economy as an integrated whole. In this perspective Indian as well as Spanish sectors were fully integrated into the system of production and distribution that—as the contemporary observer quoted initially told us so graphically—were ultimately dependent upon the labor power of the people defined as Indian by the colonial state. Further, we must add to our analysis an understanding of the operation of the colonial state, not just as a mechanism to ensure the collection of tribute and the allocation of Indian labor to the Spanish sector, although that was certainly one of its functions, but also as an essential participant in the economic process.

In any society the state is an instrument of coercion that functions to assure the ruling class its continued control of the remainder of the society. But in a society in which the labor force has not been separated from its access to the resources and means of production, laying the basis for the emergence of the labor market upon which capitalist production depends, the role of the state is even more crucial to the functioning of the economy. In this case, since people are not impelled by what we have called "natural circumstances" to offer their labor for sale, they must be forced to do so. The particular elements by which they are forced—the mechanisms of coercion—are basic to any definition of the socioeconomic formation of the society in question. In the case of colonial Peru, there was no internal dynamism fostering continued expansion of economic activity or growth. The dynamism of the economy was generated not within the system of production itself but from outside. It came through the coercive mechanisms applied by the colonial state, which maintained the flow of labor and goods to the members of Spanish society, and the distribution of the products of the Spanish economy throughout the viceroyalty. The political system of colonial Peru—official and recorded law as well as established custom—created both the market demand and the supply of goods and labor; without that political system the fragile dynamism of the economy of colonial Peru foundered and disintegrated.

In the following pages I want to survey the nature and impact of the principal levies, legal and extralegal, that constituted the specific forms of compulsion through which the Spanish sector extracted and accumulated surplus. Such surplus was generated by the native Andean sector either within their own productive system based upon the extended kin group or *ayllu*, or as temporary participants in the productive activity of Spanish enterprises. As the contemporary Spanish observer whom I quoted initially made amply clear, the members of Indian society supplied the Spanish sector with the goods and foodstuffs they consumed, provided the labor that built the economic infrastructure—the roads and bridges along which goods moved to market—and carried out factory or artisan production. Ultimately, we are forced to estimate the volume of economic surplus generated by Indian peasant society, for which there are few figures and still fewer indices of production. By looking at the articulation between the Indian economy and that of the colonial Spanish sector, we can begin to find ways to assess the volume of the economic surplus and its allocation. Our sources through the centuries have repeatedly made it clear that the economic system of colonial Peru was founded upon open exploitation and robbery, recognized and reinforced by the entire structure of colonial law and regulation. Let us take our informants at their word, and rather than deploring the exploitation and brutality that we know existed, use the data provided by that system to attempt to understand exploitation as a mechanism that determined the volume, distribution, and products of labor in colonial society.

Throughout the Spanish colonial period the labor force upon

which the members of European society depended was drawn from a peasant village economy that was built upon the production and consumption of its own necessities and that had little recourse to markets outside the community. For a variety of reasons, many of them the product of direct coercion, there was a small but steady emigration from village society to the mines, urban centers, and estates of the Spanish sector. However, that flow was a trickle rather than a flood and seems not to have increased much from the sixteenth to the nineteenth centuries. There is little sign of the development of a labor market in the course of the colonial period. There is plenty of evidence of wage labor, of course, and contrary to what was once assumed, labor was not commonly held in debt to keep it from returning to the village economy.[3] But despite the fact that we know that wage labor existed, we have little sign of any large-scale separation of the masses of the Indian population from their access to land and other productive resources during the colonial period. On the contrary, there is plenty of evidence that the state did its best to maintain the Indian village community, frequently deciding in favor of the Indian plaintiffs in disputes over land between village communities and members of Spanish society.[4]

Thus, the colonial state did not facilitate the expropriation of the Indian population from the land, thereby furthering the development of a labor market; moreover, the entire apparatus of colonial Indian administration from its elaboration in the 1560s through the 1580s was founded on the principle of retaining the traditional Andean system of production as the economic underpinning for the extraction of surplus from the members of Indian society. The role assigned the members of Andean society in colonial Peru demanded two basic conditions: (a) the Indians were to maintain their traditional structures of production, which meant preserving the Andean relations of production by means of which the members of Andean society ensured their survival and reproduction; and (b) the Indians were to provide a regular surplus to the European sector. This surplus was obtained by means of the levies placed upon the Indians by the colonial state, which either demanded goods or labor services in a regular corvée system, or forced the Indians to offer their goods or labor time in the European market in order to meet the legal and extralegal demands of the colonial state.

The traditional Andean sector was legally defined as a distinct society, or "republic," by Spanish laws and regulations. The Europeans carried out a large-scale concentration of the native population, resettling the Indians in a massive relocation program in the 1570s. This was intended to facilitate their administration and control and the appropriation of the surplus demanded by the colonial state. But despite the massive dislocation of the native population, the Spaniards preserved as much as possible the traditional patterns of access to the land, water, and other means of production of Andean society prior to the invasion of the Europeans. Although the laws regulating the new settlements specified that the Indians could retain their traditional lands if they were not more than one league (about 3 miles) from their new villages, there is no evidence that these restrictions were ever enforced by the Spanish authorities. Courts and judges ignored them until well into the eighteenth century and never questioned the principle that the members of a village community could legitimately claim as their own lands at several days' journey from their village.[5]

Spanish laws also specifically ordered that the common law, or traditional practices regulating the internal organization of Andean society, was to be observed except in cases where such practices contradicted the precepts of the crown or the Church. Members of Indian society buttressed their claims to resources and their relations with one another in disputes brought before the Spanish courts on the grounds that they had held a given area of land, or practiced a specific custom, "from time immemorial." As in Europe, established practice was the basis of common law, except that the established practice in this case was the body of custom and tradition that regulated the relations of production and reproduction of a socioeconomic formation distinct from that of its European masters. The entire body of custom and practice in Andean society was not respected. In particular, the ritual and ceremonial that reinforced community cooperation and the repair and maintenance of the resources of the community—the religious practices and beliefs of Andean society—became the focus of continual attack by the Catholic Church and its representatives. Such attacks gradually undermined the complicated edifice of social interaction and practice through which the members of Andean society carried out the production and distribution of goods and contributed to the erosion of the productive capacities of the Andean local communities. Nonetheless, the intent of the architects of the colonial state in Peru is clear: They sought to make a revived and reformed, but essentially unchanged, Andean society into the economic basis of the colonial system.

Prior to the destruction of the Inca state and the establishment of a Spanish regime in Peru, these same communities had not only ensured their own survival, but had supplied staggering amounts of surplus to the state. That surplus was primarily in the form of labor time, but the Europeans were nonetheless convinced of the large volume of surplus extracted by the Incas prior to their arrival. Francisco de Toledo, who well deserves his reputation as the Solon of the colonial system, made it his business to collect information on the nature and volume of the surplus extracted by the Incas.

Such information gave the Spaniards every basis to expect that the native Andean community could be regularly milked without exhausting its productive capacity as long as the social unit itself and its access to the resources and materials of production were maintained as much as possible as they had been prior to the arrival of the Europeans. The laws protecting the integrity of the Andean village community and its access to resources were intended to accomplish that end. The population was exploited for surplus through a series of levies, legal and illegal. The most important of these were tribute payments collected by the state; *mita*, "labor service", also collected by the state and distributed to members of Spanish society; and the *repartimiento de mercancías*, the periodic extralegal sale of goods to the Indians by the authorities of the Indian provinces. A short description of the form of each levy will give us a basis for evaluating the volume of the surplus collected in that fashion and its effect upon the relations between the Indian and the Spanish sectors in the economy.

Tribute

The members of Indian society were assessed regular payments, defined as an assessment in recognition of their status as vassals of the Spanish crown.[6] The tribute payments were the product of the state's gradual limitation and incorporation under its own authority of the lavish plunder that succeeded the European invasion of the Andes. The tribute was a specific sum in goods and specie assessed each household head by the colonial authorities from the time of Pedro de La Gasca in 1542; it was successively modified and reassessed until it was fixed in 1572 by Francisco de Toledo following the general inspection and count of the native population. It was defined as a head tax paid by all able-bodied adult men between the ages of 18 and 50. A selected number of people were exempted from the payment of tribute for specific reasons, ranging from their definition as members of the native elite—the *kurakas*, "descendants of the Inca ruling-class"—to personal infirmity and congenital illness.

Tribute assessments were based upon periodic censuses of a province or portion of a province performed by the civil administrator, the *corregidor de indios*, and his assistants. By law each *corregidor* was to carry out a census once during his term of office, which ranged from two to five years. A population count could also be ordered by the *Audiencia* at the request of the *kuraka,* the *encomendero,* or the attorney of the *Audiencia* charged with the welfare of the Indians. Until a new count was completed, remitted to the *Contaduría de Tributos* in Lima, and a new tribute assessment prepared and issued to the provincial authorities and the royal treasury officials of the district in which the province was located, the Indians were expected to pay the tribute assigned them on the books. This was true however much the actual population of the province might have changed in the interim. Further, anyone whose interests would be affected by a revision in the population figures had the right to file an objection to a new population count, which could effectively block a count for years by tying it up in litigation, despite the petition of the Indians. Both this factor and pure inertia meant that recounts were seldom, and a given census might form the basis for the tribute assessments for 20, 50, or even in some cases almost 100 years before a new count was authorized.[7]

Tribute was originally assessed and paid both in kind and in specie. Toledo converted much of the tribute assessed in kind into specie, a mechanism that was specifically intended to force the Indians to offer their labor in the Spanish market in order to obtain the precious metal demanded of them. But much continued to be collected in goods, principally cloth, coca, and foodstuffs such as *maiz,* wheat, potatoes, chickens, and eggs. All tribute, both in goods and specie, was collected twice a year in June and December and delivered to the royal treasury to officials of the district in which the province was located. The tribute assessments were valued in monetary terms in the office of the *Contaduría de Tributos,* converting payments in kind to a monetary standard, or fixed price that placed the assessment per capita according to the contemporary population figures; this ranged somewhere between four and seven pesos per person.[8]

If we are dealing with tribute in specie, we need only inquire into the distribution of that income. The Indians paid the cost of their own administration. The salaries of the provincial administrator, the *corregidor de indios,* and the attorneys and protectors of the Indians accounted for between 13 and 26% of the total value of the tribute income. Approximately one-fifth of the tribute income went to the parish priests, or *doctrineros,* as salaries. The wealth that was returned to the Indian community in the form of salaries to the ethnic chieftains or *kurakas* for their services to the state ranged from 4% to a high of 10%. By far the largest proportion of the tribute income, ranging from 40 to 60%, went to the *encomenderos* who enjoyed a fixed income that, despite its decline in the course of the colonial period, still constituted a tidy sum in the seventeenth century.[9] Despite the intermediary function of the state, which converted tribute into a pension fund to support the native aristocracy, the upper class of colonial society continued to enjoy an income derived from what may be classified as feudal or quasi-feudal rent until the eighteenth century.

But what happened to the tribute in kind? What function did that fill in the pattern of articulation between Indian and Spanish societies, and how was this surplus collected in the form of the products of the Indian economy allocated? Records from Cuzco make it possible to trace the process by which the state realized the value of tribute in kind and converted it into commodities circulating in the Spanish market.[10] After the distribution of a certain proportion of the goods to the hospitals and beneficient institutions of the city for their sustenance, announcements of the goods offered and the fixed values assigned them by the *Contaduría de Tributos* were posted by one of the attorneys of the treasury, together with the *corregidor* of the province from which the goods were collected. The goods collected in Cuzco consisted largely of *maiz*, wheat, potatoes, and fowls, usually chickens. Residents of the city bid upon the goods of a province, offering to pay the assigned face value of the goods in assayed silver.

If the state found bidders for all of the goods offered, it would realize the full fixed price of the tribute in kind, and the goods would pass from the warehouses of the state to the stores of the local merchants who dealt in such foodstuffs. But in this particular case, at least, the bidders did not immediately come forward, and after nine announcements and only two respondents, the remainder of the goods were sent to auction to be sold off in item lots to the highest bidder. In these auctions the goods were no longer offered in block units consisting of all the produce contributed by a given province; bidders were free to take, for example, only the wheat and *maiz* from Quispicanchis, or in another case, the coca from Paucartambo.

In this case the bidders were profiting from what was in effect a subsidized market. Through this market the goods extracted from the Indian economy were allocated among the Spanish residents and merchants of Cuzco, who in turn put them into circulation. This subsidized market had peculiar characteristics. Harvests vary widely in the Andes, where crop failure is an omnipresent possibility and the regular alternation of good and bad years is common. But tribute in kind was not a percentage of the harvest; it was a fixed amount that was collected no matter what the size of the crop harvested by the Indian farmer. That fixed amount went on the market each year in June, within a few weeks after the harvest. The amount collected from the Indians bore no relation either to the harvest or to the market price of the crops, and it was thrown into the market at harvest time, again without regard to market price. The actual value realized by the state from the sale of the crops undoubtedly responded to market conditions, rising in years of poor harvests and falling in the good times. So, in effect, the state subsidized the trade, with a kind of buffer not for the farmer, whose burden in effect rose in bad times relative to his total harvest, but for the dealer in grain and other foodstuffs. The merchant or middleman was protected from shortages by the regular volume of commodities provided by the state authorities through the auction of tribute goods.

Mita

The *mita*, or "labor draft", was primarily a mechanism for lowering the costs of production of the precious metals that were the cornerstone of the Spanish empire in the Americas. The *mita* ensured a constant supply of labor to the mines without depending upon the Indians or other members of colonial society to offer their labor time on the market. The *mita* was introduced by Viceroy Toledo as a solution to the crisis of production in the silver mines of Potosí. It followed the name, if not the actual practice of the *mit'a*, or "labor tax," through which the Inca state mobilized vast amounts of labor time for its massive projects. The colonial *mita*, also based upon the population statistics filed in the *Contaduría de Tributos*, took between one-sixth and one-seventh of the adult male population, according to the figures in the *Contaduría*, for six-month periods of service at tasks regarded as essential by the state.[11]

Mita service was assigned primarily to the silver mines of Potosí and the mercury mines of Huancavelica; these were arduous and deadly tasks for which few would volunteer on their own initiative. The economic function of the labor draft, therefore, at least in its conception, relates more to the production of Peru's main export goods than to the internal economic structure of the viceroyalty. By providing a substantial labor force, whose catchment area included all of southern Peru and the area of present-day Bolivia, Toledo ensured the most important miners a regular supply of labor. The *mitayos* were legally supposed to be paid according to a wage scale first established by Toledo and later revised at the end of the seventeenth century by Viceroy Duque do la Palata.[12] Considerable evidence shows, however, that as production declined in the course of the colonial period the miners converted the *mita* assignments themselves into commodities, thereby making a profit on the sale of the right to a share of the labor draft, or merely collected a fixed sum from the Indians in lieu of using their labor to dig ore—the infamous *indios de faltriquera*, or "pocket Indians."

Mita allocations were also used for other purposes, but the criteria for granting *mitayos* was the importance to the colonial state of the activity for which labor was sought, and virtually all other assignments underwrote the production of foodstuffs for the other major urban market of the viceroyalty—that of the capital in Lima—and what might be defined as the production of services and luxuries for the colonial elite. In areas outside of those that sent *mitayos* to the mines of Potosí and Huancavelica, the state assigned labor quotas to some coastal and highland *haciendas* producing for the urban market. It sent other people to work in transport and mail service, as well as to cut and transport ice from the glaciers of the coastal range to cool the drinks and food of the Lima elite.[13]

The economic function of the *mita* was fairly straightforward, and requires little further examination. It was a labor draft for the productive activities that produced the principal export goods of the viceroyalty and for other activities whose maintenance had to be subsidized by the state in one form or another. Its impact was massive. The *mita* draft was assigned only on the basis of the population native to the province in which it was counted, and thereby assumed to have access through their kin groups to lands and resources that could be used to maintain them and their families during the period of their labor turn. A migrant to the province, as an outsider without the kin ties to obtain access to land, was not liable for *mita* service. Thus the nature of the *mita* assessments constituted a push factor stimulating migration. By the eighteenth century, 40–60% of the population of the archbishopric of Cuzco, subject to the *mita* of Potosí, were *forasteros*, or "migrants from other provinces" who, by virtue of their status as migrants, were not liable to *mita* service.[14] Because the *mita* is a direct draft, assessed and assigned through state authorities, we can easily determine either the volume of the surplus labor extracted through the *mita*, or its allocation. The other levy to be examined is somewhat more complicated.

Repartimiento de Mercancías

The *repartimiento de mercancías*, or "forced sale of goods," was widely accepted and practiced not only by the provincial administrator, the *corregidor de indios,* but also by the local priests, *hacendados,* miners, and other members of provincial society, including the members of the Indian elite. But despite the fact that all, up to and including the crown and the Council of the Indies, were well aware of the practice and even included a calculation of the benefits to be obtained from the activity in estimates of the purchase price of the office of *corregidor,* the *repartimiento* was forbidden by royal ordinances and, save for a short period between 1752 and 1782, was illegal. Nonetheless, the activity was too tempting to resist. The salary of the *corregidor* was far below the calculated expenses of these officials, let alone providing enough gain for them to use their positions to advance their personal and political fortunes. Thus, from the sixteenth century the *corregidor* rapidly became the terminal point of the Spanish commercial system in the viceroyalty, a merchant-functionary who ensured the flow of currency and goods from the members of the provincial society, primarily the Indians, to the Spanish sector and beyond that, to the representatives of the great commercial houses in Lima. The function of the *corregidor,* who was administrator, policeman, and judge of first instance in his province, gave him an ideal opportunity to take on the role of merchant. In his capacity as judge and policeman, the *corregidor* was in a position to compel the Indians to pay for the goods they accepted, whether they had sought the goods or had been forced to receive them.[15]

In the mid-eighteenth century Viceroy Conde de Superunda expressed the widely accepted rationale for the mercantile practices of the provincial administrator: "Since it is well known that the provinces cannot maintain themselves witout a distribution, nor would there be anyone who would administer justice in them, these [the *repartimiento de mercancías*] have come to be tolerated."[16] In other words, the Indians needed the articles they were forced to accept; however since all Indians were defined as lazy, they had to buy the goods they needed from soneone in a position to compel them to pay their debts. Thus, in the process of filling his own coffers, the *corregidor* performed a valuable economic service by providing the members of Indian society with the goods produced by the Spanish sector.

For approximately three decades, from the middle of the eighteenth century, the *repartimiento* was legalized and the state drew up both a schedule of goods to be distributed to each province and a list of fixed prices. This list permits the calculation of the kind, the volume, and at least a minimum price for the goods distributed by the *corregidores,* almost exclusively to the Indian productive sector. Much evidence indicates that many *corregidores* were not satisfied with the mercantile activity permitted them by law and carried out considerably more than the one distribution of goods permitted them in the course of a five-year term. Still the official lists at least provide us with a minimum baseline for the calculation of the surplus extracted from the Indian sector in the form of commercial activity. Virtually every province in the viceroyalty was assigned a quota of mules, the most common item in the schedule of distribution. The other common items, assigned by volume, were iron, steel, cloth woven in the viceroyalty (*ropa de la tierra*), *guano* ("fertilizer from coastal birds"), and knives—all items that, at fair prices, can be regarded as important additions to the means of production available to the peasant producer. In addition, each province was assigned a specific amount of assorted goods, calculated by value according to assigned prices, whose value to a peasant household was far more questionable. These goods, calculated at 100% rate of profit, included cloth from Quito to the north, technically within the viceroyalty, as well as imported goods such as French linen from Rouen and Brittany, thick woolen and beaver cloth from England, *maté,* candle wax, and silk stockings for both men and women.[17]

The official price lists specified a distribution of mules in the viceroyalty whose sale prices, ranging from 25 to 40 pesos per head, totaled some 96,208 pesos. The total value of the goods to be distributed by the *corregidor* over a 5-year term was almost 6 million pesos, or approximately 1.2 million pesos per year. This is a substantial sum to be extracted from a population widely defined as marginal and outside of the productive structure of colonial society. A rough calculation of the surplus officially expected to be generated by the Indian population at the end of the eighteenth century, based upon tribute and *repartimiento,* gives us a per capita figure of 9.69 pesos per year that the state expected to realize from the Indian population.[18]

Such figures, reduced to per capita amounts, look like very little. But the multiple of the per capita calculations is extremely large. Essentially, we are dealing here with what might be called an "oil for the lamps of China" type of situation; each individual peasant household could mobilize only a relatively small amount of surplus beyond its basic subsistence needs, but the aggregate volume of those small individual contributions to the European economic sector, mediated through the *corregidor,* was substantial. Those amounts ultimately had to be generated by the Indian productive sector. Where did the Indians get the specie (or the goods that were accepted in lieu of specie, usually at a fixed rate considerably below the price the *corregidor* could hope to realize by the sale of such goods) that they were forced to hand over to the *corregidor* in payment for the goods he made them accept?

An attempt to answer that question leads us directly back to the problem of the articulation between the traditional, or Indian, productive sector and that of European society in colonial Peru. The Indians could get specie, as the organizers of the colonial system expected, by leaving their home communities at regular intervals to offer their labor to the enterprises and productive activities of the members of European society. This was the expectation and the analysis of enlightened Spaniards or members of Spanish colonial society who shared the widely held conviction that the Indians were lazy and had to be forced to work and to produce. Alonso Carrión de la Bandera, a Spanish member of the colonial bureaucracy and author of *El Lazarillo de Ciegos Caminantes,* defended both the payment of tribute and the *repartimiento de mercancías* on the grounds that both the state head tax and the forced distribution of goods made the Indians sell their labor to the Spaniards. And they did sell their labor. *Hacienda* records from the Cuzco region make it clear that the estates drew regularly upon the surrounding village communities for a labor source. *Alquilos,* "people who worked for wages," were hired by the estates at a fixed wage of two reales a day set by the colonial authorities. Wherever possible, *hacienda* managers paid their workers in goods: meat and dried beef, coca, *maiz,* honey and molasses from sugar production, cloth, potatoes and *chuño*—all goods produced within the *hacienda* itself. Although wage laborers accepted a substantial portion of their earnings in goods, they also demanded specie, usually for the payment of tribute. *Hacienda* records indicate that, in fact, most of the people hired by the *hacienda* left the estate, if not with considerable earnings, at least not in debt.[19]

Wage labor was not the only way to earn the money demanded by the state and its representatives. Other members of Indian society made profitable use of their mules, transporting the goods of the European sector to the markets, close or distant, for which they were intended. We badly need a thorough study of the *arrieros,* or "muleteers", of the colonial period. Members of Indian society at all levels worked at least part of their time at this activity, from the Indian nobility to the local villager. Tupac Amaru II, leader of the great rebellion of 1780 and a member of the elite Indian nobility of Cuzco, was active in the transport of goods between Cuzco and Potosí. Such an activity probably occupied many of the *forasteros,* "migrants from other provinces," who were consigned to the margins of the Indian productive sector by their lack of access to the goods and resources held by the village community. Given that the difficulty of moving goods from the point of production to the market is a major problem today in Peru's mountainous territory, it undoubtedly absorbed a significant proportion of the labor time and the cost of production in the colonial period as well. The accounts of the sugar *hacienda* of Pachachaca in the area of Cuzco make it clear that transport costs from the *hacienda* to Cuzco and between Cuzco and Potosí accounted for at least 40% of the disbursements of the *hacienda* between 1768 and 1774.[20]

The Indians could also adapt their own resources and turn a portion of their labor time to the production of goods for sale to the European market in order to meet the demands laid upon them. Such was the intent of the Europeans. Prior to the reorganization of native Andean society and the elaboration of the structure of Indian administration in the sixteenth century, the Spanish jurist, Juan de Matienzo, whose recommendations were read closely by the royal court, counseled the conversion of the Indian economy into a peasant sector producing for the colonial market. "Organizing them . . . and giving each one of them lands of their own and money for themselves as pay for their labor, so that they may buy llamas and cattle from Spain and other things for themselves, they will begin to like work, and will begin through that to live a civilized life."[21] In actual fact the goods that the Indians bought were for the most part not cattle but mules, iron tools, and other goods distributed by the *corregidor*. They did, however, devote a substantial part of their efforts to cattle production for the European market. The Indians of the province of Huarochirí sent beef cattle to the Lima market and to the mining area of Nuevo Potosí, now Cerro de Pasco. The Indians in the area of Ayacucho were virtually the only suppliers of beef to the urban market in the eighteenth century.[22] Other communities, whose population had dropped while their land resources remained the same, rented the land in excess of their subsistence needs to other communities, or even to members of European society. The lands most commonly rented were those that produced goods for the European market: pasturelands or relatively low lands that could be used to grow European fruits and grains. There are numerous cases of villages that rented lands from other communities and then used them to produce for the European market.[23] *Forasteros* also rented lands from the communities in which they settled, which then forced them to devote a relatively large proportion of their activity to market production in order to pay both the state levies and the land rent to their new landlords.[24]

As some members of Indian society began to accumulate lands and income well beyond their subsistence needs, this activity stimulated the internal transformation of the production relations within Indian society, and the growing internal differentiation of the native Andean community. In traditional Andean society access to productive labor was mobilized through kin ties; people who lacked such ties, or had not cultivated and maintained them, found themselves unable to obtain the aid of the other members of the community when they sought it. Migration, as well as growing social differentiation within Indian society, meant the development of a pool of available labor that could be obtained with wages, most likely in kind, by people engaged in production for the European market.

The individual case is often suspect, but there is other evidence that a substantial portion of the levies paid by the members of Indian society were generated by the diversion of a considerable amount of the efforts of the community to production for the European market. In the 1780s, a Spanish contemporary in the viceroyalty prepared a list of those provinces that yielded the most profits to the *corregidor* in the *repartimiento de mercancías*.[25] Four provinces—Conchucos, Huaylas, Lampa, and Tarma—received the highest valuations, all defined as "first class" provinces. The remarks made by the compiler of the list are extremely suggestive. Both Conchucos and Huaylas were marked high because, as the compiler stated, they were major producers of the light woolen cloth and baize that was widely used in the viceroyalty. Cloth had a ready market, although, our reporter added, the value of these goods in Lima had fallen, making them hard to sell. It is clear in this case that the *corregidor* was expected to accept the cloth produced by the Indian community in payment for the goods he distributed, converting that cloth into specie on the European market in Lima. The *corregidor* functioned as a middleman between the Indian and the European sectors.

Our rapid survey of the legal and extralegal levies imposed upon the Indians by the colonial state and its representatives makes it clear that these levies functioned to force the Indians both to offer their labor to the European sector and to orient a considerable proportion of their own internal production to the European sector. Did this activity undermine the productive capacity of the Indian village economy? There are some suggestions that three and a half centuries of extraction took their toll. The calculation of the expected profit from the *repartimiento de mercancías*, discussed earlier, noted that in some cases, the value of a particular province had fallen from its earlier level, suggesting economic decline. In ranking the province of Yauyos, for example, the author noted that "in the past an abundant distribution was obtained, but today it has become a backward and depopulated province, of the second class."[26] But the apparent decline could also have been the result of competition from other goods, implied by the falling price of rough cloth in the Lima market, which was flooded with cloth from Quito and from the rapidly growing productive centers in France and, particularly, in England. Additional indications suggest that limits to the extraction of surplus were also established by the Indians themselves. The class struggle that set the real, rather than the physiological, limit to the extraction of surplus shows up in the case of Azangaro in the 1780s. The author of the ranking noted that "although of the first class, [Azangaro] is considered among the worst because of its cold climate and the bellicose nature of its inhabitants."[27]

Summary and Conclusions

We have here an example of an economic system in which a pre-capitalist economy, oriented toward the production of specie for export, was superimposed upon another, non-European productive system primarily oriented toward the production of goods for internal distribution. Following an initial period of massive exploitation that culminated by the 1560s in a real crisis, the Spanish settlers were saved by the intervention of the colonial state and the reorganization of the system of exploitation. The authors of the structures of colonial administration in Peru did their best to maintain the native Andean community as the basic productive unit of colonial society, which would provide both labor and goods to the European economy. The system worked to a degree far greater than the originators of the colonial structure in the sixteenth century could have imagined.

By the seventeenth century, members of Spanish society had begun to move into the Indian communities, settling and even marrying there, appropriating lands and furthering the inevitable process of internal differentiation that accompanies the growth of production for the market. In 1628 a member of Spanish society tried to convince the crown to reverse its prohibition against Spaniards, *mestizos,* or mulattos living in the Indian communities.[28] From his petition it is possible to perceive the first stages of the emergence of a provincial elite, an incipient landed bourgeoisie born of both societies, Indian and European, which held the potential to draw upon the productive power of both societies. But the Council of the Indies rejected the petition and decided to maintain the division between Spanish and Indian sectors established in the sixteenth century.

Such decisions consigned this incipient class to the margins of colonial society, its autonomy and freedom of action having been undermined by its uncertain legal status and the authority over it granted to the representatives of bureaucratic power, particularly the *corregidor*. The petty commodity economy that characterized the Spanish productive system erected upon the productive power of traditional Andean society was maintained and reinforced by the political apparatus of the colonial state, which, although it could not bring a new economic system into being, could do a great deal to restrict the internal pressures toward change.

The preceding observations are highly tentative ones. I want only to insist upon two points:

1. The economy of colonial Peru was not a dual system but an integrated economic system. In this integrated system the labor power and a great deal of the actual volume of the goods that circulated in the viceroyalty was drawn from the Indian communities.

2. Through the levies the political apparatus of the colonial state played an important part in maintaining the dynamism of the colonial economic system. The demands of these levies impelled the members of Indian society to produce for the European market and to move individually into that market for limited periods in order to offer their labor to the Europeans. But these levies did not create a labor market. On the contrary, the state's efforts to preserve and maintain the Indian community also functioned to limit the development of that labor market by its protection of the Indian village community against the depredations of ambitious entrepreneurs from both sectors, Spanish and Indian.

In order to understand the origins and the mechanisms of this colonial system in Peru, a productive system oriented toward petty commodity production for a limited market, we need to return to some of the perennial topics of economic history, ignoring the traditional division that set the economic historian-anthropologist to studying the Indian sector. If we take a close look at the transport industry or cloth prooduction in the colonial period, we may find new answers to old questions. Huaylas and Conchucos were centers of cloth production. Did all of that production take place through the *obraje* system, primarily part of the Spanish productive sector? Or did the Andean community turn its traditional skills in cloth production to the prduction of cloth as a commodity with which to obtain the specie needed to pay the levies of the state? Did the Indian villagers participate in the transport of goods to the market? How did the activity of the members of the Indian elite, such as Tupac Amaru II, who built their fortunes at least in part through their participation in the transport trade, affect the internal structure of production within the Indian community? We are rapidly learning much more about the specific nature of the relations of production within the local Indian community, as young scholars teach us about the mechanisms of community reciprocity and access to labor. By drawing upon their work as well as returning to the detailed study of the articulations between the Indian community and the productive enterprises of Spanish colonial society, we can build a picture of the colonial economic system that will make it possible for us to comprehend both the productive power and the limits to growth in colonial Andean society.

Notes

[1] "Parecer del P. Manuel Toledo Leiva, rector del Colegio de la Compañía de Jésus de Huancavelica, sobre la mita de Potosí, 30 de Agosto de 1724," in Rubén Vargas Ugarte, ed., *Pareceres jurídicas en asuntos de indios* (Lima, 1951):172.

[2] W. A. Lewis, *Theory of Economic Growth* (London, 1955); see also Witold Kula, *An Economic Theory of the Feudal System* (London: New Left Books, 1976):20–23.

[3] See Pablo Macera, "Feudalismo colonial americano: el caso de las haciendas peruanas," *Acta Histórica*, 35 (Szeged, Hungary: 1971), mimeo. translation prepared for the Seminar on Peruvian Economic History by Professor Heraclio Bonilla, Universidad Católica del Peru (Lima). Also Jorge Polo y La Borda González, "Pachachaca:autoabastecimiento y comercialización." Tésis para el bachillerato en historia, Universidad Católica de Lima, 1976.

[4] See, for example, the disputes over land in the Archivo Nacional del Perú, Sección Histórica, in notes 23 and 24.

[5] "Indice del repartimiento de tasas de las provincias contenidas en este libro hechas en tiempo del exmo. Sr. D. Francisco de Toledo [copy of 1785]," Archivo General de la Nación Argentina, Sala 9: 17-2-5; also published in Carlos A. Romero, ed., "Libro de la visita general del virrey D. Francisco de Toledo, 1570–1575," *Revista Histórica*, VII, ent. II (Lima, 1924): 113–216. Material on the actual maintenance of lands far from their new settlements by the Andean community can be found in the disputes over land in the Archivo Nacional and in the Biblioteca Nacional. For specific examples, see notes 23 and 24.

[6] The laws regulating the assessment of tribute can be found in the *Recopilación de leyes de los Reynos de las Indias*, Libro VI, tit. V. *passim.*

[7] The procedure followed in assessing tribute is detailed in the *Recopilación*, Lib. VI, tit. V, ley xxi. For a summary of the date of the last census of each province, prepared in the mid-eighteenth century, which gives an idea of the time that elapsed between population counts in many provinces, see "Informe del Contador de Retasas . . . [1768]," in Antonio Porlier, "Libro de cédulas, autos acordados, y otros instrumentos pertenecientes a los indios, año de 1769 [sic.]," Book II, ff. 117–127, Yale University Library, microfilm in the Bancroft Library, University of California, Berkeley, in *Documents relating to Peru*, reel 2.

[8] See the tribute assessments in the *Tasa de la Visita General de Francisco de Toledo*, Introd. y versión paleográfica de Noble David Cook, (Lima: Univ. Nacional

Mayor de San Marcos: 1975); Antonio Vásquez de Espinosa, *Compendio y Descripción de las Indias occidentales* (Washington, D.C., Smithsonian Institution: 1948):644–670; also Archivo Nacional del Perú, Sección Histórica, Derecho Indígena, Cos. 267, 189, 287.

[9]Alfredo Moreno Cebrián, *El corregidor de indios y la economía peruana en el siglo XVIII* (Madrid:Consejo Superior de Investigaciones Cientificas: 1977):59–60.

[10]See the "Cuadro de remates de las especies que en los corregimientos de su distrito pertenecieron a esta Real Caja del Cuzco este año de [1]647" Archivo Histórico del Cuzco, document #7.

[11]On the mita, see Tomás de Ballesteros, *Tomo primero de las ordenanzas del Perú* [1685] (Lima, 1752) Libro II, tit. XIII, órden iii: "Cédula del servicio personal, 1609"; *Recopilación*, Libro VI, tít. XII, ley xxii.

[12]*Aranzel de los jornales que se han de pagar a los indios así voluntarios, mingados, alquilas, y agregados a las haciendas de españoles, como mitayos, y de obligación, en todo género de trabajo* . . . (Los Reyes, 1687). Copies of this rare publication can be found in the Biblioteca Nacional, Madrid, and in the Biblioteca de las Escuela de Derecho, Universidad de Buenos Aires, Argentina.

[13]On *mita* service other than the mines, see the "Relación que el Principe de Esquilache hace al Señor Marqués de Guadalcázar sobre el estado en que deja las provincias del Perú [1621]" in Ricardo Beltrán y Rózpide, *Colección de las memorias o relaciones que escribieron los virreyes del Perú acerca del estado en que dejaban las cosas generales del reino* (Madrid, 1921); Sebastián Francisco de Melo, "Memorandum on the mita arrangements," Archivo Nacional del Perú, Sección Histórica, Derecho Indigena, Cuaderno 287 (1726–1753) two unnumbered pages.; ANP, Seccion Historica, DI, Cuadernos 188 [1706], and 189 [1705] espec. ff. 1-1v, 6v-7, 10v-11.

[14]Oscar Cornbilt, "Society and Mass Rebellion in Eighteenth-Century Peru and Bolivia," *Latin American Affairs: St. Anthony's Papers*, no. 22 (London, 1970):24–27.

[15]For a massive amount of data on the *repartimiento de mercancías* throughout the colonial period, see Alfredo Moreno Cebrián, *El corregidor de indios y la economía peruano en el siglo XVIII*, cited note 9.

[16]Viceroy Conde de Superunda, cited in Moreno Cebrián, *El corregidor de indios*:274.

[17]The tariff lists of the legalized *repartimiento de mercanciás* have been reproduced by Moreno Cebrián in *El corregidor de indios*:317–355.

[18]Per capita figures cálculated from the tariff lists of the *repartimiento de mercanciás* in Moreno Cebrian, *El corregidor de indios* cited in note 17; tribute figures are from J. R. Fisher, *Government and Society in Colonial Peru: the Intendent System 1784–1814* (London: Athlone Press, 1970) appendix four, population statistics from the same source, appendix two.

[19]See, for example, the *hacienda* accounts in the Archivo Histórico del Cuzco, documents eight and nine.

[20]Jorge Polo y La Borda González, "Pachachaca," "Utilidades y flujo de dinero, 1768–1774," table facing page 97, unpubl. thesis cited in note 3.

[21]Juan de Matienzo, *Gobierno del Peru* [1567], edicion et etude preliminaire par Guillermo Lohmann Villena (Paris-Lima: Travaux de l'Institut Francais d'Etudes Andines, tome XI: 1967) 20.

[22]Archivo Nacional del Peru, Seccion Historica, Derecho Indigena, Co. 252, f. 111; D1, Co. 282, F. 3-3v; and "Superior Gobierno, Leg. 9, Co. 175; Biblioteca Nacional del Peru, C-2450.

[23]See, for example, Archivo Nacional del Peru, Titulos de comunidad, mandados protocolizar, Titulos de Chacalla [1711–1832]; ANP, Seccion Historica, Derecho Indigena, Co. 825, "La comunidad de Chauca contra la comunidad de Otao [1667–1749];"

ANP Tierras de Comunidad, Legajo 5, Co. 16, "Calahuaya contra Huarochirí y Yambilla [1794–1820]."

[24]See "Calahuaya contra Huarochirí y Yambilla" above; ANP, Tierras de Comunidad, Legajo 5, Co. 42, "Tambilla de Lahuaytambo contra Juan Bautista Damian [1792–1823];" ANP, Tierras de Comunidad, Legajo 5, Co. 44, "Fundacion del pueblo de Quilcamachay, [1808–1838]."

[25]Gregorio de Cangas, "Compendio historico . . . [1780], reproduced in Moreno Cebrian, *El corregidor de indios*:78–79.

[26]Ibid.:78.

[27]Ibid.:79.

[28]"Consulta del Consejo de las Indias sobre las Proposiciones que hizo el capitán Andrés de Deza pidiendo que los españoles puedan vivir libremente in pueblos de Indios, Madrid, 17 de enero de 1628," in Richard Konetzke, *Colección de documentos para la historia de la formación social de Hispanoamérica*, 1493–1810, vol. II; 1 (Madrid, 1958):308–314.

PART V

Indigenous Culture and Consciousness

Spiritual Conflict and Accommodation in New Spain: Toward a Typology of Aztec Responses to Christianity

J. Jorge Klor de Alva

Editors' Introduction

Jorge Klor de Alva questions Ricard's long-accepted thesis of the "spiritual conquest" of Mexico by showing pervasive Nahuatl resistance to true Christian conversion. Klor de Alva stresses how often natives resisted conversion and how few conversions were based on full understanding of fundamental Christian doctrine. Why else, Klor de Alva asks, would clerics have sustained such coercive tactics of evangelization? In analyzing Nahuatl metaphysical concepts, he demonstrates how Indians could accommodate Christian elements without undertaking meaningful conversion. He also reviews the evidence for a wide range of ways Indians covertly or overtly resisted Christianization.

The appearance in 1933 of Robert Ricard's *La <<conquête spirituelle>> du Mexique* had the effect of putting beyond doubt the success of the Christianization efforts in sixteenth-century New Spain. Faithfully adhering to what many interpreted as Ricard's position, more recent historians of the colonial church have claimed that, save for minor exceptions in outlying areas, the natives of Mexico converted to the new faith within the first decades after the conquest (Gómez

THE INCA AND AZTEC
STATES, 1400–1800

Canedo 1977; Kobayashi 1974; Navarrete 1978; Ulloa 1977). The documents with which Ricard and his followers have worked are primarily those of the Mendicant missionaries and other ecclesiastics, whose apologetic biases often led them to exaggerate triumphs and to minimize failures. These very sources, however, contain information that may lead us to question the accuracy of the "spiritual conquest" thesis; considered together with others, they offer an alternative view of the process of cultural change in sixteenth-century central Mexico.

There is no question with regard to the success of the Spaniards in establishing a visible church: Buildings were built, ceremonies instituted, sodalities (cofradías) founded, tithes collected, and the catechism echoed throughout most of the land. Students of the colonial church, aware of the importance of these feats, have sought primarily to explain the establishment and organization of ecclesiastical institutions, and the complex relations between these and the secular authority. The result has been a history that takes very little account of the experiences of the Native Americans in the context of the evangelization efforts.

Authenticity of Conversions

Because anthropologists and historians have paid relatively little attention to the indigenous side of the proselytization in New Spain, the distinction between outward Christianization and genuine conversion has scarcely been examined. The acceptance of some external Christian forms has been seen as tantamount to conversion; the integration of Christian values and world view have been taken for granted. Our understanding of Aztec responses to Christianity is further hampered by the lack of systematic studies of the Spanish attempts to eradicate the native religions, and of indigenous resistance to these efforts. This is in contrast to the situation in Andean studies, where a number of recent, well-documented works have elucidated both the campaign for the extirpation of "idolatry" and the methods employed by the Indians to neutralize the advance of Christianity during many decades after the conquest (Duviols 1966, 1967a,b,c, 1977; Millones 1964, 1967, 1971). However, autochthonous views of Christianity have as yet not been adequately studied for either culture area; the critical issue of the nature of the conversions therefore remains confused for both.

The spiritual encounters between Indians and Europeans in the Andean area took place under significantly different circumstances from those that prevailed in New Spain. The conquest of the Incas required more time: Communications in the Andes were more difficult, and the evangelization was dominated by Dominicans, whose doctrinaire bent led them to favor a thorough preparation. The pragmatic Franciscans in Mexico built, taught, and baptized with great enthusiasm and on a large scale. The speed and completeness of the military subjugation of central New Spain resulted in an earlier and more extensive iconoclasm than was possible in the Andes; thus, the religion of the Incas suffered less persecution than its counterpart in Mexico during the sixteenth century. It was not until 1610, almost 70 years after the commencement of the conquest of the Tawantinsuyu, that a systematic campaign to destroy the resurgent indigenous cults was initiated in Peru. Overt, widespread, militant resistance to Christianity, like that which characterized the 1565 Taki Onqoy movement among the Incas, is not found among the Aztecs, though localized rebellions occurred beyond the central area of what is now Mexico (Coll 1976; Duviols 1977:133–145; Huerta and Palacios 1967).

As a consequence of the zealous but often superficial evangelization in New Spain, many Aztecs resisted Christianity covertly. This may have led to the absence in Mexico of the *visita de las idolatrías*, which had been instituted in the Andean zone in order to destroy all vestiges of aboriginal religiosity through a full-fledged "inquisition for Indians" (Duviols 1977:176–230). The literature spawned by the *visita de las idolatrías* is replete with information detailing both sides of the spiritual warfare that intermittently gripped colonial Peru. *Visita*-like documents for New Spain are meager by comparison, but other materials were written that sought the same end. These resources, whose counterparts can also be found for the Andes, include the well-known letters and chronicles of the ecclesiastics and the works that aimed at instructing the priests on the identification and the mode of destruction of the "pernicious superstitions of the Indians." These latter texts consist of works produced by clergymen after discovering vestiges of the native cults in their bailiwicks, books of sermons especially prepared for the Mexicans, *confesionarios* for use when confessing Aztecs, and the manuals written on techniques for discovering and eradicating the ancient practices.

Other relevant sources include Inquisition records, catechisms, formal treatises on mission theory, works produced in the course of civil or ecclesiastical inspections (*visitas*), and the *Relaciones Geográficas* compiled as of 1577 in response to questionnaires formulated by the officials of the crown in Madrid. Finally, numerous secular documents in the indigenous languages are beginning to come to light.

Those written by the Aztecs themselves give us a vivid image of the extent and mode of the Christianity experienced by them. The "primordial title" from the Sula (Zollan) area south of Chalco, studied in Chapter 14 of this book, is an excellent example of the importance this untapped source will have in the future. Unfortunately, these materials have no counterpart in the Andean area since native-language texts were not produced by the Incas. I shall make use of representative examples of some of the sources mentioned here in this discussion on the Aztec responses to the new faith.

A number of authors have presented, more or less explicitly, typologies of Aztec reactions to Christianity. Wigberto Jiménez Moreno points to the variety of responses, the reasons for these reactions, and the importance of identifying them in light of specific groups, geographical regions, and historical periods (Jiménez Moreno 1958: 107–109 113–114). Pedro Carrasco also discusses these points but adds a number of important details concerning the resistance of the natives, the syncretism that often developed, and the "double religious system" that resulted when private worship continued to follow ancient patterns while veneration in the Christian mold prevailed in the public sphere (Carrasco 1975:198–203). The typology proposed in the following attempts to capture the widest possible range of Aztec responses by building on some of the distinctions described by these authors and by making use of the documentary evidence that attests to the limited success encountered in the conversion of the Indians. The study of the works produced in the sixteenth and seventeenth centuries mentioned in the preceding may lead us to modify a number of conclusions regarding the geography and chronology of the penetration of Christian ideology that have become standard in the literature on the "spiritual conquest" of New Spain.

Reliance on geographical and chronological categories alone can be misleading. This is clear from the fact that failure to convert the Indians was almost as common in Mexico City as in outlying areas and was as widespread in the late sixteenth century as in the 1530s (e.g., García Pimentel 1897). But it is generally true that the greater the isolation of the natives from Spanish influence, the less modification was suffered by the native religion; moreover, those raised to believe in the indigenous cults before the arrival of the Spaniards were more recalcitrant than the postcontact generations. The grandchildren of those raised before the conquest had forgotten, for the most part, the names of the gods and the nature of the ceremonies in the liturgy of the aristocrats. With optimism and considerable exaggeration Fray Gerónimo de Mendieta wrote during the 1850s that "today one senses no more trace [of the past idolatries] (at least wherever they obtain a sufficient doctrine), than if one thousand years had passed since their conversion" (Códice Mendieta 1892 [Vol. 5]:33). Fray Juan de Torquemada asserted a generation latter that the names of the Aztec gods were then so completely erased from their memory that of the thousands they had "there is hardly anyone who knows how some of them were called"; indeed, he adds, he has himself asked the Indians if they recognize the names of the gods "and not only have they failed to recognize them, but they have been practically astonished at hearing them" (Torquemada 1975 [Vol. 3]:53).

Caution must be used in interpreting these remarks. Aztec society was extremely hierarchical; an unbridgeable gap separated religious instruction for the rich and that for the poor, particularly in the rural areas. The native cults that survived the Spanish intrusion were composed principally of aspects of the private religious traditions of the nonprivileged classes, described by Carrasco as "the part of the aboriginal religion associated with family life: the cycle of life rites, cures, and rites which accompanied the technical activities like agriculture, hunting, etc." (Carrasco 1975:200). These were, in turn, mixed with the grossly simplified, greatly diversified, and easily mutable traces of the "great tradition" rites and beliefs that the native priests and their successors continued to practice and preach after the conquest and throughout the colonial period—though progressively augmented with stray elements from Christianity, Spanish heterodoxy, and the culture of the black slaves (Aguirre Beltrán 1963; González Obregon 1912). Therefore, ignorance of the orthodox pre-Hispanic rites and the associated pantheon of the elite class is not proof that Christianization took place successfully or otherwise.

The question of the assessment of the authenticity of conversions is ticklish. Excepting those few whose writings betray the extent to which they had accepted Christian values and a European world view, we must judge through the perceptions of others the degree to which Christian ideology penetrated the thinking of the majority. Nonetheless, the Christian image in Aztec thought is generally well reflected in the natives' reactions to the imposition of the new faith as recorded by the Spaniards and the Christianized Indians. In the first published study specifically concerned with these reactions León-Portilla advanced the following conclusions:

1. There were Náhuatl speakers who underwent authentic conversions shortly after they came in contact with the Europeans.
2. Many of the young men who studied in the College of Tlatelol-

co (between 1536 and 1550) adopted Christian ideals and attitudes, though some of their unorthodox expressions may have caused some raised brows.

3. Evidence indicates that from the start, and as late as the 1630s, a number of natives were openly hostile to the imposition of the new faith, showing both surprise and disgust at the idea of having to abandon what they considered to be the very essence of their culture.

4. A few natives carried on arguments as early as 1524; they compared the doctrines of their forefathers to the incomprehensible teachings of the missionaries, which they sometimes ridiculed. Some of these contentious Aztecs recalled the words of past sages, and as late as 1558, they threatened their hearers with dire predictions of the end of the present age and the descent of the *tzitzimime* (monsters who would eat everyone at the end of the world).

5. Whenever and wherever Spanish activity had significantly altered native routine, but not enough time had elapsed for new ways to be properly assimilated, those who found themselves *sin rumbo* (without direction) considered the possibility of remaining *nepantla*, "in the middle," a reasonable alternative.

6. In the late 1520s and 1530s some Aztecs claimed that the friars were people whose religion opposed everything that gave joy on earth. In reference to this complaint, several of them believed the moralizing of the priests was aimed only at the Indians, since the behavior of the Spaniards failed to meet the ideals preached.

7. At the same time, a few considered the existence of various religious orders to mean the existence of diverse faiths. They argued that the pre-Hispanic religion should also be worthy of being considered and accepted.

8. Some of the friars, during the second half of the sixteenth century and the beginning of the seventeenth, perceived that much of the ancient faith survived under the guise of Christian rituals. Indeed, it was a frequent practice to adopt only externally the beliefs and ways of Christianity (León-Portilla 1974:32–33).

This summary, which León-Portilla admits is far from complete, puts into perspective the complexity and variety of sentiments explicitly expressed in the documents. A number of the important issues can be supplemented by additional evidence culled from sources not discussed in his article—sources that, furthermore, reveal some of the other Nahua attitudes toward the new faith (Klor de Alva 1980b: 456–519).

Accommodation in the Christianization Process

I have reduced the many distinct modes of Aztec behavior toward Christianity to 15. For the sake of clarity and brevity I have organized these into a schema, which highlights the two basic positions: accommodation and conflict.

Accommodation

A. Complete conversion (Christianity believed and understood)
   1. Belief in Christianity with the adoption of *criollo* cultural customs.
   2. Belief in Christianity with the retention of indigenous cultural customs that were not found offensive by the Christian clergymen.
B. Incomplete conversion (Christianity believed but misunderstood)
   1. Belief in Christianity founded on the premises of the native religion with active participation only in Christian rites (external syncretism).
   2. Belief in Christianity founded on the premises of the native religion with active participation in both rites (internal syncretism).
   3. Belief in Christianity and the native religion with active participation in both rites (compartmentalization).
   4. Christianity not assimilated nor understood, and the native religion lost or disfigured. Participation in either or both rites often characterized by anomie and confusion (*nepantlism*).
C. Overt conversion only
   1. Indifference to both Christian and native religious beliefs with casual (public) participation in Christian rites.
   2. Belief in the native religion with casual (public) participation in Christian rites.

Conflict

D. Complete resistance (never baptized)
   1. Indifference to both Christian and native religious beliefs with passive resistance to Christianity.
   2. Belief in the native religion with active resistance to Christianity and active participation in indigenous rites.
   3. Belief in the native religion with passive resistance to Christianity and active participation in indigenous rites.

E. Overt conversion only
1. Belief in the native religion with voluntary active participation in indigenous rites and forced participation in Christian rites (passive resistance).
2. Belief in the native religion with voluntary active participation in indigenous rites and forced participation in Christian rites (active resistance).
F. Apostasy
1. Belief in the native religion with active participation in indigenous rites (complete abandonment of Christianity).
2. Indifference to both Christian and indigenous beliefs and rites (no participation in Christian rites and complete abandonment of Christianity).

These abstract categories are not meant to be mutually exclusive, nor can they be used to make hard and fast ethnographic classifications of group or individual behavior without specification and substantial qualifications. The basic response patterns of the Aztecs were more complex than these classes suggest. Individuals "moved" from one of these response modes to another, depending on their personal fortunes and the socioeconomic and cultural forces acting upon them. Though they were children of their parents, colonial culture changed so rapidly during the sixteenth century that generation gaps resulted, causing whole segments of the population to shift in and out of particular patterns of reaction to Christianity. The pristine cases exhibiting only the characteristics of one category were rare, but I will generalize from these since most documents only afford us a static view of individual responses.

Most of the explicit data on the success of the evangelizing effort comes from the ecclesiastical documents, though some legal documents and a few of the native poems found in the *Cantares mexicanos* manuscript also attest to this level of conversion accomplishment (León-Portilla 1974:19). The friars Motolinía and Mendieta were the principal exponents of the optimistic view. Many others agreed with them, including participants in the various church meetings held periodically during the colonial period and a number of laymen such as Hernán Cortez, Bernal Díaz del Castillo, and Suárez de Peralta (Llaguno 1963; Suárez de Peralta 1949:16). Some went so far as to suggest that the Christianity of the Indians could or did serve as an example and a source of inspiration to the less religious Spaniards (Mendieta 1971:75, 432; Motolinía 1971:141). The written works left by a number of Indians suggest not only the existence of examples of complete adoption of Christian values (A2) but also, as in the case of the historian Chimalpahin and the priest Pedro Ponce de León, an acceptance of a European world view (A1). However, very few Indians were allowed to become or could become Hispanicized enough to adopt fully the culture of the Spaniards as their own. Those who did—such as Isabel Motecuhzoma or Pablo Nazareo, another descendant of Motecuhzoma—were all drawn from the highest sector of the indigenous noble class (Paso y Troncoso 1939–1942 [Vol. 10]:109–129). Most natives who were truly Christianized accepted the new faith with an adequate understanding of its premises yet maintained many of the outward signs of native religious customs (Durán 1971; Mendieta 1971; Motolinía 1971). As a result, this group has often been erroneously identified with either those who were incompletely converted or those who had only overt conversions (B2, B3, B4, and E1) (Ricard 1966:276–281).

In the conclusions I summarized earlier, León-Portilla claims that many natives adopted Christianity only outwardly. Without changing their religious convictions, they simply borrowed from Christianity whatever elements were necessary to appear Christian. Most of the documents I have studied intimate that this was indeed commonly the case among Aztecs of both privileged and nonprivileged classes and was especially true for the latter. Whether embraced out of force, fear of punishment, political expediency, love of pomp and ceremony, or fear of the plagues, this religious stand helped to make possible the survival of the native cults among the majority of urban and rural natives (García Pimentel 1897:226; Motolinía 1971:90–92; Torquemada 1975 [Vol. 3]:45, 169–170).

Nepantlism

What made this position such an attractive and viable alternative? One reason suggested by another of the conclusions listed earlier is *nepantlism*, defined by León-Portilla as that situation in which a person remains suspended in the middle between a lost or disfigured past and a present that has not been assimilated or understood (León-Portilla 1974:24). This state is vividly described and abundantly documented in sources from the third decade in the sixteenth century to the second half of the seventeenth (Códice Franciscano 1941:91, 163; Durán 1967 [Vol. 1]:80, 199, 236–237; Motolinía 1971:439; Serna 1953:58, 350; Torquemada 1975 [Vol. 3]:61–62).

Nepantlism should not be confused with syncretism, which is, in both a historical and a psychological sense, the consequence of *nepantlism* when it is resolved under conditions that make a full conversion impossible. *Nepantlism* means that the premises of Christianity were not understood, and as a consequence only the superficial manifestations of the rites could be accepted as one's own (since most Aztecs were not free to reject Christianity outright). This was truly an anomic position: The structural base of the native faith had been dismantled, yet most people could neither convert nor keep from appearing Christian. Other circumstances contributed to the survival of some form of private autochthonous religiosity combined with a public display of Christianity: the ubiquitous disregard for adequate indoctrination; the persistent use of Latin in prayers and rituals; the lack of properly prepared or interested personnel; and the language gap, which only a minimal number of priests were able to bridge (Alva 1634:49r; García Pimentel 1897:70, 425–426; León 1611:85r; Mijangos 1966:14; Motolinía 1971:124). Those who could speak well often spoke in such an elevated style that they remained unintelligible to the masses (Villavicencio 1692:prologue).

Various authors, colonial and modern, have justly criticized the simplistic position held by those who believe that the use of indigenous customs or paraphernalia in Christian worship is necessarily (or probably) a sign of continued belief in the native cults. These authors have challenged the popular opinion that the existence of "mixed religion" or syncretism is evidenced whenever remnants of the indigenous liturgy are mixed with Christian rites (Bautista 1600:112r; Jiménez Moreno 1958:123–124, 129–230; Ricard 1966:276–281; Durán 1967 [Vol. 1]:55, 178). The problem is complex. It is obviously impossible to identify which Aztecs belong to which categories unless we have some trustworthy and explicit comments or very suggestive hints beyond a mere discovery of the appearance of indigenous elements.

The Aztecs most likely to be erroneously lumped together by the priests with those who underwent a complete religious transformation are the ones who expressed a belief in Christianity but who failed to understand its basic premises (B1, 2, 3, 4); they truly mixed native beliefs and rituals with Christian ideals and rites. Motolinía offers us the example of the Aztec elders "who are still with their idols and who hide these whenever they can; though they nevertheless approach the doctrine well, and with great devotion [approach]·the churches, and with many tears [approach] the confessions, and they marry at law and [with the official] blessing" (Códice Franciscano 1941:163; Motolinía 1971:439). However, Fray Diego Durán provides the most succinct description of the nature of *nepantlism*, that is, confused participation in both types of rites (B4).

Once I questioned an Indian regarding certain things. In particular I asked him why he had gone about begging, spending bad nights and worse days, and why, after having gathered so much money with such trouble, he offered a fiesta, invited the entire town, and spent everything. Thus I reprehended him for the foolish thing he had done, and he answered, 'Father, do not be astonished; we are still *nepantla.*' Although I understood what that metaphorical word means, that is to say, 'in the middle,' I insisted that he tell me which 'in the middle' he referred to. The native told me that, since the people were not yet well rooted in the Faith, I should not marvel at the fact that they were [still neutral]; they were governed by neither one religion nor the other. Or, better said, they believed in God and also followed their ancient heathen rites and customs [D. Durán, *Book of the Gods and Rites and the Ancient Calendar*, translated and edited by Fernando Horcasitas and Doris Heyden, pp. 410–411. Copyright © 1971 by the University of Oklahoma Press].

Those Aztecs exhibiting *nepantlism* were in the anomalous position of being unable to function in either of the two religious traditions. This state was necessarily transitory, preceding the development of the conscious bifurcation into public Christian worship along modified Spanish patterns and a greatly altered private or domestic indigenous ceremonialism that harked back to ancient ways. When the new cultural modes were established, *nepantlism* often lead to internal syncretism, which was itself the precedent to external syncretism wherever the modified native rites came to an end.

Incomplete Conversion

The stance of the indigenous priests and secular leaders in the 1524 *Libro de los colloquios* of Sahagún, who allowed themselves to be baptized because their gods had been defeated by the Christian God, is an excellent example of incomplete conversions in which aspects of Christianity are accepted but not the world view implied by them (Klor de Alva 1980a; Sahagún 1949:53–54). The extent of this condition as late as the first half of the seventeenth century is attested to by the observation of Jacinto de la Serna who writes in his *Manual de ministros de indios para el conocimiento de sus idolatrías y extirpación de ellas*:

It is very clear that this task of curing them is very difficult and so formidable that it makes me doubt as to whether it was a greater task to teach them in the beginning all the mysteries of our holy faith, or whether it will be a greater task to convert to [these mysteries] those who have apostatized from their truth, not by [their] denying [the faith] nor its principles, but by mixing with it the falseness of their superstitions [Serna 1953:350].

The incomplete conversion complex in the typology has been found in the literature to be the most widespread native response to Christianity; examples are legion. Durán and all the important Franciscan chroniclers are among those who detailed the many ways in which the indigenes betrayed this ambivalent religious posture even with regard to public worship in Christian rites. Motolinía observed that the native ritual of sweeping (whose roots go deep into the pre-Hispanic past) was a part of the ceremony that accompanied the taking of the Eucharist to the home of the sick; the ubiquitous use of fires on the eve of the Nativity also implied spiritual vestiges of non-Christian origin as did the use of extreme self-flagellation as a part of the Christian rites of self-sacrifice or in order to obtain rains or cures; and the extensive offerings made before the Christian images including the burning of *copalli* ("incense") all attest to the extensive public presence of altered aspects of native practice and, possibly, of indigenous religiosity after the initial period of catechismal instruction ended (Mendieta 1971:429; Motolinía 1971:90–98, 137, 156).

Added to these are the rigorous fasts observed by the natives that scandalized even the most ascetic friars (Motolinía 1971:137). However, Durán reminds us that, "it must be noted that the offerings of strings of ears of corn and flowers on the Day of Our Lady in September and during the festivities in that month are a survival of the [pagan] custom. But I believe they have been turned into an offering to His Divine Majesty" (Durán 1971:228). Nonetheless, the Dominican friar is quick to warn that the natives of the Cuernavaca (Cuauhnahuac), Cholula, and Tlaxcala areas still continue the ancient rite of putting banners on the fruit trees and, therefore, "let the Christian reader remember this so that when he sees it practiced he will fight against it as something smacking of idolatry. After the banners were placed upon trees, offerings were made of bread, pulque, incense, and a thousand other things. What I have described is sufficient for [the reader] to be wary" (Durán 1971:460).

Fray Bernardino de Sahagún adds that the Indians often demanded a signed seal from the confessor after their confession because, as was the case in the pre-Hispanic rite, they believed themselves immune from judicial prosecution after having confessed their crimes (Sahagún 1975:38). For a final example we have Torquemada's insistent complaint that the old Aztec ceremonies surrounding the use of incense continued, especially in the offerings made on their domestic altars (Torquemada 1975 [Vol. 2]:416).

Coercion, Dissimulation, and Resistance

The distinction between an incomplete conversion where there is only participation in Christian rites (B1) and a complete conversion where indigenous customs of a cultural not spiritual type are maintained (A2) is practically imperceptible. It is primarily a question of intention grounded on some minimal level of understanding of the Christian faith and acceptance of the ideals that support it. The fragile state of a complete conversion, when there was a retention of approved indigenous cultural customs—that is, when the individual continued to function primarily within the native social context—is shown by the ease with which the Aztecs were willing to abandon active participation in Christian ceremonies and the constant need of coercion to keep them practicing the new faith.

The need to use force, whether violent or not, to compel the natives to participate in the ceremonies of the church or to observe the rudiments of Christian polity is well documented in materials that go beyond the Inquisition sources. In some places those delinquent in attending mass were flogged (Códice Franciscano 1941:59). It was believed among some of the ruling elite of Huejotzingo that during the early years, shortly after the conquest, those who refused the Catholic faith were "tortured or burned" and that this "was done on every hand . . . in New Spain" (Anderson 1976:185). In a letter written in 1531 Archbishop Juan de Zumárraga and several other friars make clear that in their opinion the Indian "acts more out of fear than out of virtue" (García Icazbalceta 1947 [Vol. 2]:269). In 1769 Archbishop Lorenzana likewise affirmed that fear of punishment was the prime cause of virtuous behavior (Lorenzana 1770:98). Many Spaniards who lived in the intervening time concurred with this sentiment (Alarcón 1953:47; Alva 1634:2r; Durán 1967:5; García Pimentel 1897:278; Paso y Troncoso 1939–1942 [Vol. 12]:1).

This being the case, compulsion by threat or by force was systematically employed, not only to coerce the Aztecs to accept baptism (which was usually not necessary), but to compel them to hear the doctrine, attend mass, participate in the religious activities of the Christians, and, especially, to keep within the canons of Christian ethics and Spanish polity. The *Descripción del Arzobispado de México*, written in 1570 as Archbishop of Mexico Fray Alonso Montúfar's response to the inquiries concerning the state of his archdiocese put to him by the touring inspector Juan de Ovando, is perhaps our best source on the status and nature of the Christianity of the Indians living in the heart of New Spain in the last third of the sixteenth century. Here we find ample evidence of the use of force and the need for coercion to keep some semblance of Christianity among the Indians. In most towns we find *diputados* (*tequitlatos* and *tepixque*) whose job it was to gather the people for mass and for the sacraments and to punish the recalcitrants; punishment is also threatened for those who fail to bring either the unbaptized to the holy water or the young to hear the doctrine (García Pimentel 1897:62, 74–76, 89, 93, 97, 99, 143, 222). In his *Confessionario mayor* of 1569 Fray Alonso de Molina makes it a sin for a *principal* ("a local leader") to fail to gather the people for mass on holy days; the same can be found in both the *Confessionario mayor y menor* published in 1634 by the Bachiller Bartholome de Alva and that published in 1611 by the Dominican friar Martin de León titled *Camino del cielo* (Alva 1634:20r, v; León 1611:114r; Molina 1569:28v). During the early decades legislation was also implemented in an attempt to impose the Catholic faith and *policía cristiana* upon the perplexed natives (Código Penal 1953:410–411; Reyes García 1972:253).

Proposing numerous exceptions to the notion that only threats made the natives Christian, Motolinía recounts throughout his early writings how the Indians gladly attended the Christian services and devoutly partook of the sacraments. However, writing in the second half of the sixteenth century, Fray Bernardino de Sahagún was among the first to describe in detail how Motolinía had misunderstood the intentions of the natives, confusing appearances for reality (García Icazbalceta 1954:381–382). Gerónimo de Mendieta observed that neither the mere preaching of the Gospel nor the good example of the ministers was enough to persuade these "weak" people without the addition of some benign but firm coercion (Mendieta 1971:26). Indeed, Mendieta notes elsewhere, the Indians themselves confess that they needed to be chastised and compelled (Códice Mendieta 1892 [Vol. 5]:34). Both the regular and secular priests feared the consequences of being prohibited from punishing the Indians or from obliging them to attend to the Christian rituals; many of them suspected that the lack of devotion they already witnessed halfway through the century was due precisely to their own or their colleagues' laxness (Acosta 1954: 393; Códice Franciscano 1941:69; García Pimentel 1897:110, 237; Paso y Troncoso 1939–1942 [Vol. 3]:26; Sahagún 1975:582).

Ample evidence suggests that numerous Spaniards who were not priests were skeptical of the alleged Indian conversions; Mendieta himself felt compelled to answer the widespread charge that the Indians "are not truly Christians" by pointing out how devout the natives were toward the ceremonies of the church, "whereby one can deduce that in effect they are truly Christians and not [merely] in jest, as some believe" (Mendieta 1971:421, 429). Torquemada was also moved to answer the charge that the natives easily accepted any faith, whether good or bad, and, consequently, just as easily abandoned it (Torquemada 1975 [Vol. 3]:30). In his *Advertencias para los confessores* (1600) the Franciscan Juan Bautista explains that the many superstitions of the natives are not sufficient reason to accuse them of being idolaters as many people do, since the Spaniards have many superstitions themselves (Bautista 1600:lllv). However, in a letter signed in 1544, Gonzalo de Aranda advises the monarch that among the Indians, "though there are many who appear to be good Christians, there are many more who are not [and who] do not fear God nor know Him because they neither concern themselves with truths nor do they speak it, concerning themselves solely with stealing and deceiving" (Paso y Troncoso 1939 [Vol. 4]:88).

There are good reasons to believe that many priests shared similar doubts about the sincerity of the natives. The reservations of Sahagún and Diego Durán are well known but worthy of special attention (Sahagún 1975:17, 173, 189, 581; Durán 1967 [Vol. 1]:5–6, 18). Both of these friars worked closely with the Aztecs for many years, and their ethnographic bent compelled them to become well versed in their *antiguallas* ("ancient ways"). The overwhelming mass of documentation on the subject from the colonial era confirms their worst suspicions, including Sahagún's frank and penetrating admission late in the sixteenth century: "now it is almost impossible to remedy [the idolatry]" (Sahagún 1975:581).

Even if we were to agree with Mendieta, Motolinía, Gante, and others that active participation in indigenous rites was minimal, the sources would not let us conclude that this was an indication of the acceptance of Christian values and beliefs by the natives. For one thing, it appears that the priests themselves were easily fooled by the crafty Aztecs, who managed to elude the vigilant eye of the friars by taking advantage of their ignorance of the language and the indigenous customs (León 1611:95r–98v; Serna 1953:114–115; Villavicencio 1692:beginning). Furthermore, a number of sources indicate that substantial dissimulation actually took place, in spite of the external appearance of Christianity and the apparent lack of indigenous rites. Conversions where there was belief in the native religions with casual participation in Christian rites (C2) were both widespread and common throughout the sixteenth and at least the first half of the seventeenth centuries. In response to the information sought by Ovando, one particular local priest, who was apparently aware of the nature of these types of "conversions," was unwilling to assert any more than that to all *external* appearances the natives seemed to have accepted the Christian doctrine (García Pimentel 1897:59). Another priest from the same general area, just northeast of Mexico-Tenochtitlan, speaks of the Indians who worked in the mines or who lived in the outlying zones and states emphatically that they attended the sporadic sermons offered them but remained as they were as soon as the priests left (García Pimentel 1897:75). In general, in 1570 in the areas surrounding the city of Mexico, the natives apparently had such little knowledge of and interest in the new faith that many could not make the sign of the cross much less assimilate any doctrinal statements, and others were only too quick to worship their own gods under the guise of the Christian images (García Pimentel 1897:278; Sahagún 1975:704–705).

Few natives can be expected to have been neutral to both Christianity and the native faith (C1, D1, F2). These indifferent Aztecs seem to be casualties of acute cases of *nepantlism* (D1 and F2), or very Hispanicized natives who, having a low sensitivity for the spiritual, failed to adopt the faith of the Europeans (C1).

One modern historian believes that "the indigenes of the New World did not demonstrate, in general, a great capacity to resist the new faith" (Gómez Canedo 1977:63). This popular view of the natives, inherited from the Franciscan historians, needs to be reconsidered. The documents suggest it is a misinterpretation of both indigenous syncretism and the passive resistance of the Indians to Christian and Spanish customs and beliefs. It is true that—unlike the Chichimecs, Mixtecs, or Zapotecs—the Aztecs were unable to organize themselves sufficiently to undertake armed rebellions against the occupying forces (Mendieta 1971:732–733; Motolinía 1971:292–293; Paso y Troncoso 1939–1942 [Vol. 8]:230; Remesal 1619:454–455; Ricard 1966:264–266). The dense settlement of the central Mexican area also made it impossible for the Aztecs residing there to flee from the missionaries. Some did abandon their homes in the early years, and of these many returned—especially during the pestilences or out of fear of the Inquisition—pretending to be baptized or seeking baptism (Códice Franciscano 1941:80–81).

Therefore, the categories of those who resisted Christianity and were never baptized (D2, D3) were composed mostly, though not exclusively as the Inquisition records demonstrate, of Aztecs living in remote areas during and shortly after the initial postcontact period. Some passively resisted Christianity while actively participating in rites that were modeled on the ancient faith. Examples from the late sixteenth century and the early seventeenth are found in the works of Ruiz de Alarcón, Jacinto de la Serna, and the *Descripción del Arzobis-*

pado de Mexico (Alarcón 1953:passim; García Pimentel 1897:passim; Serna 1953: passim).

The persistence of postcontact indigenous ceremonies deep into the seventeenth century is confirmed by the many *confessionarios, advertencias,* and manuals for their extirpation. Not only were the native cults to be found in most isolated areas, they also enjoyed great popularity in the heart of New Spain. Writing in the 1570s, Durán minced no words on the issue:

> They are still idolaters, in spite of the many years of [Christian] teaching. . . . And I am referring to what we see, find, and discover every minute of the day, not only in villages far removed from the City of Mexico, where there would be some excuse [for idolatry] through lack of catechism. I am referring to [places] very close to Mexico, and even to the city itself. There are as many evils, superstitions, and idolatrous natives as [there were] under the old law; there are [as many] with doctors, fortune-tellers, fakers, and old men who preach their cursed religion, preventing it from falling into oblivion [D. Durán, *Book of the Gods and Rites and the Ancient Calendar,* translated and edited by Fernando Horcasitas and Doris Heyden, p. 150. Copyright © 1971 by the University of Oklahoma Press].

In a voice filled with rage against the Mendicant Orders, whose negligence he attacked, Archbishop Montúfar records in the second half of the sixteenth century that in Mexico "where the Indians ought to be better Christians, they are the worst" (García Pimentel 1897:424).

One hundred years later Jacinto de la Serna in his *Manual de ministros de indios* points out that the city of Mexico is where the "ministers of Satan" celebrate their many rites with the greatest immunity, cleverly disguising under Christian forms their various idolatries, "and I know for a fact, to our greater shame and confusion, that everyone within and outside the City [of Mexico], and throughout the kingdom is corrupted passively and actively: some because they practice all the . . . superstitions . . . ; and others passively, consenting to others making and using these" (Serna 1953:333–334).

During the colonial period many Aztec children were taught modified versions of the native beliefs and practices both at home and by self-appointed native cult leaders; these latter were usually classified by the friars as apostates (E2, F1) (Durán 1967:58, 78; Serna 1953:62; Villavicencio 1692:7). The tenacity and extent of the diffusion of the ancient beliefs led many, beside Sahagún and Durán, to suspect that there was little Christianity among the Aztecs and that with the exception of children few natives were being saved (Alarcón 1953:351; Alva 1634:1v–2r; Códice Franciscano 1941:279; García Pimentel 1897:89–222, 425, 426; Paso y Troncoso 1939–1942 [Vol. 4]:210, [Vol. 8]:76; Serna 1953:48; Villavicencio 1692:beginning). Some who despaired of eradicating the indigenous religious practices by human effort placed their faith in God as the only force who could bring this disappointing state to an end (Alarcón 1953:59; Durán 1967:79).

Overt conversions only (E1, E2) were not, therefore, isolated and insignificant phenomena. As the Inquisition records amply attest, the great number and variety of indigenous spiritual leaders—called diviners, witches, enchanters, and healers by the Christian priests—enjoyed a large following and a substantial income. They were accused of perpetuating the ancient beliefs by instigating the celebration of native rites and by preaching against Christianity (Anunciación 1577:6v; Baudot 1972:354–355; Doctrina 1548:143r; González Obregon 1912:36–51; Molina 1569:20v–21r). These self-styled Indian clerics and healers, who succeeded the precontact priests in tending to the spiritual and physical needs of the recalcitrant Aztecs, are examples of those who actively resisted the Christian faith (E2) or, less likely, those who completely abandoned the new faith after an initial acceptance (F1) (Klor de Alva 1981:passim). The penitents to whom they catered had either converted only nominally to Christianity or had apostatized; many who had incomplete conversions (B1, 2, 3, 4) also made use of their services, particularly as healers (Alarcón 1953;passim; Serna 1953:passim).

Conclusion

Sociopolitical and economic expediency, together with the simple life-style and general goodwill of the missionaries, made baptism attractive for the Aztecs; Spanish military and administrative power made it a requisite for all but the most marginalized (Klor de Alva 1979:10, 14). However, conversion in any meaningful sense demanded a radical change in values, customs, and world view. The Christian ethos was slowly accepted by some only in the course of several generations and only after the precontact mores had been sufficiently transformed by the newly evolving colonial culture.

Nonetheless, however much the interference of Spaniards and blacks altered the old patterns, many tenaciously adhered to whatever vestiges were available well into the seventeenth century and, as modern ethnography shows, into the present (Madsen 1960:passim). Sahagún asserted late in the sixteenth century that a conspiracy of silence existed on the part of both the dissimulating Indians and those who wished to keep untainted the memory of the first friars who had supposedly enjoyed overwhelming successes; as a consequence, he added, many were kept from seeing or recounting the failure of the spiritual conquest (García Icazbalceta 1954:381–383). By the time the massive campaign against the Andean religions was launched in 1610, the Indian population of New Spain was so badly decimated that few Spaniards troubled themselves any longer with the continuance of native modes of spirituality among the survivors. The various mixed castes were rapidly growing in number and developing fidelity to European values and practices. But among the Aztecs, few were wholeheartedly embracing the vision of the world implied by Christianity, many resisted it passively, most failed to meet the minimal test required of a convert (belief in one God who died to redeem humanity), and almost all mixed the colonial versions of the ancient beliefs with the Christian doctrine (García Pimentel 1897:426).

References

Acosta, José de
1954   De procuranda indorum salute. Biblioteca de Autores Españoles. Madrid: Ediciones Atlas.
Aguirre Beltrán, Gonzalo
1963   Medicina y magia. Mexico: Instituto Nacional Indigenista/Secretaría de Educación Pública.
Alarcón, Hernando Ruíz de.
1953   Tratado de las supersticiones. In Tratado de las idolatrías de las razas aborigenes de México (Vol. 2). Mexico: Ediciones Fuente Cultural. Pp. 17–180.
Alva, Bartholome de
1634   Confessionario mayor y menor en lengua mexicana. Mexico: Francisco Salvago, Impressor del Secreto del Santo Officio.
Anderson, Arthur J. O., Frances, Berdan and James Lockhart (editors)
1976   Beyond the codices. UCLA Latin American Studies Series, No. 27. Berkeley: University of California.
Anunciación, Juan de la
1577   Sermonario en lengua mexicana. Mexico: Antonio Ricardo.
Baudot, Georges
1972   Apariciones diabólicas en un texto náhuatl de Fray Andrés de Olmos. Estudios de Cultura Náhuatl **10**:349–357.
Bautista, Juan
1600   Advertencias para los confessores de los naturales. Mexico. Melchior Ocharte.
Carrasco, Pedro
1975   La transformación de la cultura indígena durante la colonia. Historia Mexicana **25**:175–203.
Códice Franciscano
1941   Nueva colección de documentos para la historia de México (Vol. 2), edited by Joaquín García Icazbalceta. Mexico: Salvador Chavez Hayhoe.

Códice Mendieta
1892   *Nueva colección de documentos para la historia de México* (Vols. 4 and 5), edited by Joaquín García Icazbalceta. Mexico: Imprenta de Francisco Díaz de León.

Código Penal u Ordenanza para el gobierno de los indios
1953   *Tratado de las idolatrías de las razas aborigenes de México.* Mexico: Ediciones Fuente Cultural.

Coll, J. Oliva de
1976   *La resistencia indígena ante la Conquista* (2nd edition). Mexico: Siglo XXI.

Doctrina cristiana en lengua española y mexicana
1548   Mexico: Juan Pablos. Biblioteca Nacional de México.

Durán, Diego
1967   *Historia de las Indias de Nueva España e islas de la tierra firme* (Vol. 1). Mexico: Editorial Porrúa.
1971   *Book of the gods and rites and the ancient calendar,* transalted and edited by Fernando Horcasitas and Doris Heyden. Norman: University of Oklahoma.

Duviols, Pierre
1966   La visite des idolatries de Concepción de Chupas. *Journal de la Société des Américanistes de Paris* 55(2).
1967a   Un inédit de Cristóbal de Albornoz: la instrucción para descubrir todas las guaccas del Pirú y sus camayos y haziendas. *Journal de la Société des Américanistes de Paris* 56(1).
1967b   La idolatriá en cifras. *Actes du Colloque d'Etudes Peruviennes.*
1967c   *Un procès d'idolatrie au Pérou* [1671] (Vol. 3). Arequipa: E.I.A.
1977   *La destrucción de las religiones andinas (Conquista y Colonia).* Mexico: Universidad Nacional Autónoma de México.

García Icazbalceta, Joaquín
1947   *Don Fray Juan de Zumárraga primer obispo y arzobispo de México* (4 vols.). Mexico: Editorial Porrúa.
1954   *Bibliografía mexicana del siglo XVI.* Mexico: Fondo de Cultura Economica.

García Pimentel, Luis (editor)
1897   *Descripción del Arzobispado de México hecha en 1570 y otros documentos.* Mexico: Joaquin Terrazas e Hijas.

Gómez Canedo, Lino
1977   *Evangelización y conquista: experiencia franciscana en Hispanoamérica.* Mexico: Editorial Porrúa.

González Obregon, Luis (editor)
1912   *Processos de indios idólatras y hechiceros.* Mexico: Archivo General de la Nación.

Huerta, María Teresa, and Patricia Palacios (editors)
1976   *Rebeliones indígenas de la época colonial.* Mexico: Secretaría de Educacíon Pública/Instituto Nacional de Antropología e Historia.

Jiménez Moreno, Wigberto
1958   Los Indígenas frente al cristianismo. In *Estudios de historia colonial.* Mexico: Instituto Nacional de Antropología e Historia.

Klor de Alva, José Jorge
1979   Christianity and the Aztecs. *San José Studies* 5:6–21.
1980a   The Aztec–Spanish Dialogues of 1524. *Alcheringa/Ethnopoetics* 4:52–193.
1980b   Spiritual Warfare in Mexico: Christianity and the Aztecs. Unpublished Ph.D.

dissertation, Department of History of Consciousness, University of California, Santa Cruz.

1981 Martín Ocelotl: clandestine cult leader. In *Struggle and Survival in Colonial America*, edited by David G. Sweet and Gary B. Nash. Berkeley and Los Angeles: University of California Press.

Kobayashi, José María
1974 *La educación como conquista (empresa franciscana en México)*. Mexico: El Colegio de Mexico.

León, Martin de
1611 *Camino del cielo en lengua mexicana*. Mexico: Diego Lopez Davalos.

León-Portilla, Miguel
1974 Testimonios nahuas sobre la conquista espiritual. *Estudios de Cultura Nahuatl* **11**:11–36.

Llaguno, José A
1963 *La personalidad jurídica del indio y el III Concilio Provincial Mexicano (1585)*. Mexico: Editorial Porrúa.

Lorenzana, Francisco Antonio
1770 *Cartas pastorales y edictos*. Mexico: Imprenta del Superior Gobierno.

Madsen, William
1960 Christo-paganism. In *Nativism and syncretism*. Middle American Research Institute, No. 19. New Orleans: Tulane University.

Mendieta, Gerónimo de
1971 *Historia eclesiástica indiana*. Mexico: Editorial Porrúa.

Mijangos, Juan de
1966 Frases y modos de hablar, elegantes y metafóricos, de los indios mexicanos. *Estudios de Cultura Nahuatl* **6**:11–27.

Millones, Luis
1964 *Un movimiento nativista del siglo XVI:el Taki ongoy* (Vol. 3). R.P.C.
1967 *Introducción al proceso de aculturación religiosa indigena*. Lima: Instituto Indigenista Peruano.
1971 *Las informaciones de Cristobal de Albornoz: Documentos para el estudio del Taki Onqoy*. Cuernavaca: Centro Cultural de Documentación.

Molina, Alonso de
1569 *Confessionario mayor en la lengua mexicana y castellana*. Mexico: Casa de Antonio Espinosa.

Motolinía, Toribio de Benavente o
1971 *Memoriales o libro de las cosas de la Nueva España y de los naturales de ella*. Mexico: Universidad Nacional Autónoma de México.

Navarette, Nicolás P
1978 *Historia de la provincia agustiniana de San Nicolás de Tolentino de Michoacan* (2 vols.), Mexico: Editorial Porrúa.

Paso y Troncoso, Francisco del (editor)
1939–1942 *Epistolario de Nueva España 1505–1818* (16 vols.). Mexico: Antigua Libería Robredo.

Remesal, Antonio de
1619 *Historia de la provincia de San Vicente de Chyapa y Guatemala*. Madrid: Francisco de Angulo.

Reyes García, Luis
1972 Ordenanzas para el gobierno de Cuauhtinchan, año 1559. *Estudios de Cultura Nahuatl* **10**:245–313.

Ricard, Robert
1933   La <<conquête spirituelle>> du Mexique. Paris: Institut d'Ethnologie.
1966   The spiritual conquest of Mexico, translated by Lesley Byrd Simpson. Berkeley
        and Los Angeles: University of California.
Sahagún, Bernardino de
1949   Coloquios y doctrina christiana. In Sterbende Götter und Christliche
        Heilsbotschaft, edited and translated by Walter Lehmann. Stuttgart: Verlag.
1975   Historia general de las cosas de Nueva España (3rd edition by Ángel Ma.
        Garibay K.), Mexico: Editorial Porrúa.
Serna, Jacinto de la
1953   Manual de ministros. In Tratado de las idolatrías de las razas aborigenes de
        México (Vol. 1). Mexico: Ediciones Fuente Cultural. Pp. 47–368.
Suárez de Peralta, Juan
1949   Tratado del descubrimiento de las Indias. Mexico: Secretaría de Educación
        Pública.
Torquemada, Juan de
1975   Monarquia indiana. (3 vols.). Mexico: Editorial Porrúa.
Ulloa, Daniel
1977   Los predicadores divididos: los dominicos en Nueva Espana, siglo XVI. Mex-
        ico: El Colegio de Mexico.
Villavicencio, Diego Jaymes Ricardo
1692   Luz y methodo de confesar idolatras y destierro de idolatrías. Puebla, Mexico:
        Diego Fernandez de León.

Views of Corporate Self and History
in Some Valley of Mexico Towns:
Late Seventeenth and Eighteenth Centuries

James Lockhart

Editors' Introduction

James Lockhart's work on late colonial Nahua historical consciousness involves hinterland villagers who claim ancient corporate autonomy
based on late colonial land titles. Purporting to be authentic copies of early
colonial originals, the documents have patently been contrived by individuals who only partially grasp what such titles ought to contain (dates,
signatures with rubrics, the identities of relevant native and colonial authorities, etc.). The numerous anachronisms reflect syncretic conceptions
of late colonial ethnic identity. By the eighteenth century, Indians attribute
roles in the autologous founding of their towns to the Spanish crown, the
Christian god, and the local patron saints; on the other hand, they cast the
prehistoric Mexica together with Spanish colonists as threatening outsiders fended off by indigenous culture heroes. Thus, the documents un-
selfconsciously express a syncretistic myth of cultural continuity.

Studies of indigenous Mesoamerican culture and society have concentrated heavily on two widely separated points in time: the contact
period, or the fifteenth–sixteenth centuries, and our own epoch, the
twentieth century. This has been so not only in the less temporally
oriented disciplines of anthropology and linguistics, but in certain
kinds of historical investigation as well. It is true that students of some

THE INCA AND AZTEC
STATES, 1400–1800

aspects of indigenous matters—social, political, and even linguistic—have by now found sources which enable them to trace patterns of continuity and change as far as the end of the colonial period. But work on indigenous views of the conquest, for example, leaps from texts like Sahagún to twentieth-century folklore. In the general area of materials for the study of indigenous thought and expression—and hence for study of expressed views of self and events—the rich codices of the immediate postconquest epoch have seemed to lead only to a select few individual native historical writers such as Chimalpahin and Tezozomoc in the later sixteenth and early seventeenth centuries, followed by a void until the recent time of collection of tales, dramas, and dances from living informants.

As the investigation of native-language sources of the colonial period proceeds, however, materials begin to come to light which are potentially revealing of indigenous historical thinking at points far into the later centuries. In this chapter I discuss some samples of one genre with this kind of potential: the type of document generally known as *títulos primordiales*, "primordial titles."

Levels of Indigenous Awareness

Let it be clear from the outset that I do not present certain documents and their implications as the sole indigenous view, even where they prove consistent internally and across samples. Within a corporate entity existing in a sedentary, differentiated society, there will always be more than one view of that entity's nature and its relation to the overall social environment. Some members of the corporation will have the specific function of dealing with external relations; as a result, they will have a quite broad, realistic conception of the outside world, as well as of their own corporation's perhaps minor role in it. For others, often the majority, the corporation tends to loom larger. Among them, a more nearly hermetic, internally centered tradition may prevail and perpetuate itself.

In central Mexican Indian towns of the middle and later colonial period, there existed an upper group who shared the Nahuatl language and the ethnicity of the rest of the local population, but stood out from it in various ways. Heirs of the preconquest nobility, they had more properties and more dependents than the average; they dominated the semiautonomous town governments; they married across town boundaries in quasi-dynastic matches, creating regional familial networks which transcended the individual towns; many of them carried on enterprises not unlike Spanish ones and sold their products in the region's broader Spanish economy; some began to intermarry with the Spaniards, who were growing in number in the main Indian towns. After 1700 it is increasingly common to find that Indians of the upper level (though they gave legal testimony through an interpreter to avoid later challenge of its validity) are described as fluent in Spanish. People like these had a very adequate grasp of the overall configuration of Spanish colonial society and government. Their own personal and official dealings took them frequently to their subprovincial capital, seat of the Spanish *alcalde mayor*, and on occasion to Mexico City itself. The many Nahuatl documents left by this group bespeak a full comprehension of Spanish legal and religious concepts and procedures, as well as an easy familiarity with the workings of the European calendar.

Although these members of the higher stratum may not have been quite as conversant with the details of Spanish royal succession as was their predecessor, the previously mentioned Amecameca historian Chimalpahin, [1] they must have understood and even, to a large extent, have shared general Spanish notions of New Spain's organization and historical process, especially in their own larger subregion and during times close to their own period, on a year-to-year, decade-to-decade basis. Since they were the dominant group, one can assert that central Mexican Indian communities as a whole had such an understanding. In fact, a relatively sophisticated grasp of supramunicipality structures and procedures may have been common at the lower levels, too, since precisely the poorest and most marginal community members spent much of their time working short stints at haciendas and other Spanish enterprises outside community borders; the same people also quite frequently changed residence from one community to another.

Nevertheless, the cross-regional view of things was not the prevalent one among the general populace of central Mexican Indian towns. From various indications it appears that the dominant group-internal lore, disseminated by the elders and only occasionally written down, took the local town or provincial unit as an autonomous, autochthonous people radically separate from all that surrounded them. Certain constituents of Spanish and Christian culture were deeply integrated into this local lore, but there was little concern with or expertise about any outside elements, be they indigenous or intrusive, except as they directly affected the local entity. In this perspective the king and the viceroy were much the same thing; except for the supposed dates of grants or surveys of local territory, the march of Spanish calendrical years passed unnoticed.

It is probably too simple to identify the dichotomy of overall views with two separate sets of people inside the Indian community. More likely, the upper group also shared in the more localized tradition but understood that it was not an appropriate mode for conducting legal business or something to be brought before the eyes of Spanish officials. The distinction would be, then, one of levels within the individual, or of different idioms for different purposes, rather than of discrete groups with divergent beliefs. A corporation-centered view, which had large components of legend, stereotype, and ignorance of the outside, thus seems to have maintained itself as a group phenomenon, despite the fact that many individual corporation members had conflicting information or thought differently part of the time.

The Written Sources

The best means presently available of obtaining access to this corporate consciousness in its late colonial form are some documents composed in Nahuatl inside the communities by people who were in some fashion literate, although not fully trained as notaries, and who wrote outside the usual Spanish-influenced documentary genres of will, sale, grant, petition, or investigation. The latter sort of documents, written by experts, make up the bulk of the colonial Nahuatl written legacy. There is also much diverse court testimony from the lips of uninstructed Indians, but most of it is in Spanish, having passed through the filter of an interpreter; even where the testimony is in Nahuatl, court procedures demanded direct responses to prepared questions, restricting spontaneous expansiveness.

Several kinds of nonprofessional Nahuatl writing have so far come to my attention. Annals kept on a more or less private basis constitute one such genre (although the authors were usually well educated and shared the broader upper-level perspectives). Also relevant are legal documents from minor or peripheral centers, where even the notaries were somewhat outside the Spanish and Nahuatl mainstream. Though based on Spanish genres, their documents varied widely from Spanish ones, partaking of local popular lore and modes of expression. Both types of writing bear on historical consciousness, but the genre most squarely confronting this issue is that already referred to as "primordial titles"—an appellation apparently not given to such documents until a very late time, possibly the nineteenth century.

It is understandable that not much advantage has been taken of the primordial titles until now. Even for those of us who rejoice in the rich local idiosyncrasies of Nahuatl documentation, the orthography of the Nahuatl originals of the titles tends to appear abominable, inept, and aberrant, a cause for puzzlement and hilarity. The language itself, once the intention of the orthography has been recognized, is often extremely obscure, whether one approaches it from "classical" or from "colonial" Nahuatl. Even the generally expert court translators had trouble with these texts, producing Spanish versions which sometimes yield no surface meaning and are frequently in grave error even when they do make sense.

Nor are these the only deterrents. The "titles" appear to deal with events of the conquest and early postconquest years; only on fairly close examination does one see that the examples which have come down to us were uniformly set on paper in the later colonial period. Though there must have been earlier oral versions, and doubtless at least some written ones too, I know of no text of this type which.in its present form dates from earlier than the latter seventeenth century. This fact leads us to another reason why primordial titles have not received much attention. As reports of certain events or justification of certain territorial claims, they are (all known to me, in any case) patently inaccurate, poorly informed, false, and even in some sense deliberately falsified, often in the most transparent fashion. (For instance, in the Tetelco title which I will discuss later, a Franciscan friar was imagined to have been present at the original occasion as a witness; not knowing his name, the writer made a signature at the end, complete with rubrics, reading *deopixqui fratzicano*, "Franciscan friar.") Spanish officials to whom such documents were presented in the colonial period usually labeled them false or ignored them entirely.

What is, then, the exact nature of these documents called titles? The notion of "title" in the colonial Spanish world went beyond the concept of a simple deed. Full title—whether to land, territory, or jurisdiction—involved not only an original grant or sale, but also an investigation on the spot to consult third parties and see if the situation was as described, and finally formal acts of giving and taking possession. Only then did the grant or sale, until that point merely virtual or hypothetical, enter into force. A Spanish notary would keep a running record of the whole proceeding, repeatedly signed by officials and witnesses; this record, appended to the original grant, order, or the like, constituted the title.

During the first postconquest generation, the viceregal government sent representatives into the countryside to establish the precise territories of the various Indian towns. This involved investigations like those just described and included the stepping out of the boundaries, setting markers, obtaining the acquiescence of people of neighboring towns, and so on. Rarely was the result fully unambiguous in a juridical sense, but the proceedings did give the community involved some legal basis for the possession of its territory. If the "primordial titles" were what many of them purport to be, they would be either the original record made by the notary present or an authorized contemporary copy. But they are not. Such originals exist in the central archives in Mexico City and probably also in the provincial centers where local administrators had their headquarters; they look like other Spanish acts of possession and bear little resemblance to our primordial titles. Apparently the originals did not stay in the towns concerned; if they did, they were lost (they may have been neglected because at that early time hardly anyone knew enough Spanish to understand them). It might seem that the records could have been given a competent translation into Nahuatl. The capability existed. But translation in colonial Mexico was mainly a one-way street; with the exception of standard religious texts and a few proclamations and ordinances, the general direction was out of indigenous languages into Spanish in order to support indigenous claims before Spanish authority. The ultimately original form of the indigenous "titles" would appear to have been not the Spanish record but a parallel record, whether in oral or written form, made by the Nahuatl speakers as interested observers of the proceedings. This version would never have had any legal standing with the Spaniards. On the other hand, the independent redaction allowed the Indians to make note of things of importance to them which Spaniards would have omitted.

As time went on, through the sixteenth century and on into the early seventeenth, other occasions presented themselves on which Spanish officials would carry out investigations of people and land, in one way or another confirming local rights. Many towns at some point underwent "congregation," or rationalization and concentration. Investigations took place periodically to review the tributary population and local resources, and others occurred at the instance of aggrieved parties. The "primordial titles" frequently add accounts of some of these subsequent occasions to the report of the original survey, or at least give a date for them. These sections seem to be in the nature of parenthetical remarks, but often the effect is to make it nearly impossible to say which occasion is being discussed (actually, we cannot presume that the later rewriters of the titles imagined different occasions located sequentially on a time continuum).

At the core of a "primordial title," then, is an account of an early local border survey, which is often overlaid with mention of subsequent surveys. The document has been prepared by local figures primarily for a local audience and has been redrafted as often as felt necessary. The style is declamatory, the tone that of advice by elders to present and future generations; much general historical material is often given, including versions of the first foundation of the town, the coming of the Spaniards, and the establishment of Christianity. Quite a few "titles" of this general type are known to exist for towns widely scattered through Mesoamerica, and a great many other examples doubtless await discovery in the archives or in their places of origin. As noted by Charles Gibson, who has already provided a succinct description of the genre, a close approximation of the entire content of the documents appears to this day in speeches given in public meetings in certain indigenous communities,[2] so that the "title" is widely diffused temporally as well as spatially.

The specific corpus under examination here consists of four texts from the Chalco region, in the southeastern arm of the Valley of Mexico (see maps at back of book). All four documents are presently preserved in the section Tierras of the Archivo General de la Nación in Mexico City. It would be possible to choose examples with a wider geographical spread, but taking several from the same subarea allows us to see some direct connections and cross-references and thus to get some sense of the degree of diffusion or common tradition involved (see Figure 14.1).

The items are as follows:

1. The first document is from San Nicolás Tetelco (also called Teteltzingo), in the far northwest of the Chalco region, subject to Mixquic yet a town in its own right, with several subdivisions. The Nahuatl text is in Tierras 1671, exp. 10, ff. 13–15, written on six very small pages made from a piece of already partially used paper, accompanied by a large map of Mixquic and Tetelco with their dependencies; the written place-names and remarks seem to be in the same hand as the document. The content relates to a Tetelco border survey, or perhaps two, dated variously at 1534, 1536, 1539, and 1556. There is no definite indication of the date of composition, except that the hand appears later than the sixteenth century. The document was presented in litigation which began in the year 1699; it was said to have been recently "found."

2. The second item is a set of documents from San Antonio Zoyatzingo (just south of Amecameca), which was subject to Tenango Tepopula despite being a full-fledged *altepetl* or city. Tierras 1665, exp. 5, ff. 166r–182v contains a series of substantial, carefully written Nahuatl texts, partially duplicating each other, telling of Zoyatzingo

Figure 14.1 Places of provenience of the sources; towns in which the titles discussed in this chapter originated designated by ●, other centers indicated by ○.

border surveys; one section purports to be a grant and act of possession. The largest text contains a full complement of added historical material, including conversations taking place among local leaders at the time of the Spanish foundation of the town. Elements of the language used, especially some Spanish loan verbs, indicate a time of composition not earlier than the second half of the seventeenth century; the documents were presented in litigation in 1699. A schematic picture-map of Zoyatzingo at the time of acknowledgment of its rights shows the territory, the church in the center, and declaiming figures at the four corners. Another diagram (called a *maban*, or "map") portrays a great hand enclosing the church of Zoyatzingo in its palm. Also included is a set of portraits of early leaders with preconquest accoutrements, apparently involved in territorial defense.

3. The third document is from San Miguel Atlauhtla (southeast of Amecameca), which not only was an *altepetl* but apparently had its own "governor" at times, even though it was in some sense subject to Amecameca. Tierras 2674, exp. 1, consists entirely of the ten-page Nahuatl *títulos primordiales* of Atlauhtla, with a nineteenth-century Spanish translation. As with the Zoyatzingo documents, there is much historical matter in addition to reports on border surveys and investigations variously dated, from 1521 forward. The document is introduced by a drawing in which an early ruler of Atlauhtla and the various barrio chiefs—dressed in European style and sporting Renaissance hats, haircuts, and beards—kneel before Charles V. The language of the

text, especially the inclusion of the Spanish particle *como*, tends to indicate a later redaction date than for the other samples; apparently the people of Atlauhtla presented the document to the authorities in Mexico City as late as the mid-nineteenth century (the translation is dated 1861), though there can be little doubt that it was written down before Mexican independence.

4. The fourth document is from Santiago Sula, on the south side of the road from Chalco to Tlalmanalco and by the latter eighteenth century considered a *formal y rigoroso pueblo*, though without a governor and in some way subject to Tlalmanalco. This is the only one of the four documents not preserved in Nahuatl. All that is left is a Spanish version made by the translator of the Royal Audiencia around 1700–1703, if one judges by the dates of the seals on the paper; for some reason this version went back to the people of Sula, who presented it again in 1778, having apparently in the meantime lost the Nahuatl original. The loss must be judged a great one, for the Sula document has by far the richest historical-legendary overlay of all the samples considered here, causing one almost to lose sight of the border measurement aspect. Still, the translation suffices for some kinds of analysis; moreover, the translator has actually reproduced the original Nahuatl of several special terms, and at times has stayed so close to the phrasing of the original that, on the basis of parallel sections in other Nahuatl documents, we could reconstruct some passages almost word for word.

I will now proceed to a more detailed thematic discussion of the kinds of material contained in these four samples. My purpose is twofold, to establish the characteristics of the genre as well as to explore the historical consciousness of people such as those who composed the documents.

Retention of Preconquest Elements

The first question that comes to mind concerns the extent and nature of preconquest elements preserved in the text. The spread is great, ranging from the lack of anything overtly pre-Columbian in the small Tetelco title to the magical transformation of the ruler into a serpent in the Sula papers. Yet certain facets of the documents repeat themselves often enough to indicate trends.

Memory of local personages and events. All four titles have as their central personages figures thought to have presided over the local entity during the generation immediately following the conquest.

These first-generation notables, or ones like them, must in fact have taken a prominent part in the various ceremonies related to the establishment of Spanish rule and religion in the Indian towns. On close inspection, however, the conquest-period leaders are sometimes seen to incorporate autochthonous figures, originators and symbols of the ethnic group. And whereas the ostensible emphasis is on relations between the local town and the outside, especially the Spanish government, the local figures sometimes embody internal subdivisions such as moieties or relate to important preconquest historical events such as invasions.

Among our samples, those from Tetelco and Atlauhtla do not go beyond simply naming the current ruler and some other notables. A trace of the autochthonous does appear in the latter document, where it is said that the story is being told by Miguel Cuauhcapoltecatl and Juana Acachiquiuhtecatl, the grandfather and grandmother of the local population. The Zoyatzingo and Sula documents, on the other hand, are well populated with ethnic representatives.

In the case of Zoyatzingo, there are three figures of major proportions: Heuhue Xohueyacatzin, (Josef Yaotepotzo) Cuauhcececuitzin, and Juan Ahuacatzin. After presentation of the basic postconquest border survey, the principal document becomes a dialogue among these three leaders. Cuauhcececuitzin, an outsider, requests land of Xohueyacatzin; Ahuacatzin variously objects, but the objections are surmounted. Clearly such transactions could not have been a postlude to a Spanish land investigation. The reference must be, in part at least, to indigenous interrelationships that date back to preconquest times.

Who are the three figures? Huehue Xohueyacatzin (Old Long-foot) not only is generally referred to without a Christian name, but shares the name of a mountain which is said in these texts to be a prominent feature of the Zoyatzingo area. In an introductory passage, Xohueyacatzin is said to have been involved in winning Zoyatzingo's territory for later generations. He is surely, then, the primary symbol of Zoyatzingo as a people and place from its first inception.

As to Juan Ahuacatzin, he appears rather late and secondarily in the dialogue; yet he has the character of a local person. Apparently he is the representative of the lower moiety; the function of this figure in legend is often to express qualifications and minority opinions, as is also exemplified in the Sula document. From colonial times to the present day the town in question has been known as Zoyatzingo. However, while some of the four sections of the town's titles refer to it as Zoyatzingo, Soyatzinco, etc. (apparently for standard Coyatzinco, or "place of the palms, diminutive"), others call it Sihuatzinco (Cihuatzinco, or "place of the woman, dim"), and in yet other sections it is called Soyasihuatzinco and Sihuasoyatzinco (i.e., a combination of the two).[3] One section, purporting to report on the situation at the time of a congregation of 1532, 1555, or 1559, pictures two individuals in a form of preconquest dress, though with postconquest names. Here don Juan Ahuacatzin represents Cihuatzinco, whereas a don Felipe, who has a surname hard to decipher and who is holding a device which might be a palm frond, represents Zoyatzingo. Apparently, for the upper moiety (Zoyatzingo), legend has bypassed the ruler of the postconquest generation and has fastened directly on the mythic autochthonous figure, while the lower moiety (Cihuatzinco) is content to use the historical figure as representative.

Our third person may well be two. The dialogue presents him first as Josef Yaotepotzo Cuauhcececuitzin, and this form is once repeated; mainly, however, he appears simply as Cuauhcececuitzin. In the diagrammatic representation of Zoyatzingo at the time of acquiring its postconquest rights, Josef Yaotepotzo stands in one corner and Cuauhcececuitzin in another. A person of the latter name was an actual historical figure of the Chalco region. Indeed, he was a major ruler, and Chimalpahin's writings repeatedly mention him as the king of Panohuayan, north of Amecameca, in the late preconquest years. He lived to meet Cortés but died not long after and may never have been baptized, since Chimalpahin gives no Christian name for him. The Cuauhcececuitzin of the Zoyatzingo account is said to be from Atzacualco, in the same part of the region as the domain of the famous king of Panohuayan, so we may suspect that the two are the same. Josef Yaotepotzo, on the other hand, may have been a separate person, more local and less renowned.

The dialogue of the Zoyatzingo titles runs approximately as follows: Old Xohueyacatzin of Zoyatzingo makes friends with Cuauhcececuitzin, who then comes to him as a supplicant. He offers him some boys and girls to serve him and asks him for a bit of land in reward for his unspecified services, land where he and his followers can settle, rest from their exertions, and be buried, land which they can leave to their descendants. Xohueyacatzin responds enthusiastically, exhorts Cuauhcececuitzin to stay, and hastens to begin preparations for distributing plots to Cuauhcececuitzin's people. At this point Ahuacatzin intervenes, not once but twice. His first group of objections is set in the framework of the Spanish organization of the town. Ahuacatzin says that the distribution must not be formless and irregular; there must be four town subdivisions (*tlaxilacalli*), and each must have its constables (*merinos*). Ahuacatzin's second objections are even easier to place in a preconquest context. He warns that Cuauhcececuitzin and his successors must never claim that they got their land by conquest. In both cases Ahuacatzin's advice is heeded, though Cuauhcececuitzin still gets the land. Further comments in the text assert that Cuauhcececuitzin came to Zoyatzingo for no special purpose, merely being tired after much moving about and founding of towns. Rumors about conquest, it is maintained, are not true. Xohueyacatzin had full rights to the territory, and the people of Zoyatzingo had nothing to fear; Cuauhcececuitzin only helped out (presumably in the defense of the land). One passage seems to imply that Cuauhcececuitzin was returning to his home to finish out his life.

No one can be sure what facts occasioned this account. One can speculate, however, that in late preconquest times Zoyatzingo may have been forced into a rather disadvantageous confederacy with more powerful outsiders, giving up some part of its territory to them. From that moment forward, the Zoyatzingo people probably told a version of the arrangement which made them the dominant partners and preserved their full autonomy. This body of material then became amalgamated with postconquest happenings, and we cannot know positively to what extent the late colonial writers were conscious of the preconquest dimension. Clearly, though, they were still smarting under the implication that any other indigenous group had ever conquered them.

In the Sula document the protagonists are much more openly and unambiguously autochthonous, yet they too are presented as being alive in the early postconquest period and receiving possession from the Spanish authorities. The figures are two brothers, the older one Martín Molcatzin (Sauce-bowl) and the younger Martín Huitzcol (Bent-thorn). It is tempting to think of them as a timeless, entirely mythic pair, who are assigned the same Christian name in order to show their underlying unity (and perhaps also because it was rather hard for the late writers to imagine anyone who was entirely without a Christian name). Yet the Zoyatzingo titles give added support to their partial historicity, twice mentioning a border shared with "Martín de Molcax of Sula." Thus we must conclude that one, if not both, of the Martíns actually flourished in Sula in the conquest generation. Nevertheless, the two also deal with a threat from the Mexica before the establishment of Tenochtitlan. As the text says, "They came from nowhere else, they are from here and were the first dwellers of this town" (despite this, their parents and grandparents were also from Sula). Martín Molcatzin bears the title of Çolteuctli, or "Quail-lord"; the original Nahuatl of "Sula" is "Çollan," or "place of the quail."

The tale of the encounter with the Mexica, inserted between the acts of possession and the full border recital, is the Sula document's outstanding feature and the most remarkable piece of later colonial legend I have yet seen. I present here a version of the principal passages, complete with their liberal admixture of postconquest elements:

Here will be seen and declared how the Mexica, before they settled the site of Mexico City, came to Sula, and they did not permit these Tenochca or Mexica, who are called Tenochtitlan people, to settle. They were walking along and came to Sula, and [the Sula people] came out to meet them, and they could not halt there. The Mexica came along the highway with trumpet and banner, and the people of Sula came there to meet them so that they would not take away their rule; those of Sula came to the defense of their town.

Then the one called Aza Persia came shouting, saying, "My lords, you here of Sula, let us make a halt here, for we are very tired and have come walking a very long way."

And then Martín Molcatzin, the Çolteuctli, answered and said, and they said to Martin Huitzcol [sic], "I and all those who are here are the dwellers of this town, and so you can go ahead, for you cannot halt here."

These two Martíns who are named here are two brothers, one called Martín Molcatzin and the other Martín Huitzcol, and they said, "Lady Ana García, we are from here and we are sons of the ancients; we were born in this valley and our grandfathers and grandmothers are from here; they came from nowhere else, and they are those of the ancient time (for their ancestors were pagans). And you, where do you come from? Perhaps you have been exiled from somewhere. Go on with you, we have our questionnaires. Just go ahead and take the highway which begins at our border . . . [here a short recital of borders and measurements] . . . And know and understand that it is not far to where you are to go; you come from a lake, and now you are very close to another lake there ahead. It could be that there would be a place for you there and you would find what you desire. You are already close to the place and they may admit you there. And so have a good trip, you are very close to a town where they might admit you and give you some place."

And when they heard what they told them, they all went away, and Ana María [sic] and her daughter called Juana García began to shout, saying "Señor, señor, you have these lands; señor Çolteuctli, we have heard what you said."

Well, my very beloved sons, I will now tell you and declare that God our lord saw fit to create him whom they call Çolteuctli, who is Martín Molcatzin, who turned himself into a serpent in the manner of a quail. The Mexica, whom they call the people of inside the water, were leaving, and got to the borders of Sula, and just where the border of the people of Sula is, they found a very large and frightful serpent in the fashion of a quail, as to its feathers, and for this reason they called it Çolcoatl [Quail-serpent], and it was all spread out there and frightful. And the Mexica were greatly taken aback, for never had they seen a serpent like that, so they were very frightened, and they went away and the people of Sula were left very content. Because if the Mexica had stayed, they would have ruled the land which the people of Sula possessed, which their ancestors and grandparents left them and which they are still possessing now.

My beloved sons, what we say here occurred this way, and understand it very well. This Martín Huitzcol wanted to feed them, and they were going to give them what they call in their language *maçatl ynenepiltzin* [deer tongue], which are a kind of small nopal cactus, and they were going to give them what they call *tlancuaxoloch* [wrinkled knee], which are beans, and as a third food they were going to give them what they call *cuentla ococolmic* [what has died off in the field], which are squash, and also what they call *cempolihuini centlamini* [what entirely disappears and ends], which is amaranth seed, and what is to be sprinkled on top of the food, what they say is pointing toward the ground, which is green chile; and then they were going to give them *cuahuitl yxpillotl* [what looks down from the tree], which are avocados—this is what they were going to give them last of all. But the older brother, who is Martín Molcatzin, did not want it to be; if they had fed them there, they would have stayed there and not gone away. God our lord orders everything, and so all the food was left behind.

The startling passage in which Ana García heads the Mexica is no simple error, since she and her daughter Juana are mentioned a second time as having brought along so many lords and vassals to no avail. Two other details in the document are directly relevant to the preceding section. At one point it is said that the whole population of Sula turned into quail and frightened the Mexica away. And at the beginning of the border recital proper it appears (though the condition of the document and the vagueness of the language make it uncertain) that the people of Sula have a border with Martín Huitzcol, as though his group were more a foreign ethnicity than a lower moiety. This is congruent with the apparently confused passage just quoted in which it is not clear whether Molcatzin is addressing himself to Huitzcol or speaking jointly with him.

Sula's version of its relation with the outside in preconquest times lacks the plausibility and possible historicity of the Zoyatzingo materials. Since no incident remotely like that narrated can have taken place, we face here legend or reshaping in a quite straightforward form. We can ask directly, therefore, what the received version shows about consciousness. Being so close to Tenochtitlan and Texcoco, Sula surely came at some time under the thorough dominance of the Triple Alliance. Also, some sixteenth-century documents of sale which the Sula people preserved demonstrate that in preconquest times and through most of the sixteenth century Tlalmanalco, or some noblemen from there, held lands inside Sula's territory. As with Zoyatzingo, Sula has inverted the situation, making itself the entirely autonomous victor, threatened only by treachery from the inside, that is, by the half-foreign subsidiary group of Huitzcol. Sula at least acknowledges the existence of the Mexica, as none of the other towns do.

No chronological dimension can be assigned to the Mexica episode, although it does occur after the Sula people have become a fixed entity with a distinct territory. The story is symbolic of outside threats successfully warded off. These threats are amalgamated; the preconquest imperial power is associated with the postconquest Garcías, who were likely early proprietors of one of the Spanish estates ringing Sula's territory by 1700. (A conflict with a neighboring hacienda brought on the litigation in which the Sula document was presented.) The means to ward off the threats are equally the postconquest questionnaire and border survey, and the preconquest powers of the totemic quail. There can be little doubt that the quail legends go back to preconquest Sula; the quail-serpent is a naturalization of the general Mesoamerican feathered serpent. Even the notion of the cry of the quail as a frightening sound has precedent in preconquest myth: when the Lord of the Dead wanted to prevent Quetzalcoatl from stealing the jade bones to create man, he sent the quail to frighten him.[4]

Thus two of our samples show evidence of preconquest historical and legendary matter circulating openly in the indigenous communities of the Chalco area in the time around 1700. There was little feeling that such matter was different in kind from postconquest beliefs and events, or that the two were in conflict; rather they were so thoroughly integrated with each other that there was an entire merging and loss of sight of the preconquest-vs.-postconquest perspective. Both kinds of elements were placed in the service of the autonomous territoriality of the local ethnic group.

In this context there is an aspect of the Zoyatzingo and Sula papers which I hardly know whether to view as a survival or as a new reaction to the colonial situation. In the Zoyatzingo titles—at the end of the conversation of Cuauhcececuitzin, Xohueyacatzin, and Juan Ahuacatzin—the latter disappears, having been enclosed by God inside the local mountain Xoxocoyoltepetl. From here he will watch after the people until he reemerges at the end of the world. This would seem to be a messianism in response to Spanish domination. But note that it is the minority representative, the objector to Cuauhcececuitzin, who goes into the mountain, and not Old Xohueyacatzin. Conceivably, then, we have here in part a reflection of the resentment of one indigenous group displaced by another. The dominant note, however, seems to be the one struck at the end of the passage—that eventually the old pagans will revive. The same is true in the Sula document, where although no messianic incident occurs, a prominent sentence asserts that "our ancient fathers," though they died, did not die, and will resuscitate on judgment day (Christian orthodoxy, of course, but surely with another dimension here).

The Chichimecs and the sweep of cultural evolution. Before the conquest, many Mesoamerican groups preserved the tradition that at a remote time they had not been sedentary people with houses and fields but had wandered about the countryside; they were also aware of repeated invasions of the settled areas by other wanderers. The general symbol of the nonsedentary was the Chichimec. How much of all this had the writers of our samples retained? In the three larger documents there are definite traces of retention of such matter, but, as we have come to expect, it is amalgamated in various ways. The three notions of an original general nonsedentary stage of existence, Chichimec invasions of the sedentary area, and a time of troubles and flight immediately after the conquest all tend to come together.

The first portion of the Zoyatzingo documents asserts that the town received confirmation of its rights to the land shortly after the conquest because the inhabitants of Zoyatzingo had not, like the people of all the other towns around, fled in fear of the Chichimecs who were everywhere entering and destroying. It is in this light that we must see the passage in the principal section of the Zoyatzingo papers to the effect that after the arrival of the Spaniards there were many people (this time possibly from Zoyatzingo too) who did not want to accept the faith and went to hide. For 7 years they dwelt in the woods, ravines, and caves, until the archbishop ordered that the recalcitrant ones be brought down forcibly from the mountains and collected, leading to a general congregation in 1555. Atlauhtla gives a version so close to Zoyatzingo's (specifying that the order came from Archbishop Zumárraga) that this must be a single tradition common to the area. The hiding place of the refugees is given in almost the same words in the two versions.[5]

Something similar appears in the Sula document. We can hardly doubt that the following passage is related to the same tradition observed for Zoyatzingo and Atlauhtla: "In the old days they did not yet know God, but worshiped whatever they felt like . . . and they went about in the wilds, hiding among the crags and in the grasslands, before they were baptized in the year of 1532." And again: "Before the faith came, they all went scattered about, hiding among the wilds and crags." But here this behavior is no mere temporary flight from Chichimecs or Spaniards, nor is it something attributed primarily to others. Rather it is an integral part of Sula's own evolution. The document begins with the creation of the world by the Christian God, proceeds to the stage of the existence of the Sula people as wild wanderers or nonsedentaries, and then tells of the coming of the Spaniards and the foundation of the town. All these happenings are seen as one related series of events. The categorization—one can hardly speak of the chronology—equates paganism with nonsedentariness, and Christianity and the Spanish king with the sedentary stage. The threat by the Mexica falls into the latter grouping, and hence it is natural that the Mexica should speak of God's will and that the Sula people should wave their Spanish titles at them.

Hints of a broader ethnicity. In what we have seen so far, almost all indigenous cultural inheritance is referred directly to the local entity. Insofar as there is recognition of nonlocal indigenous groups such as the Mexica, they are classed with the Spaniards as outside threats. Is there any evidence in the texts of Indian solidarity, referring either to past times or to the times in which the texts were written? In general, the coming of the Spaniards is a transaction between the intruders and the local group, other indigenous groups being mentioned only for their bad behavior in fleeing, resisting Christianity, and the like. Once, indeed, in the Atlauhtla document, there is mention of the exact time of the surrender of Tenochtitlan-Tlatelolco to the Spaniards in 1521. But this passage, which is without introductory context, gives every appearance of having been lifted (as something interesting about distant times) from some other text that came into the hands of the writer or a predecessor. Once again the reference to the local situation is made immediately thereafter. The writer remarks that locally too there was war, at the end of which the town acquired its rights.

Nowhere in the texts is any derivative of the Spanish word *indio* used, nor is anyone called by any other term that could be translated as "Indian." As in other colonial-period Nahuatl texts, each indigenous person or group is referred to by the name of the local ethnic-political entity: Atlauhtecatl, "person of Atlauhtla"; Coyatzincatl, "person of Zoyatzingo," etc. Only two brief and very similar passages have any implication of recognition of an overall indigenous ethnicity. In the Nahuatl of the twentieth century, *macehualli*, originally "commoner" or "vassal," has come to be the approximate referential equivalent of "Indian." Some texts of the middle and late colonial period show it already beginning to move in that direction. In the Atlauhtla document too, after a warning that Spaniards are not to take the townspeople's land, there comes the statement *"yaxca masehuali y tlali,"* "the land belongs to the commoner [or vassal, or *masehual* as the Spaniards said]"; the effect of the passage is very close to "this is Indian land." One section of the Zoyatzingo documents is nearly identical; the Spaniards are warned off, *"ca masechualtlalpan yn ticate,"* "for where we are is commoner land." But let me repeat that these words are the only hint of any arising general Indian ethnic consciousness to be found in the whole set of texts.[6]

On the other hand, there is an awareness of the larger language group. Three of the documents make some reference to Nahuatl. In the two which are preserved in that language, it is called *mexicacopa*, "in the fashion of the Mexica," a back translation from the Spanish *mexicano*. In these cases Nahuatl is seen as a defense against the prying eyes of Spaniards, though the local people are also aware that the documents will need translation in order to be brought to the attention of the authorities. Ironically, it is the Sula document, preserved only in translation, which makes the most of the language and of the language group: "God gave me these words, which are not the word of Michoacán nor of the Matlatzincas nor the Otomis, but that which we set forth and state here in our Mexican language." Here we have not the possibly Spanish-induced awareness of "Mexican," but an older Nahuatl-speaker patriotism in contradistinction to other major indigenous language groups of central Mexico. Implied here, though not fully expressed, is a view in which civilized sedentary life in the Mesoamerican sphere is restricted to a Nahuatl-speaking world of autonomous towns with their territories, surrounded by barbarians of various kinds.

Style, social concepts, and ritual. Apart from the framework of corporation and wider world, what other indigenous cultural elements do our texts demonstrate to have been retained? The vehicle of preconquest public life was a rich oratory which embodied both a manner and a highly specific set of concepts. There are strong traces of this in all the texts. Higher public discourse in general had the denomination *huehuetlatolli*, or "speech of the elders," in the preconquest Nahuatl-speaking sphere. All of our texts, even the shortest one from Tetelco, purport to be spoken by elders for the benefit of the young and those yet to be born. All retain the characteristic forms of address: "oh my children," "oh my younger brothers," etc. Formulas designating the young and future generations are preserved in full uniformity in all the titles: "those who crawl, those who drag themselves"; "those who are not yet born, [those who will come] after five or ten [years], in the time to which we look." The declamatory and metaphorical presentation typical of preconquest lore is still very much in evidence in our documents. The Zoyatzingo and Atlauhtla documents agree in calling the boundary settlement the town's "measure, seal, shield, and battle rampart." The Sula document compares its words of advice to precious stones set in gold, a standard metaphor of the old rhetoric.

Deeply embedded in that rhetoric were notions of social organization, especially of the roles of noble and commoner. In all the texts there are standard preconquest phrases denoting the dignity of rulership, here applied to the holders of municipal office in the postconquest Hispanic-style polities. All also contain standard formulas for the common people, especially the phrase "the wings and the tails," which appears in the three in Nahuatl (probably also in the Sula original, if we had it). A final section of the Sula document is directed to "you who are present, whether you are sons of lords or sons of commoners." Those who are lords and exercise the staff of office well will be fortunate, thanked by God and given bouquets of flowers by the townspeople, but if they should not heed the advice now given, they will be treated as commoners; they will go about with the carrying frame and the tumpline, and have to perform tribute labor. The preconquest stereotypes of social differentiation are thus still familiar.

The titles also betray a considerable carry-over of preconquest ritual, at least that pertaining to boundary verification. Gibson speculates that the "title" may be at least partially a preconquest genre. In view of the deviance of such documents from Spanish documentary forms and their wide range, from central Mexico to Guatemala, the suggestion is an attractive one. A preconquest original would presumably have consisted of a map with pictures and glyphs giving the date as well as the names of the places and ethnicities involved. The visual record would have been accompanied by an extensive oral recital much like the prose of the postconquest written titles. However boundary settlements were recorded, the presence in the titles of some items which would be extraneous in parallel Spanish documents indicates the existence and partial persistence of an indigenous ritual or set behavior relating to the finalization of such matters.

The most striking ritual element is that of the feast. This was given by the ruler of the town for all parties, including the elders of bordering ethnicities. Even the short Tetelco document mentions that all came to the house of don Nicolás Tlacamaçatzin for turkey and *atole*, and afterwards went to their homes in peace. The ceremonies of Atlauhtla and Zoyatzingo also end with the general feast. We have here not only a deeply ingrained custom but an act with juridical force, much like making a signature. In the Sula document, had Molcatzin fed the Mexica, he would have had to acknowledge their claims.

In the Atlauhtla and Zoyatzingo titles, wind instruments are played at every turn; the Atlauhtla document even preserves the name of the principal player, Pedro Macxochitzin. Although the Spaniards surely made use of music for important ceremonies, trumpets were not part of the general baggage of Spanish land investigations. In at least some cases, the instrument being played is apparently the indigenous conch shell trumpet, pictured in the mouth of one figure in the Zoyatzingo documents; ones looking much like it can be seen in maps and pictures of the Historia Tolteca Chichimeca.[7]

Several passages in the documents say that the local people acquired the land with effort and trouble, and for Zoyatzingo there is the specific claim that the ancestors gained their right to the town's territory "through war and dying." It appears indeed that having fought successfully for the land was a main source of legal right to it. Hence a show of war may have been part of boundary settlement ritual. In the two pictures in the Zoyatzingo materials showing the principals of the founding ceremonies, most of the dignitaries hold preconquest weapons in their hands, either the obsidian-edged sword or the bow and arrow. In the Atlauhtla document the representatives of the bordering ethnicities bring their swords to the ceremonies, and the survey is punctuated by incidents in which the neighbors temporarily threaten to make objections and want war. These sections could be an oblique reference to historical border wars, but I am more inclined to think that they refer to mock battle gestures taking place as part of border verification ritual, here reported by successors who may or may not have grasped the nature of the transaction.

Here, as elsewhere, there is more retention than awareness of retention. The people of each town know that once their ancestors were pagan, while their towns lacked saints' names, the people Christian names, and the leaders the title of "don." They know, too, that all this changed with the coming of the Spaniards and Christianity. But they view the bulk of their cultural inheritance simply as theirs, attaching little importance to whether its origin is indigenous or intrusive; rather, elements from the two spheres are freely projected upon each other.

Incorporation of Postconquest Elements

The preceding discussion anticipates much of what I have to say about the indigenous view of the postconquest period and the intrusive phenomena characteristic of it. The amalgamation of the two epochs and the two kinds of cultural elements has already been demonstrated. Certain aspects of the new era were seen as so basic or taken so much for granted that the preconquest period could no longer be imagined without them. Despite divergent beliefs such as the quail-serpent or the sojourn of Ahuacatzin in the mountain, nowhere in the titles is there any hint of disbelief in Christianity or of continuing resistance to it. Moreover, despite the intense striving for local autonomy, there is no hint of any disloyalty to the Spanish king (though knowledge about the latter personage is extraordinarily weak). Rather, God and king are seen as the ultimate support for the legitimacy of the town's claims.

How fully integrated Spanish-Christian material could be appears from the legend of the choosing of Sula's patron saint. The two oldest of all the Sula people, Miguel Omacatzin and Pedro Capolicano, decide that the choice of a saint should come from within the town. They convoke all the inhabitants and ask them to choose, but the people, saying that the two are their fathers, turn the choice back to them. That night Santiago appears in a vision to each of the two separately; when they tell each other the next day, they are fully convinced and the choice is made. The two elders are clearly the autochthonous pair in a different guise, so that the choice of the Spanish saint is an act on a level with the original foundation of the town, carried out by its deepest symbols of ethnic identity.

Postconquest historical references. Against this background let us examine the salient aspects of what the titles say about postconquest phenomena. As previously asserted, a title is built around a report on an early postconquest border survey of the local area. Certain other matter is standardly presented as more or less simultaneous with the survey: laying out the town in Spanish-style lots,[8] naming the barrios, establishing local Spanish-style officials (such as governor or alcaldes), baptizing the people, building the church, and (sometimes though not always) congregation. The whole cycle of acts has such a strong aura of a legendary first foundation and source of legitimation that, as we have seen, the Sula document quite rigorously takes it as equivalent to the origin of the town as an organized territorial entity.

In view of this, are we to imagine that the survey reports refer to any actual historical occasion or occasions at all? Apparently they do. There are several indications of authenticity in the naming of the indigenous notables said to be present at the ceremonies. First of all, they have names typical of the first postconquest generation: a Christian name plus an indigenous name, with a still quite loosely attached "don" for only a few of the most prominent. This was not at all the mode of the later colonial period. Further, in the Atlauhtla and Tetelco documents the main local figure has the same Christian name as the town's patron saint (a common congruence, which would, however, not be hard to counterfeit at a later time). Then there is some independent evidence of the existence of two of the figures mentioned. As we saw, the Martín Molcatzin so central to the Sula document receives passing mention in the Zoyatzingo titles too. More conclusively, the Atlauhtla document gives a don Tomás Quetzalmaçatzin as the representative of Amecameca at Atlauhtla's border survey, and Chimalpahin repeatedly mentions just this personage as ruling Amecameca in the early postconquest years (yet it is abundantly clear that the Atlauhtla title writers of the eighteenth century had no copy of Chimalpahin at their disposal).

As to the Spanish officials involved, only two of our samples mention an actual individual who came to the local scene, but these two do agree on a name: in Tetelco, "Do Petro de Omada"; in Zoyatzingo, "Do Pº te Omemadad." One of the Spanish translators may be right in equating this appellation with "Ahumada"; a Pedro de Ahumada (not "don") came to Mexico in 1550, in what capacity I do not presently know.[9] Although the dates supplied in the documents for postconquest events vary so widely and heap upon each other so thickly that one could reach almost any conclusion, there is a certain clustering in the 1530s for the primary border surveys and in the 1550s for congregation. I rather expect that future research on the Chalco region will show this to correspond to the facts.

The conquest proper hardly figures in the titles. It is merely signaled as "the coming of Cortés" or "the coming of the faith," something taken as a cosmic event. Only the repercussions for the immediate area are seen as something needing telling.[10] No regret is expressed about the conquest as the end of an epoch; rather, as seen earlier, there is disapproval of those who fled in the first years. The emphasis is on the first coming of outside representatives to set up the town in the new style; in the Zoyatzingo and Atlauhtla versions, a high dignitary—whether king, viceroy, or archbishop—becomes concerned in a God-like fashion about the people and sends someone out, leading to the border survey and foundation. Only the Sula document gives us a rounded picture (purely legendary, or at least composite) of the coming of the Spaniards to the town:

> When the señor Marqués brought the Catholic faith, the fathers of the order of our father St. Francis came carrying a Holy Christ in front, and the Spaniards, those with the white hides and with tubs on their heads, carrying their swords under their armpits, said they were called Spaniards and that they had been given license to establish all the towns formally, and they [the Sula people] should think what saint they wanted to be their patron, because the Catholic faith was in Mexico City already.

Spanish officials and legal concepts. At the level of the high dignitaries who send out representatives, it is apparent that the writers of the titles had no clear conception either of the individuals or of the offices. Cortés is frequently used as symbol of the Spanish advent and as source of legitimacy. However, some writers are not sure whether or not he is the same person as the Marqués (del Valle), and occasionally Viceroy Velasco is seen as having arrived jointly with him. Viceroy don Luis de Velasco is in fact a favorite figure, and after him Viceroy don Antonio de Mendoza and Archbishop Zumárraga. In Atlauhtla, Emperor Charles V enjoys great fame. But the writers so frequently mix all these figures and their titles together that the names seem to be functioning as alternate designations or different aspects of the same thing (just as gods, towns, and rulers often had multiple names in preconquest times). A viceroy may be called a king, or a king a viceroy; there is an outside seat of Spanish power, but whether it is in Spain or in Mexico City hardly matters and is hardly grasped. Consider the following examples:

[Zoyatzingo:]
 the Marqués and [the] Cortés . . .
 Cortés and don Luis de Velasco, the Marqués . . .
 the archbishop don Pedro de Ahumada . . .
 don Luis de Velasco, the Marqués del Valle . . .
 the king our lord in Mexico City, his majesty . . .
 the Viceroy de Salinas . . . [with no awareness that this is Velasco]
[Atlauhtla:]
 our great lord the viceroy emperor Charles V . . .
 the king our lord inside the water in Mexico City . . .
 the king came from Castile to Mexico City . . .
 the king don Antonio de Mendoza entered Mexico City . . .
 the king don Luis de Velasco . . .
[Tetelco:]
 don Luis de Velasco de Salinas, general

 The Spanish titles *juez* ("judge"), *visitador* ("inspector"), and *registrador* ("registrar") are also sprinkled through the texts almost haphazardly.[11]

 Essentially there is concern with these outside personae and offices only as something to appeal to in the defense of one's territory. The same is seen with certain procedural concepts of Spanish governance. A full grasp of the procedures from the inside is not sought. The local people are concerned only with the end result, confirmation of their rights, so that *merced* ("grant"), *posesión* (formal act of taking unchallenged possession), and *interrogatorio* ("questionnaire") come down to the same thing. One sheet of the Zoyatzingo papers attempts to approximate a record of the town's grant and act of possession; but while the *posesión* part does somewhat appropriately report assent by the neighboring groups, the *merced* portion bears no resemblance at all to a Spanish grant, nor does it involve anyone's giving anything to anyone. Perhaps the term acquiring the most independent existence was the Nahuatl version of the Spanish word *interrogatorio*. Since *in* is the Nahuatl article "the," the local Nahuatl speakers took the word proper to begin thereafter, resulting in written forms such as *teloca-*

dorio, derocadorio, and *delogadorio.* Even the Spanish version of the Sula document has *terrogatorio,* for the translator was demonstrably a native speaker of Nahuatl. This word then became the most basic and general one used in the area for "true title." We have seen the Sula people employing the term to the Mexica, and of Xohueyacatzin of Zoyatzingo it is said that he had nothing to fear of other local groups "because the questionnaire truly belonged to him." The map of Tetelco is prominently labeled *dodelogadorio pontzesio,* which makes little sense as literally "this is our questionnaire and act of possession"; rather the utterance is like one of the old preconquest double metaphorical phrases, with the intention "this is our title."

Christian chronology. As regards chronology, too, the years according to the European calendar are important only as they are thought to confirm a given town's claims. Two or even three mutually contradictory or individually implausible dates may be given for the same event. In one part of the Zoyatzingo papers, the Spaniards are said to have come in 945. Perhaps the most egregious example involves the previously quoted passage picturing the arrival of the Spaniards and the faith in Sula, which is dated 1607 at the beginning and 1609 at the end (despite a statement earlier that the Sula people were baptized in 1532). The events of the titles appear to take place in the timelessness of legend or dream, in which progression is short-term and any two related elements may fall together. This cannot explain, however, the utter caprice and apparent incompetence in dating or even the presence of dates at all. All Mesoamerican peoples understood well the principle of an indefinite unidirectional progression of time with the events of each consecutive year assigned a separate space. The composers of the titles doubtless also knew the principle, but they appear not to have been full masters of the European numerical system of counting the years, nor even to have grasped fully that one set of numbers was exclusive of any other. The years are there not because the writers themselves had counted them and understood them, but because they knew the authorities gave importance to them. Here even more than with the Spanish personae, offices, and procedural concepts, it seems as if the local people are using the Spanish paraphernalia as magic, as something efficacious rather than understood. They appear to have belived that if one only shouted out the right abracadabra of years, names, and titles, the genie would deliver eternally unchallenged possession of one's territory.

Christianity. As regards religious concepts, we have already noted the unorthodox legends of Sula and Zoyatzingo, as well as some vagueness about the archbishop, but the writers display a considerable grasp

of the central tenets of Christianity and of the working of the sacraments, which are standardly detailed as the rationale for building the
local church. Community identification with the church as a building
is strong; the church is felt to have been erected entirely by the people
themselves and is an important symbol of the town's existence and
relative status, as indicated in the various pictures and maps included
in the titles. Although the local Spanish friars or priests are not much
mentioned, we see their influence in various ways. Most of the documents begin with an invocation, the clerics' sermon style with its
rhetorical questions is reflected in certain passages, and they are surely
responsible for some biblical references scattered here and there. Like
material of whatever origin, the biblical enters into the general stream
of local tradition. The "Aza Persia" among the Mexica in the Sula
document seems to take his name from a biblical king. Persia has
apparently become a symbol of the exotic. Santiago is also from Persia,
"which they say is toward the east."

The lack of general history. There is very little in the titles that
could be considered under the heading of a simple account of newswor-
thy events of the past, such as the eclipses and storms so often mentioned in Nahuatl annals. The Zoyatzingo and Atlauhtla documents do
make mention of the great epidemics of the sixteenth century (the
Atlauhtla title by mistake puts the epidemic of 1576 a century later).
Even this is reported in reference to the local group and in close relation to the main subject matter. Thus in the Atlauhtla document the
loss of life is seen as an additional reason for the viceroy to favor the
town, while in the Zoyatzingo document an epidemic of 1556 comes,
very plausibly, on the heels of a congregation in 1555.

Attitudes toward individual Spaniards. If an affirmative attitude
is shown in these texts toward an overall Spanish-Christian framework, the same is not true when it comes to Spaniards as individuals.
Prominent sections of each of the three lengthier documents are given
over to admonishing the local inhabitants not to show the papers to
anyone, most especially to Spaniards, and not to let Spaniards get the
land, as will surely happen if they get at the papers. (The notion of a
secret text as a source of group power may be partially carried over
from the preconquest era.) The Zoyatzingo title warns the people to
watch lest Spaniards coming in the future should make friends with
their descendants, eat with them and become their *compadres,* then
force them to sell them land or give it to them for friendship. The Sula
document specifically denounces the Spaniards as tricky and deceitful
(*"es muy gente satírica,"* says the Nahuatl-speaker translator, probably rendering something like *"huel teca mocacayahua,"* "they greatly

deceive people"). This concern over individual Spaniards coming into the local indigenous community is not new, but in sixteenth-century Nahuatl documentation no such ready stereotype appears, and the source of concern was more likely to be other indigenous groups. With the change in the situation, particularly as Hispanic people poured out of the city into the countryside in the middle and later colonial period, the emphasis in indigenous attitudes has switched. The corporation has properly recognized the Spanish influx as the primary threat to its existence and offers resolute, blanket opposition. (Indians as individuals often felt quite differently about it, as follows in fact from the nature of the warnings alone.)

Area-wide traditions. That the town-province is the universal arena and reference point in the titles does not preclude the existence of a common tradition across the broader area, in this case the Chalco region. Each town has a similar view of itself and its surroundings. A concept such as the *terrogatorio* is area-wide (and also, so far as I have seen to date, area-specific). The similarly deviant forms of postconquest names and offices betray that the title writers consulted with one another across town boundaries. On occasion the writers incorporated whole passages from other texts; the Atlauhtla document inserts, as an afterthought and between sections, a paragraph identical to one in the Zoyatzingo title, telling in flowery language how the borders extend in the four cardinal directions and giving a date. The Tetelco people may have gone further than this; they were accused of copying their entire document from an original in Mixquic. Reciprocal influence on various points was somehow possible in the face of the fact that official Nahuatl documents and more professional writers in the same towns could have supplied conflicting and more objectively correct information. The dichotomy is seen even in the orthography. The three titles preserved in Nahuatl have deviant spellings in common which I have not seen elsewhere and which also fail to appear in eighteenth-century Nahuatl documents written by municipal officials of these very towns, included in the same dossiers as the titles (Zoyatzingo and Tetelco).[12]

If one presumes, as I do, that even in preconquest times the popular view made each city-state an entirely autonomous territorial entity, the protagonist of cultural and political movements which were really of broader scope, then little had changed by the later colonial period. God and king now supported legitimacy; but surely the towns had come to similar terms with earlier partially understood outside religious and political powers. The town-centered, atemporal view of our documents is no simple deterioration from the broad view and long chronology of the Aztec rulers or of Chimalpahin; rather the approximate equivalent to these existed in the outlook of the town officials and other notables who in the later colonial period still had supramunicipal connections, an education geared to their time, and a grasp of its complex Hispanic-Indian society.

Notes

[1]The Nahuatl text of his works is published by Günter Zimmermann as *Die Relationen Chimalpahin's zur Geschichte México's* (Hamburg, 1963–1965)

[2]*Handbook of Middle American Indians,* XV (Austin, 1975), 320–21.

[3]The only instance I have seen of outsiders calling the town anything but Zoyatzingo is reference in the title of neighboring Atlauhtla to "San Adonio Sihuatzinco."

[4]See Angel María Garibay K., *Llave del náhuatl* (3d ed., México, 1970), p. 138.

[5]Zoyatzingo:

y quactlac yn atlacon textexcala
in the woods, the ravines, the crags . . .

Atlauhtla:

quauhtla yn atlaco y tetexcalco yn oostosqui
in the woods, the ravines, the crags, the caves . . .

[6]Nowhere in the documents is the Virgin of Guadalupe even mentioned, except as the name of one of the barrios of Atlauhtla.

[7]*Historia tolteca chichimeca,* ed. by Paul Kirchoff, Lina Odena Güemes, and Luis Reyes García (México, 1976).

[8]The Spanish word *solar,* 'lot', found a home in Nahuatl very early as *xolal,* which was probably not recognized by later Nahuatl speakers as a loan. In the Zoyatzingo text (f. 175) it appears not only incorporated into a verb but with the first syllable reduplicated to indicate distributive meaning, something which could occur only with a fully assimilated root: *nexoxolaltecon,* 'laying out of the various lots occurs'.

[9]Francisco del Paso y Troncoso, ed., *Epistolario de la Nueva España,* VI (México, 1939), 5.

[10]Even the elaborate sixteenth-century narration of the conquest in the twelfth book of Sahagún's Florentine Codex concentrates overwhelmingly on the perspective from Tenochtitlan, with especially strong emphasis on Tlatelolco, where Sahagún's informants lived. *Florentine Codex: General History of the Things of New Spain,* tr. by Arthur J. O. Anderson and Charles E. Dibble, Part XIII (2d ed., Salt Lake City, 1975).

[11]One must admit that circumstances combined to make things hard for the provincial reporters. *Atlitic,* 'inside the waters', was equally applicable to Mexico City and Spain. Spaniards were in the habit of saying merely "the Marqués," meaning Cortés as Marqués del Valle; yet Velasco was the Marqués de Salinas.

[12]The principal deviation has to do with the letter *c,* which is often intruded or omitted, or used in place of *u, uh,* or *n,* or replaced by *s* even to represent [k].

15

Nahuatl Literacy

Frances Karttunen

Editors' Introduction

Unlike Andean peoples, Nahuatl speakers of central Mexico enjoyed a precolonial tradition of writing. Karttunen charts how a convergence of anthropologists, historians, and linguists on nonstandard Nahuatl texts has revised the picture of colonial Indian life in central Mexico.

Beginning with early colonial rule and continuing up to the abolition of the Royal Court of Appeals in Mexico after independence, Indian notaries wrote Nahuatl documents for litigating property ownerships, disputes, petitions, and other legal matters. Written Nahuatl was the accepted genre for public legal discourse by Indians, even in areas outside central Mexico where Nahuatl was once observed as a lingua franca for government. Karttunen suggests that the Nahuatl legal genre was a major medium for Nahuatl speakers' acculturation, even though Nahuatl litigation preserved a certain degree of autonomy in local government. Formulating arguments that could withstand appeal up the judicial hierarchy to Mexico meant adopting Spanish legal conventions and concepts, ultimately facilitating not only linguistic but also cultural assimilation into the Spanish world. Here again, as in the chapters by Borah and Stern, indigenous cultural practices collapse in unforeseen ways through articulation with the state, rather than being imposed by policy from above.

THE INCA AND AZTEC
STATES, 1400–1800

Introduction

In the year that Columbus reached the New World, Antonio de Nebrija published the first written grammar of a vernacular language. Previously, grammars such as the ancient Sanskit grammar of Pānini had only been devised to preserve archaic languages of ritual and sacred significance—languages from which the vernaculars had diverged significantly. Justifying the utility of his new type of grammar to Isabella of Spain, Nebrija suggested that it could aid in governing the heathen (Nebrija 1492–1946:prologue). Soon Spain had a vast population of heathen upon which to test this assertion, and in fact Nebrija's grammar did serve the missionary friars as a model for grammars describing hitherto unwritten languages of the Americas.

In the course of describing these newly encountered languages, compiling dictionaries, and creating instructional material for the religious conversion of the new Spanish subjects, a surprisingly large number of Spaniards, at first mainly friars, acquired fluency in New World languages. Their concerns extended beyond simple evangelism to an intense interest in the cultures that lay in ruins all about them. From this concern arose the vast and detailed ethnographic works that document New World civilizations in the first quarter of the sixteenth century (Sahagún 1950–1969). Although these collections were dictated by the survivors of the conquest, they were created, glossed, and annotated under the direction of Europeans and so can be classed together with the native-language breviaries, confessional guides, didactic theatricals (Horcasitas 1974), and other such works as literature created for the interaction of Europeans and Indians. The impetus came from the Spanish side.

Beginning at the very same time, a second body of writing in Nahuatl came into being. These are documents written by native speakers for other native speakers in Spanish-based orthography. Although these documents often came to be presented before Spaniards in the course of litigation, they were created primarily for use among Nahuatl speakers. Upon contact with Europeans, a sector of the Indian population had become literate and remained literate on its own initiative so long as literacy had a functional role in indigenous communities.

There is a clear contrast between these two bodies of Nahuatl writing. The first has preserved for us what is known as "Classical Nahuatl"—the highly formal and sytlized tecpillatolli ("lordly speech") of poetry, oration, and ritual—which was learned through long training and memorization. It also created a standard exemplified in Molina's great sixteenth-century dictionary (Molina 1571/1970) and a whole series of grammars culminating in Carochi's comprehensive masterwork of the mid-seventeenth century (Carochi 1645). Beginning with the 1539 Nahuatl religious guide, which is believed to be the first book printed in the Americas (Horcasitas 1979:94; Schwaller 1973:69), works in Nahuatl produced from within the church have adhered to this standard with the great consistency so admired by Jorge Klor de Alva.

In contrast, the other sort of Nahuatl writing, which James Lockhart and I call "Colonial Nahuatl," appears chaotic. Spelling conventions in particular vary wildly not only across documents but within individual documents. So far as we can tell, with the possible exception of Chimalpahin, no Indian ever owned or consulted Molina's dictionary. Yet the very fact that the people who wrote Colonial Nahuatl were not constrained by a standard led them to create records of the fine details of their actual speech and hence the geographic and historical variation of Nahuatl. Through them it has been possible to document important changes in the language over the whole colonial period and the concomitant changes in the circumstances of the Indians themselves.

In the past decade or so scholars have begun to realize the full extent and potential of postconquest documentation written in Nahuatl and other Mesoamerican languages. Anthropologists, who have a long-standing tradition of association with linguists, have taken the lead in this, particularly Pedro Carrasco and Fernando Horcasitas. Insisting as they do that we must know what Indians said about themselves in their own languages within the context of their own cultures, they stand as a bridge between linguists and historians, who until recently have perceived little common ground. In this particular area, however, the interests of linguists and historians directly converge. Linguistic studies of Indian texts, showing not only what was said but how it was said, can reveal trends and patterns that run parallel to those seen in various kinds of historical research and can also throw much direct light on cultural and social history. The dialogues between historians and anthropologists, on the one hand, and between anthropologists and linguists, on the other, here become a conversation among us all.

Preconquest Precedents

In Mesoamerica and in Peru the Europeans encountered indigenous high cultures in which mathematical calculation and record keeping occupied a role of central importance, but only in Mesoamerica was there anything like writing. The Maya, Mixtec, Nahua, and other peoples kept records carved in stone and painted on paper. The manufacture of paper was an important commercial industry; many towns lived and thrived on paper production. It also.had its ceremonial aspects. Not only were records kept on paper, but paper was offered in sacrifice along with other precious things such as fine food, quetzal feathers, and human blood. The attitudes toward paper and what was recorded on it were set down soon after the conquest in considerable detail, and from this we know that the writing of things and the interpretation of what was written was an occupation of great prestige. The tradition of conventional abstract representation was protected, developed, shared, and highly regarded among the Mesoamerican peoples. The Spaniards destroyed great quantities of the paper records, but from the remaining ones and from those produced immediately after the conquest, we can tell much about how they were used and interpreted.

There is a world of difference between Mesoamerica and Peru in this respect. The Andean culture completely lacked this tradition of representation on paper. The thing generally understood to be its closest analogue was the *Khipu*, a knotted cord that could be "read" by an interpreter. Unfortunately, the details of knotting the cord and interpreting the knots have not been described in any satisfying way, and the direct relationship to linguistic phenomena (sound segments, syllables, words) is much in doubt. In Chapter 16 of this volume Zuidema presents other examples of ways in which the Andeans kept records, and these seem even less directly linguistic. Hence, in the Andes there were no precedents with which to identify European alphabetic writing, and I believe that it is as a direct result of this that so little colonial documentation in written Quechua exists.

Mesoamerican indigenous writing was a mixed system. The symbols comprised at least the following: (a) a complex and precise vigesimal number system, (b) direct pictorial representation, and (c) indirect representation of the phonetic value of individual syllables. A syllabic writing system is a significant advance over a pictorial one and prepares the way for the adoption of an alphabetic one, but there is no evidence that any Mesoamerican people had moved on to writing complex discourses in glyphs. Until the conquest, their representations were largely restricted to dates, personal names, place names, and records of events.

With respect to phonetic representation, Mesoamerican texts and inscriptions were always mixed. There is none known, no matter how brief, that is composed entirely of symbols representing individual syllable values, although some scholars, such as Floyd Lounsbury and Linda Schele, believe the potential was always there. Amidst pictures of rabbits that really represent rabbits; hills that represent hills; and water symbols that represent springs, rivers, tears, etc., there are some other pictures that represent sound rather than content. Just as in English one could represent the pronoun *I* with a picture of an eye, so incorporated into the representation of a Nahuatl name one finds, for instance, a picture of buttocks to represent the honorific element. The stem of *buttocks* is *tzīn-*, and the honorific is a suffix *-tzīn*. The Nahuatl locative *-tlan* common to so many place names is conventionally represented by a mouthful of teeth: *tlan-*. (In the dictionary citation form *tlantli*, the *-tli* is a suffix.) In both these cases the thing pictured is homophonous with the thing intended—that is, both have the same pronunciation—and the substitution is effected because it is more easily drawn than the semantically abstract thing it represents.

Beyond this, there is some evidence that there was development in the direction of further abstraction: The drawn object represented a syllable only partially its homophone. Distinctive tone in Mayan languages might be ignored and likewise distinctive vowel length in Nahuatl. Here again there is a move to arbitrariness, from literal pictorial representation to a type of writing system.

But no Mesoamerican group had developed a full syllabary by the time of the conquest. Compared with the syllabic Egyptian hieroglyphic writing system, all Mesoamerican systems were narrowly restricted in the information they conveyed; they were pervasively pictorial. Because the messages were few (e.g., a certain person named W was born on date X at the town of Y and was interred at Z), the creator of the text or inscription could invest much ingenuity in elaborating the symbols conveying the message. Within certain conventions the artist creating glyphs sought the most subtle and artful way of expressing his message. Thus, far from informative communicative writing, Mesoamerican texts—particularly the Mayan inscriptions—stand as intricate puzzles constructed on predictable messages.

Interpretation of the painted codices depended on intensive memorization by select groups of individuals under instruction in special institutions. Literacy in preconquest Mesoamerica was not a general skill that could be internalized and used productively; transmission of the extensive bodies of hymns, poems, and chronicles was essentially oral. The prestige accruing from the creation of the written—or rather, painted—page was great, however, and this Mesoamerican attitude, together with the approach to syllabic writing already achieved, produced a ready receptivity to alphabetic writing as introduced by the Spanish friars in the second quarter of the sixteenth century.

Postconquest Developments

Although its place in Christian iconography is relatively minor, the book should be nearly as central a symbol of the church as the cross. The Europeans brought books with them and immediately began creating new ones. To expedite instruction and inquiry, they compiled dictionaries, wrote grammars, translated religious works, composed sermons, and created confessionary guides. Pictures from the mid-sixteenth century already show Indians gathered around friars in monastery atrios with books on their laps (McAndrew 1965:295, 626). Moreover, sons of noble families were brought together by the Franciscans, instructed in reading and writing along with Christian doctrine, and sent back out to preach to their people. Through direct and indirect contact with Spanish friars, writing passed into Indian hands at an early date and quickly came to live a life of its own independent of the church.

Although there are colonial documents in existence today written in Yucatecan Maya, Otomí, Mixtec, and other languages, the number of known documents in these languages is rather small. On the other hand, there is such profusion of written Nahuatl that samples are available for virtually every decade from the conquest down to the inception of Mexican independence. By the end of the first half-century of Spanish presence in Mesoamerica, every central Mexican community of any size and importance had a native notary who kept records, generally in Nahuatl. The notarial tradition was self-perpetuating at the local level; sometimes the same family would provide the notary for generations. In some communities the notary was the only person who could read and write. In others, such as Amecameca, literacy was clearly widespread (Karttunen and Lockhart 1978). But in either case, notary succeeded notary within the community through generations and centuries. Thanks to this we have texts without a break from the 1540s to the end of the colonial period. No other Indian language is so documented.

The subject matter of the notarial records is mundane, far from the metaphorical and often obscure language of the "Classical Nahuatl" tradition. It has to do with stewardship or ownership of property, settlement of disputes, petitions, and other legal matters where ambiguity was anathema. Much verbatim testimony is recorded, showing what everyday speech was like. When Juan Vicente, *alcalde* of Ja-lostitlan complained of being beaten, he said the priest replied, "Yes, I beat you and splintered your staff, and I will break your whole head" (Anderson *et al.* 1976:167). Leonor Magdalena accused her daughter-in-law of following her around, beating her, and generally behaving as a *loca* (Karttunen and Lockhart 1976:105). Juan Gregorio justified his appropriation of his cousin's land on the grounds that he had irresponsibly leased it to "really stupid people" (Karttunen and Lockhart 1978:168).

Of the texts produced in great abundance by the local notaries, the number from the immediate area of Mexico-Tenochtitlan dwindles with time as the indigenous population died off or was assimilated in what had become a Spanish city. Nearby Xochimilco and Milpa Alta and many towns of the neighboring states of Morelos, Puebla, and Tlaxcala remained Indian, providing us with numerous texts whereby we can compare the details of speech of these communities at various points in the colonial period with modern Nahuatl currently spoken. Generally, Nahuatl survived best and longest in inaccessible places where contact with Spanish was minimal. But contact was nowhere absent, and these texts reflect over decades and centuries the internal adjustments Nahuatl made because of the proximity of Spanish and the translation that went on between the two languages.

Because Spanish and Nahuatl have now been in continual contact for over 400 years, there has been constant opportunity for Nahuatl speakers to return to Spanish to augment or eliminate older lexical and grammatical borrowings. As a result, modern Nahuatl is overlaid with contact phenomena of different periods. Some earlier material has been replaced or discarded, while other things remain as relics. Given only texts of modern Nahuatl, we would have a difficult task in reconstructing the sequence by which it acquired its various types of Hispanisms. The written texts of the colonial period, however, give us a view of the evolution of Nahuatl since the conquest. Happily for us, a clear picture emerges that is in accord with descriptive work done with other languages in apparently similar circumstances: Comanche, Huave, and Popoluca (Casagrande 1955; Diebold 1964; Law 1961:561).

Rarely are the effects of language contact situations so clear. This is true largely because of the unique isolation of the Americas from the rest of the world prior to the sixteenth century. We know exactly when and under what circumstances contact with Spanish began. The fact that the languages are so typologically dissimilar is very helpful. Most helpful of all are the notarial texts.

Nahuatl started with no previous experience of Spanish or any language like it. It did exist in contact with many languages belonging to other language families. These languages had come to share many common typological features in spite of their heterogeneous ancestry. But Nahuatl shows no evidence of having had strategies for borrowing from its neighbors. Apparently the diffusion of linguistic areal features in Mesoamerica was quite ancient and widespread; it was certainly unconscious, a slow osmosis rather than a matter of daily confrontation. For a long time, too, Nahuatl had been in the position of donor, not recipient.

Comparing Nahuatl with Comanche, Huave, Popoluca, and in a very preliminary way with Yucatecan Maya, one does not find any real differences in type of response to contact with Spanish. According to the best of evidence at hand, they all moved through a set sequence of linguistic accommodations. This is also true across Nahuatl dialects, which otherwise vary among themselves to some considerable extremes due to historical and geographical separation. With respect to Spanish language contact phenomena, the diverse Nahuatl dialects are monolithic; one finds no startling deviances. What is variable is not what happened or the order in which it happened, but the rate at which it happened. Nahuatl of the central Mexican highlands moved through this set sequence much further and faster than Nahuatl spoken in remote areas, and Nahuatl as a unitary language moved through the sequence far ahead of socially and geographically more isolated languages of Mesoamerica. At mid-seventeenth century a cluster of significant steps along the scale reflects the increased pressure of daily contact, translation, and large-scale bilingualism. The abundance of documents leading to and through this period makes it possible to date a qualitative change in the nature of Nahuatl and Spanish language contact.

Figure 15.1 summarizes Spanish contact phenomena as they appear in the Nahuatl texts. It represents a certain amount of averaging and rounding off; some Nahuatl communities have been more in contact with Spanish than others, and some individuals have always been more conservative in speech than others. But the figure is based on generalizations from literally hundreds of colonial documents written by local notaries in both central and peripheral Nahuatl-speaking areas. James Lockhart and I have documented these developments at length and in detail elsewhere (Karttunen and Lockhart 1976).

The first manifestations of Nahuatl and Spanish contact have to do with Nahuatl nouns. Extension of lexical meaning was typical of Nahuatl in the earliest years after the conquest, just as it has been of other languages in similar situations. Nahuatl speakers had to find

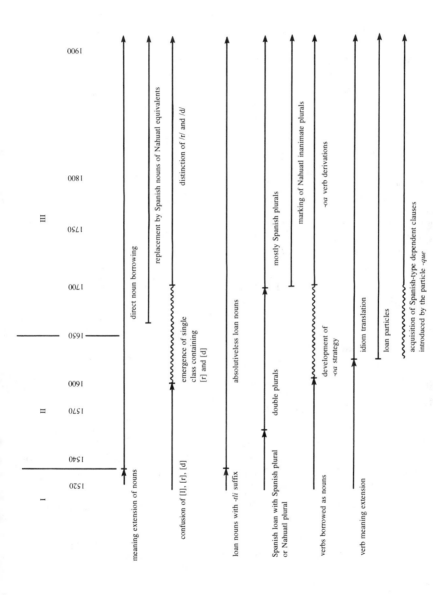

Figure 15.1 The chronology of Nahuatl contact strategies.

some way to talk about the many new things the Spaniards brought along with them, and for the most part they did so out of the resources of their own language. Nahuatl extended the sense of its word for "cotton" to "wool" and thence to "sheep," and *tepoztli* "copper" came to mean " 'workable metal from which instruments are made," specifically "iron," which is its universal and exclusive sense today.

Molina's dictionary of 1571 records some of the original extensions involving *maçātl*, "deer," for "horse" and descriptions such as "seat upon a horse" for "saddle," but these were already archaisms that had been replaced in actual usage by *caballo* and *silla* (Molina 1571/1970). Nahuatl had already moved on from using extensions, descriptions, and circumlocutions to direct noun borrowing. For nouns this change happened so quickly that by 1540 there was a substantial core of loan vocabulary of just the sort one would expect: names for introduced artifacts, plants, and animals; words for European religious, legal, and economic concepts. But not a single verb borrowed as a verb is attested for the entire sixteenth century.

The first direct noun borrowings into Nahuatl were strongly assimilated into the language, not only phonetically, as we can tell from deviant spellings, but morphologically. A handful of relic forms of the very oldest Spanish loans end in the Nahuatl absolutive suffix -*tli:* *camisatli* < *camisa* "shirt"; *cuentaxtli* < *cuenta(s)* "rosary bead"; *xayotli* < *sayo* "coat". But as the flood of loan words swelled to grand proportions, the absolutive suffix lost its productivity, and Nahuatl came to have two large noun classes: those with absolutive marking, mainly native Nahuatl nouns, and those unmarked for the absolutive, mainly—but not exclusively—Spanish loanwords.

A third effect of Spanish contact upon Nahuatl nouns in the sixteenth century was the beginning of a series of adjustments in the system of plural marking. Nahuatl differed from Spanish in that only animate nouns were overtly marked in the plural. Inanimate nouns had no special plural form. In the early period of contact, Spanish loan nouns appeared in texts with either a Spanish or a Nahuatl plural suffix rather unpredictably. Generally inanimate Spanish loan words went completely unmarked even in contexts where they were unambiguously plural, as after numbers. Then, in the latter half of the sixteenth century and on into the seventeenth century, double plurals were in use. During this period, Spanish loan nouns in the singular had their regular singular forms, while their corresponding plurals often bore both the Spanish and a Nahuatl plural suffix. Nahuatl had its own precedent for redundant plural marking in those of its animate nouns that form their plurals by reduplicating part of the stem and adding a plural suffix for good measure: *cih-* "hare" > *cīcih-tin* "hares" In the peculiar Spanish double plurals we can see another case of Nahuatl extending some pattern of its own to intrusive new material.

Noun borrowing had some linguistic consequences for Nahuatl beyond enlarging its lexicon. It eventually brought new sound classes into the language. Although certain sound substitutions remain characteristically Nahuatl, for general purposes the confusion of [l], [r], and [d] in Spanish words was already becoming an anachronism in notarial texts by the mid-seventeenth century. Once [r] and [d] were perceived as different from [l], they went on to be differentiated from one another. When they all got sorted out, Nahuatl had gained via borrowing the distinct sound classes /r/ and /d/, which it had not had earlier.

As long as the Spanish /l/-/r/-/d/distinction remained problematical to Nahuatl speakers, along with several other major phonological distinctions, loanwords made their way into Nahuatl in often nearly unrecognizable assimilated forms (Karttunen and Lockhart 1976:Chapter 1). In fact, the whole early period of contact in the sixteenth century can be thought of as a time of assimilation to Nahuatl. Meaning extension is a sort of lexical assimilation, where Spanish concepts were fit into existing vocabulary. Then there is the phonetic assimilation. Spanish words were heard and borrowed in terms of Nahuatl phonology. Finally, the early extension of the *-tli* absolutive suffix and the use of redundant double plural marking for Spanish animate loan nouns and no marking at all for inanimate loan nouns can be thought of as a type of morphological assimilation. In the beginning Spanish was fit to the Procrustean bed of Nahuatl linguistic structure.

After the great switch to direct noun borrowing with its attendant consequences, Nahuatl entered a relatively stable period that lasted until the mid-seventeenth century. Then a cluster of new developments marks some change in Nahuatl/Spanish contact.

As more and more aspects of Spanish culture found their way into the Indian world, direct intercultural noun borrowing continued. From this point on, however, the process became more than just augmentative. After 1650, Spanish loan nouns began replacing Nahuatl equivalents for blood relations, cardinal directions, and other basic vocabulary. The double plurals fell from use, and henceforth Spanish loan nouns more often than not appeared with their simple Spanish plural suffixes. The animate/inanimate distinction for plural marking was relaxed and extended even to native vocabulary, so that trees and houses as well as rabbits and grandparents were overtly pluralized (Karttunen 1978).

Although extension of meaning came to a near halt very early for Nahuatl nouns, it had continued on into the seventeenth century for verbs. The first strategies Nahuatl developed for borrowing verbs were (a) to derive Nahuatl verbs from Spanish nouns, and (b) to treat the Spanish infinitive as a noun. At about the time that Nahuatl was developing a distinct phonological class /r/, Spanish verbs finally began to be borrowed as verbs by attaching the suffix -oa to the Spanish infinitive, which ends in /r/. (This relative lateness and overall lower frequency of verb borrowing when compared with noun borrowing is typical of all well-documented language contact situations).

By the time the -oa convention was developed, some Nahuatl verbs had attained equivalence with certain high-frequency basic Spanish verbs by meaning extension; these remained in use, continuing on in both their original literal meanings and their new Spanish-equivalent meanings. These include equivalents for *tener, deber, pasar, parecer,* and *faltar*—verbs that have highly idiomatic uses in Spanish. As soon as the Nahuatl verb had been extended to equivalence with the literal meaning of the Spanish verb, it began to appear in Nahuatl translations of the full range of Spanish idioms, often replacing native Nahuatl grammatical constructions. This process is well attested for *tener* and *deber* equivalents in the eighteenth century (Karttunen and Lockhart 1976:43–48). The other equivalences and idiom translations so characteristic of modern texts may also date from that time.

Again, at about the same time as double plurals were being abandoned, the /r/ and /d/ distinction was being made, the -oa convention for verbs was developing, and idiom translation was getting underway, Spanish particles such as *hasta, como,* and *mientras* began to appear regularly in Nahuatl. Generally this type of uninflected function word (as opposed to content words such as nouns and verbs) is resistant to borrowing, and a linguist would expect even more resistance when the languages involved are as typologically dissimilar as Spanish and Nahuatl, since Spanish has these particles as prepositions and clause introductory particles, while Nahuatl has its closest equivalents in postpositions bound by possessive prefixes. Yet what we find is that Nahuatl borrowed particles unlike its own from Spanish while retaining Nahuatl particles where there is a strong Nahuatl/Spanish equivalence. There was nothing like Spanish *hasta* in Nahuatl, and the particle was borrowed early, appearing with high frequency ever since. On the other hand, Nahuatl *īpampa* has almost the same semantic range as *porque,* and we have yet to find a single example of *porque* in colonial texts, although it occurs in modern Nahuatl. This parallels and is roughly simultaneous with the two stages of noun borrowing:

earlier borrowing of the new and different and later replacement of native vocabulary.

Finally, there is the emergence of Spanish-modeled dependent clauses introduced by *que* (or sometimes by its back translations *tle* and *inīn*). The use of *que* as a relative pronoun and as a clause complementizer in Nahuatl followed on the heels of particle borrowing. Although this addition to the fundamental syntactic machinery of Nahuatl is difficult to date from its inception, it is characteristic of Nahuatl as it is spoken today.

Thus, there have been two great breakthroughs in Nahuatl's long relationship with Spanish. The first came by the second half of the sixteenth century when Nahuatl began borrowing Spanish nouns directly, quickly leaving behind the stage in which a breaker and trainer of horses was called a *maçāmachtiāni* "deer master." Many Native American languages stayed with this first stage much longer, and some are still there today. For Nahuatl speakers the brevity of the first period was due to the intrusion of large numbers of Spaniards into central Mexico and the daily confrontation and interaction with them. Furthermore, in spite of epidemics and depopulation, Nahuatl speakers continued to outnumber Spaniards for a long time, so that the indigenous language was maintained rather than quickly obliterated. Had the missionary friars succeeded in separating Indians and Spaniards in respective communities, the next stage would have been a long time in coming.

The second breakthrough came in the seventeenth century, mainly in the latter half, when a convention for borrowing Spanish verbs developed, idiom translation was underway, Spanish nouns began replacing Nahuatl fundamental vocabulary, and Spanish particles began to appear with high frequency and to bring significant syntactic change in tow. By the first decade or so of the eighteenth century Nahuatl was capable of absorbing and expressing succinctly anything Spanish had to offer. This acceleration in accommodation to Spanish strongly suggests that at this point, and not earlier, there was widespread bilingualism and nontraumatic daily contact between Indians and Europeans.

In no way should this change from strong assimilation of Spanish into Nahuatl to structural accommodation by Nahuatl—together with the leaving behind of certain preconquest trappings and styles—be equated with deterioration of the indigenous language. On the contrary, this process of keeping up with the times shows the vitality and flexibility of the language. Colonial Nahuatl of the eighteenth century is fine high Nahuatl; its characteristic overall linguistic structure is intact and supplemented by the best and most useful that Spanish had to offer. Nor did Nahuatl become moribund toward the end of the colonial period. Although, as we shall see, the tradition of Nahuatl literacy was lost during the nineteenth century, the language went on being spoken and continues today. From a linguistic point of view, modern spoken Nahuatl resembles sixteenth-century Nahuatl more than it differs, and the danger to it has not been from internal decay but from the decision on the part of communities and individuals to let Nahuatl go in favor of Spanish.

The Implications of Nahuatl Literacy

A characteristic of postconquest Indian writing is the complexity of the context in which it is embedded. The choice of one language and mode of literacy rather than another at the start of the colonial period, and the role of that language once chosen, depended on the distribution of ethnicities and sociopolitical entities throughout Mesoamerica. Preconquest writing systems were an indispensable precedent for postconquest literacy, and the strands of their influence can be traced far into the colonial period.

Although the Spaniards had, in principle, uniform intentions toward all their new subjects—to reveal to them the errors of their pagan ways and to lead them into the true faith as perceived by the Roman Church—their successes were uneven to say the least. In addition to the fact that some indigenous languages were more unwritten than others, living patterns and socioeconomic organization were also important. The sedentary agricultural people of the New World, who had their own hierarchical government with trade and tribute systems, were easier to take over than small, mobile hunting groups that could never be pinned down and controlled. Because of the characteristic community pattern of Nahuatl speakers and because of the historical events just prior to the conquest, it was inevitable that Nahuatl should be the principal intermediary language between the Europeans and the peoples of Mesoamerica.

Consider the context. Traditionally, Nahuatl has also gone by the names Mexican and Aztec. If one strictly equates the Aztecs with the Mexica, then neither of these alternative names is accurate. Nahuatl was dominant at the time of the conquest not only or even principally because of the vast sphere of Mexica influence that extended itself at that time from their midlake city. The Mexica did not rule an empire in the sense we know. Nowhere were there frontiers that encircled solidly Mexica territories. On the contrary, throughout central Mexico were cities and towns, large and small, which were distinct from the Mexica, often independent of them, and in some cases their mortal enemies. Yet the people of these communities—Texcocans, Tlaxcalans, Cholulans, Tlahuica, and countless others—spoke the same language. Moreover, the legendary predecessors of the Mexica, those Toltecs whose high culture they idealized, almost certainly were historically speakers of a variety of Nahuatl, and the wild and barbarous Chichimecs to the north, of whom the Mexica had been one group, spoke related Aztecan languages. Quite probably this linguistic unity was one important factor that made it possible for one group after another to rise to prominence. Due to the preconquest mobility of groups of people in Mesoamerica and to the degree of mutual intelligibility of Nahuatl dialects, there was widespread diffusion of material culture and vocabulary, which was not linked to conquest and imposition.

With all its varieties taken together, Nahuatl was still just one language among many; it coexisted with Mixtec, Zapotec, Tarascan, Popoluca, Otomí, and several Mayan languages. But in the century or so before European contact, Nahuatl had become the prestige language, used as a lingua franca among speakers of these other languages and reflected in place names and inscriptions.

Examining detailed maps of Mesoamerica, one notes that even in some Maya areas the place names are almost exclusively Nahuatl. This does not necessarily mean that they were occupied by speakers of the language. Apparently these places had (and many still have) names in the local indigenous language as well as names they acquired from Nahuatl-speaking people. But the Spaniards became proficient in Nahuatl before they mastered other languages. For this reason the Nahuatl name became the official postconquest name, so registered not by the locals or even necessarily by Nahuatl speakers, but by the Spaniards. The universality of this is one measure of the prevalence and prestige of Nahuatl in Mesoamerica, but it says less than one might think about demography and politics.

The Toluca valley immediately to the west of the Valley of Mexico is a case in point. Until just a short time before the conquest it was an Otomanguean valley; its residents spoke Otomanguean languages such as Otomí, Matlazinca, and Mazahua. But from the colonial period we have not only masses of documentation in Nahuatl but Nahuatl church inscriptions, which are a great rarity. One would form the impression that Toluca was a Nahua bastion. Yet today the surviving Nahuatl-speaking communities are relatively few among the valley's many Otomí, Matlazinca, and Mazahua communities. What this surely means is that Toluca was and has remained inhabited by the same stock of Otomanguean speakers. Conquest by the Mexica brought to Toluca a relatively small proportion of high-prestige Nahuatl speakers who had primary contact with the succeeding conquerors, the Spanish. The Nahuatl speakers, not the local indigenous group, had the predisposition to literacy as well as the organization and the social standing that made it possible for them to function within Spanish conventions and turn them to their own purposes. These very advantages brought about the total assimilation of the Nahuas into the Spanish world and left behind the great Otomanguean lake barely ruffled by the wind of conquest.

Although the voluminous Nahuatl documentation from the Toluca valley is a legacy of Mexica expansionism, one cannot narrowly identify Nahuatl with the Mexica, that group of Nahuatl speakers who happened to be dominant when Cortés arrived. There were Nahuatl speakers who were the enemies of the Mexica, Nahuatl speakers subjugated to the Mexica, and quite possibly Nahuatl speakers who had never heard of the Mexica. The emergence of Nahuatl as the primary indigenous language of postconquest use in interaction with the Spanish was significant for all Nahuatl speakers, not just that group dominating political and economic structures in the first quarter of the sixteenth century. The adoption of their language for legal and clerical purposes put other Nahuatl speakers on an equal footing with the Mexica.

The unity of the Nahuatl language in some sense transcended ephemeral political organization. This is not to deny the intense local chauvinism of indigenous groups or to ignore the claims that Nahuatl speakers make about the unintelligibility of their neighbors' dialects. But when there has been a pressing need, Nahuatl speakers have been able to understand other Nahuatl speakers and to make themselves understood by them in a way they have not been able to with speakers or entirely separate languages—for example, Otomí speakers or Huastec speakers—without resort to full-scale bilingualism. Thus, the colonial legal documentation had a function that kept it viable all over Mexico, not just within the remains of Mexica structures. Records were kept in Nahuatl because in case of litigation they could be sent all the way to Mexico City if necessary, and they would be understood and respected as valid evidence even if they came from faraway Chiapas and were in such a deviant Nahuatl that at first it strikes the reader as a pidgin (Anderson *et al.* 1976:190–195). In some cases there are hints that testimony recorded in Nahuatl was in fact taken from witnesses whose language was something else, Nahuatl rather than Spanish serving as the language of documentation (Anderson *et al.* 1976:166, note). Moreover, quite aside from the potential of appeal to Spanish courts, Nahuatl-language documentation functioned within the community, being constantly presented and cosulted in local dealings.

For Nahuatl speakers of the colonial period a major consequence of Nahuatl literacy was that they could and did make vigorous use of colonial Mexican courts. Though the legal system may have been at times slow, inefficient, corrupt, and partial (and there is plenty of evidence of bare-faced lying on all sides), still it settled disputes among Indians, among Spaniards, and between the two. It was by no means a hopeless, impenetrable snarl to Nahuatl speakers; had it been, no one would have patronized the notaries. The courts gave satisfaction often enough to keep everyone in business.

Adopting legal conventions, the Nahuatl of the notaries continued for a long time to evolve in its own terms, enriching itself by drawing on Spanish without at all deteriorating or being corrupted. A fine example of excellent colonial Nahuatl is the record of suit and countersuit filed by two cousins in Amecameca in 1746. All the Spanish legal formulas are turned to Nahuatl use. Notaries are called in to identify a deceased colleague's handwriting, and there is verbatim testimony by witnesses in blunt, colloquial language. The proceedings were carried out by and for Nahuatl speakers in the total absence of Spaniards (Karttunen and Lockhart 1978).

The Amecameca suit illustrates the high degree of autonomy achieved at the local level. The whole matter was handled within the Indian community; the investigation was carried out in Nahuatl, and the court record was made by one of several resident Nahuatl-speaking notaries. There is no evidence of any translation being made or any Spaniard consulted. In the face of such total competence, Indian communities were left to look after themselves, and in the absence of outside interference, indigenous structures survived and functioned throughout the colonial period.

Literacy not only made it possible for Nahuatl speakers to manage their own affairs with a degree of autonomy during the colonial period, it also served as a vehicle to carry forward indigenous genres of literature. Over the whole postconquest period the genres of attested Nahuatl writing are the following: the *huehuetlatolli* (maxims for proper deportment, literally "words of the elders"), songs/poems, histories and annals, *padrones* (census and tribute records), correspondence, and the whole range of legal documentation (from the elegant formalities of the Amecameca document to such pieces of naivete as the founding legends exemplified in Chapter 14 in this volume). All of these to some degree carry on preconquest precedents. In the case of what is known as Classical Nahuatl, they are the only surviving artifacts of a complex oral tradition that was virtually destroyed in the sixteenth century.

There are a number of different collections of *huehuetlatolli*, much alike in content but sufficiently different in detail to make it clear that they form a genre and are not from a single canonical body of maxims. All are quite early, the latest perhaps being the one preserved at the Bancroft Library and dating from the first half of the seventeenth century (Garibay 1943:31–53, 1943:81–107).

The great songs or poems of the high Aztec culture continued to be composed for a brief time after the conquest. In some cases they were altered to serve the Christian faith. Other songs record the events of the conquest. Many mention Cortés. The tradition, if not the formal style, lives on even today in the *relaciones* that accompany dance dramas performed by Indians throughout Mexico. Although these dialogues are primarily transmitted orally, they have also been redacted from time to time over centuries, and written versions are carefully preserved and guarded locally.

As for those poems created within the canons of postconquest convention, the two major collections—the mss. *Cantares mexicanos* and *Romances de los señores de la Nueva España*—contain enough patent copyist's errors to prove beyond doubt that they were drawn from other written sources in the sixteenth century (Karttunen and Lockhart 1980). These poems appear to be the most personal expressions of human concerns to be found in written Nahuatl. As Miguel León-Portilla so lucidly sets forth (León-Portilla 1974), they come to terms with fundamental questions of intellect versus myth, the transitory nature of mortal existence, and the enigma of death. But taken in the context of the whole body of Classical Nahuatl poetry, what seem like highly personal and suggestive lyric poems turn out to be particularly felicitous concatenations of stock Nahuatl poetic building blocks to be found repeated over and over again in less profound poems. Postconquest literacy had no role in creating these poems, only in preserving them at the brink of the destruction of classical oral tradition. Their survival into colonial times was as brief as that of the *huehuetlatolli*.

In the histories and annals, which range from the most elevated to the most humble, we see a continuation of Mesoamerican record keeping. From this genre proceeded the great histories such as that of Chimalpahin, but in the colonial period it also provided a context for personal observation as in the almost chatty annals of Juan Bautista and the gripping descriptions of events in the annals of Puebla, where the writer says that a pirate attack on Veracruz was the most disturbing local event since the coming of the Faith (Karttunen and Lockhart 1976:112–116).

The *padrones* are the quintessence of record keeping. Here was a merging of parallel European and Mesoamerican procedures from which we can learn in detail the constituencies of Nahua communities and individual households. But as the separation of European and Indian communities deteriorated and matters grew ambiguous, *padrones*, too, generally ceased to be created.

The scope of correspondence is surprisingly limited. Relatively little of a personal nature has been found aside from some letters between members of the Moteuczoma family, and even these are mainly business letters. Other letters are between towns and high officials or from one town council to another (see the appended sample business letter).

The legal documentation was the single most vital genre of written Nahuatl. Because of its purposefulness, it survived the other genres to the end of the colonial period.

There was an evolution in the physical appearance of Nahuatl documents as well as in their language and subject matter. The pictorial tradition continued on for many generations in illustrated tribute lists and conventionalized maps. The little footprints, which in the great codices show the wanderings of ancestral groups, trudge on through colonial boundary descriptions and house plans. Quantities of pesos appear as circles, and the installation and deaths of bishops are signified with mitres. Even annals of the eighteenth century were illustrated: those of Tlaxcalla with elaborate year signs—an elegant rabbit every fourth year quite overwhelming the text beside it—and those of Puebla with a rat, a smoking volcano, a dead king, and more to mark various calamities.

Early in the colonial period there began a reversal of the relative weight of the pictorial and textual components. In the mid-sixteenth-century Codex Osuna, the council of Mexico City expresses its complaints primarily through graphic means: pictures of individuals and buildings, numbers in the preconquest notation, and stylized drawings of items delivered. In some cases a whole page of pictorial material has only a few written Nahuatl words to accompany it, and they for the most part give no additional information. Yet long before the end of the century such documents were becoming rarer, and similar complaints were expressed entirely in written Nahuatl. Gradually over the colonial period there is a diminution of the preconquest elements; finally annals were no longer kept, lists ceased to be illustrated, and maps and plans adopted the developing European conventions.

A danger to Nahuatl inherent in such proficiency with Spanish conventions was total assimilation into the Spanish world, .as happened fairly early in what had been Tenochtitlan and as in the case of the Toluca Nahuatl speakers mentioned earlier. Paradoxically, as individuals and communities become more and more adept at moving back and forth between the Spanish language-and-culture complex and their own, establishing equivalences between them, they have less and less pressing need for Nahuatl; it has been and remains easier to let Nahuatl go than to maintain it. The continuing process is well documented for modern Nahuatl-speaking communities today (Hill and Hill 1978, 1979). Internal social change, rather than the endlessly shifting official policy on indigenous language maintenance so thoroughly documented by Shirley Brice Heath (1972), has determined the fortunes of Nahuatl over the years.

Language loss did not wipe out Nahuatl during the colonial period, although it skimmed off the wellborn and the city dwellers. In predominantly Indian communities it has lived on until today. A condition for language loss is a period of bilingualism, however brief, during which dominance switches from one language to the other. Another condition is a genuine possibility of assimilation. Even into this century Nahua communities have had many monolingual Nahuatl speakers. Although their language has been greatly influenced by Spanish, much or even all the Spanish influence has been secondhand. Only in the last few generations has Spanish contact been so pervasive and opportunities in the Spanish-speaking world sufficiently within reach that whole Nahua communities have become generationally bilingual and the children have switched to Spanish dominance. Now language loss really is upon them. In a nonthreatening situation where all the social and economic benefits are to be reaped through Spanish and where virtually no one in the local community must perforce communicate with another exclusively in Nahuatl, there is no longer motivation for young children to master the language of their grandparents. Insofar as the lot of Nahuatl speakers today is the common lot of all Mexicans, their language itself serves no pressing vital purpose in modern Mexico.

The tradition of literacy died much earlier and of the same causes. In fact it died with the colonial period. The danger to written Nahuatl was its concentration in the hands of professionals. Literacy continued as a specialty, as it had been with the painted codices of preconquest times. In the Nahua world written language had a public rather than a personal function, and that function did not really evolve into anything different and more European. There was no tradition of reading and writing for personal expression and for pleasure as in the European world. People did not carry on private correspondence, and books were not common personal property. There is no definite evidence that prior to the twentieth century any woman was ever literate in Nahuatl.

To be written down in Nahuatl a matter had to be pragmatic; more than any of the other types of Nahuatl writing, legal documentation met that criterion. Toward the end of the colonial period, however, gradual internal change at the local level had placed on the town councils people who spoke Spanish as well as or better than Nahuatl. By the time Mexico gained its independence and the Royal Court of Appeals in Mexico City went out of existence, notarial Nahuatl ceased to be genuinely and immediately useful. Depending on their individual skills, the notaries switched to Spanish (Lockhart 1980) or went out of business and took virtually the entire Nahuatl writing tradition with them. After three centuries Nahuatl ceased to be a written language. Efforts since then to restore it have met with no lasting success. This is hardly surprising, since no new function for written Nahuatl has arisen that is broadly meaningful within the specifically Nahua culture.

Appendix

This is a letter from a set of early seventeenth-century Coyoacan papers in an unclassified bundle in the Archivo General de Notarías, Mexico City. A group of officials of one subtown wrote to another requesting aid in meeting their obligations. The first section of the letter is typical of the elaborate traditional greetings exchanged among Nahuatl speakers. Although the content is Christian, the style is indigenous. After the relatively long salutation, the matter at hand is stated succinctly and the letter brought to a close. Notice the italicized Spanish loan words.

Ma tt° dios amechmochicahuilitzino yn amehuatzitzin yn cenca mahuiztililoni Yn onpa tochantzinco tenanitla quen amechmoyetztilitica yn tt° *dios* Cuix achitzin qualli cuix noço amo cuix ceme cocoliztli amotetzinco oquimotlalili yn *dios* cuix noço amo camo huel toconmati auh yntla achitzin qualli ma yc tictotlatlauhtilica yn tt° *dios—amen—*ett[a]
auh ca nican catqui yc tocōtlacahuilohua yn tix in toyollo yn amotechcopatzinco totech ohuetztico *Palançio*tequitl techitlanilia *peras* yhuā *albarcoques* auh yn axca cuix huel tihuelitizque cana ome *toce*natzin *peras* tlachcuitl tepitzitzin yhuan macuilli *albarcoquez* yntla tihuelitizque ma cēca tocnopiltiz tomacehualtiz yn amotepalehuiliz tetlaçotlaliztzin ca yn iquac quenmania yntla itla amotetzinco

monequiz ca no totlapalehuizque ca ye ixquich yn āquimocaquitia ma tt° *dios*
amechmochicahuilitzino onpa tiquitlani tepixqui yhuā ome tlamama conitqui ta-
mauh axca otitlacuiloque *viernez*

Cenca tamechontotlaçotilia

pablo thaniel *Regidor*   p° hernandez *alhuacil maior*
juº de la Cruz *rejidor*

On the outside of the letter is written:

quimotilizque amatzintli y cenca mahuiztililoni *señores* matheotzin yhuā
yehuatzin thomas de aquinotzi yn onpa tochantzinco tenanitla S. jacinto

Most esteemed sirs, may our Lord God give you health. How is the Lord God
causing you to fare there at our home of Tenanitla? Are things at all good or not so
good? Has God brought down sickness upon you or not? We can't know, but we pray
to our Lord God that you should be a bit well. Amen. Etc.

And here is why we invoke your compassionate aid. The palace duty has fallen
to us . They are demanding pears and apricots of us, but right now we can come up
with only two dozen miserable little pears and five apricots. If we could, we would
be very much indebted to your generosity, and if you are ever in need, we will aid
you too. This is all we have to inform you of. May our Lord God give you health. We
are requesting there a ward chief and two bearers to carry it. We have written today,
Friday.

With great affection for you,

Pablo Daniel, regidor   Pedro Hernandez, alguacil mayor

Juan de la Cruz, regidor
The most esteemed gentlemen Mateo and Thomas de Aquinas are to see this letter
there in our home of Tenanitla San Jacinto.

References

Anderson, Arthur J. O., Frances Berdan, and James Lockhart
  1976   *Beyond the codices.* Berkeley and Los Angeles: University of California Press.
Carochi, Horacio
  1645   *Arte de la lengua mexicana.* México: Juan Ruiz.
Casagrande, Joseph B.
  1954,   Comanche linguistic acculturation. *International Journal of American Lin-*
  1955   *guistics* **20–21**:140–151, 217–237.
Diebold, A. Richard
  1964   Incipient bilingualism. In *Language in culture and society,* edited by Dell
          Hymes. New York: Harper. Pp. 485–508.
Garibay K., Angel Ma.
  1943   Huehuetlatolli, Documento A. *Tlalocan* **1** (1–2):31–53, 81–107.
Heath, Shirley Brice
  1972   *Telling tongues: language policy in Mexico, colony to nation.* New York:
          Teachers College Press.

Hill, Jane H., and Kenneth C. Hill
1978   Honorific usage in modern Nahuatl. *Language* **54**(1):123–155.
1980   Mixed grammar, purist grammar, and language attitudes in Nahuatl. *Language in Society* **9**:321–348.
Horcasitas, Fernando
1974   *El teatro náhuatl: epocas novohispana y moderna.* México: Instituto de Investigaciones Históricas.
1979   *The Aztecs then and now.* México: Minutiae Mexicana.
Karttunen, Frances
1978   The development of inanimate plural marking in postconquest Nahuatl. *Texas Linguistic Forum* **10**:21–29.
Karttunen, Frances, and James Lockhart
1976   Nahuatl in the middle years: language contact phenomena in texts of the colonial period. Berkeley and Los Angeles: University of California Press.
1978   Textos en náhuatl del siglo XVIII: un documento de Amecameca, 1746. *Estudios de Cultura Náhuatl* **13**:153–175.
1980   La estructura de la poesía náhuatl vista por sus variantes. *Estudios de Cultura Náhuatl* **14**:15–64.
Law, Howard W.
1961   Linguistic acculturation in Isthmus Nahuat. In *A William Cameron Townsend en el vigésimoquinto aniversario del Instituto Lingüístico de Verano.* México: Summer Institute of Linguistics. Pp. 555–562.
León-Portilla, Miguel
1974   La filosofía náhuatl estudiada en sus fuentes. Serie de Cultura Náhuatl, Monografías 10. Mexico: Instituto de Investigaciones Históricas.
Lockhart, James
1980   A language transition in eighteenth-century Mexico: the change from Nahuatl to Spanish recordkeeping in the Valley of Toluca. Manuscript.
Molina, fray Alonso de
1970   *Vocabulario en lengua castellana y mexicana y mexicana y castellana* [1571]. México: Editorial Porrúa.
McAndrew, John
1965   *The open-air churches of sixteenth-century Mexico.* Cambridge, Massachusetts: Harvard University Press.
Nebrija, Elio Antonio de
1946   *Gramatica castellana* [1492]. Madrid: Edición de la Junta del Centenario.
Sahagún, Fray Bernadino de
1950–   *Florentine codex: general history of the things of New Spain,* translated by
1969   Arthur J. O. Anderson and Charles Dibble. Salt Lake City: University of Utah Press, and Santa Fe, New Mexico: School of American Research.
Schwaller, John Frederick
1973   A catalogue of pre-1840 Nahuatl works held by the Lily Library. *Indiana University Bookman* **11**:69–88.

16

Bureaucracy and Systematic Knowledge in Andean Civilization

R. Tom Zuidema

Editors' Introduction

Reconstructing prehistoric Andean conceptual systems requires bold imagination because there is scant documentation in the native language. How did the Incas organize their state without a system of writing? In this chapter Tom Zuidema finds that textiles, foremost among other media, record tabular orderings between time and space in the realms of politics, religion, and cosmology.

Khipu (quipu), or knotted strings, were not the only Andean technique for recording systematic knowledge. Zuidema suggests that sightlines radiating from the Temple of the Sun in Cuzco formed part of a network extending throughout the Inca realm, which coordinated planting, irrigation, and state ritual with calendrics and astronomy. The intricate patterns of Andean textiles, Zuidema believes, symbolized how social and political statuses fit into such an overarching cosmological scheme. With the system he also correlates myths of origin and the interconnected cultus of water and of ceremonial state redistribution of sacrifical blood. Zuidema thus postulates Andean ceremonial and cosmological ideas comparable in sophistication and scope to those we know to have developed in Mesoamerica with writing. The notion that nonliterate Andean peoples achieved sophisticated systematic knowledge runs counter to Goody's claim (in *The Domestication of the Savage Mind*) that writing is a prerequisite for scientific classification and cumulative knowledge.

THE INCA AND AZTEC
STATES, 1400–1800

A text on
Order in the domain of an Inca housewife
and
an Andean recipe to make children grow:
. . . and when I found among other (priests of the huacas) this occupation in the valley of Yucay, I wanted to know what they used for this, and they said that they collected dirt of the house when they swept it, and foam of (the water of) the river, and some wild herbs, and with these they applied certain fumes to them (the children), saying that, just like all that grows without anybody understanding how and although it is a nuisance to everybody, the child would grow too [Polo de Ondegardo, Relacion p. 113].

The feast of *Situa:*
The reason why they celebrated it this month (of September), was because then it started to rain, and with the first water there would be some illnesses. . . .
First they had the foreigners leave town, and those who had their earlobes broken or who had any damage or imperfection on their body, like hunchbacks, lames and cripples. . . . They also threw out the dogs. . . .
They waited till the New Moon came out and when they saw her, they shouted, with fagots of fire in their hands, saying: "Illnesses, disasters, calamities go away from this land!"; and all repeating "Let evil go away!"
And then, when 400 warriors of the different lineages were running out of town, shouting "Let evil and illness go away", "there was a general lavation in the whole city, the inhabitants going to the wells and rivers to bathe, each person in his own *ceque,* saying that in this way the illnesses would leave them".
After this, "they anointed their faces, the threshholds of the doors to their houses and the places where they kept their food and dresses, saying that no illnesses would enter that house". "After this they ate and drank the best food and chicha that they could make, because they thought that those who would not be content and eat and drink splendidly, would have bad luck and problems throughout the whole year. They would not quarrel . . . and not ask debts, because who was angry and quarrelsome this date would be it the whole year [Cobo XIII, ch. 29].

Introduction

Recent ethnohistorical studies on Mesoamerican and Andean civilizations concentrate on the analysis of specific problems based on regional documents. In the case of the Inca empire, this change of approach constitutes a reaction to the assumption that data, collected by chroniclers on or in Cuzco, would give information on the Inca empire or on Andean civilization as a whole. Fieldwork in Cuzco enabled me, however, to discern the specific character in the chroniclers' data of the sixteenth and seventeenth centuries that refer to Cuzco and its immediate surroundings. These data allow us to discover and analyze more rigorously a type of data on Andean culture that can hardly be studied in documents on other parts of Peru that have a more provincial character.

The data deal with classificatorial systems of a level of sophistication that, due to the unique position of Cuzco as the Inca capital, can probably be studied only in the ethnohistorical record in Cuzco. A study of this intricate ritual and social pattern is essential for an understanding of other regional cultures, which were directly or indirectly affected by Cuzco. For example, look at the calendar that was used for organizing Inca administration. Even if we assume that only the capital needed the intricate and precise calendar, the imposition of such a calendar throughout the empire directly affected other cultures. Continuing with our example, the uniqueness of our data on Cuzco is no reason to question the deep roots of such an intricate calendar in Andean civilization. The dichotomy of a "Great Tradition" and more provincial ones existed for, at least, some 2000 years. One cannot be understood without the other.

This chapter deals with a sophisticated system of exact measurement of space—a system that, in its relation to the state calendar, involves the measurement of space in the whole empire. The measurement was based on a system of 41 sightlines going out from the Temple of the Sun in Cuzco toward its immediate horizon. The Incas were, however, interested in extending these sightlines beyond the horizon; an interest that led them to extend these lines or *ceques* to the confines of their empire. In this chapter I consider the question of why the Incas were interested in such a complex classification system. The system needed a great ability of empirical verification and, at first glance, seems to go far beyond any practical needs. What were the intellectual motivations that led to the exploration of this area of exact knowledge? To what other elements of culture was it related? What "practical" uses were made of these measurements? Finally, how was this knowledge stored and transmitted?

I then test the hypothesis that Jack Goody put forward in *The Domestication of the Savage Mind* (1977). Goody analyzes the potential of literacy for the cumulation of knowledge and its importance for the history of the scientific endeavor in its broadest context. In this way he intends to overcome the dichotomies into which anthropological thinking so many times seems to fall:

abstract and scientific thought or knowledge	to	mythical, magical, or intuitive thought or knowledge.

Goody argues that, although rational thought is possible in an oral, preliterate society, the introduction of writing, especially alphabetic writing, enables the inspection of a text and reflection upon it. In general it leads to the storage and gradual accumulation of knowledge. Therefore, it is not accidental that major steps in the development of what we now call "science" followed the introduction of. major changes in the channels of communication in Babylonia (writing), Ancient Greece (alphabet), and Western Europe (printing) (Goody 1977:51). He concludes that tables, lists, formulas, and recipes are basically graphic devices, used far more in literate than in oral societies. Literacy develops another way of thinking, even in those segments of literate societies where no writing is used. With respect to Durkheim and Mauss's discussion of "primitive classifications" as based on Cushing's work among the Zuni, Goody points out that the table of their clan system is a deliberate literary elaboration by the ethnographer on the basis of only partial mythical stories that nowhere are found together within one great myth.

Goody recognizes in the end that he too tends to drop into a dichotomous treatment of utterance versus text, or the oral versus the written. He certainly has not studied the "prehistory" of writing. Whenever he mentions that classificatorial systems or tables are not absent from oral societies, he immediately falls back to a contrast of their more elaborate use in literate societies. When discussing "redistributive" economies such as those centered upon palaces and temples (1977:82–83), Goody writes:

> Whilst state systems approximating to this kind of elaboration did arise in Central America, without the advent of true writing system (Gelb 1963:57–58) but using a system of recording by means of knotted ropes, the complexities of which are only just being understood, it is clear that the presence of writing both facilitated and promoted the development of such an economy as well as the polity that organized it.

We can forego Goody's garbled reference to Peruvian *quipus* as "knotted ropes" from Central America. But we must express a basic reservation and criticism against his handling of literacy as the causal factor in the origin of rational and scientific thought. His two major ethnographic examples are the modern Lo Daaga and the Sumerians. He takes the first as an example of a nonliterate culture. It exists, however, in the context of surrounding literate ones. It cannot serve, therefore, as a valid test case. In the example of Sumerian culture Goody does not ask the essential questions: Did rational thought and inspection result from writing, and thus, did writing have its origin elsewhere? Or, did the existence of the former help in the formation of a notational system? To answer this question, we find the ideal test case in the situation in the Andes, especially at the time of Inca culture when it could be documented by the Spaniards. Here we have a major, well-administered empire that was far beyond the stage of first urban development. Although it had a well-developed interest in rational thought and empirical verification and various means of using intricate tables and lists, the culture did not have writing. The particular direction of cultural development in Mesopotamia may have led to a discovery of writing. The discovery of notational systems in a far wider area of the Near East from approximately 6000 B.C. indicates that the discovery of writing had a much longer and more complicated prehistory than represented in such a superficial way by Goody. It seems, moreover, reasonable to suppose that the discovery of writing in the other areas of the Old World where civilization arose (such as Egypt, Indus, and China) went much faster, following the lead of the Sumerians. Andean civilization is our most independent test case for checking the hypothesis that writing is the necessary correlate in the development of rational thought, tables, etc. Based on the Inca example, my conclusion is that writing is not the necessary correlate. Their development precedes the origin of writing and is independent of it.

In this chapter I argue that the Andean form of exact knowledge did not originate in the context of what anthropologists have analyzed mostly as Andean or Inca systems of measurement. Let me first mention, therefore, the material that Maria Rostworowski has collected on this subject (Rostworowski 1978). Measurements of distance, surface, or volume have a very relative value. For instance, when it was to indicate a measurement of distance identified by the Spaniards as roughly equivalent to a "league," the *tupu* was longer or shorter according to the terrain that had to be traversed. As a measurement of space, the *tupu* corresponded to the land needed to support a family without children, but the quality of the land was a variable. Looking over the material, one reaches the conclusion that no single measurement can be used to begin to build a precise system of measurement.

A more fruitful introduction to our subject is found in Guaman Poma's description of Inca officials and functionaries, specifically the ones that he calls *hucha quipoc* (Guaman Poma 1980:360, 361). They were the official Inca accountants attached to the secretaries of the Inca king. The word *quipu* refers to the system of knotted chords on which the Incas recorded all numerical information. A drawing of the *hucha quipoc* (Figure 16.1) shows him, not only with such a *quipu*, but also with a board, called *tabla* in Spanish, a kind of abacus that Radicati (1979) takes as an example of *yupanu*. This author has studied intensively the theme of *quipus* and gameboards (*yupanu*) and their

Figure 16.1 The accountant *hucha quipoc* with his *quipu* and *tabla* or abacus. (After Guaman Poma 1980:360, 361.)

place in Andean culture. Marcia and Robert Ascher have indicated in various publications (1975, 1980) the existence of sophisticated algebraic concepts in the construction of a *quipu*. The text of Guaman Poma says that the *hucha quipoc* counted "from 100,000, 10,00, [not 1000?], 100 coming to one" and that he had to report everything that occurred in the "kingdom," that is, about "the feasts and sundays and months, years in each city, town and village." The primary concerns were counting and chronology: the business of how local calendars were integrated into the state calendar. Only the study of the Inca calendar—a calendar that our recent studies on this subject (Aveni 1981; Zuidema 1981a, 1982a,b) reveal to be far more sophisticated than suspected before—based on careful Inca astronomical observations in Cuzco itself, can help us to realize the importance of the *hucha quipoc* and the secretaries of the Inca and the scope of their administrative knowledge.

Why were these *quipu* specialists referred to by the word *hucha*, a term that in the first place means "sin"? A discussion of this concept will lead us to conclude that the development of an Andean interest in exact and systematic knowledge was motivated not by an involvement in measurements such as the ones mentioned earlier (e.g., *tupu*) but by moral and abstract concepts such as "sin," "secret," "health," "obligation," and "order." They led the Incas to explore the boundaries of knowledge. The abstract system that they developed then helped them in the solution of practical problems. I shall analyze here the concept of *hucha* and how this led the Incas to an interest in measuring straight lines over long distances.

Hucha

Whereas the earlier dictionaries of Quechua by Santo Tomas (1561) and the anonymous one edited by Ricardo (1586) only mention *hucha* and words derived from it with the meaning of "sin," the dictionaries of Gonzalez Holguín (1608/1952) on Quechua and Bertonio (1612) on Aymara analyze the concept in far more depth.

Gonzalez Holguín mentions two synonymous terms:

Hucha, or *Cama*: sin ("peccado"); business, occupation or work ("negocio"); contract, dispute, debate ("pleito")
Runaphuchan: sin [i.e., translated literally, the sin of man]
Dioshucha: the business of God
Runahucha: dispute [i.e., of man], without genitive

The distinction "with or without genitive" is explained further in the context of

> *Qquelcca huchayachak:* The secretary of letters; and observe that in (hucha) used in sin has genitive with (p) and for dispute or business not.

The sense of "business" is clarified in the term:

> *Huachacta camacta yachak,* or *hucha yachak:* the secretary of the Inca, or consultant of his business or secrets to whom he revealed his resolutions in order that he [the secretary] would command it to the executors.

We can draw two conclusions about these data:

1. The terms *hucha quipoc,* used by Guaman Poma for one of the lowest ranks (Zuidema 1981b), and *huchayachak,* secretary of the Inca, belong to the same context. They refer to specialists who classify and count matters of interest to the Inca and government. A first way of doing this is to place these matters in a calendrical context.

2. Recognizing the distinction between *hucha,* "sin," and *hucha* "dispute or business," and recognizing the distinction in their grammatical use, we see that they still have a basic property in common. Both concepts involve an element of hiddenness that has to be revealed and that creates, for that reason, an insecure and dangerous situation. "Sin," as we shall see, affects the well-being of society and has to be confessed in order to be neutralized and classified. A decision of the Inca, on the other hand, is first heard by his secretary alone. He might be the only person in this secret situation who is aware of the vacillations of the Inca and who is allowed to discuss and dispute the coming decision with him. Once the decision had been taken and was following the chain of command, it reached the *hucha quipoc* as an already classified and resolved matter. The latter person also collected material at the other end of the hierarchy. Ultimately, again alone, the Inca decided upon the situation. "Classified material," in the Inca sense, meant the opposite of what it is in Western culture: It was the material that was decided upon, organized in categories, and open to the people.

Besides *hucha,* the term *cama,* given as a synonym, defines best the wide range of reference of both terms (see also Taylor 1974–1976; Duviols 1978). Let us look for a moment at *cama* and its different meanings (selected from Gonzalez Holguín, but not in exactly the same order):

1. *Cama:* sin ("pecado") or fault or guilt ("culpa")
2. *Camachini:* to order; to consult, what has to be ordered

Camani: to have fruit; to produce; to create
Camak: God; God, the Creator
3. *Camani:* to measure grain, or *Tupuni*
Camaycucuni (or *Camallicuni, tupucini*): to fit a dress
4. *Cama:* according to
Camaycama: according to my merits
Camy niyquicama: according to your office, your knowledge or talent

In these two expressions the first use of *camay* refers to "merit, office, knowledge, talent" and the second use to the suffix *-cama,* "according to."

5. *Camak:* God; God, the Creator
Camachic, camachicuc: Governor . . . , he who orders or he who rules.
6. *Camay* (or *suyuy*): the task in the work
Camay: my obligation
Camaricuk: he who gets something ready or who will get ready
Camayok: official; he who is in charge of an estate or a piece of land

From the use of this word in the literature—documents and chronicles—I would conclude that the word *camayok* is used for any official or specialist who is put in charge of any job.

We notice the great importance of *cama* and its derivations—and by implication the term *hucha*—for the general concepts of "order" and "creation of order," the primordial stage of "disorder" or "secrecy," and "sin" out of which order was created. The concept approximately translated by "sin" and the great Andean concern with "sin" led to the more general use of both words.

Cobo explains in general terms (1956 [Vol. XIII, Chapter 24]) that it was sin not only to kill and to steal but also to be careless in the cult of the *huacas* (places of worship), to forget celebrating the (calendrical) feasts, and to speak badly about the Inca. When the king was sick or suffered misfortune, its cause was in the sins of his subjects. An important myth from central Peru, which discusses the concept of "royalty" (Avila 1967: Chapter 5), describes a king who fell ill because of the adultery of his wife. For that reason he lost the following of his subjects and his royal power. The health of the king and his government was in direct correlation to his knowledge of *hucha* and to his ability to remove it from any part of his territory—whether its cause was a person, an organization of people, or the *huaca* by which they were represented. This was the reason why a king at the time of his ascent to the throne and later at regular intervals assessed the standing of all the *huacas* in his empire. (For a modern example of such reevaluations of *huacas*, see Martinez 1976:267–279.) The classification of sociopolitical units in the Inca empire was done by way of the *huacas* representing each unit (Albornoz 1967:18, 20, 37).

Essential to the ability of handling *hucha* was the act of speaking it out to a confessor. It was done not only for a person's own illness but also for that of a wife, husband, or child; important people such as one's *cacique;* and, in final instance, the Inca himself. The person was then absolved by ablution in a river, which would carry away the sin as dirt and illness and ultimately deliver it to the ocean.

The *hucha* ritual was intertwined with the cult of water. This element comes out most clearly in the *Situa* ritual. In August the earth has been plowed, "opened," freeing illnesses from the Underworld. Also, in order to expect a good harvest, the people had to be without sin themselves. Therefore, in September, the first act of *Situa* was to have the illnesses expelled from town toward the four directions of the empire by 400 warriors, who would throw them into the first big rivers, the Villcanota and the Apurimac, which carried them away toward the ocean. Then each *ayllu*, or "social group," according to its *ceque*, or "direction," went out of town in order to clean a source from which water was leading into town or valley. Water had a double function of purification: Certain rivers carried *hucha* away from town, while others purified the town itself. *Ceques* could have the two functions or one of the two. The *ceque* with the first function could go over the horizon of Cuzco to reach the end point; a *ceque* with the second function generally would not have to.

The confessor could request the use of a hunchback, who, after the sins of the person had been washed off in the river, would flagellate him with nettles. The hunchback himself was not affected by the sins. In contrast, the Inca king and the high nobility could not use such persons. The king was allowed, without mediation, to confess directly to the Sun. Probably within the system of the Incaic cult to the sun, the letter was the purest element in existence. Even though confession relieved the Inca from his *hucha*, it remained hidden from all the other people in his empire. The state of hiddenness of his confessed sin was like the counsel that he took from his secretary *huchayachak*.

Againt this background we can understand the most important imperial ritual, the *capac hucha*, or "royal *hucha*" (Duviols 1976; Rostworowski 1970; Zuidema 1973, 1978a). Here we find the most explicit reference to the concept of straight directions over long distances. In the *capac hucha* ritual the king could allow any social group or its *curaca* in the empire to send an immaculate child, without birthmarks, to Cuzco or any other ritual center. There it would be sacrificed, or from there it would be redistributed to another place, including its place of origin, to be sacrificed. In an actual ritual, which was remembered by people and described by Hernandez Principe in 1624 (Zuidema 1973, 1978a,b), an *aclla,* or "chosen virgin," was sent by her father, a local *curaca,* or "chief," to Cuzco where she participated with the Inca in the December solstice rituals. Finding an immaculate child was a rare event, and the father had taken the opportunity to offer his child to the Inca. The former had made himself meritorious to the Inca by organizing the help of the neighboring towns to build an important irrigation canal. For this act the Inca honored the *curaca* by sending the daughter back and allowing the father to sacrifice and bury her on a mountaintop, where she could be worshipped from visible surrounding mountains belonging to the towns who had collaborated in building the canal. The father was elevated in rank as *curaca* over all these towns. The girl, who had been dedicated to the sun, was worshipped especially at the beginning and end of the agricultural season. Through the mouth of her younger brothers and their descendants, who would speak in a falsetto voice, she came to be consulted by her worshippers as a goddess of the earth and as an oracle.

The analysis of the *capac hucha* ritual may give us one of the most critical instruments for studying pre-Spanish political organization, especially where it concerns defining territorial and hierarchical limits of power. Hernandez Principe claims that every *curacazgo*—its origin and the circumscription of its political rights and obligations—was based on the initial sacrifice of a *capac hucha.* In the particular case of two towns, he gives full lists of the *capac huchas* that they had carried out in their past, and he defines for every case its purpose in terms of the rank and political role of its *ayllu.* A traveling *aclla* or *capac hucha* could be accompanied only by the people whose territory it passed. The document discussed by Maria Rostworowski illustrates this point well. Here is the legal case of people who in this way trespassed their border and who thereby obtained impunity in occupying new land.

The most visual and explicit expression of the *capac hucha* ritual was the solumn way in which the *aclla* traveled to and from Cuzco. Molina (1943) gives us the most vivid description (pp. 69–78). He first says that from each town and village and group of people in each of the four provinces of the empire children were sent to Cuzco with offerings of cloth, llamas, golden and silver llamas, and *mullu* (shells). From here the king sent them back to the principal *huacas* in order to be sacrificed.

> They made this sacrifice at the beginning of the reign of the Lord so that the *huacas* would give him much health and would keep his territories in peace and rest, and that he would reach an old age, and that he would live without any sickness, in such

a way that not a single *huaca* or place of praying or of worship, as small as it was, would remain without sacrifice, because it was already ordered and agreed upon what had to be sacrificed in each place. The reason why they wanted that all the *huacas*, places of worship, trees, wells, mountains and lakes would obtain part of the sacrifice, was that they held it as an omen that no one would be missed, in order that the one that was missed in the sacrifice would not be angry and out of angriness would punish the Inca. And if they came to some mountains that were very difficult, that they would not climb, then they would throw the sacrifice from where they could throw it with their slings. [For this last element, see also Rostworowski 1970.]

Molina then describes the *quipucamayoc* who took account of the *huacas*, the way of sacrificing the children, and the prayers. He also describes how he had made a list of all the *huacas* around Cuzco, the *"Relacion de las huacas,"* which is, in fact, a reference to the system of 41 *ceques* and the 328 *huacas* organized by them, as preserved in the chronicle of Cobo. The two following quotations describe the actual traveling of the *acllas*, called *capaccocha* (*capac hucha*) and also *cachague:*

And so it was that all the people that went with the capaccocha, called by another name *cachagues*, . . . separated from each other, not going by the royal road, straight, without turning off to any place, crossing the gorges and mountains that they had in front of them, until each came to the place where they were waited for to receive the sacrifices mentioned; they walked by stretches; they shouted, that was started by an Indian trained for this purpose and when he began all would follow in shouting, asking the Creator that the Inca would always conquer and not be conquered and that he always would live in peace and safety.

But the Inca (himself) and the old and young llamas went by the royal road (that is, not following the straight direction). Molina then describes the children, the accounting of all the sacrifices, and the procedures of elevating and lowering the *huacas* in rank. Finally, he says:

They held this worship in such high esteem, called *capaccocha* or *cachaguaco*, that when they traveled through the uninhabited areas or other places and met with someone, these would not dare to raise their eyes and look, but they would prostrate themselves on the ground till they had passed. And in the villages with people through which they passed, these would not leave their houses staying with great respect and humility until the capaccocha had passed by. It was also the case that when they subjected and conquered some nations, they took and chose of the most beautiful [children] that they could find and they brought them to Cuzco, where they sacrificed them to the Sun, for the victory that they had obtained. They also said that every time that something was the best and most beautiful of its kind, that they would worship it and give it a huaca and place of worship. They worshipped all the mountaintops and offered salt and other things because they said that when they went up a hillside, and reached the top, that there they rested from the work of climbing; they called [this restplace] *apachita*.

From the words of Molina, one would have to conclude that the *aclla* traveled, literally, in a straight direction. Moreover, he links the system of *capac hucha* explicitly to the idea of *ceque:* first by mentioning the system of *ceque* directions in Cuzco itself and, second, by using the word *cachague.* (From the faulty copying it is difficult to know the meaning of the two endings, *-es* and *-co,* in the two instances where Molina refers to the word.) The same word, written *cachaui* (*cacha-hui*), is used by Albornoz for the offerings, including sacrifices of children placed around *huacas.* (The same description, although the Quechua word is not used, is given by Hernandez Principe [see Zuidema 1973]). The word is derived from *cacha,* or "messenger," and Albornoz gives *ceque* as a synonym.

Our data from Molina refer to three contexts of *ceques:* The first is composed of the offerings, *ceque* or *cachahui,* that are in direct, visual contact to the *huaca* that is worshipped. The second context is that of the *ceque* system of Cuzco. Here the *ceques* are sightlines covering the whole valley, and, because of their longer extension, various *huacas* as *cachahuis* are organized along each *ceque,* worshipping the center of the system. In this case, certain *ceques* went beyond the immediate horizon, extending the concept of visual connection by way of the concept of straight line or direction. However, the system is still kept within a local context. The third context is that of the *capac hucha.* Here the visual connection is expanded by the act of the *aclla* actually traveling as a *cachahui* ("messenger") or *ceque* between two distant points. The visual aspect was not lost. By traveling in a straight line, not avoiding mountains, visible long-distance connections were kept in mind. Finally, Molina's discussion of climbing high mountains and the use of *apachitas,* or "mountain passes," is a direct reference not only to the connection of horizon points to the center (see, for instance, the chronicle of the Agustinos [1557/1952:78] on Huamachuco) but also to the visual connection it allowed between two valleys.

Although I analyzed the hierarchy of *ceques* from Molina's description, he does not mention it explicitly. Also he does not mention here the aspect of ablution and water (although he does so in relation to the *Situa* feast). Both facts come out more clearly in a description by Murúa (1613/1962 [Vol. II]: Chapter 29; Murúa was a later chronicler, but he probably got this data from an earlier source, which could be Polo de Ondegardo) of pilgrimages by priests. He excludes women from these pilgrimages, but otherwise his description is very similar to that of the *capac hucha* ritual. The priests would

walk straight, without looking sideways. At regular intervals they stopped and prayed on their knees, saying "let the Sun be young; let the moon be a young girl and not turn back, let the earth be in peace and the Inca live for many years, let he reach an old age, and not fall sick and not stumble and fall; let him live long and watch [after] us and rule us.

They would sleep where the night caught them, be it on a plain or on a mountainside up or down, and they would offer blood of llamas that they carried along to high and low mountains. This they did so that it would rain and snow. On the mountains where it was difficult to reach the top, they threw the blood in some earthen vessels with blood, well closed, and they threw them with their slings, high, so they would break and spill the blood.

With these offerings went a nobleman of the counsel of the Inca, to oversee how they sacrificed in the villages. And when they reached the Incas who are at the coast of the sea, having sacrificed what they brought them, they put other things in bags and after many ceremonies, they threw them in the sea, and thus they went back to Cuzco.

Murúa makes a direct reference to the importance of the mountains as sources of rain and snow and to the water in rivers and canals deriving from there. The ultimate source of water was the ocean. High snow-capped mountains, even the distant ones, had a great importance in providing water for rivers that irrigated lands. Albornoz (1967:20, 21), Guaman Poma (1980:282) and Avila (1967:Chapter 22) give a strict hierarchical classification of these mountains; Guaman Poma and Albornoz also provide lists of individual ones.

On the basis of these data we can conclude that all the mountains and *huacas* in the whole empire were important for the health of the Inca and his government. We also should recognize the importance of their organization, carried out by extending the visual relationship into a concept of direct relationship between *huaca* and center (the Inca and Cuzco). This was expressed by way of a straight line in a certain direction. I finish this section with a statement and accompanying drawing (Figure 16.2) from Guaman Poma (1980:263, 264):

> In time of the Inca [the King Tupa Yunga Yupangui] spoke with the *huacas* and stones and demons and knew because of them the past and the future of them and of the whole world and how the Spaniards would come to govern, and because of that the Ynga called himself *Viracocha Ynga*, but otherwise he did not teach them about God although they say that he said that there was another Great Lord.

Tupa Yupanqui spoke with all the *huacas* in his empire, which in the time of his son Huaina Capac, just before the Spanish conquest, they refused to do. Tupa Yupanqui spoke to the visible and to the distant, invisible *huacas*. They told him about the past and the future, those times that the king by personal experience could not know. The spatial distance of existing *huacas*, which were invisible but which affected his own existence, allowed him to know things distant in time. He learned of a calamity to come, that is, the Spanish conquest.

Figure 16.2 Tupa Yupanqui, adopting the name of his grandfather Viracocha Inca, talks to all the *huacas* in the empire and asks them about the past and the future. (After Guaman Poma 1980:263, 264.)

It was a calamity (*hucha*) caused by the discord (*hucha*) during the time of Huaina Capac's reign. He learned, too, of how this king split his government over his two sons Huascar and Atahuallpa. (This is the explanation found in Avila [1967:Chapter 14], and in Santacruz Pachacuti [1950:247]). Tupa Yupanqui, consulting the *huacas* as an oracle, adopted the name of his grandfather the king Viracocha Inca. By implication he referred to the God Virachocha, the Creator god. In his capacity as God of the Ocean (Polo de Ondegardo 1917:110) he was addressed as *Con Ticci Viracocha* (*Ticci*, "foundation"; but also, in modern Quechua, "dirt and mud"). To the ocean went ultimately the *hucha*—the guilt, illness and dirt of men. From there came the Spaniards, called *Viracocha*, and from there came the knowledge of past, future, invisible distance, and *hucha*. Guaman Poma expresses the identity of distant time and distant space; both concepts of time and space are included in the Quechua word *pacha*.

The Straightness of Ceques

Molina's description points to three types of *ceques* according to their length. The straightness of the first type—where an unambiguous visual relationship existed between *huaca* and sacrifice, called *cachahui* or *cachahua* and *ceque*—does not need to be accounted for (see also Zuidema 1978a,b for a documentation of three such cases). In the second type, the 41 *ceques* of Cuzco, our research of the last years supports the conclusion that the *ceques* were straight. Here I shall give an example of one *ceque* that in its major part went beyond the horizon. *Ceques* of the third type, the long-distance ones, are referred to in various places in the chronicles, but only one case is well documented. I shall give this as the second example. Both examples refer to *ceques* that had practical astronomical significance to the Incas. Although the *ceque* system of Cuzco as a whole, with its numbers of *ceques* and *huacas*, was a system used also for computing time (Zuidema 1977b, 1982a,b), we do not have to suppose that every *ceque* was used in relation to measuring rises and sets of sun, moon, or stars. In this respect we have pertinent data of certain *ceques*. Elsewhere we (Zuidema 1981a; Aveni 1981) discuss and document these data. Here I use our conclusions in order to discuss the straightness of the *ceques*.

One essential feature, stated as a warning, should be made explicit about the astronomical observations in Cuzco. Although the *ceque* system was based on a system of sightlines from Coricancha, the central Temple of the Sun in Cuzco, and although certain *huacas* on its horizon had a well-described astronomical function in terms of sunrise and sunset, only in one case did the Temple of the Sun itself function as the observatory. In all other cases the observation was made from another place, not this temple. With one exception, the astronomical value of certain *huacas* on the horizon derived from their position not toward Coricancha but toward another observatory. The actual location of the *huacas* of the two *ceques* to be used in the argument here are explained in relation to a map of each. Here I shall concentrate on the arguments themselves.

Eighth Ceque of Chinchaysuyu, with Thirteen Huacas (Ceque IIb, Payan)

The example of this *ceque* is important for two reasons (see Figure 16.3). First, its part toward the horizon from Coricancha is much shorter (about 2.5 km) than the part beyond (approximately 10 km). Second, defining its straightness is confirmed completely by a calendrical argument. When the sun at sunset reached the horizon point of this *ceque*, as observed from a building on the main plaza of Cuzco, it was the official date that defined the first lunar month of the Inca agricultural year. This date, August 18, marked the time when the sun goes through nadir (defined by looking back from the place of sunrise when the sun goes through zenith, both dates being half a year apart) (Zuidema 1981a).

Discussion

The *huacas* that could be located precisely, were the thirteenth (last), the twelfth, ninth, and fourth. The sixth is also known.

The name *Collana sayhua*, "the first, principal (territorial) marker," of the thirteenth *huaca*, only reserved for this *huaca*, indicates its very important position in the *ceque* system. Assuming its function for throwing out *hucha*, "illness," into the river, it is ideally suited for this purpose. Close to Sicllabamba, the river draining the valley of Poroy and Puquiura west of Cuzco breaks through a gorge in between two rocky hills. Here I found the remains of Incaic ruins.

The name and place of the twelfth *huaca*, Poroypuquio, "the well of (the village of) Poroy," is still known. Here I found the archaeological remains of two Spanish mills, mentioned in the description locating this *huaca* as belonging to a sixteenth-century Spaniard, Juan Julio (Hojeda), who is also mentioned in other documents as the owner of watermills.

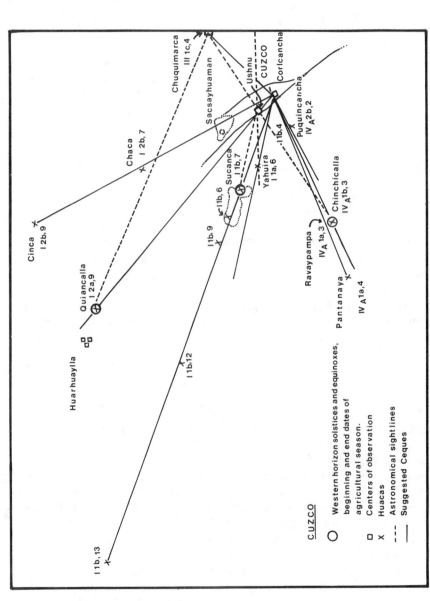

Figure 16.3 Eight *ceque* of Chinchaysuyu, "called Payan, being the second and there were 13 *guacas.*"

1. Illanguarque, "a small house close to the temple of the Sun." Not identified.

2. "A *chacra* ("field") of (dedicated to) Huanacauri." Not identified.

3. A well callded Aacaypata (or possibly Ancaypata), "close to where is now the house of the Cabildo." Apparently, the Cabildo was at some time where is now the house of Garcilaso (see next *huaca*) is located too.

4. Cugitalis, "a plain where Garcilaso built his house." The house, on the southwest side of the Plaza de Regocijo still exists and is identified. Although we do not know how extensive was the plain, at least it was on the *ceque*. Perhaps the name, copied as cugitalis refers to the word *cusi* in *cusipata*, the Inca name of the same Plaza where both *huacas* (3) and (4) are located.

5. A *chacra* called chaguaytapata in Carmenga. Carmenca is the Inca name of the neighborhood now called Santa Ana. The *ceque* passes over it.

6. The well called Orocotopuquio, in Carmenga. The gorge known today as Coto runs from the mountain mentioned in (7) towards the northeast. I cannot make sense of the word *oro* in this context. Perhaps it is misspelled for *orco*, "moutain," that is, the mountain from where the gorge came down.

7. Sucanca. "A mountain along which runs the irrigation canal from Chinchero." The canal, in fact, passed (until 1950) around this mountain, still known with the Inca name Picchu. As such it cannot identify exactly the location of Sucanca. Its gentle slope toward the north serves, however, best the astronomical purpose of Sucanca.

8. A house called Mamararoy. Not identified.

9. Urcoscalla (*urco*, "mountain"; *calla*, "a *huaca* from where one worships another huaca")(Arriaga), "Those who walked to Chinchaysuyu lost sight of Cuzco here." The *ceque* passes over a hill south, and very close to, the pass Arcopunco that is still considered as the last and first place from where one sees Cuzco.

10. Catachilla, "a well in the first plain going down on the road to *Chinchaysuyu*." Not identified. The name Catachillay is also used for the constellation of the Pleiades. As seen from Coricancha, the direction of this *ceque* is some 2° south of their setting point (see Zuidema 1982a).

11. "Another well close to the one mentioned before, called Aspadquiri." Not identified. The plain on which both, no. 10 and no. 11, are located is, however, on this *ceque*.

12. A well called Poroypuqui, close to the mill of Juan Julio (Hojeda). The name of this precise location still exists and is close to the ruins of an old Spanish watermill.

13. "The last *huaca* of this *ceque* was called Collana Sayba." "It was a marker on a mountain at the beginning of Sicllabamba, as end and border of the *huacas* of this "*ceque*." The old house of the *hacienda* Sicllabamba still identifies this place. The "beginning of Sicllabamba" is probably reckoned from the old, and modern, road to Chinchaysuyu. Close to it, in between the road and the *hacienda* house, is a very conspicuous double hill, with the river from Poroy running in between. As end of the *ceque* it is an ideal place for throwing the offerings of this *ceque* into the river. Around the first hill, closest to Cuzco, is a heavy wall, probably colonial. But at the foot of it and close to the river, were found the remains of a well-built Inca structure.

Huacas 13, 12, and 9 identify the *ceque* as straight and indicate its exact direction. Calculating the location of (7) gives a completely satisfactory estimate, taking into consideration its astronomical function. The plains mentioned in (4), (10), and (11) and the neighborhood Carmenca in (5) and (6) do not allow a precise identification of the *ceque*, but they do conform completely to it. *Huacas* (2), (3), and (8) are not identified; from their description we can say, however, that much that it does not contradict the direction of the *ceque*.

The ninth huaca, Urcoscalla, "the mountain (urco) from where one worships (calla) another huaca," mentioned as the place where travelers to Chinchaysuyu lost sight of Cuzco, should be the pass today known as Arcopuncu, "the gate (Q. puncu) of the arches (Sp. ·arco) (of the Spanish aquaduct)." The same comment of "losing sight of Cuzco" was given on Arcopuncu in colonial times and is given today. The ceque as a straight line passes over the hillside (the "urco" of Urcoscalla) overlooking, and very close to, this point.

The site of the fourth huaca, Cugitalis, is identified by the house of the chronicler Garcilaso de la Vega, a house still in existence. The ceque as straight line passes along this house. Because of its extension and relative closeness to Coricancha, it cannot be used as a precise indicator of direction.

In the case of the well Orocotopuquio, the sixth huaca, the small affluent to the water coming from Ticatica to Cuzco, today still is known as Coto, which is derived from the hill on which the seventh huaca, Sucanca, the horizon point of our interest, is located. The description of Coto agrees with our ceque, but does not define it more sharply.

As the thirteenth huaca seemed to be the most important one of this ceque, Aveni and I traced the straight line between this point and Coricancha. A transit and a map were used, but otherwise the method was by trial and error. The direction passes exactly over the twelfth and ninth huacas. In this way we defined the horizon point in this direction, and we checked to see if this point could be the location of the seventh huaca, Sucanca, toward which the Incas made their astronomical observation. Having located by independent means the Inca observatory and having defined the Inca astronomical theory on which the observation was based, we could confirm the identity of Sucanca with the horizon point of the ceque.

From these results we cannot conclude that the only or principal purpose of the Incas in defining the direction of this ceque was its application for the astronomical observation. Probably it was not. By locating the horizon point or passage and using the two huacas, Coricancha and Collanasayhua, people of the valley of Cuzco, as well as those of the valley of Poroy and Puquiura, were able to define sharply the direction toward each other, even if these huacas were invisible to each other. Knowing these specific points, one could extend the ceque greatly in both directions. A practical advantage to the Incas of this ceque was that it passed a convenient place on the horizon from Cuzco for making an astronomical observation, if one adjusted the location of the observatory accordingly. As the location of the latter and the type of observation were reconstructed independently, they afford us with a confirmation that the Incas did use the property of straightness of the *ceque*. But the straightness itself was reconstructed from locating its *huacas*.

The Long-Distance Ceque from Cuzco (Huanacauri) to the Temple of Tiahuanaco Over That of Villcanota

Whereas in the case of the local *ceque* to Collanasayhua we were considering a distance of about 12.5 km, this example refers to an aerial distance of approximately 300 km to Tiahuanaco and about 100 km to Villcanota (see Figures 16.4 and 16.5). The specific data on this *ceque* are comprised, first, in the detailed description of a *capac hucha* type pilgrimage to Villcanota and, second, in mythical–ritual data about the astronomical significance of Huanacauri, Villcanota and Titicaca-Tiahuanaco. Moreover, many other mythical and ritual data elaborate upon the significance of this *ceque*. Let me start with the second group of specific data (see Figure 16.4).

For the Incas the common element in the religious significance of Huanacauri, Villcanota, and Tiahuanaco was that all three were related to the "birth of the sun" and the creation of the world and that they were aligned to each other in an exact southeasterly direction. I shall not discuss here the exact calendrical—astronomical meaning of the concept "birth of the sun"; I shall only point out that it was the common direction that defined the concept and not the location per se.

Discussion

Villcanota, today called La Raya in Spanish, is the continental divide between two rivers: one, also called Villcanota, flows toward Cuzco in the northwest and the other flows southeast into Lake Titicaca. Villcanota is translated in Aymara as "the house of the sun," meaning the "house where the sun was born." Various rituals, celebrated here, commemorated this idea, and here one Inca king placed "two clubs of gold and silver with lines and heaps of stones" (Santacruz Pachacuti 1950:251) describing a horizon point or *sucanca*, of astronomical use to the Incas.

The island of Titicaca, also called "of the sun," in Lake Titicaca, and the pre-Inca ruins of the city of Tiahuanaco are, together or individually, mentioned in different versions of the myth about the birth of the sun from a subterranean room from the underworld, and about the creation of man, at the same time. After his creation, the God Vir-

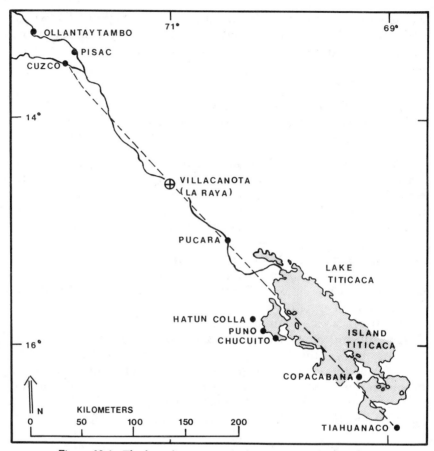

Figure 16.4   The long-distance *ceque* from Cuzco to Tiahuanaco.

acocha travels "straight" (Betanzos 1880:Chapter 2) along the direction from Tiahuanaco, passing the pre-Inca city of Pucara, and Villcanota and Cuzco to Ecuador. Pucara, Villcanota, and Huanacauri conform closely to this direction, but the island of Titicaca is somewhat off. In a more detailed discussion I will argue that the area including the island of the sun, the temple of the sun in Copacabana, and the sacred peninsula of Copacabana was represented by Tiahuanaco on the long-distance ceque extending from these points over Huanacauri to Ecuador.

Huanacauri, in the local context of the valley of Cuzco, represented the concept of "birth of the sun," referring to the primordial and

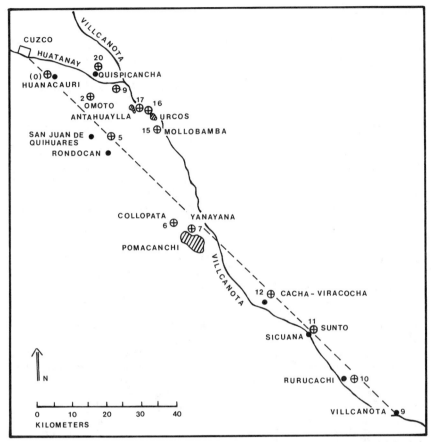

Figure 16.5 The 21 stations of the pilgrimage route to Villcanota. The names of the first and last *huacas*, Sucanca, indicate that they were astronomical horizon points. *Huacas* nos. 0, 5 (probably), 7, 9, 10, 11, and 12 can be identified as being on or close to the straight line from Cuzco to Villcanota and then to Pucara and Tiahuanaco. *Huacas* 0, 5, and 7 are on the way to Villcanota (9); 10, 11, and 12 are on the way back. *Huacas* 0 and 1 to 8 follow the road through the mountains: *huacas* 9 to 15 are in the valley of the Villcanota river and *huacas* 16 to 20 go toward the Huatanay valley.

Description by Cristobal de Molina	Modern identification
0. (Mountain Huanacauri)	(On the day when the pilgrimage started, other priests went to Huanacauri)
1. mountain Sucanca	?
2. mountain Omotoyanacauri	Mountain Mutu
3. mountain Capac vilca	?
4. mountain Queros Huanacauri	?

(continued)

Figure 16.5 (*continued*)

Description by Cristobal de Molina	Modern identification
5. mountain Rontoca, that is in Quiguares	The mountain should be found as indicated above the modern towns of Rondocan and San Juan de Quihuares.
6. mountain Collopata, in Pumacancha, 14 "leguas" from Cuzco	Mountain Cullopata, near lake Pomacanchi
7. plain of Yana yana	Hamlet and plain of Yanapampa, near lake Pumacanchi
8. mountain Cuti in the puna of Pomacanche	?; puna is probably in between lake Pumacanchi and river Villcanota
9. Villcanota, 26 "leguas" from Cuzco	La Raya, highest point between Cuzco and Lake Titicaca.
10. plain near Rurucachi	Plain near (former hacienda and village of) Lurucachi
11. mountain Sunto, near Sicuana, in Cacha	Mountain Suntu, just above Sicuani
12. mountain Cacha-Viracocha	Mountain above town of San Pedro de Racchi and Inca temple of Viracocha
13. mountain Yacalla huaca	?
14. mountain Virauma, in plain near Quiquijana	Modern town of Quiquijana
15. Mollobamba	Village of Mollobamba, just South of Urcos
16. mountain Urcos Viracocha, in Urcos	Mountain Viracocha, just North of Urcos
17. plain of Antahuayla	Plain of modern town of Andahuaylillas
18. plain of Pati, close to Antahuayla	?
19. plain of Acahuara	Hamlet Huacarpay (?) near lake Muyna or Huacarpay
20. mountain above town of Quispicancha	Village of Quispicanchi
21. mountain Sucanca	Probably on top of (20) (see Zuidema 1981a)

first sunrise, the origin of the world and the establishment of social order after the Flood, *in casu* the establishment of Inca government in Cuzco (Molina 1943; Santacruz Pachacuti 1950:214–216). As seen from Coricancha, Huanacauri is 1° off to the south from the southeast to Villcanota and Tiahuanaco. The discrepancy is minor, but the relationship between town and mountain might also be considered in a different way. According to the origin myth of the Incas, their first ancestor established himself as king of Cuzco in Huanacauri, claiming the territory as seen from here into all directions toward the horizon

(Cavello Valboa [Vol. III]:Chapter 9). He also threw stones into the four directions; not only to confirm his rights of possession (as was done in similar medieval-European and colonial-Spanish acts) but also to shape the mountains on the horizon according to his claim and wishes (Betanzos 1880:Chapter 3). Huanacauri, being the highest mountain bordering the valley of Cuzco (3950 m, some 700 m higher than the city) allows a distant visibility of the horizon and the claim of land was indeed extensive. My further discussion here supports the conclusion that Huanacauri should be taken as the place marked on the direction to Tiahuanaco. Cuzco was "hooked onto" (Zuidema 1981a) this interlocal ceque by way of its local ceque II2a. In this interpretation, then, Coricancha was "off" by 1^0 from the interlocal ceque, not Huanacauri.

The Inca concept that Huanacuari, Villcanota, and Tiahuanaco were aligned in a straight line is confirmed by the ritual use that they made of the part between Huanacauri and Villcanota (Figure 16.5). On the day of the June solstice, when the Inca king himself celebrated this event in a temple north of Cuzco, priests went from Coricancha early in the morning to celebrate the sunrise on Huanacauri. The explicit purpose of this visit on this day and hour is proven by the fact that later, at noon, they would celebrate the sun passing the meridian in Coricancha. Again later, just before sunset, they would celebrate at a place northwest of Cuzco. On the same day other priests started a pilgrimage to Villcanota, where "the sun was born" (Molina 1573/1943: 26, 27). The pilgrimage followed most closely the pattern as described by Murúa, quoted on pages 431–432. The priests rested at 21 stations—9 on the way down and 12 on the way back. The purpose of the pilgrimage was to mark the border of the region that administratively belonged to the city of Cuzco proper (Santacruz Pachacuti 1950:233) and to celebrate the fact that here one king had "invented" the ritual custom of "drinking to the sun" (Guaman Poma 1980:100, 101, 149, 150; Santacruz Pachacuti 1950:231) in reference to the sun's mythical birth.

The interest in water is also stressed by the fact that the priests on their way back from this place, which was also the birthplace of the river Villcanota, would strictly follow the river itself. Besides being the goal of male priests, the Villcanota sanctuary was the end point of a *capac hucha* pilgrimage (Santacruz Pachacuti 1950:233).

The priests would travel through the mountains to Villcanota and follow the river on their way back. Most of the place names for the 21 stations of the pilgrimage route are given in Figure 16.5. Stations 5 and

7, used on the way to the Villcanota sanctuary, and stations 10, 11, and 12, used on the way back, all keep close to the direction of the ceque. Station 6, Collopata, a small hill somewhat off the ceque, identifies a large plain that is included on it. Comment is needed about the last six stations and the first two.

Descriptions of modern rituals of people addressing themselves (i.e., traveling) to a shrine, make clear that traveling to the shrine is done in as direct a way as possible; returning from the shrine, however, is done in a nonritual way—by following the normal road (e.g., Bastien 1978:Chapter 9). The same idea might have been expressed in the Inca distinction of the *capac hucha* traveling in a straight direction, while the Inca accompanied him on a normal road. The priests returning from Villcanota first followed the river and then, at the point where the Huatanay River from Cuzco joins the Villcanota, going up by way of the first. Stations 10 and 12 were still situated in the Villcanota Valley itself and, because they were probably also used on the way down, the straight direction could be kept; however, stations 15–21 were off the *ceque* for the reasons indicated.

Stations 1 and 21, the first and the last, were called *sucanca*, and were horizon points from Cuzco used for astronomical purposes. Station 1 was located on Omoto Mountain (number 2 on the map in Figure 16.5) and station 21 on Quispicancha Mountain (number 20). From Cuzco, the December solstice sunrise was observed behind station 1. The sunrise at station 21 indicated the times (October 30 and February 13) when the sun went through zenith (Zuidema 1981a). The priests, then, did not start their pilgrimage on the *ceque* itself, but turned to it immediately after leaving. Nonetheless, on the same morning when they started, other priests, celebrating the same cosmological event, went to Huanacauri, which was the beginning point of this long-distance ceque.

The empirical data on this pilgrimage are precise and do confirm the intent, expressed by Molina and Murúa, about the straightness of the direction traveled in a ritual way by either *capac hucha* or priests. The very long distance between Huanacauri and Villcanota, and from here to Pucara and Tiahuanaco, might make us hesitant in accepting this conclusion. I should point out, therefore, the fact that any person who travels on foot through the Andes is able to distinguish, on days of clear visibility, high mountains at distances of 100 km and beyond. The distance between Huanacauri and Villcanota, for instance, can be estimated quite exactly using other mountains situated in between or close to the direction. In this case, mountains 5, 6, 8, and 11 (Figure 16.5) probably served the purpose. Using similar methods, directions are still given to travelers by Andean people.

The *ceque* direction from Huanacauri to Villcanota and Tiahuana-co had a paradigmatic value to the Incas; this is the reason why we have so many references to it from myth, ritual, Inca dynastic history, and political ideology. The direction is still vividly alive in spatial concepts of present-day Andean peoples in southern Peru (Condori 1977:19; Urbano 1974). References to other examples of long-distance *ceques* show, however, that it was not the only direction of interest to the Incas.

Technically, observing and calculating a direction over a long distance in the Andes is not difficult. The importance of analyzing this type of Andean data is the fact that an administrative center like Cuzco was intent on registering and classifying methodically this information, refining the technique of measurement, and extending measurements covering the whole extension of the empire. The technique of using sightlines in a local context for the purpose of surveying and mapping irrigation canals and regulating their flow of water is attested for Cuzco (Zuidema 1978b) and was already suggested by Craig and Psuty (1968) for lines in the desert of Pisco. Directions of winds as indicators of different types of weather are still today defined by mountains on the horizon (Barthel 1959; Mariscotti de Görlitz 1978; Zuidema 1976). But these practical uses were no reason in themselves to expand the directions over long distances. Moreover, long-distance *ceques* are probably not the only possible means for an imperial government to organize the input of data on political organization. Rather, the metaphysical concerns with sin, illness, and health affecting a state and its ruler developed this intellectual interest into exact and precise knowledge. In this way the Incas intended to control not only the unknown outside but also the unknown past and future.

The Use of Tables in Andean Culture

The similarity of the *ceque* system to a *quipu* has been observed by different people. It should be pointed out, therefore, that the *ceque* system of Cuzco actually was recorded from a *quipu* (Molina 1573/1943: 75). The organizing principles regulating the very complex structure of the *ceque* system (Zuidema 1964, 1973, 1977b) were in direct correlation to the system that organized this *quipu*. A comparison to the mathematical orders found by M. and R. Ascher (1980, 1981) in *quipus* is therefore of immediate interest. Furthermore, as projected onto the landscape, the *ceque* system of Cuzco—with all the calendrical rituals carried out in relation to the huacas and ceques mentioned by it—was itself a table, like the *quipu* explaining it. The visibility of all the *ceques* from one center meant that a person located in the Temple of the Sun had before him "an open book." The *ceques* organized space as a map and made the inspection of and reflection upon it as possible as if the person were seeing an actual map.

Besides the *quipus* and their application through *ceques* onto the landscape, Andean cultures had many other expressive media to use for representation in tables. Especially important in this respect were textiles and wooden or metal beakers. Let me elaborate on the example of textiles.

Our data on *capa hucha* in general and those on the long-distance *ceque* from Cuzco to Tiahuanaco in particular repeatedly mention textiles and their classificatorial use. Each of the four *suyus* ("provinces") of the empire, each town, and also each *huaca* had its particular type of dress (Albornoz 1967:17, 21, 27). When the Inca transferred a group of people from one part of the country to another, he would give them a new *guaca pacarisca*, "huaca of origin." The consecration of the new *huaca* was carried out by transferring the interest of worship from the original *huaca* to the new one. If the *huaca* was a well of water, this was done by ceremonially carrying water in a beaker from the old *huaca* to the new. If the *huaca* was a stone, the worship was transferred by way of a dress that belonged to the new *huaca*. For this reason, the dress was called *capaccocha* (*capac hucha*). Albornoz warns, therefore, that the "extirpators of the idolatries" should be especially careful to destroy these dresses, not the stones; given the dress, one could easily consecrate a new stone as *huaca* (Albornoz 1967:21, 37).

At least three major rituals describe the use of beakers with holy water for linking Cuzco to the continental divide in Villcanota and to a well on top of the Island of the Sun in Lake Titicaca. But especially data on textiles allow us a careful analysis of Albornoz's statement on the connection between textile, stone (i.e., dry) *huaca*, origin, on the one hand, and *capac hucha, ceque,* and *cachahui* (or *cachahua*), on the other. We must assume that the *huaca*, as stone, itself was related to the inherent idea of "origin." But the property of pattern in a textile gave it expression, a "translation" that related the stone to the people who worshipped it and to the *aclla* as *capac hucha* who traveled to her destination representing the *huaca* and its people.

Various myths and mythical histories structured around the direction to Villcanota, Pucara, and Tiahuanaco concentrate on the connection of stone and textile. After the Flood, the "Creator of all things" in Tiahuanaco "created from clay all the nations, painting on them the dresses that every one of them had to wear." Then he sent them away, underground, in order to come out at the places where they were going to live, so that "each nation was wearing the dress that belonged to their *huaca*." He himself then traveled straight (Betanzos 1551–1880: Chapter 2) to Cuzco and further to Ecuador with two sons. One was called Imaymana Viracocha "Viracocha of all the things (created)" and the other Tocapu Viracocha, "Viracocha of the *tucapu*-designs in ceremonial dresses" (Molina 1943:8–13). The name of the one son, procreated by Viracocha, symbolizes the idea of his creation of "all the things," while that of the other reflects their projection onto textiles. *Tocapus* are rectangular, mostly abstract, patterns of considerable variation that are combined on certain textiles in rows, columns, or diagonals. Examples of colonial art show them also on *queros*, wooden beakers. In the myth of Molina, people were sent out, as *mitimaes*, from Tiahuanaco to their place of destination into all directions; each probably went according to his specified *ceque* (Guaman Poma 1980:84, 85). The reverse was true in the actual government of the Inca empire. *Capac hucha*, as dress and as *aclla*, were sent to the court in Cuzco, together with functionaries as representatives of local governments. They would also take with them the *huaca* that had to stay in Cuzco for a year.

We expect, therefore, that especially textiles, representing local governments were kept in Cuzco. In his drawings Guaman Poma gives us a good idea of the heraldic value of these local distinctions in dresses and of how they established a one-to-one relation between dress and group.

There stand out, however, two types of dress that were used especially at the court in Cuzco. Both types use extensively *tocapu* designs. In the first type the *tocapu* designs occur at the height of the waist and form a V-shaped collar. Other symbols such as crowns, decapitated enemy-heads, and shields with heraldic designs complete the decoration. The overall pattern expresses a centripetal, concentric order, having the person who wears the dress in the center of it. Ethnohistorical data and drawings of Guaman Poma recognize these as royal dresses, worn by the king during the most important state rituals, especially those of the solstices. The iconography had an eminently political, hierarchical character. A particular point of interest of these dresses is that the origin of their overall pattern can be traced back to textiles from the times of the earlier Huari empire.

The other type of dress has the whole surface covered with *tocapu* designs. We know of one splendid example that was found on the Island of the Sun (Bandelier 1910), suggesting its use by the High Priest of the Sun there. The front side is covered with *tocapu* designs and the backside with the pattern of a jaguar skin. Another equally beautiful example has been analyzed by Barthel (1971). All examples of this type show a much more random distribution of the *tocapus*. Barthel, in his example, was able to systematize the designs to a series of 24. Analyzing distributional patterns, frequency of designs, and regular relationships between certain *tocapus*, Barthel concluded that the use of the *tocapus* on this textile conforms best to that of signs in a writing system. It may be that certain frequent signs had a word value. Barthel certainly makes it abundantly clear that these textiles have a highly complex but well thought-out order of *tocapu* designs. But I agree with David Rojas (currently the most serious student of *tocapus* in Peru) that these designs represent, in the first place, heraldic values, corresponding to political groups.

Certain *tocapu* designs are easily recognizable as miniature representations of whole textiles; these textiles are of certain types that actually do exist and that can be found in the drawings of Guaman Poma as representing specific sociopolitical units. Compared to the vertical and concentric political hierarchy found on the first type of textiles, the more random order of the second type might reflect a horizontal concept, expressing an exhaustive priestly interest in *huacas* and their potential power of *hucha*, which might lead to a geographic pattern of actual distribution of *huacas* and their social groups. Both types of dresses were like the ornate cloths that medieval kings sometimes wore over their armor, which had the coat-of-arms of their subject noblemen woven into them. The data that I have brought together on dresses as *capac hucha* and as *ceque* will allow us to study both types of Inca dresses as similar, highly intricate tables of heraldic and political information.

Another use of textiles as tables was for calendrical purposes. Kosok (1965) suggested the importance of an Inca textile as a representation of a calendar, and Zerries (1968) similarly described a Huari textile.

In the first example, rectangular designs count the days of a full year by way of a sidereal lunar sequence; the second example uses circles for the days of the year, integrating a sequence of "weeks" of 10 days (columns of 10 circles) and months of 30 days (3 columns corresponding to 1 of 12 frontal figures like on the gate of Tiahuanaco) to a very intricate sequence of diagonals of circles distinguished by five different colors (Zuidema 1977b). I introduced the theme of systematic knowledge in the Andes with the example of the *hucha quipoc*, who, using *quipu* and *abacus*, registered political entities by way of a spatial distribution of *huacas* and a temporal distribution of calendrical feasts.

We can conclude now that while the abacus of the *hucha quipoc* probably was used for carrying out actual calculations of adding, subtracting, etc., and the quipu was used for registering numbers, textiles were probably the best medium in the Andean context for exposing political, religious, cosmological, and calendrical orders in the form of tables.

Conclusions

Writing has been associated generally with the rise of civilization. Goody tried to build a theory in general anthropological terms on this idea. As his examples derived only from the Old World—where it cannot be assumed that writing in Sumeria, Egypt, Indus, or China developed completely independently from each other—he did not ask the question if writing was a *conditio sine qua non* for the development of rational thought, the use of tables, or a scientific interest. As we cannot use writing as the only criterion for estimating such a development, we can better evaluate Inca culture by placing it in a comparative framework. For instance, Wheatley's (1971) study of the origin of the city and its development as a ceremonial center takes a broader range of factors into account (Wheatley 1971:Chapter 4). The role of Cuzco in the Inca empire and that of earlier capitals in the central Andes fit squarely within this general typology. While a provincial Inca city such as Huanucopampa might conform to his "dispersed ceremonial center," the city of Cuzco reached the stage of "the compact city" (Wheatley 1971:322–323).

The interest of the Incas in *ceques*, which defined exact directions to the borders of the empire, also agrees with a feature generally found in urban ceremonial centers. In his paragraph on "cardinal orientation and axiality," Wheatley offers the following example of:

the ceremonial and administrative complex of Yasódharapura, laid out by Jayavarman VII of Cambodia at the end of the 12th century A.D. The centrally situated temple-mountain, known today as Bayon, consisted essentially of a central quincunx of towers, representing the five peaks of Mount Meru, axis of the world, surrounded by forty-nine smaller towers, each of which represented a province of the empire. According to Paul Mus's elucidation of the symbolism of this structure, the chapels below the smaller towers housed statues of apotheosized princes and local gods, connected with the provinces of the empire, so that the Bayon as a whole constituted a pantheon of the personal and regional cults practised in the various parts of the kingdom. By thus assembling them at the sacred axis of Kambujadesa, the point where it was possible to effect an ontological passage between the worlds so that the royal power was continually replenished by divine grace from on high, Jayavarman brought these potentially competitive forces under his own control."

Jayavarman had "his own face, in the likeness of Vajradhara carved on each of the four sides of each of the fifty-four towers of the Bayon, (thereby) ensuring the projection of divine power, of which he was the transmitter, to the four quarters of his kingdom [Wheatley 1971:432, 434].

We do not know if in Cambodia a specific relationship was sought between capital and provincial towns in terms of degrees of the compass. Bringing competitive forces under control was, however, much like the interest of the Incas, where the concept of *hucha* led to the establishment of the *ceque* system.

Even though Andean culture and that of the Yoruba are the only ones mentioned by Wheatley that did not have writing, the Incas were not inhibited in developing a scientific curiosity. Their curiosity resulted in a state calendar that completely met the demands of a bureaucracy equal to that of other kingdoms or empires.

As the ability of the Incas in extending straight directions beyond the horizon has been an essential part in my argument, I would like to contrast my conclusions to the opinions of McCluskey (1977) as expressed in his study of Hopi astronomy. Given his interest as a historian of science, McCluskey found in the Hopi an ideal test case for studying the extent to which their calendar was based on actual and precise astronomical observation. A chant recorded at Oraibi, in 1901, refers to exact information on where the sun rises or sets as the plants are planted and develop. The Hopi calendar integrates the celebration of festivals based on solar observations, and observations of a new moon. Combining an analysis of the festivals with that of the list of recorded dates in terms of the Western calendar, McCluskey admirably solves his well-defined problem. In the local context of a village, the Hopi solve an intricate problem of solar-lunar integration in a way similar to the Incas.

McCluskey then concludes by explaining why the Hopi calendar should be considered to be based upon prescientific astronomy. "First," he says (1977:190, 191), "it is directed almost entirely toward practical ends . . . as it regulates religious festivals explicitly concerned with the success of crops. . . . Secondly, the two major conceptual constructs employed by the Hopi, the four directions and the cycle of the year, are not consciously expressed in theoretical terms, but in the theological terms of Sacred Space and Sacred Time." We can question McCluskey's concept of "sacred" and why this should not be considered as a conscious expression in theoretical terms of "space" and "time." Whatever "sacred" means, it is an abstract construct that uses empirically observed data on the relationship between sun, moon, and planting times. But, accepting his criteria for the moment, we might try to define the type of Inca astonomical and calendrical interest.

We can choose four properties of the *ceque* system to define its specific character:

1. The statement of chroniclers about the use of the *ceque* system and its *quipu* as a calendrical computing device. This is confirmed by two facts: (*a*) *ceques* as sightlines do not go only to sunrise and sunset points, but into all directions, and (*b*) the numbers represented by the *ceques* and the *huacas* on *ceques* include calendrical information (Zuidema 1977a: 241–250, 1982a,b).

2. The cosmological concepts of *hucha, cama, ceque,* etc. and their derivations, which relate to specific bureaucratic and calendrical notions of order in space and time, "consciously expressed in theoretical terms."

3. The fact that *ceques* go as sightlines not just to the immediate horizon but extend beyond it, demonstrating that they are not limited to a practical, empirical purpose in one locality. They also express a more abstract interest beyond the restriction of local space and time.

4. The integration of local calendars into a state calendar. This state calendar is obtained by the observation of astronomical phenomena that are not dependent on local agricultural cycles. I will elaborate on this point as a confirmation of the third.

The argument is based on the results of fieldwork carried out by Aveni and myself (Zuidema 1981a). The observation of the *sucanca* on the local ceque IIb defined sunset on the days when the sun goes through nadir. This observation was obtained by reversing the observation from this *sucanca* towards sunrise on the days when the sun goes through the zenith. This point was defined by another *huaca,* to the east, also called *sucanca.* This second *sucanca* was discussed as the last *huaca* in relation to the pilgrimage that defined the interlocal ceque to Villcanota and Tiahuanaco. Although carried out during the June solstice, the pilgrimage started from the *sucanca* that defined sunrise during the December solstice and ended at the *sucanca* that defined sunrise during passage of the zenith. The dates of the latter event, October 30 and February 13, are only valid for the latitude of Cuzco. We know that the Incas in Titicaca and Tiahuanaco measured the local times of zenith passage (November 6 and February 6) and that these times had a particular significance to them in terms of their own local calendar, because they divide the year in eight almost equal parts. I conclude therefore that the pilgrimage was a conscious effort to integrate "local Cuzco time" to "interlocal Tiahuanaco time." While

Cuzco has a latitude of 13½° south of the equator and Tiahuanaco one of 16½°, we know that the Incas measured passage of the zenith of the sun in Huanucopampa, at a latitude of 10°, again at other times of the year. We can give credence, then, to the chroniclers who state that one of the reasons of the Inca conquest towards Ecuador was their interest and cosmological concern to observe an "ideal" zenith passage: that is, to find the place where the times of the equinoxes and zenith passages coincide, and where the sun will go straight up and down. This occurs, of course, close to the place where the Incas founded their last provincial capital, Quito.

With these criteria we can define a hypothesis of a theoretical astronomical interest on the part of the Incas. Their goal was the integration of local calendars into a state calendar. The interest was focused not on the local relationships of calendar and agricultural needs but on the knowledge that despite the observation of the solstices and of the lunar cycle, the times of zenith passage are not everywhere the same. Interlocal *ceques*, such as those from Huanacauri to Tiahuanaco, were instrumental in codifying this knowledge. The hypothesis defines an interest that is more than "prescientific." We can measure the scientific accomplishment of the Incas against that of other American calendars, such as the Hopi, whose existence go back to times before direct contact of America with Europe in the sixteenth century.

This is as far as we can go if we do not want to make an ethnocentric use of the terms "prescientific" and "scientific." But McCluskey goes far beyond this necessary restriction. To his second conclusion he adds the following two remarks:

> Related to this absence of theory is the absence of continuous quantification, with the counting of the passage of a specific number of days or nights (seldom exceeding 16) substituting for the measurement of duration in time and with observation against discrete landmarks substituting for the measurement of position in space.

The sting is in the second remark. It refers to the introduction of his conclusions where he says, "Despite its complexity Hopi astronomy had an entirely different orientation then the scientific astronomy of the Greek or Babylonians." What he means by this was stated already at the outset in his article:

> The use of horizon observations as a means of regulating the calendar is best adapted to a sedentary society that has the opportunity to identify suitable local landmarks denoting the seasons of the year or to erect markers for this purpose. Nomadic or cosmopolitan societies, on the other hand, would tend to use an astronomical sys-

tem that is valid over an extended geographic area, hence the concern of the Greek and the Egyptians with heliacal risings of stars as a means for regulating the calendar. Since the calendar of an expanding society is almost certain to be portable, it is not likely to be based upon horizon observations.

McCluskey seems to assume that a culture has a free choice among different astronomical systems according to its sociological needs. He does not consider that the direction of intellectual development is conditioned by certain historical constraints. As his judgment from the Graeco-Roman (and by implication from the modern Western) point-of-view applies to the Inca case, as it does to the Hopi one, we observe that the Incas had an expanding society, strongly cosmopolitan in its practices of herding, economic redistribution, warfare, and resettlement of entire populations. In astronomy they combined horizon observation with an extensive knowledge of heliacal risings, settings, and midnight culminations of stars (Zuidema and Urton 1976). They even had certain notions about position in space (Urton 1981; Zuidema 1982a,b). But their portable calendar was based on expanding the notion of horizon observation, not on the other notions.

The data completely belie McCluskey's assumptions and expose their fallacies. The example of societies in the Middle East and the Mediterranean that expanded through empire building demonstrates a historical, not a logical or even necessary, connection to an astronomy based on the use of the ecliptic. Andean astronomical knowledge expanded by using the notion of long-distance *ceque.* "Scientific" was the ability to do this.

This chapter is a response to, and a reflection upon, the original subtitle of the conference for which it was written: "Historical Consciousness of the Incas and Aztecs, 1400–1800." I dealt here with the pre-Spanish part of this period in the Andes.

Elsewhere I have pointed out (Zuidema 1978b) the methodological difficulties of studying Inca history, where no historical records exist and where the concept of Inca dynasty, as the chroniclers described it, was heavily influenced by European dynastic concepts. The overriding Andean interest was in mummy worship; it expressed political and hierarchical concerns, not those of dynasty. But all data on the pre-Spanish past are known through the European construct of such a dynasty. They need, therefore, to be checked very critically against data that do not derive from such a Western historical model. In order to understand "consciousness" at the level where "historical consciousness" of the Inca state is thought to be—that is, primarily at the imperial court of the Inca kings—we have first to study the pre-Spanish concepts of space and time.

The purpose of this chapter was to bring to the fore some of the most salient examples of these concepts. They played an essential role in the building up of an Inca state bureaucracy, which influenced sociopolitical systems on all levels and in all parts of the empire. But only in Cuzco can we study, with enough technical detail, their use in intricate systems of spatial and calendrical order. These systems confirm that rational thought, the use of tables (in the form of *quipus*, abacus, and textiles), a developing scientific interest, and the ability to inspect and reflect played a role here no less then in any other comparable civilization of the world. They give a glimpse of the type of consciousness that existed in the Inca world.

Acknowledgments

This chapter is part of the research on Inca astronomy and the Inca calendar that I have conducted since 1973 with grants from the National Science Foundation, the Social Science Research Council, the American Council of Learned Societies, and the University of Illinois. Together with A. F. Aveni, I had support from Organization Earthwatch. Substantial rewriting was done during 1980–1981 with the help of a Guggenheim fellowship. I thank all these institutions for their moral and financial support.

References

Agustinos
    1952   Religion en Huamachuco [1557]. *Los pequeños grandes libros de Historia Americana* (Serie 1, Vol. 17), Director, Francisco A. Loayza. Lima: Librería e Imprenta D. Miranda.
Albornoz
    1967   Un inédit de Cristobal de Albornoz: La instrucción para descubrir todas las guacas del Piru y sus camayos y haziendas. *Journal de la Société des Américanistes* **56.**
Alcaya, Diego Felipe de
    1961   Relación cierta . . . In *Cronistas Cruceños del Alto Peru Virreinal,* edited by H. Sanabria Fernandez. Santacruz de la Sierra, Bolivia: Publicaciones de la Universidad Gabriel René: Moreno. Pp. 47–68.
Anonymous
    1951   Vocabulario y phrasis en la lengua general de los indios del Perú, llamada Quichua [1586] Edited by G. Escobar Risco. Lima: Universidad Nacional Mayor de San Marcos.
Ascher, Marcia, and Robert Ascher
    1957   The quipu as a visible language. *Visible Language* **9**(4).
    1980   *Code of the quipu data book.* Ann Arbor, Michigan: University Microfilm International.
    1981   Code of the Quipu: A study in media, mathematics, and culture. Ann Arbor: University fo Michigan Press.

Aveni, A. F. (editor)
1977   *Native American astronomy.* Austin: University of Texas Press.
Aveni, A. F.
1981   Horizon astronomy in Incaic Cuzco. In *Archaeoastronomy in the Americas,*
        edited by R. A. Williamson. Los Altos, California: Ballena Press/Center for
        Archaeoastronomy Cooperative Publication. Pp. 305–318.
Avila, Francisco de
1967   *Francisco de Avila* [1608], translated by H. Trimborn. Berlin: Gebr. Mann
        Verlag.
Bandelier, Adolph F.
1910   *The islands of Titicaca and Koati.* New York: The Hispanic Society of
        America.
Barthel, Thomas S.
1959   Ein Frühlingsfest der Atacameños. Zeitschrift Für Ethnologie **84**(1):25–45.
1971   Viracochas Prunkgewand. *Tribus* **20**:63–124.
Bastien, Joseph W.
1978   *Mountain of the condor: metaphor and ritual in an Andean ayllu.* St. Paul:
        West Publishing.
Betanzos, Juan de
1880   Suma y Narración de los Incas . . . [1551]. *Biblioteca Hispano-Ultramarina*
        (Vol. 5). Madrid: Imprenta de Manuel G. Hernández.
Cabello Valboa, Miguel
1951   *Miscelanea Antártica* [1586]. Lima: Universidad nacional mayor de San
        Marcos.
Condori Mamani
1977   Gregorio Condori Mamani, autobiografía: biblioteca de la tradición oral An-
        dina (Vol. 2), edited by R. Valderrama Fernandes and Carmen Escalante
        Gutierrez. Cuzco: Centro de Estudios Rurales Andinos "Bartolomé de las
        Casas."
Cieza de León, Pedro de
1967   El señorío de los Incas [1551]. *Fuentes e investigaciones para la historia del
        Peru.* Lima: Instituto de Estudios Peruanos.
Cobo, Bernabé
1956   Historia del Nuevo Mundo [1653]. Madrid: Biblioteca de Autores Españoles.
Craig, Alan K., and Norbert P. Psuty
1968   *The Paracas papers: studies in marine desert ecology* (Vol. 1, No. 2). Boca
        Raton: Florida Atlantic University.
Duviols, Pierre
1967   Un inédit de Cristobal de Albornoz: La instrucción para descubrir todas las
        guacas del Piru y sus camayos y haziendas. *Journal de la Société des Améri-
        canistes* **56.**
1976   La Capaccocha. *Allpanchis* **9.**
1978   Camaquen upani: un concept animiste des anciens Péruviens. In *Ame-
        rikanistische Studien,* edited by R. Hartmann and U. Oberem. St. Augustin:
        Festschrift für Hermann Trimborn.
Gasparini, Graziano, and Luise Margolies
1977   *Arquitectura Inka.* Caracas: Centro de Investigaciones Históricas y Estéticas,
        Facultad de Arquitectura y Urbanismo, Universidad Central de Venezuela.
Gonzalez Holguín, Diego
1952   *Vocabulario de la lengua general de todo el Peru llamada lengua Qquichua o
        del Inca* [1608]. Lima: Imprenta Santa Maria.

Goody, Jack
1977 The domestication of the savage mind. London and New York: Cambridge University Press.

Guaman Poma de Ayala, Felipe
1980 El primer nueva corónica y buen gobierno [1615], edited by J. V. Murra and R. Adorno. Mexico, D.F.: Siglo Veintiuno.

Hartung, Horst
1971 *Die Zeremonialzentren der Maya.* Graz: Akademische Druck und Verlaganstalt.

Hawkins, Gerald S.
1974 *Prehistoric desert markings in Peru.* National Geographic Society research reports, 1967 Projects. Washington, D.C.: National Geographic Society. Washington, D.C. Pp. 117–144.

Kosok, P.
1965 *Life, land and water in ancient Peru.* New York: Long Island University Press.

Mariscotti de Görlitz, Ana María
1978 *Pachamama Santa Tierra.* Berlin: Gebr. Mann. Verlag.

Martinez, A. Gabriel.
1976 El sistema de los uywiris en Isluga. In *Homenaje al Dr. Gustavo le Paige.* Antofagasta, Chile: S. I. Universidad del Norte.

McCluskey, S.
1977 The astronomy of the Hopi Indians. *Journal for the History of Astronomy* **8**:174–195.

Métraux, Alfred
1934 Contribution au folklore Andin. *Journal de la Société des Américanistes* **26**:67–102.

1967 Les Indiens Uro-Cipaya de Carangas [1935]. *Journal de la Société des Américanistes* **27**:111–128, 325–415. (Reprinted in part in *Religions et magies indiennes d'Amérique du Sud.* Paris: Gallimard.)

Molina, Cristobal de
1943 Relación de las fábulas y ritos de los Incas [1573]. *Los pequeños grandes libros de historia Americana,* serie 1. (Vol. IV). Lima: Lib. e Imprenta D. Miranda.

Murra, John V.
1975 Las etno-categorías de un khipu estatal [1973]. In *Formaciones economicas y politicas del mundo Andino.* Lima: Instituto de Estudios Peruanos.

Murúa, Martín de
1962 Historia general del Perú [1613]. Colección Joyas Bibliograficas. Bibliotheca Americana Vetus (2 vols.). Madrid: Instituto Gonzalo Fernández de Oviedo.

Polo de Ondegardo, Juan
1917 Del linage de los Ingas y como conquistaron. Coleccion de libros y documentos referentes a la historia del Peru, serie 1, (Vol. 4), Lima, pp. 95–138.

Porras Barrenechea, R. (editor)
1961 Acta de la fundacion del Cuzco [23 de Marzo 1534]. In *Antologia del Cuzco.* Lima: Liberia Internacional del Peru. Pp. 77–85.

Radicati di Primeglio, Carlos
1965 La "seriación" como posible clave para descifrar los quipus extra-numerales. *Documenta* **4**:112–215.

1979 El sistema contable de los Incas. Lima: Studium.

Ramos Gavilán, Fray Alonso
1976 Historia de Nuestra Señora de Copacabana [1621]. La Paz: Cámara Nacional de Comercio, Cámara Nacional de Indústrias.

Reiche, María
1968   *Mystery on the desert.* Stuttgart: Offizindruck AG.
Rostworowski de Diez Canseco, María
1960   Pesos y medidas en el Perú pre-hispánico. Lima: Imprenta Minerva.
1970   Etnohistoria de un valle costeño durante et Tahuantinsuyu. *Revista del Museo Nacional (Lima)* **35.**
1978   *Mediciones y computos en el antiguo Peru.* Valladolid: Cuadernos Prehispanicos.
Santacruz Pachacuti Yamqui Salcamaygua, Joan de
1950   Relación de antigüedades deste reyno del Piru [approximately 1613]. Reproducción de la edición Marcos Jimenez de la Espada. In *Tres relaciones de antigüedades peruanas.* Asunción del Paraguay: Editorial Guarania. Pp. 207–281.
Santo Tomás, Domingo de
1951   Lexicon, o vocabulario de la lengua general del Peru [1560]. Facsimil edition by Raul Porras Barrenechea. Lima: Universidad Nacional Mayor de San Marcos.
Sarmiento de Gamboa, Pedro
1947   *Historia de los Incas* [1572]. Buenos Aires: Emece.
Taylor, Gerald
1974–1976   *Camay, Camac* et *Camasca* dans le manuscrit Quechua de Huarochiri. *Journal de la Société des Américanistes* **63:**231–244.
Trimborn, Hermann
1959   *Archäologische Studien in den Kordilleren Boliviens* (Baessler-Archiv, Neue Folge, Beiheft 2). Berlin: Dietrich Reimer Verlag.
Urbano, H. O.
1974   Le temps et l'espace chez les paysans des Andes péruviennes. *Boletín del Instituto Francés de Estudios Andinos* **3**(3).
Urton, Gary
1981   *At the crossroads of the earth and the sky: an Andean cosmology.* Austin: University of Texas Press.
Valderrama Fernandez, Ricardo, and Carmen Escalante Gutierrez
1977   *Gregorio Condori Mamani, Autobiografía: Biblioteca de la Tradición Oral Andina* (Vol. 2). Cuzco: Centro de Estudios Rurales Andinos "Bartolomé de las Casas."
Vernant, J. P.
1969   *Mythe et Pensée chez les Grecs.* Paris: Máspero.
1975   *Les origines de la pensée grecque.* Paris: Presses Universitaires de France.
Wachtel, N.
1973   Compte-rendu de Mission en Bolivie. Private edition.
1976   Le système d'irrigation des Chipayas. *INSERM* **63:**87–116.
Wheatley, Paul
1971   *The pivot of the four quarters: a preliminary enquiry into the origins and character of the ancient chinese city.* Chicago: Aldine.
Zerries, O.
1968   *Catalog Mexico-Peru 1968.* Munich: Museum of Anthropology. (no. 630, fig. 91).
Zuidema, R. T.
1964   The ceque system of Cuzco: The social organization of the capital of the Inca. Leiden: E. L. Brill.
1973   La parenté et le culte des ancêtres dans trois communautés péruviennes: un compte-rendu de 1622 par Hernandez Principe. In *Signes et langages des*

Amériques: recherches amérindiennes au Québec (Montreal) **3** (1 - 2):129–145.

1976 Mito, Rito, Calendario y Geografía en el Antiguo Peru. Actes du Congrés International des Américanistes, Congrés du Centenaire, 42nd, 1976. Vol. IV:347–357.

1977a The Inca kinship system: a new theoretical view. In *Andean kinship and marriage* (Special Publication No. 7), edited by R. Bolton and E. Mayer. Washington, D.C.: American Anthropological Association. Pp. 240–281.

1977b The Inca calendar. In *Native American astronomy*, edited by A. F. Aveni. Austin: University of Texas Press. Pp. 219–259.

1978a Shafttombs and the Inca Empire. *Journal of the Steward Anthropological Society* **9** (1–2):133–177.

1978b Lieux sacrés et irrigation: tradition historique, mythes et rituels au Cuzco. In *Annales: economies sociétés civilizations* (Nos. 5–6).

1981a The Inca observation of the solar and lunar passages through zenith and anti-zenith. In *Archaeoastronomy in the americas*, edited by R. A. Williamson. Los Altos, California: Ballena Press/Center for Archaeoastronomy cooperative Publication. Pp. 319–342.

1981b Hierarchy and space in Incaic social organization. *Ethnohistory.*

1982a Catachillay: The role of the Pleiades and of the Southern Cross and α and β Centauri in the calendar of the Incas. In *Ethnoastronomy and Archaeoastronomy in the American tropics*, edited by A. F. Aveni and G. Urton. New York: The New York Academy of Sciences (Volume 385 of the Annals).

1982b The sidereal lunar calendar of the Incas. In *New World Archaeoastronomy*, edited by A. F. Aveni. Cambridge: Cambridge University Press. Pp. 59–107.

Zuidema, R. T., and G. Urton

1976 La constelación de la llama en los Andes Peruanos. *Allpanchis Phuturinga* **9**:59–119.

Afterword

Renato I. Rosaldo

Teaching a joint course on Latin America, George Collier and I strayed far from our research areas in the uplands of Chiapas, Mexico, and northern Luzon, Philippines. Problems of indigenous state formation and the imposition of Spanish colonial rule especially captured our imagination in the classroom and in the end led us to convene a conference on the Incas and Aztecs. Indeed, the conference in part was a response to the arduous task of piecing together lectures on Nuclear America in the period 1200–1800. The quest for books and journals located in far-flung library niches seemed to be a symbolic representation of the barriers separating disciplines, methods, and sources of data that should go together. The usual problems of national boundaries and historical periods were compounded by divisions among archaeologists, ethnohistorians, colonial historians, linguists, and cultural anthropologists. The effort to gain a larger synthetic view of Nuclear America in this period suffered further from the all too frequent inclination of specialists to write for other specialists with little sense that amateurs could be looking on in search of answers or, at any rate, clear formulations of major questions.

Among divisions separating Nuclear Americanists, the Spanish conquest looms as the greatest. From perusing the literature one could almost imagine that continents rather than historical phases separated the Spanish empire from the Inca and Aztec states. In almost equal measure, though, comparisons between Mesoamerica and the Andes have suffered from the demand of area specialists that one must know everything in order to say anything. Surely updated systematic comparisons between the two areas could sharpen old questions and open new ones. Even such a simple procedure as mapping in time and space the spread of empire, the development of key institutions, and the delineation of major transitions could pinpoint fresh problems as well as gaps in knowledge. Juxtaposing such maps, for example, with developmental models of the spread of empire and the imposition of colonial rule could highlight disparities in rates and modes of transformation within and between regions in both Mesoamerica and the Andes.

One set of comparisons in this vein could align Spanish conquests in a temporal series beginning with the reconquest of the Iberian peninsula, moving through Mexico and Peru, and ending in the Philippines. Each conquest in this series built upon its predecessors by borrowing already developed institutions, remolding them, or even inventing new ones through successive confrontations with *indios*. Working within this framework, one could compare, among other things, the nature of indigenous political systems, sources of material gain for colonizers, modes of rewarding loyal followers, the Spanish jural–political administration, notions of legitimate rule, and the sense of religious mission. Such analyses could clarify, for example, the ways in which Philippine colonization both differed and derived from its predecessors. In the Philippines neither *encomiendas* nor *haciendas* played as large a part as they did in Hispanic America. Instead, the lack of substantial mineral wealth plus earlier religious attacks on secular rule over *indios* (as Filipinos were also called) permitted the Church to gain a virtual monopoly over the crown's subjects in the hinterlands. Manila itself became a center more of trade than rule and provided the link via the galleon bearing its name between the Far East and Acapulco.

The story of colonization, however, becomes even more intelligible when told from the vantage point both of subject populations and of their rulers. In the Philippine island world the Spanish encountered rather different social formations from those in Mesoamerica and the Andes. Early reports of this encounter described a hierarchical ordering of social relations divided into rulers, ruled, and slaves. But nobody reported the awe their predecessors had felt before the Incas and Aztecs, whose indigenous states, it seemed, compared favorably with their own. Thus, among the other factors already enumerated, the failure of the Spanish in the Philippines to find polities organized so as to facilitate indirect rule on a large scale in part determined the course of their relatively light-handed colonial regime.

Yet to say that Filipinos provoked less Spanish awe (not to mention ire) than Incas and Aztecs hardly even begins to describe the workings of their political systems. The descriptive categories Spanish writers employed—rulers, ruled, slaves—pose a classic dilemma in confrontations between alien cultures. The Spanish inevitably used their own categories to (mis)interpret the novel social formations they encountered. In addition to blatant category mistakes, their accounts simply did not contain the kinds of data that modern readers require for understanding the nature of rank and power in such societies. Yet these Spanish writings, in the Philippine case as elsewhere, remain the primary source of knowledge about indigenous polities of the time. Even after discovering and perusing fresh sources (such as the *visitas* John Murra so skillfully elucidates), any attempt to use Spanish writings in understanding precolonial indigenous societies must remain incomplete, condemned to gaps in information. Hence our analyses of precolonial social formations become intelligible only when we use theoretical constructs, albeit with caution and tact, for reading between the lines of the partial evidence provided by history.

Selecting apt constructs, of course, requires an accurate appraisal of comparable political systems elsewhere in the world. Surely one can hasten to say that early modern European categories more readily conceal than reveal the political realities they purport to represent. Thus Montaigne's famous ruminations on cannibals and kings and his magnanimous humanitarian gestures equating Inca and Aztec civilizations with those of Europe involve a category mistake more likely to distort than to illuminate other polities. Similarly, a number of modern concepts—including class, the state, bureaucracy, and power in the sense of a monopoly on the legitimate use of violence—should be applied with caution, if at all. Recall the infamous debates of the 1930s concerning whether the Inca state more nearly resembled a totalitarian (often Stalinist) regime or a socialist utopia. Facile, often faddish, analogies have already proven so debilitating that one almost wishes to say the Incas and Aztecs resemble nobody nearly so much as themselves, thereby calling an end to comparisons.

Indeed, finding apt comparisons for systems of rank and power in chiefdoms and precapitalist state formations proves challenging precisely because their contours elsewhere have been surveyed more sporadically than systematically. Within anthropology one thinks of Louis Dumont on Homo Hierarchicus in South Asia, Lloyd Fallers on Bantu bureaucracies, Clifford Geertz on the Balinese theater state, Irving Goldman on rank in Polynesia, and perhaps a handful of others. But such exemplary studies remain few and far between, more a source of suggestive hypotheses than refined theory. At the same time, aptly chosen comparisons could prove fertile in suggesting productive questions for analysis. From this perspective, studying the Incas and Aztecs becomes part of the wider theoretical task of understanding rank and power in precapitalist polities.

Consider, for example, Craig Morris's archaeological discovery that stone structures along Inca roadways housed containers for food and drink rather than the military garrisons or administrative officials envisioned by those who saw the Inca state as an imperial machine run on brute force and tight bureaucratic control. This certainly weakens the totalitarian state hypothesis. Indeed one hopes that in general the question (often posed implicitly) of why the Incas and Aztecs never developed modern state mechanisms, including foremost among other things large standing armies and administrative bureaucracies, can finally be laid to rest. This unproductive line of questioning can only be speculative and teleological.

The development of the Inca and Aztec states has been best elucidated by asking what they evolved *from* rather than what they were moving *toward*. One can readily sketch certain features of local ranking systems that preceded indigenous state formations. High rank involved the capacity to amass and the obligation to give away large amounts of food and drink. In a circular process where one thing implied another, the higher one's status the more one gave, and the more one gave the greater one's following. Thus, these polities inextricably fused one's social rank, the capacity and the obligation to give feasts, and certain rights in a following of people. Because ceremonial feasts had a sacred character, rank and religion also became close associates. Thus the sense in which the Inca Empire took over forms of social rank that previously operated only on more local levels.

What Morris has discovered indicates both formal continuity in ceremonial feast-giving and a marked shift in its local consequences. When high-ranking Incas used these stone structures to give ceremonial feasts, they did so not for the local community as a whole but for its elite. Entertaining local elites involved securing both their loyalty and their capacity to marshal labor as a form of state tribute. If redistributive mechanisms formerly included the entire local community (to telescope a vastly more protracted process), they now redefined social relations along two new vectors: One deepened, indeed recast, the boundary between local elite and nonelite, and the other siphoned labor and its products beyond local social and territorial limits. Through this process the world became wider and more stratified.

The recent trend toward studying sub-imperial units rather than the centers of rule promises to sharpen these analyses in a number of ways. To begin, they highlight the gap between how the Incas and

Aztecs (and indeed the Spanish) depicted monolithic empire from the capitals and how they implemented it in the provinces. For this entire period of empire—Inca, Aztec, and Spanish—the guiding principle seems to have been: Use indirect rule whenever possible. One can infer that rulers on the whole preferred subject populations that could both provide tribute to the state and feed, clothe, house, and govern themselves. The ideal, in other words, was a self-sufficient peasantry capable of producing a certain amount of surplus (whether in labor or kind).

Surely modes of incorporating local systems into encompassing state formations displayed considerable variation. Especially under systems of indirect rule, continuities of social form could mask deep discontinuities in social relations, as already shown for ceremonial feasting and as suggested by Karen Spalding's vigorous rejection of the dual economy model for the colonial era. Studies particularly strategic from this perspective have concentrated on local elites and the forces set in motion to alter their positions through the imposition of indirect rule. Whereas, once upon a time, local elites pooled and redistributed goods and services among a group of followers, with the coming of empire they found themselves compelled to bend the old system, all the while appearing to change nothing. Januslike, local leaders faced in two directions, struggling to maintain an old following, while milking them to provide tribute for a new elite. In the meantime their position shifted from the top to the middle, from leader to broker. Investigations of the movement from big-man to middleman, including the historical vicissitudes of local elites, could provide a point of departure for understanding key transitions in Nuclear America during the period of 1200–1800.

Seen from the perspective of local systems, this volume suggests a tentative generalization about these processes of incorporation into the imperial state. The most developed local political economies proved the most likely, on the one hand, to survive imperial rule with their traditional social forms intact. On the other hand, they most easily lent themselves to subjugation from above probably because their very unification provided a single organizing node to capture as contrasted with the myriad foci of less centralized polities. Arguably, less developed local systems could not be assimilated as such and had to be destroyed and reconstructed before coming under the sway of imperial rule and the exaction of tribute. Such at any rate appears to be the moral of Franklin Pease's chapter, which contrasts the fates of the Lupacas and the Chachapoyas, or the enduring ethnic kingdom versus the more shadowy people of the tropical forest frontier.

Overall, my concern is to keep the larger view in mind. Detailed studies, like those included here, must be balanced by periodic attempts at synthesis: the constant mapping and remapping, as I already suggested, of the spread of empire in order to better delineate major changes. The problem of significant change, of course, can be explored productively through a number of topics here passed over in silence. Litigation, for example, both in its immediate results and long-term unintended consequences, has provided incisive analyses of shifting interethnic relations during the colonial era. Both before and after the Spanish conquest religious cosmologies and forms of state power appear intimately related, if relatively understudied. Thus, aside from the shifting fortunes of local elites, a number of other substantive topics lend themselves to studying relations to inequality. How are relations of inequality conceived, exercised in practice, and transformed through time? Such central questions, explicitly formulated, can sharpen further investigations of rank and power among the Incas and Aztecs from the period of state formation through major transitions in imperial rule to key shifts under the colonial regime.

Index

A

Aclla, see Chosen women
Administrative centers, 155–156
  ceremonial functions, 162
  facilities, 157, 158
  Inca empire, 14
  military force, 160
  military supplies, 158
  residences, 163
Administrative records, *see* Source
  materials
Agriculture, 25
  in colonies, 218
  crops, 246, 248, 250
  tools, 26
  Valley of Mexico, 45
Animals, domestic, 26
Appeal, *see* Litigation, appeal
Aristocracy, *see* Elites
Articulation
  Canta, 246–248
  Caraveli, 248–249
  Chupaychu, 240–246
  ethnic groups, 175, 190, 237–238
  levels, 182, 186
  Lupaca, 254–256
  marginal groups, 188–189
  state and local, 155, 167, 168,
    238
  state and region, 165–168
  varieties, 173, 184–190
Artisans, 25, 27, 29, 31, 251; *see also*
  Camayos
  decimal administration, 130

B

Bilingualism
  elites', 369
  Nahuatl speakers', 414
Black Legend, 289–290, 322
Books, and evangelization, 400
Brokers, and litigation, 273
Bureaucracy, *see* Imperial administration

C

Calendars, 30, 421, 425–426, 448,
  450–451
Calpulli, 29, 30
Cama, see Moral concepts, order
Camayos, 102–105; *see also yanaconas*,
  104
  country of origin, 102–103
  as garrisons, 105
  occupational specialists, 102
  resettled near Cuzco, 104
  resettlement, 103
  self-supporting, 103
  after Spanish conquest, 111
  specialized occupations, 96
Capitalism, *see* Economy, colonial, capitalist versus precapitalist

A

Astronomy, 425, 434–435, 438–439, 444,
  450–453
Ayllu, 29, 30
  and colonial levies, 302
  decimal administration, 129–131
Azcapotzalco, fall, 55

Census
  basis for tribute, 328–329
  categories, 127
  revision to avoid levies, 300–305
Ceque system, 430–431, 434–435
  and cult of water, 428
  in imperial administration, 421,
    449–450
  long-distance, 439–445, 451
  relation to quipu, 445–446, 451
  straightness, 434–439, 443–444
  variations, 434
Ceremony, see Ritual
Chachapoyas, 188–190
Chicha, 166
Chichimecs, migration, 46
Chimor, 186–188
  conquest by Inca, 187
Chinampas, 45
Chosen women, 31, 107–108, 247, 251,
    429–431
  awarded as brides, 108
Christianity
  acceptance, 386
  and corporate consciousness, 390–391
  imposition, 268
  native interpretations, 382
  responses, 345–363
  Patron saints, 386–387
Church jurisdiction, 269
Cihuacoatl, see Succession, and role of
    stand-in
City states
  basic Mesoamerican units, 6, 9
  development, 45
  early autonomy, 45
  early Mexican development, 46–48
  expansion, 54
  rivalry, 55
  subordination, 56
  Valley of Mexico, 44; see also Sub-
    imperial organization
Civilizations
  comparisons, 1, 23–39, 459–464
  typologies, 2, 4
Class, see Stratification
Clothing, see also Textiles; Weaving
  given to camayos by Inca, 102
  required of Inca subjects, 111

Coca, 252–253
  produced by camayos, 104
Cochabamba, 199–222
  colonization by Inca, 199–222
Codices, 399
Coercion, see Power, coercive
Colonial administration
  corruption, 299
  crown policy, 268
  financed by tribute, 329–330
  Indians, 267
  reforms by Toledo, 292–293
  viewed by Indians, 388–390
Colonies, ethnic composition, 219
Colonization, 179–180, 219
  in empires, 36
  Inca, 15, 199–222
  large-scale, 202
  Spanish, 460
  variations, 217–222
Commerce, see Economy, circulation;
    see also Repartimiento de
    mercancías
Commoners, 28
Communal labor, see Labor, communal
Communications, 153, 155–156
Comparisons
  Aztec and Inca, 1, 24–39
  Mesoamerican and Andean civiliza-
    tion, 23–24, 459–464
Concepts, see also Moral concepts; Nu-
    merical concepts; Quadripartite con-
    cepts; Spatial concepts; Status;
    Tabular concepts; Temporal
    concepts
  decimal, see Decimal administration
  for ethnicity, 210
  history, see Historical consciousness
  for jurisdiction, 211
  land, 205–206
  mathematical, 449
  measurement, 423
  pictographic, 398
  textiles as tables, 446–449
  use of tables, 445–449
Confession, see Moral concepts,
    confession
Conquest
  chaos, 111

continuities, 10
in empires, 36
impact, 10
legitimation, 183
Spanish, 460
Continuities
allowed by Nahuatl literacy, 411
despite conquest, 221–222
native thought, 10
religion, 348–349, 356, 360–362
sub-imperial, 9–10, 185–186, 257
Conversion, 345
authenticity, 346–350
forced, 357–358
incomplete, 355–356
pretended, 358–360
types, 349–350
versus Christianization, 346, 353
Corporate consciousness, 367–393
and churches, 390–391
source materials, 370–375
symbols of primordiality, 376–386
Corporate groups, 29–31
Corporate ruling class
coalitions, 72
development, 48–54, 63, 66, 70
expansion, 72
ideology, 67, 75, 77
segmentation, 82
succession, *see* Succession
Toltec descent, 48–49, 53, 65
usurpation, 69
Cosmology, 439–445, 451
persistence, 10
Costume, *see* Textiles
Crafts, *see* Artisans
Criminal law, applied to Indians, 276–277
Crops, *see* Agriculture, crops
Cultural unification, Inca, *see* Inca cultural unification
Curacas
claiming royal status, 112
decimal administration, 144
installed by Inca, 188
labor service, 120
mita, 295
rank in decimal administration, 124
rivalries, 308, 309
after Spanish conquest, 121, 142–143

Custom
before the law, 275
changes under colonial rule, 268–279, 327
legal standing, 267
preserved by colonial policy, 327

D

Decimal administration, 16, 119–147, 168, 237, 240, 425
censuses, 124
documentation, 120
Lupaca, 133–135
officers, 124
origins, 121
prevalence, 126
ranks, 125
succession, 125
tributaries, 123
Demographic decline, and levies, 304
Demographic growth, and formation of empire, 47
Valley of Mexico, 44–45
Descent, 30
corporate groups, 29
Dress, *see* Textiles
Dual division, 131, 211–213
Andean, 128, 130
Lupaca, 129
preimperial, 134
Dynasties, *see* Corporate ruling class

E

Ecological diversity, *see* Environment
Economic exchange, city-states, 45
Economy, 24–33
circulation, 25–26, 32–33, 37, 45; *see also Repartimiento de mercancías*
Inca versus Aztec, 38
colonial, 321–340
articulation of sectors, 325, 335
capitalist versus precapitalist, 13, 322, 323
circulation of goods, 333–334
circulation of tribute goods, 330
dual versus integral, 321, 323–324, 339

Economy colonial (*continued*)
  limits to growth, 338, 340
  politically organized, 325
  precapitalist, 338
  sectors, 324, 326–327
  political organization, 24, 32, 34
Education, and Inca cultural unification, 95–96
Elites, 28, 30; *see also* Corporate ruling class; *Curacas*; Royalty; Rulers
  colonial factions, 297–299
  colonial natives, 269
  native concepts, 384
  pipiltin, 49
  provincial, 95–96, 124, 135, 142, 144, 165
  subimperial, 16, 121
  surviving Spanish conquest, 142–144
  Toltec descent, 48
Empire
  by conquest, 55
  comparative study, 1–4
  dissolution, 78
  expansion, 51, 72
  formation, 47, 54–56; *see also* Political evolution
  illegitimate, 183
  incorporation of bands, 50
  spatial organization, 432
  subimperial foundations, 8
  utopian, 183
Encomienda distribution, 143
Environment, 26
  altitude, 36
  diversity, 9, 26; *see also* Vertical archipelago
Estate, *see* Stratification, estates
Ethnicity, 30, 367; *see also* Inca cultural identity
  articulation, 4, 7, 175
  Cochabamba, 206–210
  colonies, 181
  corporate groups, 30
  costume, 111
  in empire, 173–190
  evidence for existence, 189
  native concepts, 383
  persistence, 257
  politics under colonial exploitation, 13

  preservation, 94
  schema for, 210
Ethnohistory
  methods, 3, 5
  trends, 1, 4–8, 459, 462–464; *see also* Source materials
Evangelization, *see also* Conversion; Resistance
  accommodations, 351
  forced, 357–358
  and language, 396
  and literacy, 400
  New Spain versus Peru, 347
  response varieties, 348
  use of *linqua franca*, 113
Exploitation
  abetted by litigation, 310
  colonial economy, 325
  by colonial elites, 299
  by *curacas*, 309
  legal mechanisms, 293
  and litigation, 291
  mechanisms, 291; *see also* Labor, forced; Levies
Exports, produced by forced labor, 332

F

Factionalism
  Indians, 308–309
  reinforced by litigation, 310
Family, *see* Household
Federations, bands, 47
Fortifications, 160
  garrisoned by *camayos*, 105
Frontier, northern Mesoamerica, 46

G

Garrisons, 161
Genres, native, 411–412
Government in exile, Inca, 112
Governors, Inca, 143–144
Grammars, unwritten languages, 396
Guard duty, *camayos*, 105

H

Herding, 242
  for Inca, 251

Historical consciousness, 367–393,
    453–454
  Chichimecs, 381–382
  Christianity, 382
  chronology, 390
  of individual colonists, 391
  legends of origin, 376–380
  Mexica, 380–381
  prehispanic era, 375–386
  Spanish conquest, 388
  Spanish King, 386, 389
  Spanish officials, 388–390
  Toltecs, 381
  warfare, 386
Historical records, Nahuatl, 412
History, revision, 69, 112
Household, self-sufficiency, 27, 31
Huacas, see Ritual, huacas
Huamanga, 291, 317–320
Huanuco Pampa, 155, 157–161, 164, 165, 167
Huanuco, labor service, 135–138
Hucha, see Moral concepts, sin
Hydraulic civilization, 17, 24, 38
  Wittfogel, 4, 24, 38

I

Idolatry, see Religion, native, persistence;
    see also Taqui Oncoy movement
Imperial administration, 168–169; see
    also Ceque system; Record keeping
  calendrical, 421
  infrastructure, 153–154, 157
  provinces, 141–144, 155
  and systematic knowledge, 419–454
Imperial authority, provinces, 141–144
Imperial colonization, 202–205
Imperial development, 13–17
  preexisting bases, 12
Imperial organization, 35, 56–58, 153;
    see also Colonization; Conquest;
    Decimal administration
  administration, 35
  complexity, 190
  concepts, 445
  indirect rule, 463
  labor service, 141
  new models, 2
  systematic knowledge, 454
  textiles, 446–449

Inca cultural identity, 93–114
  and camayo status, 105
  chosen women, 108
  creation, 94
  growth in colonial era, 112–114
  rebellion, 112–113
  religion, 108–110
  Spanish colonial policies, 112–114
  yanacona service, 102
Inca cultural unification, 93–110
  education, 95–96
  language, 95–96, 111
  yanacona status, 97–102
Indirect rule, 165, 237–238, 257,
    463–464
Industry, 26
Inheritance, imposed Spanish categories,
    275
Irrigation, 45, 429, 445; see also
    Hydraulic civilization

J

Justice, as exploitation, 311

K

Khipu, see Quipu
Kingship, symbolic role, 73
Kinship
  in Aztec ruling class, 85
  in corporate groups, 30
  and stratification, 30
  Valley of Mexico dynasties, 58

L

Labor
  in colonial economy, 321–322
  communal, 31
  direct exploitation, 306–307
  exchange, 31
  organization, 214
  wage, 335
Labor service, 15, 25, 27, 28, 31, 120; see
    also Mita; Obrajes
  categories, 138
  colonial, 289
  construction, 254
  decimal organization, 136

Labor service (*continued*)
exemptions, 102, 122
forced, 296, 325–326
avoidance, 298
Huanuco, 135–138
to Inca persons, 242
Lupaca, 135, 138–141
military, 161
permanent, 122, 136
provisioning, 215
rewards, 167
rotating, 213
seasonal, 244
under Spanish colonial rule, 113
types and amounts, 136–141, 240–256
Land
alienated by Inca, 238
categories, 205–206
colonial policies, 294
conflicts, 271
corporate, 377–378
cultivated for elites, 215
cultivated for state, 214–215, 248
distribution by Inca, 205
divisions in Cochabamba, 206–210
given to *camayos* by Inca, 102
litigation by Indians, 294
native versus Spanish categories,
270–271
tenure, 25
Language
borrowing, 401, 407
change, 407
Nahuatl clauses, 403, 407
Nahuatl nouns, 402–405
Nahuatl phonology, 403, 405–406
Nahuatl plurals, 403–405
Nahuatl verbs, 403, 406
preconquest, 402
contact, 401
Nahuatl–Spanish, 402–408
decimal administration, 131
diversity and colonization, 396
groups
native concepts, 383–384
organization, 134
and Inca cultural unification, 95–96,
111
loss, Nahuatl, 414

Law
European categories, 265–266
for Indians, 265–267, 283–285
Leaders
appointed by Inca, 110
preserved in Inca provinces, 110
regional, 14
Leadership, 238
hereditary elites, 52
theocratic basis among Aztecs, 51
Legal institutions, social significance,
291–311
Legal reforms, Toledo, 293
Legal tactics, of Indians, 299–305
Legends of origin, *see* Historical
consciousness
Levies
basis of colonial economy, 321,
328–329
in colonial economy, 339; *see also*
*Mita; Repartimiento de mercan-
cías; Tribute*
colonial era, 337
extraction of surplus, 326
Lingua franca
Nahuatl, 395, 408, 410
Quechua, 111, 113
Linguistic unity, central Mexico,
408–409
Literacy, *see also* Nahuatl; Systematic
knowledge
in litigation, 396, 411
preconquest, 397–400
Litigation, 6, 464
accommodation to Indian cases, 274
administrative, 277
appeal, 272–274, 278–279
attorneys for Indians, 282
criminal, 276–277
fees, 273, 280–281
Indian witnesses, 279
by Indians, 6, 265, 290, 292–311
Indians versus Indians, 307–311
informal procedures, 279
labor, 294
land, 294
and literacy, 395, 411
native, 272–285
as politics, 289, 296

by the poor, 281–282
reforms, 277–285
simplification, 278–280
social significance, 291–311
Spanish usage by Indians, 273
strategic, 6
types, 274
Livestock, and Spanish grazing law, 275
Loyalty
holding of hostages, 95
ideological basis, 15
to kingship, 70
and new status in state, 97
provincial, preserved under Inca rule, 110
state, 15
to state, *camayo* status, 105
and state redistribution, 166
Lupaca, 127–144, 185–186, 254–256
administration, 127–144

M

Maps, 374
Markets, 29, 32, 37, 45
production by Indians, 336–337
subsidized by tribute, 330–331; see *also* Economy, circulation
Marriage alliances, dynasties, 52–53, 74–75
Merchants, 29
Migration, see *also* Mitimas
Aztec, 51
forced, 177, 179
return, 180
types, 176–181
Military
arms, 160
development of empire, 14
exaggeration of, 161
organization, 27, 29, 77
supplies, 158
Mining, 240, 246, 255; see *also* Mita
Huancavelica, 305–306
Miserables, jurisdiction for Indians, 266, 284–285
Mita, 113–114, 289, 328, 331–332; see *also* Labor service
colonial, 221, 294–295

diverted from mining, 332
exemptions, 295
levies, 237–257, 300–305
Mitimas, 105–107, 176, 179, 213
antiquity, 199
Cochabamba, 199–222
colonists, 105–106
estimated numbers, 107
ethnic, 110, 202, 220
places of origin, 201–204
provincial administrators, 105, 106
relocated ethnics, 96
spies, 110
supervisory, 214
Mobility, social, 28
Money, 32
Moral concepts
and abstract thought, 425
confession, 428
and imperial organization, 425, 445, 450
order, 426–427, 434
sin, 425–434
Myths of origin, 439–443; see *also* Primordial titles

N

Nahuatl
genres, 411–412
language change, see Language change, Nahuatl
as *lingua franca*, 395, 408, 410
literacy, 395–416
demise, 414–415
place names, 409
poetry, 412
writing, 368, 370–375, 395–416
classical, 396–397
colonial, 397
variations, 401
Native categories, 7; see *also* Corporate consciousness; Ethnicity; Historical consciousness; World view
methods for studying, 7
variations, 368–370
Nepantlism, 353–355
versus syncretism, 354
Nobility, 28, 30; see *also* Elites
native concepts, 384

Nobility of natives, colonial, 269
Notarial records, Nahuatl, 411
Notaries, native, 400
Numerical concepts, 29, 123–124, 126,
   398, 452; see also Decimal; Dual;
   and Quadripartite concepts

O

Obrajes, 297
Officials, local versus regional or royal,
   298
Oracles, Inca realm, 109

P

Paper, 398
Patrons and clients
   encomenderos, 297–298
   Indians, 297–299
Patron saints, see Christianity
Periodization, spanning the conquest, 10,
   459
Pilgrimage, see Ritual, pilgrimage
Poetry, Nahuatl, 412
Political actors, Indians, 291
Political centralization, 17, 33, 37,
   64–65, 70, 83
   dynastic succession, 66
   Inca and Aztec differences, 37–38
   inducements, 74
   succession, 70, 83
Political economy, 37
   Inca and Aztec, 3
Political evolution, 17, 34, 45, 63, 462,
   464
   Aztec, 63–84
   empires, 12
   Inca, 215, 221, 257
   Inca and Aztec, 39
   Mesoamerica, 43–44
Political fragmentation
   Mesoamerica, 36
   Valley of Mexico, 46, 57
Political organization
   comparison, 460–462
   concepts, 460–462
   in empires, 4, 11–13
   instability, 74
   models, 460

systems, 33–36
   territorial integration, 34
   varieties, 460
Population, city-states, 44
Population decline, Chimor, 187
Power
   centralization, 72
   coercive, 16, 182–183, 324
   compliance, 181
   concentration, 67
   consent, 181–182
   diffusion, 72
   diffusion through fraternal succession,
      71
   management by elites, 65
   normative, 15–16, 73–74
   remunerative, 14–16, 74
   shifts under empire, 16
   sources, 66
   state, exaggeration, 237
   types, 14
Precapitalist sectors, articulation, 13
Preimperial organization, 133–134
   enduring, 185–186
Preservation of Indians, crown policies,
   267–268
Primordial titles, 6, 348, 368, 371–375
   kept in towns, 372
   language, 374
   originals, 371–372
   protagonists, 375–386
   rhetoric, 384
   structure and style, 372–373
Private property, Indians, 309–310
Production, 25–6
   commoners, 31
   households, 25, 32
   kin versus market relations, 337
   material factors, 24–25
   social relations, 24
   structures preserved by colonial policy,
      326–327, 338
   units, 31–32
Protector of Indians, 282, 293
Provincial administration, 122
   encomenderos, 143
Provincial elites, 144, 165; see also
      Curacas
   decimal administration, 124, 135
   restrictions, 142

Provincial nobility
  education by Inca, 95
  Inca confirmation, 96
Provincial organization, 129
  Lupaca, 128
  subdivisions, 132–133
Public works, 25–26, 31–33

Q

Quadripartite concepts, 211–213, 244
Quipu, 27, 127–128, 130, 161, 237, 398,
  419, 422–425, 445–446
  categories, 7, 240
  decimal administration, 129
  keepers, 239

R

Rebellion
  Inca policies for preventing, 94
  suppression by Toledo, 113
Reciprocity, traditional, 155, 168
Record keeping, administrative centers,
  7, 162, 398, 423–425; *see also Quipu*
Redistribution, state, 15, 155–156,
  166–167, 169, 174, 215–217, 462
Regional centers, Mexico, 44
Regional culture, 392
Regional organization, 11
  Mexican city-states, 48
Regional variation, 5
Religion; *see also* Christianity; Conversion; Evangelization; *Nepantlism*;
  Ritual
  and dynastic rule, 48
  Inca state, 108–110
  persecuted by Spanish, 114
  persistence, 348–349, 356, 360–362
  political organization, 34
  of provinces under Inca rule, 109
  revitalization, *see Taqui Oncoy*
    movement
  surplus distribution, 33
  syncretism, 354
Repartimiento de mercancías, 328,
  332–338
  legal status, 333
Resettlement
  camayos, 103

Indians, 270
Valley of Mexico, 47
Resistance
  to Christianity, 345–363
  colonial Indians, 7
  covert, 347
  Indian incapacity, 311
  to *mita*, 295
  passive versus active, 360
Ritual; *see also* Religion
  administrative centers, 155, 162
  chicha consumption, 166
  cult of Sun, 439–445, 451–452
  cult of water, 428–429, 432, 443, 446
  feasts, 385
  huacas, 428–438, 446
  pilgrimage, 441, 443–444, 451
  and political loyalty, 166
  in primordial titles, 385–386
  and stratification, 462
  use of textiles, 446–447
Roads, 153, 154–156
  labor for construction, 245
Royalty, *see also* Elites
  claimants after conquest, 111–112
  establishment, 52
  lineages, 30
  religious basis, 48
Rulers, 28, 30
  hereditary, 50
  local, 56–57
  symbolic legitimation, 73

S

Sacrifice, human, 109–110, 256, 428–429
Saya division, *see* Dual division
Schools, *see* Education
Science, *see* Systematic knowledge
Servility, under the Inca, 97
Settlement
  colonial, 269
  Valley of Mexico, 44
Shrines
  Inca state, 108
  labor service, 245
Sight lines, *see Ceque* system
Slavery, 29; *see also* Servility
  colonial, 290
  as criminal penalty, 276

Slavery (*continued*)
  Indians, 271–272
  Spanish categories, 272
Source materials, 3, 5, 174, 178–179,
    184, 200; *see also* Primordial titles;
    Visitas
  administrative records, 120
  biases, 184, 346
  central versus provincial, 420
  confesionarios, 347
  corporate consciousness, 370–375
  ecclesiastical, 347, 352–353
  impact, 2
  Nahuatl, 370–371
  native concepts, 368
  native language, 397
  notarial records, 400–401
  provincial, 239
  questionnaires, 144
  sub-imperial, 3
  written, 7
Spatial concepts, 428, 432–433, 439,
    450–451; *see also Ceque* system
Spiritual conquest, 7
State formation, theories, 64
State generosity, *see* Redistribution, state
State institutions, *see also* Imperial ad-
    ministration; Sub-imperial
    administration
  aggrandized by Inca, 200
  theory versus practice, 5
Status, native concepts, 384
Storehouses, 31, 157–158
Stratification, 3, 28–29, 384
  colonial class change, 338–339
  commoners, 28
  estates, 3, 25, 28
  and governance, 33
  and kinship, 30
  sub-imperial, 4
  Tenochtitlan, 66
Sub-imperial organization, 2, 8, 37, 39,
    462–463
  administration, 163
    by *mitimas*, 105, 106
  Cochabamba, 210
  concepts, 427–428
  continuities, 8–11, 110–111
  enduring, 9–10
  leadership, *see* Elites, sub-imperial

preservation, 12
sources, 5
Succession, 65
  concentration of power, 67
  during interregnum, 78–83
  dynastic, of Aztecs, 68
  election, 76
  filial, 67
  filial to fraternal, 67–68, 70, 83
  fraternal, 67–75
    instability, 74
  Goody, 70, 73, 79
  legitimate, 83
  military leaders, 77
  rivalry, 78–79
  role of stand-in, 78, 79–81, 83
  selection, 75–78
  uncertain, 67, 70, 73, 77
  usurpers, 69
Sun, *see* Ritual, cult of Sun
Supremacy, Aztec, 56
Surplus appropriation, 25
  colonial economy, 325, 328
  by colonial state, 13
  Repartimiento de mercancías, 334
  by state, 32–33
Systematic knowledge
  Andean, 419–454
  with literacy, 422
  without literacy, 419, 422–423, 449

T

Tabular concepts, 445–449
Taqui Oncoy movement, 112–113
Temporal concepts, 28, 180, 390,
    450–451; *see also* Calendars
Tenochtitlan, 63–84
  foundation, 44
  stratification, 66
Teotihuacan, 44
  collapse, 46
Textiles, 31; *see also* Clothing
  and calendars, 448
  as classification, 446–449
  designs, 447–448
  and imperial organization, 446–449
Tlatelolco, foundation, 44
Tlatoani, see Royalty
Toltec empire, decline, 44, 46

Towns
 founding, 387
 imposed polities, 269
 viewed as autochthonous, 369; *see also*
  Primordial titles
Transportation, in colonial economy, 335
Tributaries, hereditary, 123
Tribute, 15, 25, 28, 120, 129; *see also*
  Labor service
 administration, 58–59
 colonial, 328–331
 decimal administration, 121–123
 exemptions, 304, 328
 expansion of empire, 72
 Huamanga, 317–320
 in kind, 238–239, 245, 248, 252
 in kind versus in specie, 329
 levies, 300–305
 redistribution, 57
 subjugated city-states, 56
 Valley of Mexico, 58–59
Triple Alliance, formation, 56

V

Variation, sub-imperial, 4
Vertical archipelago, 11, 176, 201; *see
 also* Colonies
 Uru, 204
Visitas, 7, 120, 154, 239–257

W

Warehouses, *see* Storehouses
Warfare

native concepts, 386
 political organization, 34
 Valley of Mexico, 47
Water, *see* Ritual, cult of water
Weaving, 244, 248, 256; *see also* Textiles
Wittfogel, *see* Hydraulic civilization,
  Wittfogel
World view
 native elites', 368–369
 ordinary Indians', 369
Writing, 27; *see also* Codices; Nahuatl
  writing
 colonial era, 400–408
 Nahuatl pictorial conventions, 413
 phonetic, 398–399
 syllabic, 399

Y

Yanaconas, 96–102, 220
 attached to temples, 101
 civic status, 96
 exempt from *curaca* authority, 99
 of Guayna Capac, 99–100
 hereditary status, 100
 high administrative posts, 99–101
 honored retainers, 98–100
 numbers, 101
 personal service to Spanish, 98
 retainers to Inca governors, 101
 retainers to Inca ruler, 101
 after Spanish conquest, 111

STUDIES IN ANTHROPOLOGY

Under the Consulting Editorship of E. A. Hammel,
UNIVERSITY OF CALIFORNIA, BERKELEY

Andrei Simić, THE PEASANT URBANITES: A Study of Rural-Urban Mobility in Serbia

John U. Ogbu, THE NEXT GENERATION: An Ethnography of Education in an Urban Neighborhood

Bennett Dyke and Jean Walters MacCluer (Eds.), COMPUTER SIMULATION IN HUMAN POPULATION STUDIES

Robbins Burling, THE PASSAGE OF POWER: Studies in Political Succession

Piotr Sztompka, SYSTEM AND FUNCTION: Toward a Theory of Society

William G. Lockwood, EUROPEAN MOSLEMS: Economy and Ethnicity in Western Bosnia

Günter Golde, CATHOLICS AND PROTESTANTS: Agricultural Modernization in Two German Villages

Peggy Reeves Sanday (Ed.), ANTHROPOLOGY AND THE PUBLIC INTEREST: Fieldwork and Theory

Carol A. Smith (Ed.), REGIONAL ANALYSIS, Volume I: Economic Systems, and Volume II: Social Systems

Raymond D. Fogelson and Richard N. Adams (Eds.), THE ANTHROPOLOGY OF POWER: Ethnographic Studies from Asia, Oceania, and the New World

Frank Henderson Stewart, FUNDAMENTALS OF AGE-GROUP SYSTEMS

Larissa Adler Lomnitz, NETWORKS AND MARGINALITY: Life in a Mexican Shantytown

Benjamin S. Orlove, ALPACAS, SHEEP, AND MEN: The Wool Export Economy and Regional Society in Southern Peru

Harriet Ngubane, BODY AND MIND IN ZULU MEDICINE: An Ethnography of Health and Disease in Nyuswa-Zulu Thought and Practice

George M. Foster, Thayer Scudder, Elizabeth Colson, and Robert Van Kemper (Eds.), LONG-TERM FIELD RESEARCH IN SOCIAL ANTHROPOLOGY

R. H. Hook (Ed.), FANTASY AND SYMBOL: Studies in Anthropological Interpretation

Richard Tapper, PASTURE AND POLITICS: Economics, Conflict and Ritual Among Shahsevan Nomads of Northwestern Iran

George Bond, Walton Johnson, and Sheila S. Walker (Eds.), AFRICAN CHRISTIANITY: Patterns of Religious Continuity

Philip Burnham, OPPORTUNITY AND CONSTRAINT IN A SAVANNA SOCIETY: The Gbaya of Meiganga, Cameroon

John Comaroff (Ed.), THE MEANING OF MARRIAGE PAYMENTS

Michael H. Agar, THE PROFESSIONAL STRANGER: An Informal Introduction to Ethnography

Robert J. Thornton, SPACE, TIME, AND CULTURE AMONG THE IRAQW
OF TANZANIA

Linda S. Cordell and Stephen Beckerman (Eds.), THE VERSATILITY OF
KINSHIP

Peggy F. Barlett (Ed.), AGRICULTURAL DECISION MAKING: Anthropological Contributions to Rural Development

Thayer Scudder and Elizabeth Colson, SECONDARY EDUCATION AND
THE FORMATION OF AN ELITE: The Impact of Education
on Gwembe District, Zambia

Eric B. Ross (Ed.), BEYOND THE MYTHS OF CULTURE: Essays in Cultural
Materialism

Gerald D. Berreman (Ed.), SOCIAL INEQUALITY: Comparative and Developmental Approaches

Karla O. Poewe, MATRILINEAL IDEOLOGY

J. D. Lewis-Williams, BELIEVING AND SEEING: Symbolic Meaning in Southern San Rock Paintings

David Riches, NORTHERN NOMADIC HUNTER-GATHERERS: A Human-
istic Approach

George A. Collier, Renato I. Rosaldo, and John D. Wirth (Eds.), THE INCA
AND AZTEC STATES, 1400-1800: Anthropology and History

in preparation

Raymond B. Hames and William T. Vickers (Eds.), ADAPTIVE RESPONSES
OF NATIVE AMAZONIANS

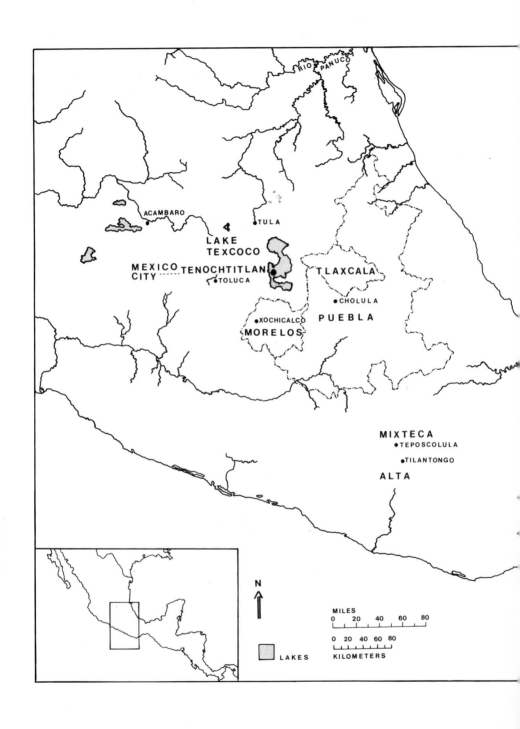